23-38

Education
for
What?

Readings in the Ends and Means of Education

Edited by
Charles H. Monson, Jr.
University of Utah

Houghton Mifflin Company · Boston
New York Atlanta Geneva, Illinois Dallas Palo Alto

To
Sharon, Kenneth, Margene, Ronald
Children and Teachers

Foreword

There is an aching unease in the American spirit. We have a distinct, articulable sense of living in apocalyptic times, when a nation's destiny seems so unnervingly near, so volcanically present, so conceivably terminal! Events are piling up around us faster than we can sort them out and arrange them properly in the logic of our lives. Even the logic shows signs of strain, groaning under the weight of insanity and mayhem run amok in a so-called rational and scientific age, rendering future sorting operations uncomfortably pointless. The whole thing, we feel, could come unstuck in a twinkling.

A standard and popular response to all this, in our and other times, is strident and loudly announced despair. We are in difficulty steering through this world. So we may as well let go of the tiller altogether and give up! There is, I suppose, a certain creditable honesty to this answer, a kind of inverse courage in being able to admit that the world is just too much, rather beyond—in the lingo of the social psychologist—the reach of coping.

Another and opposite response, also standard and popular but not so courageous, is a dogged determination to stay with it, a faith that maybe what we need is not a new compass setting for the tiller or some grand shift in living strategy, but simply the application of more, and then more, and then still more of the conventional wisdom of our traditions. If upheaval portends on every side, let us keep faith with our institutions, shield them from excessive dissent, and redouble our efforts to make sense of the present scheme of things.

Neither of these responses has ever appealed to those who call themselves educators. Education is, for the most part, a business of the young. And when you work with the young, you are never free of the innocence and romanticism of that period. Youth is not an age, but a condition, and educators are forever contaminated by that condition: an exuberant idealism which doggedly goes on believing that the world can be made better, more livable, more humane. Youth will neither give up nor stand pat. They will never permit their teachers to do so either.

What we need, the young seem to be saying, is a wrenching realignment of our values and priorities. If there is an apocalyptic dimension in our experience, maybe, as with Brutus, it lies in ourselves and not in the world's events. What needs changing is not the world, not even the major institutions by which we manage the world, but rather the spirit of meaning we bring to these institutions, the jobs we give them to do, the kind of world we want them to help us create.

Our task is therefore primarily *educational*, not political or religious or economic or technological. Today we turn to the educational enterprise—not to Congress, nor to God, nor to General Motors, nor to the Jet Propulsion Laboratory—to organize the long and arduous task of reclaiming our own time and of, who knows, maybe even saving our civilization.

If we turn to education, we are obviously in need of ideas with a very large sweep, the kind of ideas which offer hypotheses for change on a grand scale. If we ask, in our epoch of revolutionary upheaval, "Education for What?" we are not likely to be satisfied with anything less than revolutionary answers.

Mr. Monson has collected this kind of answers here. And since revolutionism has no century, no period all its own, he wisely gives us radical educational proposals from all of Western thought, past and present. Here is, if I may say so, a sort of handbook for educational revolutionaries, a manual of insights any teacher or educator should keep in his hip pocket for quick reference or angry inspiration while riding home on the bus or subway.

Revolutions are customarily made in the streets, but there is need for an occasional planning session in the strategy room back at headquarters. The first round of discussions may as well start with this provocative and stimulating book.

Van Cleve Morris

Preface

More than any other single institution the American school reflects the multiplicity of purposes and diversity of hopes which characterize American society. A school is expected to preserve and transmit America's heritage and at the same time to prepare students to live in an unknown future. A teacher is expected to treat every child in a classroom of forty as unique. The educational enterprise should not be involved in politics and yet it depends on the political processes for its funding and is expected to help students become better citizens. It must prepare students to enter a vocation as well as to treat clear thinking as an end in itself. It must help students to develop "good characters" and adopt "upstanding ideals" while having respect for the multiplicity of value systems implied by an open society. And in between times the schools are expected to help bring about social change, relate disparate bits of knowledge into a coherent whole, encourage self-expression, improve social behavior, obtain new knowledge, innovate, preserve, challenge, and discipline, all at once—and at the smallest possible cost.

Measured against this multiplicity—and potential inconsistency—of goals, the modern American school must be judged to be an expensive failure. It does not, and perhaps cannot, do all that is expected of it. But the fact that the schools are expected to both preserve and change, encourage freedom and establish discipline, be vocational and academic, is a sure, although subtle, sign of the modern school's spectacular success. What other institution is expected to do so much? A church? A corporation? A newspaper? An athletic team? Of the institutions which compose a society, only the diversity of government approaches the diversity of educational purposes. As Jacques Barzun says: "Education is to do everything that the rest of the world leaves undone."

The fact is that the schools have become the central repository of modern man's aspirations. And this is the kind of environment in which a teacher teaches.

Whether he is new or experienced at his job, every teacher knows the push and pull resulting from this multiplicity of purposes. He may want to help his students develop the skills he believes they must have next year and yet he is sure to hear them complain about the irrelevance of what he is teaching. Or he may view the school as an instrument for bringing about social change; that is, until the parents and taxpayers tell him to "stick to his teaching." He may want to try out a new idea, such as abandoning grades, but then he also has to contend with a principal or dean who may think otherwise.

What is a teacher to do when faced with these conflicting interests? The question will be faced by every teacher, and it is much easier to ask than to answer, for it brings him to the question of the purpose of his teaching, the problem of what he thinks education is for. Such a question involves, at the least, problems concerning proficiency in a subject matter and skills in pedagogy, but more importantly, it also involves a man's conception of himself, what he thinks he is doing with his life, and this kind of question is so important, so fundamental in a man's thinking that, paradoxically, it is frequently unanswerable; sometimes it is even unaskable.

This is why no book, no teacher, no colleague, no student—not even a husband or wife or close friend—can come to grips with the teacher's most important problems, although each in his own way can help. Dialogue allows close friends to serve as sounding boards, foils, or gadflies. Student reactions can serve as a test of one's self-image and achievements, or lack of these. A thoughtful teacher can sharpen the questions and clarify the answers of a student, even stretch his mind's understanding. And what can a book do? Well, a book can present a variety of alternative answers in the richness and complexity of a thoughtful man's writings, exhibiting not only *what* he believes and *why*, but *how* he would exemplify those beliefs in the classroom as well.

In all these ways and a hundred others every thoughtful and observant teacher will discover, each of us should gradually come to answer for ourselves the most important question we need to ask, "Education for What?"

Many of the selections in this book are contemporary, for that is where the action is in the searching self-analysis which is now going on in the educational enterprise. But the shrillness of the present must not blind us to the wisdom of the past, so this book begins with traditions before considering criticisms. Both the past and the present should be considered thoughtfully, but better still, critically. This is why you should read each author initially *to understand what he says* about the purposes of education and the means for achieving those ends. You also need to think about what you have read, and to talk with teachers and friends about each author's ideas to determine whether you agree with them. Comprehension and evaluation, reading and discussion, thought and argument; these are the tools with which you should attack *every* selection in this book. Comments to help guide your reading precede each selection while questions for further discussion follow.

Finally, I should acknowledge my gratitude to those who have advised me during the preparation of this book. My philosophy colleagues were Sterling M. McMurrin and Waldemer P. Read; my education colleagues, Stephen P. Hencley, Elliott D. Landau, Joseph C. Bentley and Walter Hahn. I wish to make a special acknowledgment to William D. MacDonald of Houghton Mifflin Company and to Van Cleve Morris who helped to shape the book's contemporary conception. Most importantly, I am grateful to those many students who, during the past fifteen years, have helped me to learn of my own educational failures and successes; they have been my teachers just as much as I have been theirs.

Charles H. Monson, Jr.

Contents

Part Three
Some Thoughts on the Art of Successful Teaching

Part One
Some
Traditional
Views

Prologue: Which Way Is Wisdom?

So here you are in the foothills of the educational enterprise, looking for a path to wisdom. Already you have come a long way, as even a cursory glance backwards indicates, but as you look ahead the obstacles, blind alleys and steep ascent look forbidding indeed. Could the future ever have looked so challenging before?

Perhaps you are beginning to notice things you've never seen before, how some leaders can take their group safely over a chasm of insecurity or around a boulder of prejudice and how others proceed slowly, deliberately along well-worn paths. Perhaps you are beginning to be aware of the fact that different leaders take different paths, and perhaps you are wondering which path most suits your own climbing talents and interests. So here you are reconnoitering, examining the terrain, looking for a trail.

Over on the left is a path marked "To Rousseau's Roost," and at the bottom the sign: "All guides stay here; students must learn to climb by themselves." A short way up that path is a branching trail which begins with a sign saying: "Let children pick the flowers, feel the rocks, listen to the birds" and it is signed Maria M. And a little farther up still another branch indicated by the sign: "This way to intelligent problem solving," and in small letters at the bottom "Observe the facts," signed J. Dewey.

As you gaze up these paths you see signs saying "Let each man do his own thing," and "Don't tyrannize the children," and you hear people on the trail shouting, "Freedom, freedom, freedom." You also hear of skinned knees and frustrations and you soon see some bedraggled students coming back along the path looking for a guide. You wonder whether everyone can find wisdom by self-initiative alone, and whether there are any openings for "teachers" in Rousseau's Roost, but nothing ventured, nothing gained, so you resolve to try the path, keeping a close watch for both the exhilarations and the obstacles of self-learning.

Nearby is another path with the simple sign: "Values." Have you ever seen such a sign in education land before? And then you remember the times you marched in straight lines, were told not to cheat, were required to listen, and you realize you must have missed seeing that sign, for it was there all along—or perhaps it was hidden by the underbrush. However, you can only see far enough up that path to determine that it has two branches. The right branch is advertised by a young man, neatly dressed, with button-down collar, who proclaims, "Preserve what is proven; hold fast to the past; trod the tried and the true," and you observe that his path is well worn from the passage of many feet. On the left, the hawker is slightly disheveled, with sandals and beads, and he shouts, "Look to the future; abandon all that's wrong; renew, revitalize, reconstruct." And a little farther along this path is the sign: "Let the schools do it!" You wonder whether you have the time and interest to trod this path, but you wonder, also, whether you can resist looking at Kalinen and Brameld.

Still a third path vies for your recognition alongside the paths leading to self-reliance and values. This path is marked "Subject Matter." Here, guides stand ready to lead you through the labyrinths of the known and to confront you at the proper time with the unknown. They have covered the terrain, know the material, and are prepared to save you time and money by passing on to you what they have spent a lifetime learning for themselves. All they ask is that you hold their hand, at least initially, and let them help you to climb. Spencer's climb offers the most variety, although the method for climbing, the study of science, is the same for each discipline. Plato's prisoners ascend toward wisdom by studying mathematics, and those who follow his path soon find themselves in Newman's narrow gorge named "The disciplined mind." And if you look closely, the path leading to Martin's "liberal education" almost seems to end at Rousseau's Roost.

Finally, hidden away in the foliage is a small sign reading: "What are four metaphors for?" A joker in the crowd, no doubt.

So, you've given the terrain a quick glance, and determined what paths are available. Now is the time for you to begin climbing and exploring each of them! And when you look back, you'll probably discover the ascent wasn't so steep after all.

1 The Education of Emile

Jean Jacques Rousseau

*If you had the opportunity to raise a child from infancy, educating him in
what you consider the best possible way, what would you do? Hire expensive
tutors? Send him to a private school? Enroll him in the public schools? Or
would you let him develop naturally, without outside guidance or control, as
Rousseau advocates? This philosophy of education has been called "the supreme example of learning to do by doing," and notice how Emile learns about
geography and history, science and art, in the process. Rousseau believes that
Emile will never "form inaccurate or confused ideas," and that this fifteen-
year-old boy who "thinks not of others but of himself . . . who depends on
himself alone" is the product of an ideal education. After you have read this
selection, ask yourself whether you agree with Rousseau.*

As I said before, man's education begins at birth; before he can speak or
understand he is learning. Experience precedes instruction; when he recognises his
nurse he has learnt much. The knowledge of the most ignorant man would surprise
us if we had followed his course from birth to the present time. If all human
knowledge were divided into two parts, one common to all, the other peculiar to
the learned, the latter would seem very small compared with the former. But we
scarcely heed this general experience, because it is acquired before the age of reason.
Moreover, knowledge only attracts attention by its rarity, as in algebraic equations
common factors count for nothing. Even animals learn much. They have senses and
must learn to use them; they have needs, they must learn to satisfy them; they must
learn to eat, walk, or fly. Quadrupeds which can stand on their feet from the first
cannot walk for all that; from their first attempts it is clear that they lack confidence.
Canaries who escape from their cage are unable to fly, having never used their wings.
Living and feeling creatures are always learning. If plants could walk they would
need senses and knowledge, else their species would die out. The child's first mental
experiences are purely affective, he is only aware of pleasure and pain; it takes him
a long time to acquire the definite sensations which show him things outside himself, but before these things present and withdraw themselves, so to speak, from his
sight, taking size and shape for him, the recurrence of emotional experiences is
beginning to subject the child to the rule of habit. You see his eyes constantly follow
the light, and if the light comes from the side the eyes turn towards it, so that one
must be careful to turn his head towards the light lest he should squint. He must
also be accustomed from the first to the dark, or he will cry if he misses the light.
Food and sleep, too, exactly measured, become necessary at regular intervals, and
soon desire is no longer the effect of need, but of habit, or rather habit adds a fresh
need to those of nature. You must be on your guard against this.

From the book *Emile; Or, Education* by Jean Jacques Rousseau. Translated by Barbara
Foxley. Everyman's Library Edition. Reprinted by permission of E. P. Dutton & Co., Inc.,
and J. M. Dent & Sons Ltd.

The only habit the child should be allowed to contract is that of having no habits; let him be carried on either arm, let him be accustomed to offer either hand, to use one or other indifferently; let him not want to eat, sleep, or do anything at fixed hours, nor be unable to be left alone by day or night. Prepare the way for his control of his liberty and the use of his strength by leaving his body its natural habit, by making him capable of lasting self-control, of doing all that he wills when his will is formed.

As soon as the child begins to take notice, what is shown him must be carefully chosen. The natural man is interested in all new things. He feels so feeble that he fears the unknown: the habit of seeing fresh things without ill effects destroys this fear. Children brought up in clean houses where there are no spiders are afraid of spiders, and this fear often lasts through life. I never saw peasants, man, woman, or child, afraid of spiders.

Since the mere choice of things shown him may make the child timid or brave, why should not his education begin before he can speak or understand? I would have him accustomed to see fresh things, ugly, repulsive, and strange beasts, but little by little, and far off till he is used to them, and till having seen others handle them he handles them himself. If in childhood he sees toads, snakes, and crayfish, he will not be afraid of any animal when he is grown up. Those who are continually seeing terrible things think nothing of them. . . .

I have observed that children are rarely afraid of thunder unless the peals are really terrible and actually hurt the ear, otherwise this fear only comes to them when they know that thunder sometimes hurts or kills. When reason begins to cause fear, let use reassure them. By slow and careful stages man and child learn to fear nothing.

In the dawn of life, when memory and imagination have not begun to function, the child only attends to what affects its senses. His sense experiences are the raw material of thought; they should, therefore, be presented to him in fitting order, so that memory may at a future time present them in the same order to his understanding; but as he only attends to his sensations it is enough, at first, to show him clearly the connection between these sensations and the things which cause them. He wants to touch and handle everything; do not check these movements which teach him invaluable lessons. Thus he learns to perceive the heat, cold, hardness, softness, weight, or lightness of bodies, to judge their size and shape and all their physical properties, by looking, feeling,[1] listening, and, above all, by comparing sight and touch, by judging with the eye what sensation they would cause to his hand.

It is only by movement that we learn the difference between self and not self; it is only by our own movements that we gain the idea of space. The child has not this idea, so he stretches out his hand to seize the object within his reach or that which is a hundred paces from him. You take this as a sign of tyranny, an attempt to bid the thing draw near, or to bid you bring it. Nothing of the kind, it is merely

---

[1] Of all the senses that of smell is the latest to develop in children; up to two or three years of age they appear to be insensible of pleasant or unpleasant odours; in this respect they are as indifferent or rather as insensible as many animals.

that the object first seen in his brain, then before his eyes, now seems close to his arms, and he has no idea of space beyond his reach. Be careful, therefore, to take him about, to move him from place to place, and to let him perceive the change in his surroundings, so as to teach him to judge of distances.

When he begins to perceive distances then you must change your plan, and only carry him when you please, not when he pleases; for as soon as he is no longer deceived by his senses, there is another motive for his effort. This change is remarkable and calls for explanation.

The discomfort caused by real needs is shown by signs, when the help of others is required. Hence the cries of children; they often cry; it must be so. Since they are only conscious of feelings, when those feelings are pleasant they enjoy them in silence; when they are painful they say so in their own way and demand relief. Now when they are awake they can scarcely be in a state of indifference; either they are asleep or else they are feeling something.

All our languages are the result of art. It has long been a subject of inquiry whether there ever was a natural language common to all; no doubt there is, and it is the language of children before they begin to speak. This language is inarticulate, but it has tone, stress, and meaning. The use of our own language has led us to neglect it so far as to forget it altogether. Let us study children and we shall soon learn it afresh from them. Nurses can teach us this language; they understand all their nurslings say to them, they answer them, and keep up long conversations with them; and though they use words, these words are quite useless. It is not the hearing of the word, but its accompanying intonation that is understood.

To the language of intonation is added the no less forcible language of gesture. The child uses, not its weak hands, but its face. The amount of expression in these undeveloped faces is extraordinary; their features change from one moment to another with incredible speed. You see smiles, desires, terror, come and go like lightning; every time the face seems different. The muscles of the face are undoubtedly more mobile than our own. On the other hand the eyes are almost expressionless. Such must be the sort of signs they use at an age when their only needs are those of the body. Grimaces are the sign of sensation, the glance expresses sentiment.

As man's first state is one of want and weakness, his first sounds are cries and tears. The child feels his needs and cannot satisfy them, he begs for help by his cries. Is he hungry or thirsty? there are tears; is he too cold or too hot? more tears; he needs movement and is kept quiet, more tears; he wants to sleep and is disturbed, he weeps. The less comfortable he is, the more he demands change. He has only one language because he has, so to say, only one kind of discomfort. In the imperfect state of his sense organs he does not distinguish their several impressions; all ills produce one feeling of sorrow.

These tears, which you think so little worthy of your attention, give rise to the first relation between man and his environment; here is forged the first link in the long chain of social order.

When the child cries he is uneasy, he feels some need which he cannot satisfy; you watch him, seek this need, find it, and satisfy it. If you can neither find it nor satisfy it, the tears continue and become tiresome. The child is petted to quiet him, he is rocked or sung to sleep; if he is obstinate, the nurse becomes impatient and threatens him; cruel nurses sometimes strike him. What strange lessons for him at his first entrance into life! . . .

The child's first tears are prayers, beware lest they become commands; he begins by asking for aid, he ends by demanding service. Thus from his own weakness, the source of his first consciousness of dependence, springs the later idea of rule and tyranny; but as this idea is aroused rather by his needs than by our services, we begin to see moral results whose causes are not in nature; thus we see how important it is, even at the earliest age, to discern the secret meaning of the gesture or cry.

When the child tries to seize something without speaking, he thinks he can reach the object, for he does not rightly judge its distance; when he cries and stretches out his hands he no longer misjudges the distance, he bids the object approach, or orders you to bring it to him. In the first case bring it to him slowly; in the second do not even seem to hear his cries. The more he cries the less you should heed him. He must learn in good time not to give commands to men, for he is not their master, nor to things, for they cannot hear him. Thus when the child wants something you mean to give him, it is better to carry him to it rather than to bring the thing to him. From this he will draw a conclusion suited to his age, and there is no other way of suggesting it to him. . . .

Reason alone teaches us to know good and evil. Therefore conscience, which makes us love the one and hate the other, though it is independent of reason, cannot develop without it. Before the age of reason we do good or ill without knowing it, and there is no morality in our actions, although there is sometimes in our feeling with regard to other people's actions in relation to ourselves. A child wants to overturn everything he sees. He breaks and smashes everything he can reach; he seizes a bird as he seizes a stone, and strangles it without knowing what he is about.

Why so? In the first place philosophy will account for this by inbred sin, man's pride, love of power, selfishness, spite; perhaps it will say in addition to this that the child's consciousness of his own weakness makes him eager to use his strength, to convince himself of it. But watch that broken down old man reduced in the downward course of life to the weakness of a child; not only is he quiet and peaceful, he would have all about him quiet and peaceful too; the least change disturbs and troubles him, he would like to see universal calm. How is it possible that similar feebleness and similar passions should produce such different effects in age and in infancy, if the original cause were not different? And where can we find this difference in cause except in the bodily condition of the two. The active principle, common to both, is growing in one case and declining in the other; it is being formed in the one and destroyed in the other; one is moving towards life, the other towards death. The failing activity of the old man is centered in his heart, the child's overflowing activity spreads abroad. He feels, if we may say so, strong enough to give life to all about him. To make or to destroy, it is all one to him; change is what he seeks, and all change involves action. If he seems to enjoy destructive activity it is only that it takes time to make things and very little time to break them, so that the work of destruction accords better with his eagerness.

While the Author of nature has given children this activity, He takes care that it shall do little harm by giving them small power to use it. But as soon as they can think of people as tools to be used, they use them to carry out their wishes and to supplement their own weakness. This is how they become tiresome, masterful, imperious, naughty, and unmanageable; a development which does not spring from a natural love of power, but one which has been taught them, for it does not need much experience to realise how pleasant it is to set others to work and to move the world by a word.

As the child grows it gains strength and becomes less restless and unquiet and more independent. Soul and body become better balanced and nature no longer asks for more movement than is required for self-preservation. But the love of power does not die with the need that aroused it; power arouses and flatters self-love, and habit strengthens it; thus caprice follows upon need, and the first seeds of prejudice and obstinacy are sown.

First Maxim.—Far from being too strong, children are not strong enough for all the claims of nature. Give them full use of such strength as they have; they will not abuse it.

Second Maxim.—Help them and supply the experience and strength they lack whenever the need is of the body.

Third Maxim.—In the help you give them confine yourself to what is really needful, without granting anything to caprice or unreason; for they will not be tormented by caprice if you do not call it into existence, seeing it is no part of nature.

Fourth Maxim.—Study carefully their speech and gestures, so that at an age when they are incapable of deceit you may discriminate between those desires which come from nature and those which spring from perversity.

The spirit of these rules is to give children more real liberty and less power, to let them do more for themselves and demand less of others; so that by teaching them from the first to confine their wishes within the limits of their powers they will scarcely feel the want of whatever is not in their power.

This is another very important reason for leaving children's limbs and bodies perfectly free, only taking care that they do not fall, and keeping anything that might hurt them out of their way.

We have now reached the second phase of life; infancy, strictly so-called, is over; for the words *infans* and *puer* are not synonymous. The latter includes the former, which means literally "one who cannot speak"; thus Valerius speaks of *puerum infantem*. But I shall continue to use the word child (French *enfant*) according to the custom of our language till an age for which there is another term.

When children begin to talk they cry less. This progress is quite natural; one language supplants another. As soon as they can say "It hurts me," why should they cry, unless the pain is too sharp for words? If they still cry, those about them are to blame. When once Emile has said, "It hurts me," it will take a very sharp pain to make him cry.

If the child is delicate and sensitive, if by nature he begins to cry for nothing, I let him cry in vain and soon check his tears at their source. So long as he cries I will not go near him; I come at once when he leaves off crying. He will soon be quiet when he wants to call me, or rather he will utter a single cry. Children learn the meaning of signs by their effects; they have no other meaning for them. However much a child hurts himself when he is alone, he rarely cries, unless he expects to be heard.

Should he fall or bump his head, or make his nose bleed, or cut his fingers, I shall show no alarm, nor shall I make any fuss over him; I shall take no notice, at any rate at first. The harm is done; he must bear it; all my zeal could only frighten him more and make him more nervous. Indeed it is not the blow but the fear of it which distresses us when we are hurt. I shall spare him this suffering at least, for he will certainly regard the injury as he sees me regard it; if he finds that I hasten anxiously to him, if I pity him or comfort him, he will think he is badly hurt. If he finds I take no notice, he will soon recover himself, and will think the wound is healed when it ceases to hurt. This is the time for his first lesson in courage, and by bearing slight ills without fear we gradually learn to bear greater.

I shall not take pains to prevent Emile hurting himself; far from it, I should be vexed if he never hurt himself, if he grew up unacquainted with pain. To bear pain is his first and most useful lesson. It seems as if children were small and weak on purpose to teach them these valuable lessons without danger. The child has such a little way to fall he will not break his leg; if he knocks himself with a stick he will not break his arm; if he seizes a sharp knife he will not grasp it tight enough to make a deep wound. So far as I know, no child, left to himself, has ever been known to kill or maim itself, or even to do itself any serious harm, unless it has been foolishly left on a high place, or alone near the fire, or within reach of dangerous weapons. What is there to be said for all the paraphernalia with which the child is surrounded to shield him on every side so that he grows up at the mercy of pain, with neither courage nor experience, so that he thinks he is killed by a pin-prick and faints at the sight of blood?

With our foolish and pedantic methods we are always preventing children from learning what they could learn much better by themselves, while we neglect what we alone can teach them. Can anything be sillier than the pains taken to teach them to walk, as if there were any one who was unable to walk when he grows up through his nurse's neglect? How many we see walking badly all their life because they were ill taught?

Emile shall have no head-pads, no go-carts, no leading-strings; or at least as soon as he can put one foot before another he shall only be supported along pavements, and he shall be taken quickly across them.[2] Instead of keeping him mewed up in a stuffy room, take him out into a meadow every day; let him run about, let him struggle and fall again and again, the oftener the better; he will learn all the sooner to pick himself up. The delights of liberty will make up for many bruises. My pupil will hurt himself oftener than yours, but he will always be merry; your pupils may receive fewer injuries, but they are always thwarted, constrained, and sad. I doubt whether they are any better off.

As their strength increases, children have also less need for tears. They can do more for themselves, they need the help of others less frequently. With strength comes the sense to use it. It is with this second phase that the real personal life has

[2] There is nothing so absurd and hesitating as the gait of those who have been kept too long in leading-strings when they were little. This is one of the observations which are considered trivial because they are true.

its beginning; it is then that the child becomes conscious of himself. During every moment of his life memory calls up the feeling of self; he becomes really one person, always the same, and therefore capable of joy or sorrow. Hence we must begin to consider him as a moral being.

Although we know approximately the limits of human life and our chances of attaining those limits, nothing is more uncertain than the length of the life of any one of us. Very few reach old age. The chief risks occur at the beginning of life; the shorter our past life, the less we must hope to live. Of all the children who are born scarcely one half reach adolescence, and it is very likely your pupil will not live to be a man.

What is to be thought, therefore, of that cruel education which sacrifices the present to an uncertain future, that burdens a child with all sorts of restrictions and begins by making him miserable, in order to prepare him for some far-off happiness which he may never enjoy? Even if I considered that education wise in its aims, how could I view without indignation those poor wretches subjected to an intolerable slavery and condemned like galley-slaves to endless toil, with no certainty that they will gain anything by it? The age of harmless mirth is spent in tears, punishments, threats, and slavery. You torment the poor thing for his good; you fail to see that you are calling Death to snatch him from those gloomy surroundings. Who can say how many children fall victims to the excessive care of their fathers and mothers? They are happy to escape from this cruelty; this is all that they gain from the ills they are forced to endure: they die without regretting, having known nothing of life but its sorrows.

There is such a thing as excessive severity as well as excessive indulgence, and both alike should be avoided. If you let children suffer you risk their health and life; you make them miserable now; if you take too much pains to spare them every kind of uneasiness you are laying up much misery for them in the future; you are making them delicate and over-sensitive; you are taking them out of their place among men, a place to which they must sooner or later return, in spite of all your pains. You will say I am falling into the same mistake as those bad fathers whom I blamed for sacrificing the present happiness of their children to a future which may never be theirs.

Not so; for the liberty I give my pupil makes up for the slight hardships to which he is exposed. I see little fellows playing in the snow, stiff and blue with cold, scarcely able to stir a finger. They could go and warm themselves if they chose, but they do not choose; if you forced them to come in they would feel the harshness of constraint a hundredfold more than the sharpness of the cold. Then what becomes of your grievance? Shall I make your child miserable by exposing him to hardships which he is perfectly ready to endure? I secure his present good by leaving him his freedom, and his future good by arming him against the evils he will have to bear. If he had his choice, would he hesitate for a moment between you and me?

Do you think any man can find true happiness elsewhere than in his natural state; and when you try to spare him all suffering, are you not taking him out of his natural state? Indeed I maintain that to enjoy great happiness he must experience slight ills; such is his nature. Too much bodily prosperity corrupts the morals. A man who knew nothing of suffering would be incapable of tenderness towards his fellow-creatures and ignorant of the joys of pity; he would be hard-hearted, unsocial, a very monster among men.

Do you know the surest way to make your child miserable? Let him have everything he wants; for as his wants increase in proportion to the ease with which they are satisfied, you will be compelled, sooner or later, to refuse his demands, and this unlooked-for refusal will hurt him more than the lack of what he wants. He will want your stick first, then your watch, the bird that flies, or the star that shines above him. He will want all he sets eyes on, and unless you were God himself, how could you satisfy him? . . .

I return to practical matters. I have already said your child must not get what he asks, but what he needs;[3] he must never act from obedience, but from necessity.

The very words *obey* and *command* will be excluded from his vocabulary, still more those of *duty* and *obligation;* but the words strength, necessity, weakness, and constraint must have a large place in it. Before the age of reason it is impossible to form any idea of moral beings or social relations; so avoid, as far as may be, the use of words which express these ideas, lest the child at an early age should attach wrong ideas to them, ideas which you cannot or will not destroy when he is older. The first mistaken idea he gets into his head is the germ of error and vice; it is the first step that needs watching. Act in such a way that while he only notices external objects his ideas are confined to sensations; let him only see the physical world around him. If not, you may be sure that either he will pay no heed to you at all, or he will form fantastic ideas of the moral world of which you prate, ideas which you will never efface as long as he lives.

"Reason with children" was Locke's chief maxim; it is in the height of fashion at present, and I hardly think it is justified by its results; those children who have been constantly reasoned with strike me as exceedingly silly. Of all man's faculties, reason, which is, so to speak, compounded of all the rest, is the last and choicest growth, and it is this you would use for the child's early training. To make a man reasonable is the coping stone of a good education, and yet you profess to train a child through his reason! You begin at the wrong end, you make the end the means. If children understood reason they would not need education, but by talking to them from their earliest age in a language they do not understand you accustom them to be satisfied with words, to question all that is said to them, to think themselves as wise as their teachers; you train them to be argumentative and rebellious; and whatever you think you gain from motives of reason, you really gain from greediness, fear, or vanity with which you are obliged to reinforce your reasoning.

Most of the moral lessons which are and can be given to children may be reduced to this formula:

Master. You must not do that.

Child. Why not?

[3] We must recognise that pain is often necessary, pleasure is sometimes needed. So there is only one of the child's desires which should never be complied with, the desire for power. Hence, whenever they ask for anything we must pay special attention to their motive in asking. As far as possible give them everything they ask for, provided it can really give them pleasure; refuse everything they demand from mere caprice or love of power.

Master. Because it is wrong.
Child. Wrong! What is wrong?
Master. What is forbidden you.
Child. Why is it wrong to do what is forbidden?
Master. You will be punished for disobedience.
Child. I will do it when no one is looking.
Master. We shall watch you.
Child. I will hide.
Master. We shall ask you what you were doing.
Child. I shall tell a lie.
Master. You must not tell lies.
Child. Why must not I tell lies?
Master. Because it is wrong, etc.

That is the inevitable circle. Go beyond it, and the child will not understand you. What sort of use is there in such teaching? I should greatly like to know what you would substitute for this dialogue. It would have puzzled Locke himself. It is no part of a child's business to know right and wrong, to perceive the reason for a man's duties. . . .

It is very strange that ever since people began to think about education they should have hit upon no other way of guiding children than emulation, jealousy, envy, vanity, greediness, base cowardice, all the most dangerous passions, passions ever ready to ferment, ever prepared to corrupt the soul even before the body is full-grown. With every piece of precocious instruction which you try to force into their minds you plant a vice in the depths of their hearts; foolish teachers think they are doing wonders when they are making their scholars wicked in order to teach them what goodness is, and then they tell us seriously, "Such is man." Yes, such is man, as you have made him. Every means has been tried except one, the very one which might succeed — well-regulated liberty. Do not undertake to bring up a child if you cannot guide him merely by the laws of what can or cannot be. The limits of the possible and the impossible are alike unknown to him, so they can be extended or contracted around him at your will. Without a murmur he is restrained, urged on, held back, by the hands of necessity alone; he is made adaptable and teachable by the mere force of things, without any chance for vice to spring up in him; for passions do not arise so long as they have accomplished nothing.

Give your scholar no verbal lessons; he should be taught by experience alone; never punish him, for he does not know what it is to do wrong; never make him say, "Forgive me," for he does not know how to do you wrong. Wholly unmoral in his actions, he can do nothing morally wrong, and he deserves neither punishment nor reproof.

Already I see the frightened reader comparing this child with those of our time; he is mistaken. The perpetual restraint imposed upon your scholars stimulates their activity; the more subdued they are in your presence, the more boisterous they are as soon as they are out of your sight. They must make amends to themselves in some way or other for the harsh constraint to which you subject them. Two schoolboys from the town will do more damage in the country than all the children of the village. Shut up a young gentleman and a young peasant in a room; the former will have upset and smashed everything before the latter has stirred from his place. Why is that, unless that the one hastens to misuse a moment's licence, while the other, always sure of freedom, does not use it rashly. And yet the village children, often flattered or constrained, are still very far from the state in which I would have them kept.

Let us lay it down as an incontrovertible rule that the first impulses of nature are always right; there is no original sin in the human heart, the how and why of the entrance of every vice can be traced. The only natural passion is self-love or selfishness taken in a wider sense. This selfishness is good in itself and in relation to ourselves; and as the child has no necessary relations to other people he is naturally indifferent to them; his self-love only becomes good or bad by the use made of it and the relations established by its means. Until the time is ripe for the appearance of reason, that guide of selfishness, the main thing is that the child shall do nothing because you are watching him or listening to him; in a word, nothing because of other people, but only what nature asks of him; then he will never do wrong.

I do not mean to say that he will never do any mischief, never hurt himself, never break a costly ornament if you leave it within his reach. He might do much damage without doing wrong, since wrong-doing depends on the harmful intention which will never be his. If once he meant to do harm, his whole education would be ruined; he would be almost hopelessly bad.

Greed considers some things wrong which are not wrong in the eyes of reason. When you leave free scope to a child's heedlessness, you must put anything he could spoil out of his way, and leave nothing fragile or costly within his reach. Let the room be furnished with plain and solid furniture; no mirrors, china, or useless ornaments. My pupil Emile, who is brought up in the country, shall have a room just like a peasant's. Why take such pains to adorn it when he will be so little in it? I am mistaken, however; he will ornament it for himself, and we shall soon see how.

But if, in spite of your precautions, the child contrives to do some damage, if he breaks some useful article, do not punish him for your carelessness, do not even scold him; let him hear no word of reproval, do not even let him see that he has vexed you; behave just as if the thing had come to pieces of itself; you may consider you have done great things if you have managed to hold your tongue.

May I venture at this point to state the greatest, the most important, the most useful rule of education? It is: Do not save time, but lose it. I hope that every-day readers will excuse my paradoxes; you cannot avoid paradox if you think for yourself, and whatever you may say I would rather fall into paradox than into prejudice. The most dangerous period in human life lies between birth and the age of twelve. It is the time when errors and vices spring up, while as yet there is no means to destroy them; when the means of destruction are ready, the roots have gone too deep to be pulled up. If the infant sprang at one bound from its mother's breast to the age of reason, the present type of education would be quite suitable, but its natural growth calls for quite a different training. The mind should be left undisturbed till its faculties have developed; for while it is blind it cannot see the torch you offer it, nor can it follow through the vast expanse of ideas a path so faintly traced by reason that the best eyes can scarcely follow it.

Therefore the education of the earliest years should be merely negative. It consists, not in teaching virtue or truth, but in preserving the heart from vice and from the spirit of error. If only you could let well alone, and get others to follow your example; if you could bring your scholar to the age of twelve strong and healthy, but unable to tell his right hand from his left, the eyes of his understanding would be open to reason as soon as you began to teach him. Free from prejudices and free from habits, there would be nothing in him to counteract the effects of your labours. In your hands he would soon become the wisest of men; by doing nothing to begin with, you would end with a prodigy of education.

The whole course of man's life up to adolescence is a period of weakness; yet there comes a time during these early years when the child's strength overtakes the demands upon it, when the growing creature, though absolutely weak, is relatively strong. His needs are not fully developed and his present strength is more than enough for them. He would be a very feeble man, but he is a strong child.

What is the cause of man's weakness? It is to be found in the disproportion between his strength and his needs. It is our passions that make us weak, for our natural strength is not enough for their satisfaction. To limit our desires comes to the same thing, therefore, as to increase our strength. When we can do more than we want, we have strength enough and to spare, we are really strong. This is the third stage of childhood, the stage with which I am about to deal. I still speak of childhood for want of a better word; for our scholar is approaching adolescence, though he has not yet reached the age of puberty.

About twelve or thirteen the child's strength increases far more rapidly than his needs. The strongest and fiercest of the passions is still unknown, his physical development is still imperfect and seems to await the call of the will. He is scarcely aware of extremes of heat and cold and braves them with impunity. He needs no coat, his blood is warm; no spices, hunger is his sauce, no food comes amiss at this age; if he is sleepy he stretches himself on the ground and goes to sleep; he finds all he needs within his reach; he is not tormented by any imaginary wants; he cares nothing what others think; his desires are not beyond his grasp; not only is he self-sufficing, but for the first and last time in his life he has more strength than he needs. . . .

This interval in which the strength of the individual is in excess of his wants is, as I have said, relatively though not absolutely the time of greatest strength. It is the most precious time in his life; it comes but once; it is very short, all too short, as you will see when you consider the importance of using it aright.

He has, therefore, a surplus of strength and capacity which he will never have again. What use shall he make of it? He will strive to use it in tasks which will help at need. He will, so to speak, cast his present surplus into the storehouse of the future: the vigorous child will make provision for the feeble man; but he will not store his goods where thieves may break in, nor in barns which are not his own. To store them aright, they must be in the hands and the head, they must be stored within himself. This is the time for work, instruction, and inquiry. And note that this is no arbitrary choice of mine, it is the way of nature herself. . . .

Brought up in the spirit of our maxims, accustomed to make his own tools and not to appeal to others until he has tried and failed, he will examine everything he sees carefully and in silence. He thinks rather than questions. Be content, therefore, to show him things at a fit season; then, when you see that his curiosity is thoroughly aroused, put some brief question which will set him trying to discover the answer.

On the present occasion when you and he have carefully observed the rising sun, when you have called his attention to the mountains and other objects visible from the same spot, after he has chattered freely about them, keep quiet for a few minutes as if lost in thought and then say, "I think the sun set over there last night; it rose here this morning. How can that be?" Say no more; if he asks questions, do not answer them; talk of something else. Let him alone, and be sure he will think about it.

To train a child to be really attentive so that he may be really impressed by any truth of experience, he must spend anxious days before he discovers that truth. If he does not learn enough in this way, there is another way of drawing his attention to the matter. Turn the question about. If he does not know how the sun gets from the place where it sets to where it rises, he knows at least how it travels from sunrise to sunset, his eyes teach him that. Use the second question to throw light on the first; either your pupil is a regular dunce or the analogy is too clear to be missed. This is his first lesson in cosmography. . . .

His geography will begin with the town he lives in and his father's country house, then the places between them, the rivers near them, and then the sun's aspect and how to find one's way by its aid. This is the meeting place. Let him make his own map, a very simple map, at first containing only two places; others may be added from time to time, as he is able to estimate their distance and position. You see at once what a good start we have given him by making his eye his compass.

No doubt he will require some guidance in spite of this, but very little, and that little without his knowing it. If he goes wrong let him alone, do not correct his mistakes; hold your tongue till he finds them out for himself and corrects them, or at most arrange something, as opportunity offers, which may show him his mistakes. If he never makes mistakes he will never learn anything thoroughly. Moreover, what he needs is not an exact knowledge of local topography, but how to find out for himself. No matter whether he carries maps in his head provided he understands what they mean, and has a clear idea of the art of making them. See what a difference there is already between the knowledge of your scholars and the ignorance of mine. They learn maps, he makes them. Here are fresh ornaments for his room.

Remember that this is the essential point in my method—Do not teach the child many things, but never to let him form inaccurate or confused ideas. I care not if he knows nothing provided he is not mistaken, and I only acquaint him with truths to guard him against the errors he might put in their place. Reason and judgment come slowly, prejudices flock to us in crowds, and from these he must be protected. But if you make science itself your object, you embark on an unfathomable and shoreless ocean, an ocean strewn with reefs from which you will never return. When I see a man in love with knowledge, yielding to its charms and flitting from one branch to another unable to stay his steps, he seems to me like a child gathering shells on the sea-shore, now picking them up, then throwing them aside for others which he sees beyond them, then taking them again, till overwhelmed by their number and unable to choose between them, he flings them all away and returns empty handed.

Time was long during early childhood; we only tried to pass our time for fear of using it ill; now it is the other way; we have not time enough for all that would be of use. The passions, remember, are drawing near, and when they knock at the door your scholar will have no ear for anything else. The peaceful age of intelligence is so short, it flies so swiftly, there is so much to be done, that it is madness to try to make your child learned. It is not your business to teach him the various sciences, but to give him a taste for them and methods of learning them when this taste is more mature. That is assuredly a fundamental principle of all good education.

This is also the time to train him gradually to prolonged attention to a given object; but this attention should never be the result of constraint, but of interest or desire; you must be very careful that it is not too much for his strength, and that it is not carried to the point of tedium. Watch him, therefore, and whatever happens, stop before he is tired, for it matters little what he learns; it does matter that he should do nothing against his will.

If he asks questions let your answers be enough to whet his curiosity but not enough to satisfy it; above all, when you find him talking at random and overwhelming you with silly questions instead of asking for information, at once refuse to answer; for it is clear that he no longer cares about the matter in hand, but wants to make you a slave to his questions. Consider his motives rather than his words. This warning, which was scarcely needed before, becomes of supreme importance when the child begins to reason. . . .

Undoubtedly the notions of things thus acquired for oneself are clearer and much more convincing than those acquired from the teaching of others; and not only is our reason not accustomed to a slavish submission to authority, but we develop greater ingenuity in discovering relations, connecting ideas and inventing apparatus, than when we merely accept what is given us and allow our minds to be enfeebled by indifference, like the body of a man whose servants always wait on him, dress him and put on his shoes, whose horse carries him, till he loses the use of his limbs. Boileau used to boast that he had taught Racine the art of rhyming with difficulty. Among the many short cuts to science, we badly need some one to teach us the art of learning with difficulty.

The most obvious advantage of these slow and laborious inquiries is this: the scholar, while engaged in speculative studies, is actively using his body, gaining suppleness of limb, and training his hands to labour so that he will be able to make them useful when he is a man. Too much apparatus, designed to guide us in our experiments and to supplement the exactness of our senses, makes us neglect to use those senses. The theodolite makes it unnecessary to estimate the size of angles; the eye which used to judge distances with much precision, trusts to the chain for its measurements; the steel yard dispenses with the need of judging weight by the hand as I used to do. The more ingenious our apparatus, the coarser and more unskilful are our senses. We surround ourselves with tools and fail to use those with which nature has provided every one of us.

But when we devote to the making of these instruments the skill which did instead of them, when for their construction we use the intelligence which enabled us to dispense with them, this is gain not loss, we add art to nature, we gain ingenuity without loss of skill. If instead of making a child stick to his books I employ him in a workshop, his hands work for the development of his mind. While he fancies himself a workman he is becoming a philosopher. Moreover, this exercise has other advantages of which I shall speak later; and you will see how, through philosophy in sport, one may rise to the real duties of man.

Emile's knowledge is confined to nature and things. The very name of history is unknown to him, along with metaphysics and morals. He knows the essential relations between men and things, but nothing of the moral relations between man and man. He has little power of generalisation, he has no skill in abstraction. He perceives that certain qualities are common to certain things, without reasoning about these qualities themselves. He is acquainted with the abstract idea of space by the help of his geometrical figures; he is acquainted with the abstract idea of quantity by the help of his algebraical symbols. These figures and signs are the supports on which these ideas may be said to rest, the supports on which his senses repose. He does not attempt to know the nature of things, but only to know things in so far as they affect himself. He only judges what is outside himself in relation to himself, and his judgment is exact and certain. Caprice and prejudice have no part in it. He values most the things which are of use to himself, and as he never departs from this standard of values, he owes nothing to prejudice.

Emile is industrious, temperate, patient, stedfast, and full of courage. His imagination is still asleep, so he has no exaggerated ideas of danger; the few ills he feels he knows how to endure in patience, because he has not learnt to rebel against fate. As to death, he knows not what it means; but accustomed as he is to submit without resistance to the law of necessity, he will die, if die he must, without a groan and without a struggle; that is as much as we can demand of nature, in that hour which we all abhor. To live in freedom, and to be independent of human affairs, is the best way to learn how to die.

In a word Emile is possessed of all that portion of virtue which concerns himself. To acquire the social virtues he only needs a knowledge of the relations which make those virtues necessary; he only lacks knowledge which he is quite ready to receive.

He thinks not of others but of himself, and prefers that others should do the same. He makes no claim upon them, and acknowledges no debt to them. He is alone in the midst of human society, he depends on himself alone, for he is all that a boy can be at his age. He has no errors, or at least only such as are inevitable; he has no vices, or only those from which no man can escape. His body is healthy, his limbs are supple, his mind is accurate and unprejudiced, his heart is free and untroubled by passion. Pride, the earliest and the most natural of passions, has scarcely shown itself. Without disturbing the peace of others, he has passed his life contented, happy, and free, so far as nature allows. Do you think that the earlier years of a child, who has reached his fifteenth year in this condition, have been wasted?

Questions for Discussion

1. Describe some of the specific procedures, as well as the general principles on which those specific recommendations rest, which Rousseau advocates for teaching Emile. Do you think these procedures actually would produce the kind of educated person Rousseau would like?
2. Is Rousseau's theory an example of learning to do by doing? In this sense, what is meant by "doing"?
3. Is this theory compatible with a formal educational system which includes classrooms, courses, textbooks, examinations, etc.? If not, could any of his ideas be incorporated into the formal system? Be specific.
4. Is self-expression a worthy goal of the educational enterprise, or is some other purpose more advisable? How do you decide what is a worthy purpose?

2 The Children's House

María Montessori

Maria Montessori began her educational career by working with children of low intelligence in Italy during the first part of this century. She discovered that these children learned by seeing and feeling as well as listening, and she organized her classroom like a house for children, complete with appropriate furniture and games, equipment and activities. She taught her students by asking them to walk on lines, by learning to listen to the silence, by placing cylinders inside each other, by feeling different textures. And what did she hope to accomplish? To help children "show a love of work," a "calm and orderliness in their movements," a "spontaneous discipline," a "perfect organization of work permitting the possibility of self-development." When she became the Italian Minister of Education in the early 1920's, she attempted to apply many of these same ideas to the entire educational system. Do you think they should be implemented in the school system or, more modestly and realistically, in your own classroom?

The "Children's House" is the environment which is offered to the child that he may be given the opportunity of developing his activities. This kind of school is not of a fixed type, but may vary according to the financial resources at disposal and to the opportunities afforded by the environment. It ought to be a real house; that is to say, a set of rooms with a garden of which the children are the masters. A garden which contains shelter is ideal, because the children can play or sleep under them, and can also bring their tables out to work or dine. In this way they may live almost entirely in the open air, and are protected at the same time from rain and sun.

The central and principal room of the building, often also the only room at the disposal of the children, is the room for "intellectual work." To this central room can be added other smaller rooms according to the means and opportunities of the place: for example, a bathroom, a dining room, a little parlor or common-room, a room for manual work, a gymnasium and rest-room.

The special characteristic of the equipment of these houses is that it is adapted for children and not adults. They contain not only didactic material specially fitted for the intellectual development of the child, but also a complete equipment for the management of the miniature family. The furniture is light so that the children can move it about, and it is painted in some light color so that the children can wash it with soap and water. There are low tables of various sizes and shapes— square, rectangular and round, large and small. The rectangular shape is the most common as two or more children can work at it together. The seats are small wooden chairs, but there are also small wicker armchairs and sofas.

From *Dr. Montessori's Own Handbook* by Maria Montessori, originally published in 1914. Published since 1964 by Robert Bentley, Inc., Cambridge, Mass.

In the working-room there are two indispensable pieces of furniture. One of these is a very long cupboard with large doors. It is very low so that a small child can set on the top of it small objects such as mats, flowers, etc. Inside this cupboard is kept the didactic material which is the common property of all the children.

The other is a chest of drawers containing two or three columns of little drawers, each of which has a bright handle (or a handle of some color to contrast with the background), and a small card with a name upon it. Every child has his own drawer, in which to put things belonging to him.

Round the walls of the room are fixed blackboards at a low level, so that the children can write or draw on them, and pleasing, artistic pictures, which are changed from time to time as circumstances direct. The pictures represent children, families, landscapes, flowers and fruit, and more often Biblical and historical incidents. Ornamental plants and flowering plants ought always to be placed in the room where the children are at work.

Another part of the working-room's equipment is seen in the pieces of carpet of various colors—red, blue, pink, green and brown. The children spread these rugs upon the floor, sit upon them and work there with the didactic material. A room of this kind is larger than the customary class-rooms, not only because the little tables and separate chairs take up more space, but also because a large part of the floor must be free for the children to spread their rugs and work upon them.

In the sitting-room, or "club-room," a kind of parlor in which the children amuse themselves by conversation, games, or music, etc., the furnishings should be especially tasteful. Little tables of different sizes, little armchairs and sofas should be placed here and there. Many brackets of all kinds and sizes, upon which may be put statuettes, artistic vases or framed photographs, should adorn the walls; and, above all, each child should have a little flower-pot, in which he may sow the seed of some indoor plant, to tend and cultivate it as it grows. On the tables of this sitting-room should be placed large albums of colored pictures, and also games of patience, or various geometric solids, with which the children can play at pleasure, constructing figures, etc. A piano, or, better, other musical instruments, possibly harps of small dimensions, made especially for children, completes the equipment. In this "club-room" the teacher may sometimes entertain the children with stories, which will attract a circle of interested listeners.

The furniture of the dining-room consists, in addition to the tables, of low cupboards accessible to all the children, who can themselves put in their place and take away the crockery, spoons, knives and forks, table-cloth and napkins. The plates are always of china, and the tumblers and water-bottles of glass. Knives are always included in the table equipment.

The Dressing-room. Here each child has his own little cupboard or shelf. In the middle of the room there are very simple washstands, consisting of tables, on each of which stand a small basin, soap and nail-brush. Against the wall stand little sinks with water-taps. Here the children may draw and pour away their water. There is no limit to the equipment of the "Children's Houses" because the children themselves do everything. They sweep the rooms, dust and wash the furniture, polish the brasses, lay and clear away the table, wash up, sweep and roll up the rugs, wash a few little clothes, and cook eggs. As regards their personal toilet, the children know how to dress and undress themselves. They hang their clothes on little hooks, placed very low so as to be within reach of a little child, or else they fold up such articles of clothing, as their little serving-aprons, of which they take great care, and lay them inside a cupboard kept for the household linen.

In short, where the manufacture of toys has been brought to such a point of complication and perfection that children have at their disposal entire dolls' houses, complete wardrobes for the dressing and undressing of dolls, kitchens where they can pretend to cook, toy animals as nearly lifelike as possible, this method seeks to give all this to the child in reality—making him an actor in a living scene.

The technique of my method as it follows the guidance of the natural physiological and psychical development of the child, may be divided into three parts:

Motor education.

Sensory education.

Language.

The care and management of the environment itself afford the principal means of motor education, while sensory education and the education of language are provided for by my didactic material.

The didactic material for the education of the senses consists of:

(a) Three sets of solid insets.

(b) Three sets of solids in graduated sizes, comprising:
   (1) Pink cubes.
   (2) Brown prisms.
   (3) Rods: (a) colored green; (b) colored alternately red and blue.

(c) Various geometric solids (prism, pyramid, sphere, cylinder, cone, etc.).

(d) Rectangular tablets with rough and smooth surfaces.

(e) A collection of various stuffs.

(f) Small wooden tablets of different weights.

(g) Two boxes, each containing sixty-four colored tablets.

(h) A chest of drawers containing plane insets.

(i) Three series of cards on which are pasted geometrical forms in paper.

(k) A collection of cylindrical closed boxes (sounds).

(l) A double series of musical bells, wooden boards on which are painted the lines used in music, small wooden discs for the notes.

(Didactic material for the preparation for writing and arithmetic:)

(m) Two sloping desks and various iron insets.

(n) Cards on which are pasted sandpaper letters.

(o) Two alphabets of colored cardboard and of different sizes.

(p) A series of cards on which are pasted sandpaper figures (1, 2, 3, etc.).

(q) A series of large cards bearing the same figures in smooth paper for the enumeration of numbers above ten.

(r) Two boxes with small sticks for counting.

(s) The volume of drawings belonging specially to the method, and colored pencils.

(t) The frames for lacing, buttoning, etc., which are used for the education of the movements of the hand.

The education of the movements is very complex, as it must correspond to all the coordinated movements which the child has to establish in his physiological organism. The child, if left without guidance, is disorderly in his movements, and these disorderly movements are the special characteristic of the little child. In fact, he "never keeps still," and "touches everything." This is what forms the child's so-called "unruliness" and "naughtiness."

The adult would deal with him by checking these movements, with the monotonous and useless repetition "keep still." As a matter of fact, in these movements the little one is seeking the very exercise which will organize and coordinate the movements useful to man. We must, therefore, desist from the useless attempt to reduce the child to a state of immobility. We should rather give "order" to his movements, leading them to those actions towards which his efforts are actually tending. This is the aim of muscular education at this age. Once a direction is given to them, the child's movements are made towards a definite end, so that he himself grows quiet and contented, and becomes an active worker, a being calm and full of joy. This education of the movements is one of the principal factors in producing that outward appearance of "discipline" to be found in the "Children's Houses." I have already spoken at length on this subject in my other books.

Muscular education has reference to:

The primary movements of everyday life (walking, rising, sitting, handling objects).

The care of the person.

Management of the household.

Gardening.

Manual work.

Gymnastic exercises.

Rhythmic movements.

Among the gymnastic exercises that which must be considered the most important is that of the "line." A line is described in chalk or paint upon a large space of floor. Instead of one line, there may also be two concentric lines, elliptical in form. The children are taught to walk upon these lines like tight-rope walkers, placing their feet one in front of the other. To keep their balance they make efforts exactly similar to those of real tight-rope walkers, except that they have no danger with which to reckon, as the lines are only drawn upon the floor. The teacher herself performs the exercise, showing clearly how she sets her feet, and the children imitate her without any necessity for her to speak. At first it is only certain children who follow her, and when she has shown them how to do it, she withdraws, leaving the phenomenon to develop of itself.

The children for the most part continue to walk, adapting their feet with great care to the movement they have seen, and making efforts to keep their balance so as not to fall. Gradually the other children draw near and watch and also make an attempt. Very little time elapses before the whole of the two ellipses or the one line is covered with children balancing themselves, and continuing to walk round, watching their feet with an expression of deep attention on their faces.

Music may then be used. It should be a very simple march, the rhythm of which is not obvious at first, but which accompanies and enlivens the spontaneous efforts of the children.

When they have learned in this way to master their balance the children have brought the act of walking to a remarkable standard of perfection, and have acquired, in addition to security and composure in their natural gait, an unusually graceful carriage of the body. The exercise on the line can afterwards be made more complicated in various ways. The first application is that of calling forth rhythmic exercise by the sound of a march upon the piano. When the same march is repeated during several days, the children end by feeling the rhythm and by following it with movements of their arms and feet. They also accompany the exercises on the line with songs.

Little by little the music is *understood* by the children. They finish, as in Miss George's school at Washington, by singing over their daily work with the didactic material. The "Children's House," then, resembles a hive of bees humming as they work.

As to the little gymnasium, of which I speak in my book on the "Method," one piece of apparatus is particularly practical. This is the "fence," from which the children hang by their arms, freeing their legs from the heavy weight of the body and strengthening the arms. This fence has also the advantage of being useful in a garden for the purpose of dividing one part from another, as, for example, the flower-beds from the garden walks, and it does not detract in any way from the appearance of the garden.

My didactic material offers to the child the *means* for what may be called "sensory education."

In the box of material the first three objects which are likely to attract the attention of a little child from two and a half to three years old are three solid pieces of wood, in each of which is inserted a row of ten small cylinders, or sometimes discs, all furnished with a button for a handle. In the first case there is a row of cylinders of the same height, but with a diameter which decreases from thick to thin. In the second, there are cylinders which decrease in all dimensions, and so are either larger or smaller, but always of the same shape.

Lastly, in the third case, the cylinders have the same diameter but vary in height, so that, as the size decreases, the cylinder gradually becomes a little disc in form.

The first cylinders vary in two dimensions (the section); the second in all three dimensions; the third in one dimension (height). The order which I have given refers to the degree of *ease* with which the child performs the exercises.

The exercise consists in taking out the cylinders, mixing them and putting them back in the right place. It is performed by the child as he sits in a comfortable position at a little table. He exercises his hands in the delicate act of taking hold of the button with the tips of one or two fingers, and in the little movements of the hand and arm as he mixes the cylinders, *without letting them fall and without making too much noise* and puts them back again each in its own place.

In these exercises the teacher may, in the first instance, intervene, merely taking out the cylinders, mixing them carefully on the table and then showing the child that he is to put them back, but without performing the action herself. Such intervention, however, is almost always found to be unnecessary, for the children *see* their companions at work, and thus are encouraged to imitate them.

They like to do it *alone;* in fact, sometimes almost in private for fear of inopportune help.

But how is the child to find the right place for each of the little cylinders which lie mixed upon the table? He first makes trials; it often happens that he places a cylinder which is too large for the empty hole over which he puts it. Then, changing its place, he tries others until the cylinder goes in. Again, the contrary may happen; that is to say, the cylinder may slip too easily into a hole too big for it. In that case it has taken a place which does not belong to it at all, but to a larger cylinder. In this way one cylinder at the end will be left out without a place, and it will not be possible to find one that fits. Here the child cannot help seeing his mistake in concrete form. He is perplexed, his little mind is faced with a problem which interests him intensely. Before, all the cylinders fitted, now there is one that will not fit. The little one stops, frowning, deep in thought. He begins to feel the little buttons and finds that some cylinders have too much room. He thinks that perhaps they are out of their right place and tries to place them correctly. He repeats the process again and again, and finally he succeeds. Then it is that he breaks into a smile of triumph. The exercise arouses the intelligence of the child; he wants to repeat it right from the beginning and, having learned by experience, he makes another attempt. Little children from three to three and a half years old have repeated the exercise up to *forty* times without losing their interest in it.

If the second set of cylinders and then the third are presented, the *change* of shape strikes the child and reawakens his interest.

The material which I have described serves to *educate the eye* to distinguish *difference in dimension,* for the child ends by being able to recognize at a glance the larger or the smaller hole which exactly fits the cylinder which he holds in his hand. The educative process is based on this: that the control of the error lies in *the material itself,* and the child has concrete evidence of it.

The desire of the child to attain an end which he knows, leads him to correct himself. It is not a teacher who makes him notice his mistake and shows him how to correct it, but it is a complex work of the child's own intelligence which leads to such a result.

Hence at this point there begins the process of auto-education.

The aim is not an external one, that is to say, it is *not* the object that the child should learn how to place the cylinders, and that *he should know how to perform an exercise.*

The aim is an inner one, namely, that the child train himself to observe; that he be led to make comparisons between objects to form judgments, to reason and to decide; and it is in the indefinite repetition of this exercise of attention and of intelligence that a real development ensues.

During the same period the child can be doing other exercises. Among the material is to be found a small rectangular board, the surface of which is divided into two parts—rough and smooth. The child knows already how to wash his hands with cold water and soap; he then dries them and dips the tips of his fingers for a few seconds in tepid water. Graduated exercises for the thermic sense may also have their place here, as has been explained in my book on the "Method."

After this, the child is taught to pass the soft cushioned tips of his fingers *as lightly as possible* over the two separate surfaces, that he may appreciate their difference. The delicate movement backwards and forwards of the suspended hand, as it is brought into light contact with the surface, is an excellent exercise in control. The little hand, which has just been cleansed and given its tepid bath, gains much in grace and beauty, and the whole exercise is the first step in the education of the "tactile sense," which holds such an important place in my method.

When initiating the child into the education of the sense of touch, the teacher must always take an active part the first time; not only must she show the child "how it is done," her interference is a little more definite still, for she takes hold of his hand and guides it to touch the surfaces with the finger-tips in the lightest possible way. She will make no explanations; her words will be rather to *encourage* the child with his hand to perceive the different sensations.

When he has perceived them, it is then that he repeats the act by himself in the delicate way which he has been taught.

After the board with the two contrasting surfaces, the child is offered another board on which are gummed strips of paper which are rough or smooth in different degrees.

Graduated series of sandpaper cards are also given. The child perfects himself by exercises in touching these surfaces, not only refining his capacity for perceiving tactile differences which are always growing more similar, but also perfecting the movement of which he is ever gaining greater mastery.

Following these is a series of stuffs of every kind: velvets, satins, silks, woolens, cottons, coarse and fine linens. There are two similar pieces of each kind of stuff, and they are of bright and vivid colors.

The child is now taught a new movement. Where before he had to *touch*, he must now *feel* the stuffs, which, according to the degree of fineness or coarseness from coarse cotton to fine silk, are felt with movements correspondingly decisive or delicate. The child whose hand is already practised finds the greatest pleasure in feeling the stuffs, and almost instinctively, in order to enhance his appreciation of the tactile sensation he closes his eyes. Then, to spare himself the exertion, he blindfolds himself with a clean handkerchief, and as he feels the stuffs, he arranges the similar pieces in pairs, one upon the other, then, taking off the handkerchief, he ascertains for himself whether he has made any mistake.

This exercise in *touching* and *feeling* is peculiarly attractive to the child, and induces him to seek similar experiences in his surroundings. A little one, attracted by the pretty stuff of a visitor's dress, will be seen to go and wash his hands, then to come and touch the stuff of the garment again and again with infinite delicacy, his face meanwhile expressing his pleasure and interest.

The great pleasure which the children derive from the recognition of *objects* by touching their form corresponds in itself to a sensory exercise.

My psychologists have spoken of the *stereognostic* sense, that is, the capacity of recognizing forms by the movement of the muscles of the hand as it follows the outlines of solid objects. This sense does not consist only of the sense of touch, because the tactile sensation is only that by which we perceive the differences in quality of surfaces, rough or smooth. Perception of form comes from the combination of two sensations, tactile and muscular, muscular sensations being sensations of movement. What we call in the blind the tactile sense is in reality more often the stereognostic sense. That is, they perceive by means of their hands the *form of bodies*.

It is the special muscular sensibility of the child from three to six years of age who is forming his own muscular activity which stimulates him to use the stereognostic sense. When the child spontaneously blindfolds his eyes in order to recognize various objects, such as the plane and solid inserts, he is exercising this sense.

There are many exercises which he can do to enable him to recognize with closed eyes objects of well defined shapes, as, for example, the little bricks and cubes of Froebel, marbles, coins, beans, peas, etc. From a selection of different objects mixed together he can pick out those that are alike, and arrange them in separate heaps.

In the didactic material there are also geometrical solids—pale blue in color—a sphere, a prism, a pyramid, a cone, a cylinder. The most attractive way of teaching a child to recognize these forms is for him to touch them with closed eyes and guess their names, the latter learned in a way which I will describe later. After an exercise of this kind the child when his eyes are open observes the forms with a much more lively interest. Another way of interesting him in the solid geometrical forms is to make them move. The sphere rolls in every direction; the cylinder rolls in one direction only; the cone rolls around itself; the prism and the pyramid, however, stand still, but the prism falls over more easily than the pyramid.

To quicken the child's attention in special relation to sounds there is a most important exercise which, contrary to all attempts made up to this time in the practise of education, consists not in producing but in eliminating, as far as possible, all sounds from the environment. My "lesson of silence" has been very widely applied, even in schools where the rest of my method has not found its way, for the sake of its practical effect upon the discipline of the children.

The children are taught "not to move"; to inhibit all those motor impulses which may arise from any cause whatsoever, and in order to induce in them real "immobility," it is necessary to initiate them in the *control* of all their movements. The teacher, then, does not limit herself to saying, "Sit still," but she gives them the example herself, showing them how to sit absolutely still; that is, with feet still, body still, arms still, head still. The respiratory movements should also be performed in such a way as to produce no sound.

The children must be taught how to succeed in this exercise. The fundamental condition is that of finding a comfortable position, i.e., a position of equilibrium. As they are seated for this exercise, they must therefore make themselves comfortable either in their little chairs or on the ground. When immobility is obtained, the room if half-darkened, or else the children close their eyes, or cover them with their hands.

It is quite plain to see that the children take a great interest in the "silence"; they seem to give themselves up to a kind of spell: they might be said to be wrapped in meditation. Little by little, as each child, watching himself, becomes more and more still, the silence deepens till it becomes absolute and can be felt, just as the twilight gradually deepens whilst the sun is setting.

Then it is that slight sounds, unnoticed before, are heard; the ticking of the clock, the chirp of a sparrow in the garden, the flight of a butterfly. The world becomes full of imperceptible sounds which invade that deep silence without disturbing it, just as the stars shine out in the dark sky without banishing the darkness of the night. It is almost the discovery of a new world where there is rest. It is, as it were, the twilight of the world of loud noises and of the uproar that oppresses the spirit. At such a time the spirit is set free and opens out like the corolla of the convolvulus.

And leaving metaphor for the reality of facts, can we not all recall feelings that have possessed us at sunset, when all the vivid impressions of the day, the brightness and clamor, are silenced? It is not that we miss the day, but that our spirit expands. It becomes more sensitive to the inner play of emotions, strong and persistent, or changeful and serene. . . .

The special importance of the sense of hearing comes from the fact that it is the sense organ connected with speech. Therefore, to train the child's attention to follow sounds and noises which are produced in the environment, to recognize them and to discriminate between them, is to prepare his attention to follow more accurately the sounds of articulate language. The teacher must be careful to pronounce clearly and completely the sounds of the word when she speaks to a child, even though she may be speaking in a low voice, almost as if telling him a secret. The children's songs are also a good means for obtaining exact pronunciation. The teacher, when she teaches them pronounces slowly, separating the component sounds of the word pronounced.

But a special opportunity for training in clear and exact speech occurs when the lessons are given in the nomenclature relating to the sensory exercises. In every exercise, when the child has recognized the differences between the qualities of the objects, the teacher fixes the idea of this quality with a word. Thus, when the child has many times built and rebuilt the tower of the pink cubes, at an opportune moment the teacher draws near him, and taking the two extreme cubes, the largest and the smallest, and showing them to him, says, "This is large"; "This is small." The two words only, large and small, are pronounced several times in succession with strong emphasis and with a very clear pronunciation, "This is large, large, large"; after which there is a moment's pause. Then the teacher, to see if the child has understood, verifies with the following tests: "Give me the large one. Give me the small one." Again, "The large one." "Now the small one." "Give me the large one." Then there is another pause. Finally, the teacher, pointing to the objects in turn asks, "What is this?" The child, if he has learned, replies rightly, "Large," "Small." The teacher then urges the child to repeat the words always more clearly and as accurately as possible. "What is it?" "Large." "What?" "Large." "Tell me nicely, what is it?" "Large."

Large and small objects are those which differ only in size and not in form; that is, all three dimensions change more or less proportionally. We should say that a house is "large" and a hut is "small." When two pictures represent the same objects in different dimensions one can be said to be an enlargement of the other.

When, however, only the dimensions referring to the section of the object change, while the length remains the same, the objects are respectively "thick" and "thin."

We should say of two posts of equal height, but different cross-section, that one is "thick" and the other is "thin." The teacher, therefore, gives a lesson on the brown prisms similar to that with the cubes in the three "periods" which I have described:

Period 1. Naming. "This is thick. This is thin."

Period 2. Recognition. "Give me the thick. Give me the thin."

Period 3. The Pronunciation of the Word. "What is this?"

There is a way of helping the child to recognize differences in dimension and to place the objects in correct gradation. After the lesson which I have described, the teacher scatters the brown prisms, for instance, on a carpet, says to the child, "Give me the thickest of all," and lays the object on a table. Then, again, she invites the child to look for the thickest piece among those scattered on the floor, and every time the piece chosen is laid in its order on the table next to the piece previously chosen. In this way the child accustoms himself always to look either for the thickest or the thinnest among the rest, and so has a guide to help him to lay the pieces in gradation.

By means of these lessons the child comes to know many words very thoroughly—large, small; thick, thin; long, short; dark, light; rough, smooth; heavy, light; hot, cold; and the names of many colors and geometrical forms. Such words do not relate to any particular object, but to a psychic acquisition on the part of the child. In fact, the name is given after a long exercise, in which the child, concentrating his attention on different qualities of objects, has made comparisons, reasoned, and formed judgments, until he has acquired a power of discrimination which he did not possess before. In a word, he has refined his senses; his observation of things has been thorough and fundamental; he has changed himself. . . .

The success of these results is closely connected with the delicate intervention of the one who guides the children in their development. It is necessary for the teacher to guide the child without letting him feel her presence too much, so that she may be always ready to supply the desired help, but may never be the obstacle between the child and his experience.

A lesson in the ordinary use of the word cools the child's enthusiasm for the knowledge of things, just as it would cool the enthusiasm of adults. To keep alive that enthusiasm is the secret of real guidance, and it will not prove a difficult task, provided that the attitude towards the child's acts be that of respect, calm and waiting, and provided that he be left free in his movements and in his experiences.

Then we shall notice that the child has a personality which he is seeking to expand; he has initiative, he chooses his own work, persists in it, changes it according to his inner needs; he does not shirk effort, he rather goes in search of it, and with great joy overcomes obstacles within his capacity. He is sociable to the extent of wanting to share with everyone his successes, his discoveries, and his little triumphs. There is therefore no need of intervention. "Wait while observing." That is the motto for the educator.

Let us wait, and be always ready to share in both the joys and the difficulties which the child experiences. He himself invites our sympathy, and we should respond fully and gladly. Let us have endless patience with his slow progress, and show enthusiasm and gladness at his successes. If we could say: "We are respectful and courteous in our dealings with children, we treat them as we should like to be

treated ourselves," we should certainly have mastered a great educational principle
and undoubtedly be setting an example of good education.

What we all desire for ourselves, namely, not to be disturbed in our work, not
to find hindrances to our efforts, to have good friends ready to help us in times of
need, to see them rejoice with us, to be on terms of equality with them, to be able
to confide and trust in them—this is what we need for happy companionship. In
the same way children are human beings to whom respect is due, superior to us by
reason of their "innocence" and of the greater possibilities of their future. What
we desire they desire also.

As a rule, however, we do not respect our children. We try to force them to follow
us without regard to their special needs. We are overbearing with them, and above
all, rude; and then we expect them to be submissive and well-behaved, knowing all
the time how strong is their instinct of imitation and how touching their faith in and
admiration of us. They will imitate us in any case. Let us treat them, therefore, with
all the kindness which we would wish to help to develop in them. And by kindness
is not meant caresses. Should we not call anyone who embraced us at the first time
of meeting rude, vulgar and ill-bred? Kindness consists in interpreting the wishes of
others, in conforming one's self to them, and sacrificing, if need be, one's own
desire. This is the kindness which we must show towards children.

To find the interpretation of children's desires we must study them scientifically,
for their desires are often unconscious. They are the inner cry of life, which wishes
to unfold according to mysterious laws. We know very little of the way in which it
unfolds. Certainly the child is growing into a man by force of a divine action similar
to that by which from nothing he became a child.

Our intervention in this marvelous process is *indirect;* we are here to offer to this
life, which came into the world by itself, the means necessary for its development,
and having done that we must await this development with respect.

Let us leave the life *free* to develop within the limits of the good, and let us
observe this inner life developing. This is the whole of our mission. Perhaps as we
watch we shall be reminded of the words of Him who was absolutely good, "Suffer
the little children to come unto Me." That is to say, "Do not hinder them from
coming, since, if they are left free and unhampered, they will come." . . .

The child who has completed all the exercises above described, and is thus prepared for an advance towards unexpected conquests, is about four years old.

He is not an unknown quantity, as are children who have been left to gain
varied and casual experiences by themselves, and who therefore differ in type and
intellectual standard, not only according to their "natures," but especially according
to the chances and opportunities they have found for their spontaneous inner
formation.

Education has determined an environment for the children. Individual differences to be found in them can, therefore, be put down almost exclusively to each
one's individual "nature." Owing to their environment which offers means adapted
and measured to meet the needs of their psychical development, our children have
acquired a fundamental type which is common to all. They have coordinated their
movements in various kinds of manual work about the house, and so have acquired
a characteristic independence of action, and initiative in the adaptation of their

actions to their environment. Out of all this emerges a personality, for the children have become little men, who are self-reliant.

The special attention necessary to handle small fragile objects without breaking them, and to move heavy articles without making a noise, has endowed the movements of the whole body with a lightness and grace which are characteristic of our children. It is a deep feeling of responsibility which has brought them to such a pitch of perfection. For instance, when they carry three or four tumblers at a time, or a tureen of hot soup, they know that they are responsible not only for the objects, but also for the success of the meal which at that moment they are directing. In the same way each child feels the responsibility of the "silence," of the prevention of harsh sounds, and he knows how to cooperate for the general good in keeping the environment, not only orderly, but quiet and calm. Indeed, our children have taken the road which leads them to the mastery of themselves.

But their formation is due to a deeper psychological work still, arising from the education of the senses. In addition to ordering their environment and ordering themselves in their outward personalities, they have also ordered the inner world of their minds.

The didactic material, in fact, does not offer to the child the "content" of the mind, but the order for that "content." It causes him to distinguish identities from differences, extreme differences from fine gradations, and to classify, under conceptions of quality and of quantity, the most varying sensations appertaining to surfaces, colors, dimensions, forms and sounds. The mind has formed itself by a special exercise of attention, observing, comparing, and classifying.

The mental attitude acquired by such an exercise leads the child to make ordered observations in his environment, observations which prove as interesting to him as discoveries, and so stimulate him to multiply them indefinitely and to form in his mind a rich "content" of clear ideas.

Language now comes to fix by means of exact words the ideas which the mind has acquired. These words are few in number and have reference, not to separate objects, but rather to the order of the ideas which have been formed in the mind. In this way the children are able to "find themselves," alike in the world of natural things and in the world of objects and of words which surround them, for they have an inner guide which leads them to become active and intelligent explorers instead of wandering wayfarers in an unknown land.

These are the children who, in a short space of time, sometimes in a few days, learn to write and to perform the first operations of arithmetic. It is not a fact that children in general can do it, as many have believed. It is not a case of giving my material for writing to unprepared children and of awaiting the "miracle."

The fact is that the minds and hands of our children are already prepared for writing, and ideas of quantity, of identity, of differences, and of gradation, which form the bases of all calculation, have been maturing for a long time in them.

One might say that all their previous education is a preparation for the first stages of essential culture—writing, reading, and number, and that knowledge comes as an easy, spontaneous, and logical consequence of the preparation—that it is in fact its natural conclusion.

We have already seen that the purpose of the word is to fix ideas and to facilitate the elementary comprehension of things. In the same way writing and arithmetic now fix the complex inner acquisitions of the mind, which proceeds henceforward continually to enrich itself by fresh observations. . . .

A brief description such as this, of the means which are used in the "Children's House," may perhaps give the reader the impression of a logical and convincing system of education. But the importance of my method does not lie in the organization itself, but in the effects which it produces on the child. It is the child who proves the value of this method by his spontaneous manifestations, which seem to reveal the laws of man's inner development. Psychology will perhaps find in the "Children's Houses" a laboratory which will bring more truths to light than thus hitherto recognized; for the essential factor in psychological research, especially in the field of psychogenesis, the origin and development of the mind, must be the establishment of normal conditions for the free development of thought.

As is well known, we leave the children free in their work, and in all actions which are not of a disturbing kind. That is, we eliminate disorder, which is "bad," but allow to that which is orderly and "good" the most complete liberty of manifestation.

The results obtained are surprising, for the children have shown a love of work which no one suspected to be in them, and a calm and an orderliness in their movements which, surpassing the limits of correctness, have entered into those of "grace." The spontaneous discipline, and the obedience which is seen in the whole class, constitute the most striking result of our method.

The ancient philosophical discussion as to whether man is born good or evil is often brought forward in connection with my method, and many who have supported it have done so on the ground that it provides a demonstration of man's natural goodness. Very many others, on the contrary, have opposed it, considering that to leave children free is a dangerous mistake, since they have in them innate tendencies to evil.

I should like to put the question upon a more positive plane.

In the words "good" and "evil" we include the most varying ideas, and we confuse them especially in our practical dealings with little children.

The tendencies which we stigmatize as evil in little children of three to six years of age are often merely those which cause annoyance to us adults when, not understanding their needs, we try to prevent their every movement, their every attempt to gain experience for themselves in the world (by touching everything, etc.). The child, however, through this natural tendency, is led to coordinate his movements and to collect impressions, especially sensations of touch, so that when prevented he rebels, and this rebellion forms almost the whole of his "naughtiness."

What wonder is it that the evil disappears when, if we give the right means for development and leave full liberty to use them, rebellion has no more reason for existence?

Further, by the substitution of a series of outbursts of joy for the old series of outbursts of rage, the moral physiognomy of the child comes to assume a calm and gentleness which make him appear a different being.

It is we who provoked the children to the violent manifestations of a real struggle for existence. In order to exist according to the needs of their psychic development they were often obliged to snatch from us the things which seemed necessary to them for the purpose. They had to move contrary to our laws, or sometimes to struggle with other children to wrest from them the objects of their desire.

On the other hand, if we give children the means of existence, the struggle for it disappears, and a vigorous expansion of life takes its place. This question involves a hygienic principle connected with the nervous system during the difficult period when the brain is still rapidly growing, and should be of great interest to specialists in children's diseases and nervous derangements. The inner life of man and the beginnings of his intellect are controlled by special laws and vital necessities which cannot be forgotten if we are aiming at health for mankind.

For this reason, an educational method, which cultivates and protects the inner activities of the child, is not a question which concerns merely the school or the teachers; it is a universal question which concerns the family, and is of vital interest to mothers.

To go more deeply into a question is often the only means of answering it rightly. If, for instance, we were to see men fighting over a piece of bread, we might say: "How bad men are!" If, on the other hand, we entered a well-warmed eating-house, and saw them quietly finding a place and choosing their meal without any envy of one another, we might say: "How good men are!" Evidently, the question of absolute good and evil, intuitive ideas of which guide us in our superficial judgment, goes beyond such limitations as these. We can, for instance, provide excellent eating-houses for an entire people without directly affecting the question of their morals. One might say, indeed, that to judge by appearance, a well-fed people are better, quieter, and commit less crime than a nation that is ill-nourished; but whoever draws from that the conclusion that to make men good it is enough to feed them, will be making an obvious mistake.

It cannot be denied, however, that nourishment will be an essential factor in obtaining goodness, in the sense that it will eliminate all the evil acts, and the bitterness caused by lack of bread.

Now, in our case, we are dealing with a far deeper need—the nourishment of man's inner life, and of his higher functions. The bread that we are dealing with is the bread of the spirit, and we are entering into the difficult subject of the satisfaction of man's psychic needs.

We have already obtained a most interesting result, in that we have found it possible to present new means of enabling children to reach a higher level of calm and goodness, and we have been able to establish these means by experience. The whole foundation of our results rests upon these means which we have discovered, and which may be divided under two heads—the organization of work, and liberty.

It is the perfect organization of work, permitting the possibility of self-development and giving outlet for the energies, which procures for each child the beneficial and calming satisfaction. And it is under such conditions of work that liberty leads to a perfecting of the activities, and to the attainment of a fine discipline which is in itself the result of that new quality of calmness that has been developed in the child.

Freedom without organization of work would be useless. The child left free without means of work would go to waste, just as a new-born baby, if left free without nourishment, would die of starvation. The organization of the work, therefore, is the corner-stone of this new structure of goodness; but even that organization would be in vain without the liberty to make use of it, and without freedom for the expansion of all those energies which spring from the satisfaction of the child's highest activities.

Has not a similar phenomenon occurred also in the history of man? The history of civilization is a history of successful attempts to organize work and to obtain liberty. On the whole, man's goodness has also increased, as is shown by his progress from barbarism to civilization, and it may be said that crime, the various forms of wickedness, cruelty and violence have been gradually decreasing during this passage of time.

The criminality of our times, as a matter of fact, has been compared to a form of barbarism surviving in the midst of civilized peoples. It is, therefore, through the better organization of work that society will probably attain to a further purification, and in the meanwhile it seems unconsciously to be seeking the overthrow of the last barriers between itself and liberty.

If this is what we learn from society, how great should be the results among little children from three to six years of age if the organization of their work is complete, and their freedom absolute? It is for this reason that to us they seem so good, like heralds of hope and of redemption.

If men, walking as yet so painfully and imperfectly along the road of work and of freedom, have become better, why should we fear that the same road will prove disastrous to the children?

Yet, on the other hand, I would not say that the goodness of our children in their freedom will solve the problem of the absolute goodness or wickedness of man. We can only say that we have made a contribution to the cause of goodness by removing obstacles which were the cause of violence and of rebellion.

Questions for Discussion

1. Briefly, describe each of the general educational principles which are implied by the activities described in "The Children's House." Are they consistent with each other? Could you develop the educational philosophy at which Miss Montessori hints by combining these principles into a carefully reasoned and coherent statement?
2. Are any—or all—of the techniques described in this selection applicable to elementary school classes? To high school classes? To university classes? Be imaginative, and be specific!
3. Are there any assumptions concerning the nature of man or the purpose of life in this selection?
4. Describe the similarities and differences between Miss Montessori's and Rousseau's ideas on education.

3 Pragmatic Education

John Dewey

Probably the most famous and influential of all American philosophers, John Dewey, sees education occurring in a social context. He thinks that the school should be like an ideal home, and that the concerns of the classroom should extend into the family and community, each posing problems to, and learning from, the others. He also believes that learning must grow out of the "problematic situations" in which students find themselves, and that "the old education" in which a teacher determines what the child will learn, and how, is quite inadequate. Notice how Dewey uses Rousseau's principles to teach factual knowledge, such as cooking eggs, to students, as well as the ways in which he organizes the classroom and curriculum to bring about his aim of helping students to become "intelligent problem-solvers." When you have finished reading this selection look about your own educational environment to notice what elements of pragmatic education you are experiencing.

Profound differences in theory are never gratuitous or invented. They grow out of conflicting elements in a genuine problem—a problem which is genuine just because the elements, taken as they stand, are conflicting. Any significant problem involves conditions that for the moment contradict each other. Solution comes only by getting away from the meaning of terms that is already fixed upon and coming to see the conditions from another point of view, and hence in a fresh light. But this reconstruction means travail of thought. Easier than thinking with surrender of already formed ideas and detachment from facts already learned is just to stick by what is already said, looking about for something with which to buttress it against attack.

Thus sects arise: schools of opinion. Each selects that set of conditions that appeals to it; and then erects them into a complete and independent truth, instead of treating them as a factor in a problem, needing adjustment.

The fundamental factors in the educative process are an immature, undeveloped being; and certain social aims, meanings, values incarnate in the matured experience of the adult. The educative process is the due interaction of these forces. Such a conception of each in relation to the other as facilitates completest and freest interaction is the essence of educational theory.

But here comes the effort of thought. It is easier to see the conditions in their separateness, to insist upon one at the expense of the other, to make antagonists of them, than to discover a reality to which each belongs. The easy thing is to seize upon something in the nature of the child, or upon something in the developed consciousness of the adult, and insist upon *that* as the key to the whole problem.

From John Dewey, *The Child and the Curriculum* (Chicago: University of Chicago Press, 1900) and *The School and Society* (Chicago: University of Chicago Press, 1902). Reprinted by permission of the University of Chicago Press and Mrs. John Dewey.

When this happens a really serious practical problem—that of interaction—is transformed into an unreal, and hence insoluble, theoretic problem. Instead of seeing the educative steadily and as a whole, we see conflicting terms. We get the case of the child *vs.* the curriculum; of the individual nature *vs.* social culture. Below all other divisions in pedagogic opinion lies this opposition.

The child lives in a somewhat narrow world of personal contacts. Things hardly come within his experience unless they touch, intimately and obviously, his own well-being, or that of his family and friends. His world is a world of persons with their personal interests, rather than a realm of facts and laws. Not truth, in the sense of conformity to external fact, but affection and sympathy, is its keynote. As against this, the course of study met in the school presents material stretching back indefinitely in time, and extending outward indefinitely into space. The child is taken out of his familiar physical environment, hardly more than a square mile or so in area, into the wide world—yes, and even to the bounds of the solar system. His little span of personal memory and tradition is overlaid with the long centuries of the history of all peoples.

Again, the child's life is an integral, a total one. He passes quickly and readily from one topic to another, as from one spot to another, but is not conscious of transition or breaks. There is no conscious isolation, hardly conscious distinction. The things that occupy him are held together by the unity of the personal and social interests which his life carries along. Whatever is uppermost in his mind constitutes to him, for the time being, the whole universe. That universe is fluid and fluent; its contents dissolve and re-form with amazing rapidity. But, after all, it is the child's own world. It has the unity and completeness of his own life. He goes to school, and various studies divide and fractionize the world for him. Geography selects, it abstracts and analyzes one set of facts, and from one particular point of view. Arithmetic is another division, grammar another department, and so on indefinitely.

Again, in school each of these subjects is classified. Facts are torn away from their original place in experience and rearranged with reference to some general principle. Classification is not a matter of child experience; things do not come to the individual pigeonholed. The vital ties of affection, the connecting bonds of activity, hold together the variety of his personal experiences. The adult mind is so familiar with the notion of logically ordered facts that it does not recognize—it cannot realize—the amount of separating and reformulating which the facts of direct experience have to undergo before they can appear as a "study," or branch of learning. A principle, for the intellect, has had to be distinguished and defined; facts have had to be interpreted in relation to this principle, not as they are in themselves. They have had to be regathered about a new center which is wholly abstract and ideal. All this means a development of a special intellectual interest. It means ability to view facts impartially and objectively, that is, without reference to their place and meaning in one's own experience. It means capacity to analyze and to synthesize. It means highly matured intellectual habits and the command of a definite technique and apparatus of scientific inquiry. The studies as classified are the product, in a word, of the science of the ages, not of the experience of the child.

These apparent deviations and differences between child and curriculum might be almost indefinitely widened. But we have here sufficiently fundamental divergences: first, the narrow but personal world of the child against the impersonal but infinitely extended world of space and time; second, the unity, the single whole-heartedness of the child's life, and the specializations and divisions of the curriculum; third, an abstract principle of logical classification and arrangement, and the practical and emotional bonds of child life.

From these elements of conflict grow up different educational sects. One school fixes its attention upon the importance of the subject-matter of the curriculum as compared with the contents of the child's own experience. It is as if they said: Is life petty, narrow, and crude? Then studies reveal the great, wide universe with all its fulness and complexity of meaning. Is the life of the child egoistic, self-centered, impulsive? Then in these studies is found an objective universe of truth, law, and order. Is his experience confused, vague, uncertain, at the mercy of the moment's caprice and circumstance? Then studies introduce a world arranged on the basis of eternal and general truth; a world where all is measured and defined. Hence the moral: ignore and minimize the child's individual peculiarities, whims, and experiences. They are what we need to get away from. They are to be obscured or eliminated. As educators our work is precisely to substitute for these superficial and casual affairs stable and well-ordered realities; and these are found in studies and lessons.

Subdivide each topic into studies; each study into lessons; each lesson into specific facts and formulae. Let the child proceed step by step to master each one of these separate parts, and at last he will have covered the entire ground. The road which looks so long when viewed in its entirety is easily traveled, considered as a series of particular steps. Thus emphasis is put upon the logical subdivisions and consecutions of the subject-matter. Problems of instruction are problems of procuring texts giving logical parts and sequences, and of presenting these portions in class in a similar definite and graded way. Subject-matter furnishes the end, and it determines method. The child is simply the immature being who is to be matured; he is the superficial being who is to be deepened; his is narrow experience which is to be widened. It is his to receive, to accept. His part is fulfilled when he is ductile and docile.

Not so, says the other sect. The child is the starting-point, the center, and the end. His development, his growth, is the ideal. It alone furnishes the standard. To the growth of the child all studies are subservient; they are instruments valued as they serve the needs of growth. Personality, character, is more than subject-matter. Not knowledge or information, but self-realization, is the goal. To possess all the world of knowledge and lose one's own self is as awful a fate in education as in religion. Moreover, subject-matter never can be got into the child from without. Learning is active. It involves reaching out of the mind. It involves organic assimilation starting from within. Literally, we must take our stand with the child and our departure from him. It is he and not the subject-matter which determines both quality and quantity of learning.

The only significant method is the method of the mind as it reaches out and assimilates. Subject-matter is but spiritual food, possible nutritive material. It cannot digest itself; it cannot of its own accord turn into bone and muscle and blood. The source of whatever is dead, mechanical, and formal in schools is found precisely in the subordination of the life and experience of the child to the curriculum. It is because of this that "study" has become a synonym for what is irksome, and a lesson identical with a task.

This fundamental opposition of child and curriculum set up by these two modes of doctrine can be duplicated in a series of other terms. "Discipline" is the watchword of those who magnify the course of study; "interest" that of those who blazon "The Child" upon their banner. The standpoint of the former is logical; that of the latter psychological. The first emphasizes the necessity of adequate training and scholarship on the part of the teacher; the latter that of need of sympathy with the child, and knowledge of his natural instincts. "Guidance and control" are the catchwords of one school; "freedom and initiative" of the other. Law is asserted here; spontaneity proclaimed there. The old, the conservation of what has been achieved in the pain and toil of the ages, is dear to the one; the new, change, progress, wins the affection of the other. Inertness and routine, chaos and anarchism, are accusations bandied back and forth. Neglect of the sacred authority of duty is charged by one side, only to be met by counter-charges of suppression of individuality through tyrannical despotism.

Such oppositions are rarely carried to their logical conclusion. Common-sense recoils at the extreme character of these results. They are left to theorists, while common-sense vibrates back and forth in a maze of inconsistent compromise. The need of getting theory and practical common-sense into closer connection suggests a return to our original thesis: that we have here conditions which are necessarily related to each other in the educative process, since this is precisely one of interaction and adjustment.

What, then, is the problem? It is just to get rid of the prejudicial notion that there is some gap in kind (as distinct from degree) between the child's experience and the various forms of subject-matter that make up the course of study. From the side of the child, it is a question of seeing how his experience already contains within itself elements—facts and truths—of just the same sort as those entering into the formulated study; and, what is of more importance, of how it contains within itself the attitudes, the motives, and the interests which have operated in developing and organizing the subject-matter to the plane which it now occupies. From the side of the studies, it is a question of interpreting them as outgrowths of forces operating in the child's life, and of discovering the steps that intervene between the child's present experience and their richer maturity.

Abandon the notion of subject-matter as something fixed and ready-made in itself, outside the child's experience; cease thinking of the child's experience as also something hard and fast; see it as something fluent, embryonic, vital; and we realize that the child and the curriculum are simply two limits which define a single process. Just as two points define a straight line, so the present standpoint of the child and the facts and truths of studies define instruction. It is continuous reconstruction, moving from the child's present experience out into that represented by the organized bodies of truth that we call studies.

On the face of it, the various studies, arithmetic, geography, language, botany,

etc., are themselves experience—they are that of the race. They embody the cumulative outcome of the efforts, the strivings, and the successes of the human race
generation after generation. They present this, not as a mere accumulation, not as
a miscellaneous heap of separate bits of experience, but in some organized and
systematized way—that is, as reflectively formulated.

Hence, the facts and truths that enter into the child's present experience, and
those contained in the subject-matter of studies, are the initial and final terms of
one reality. To oppose one to the other is to oppose the infancy and maturity of
the same growing life; it is to set the moving tendency and the final result of the
same process over against each other; it is to hold that the nature and the destiny
of the child war with each other.

If such be the case, the problem of the relation of the child and the curriculum
presents itself in this guise: Of what use, educationally speaking, is it to be able to
see the end in the beginning? How does it assist us in dealing with the early stages
of growth to be able to anticipate its later phases? The studies, as we have agreed,
represent the possibilities of development inherent in the child's immediate crude
experience. But, after all, they are not parts of that present and immediate life.
Why, then, or how, make account of them?

Asking such a question suggests its own answer. To see the outcome is to know
in what direction the present experience is moving, provided it move normally and
soundly. The far-away point, which is of no significance to us simply as far away,
becomes of huge importance the moment we take it as defining a present direction
of movement. Taken in this way it is no remote and distant result to be achieved,
but a guiding method in dealing with the present. The systematized and defined
experience of the adult mind, in other words, is of value to us in interpreting the
child's life as it immediately shows itself, and in passing on to guidance or direction.

Let us look for a moment at these two ideas: interpretation and guidance. The
child's present experience is in no way self-explanatory. It is not final, but transi-
tional. It is nothing complete in itself, but just a sign or index of certain growth-
tendencies. As long as we confine our gaze to what the child here and now puts
forth, we are confused and misled. We cannot read its meaning. Extreme deprecia-
tions of the child morally and intellectually, and sentimental idealizations of him,
have their root in a common fallacy. Both spring from taking stages of a growth or
movement as something cut off and fixed. The first fails to see the promise contained in feelings and deeds which, taken by themselves, are uncompromising and
repellent; the second fails to see that even the most pleasing and beautiful exhibitions are but signs, and that they begin to spoil and rot the moment they are
treated as achievements.

What we need is something which will enable us to interpret, to appraise, the
elements in the child's present puttings forth and fallings away, his exhibitions of
power and weakness, in the light of some larger growth-process in which they have
their place. Only in this way can we discriminate. If we isolate the child's present
inclinations, purposes, and experiences from the place they occupy and the part
they have to perform in a developing experience, all stand upon the same level;
all alike are equally good and equally bad. But in the movement of life different
elements stand upon different planes of value. Some of the child's deeds are symp-

toms of a waning tendency; they are survivals in functioning of an organ which has done its part and is passing out of vital use. To give positive attention to such qualities is to arrest development upon a lower level. It is systematically to maintain a rudimentary phase of growth. Other activities are signs of a culminating power and interest; to them applies the maxim of striking while the iron is hot. As regards them, it is perhaps a matter of now or never. Selected, utilized, emphasized, they may mark a turning-point for good in the child's whole career; neglected, an opportunity goes, never to be recalled. Other acts and feelings are prophetic; they represent the dawning of flickering light that will shine steadily only in the far future. As regards them there is little at present to do but give them fair and full chance, waiting for the future for definite direction.

Just as, upon the whole, it was the weakness of the "old education" that it made invidious comparisons between the immaturity of the child and the maturity of the adult, regarding the former as something to be got away from as soon as possible and as much as possible; so it is the danger of the "new education" that it regard the child's present powers and interests as something finally significant in themselves. In truth, his learnings and achievements are fluid and moving. They change from day to day and from hour to hour.

It will do harm if child-study leaves in the popular mind the impression that a child of a given age has a positive equipment of purposes and interests to be cultivated just as they stand. Interests in reality are but attitudes toward possible experiences; they are not achievements; their worth is in the leverage they afford, not in the accomplishment they represent. To take the phenomena presented at a given age as in any way self-explanatory or self-contained is inevitably to result in indulgence and spoiling. Any power, whether of child or adult, is indulged when it is taken on its given and present level in consciousness. Its genuine meaning is in the propulsion it affords toward a higher level. It is just something to do with. Appealing to the interest upon the present plane means excitation; it means playing with a power so as continually to stir it up without directing it toward definite achievement. Continuous initiation, continuous starting of activities that do not arrive, is, for all practical purposes, as bad as the continual repression of initiative in conformity with supposed interests of some more perfect thought or will. It is as if the child were forever tasting and never eating; always having his palate tickled upon the emotional side, but never getting the organic satisfaction that comes only with digestion of food and transformation of it into working power.

As against such a view, the subject-matter of science and history and art serves to reveal the real child to us. We do not know the meaning either of his tendencies or of his performances excepting as we take them as germinating seed, or opening bud, of some fruit to be borne. The whole world of visual nature is all too small an answer to the problem of the meaning of the child's instinct for light and form. The entire science of physics is none too much to interpret adequately to us what is involved in some simple demand of the child for explanation of some casual change that has attracted his attention. The art of Raphael or of Corot is none too much to enable us to value the impulses stirring in the child when he draws and daubs.

So much for the use of the subject-matter in interpretation. The further employment in direction or guidance is but an expansion of the same thought. To interpret the fact is to see it in its vital movement, to see it in its relation to growth. But to view it as part of a normal growth is to secure the basis for guiding it. Guidance is not external imposition. *It is freeing the life-process for its own most adequate fulfilment.* What was said about disregard of the child's present experience because of its remoteness from nature experience; and of the sentimental idealization of the child's naïve caprices and performances, may be repeated here with slightly altered phrase. There are those who see no alternative between forcing the child from without, or leaving him entirely alone. Seeing no alternative, some choose one mode, some another. Both fall into the same fundamental error. Both fail to see that development is a definite process, having its own law which can be fulfilled only when adequate and normal conditions are provided. Really to interpret the child's present crude impulses in counting, measuring, and arranging things in rhythmic series involves mathematical scholarship—a knowledge of the mathematical formulae and relations which have, in the history of the race, grown out of just such crude beginnings. To see the whole history of development which intervenes between these two terms is simply to see what step the child needs to take just here and now; to what use he needs to put his blind impulse in order that it may get clarity and gain force.

If, once more, the "old education" tended to ignore the dynamic quality, the developing force inherent in the child's present experience, and therefore to assume that direction and control were just matters of arbitrarily putting the child in a given path and compelling him to walk there, the "new education" is in danger of taking the idea of development in altogether too formal and empty a way. The child is expected to "develop" this or that fact or truth out of his own mind. He is told to think things out, or work things out for himself, without being supplied any of the environing conditions which are requisite to start and guide thought. Nothing can be developed from nothing; nothing but the crude can be developed out of the crude—and this is what surely happens when we throw the child back upon his achieved self as a finality, and invite him to spin new truths of nature or of conduct out of that. It is certainly as futile to expect a child to evolve a universe out of his own mere mind as it is for a philosopher to attempt that task. Development does not mean just getting something out of the mind. It is a development of experience and into experience that is really wanted. And this is impossible save as just that educative medium is provided which will enable the powers and interests that have been selected as valuable to function. They must operate, and how they operate will depend almost entirely upon the stimuli which surround them and the material upon which they exercise themselves. The problem of direction is thus the problem of selecting appropriate stimuli for instincts and impulses which it is desired to employ in the gaining of new experience. What new experiences are desirable, and thus what stimuli are needed, it is impossible to tell except as there is some comprehension of the development which is aimed at; except, in a word, as the adult knowledge is drawn upon as revealing the possible career open to the child. . . .

I may have exaggerated somewhat in order to make plain the typical points of the old education: its passivity of attitude, its mechanical massing of children, its uniformity of curriculum and method. It may be summed up by stating that the center of gravity is outside the child. It is in the teacher, the textbook, anywhere and everywhere you please except in the immediate instincts and activities of the child himself. On that basis there is not much to be said about the *life* of the child. A good deal might be said about the studying of the child, but the school is not the place where the child *lives*. Now the change which is coming into our education is the shifting of the center of gravity. It is a change, a revolution, not unlike that introduced by Copernicus when the astronomical center shifted from the earth to the sun. In this case the child becomes the sun about which the appliances of education revolve; he is the center about which they are organized.

If we take an example from an ideal home, where the parent is intelligent enough to recognize what is best for the child, and is able to supply what is needed, we find the child learning through the social converse and constitution of the family. There are certain points of interest and value to him in the conversation carried on: statements are made, inquiries arise, topics are discussed and the child continually learns. He states his experiences, his misconceptions are corrected. Again the child participates in the household occupations, and thereby gets habits of industry, order and regard for the rights and ideas of others, and the fundamental habit of subordinating his activities to the general interest of the household. Participation in these household tasks becomes an opportunity for gaining knowledge. The ideal home would naturally have a workshop where the child could work out his constructive instincts. It would have a miniature laboratory in which his inquiries could be directed. The life of the child would extend out of doors to the garden, surrounding fields, and forests. He would have his excursions, his walks and talks, in which the large world out of doors would open to him.

Now, if we organize and generalize all of this, we have the ideal school. There is no mystery about it, no wonderful discovery or pedagogy or educational theory. It is simply a question of doing systematically and in a large, intelligent, and competent way what for various reasons can be done in most households only in a comparatively meager and haphazard manner. In the first place, the ideal home has to be enlarged. The child must be brought into contact with more grown people and with more children in order that there may be the freest and richest social life. Moreover, the occupations and relationships of the home environment are not specially selected for the growth of the child, the main object is something else, and what the child can get out of them is incidental. Hence the need of a school. In this school the life of the child becomes the all-controlling aim. All the media necessary to further the growth of the child center there. Learning? certainly, but living primarily, and learning through and in relation to this living. When we take the life of the child centered and organized in this way, we do not find that he is first of all a listening being; quite the contrary.

The statement so frequently made that education means "drawing out" is excellent, if we mean simply to contrast it with the process of pouring in. But, after all, it is difficult to connect the idea of drawing out with the ordinary doings of the child of three, four, seven, or eight years of age. He is already running over, spilling over, with activities of all kinds. He is not a purely latent being whom the adult has to approach with great caution and skill in order gradually to draw out some hidden germ of activity. The child is already intensely active, and the question of education is the question of taking hold of his activities, of giving them direction. Through direction, through organized use, they tend toward valuable results, instead of scattering or being left to merely impulsive expression.

If we keep this before us, the difficulty I find uppermost in the minds of many people regarding what is termed the new education is not so much solved as dissolved; it disappears. A question often asked is: If you begin with the child's ideas, impulses, and interests, all so crude, so random and scattering, so little refined or spiritualized, how is he going to get the necessary discipline, culture, and information? If there were no way open to us except to excite and indulge these impulses of the child, the question might well be asked. We should either have to ignore and repress the activities or else to humor them. But if we have organization of equipment and of materials, there is another path open to us. We can direct the child's activities, giving them exercise along certain lines, and can thus lead up to the goal which logically stands at the end of the paths followed.

"If wishes were horses, beggars would ride." Since they are not, since really to satisfy an impulse or interest means to work it out, and working it out involves running up against obstacles, becoming acquainted with materials, exercising ingenuity, patience, persistence, alertness, it of necessity involves discipline—ordering of power—and supplies knowledge. Take the example of the little child who wants to make a box. If he stops short with the imagination or wish, he certainly will not get discipline. But when he attempts to realize his impulse, it is a question of making his idea definite, making it into a plan, of taking the right kind of wood, measuring the parts needed, giving them the necessary proportions, etc. There is involved the preparation of materials, the sawing, planing, the sandpapering, making all the edges and corners to fit. Knowledge of tools and processes is inevitable. If the child realizes his instinct and makes the box, there is plenty of opportunity to gain discipline and perseverance, to exercise effort in overcoming obstacles, and to attain as well a great deal of information.

So undoubtedly the little child who thinks he would like to cook has little idea of what it means or costs, or what it requires. It is simply a desire to "mess around," perhaps to imitate the activities of older people. And it is doubtless possible to let ourselves down to that level and simply humor that interest. But here, too, if the impulse is exercised, utilized, it runs up against the actual world of hard conditions, to which it must accommodate itself; and there again come in the factors of discipline and knowledge. One of the children became impatient, recently, at having to work things out by a long method of experimentation, and said "Why do we bother with this? Let's follow a recipe in a cookbook." The teacher asked the children where the recipe came from, and the conversation showed that if they simply followed this they would not understand the reasons for what they were doing. They were then quite willing to go on with the experimental work. To follow that work will, indeed, give an illustration of just the point in question. Their occupation happened that day to be the cooking of eggs, as making a transition from the cooking of vegetables to that of meats. In order to get a basis of comparison they first summarized the constituent food elements in the vegetables and made a preliminary comparison with those found in meat. Thus they found that the woody

fiber or cellulose in vegetables corresponded to the connective tissue in meat, giving
the element of form and structure. They found that starch and starchy products
were characteristic of the vegetables, that minerals salts were found in both alike,
and that there was fat in both—a small quantity in vegetable food and a large
amount in animal. They were prepared then to take up the study of albumen as the
characteristic feature of animal food, corresponding to starch in the vegetables, and
were ready to consider the conditions requisite for the proper treatment of albumen
—the eggs serving as the material of experiment.

They experimented first by taking water at various temperatures, finding out
when it was scalding, simmering, and boiling hot, and ascertained the effect of the
various degrees of temperature on the white of the egg. That worked out, they were
prepared, not simply to cook eggs, but to understand the principle involved in the
cooking of eggs. I do not wish to lose sight of the universal in the particular incident. For the child simply to desire to cook an egg, and accordingly drop it in water
for three minutes, and take it out when he is told, is not educative. But for the
child to realize his own impulse by recognizing the facts, materials, and conditions
involved, and then to regulate his impulse through that recognition, is educative.
This is the difference, upon which I wish to insist, between exciting or indulging an
interest and realizing it through its direction. . . .

If you observe little children, you will find they are interested in the world of
things mainly in its connection with people, as a background and medium of human concerns. Many anthropologists have told us there are certain identities in the
child interests with those of primitive life. There is a sort of natural recurrence of
the child mind to the typical activities of primitive peoples; witness the hut which
the boy likes to build in the yard, playing hunt, with bows, arrows, spears, and so
on. Again the question comes: What are we to do with this interest—are we to ignore
it, or just excite and draw it out? Or shall we get hold of it and direct it to something ahead, something better? Some of the work that has been planned for our
seven-year-old children has the latter end in view—to utilize this interest so that it
shall become a means of seeing the progress of the human race. The children begin
by imagining present conditions taken away until they are in contact with nature at
first hand. That takes them back to a hunting people, to a people living in caves or
trees and getting a precarious subsistence by hunting and fishing. They imagine as
far as possible the various natural physical conditions adapted to that sort of life;
say, a hilly, woody slope, near mountains, and a river where fish would be abundant. Then they go on in imagination through the hunting to the semi-agricultural
stage, and through the nomadic to the settled agricultural stage. The point I wish
to make is that there is abundant opportunity thus given for actual study, for inquiry which results in gaining information. So, while the instinct primarily appeals
to the social side, the interest of the child in people and their doings is carried on
into the larger world of reality. For example, the children had some idea of primitive weapons, of the stone arrowhead, etc. That provided occasion for the testing of
materials as regards their friability, their shape, texture, etc., resulting in a lesson in
mineralogy, as they examined the different stones to find which was best suited to the
purpose. The discussion of the iron age supplied a demand for the construction
of a smelting oven made out of clay and of considerable size. If the children did

not get their drafts right at first, the mouth of the furnace not being in proper relation to the vent as to size and position, instruction in the principles of combustion, the nature of drafts and of fuel, was required. Yet the instruction was not given ready-made; it was first needed, and then arrived at experimentally. Then the children took some material, such as copper, and went through a series of experiments, fusing it, working it into objects; and the same experiments were made with lead and other metals. This work has been also a continuous course in geography, since the children have had to imagine and work out the various physical conditions necessary to the different forms of social life implied. What would be the physical conditions appropriate to pastoral life? to the beginning of agriculture? to fishing? What would be the natural method of exchange between these peoples? Having worked out such points in conversation, they have afterward represented them in maps and sand-molding. Then they have gained ideas of the various forms of the configuration of the earth, and at the same time have seen them in their relation to human activity, so that they are not simply external facts but are fused and welded with social conceptions regarding the life and progress of humanity. The result, to my mind, justifies completely the conviction that children, in a year of such work (of five hours a week altogether), get infinitely more acquaintance with facts of science, geography, and anthropology than they get where information is the professed end and object, where they are simply set to learning facts in fixed lessons. As to discipline, they get more training of attention, more power of interpretation, of drawing inferences, of acute observation and continuous reflection, than if they were put to working out arbitrary problems simply for the sake of discipline. . . .

Every study or subject thus has two aspects: one for the scientist as a scientist; the other for the teacher as a teacher. These two aspects are in no sense opposed or conflicting. But neither are they immediately identical. For the scientist, the subject-matter represents simply a given body of truth to be employed in locating new problems, instituting new researches, and carrying them through to a verified outcome. To him the subject-matter of the science is self-contained. He refers various portions of it to each other; he connects new facts with it. He is not, as a scientist, called upon to travel outside its particular bounds; if he does, it is only to get more facts of the same general sort. The problem of the teacher is a different one. As a teacher he is not concerned with adding new facts to the science he teaches; in propounding new hypotheses or in verifying them. He is concerned with the subject-matter of the science as *representing a given stage and phase of the development of experience*. His problem is that of inducing a vital and personal experiencing. Hence, what concerns him, as teacher, is the ways in which that subject may become a part of experience; what there is in the child's present that is usable with reference to it; how such elements are to be used; how his own knowledge of the subject-matter may assist in interpreting the child's needs and doings, and determine the medium in which the child should be placed in order that his growth may be properly directed. He is concerned, not with the subject-matter as such, but with the subject-matter as a related factor in a total and growing experience. Thus to see it is to psychologize it.

It is the failure to keep in mind the double aspect of subject-matter which causes the curriculum and child to be set over against each other as described in our early pages. The subject-matter, just as it is for the scientist, has no direct relationship to the child's present experience. It stands outside of it. The danger here is not a merely theoretical one. We are practically threatened on all sides. Textbook and teacher vie with each other in presenting to the child the subject-matter as it stands to the specialist. Such modification and revision as it undergoes are a mere elimination of certain scientific difficulties, and the general reduction to a lower intellectual level. The material is not translated into life-terms, but is directly offered as a substitute for, or an external annex to, the child's present life.

Three typical evils result: In the first place, the lack of an organic connection with what the child has already seen and felt and loved makes the material purely formal and symbolic. There is a sense in which it is impossible to value too highly the formal and the symbolic. The genuine form, the real symbol, serve as methods in the holding and discovery of truth. They are tools by which the individual pushes out most surely and widely into unexplored areas. They are means by which he brings to bear whatever of reality he has succeeded in gaining in past searchings. But this happens only when the symbol really symbolizes—when it stands for and sums up in shorthand actual experiences which the individual has already gone through. A symbol which is induced from without, which has not been led up to in preliminary activities, is, as we say, a *bare* or *mere* symbol; it is dead and barren. Now, any fact, whether of arithmetic, or geography, or grammar, which is not led up to and into out of something which has previously occupied a significant position in the child's life for its own sake, is forced into this position. It is not a reality, but just the sign of a reality which *might* be experienced if certain conditions were fulfilled. But the abrupt presentation of the fact as something known by others, and requiring only to be studied and learned by the child, rules out such conditions of fulfilment. It condemns the fact to be a hieroglyph: it would mean something if one only had the key. The clue being lacking, it remains an idle curiosity, to fret and obstruct the mind, a dead weight to burden it.

The second evil in this external presentation is lack of motivation. There are not only no facts or truths which have been previously felt as such with which to appropriate and assimilate the new, but there is no craving, no need, no demand. When the subject-matter has been psychologized, that is, viewed as an outgrowth of present tendencies and activities, it is easy to locate in the present some obstacle, intellectual, practical, or ethical, which can be handled more adequately if the truth in question be mastered. This need supplies motive for the learning. An end which is the child's own carries him on to possess the means of its accomplishment. But when material is directly supplied in the form of a lesson to be learned as a lesson, the connecting links of need and aim are conspicuous for their absence. What we mean by the mechanical and dead in instruction is a result of this lack of motivation. The organic and vital mean interaction—they mean play of mental demand and material supply.

The third evil is that even the most scientific matter, arranged in most logical fashion, loses this quality, when presented in external, ready-made fashion, by the time it gets to the child. It has to undergo some modification in order to shut out some phases too hard to grasp, and to reduce some of the attendant difficulties. What happens? Those things which are most significant to the scientific man, and most valuable in the logic of actual inquiry and classification, drop out. The really thought-provoking character is obscured, and the organizing function disappears. Or, as we commonly say, the child's reasoning powers, the faculty of abstraction and generalization, are not adequately developed. So the subject-matter is evacuated of its logical value, and, though it is what it is only from the logical standpoint, is presented as stuff only for "memory." This is the contradiction: the child gets the advantage neither of the adult logical formulation, nor of his own native competencies of apprehension and response. Hence the logic of the child is hampered and mortified, and we are almost fortunate if he does not get actual non-science, flat and commonplace residua of what was gaining scientific vitality a generation or two ago—degenerate reminiscence of what someone else once formulated on the basis of the experience that some further person had, once upon a time, experienced.

The train of evils does not cease. It is all too common for opposed erroneous theories to play straight into each other's hands. Psychological considerations may be slurred or shoved to one side; they cannot be crowded out. Put out of the door, they come back through the window. Somehow and somewhere motive must be appealed to, connection must be established between the mind and its material. There is no question of getting along without this bond of connection; the only question is whether it be such as grows out of the material itself in relation to the mind, or be imported and hitched on from some outside source. If the subject-matter of the lessons be such as to have an appropriate place within the expanding consciousness of the child, if it grows out of his own past doings, thinkings, and sufferings, and grows into application in further achievements and receptivities, then no device or trick of method has to be resorted to in order to enlist "interest." The psychologized is of interest—that is, it is placed in the whole of conscious life so that it shares the worth of that life. But the externally presented material, conceived and generated in standpoints and attitudes remote from the child, and developed in motives alien to him, has no such place of its own. Hence the recourse to adventitious leverage to push it in, to factitious drill to drive it in, to artificial bribe to lure it in.

Three aspects of this recourse to outside ways for giving the subject-matter some psychological meaning may be worth mentioning. Familiarity breeds contempt, but it also breeds something like affection. We get used to the chains we wear, and we miss them when removed. 'Tis an old story that through custom we finally embrace what at first wore a hideous mien. Unpleasant because meaningless, activities may get agreeable if long enough persisted in. *It is possible for the mind to develop interest in a routine or mechanical procedure if conditions are continually supplied which demand that mode of operation and preclude any other sort.* I frequently hear dulling devices and empty exercises defended and extolled because "the children take such an 'interest' in them." Yes, that is the worst of it; the mind, shut out from worthy employ and missing the taste of adequate performance, comes down to the level of that which is left to it to know and do, and perforce takes an interest in a cabined and cramped experience. To find satisfaction in its own exercise is the normal law of mind, and if large and meaningful business for the mind be denied, it tries to content itself with the formal movements that remain to it—and too often succeeds, save in those cases of more intense activity which cannot accommodate themselves, and that make up the unruly and *declassé* of our school product.

An interest in the formal apprehension of symbols and in their memorized reproduction becomes in many pupils a substitute for the original and vital interest in
reality; and all because, the subject-matter of the course of study being out of relation to the concrete mind of the individual, some substitute bond to hold it in
some kind of working relation to the mind must be discovered and elaborated.

The second substitute for living motivation in the subject-matter is that of con-
trast-effects; the material of the lesson is rendered interesting, if not in itself, at
least in contrast with some alternative experience. To learn the lesson is more interesting than to take a scolding, be held up to general ridicule, stay after school,
receive degradingly low marks, or fail to be promoted. And very much of what
goes by the name of "discipline," and prides itself upon opposing the doctrines of
a soft pedagogy and upon upholding the banner of effort and duty, is nothing more
or less than just this appeal to "interest" in its obverse aspect—to fear, to dislike
of various kinds of physical, social, and personal pain. The subject-matter does not
appeal; it cannot appeal; it lacks origin and bearing in a growing experience. So
the appeal is to the thousand and one outside and irrelevant agencies which may
serve to throw, by sheer rebuff and rebound, the mind back upon the material from
which it is constantly wandering.

Human nature being what it is, however, it tends to seek its motivation in the
agreeable rather than in the disagreeable, in direct pleasure rather than in alternative pain. And so has come up the modern theory and practice of the "interesting,"
in the false sense of that term. The material is still left; so far as its own characteristics are concerned, just material externally selected and formulated. It is still just so
much geography and arithmetic and grammar study; not so much potentiality of
child-experience with regard to language, earth, and numbered and measured reality.
Hence the difficulty of bringing the mind to bear upon it; hence its repulsiveness;
the tendency for attention to wander; for other acts and images to crowd in and
expel the lesson. The legitimate way out is to transform the material; to psychologize
it—that is, once more, to take it and to develop it within the range and scope of
the child's life. But it is easier and simpler to leave it as it is, and then by trick
of method to *arouse* interest, to *make* it *interesting*; to cover it with sugar-coating;
to conceal its barrenness by intermediate and unrelated material; and finally, as it
were, to get the child to swallow and digest the unpalatable morsel while he is enjoying tasting something quite different. But alas for the analogy! Mental assimilation is a matter of consciousness; and if the attention has not been playing upon
the actual material, that has not been apprehended, nor worked into faculty.

How, then, stands the case of Child *vs.* Curriculum? What shall the verdict be?
The radical fallacy in the original pleadings with which we set out is the supposition
that we have no choice save either to leave the child to his own unguided spontaneity or to inspire direction upon him from without. Action is response; it is
adaptation, adjustment. There is no such thing as sheer self-activity possible—because all activity takes place in a medium, in a situation, and with reference to its
conditions. But, again, no such thing as imposition of truth from without, as inser-
tion of truth from without, is possible. All depends upon the activity which the
mind itself undergoes in responding to what is presented from without. Now, the
value of the formulated wealth of knowledge that makes up the course of study is

that it may enable the educator *to determine the environment of the child* and thus by indirection to direct. Its primary value, its primary indication, is for the teacher, not for the child. It says to the teacher: Such and such are the capacities, the fulfilments, in truth and beauty and behavior, open to these children. Now see to it that day by day the conditions are such that *their own activities* move inevitably in this direction, toward such culmination of themselves. Let the child's nature fulfil its own destiny revealed to you in whatever of science and art and industry the world now holds as its own.

Questions for Discussion

1. Describe Dewey's criticisms of traditional education. Are his criticisms justified?
2. In what specific ways do you find that the educational ideas, advocated by Dewey, are similar to or different from those advocated by Rousseau and Montessori?
3. What particular kinds of curriculum, teaching methods, and examination procedures are implied by Dewey's ideas on education?
4. Well, did you look at your own learning environment? Is it infused with pragmatic educational principles? If so, do you like them?

4 Education As Reconstruction

Theodore Brameld

If the school should be intimately involved with the problems of the community, as Dewey said, then should the school seek to change the values of the community, or should it preserve and enhance those values? The next two selections explore that question.

Brameld points out two of the important purposes which should guide teachers today: "To channel the energies of education toward the reconstruction of the economic system . . . and the establishment of a genuine international order." He stands, then, for the schools acting as change agents in the society. But, why should the schools be instruments for bringing about change? Should that change be for the purposes Brameld advocates? How can the school bring about a change in the society? Notice how Brameld uses his five "buttresses" for an educational philosophy to provide answers to these questions.

We have now perhaps sampled enough of the difficulties integral with the central educational-political problem of our time, so that we may turn to certain more positive considerations. The aim of these considerations—besides helping to clarify the rather oversimplified generalizations already outlined—is again the central one of bridge building: of providing a continuous and trustworthy span between the two shores of common enlightenment and objective social achievement. The blueprint of such a span may be considered around at least five buttresses. These may be called, respectively, an adequate theory of human nature; an adequate theory of social forces; an adequate theory of the state; an adequate theory of government; and an adequate theory of normative commitment. Each of these is connected with the others by the two great cables of an adequate theory of education and of politics.

Of all five philosophic buttresses, the first, concerning human nature, is thus far the most satisfactory in its present stage of formulation. By both anticipating and utilizing the investigations of modern experimental psychology, philosophers of a naturalistic and organismic preference have been converging for at least two generations toward the guiding hypothesis that human beings are best characterized in terms of a complex, dynamic fusion of drives. This hypothesis, to which the gestalt, functional, behaviorist, Freudian, and other psychologies have all contributed richly, has now reached sufficient crystallization for us confidently to declare that educational method could and should become transformed—transformed in so far, that is to say, as child development, emotional-intellectual growth, and other vital aspects of learning-as-living in their more individualized emphases are properly concerned.

From pp. 61–194 in *Ends and Means in Education: A Midcentury Appraisal* by Theodore Brameld. Copyright, 1950 by Harper & Row, Publishers, Incorporated. Reprinted by permission of the publishers.

In the perspective of our theme, this fruitful approach to human nature has both its positive and negative aspects. Positively, it supports the prime political assumption of democracy that people of every race, nationality, religion, or social status are sufficiently alike in their basic structures, energies, potential abilities, to reach a vastly higher level of competence, self-reliance, and achievement than social opportunity has thus far typically offered. Or, still more relevantly, the capacities of human beings for appreciating the requisites of complete self-government are now proving to be, not merely a pleasant sentiment, but a demonstrable expectation—an expectation supported even by scientific recognition that the desire for self-government, as one form of participation, is itself a basic drive of man. The problem for us thus becomes one of charging these capacities with the kind of educational energy which no longer conceals or warps economic and similar meanings, but rather reveals and translates them into democratic institutions consistent with such meanings.

Negatively, however, the contemporary theory of human dynamics has largely failed to cope with just this problem of translation. For the most part it has neither asked nor answered forthrightly the crucial question of what kind of humane order is essential so that human potentialities may flower to the maximum. In the degree of its concentration upon the psychological aspects of education to the neglect of the sociological, we venture the severe criticism that recent educational theory becomes thus far an irresponsible theory. It has not clearly recognized—rather it has evaded—the direct and logical consequence of its own priceless contribution; namely, the double necessity at once to destroy and to create social arrangements according to whether these frustrate or release for satisfaction the wants of the largest possible majority of men.

The need of a second buttress, an adequate theory of social forces, follows in part from the first. In order that human nature may reach the heights of fulfillment of which we now know it is capable, we are required not only to reconstruct institutional patterns but to analyze, utilize, or paralyze, as the case may be, those forces in our culture which accelerate or retard such reconstruction.

Here educational theory thus far has been woefully weak, so weak that we can scarcely point to a single outstanding educational contribution even remotely comparable to those bearing upon human nature. Take this instance: one of the most seminal, if not the single most seminal, of American contributors to a theory of social forces is still scarcely known to the teachers of our public schools, or perhaps even to most of us who teach these teachers. We refer, of course, to Thorstein Veblen.

To the extent that such a theory becomes adequate, it will surely recognize, for example, the potency of the unrational in all kinds of group relationships. It will diagnose and measure the stubborn ethnocentric allegiances and intergroup conflicts incipiently or overtly manifested in virtually all racial, national, religious clusterings. It will face head-on the flamboyant issue of the struggle between economic classes in all its subtle as well as obtuse forms. It will acquaint citizens, young and old, with the surreptitious and devious exertions of the forces which shape public opinion. It will ask and seek to answer the persistent question of how the still largely latent, yet also tremendous and constructive, power of the common peoples may be released and directed through democratic means in behalf of the building of a world-wide democratic culture.

A theory of the state, the third foundation required by our blueprint, has likewise been anticipated. The unrational factor in social forces, to take one instance, is demonstrated only too tragically by the pressures exerted by one state against another—pressures which, when resisted too heavily by counterpressures, generate war.

Yet it is this very power potential in the state which requires equally realistic appraisal by educational theory. Aside from the complicated question of whether supreme coercive power is not the prime differentiating quality of statehood, it is difficult any longer to deny that no state is actually a state which cannot authorize and enforce obedience to its own mandates. Such authorization and enforcement may, to be sure, assume a variety of organizational forms. Thus in an autocracy or oligarchy power is exercised over, rather than by, majorities—a kind of exercise which, under other guises, still characterizes too many modern states. Supreme coercive power need not and certainly should not, however, be of this kind: rather a compelling requirement of which education should be cognizant today is to guarantee that such power is exercised in behalf of and exclusively for the widest obtainable compass of peoples on an *international* plane. In short, a theory of the state appropriate to the revolutionary conditions thrust upon us by the dubious alliance of economics, militarism, and natural science needs to embrace the coercive powers of separate states by a still more coercive power—a supremely enforceable power over all states. It is not too much to insist, if life itself remains precious to men, that international sovereignty is the first item on civilization's agenda for survival.

It follows that a philosophy of education integrated with a philosophy of the state will also include a defensible conception of the relations of parts to the whole. Within America, the demand is, of course, that of establishing a functional association between the "pluralism" of localities, states, and regions, on the one hand, and the "monism" of the nation, on the other hand. Again, however, this demand is by no means confined to America alone: a far more urgent imperative, we reiterate, is for a whole never yet achieved in history—a *world* which is whole.

At least one other familiar, though important, constituent should be added to our third buttress. This is the theory of the positive welfare state of public service as a much more urgent approach to our closely knit industrial culture than the negative state of our *laissez-faire* past. The state, in other words, has a growing number of constructive duties to perform in behalf of popular well-being; and it is one of education's cutting edges to analyze these duties as exactly as possible. Thus, to select a particularly controversial illustration, education, instead of assuming as a matter of course that federal direction of the schools must be rejected a priori as contrary to the whole tradition of local autonomy, should scrupulously consider the case for such direction. In the same way that the service state now begins, even in America, to recognize its national obligations to the unemployed, the sick, or the aged, and to establish standards appropriate to human welfare, so it should begin also to recognize such obligations and standards in the education of all citizens. The core issue here is not federal *versus* local control: it is whether federal control can be more efficient and more effective at the same time that it is indisputably responsible to the majority. To learn how to provide wide two-way traffic lanes between centralized authority and decentralized administration, according to principles roughly analogous to those which the Tennessee Valley Authority has already experimentally provided, is another of education's high priority tasks.

The fourth great theoretical need is an adequate theory of government. If the state be differentiated in terms of supreme coercive power, governments are the refined instruments and expressions of that power. For our own age the problem, we have urged, is to guarantee for the first time in history a government which *in action* is therefore completely the organization and agent of the widest possible range of common interests—in brief, an unqualifiedly *democratic* government.

The complexity of this problem has also been glossed over by some educational theorists. They have failed to appreciate that in a world of deep-seated conflict self-government is not necessarily identifiable with some abstract government of all or for all. Indeed, any dialectical definition of "majority" implies the polar fact of a minority whose own interests, or at least whose interpretation of such interests, differ from the majority's. Hence, we need here to perceive that the final import of majority rule for our period, if not for all periods, is to express and guarantee the largest obtainable consensus upon the largest quantity and richest quality of interests among the earth's peoples at any given time—a consensus springing always from the drives of human nature, individually and socially, and producing institutional arrangements, especially of the service state and government, through which those drives may be released.

Meanwhile, minority dissent consists of two main types. There is the dissent of those who, because of some heavy stake in traditional structures, exert every effort to thwart the will of the majority. They are likely to be, in our generation, the same forces of contraction which engineer the steam-shovels of public opinion to dig the void deeper. Second, there is the minority which dissents, not so much because it disagrees with the central aims of the majority, as because it is unconvinced of a particular means to their attainment and thus may prefer an alternative means. The importance of the service performed by this second type of minority can scarcely be overstressed: so long as judgments of the majority are not sanctified as absolutes they will continue to need salutary critiques of their own fallibility.

Another aspect of almost equal importance to an adequate theory of government is that of the proper role of democratic leadership. In light of the principles considered thus far, this role is a double one. On one side, democratic leaders carry out majority-formulated policies by expertly translating these into the specifics of legislative operation, executive application, judicial interpretation, a process during which leaders aim in every possible way to maintain close communication with their constituents to whom they are at every step responsible. On the other side, leaders are equally articulators and suggesters, that is to say, "pointers" who continually help people to perceive more exactly, more generously, their own best interests. Here is a role so suitable also to the democratic teacher that he himself becomes, in this sense, a democratic leader.

Fifth, a philosophy of education-as-politics should embrace an adequate theory of normative commitment.

Let us return for a moment to an earlier remark to the effect that educational theory, especially of one influential type, emphasizes methodology to such an extent as to squeeze all other considerations to minute proportions. That this, too, is a form of commitment has often been pointed out; indeed, certain of its most eloquent spokesmen are at times evangelistic in their fervent glorification of the scientific method as the be-all and end-all of democracy itself. As others, however, have also pointed out, such commitment is paradoxical. Since one of its most passionate beliefs is that we must at all cost avoid any sort of philosophy which gives itself too wholeheartedly to precise, future-oriented goals, therefore its own professed concern with ends somehow seems to dissolve usually into some renewed formulation of scientific means.

This avoidance, though it springs from a legitimate hostility to dogmatism and indoctrination, is no longer tenable. Actually, if we view educational philosophy in the setting of the history of ideas, we find that from Plato onward the attempt to interpret an age philosophically has been, and properly, the attempt to incorporate in one sweeping panorama both the necessary means and dominant ends of that age. In this respect, if no other, we would plead for a revivification of the great tradition of philosophy—a tradition which, applied to current education, would suggest that one pressing obligation is to construct *both* a potent methodology of social transformation and grand-scale designs for the future order.

Please do not misunderstand. This is no plea for a retrogression to the metaphysical systems of either ancient or modern history. We are asserting, rather, that men stand today in a unique intellectual position to build a theory of cultural commitment which is in complete accord with the canons of naturalism, empiricism, and of experimental method. More exactly, the theory now needed might be named one of "defensible partiality"—partiality to crystallized ends which fuse at every point with the deepest cravings of the largest possible majority; at the same time ends steadily exposed to the bright light of maximum evidence, of continuous public inspection, of a free flow of communication. Unlike the ends of dogmatic doctrine, therefore, they are defensible in the way that outcomes of scientific investigation are defensible. Yet they are also definite and strong in the way that convictions should be definite and strong.

In our present setting, the need then is for commitment, first of all, to the end of that kind of world order where all such creations of man's inventive genius as atomic energy are brought under completely public control. Such an end, delineated into the specifics of human experience, requires the utmost cooperation of every department of learning: of politics, certainly, but likewise of all the social sciences; of physics, but likewise of all the natural sciences; of education, but likewise of all great religions and arts. The service that philosophy should render here becomes comparable in our time to that of such critical periods of both danger and promise as the fifth century B.C., or the seventeenth A.D.: the paramount service of viewing and testing the ends of life as a whole, of audacious and cosmic vision. . . .

The kind of education here being discussed encourages students, teachers, and all

members of the community not merely to *study* knowledge and problems considered crucial to our period of culture, but *to make up their minds* about promising
solutions, and then to act concertedly. Its emphasis on *commitment* to agreed-upon,
future-looking goals thus raises once more the old problem of bias and indoctrination.

Is it not true, the critic may ask, that the teacher who believes in the purposes of
national and international reconstruction, who accepts the dominant value of self-
realization, who infers that the majority of people should agree with his own judge-
ment that the present junction of forces demands the choice of a socialized democracy—is it not true that such a philosophy repudiates the ideal of academic freedom,
of fairness to "all sides of all questions"?

Stated thus academically the issue is important enough. It becomes still more important when we view it again through the lens of our cultural crisis. For then we
perceive that the question is ultimately whether public educaton should become the
dedicated ally of certain social forces and aims, or whether education should remain
so far as possible neutral and impartial, true to the liberal ideal of academic freedom at its best. Will the "democratic way of life" ultimately be served by emulating
in any way the fixed educational systems of certain countries? Yet if public education does not do so, can it possibly succeed in building a generation of citizens who
deeply believe in their own future? Is one of liberal democracy's greatest weaknesses
perhaps its very pride in open-mindedness and tolerance—with all their accompanying vacillations, uncertainties, confusions—by contrast with which millions of young
citizens elsewhere in the world seem now to be acquiring an absolute social devotion,
loyalty, and purposefulness which serve as bulwarks of strength to those
countries?

The preceding interpretation of philosophical and educational principles, however superficially treated, should already have provided the outlines of an answer
to such a challenge. This answer, in essence, is unequivocal opposition to indoctrination; and equally unequivocal support of academic freedom, in the sense of
impartial and thorough study of all kinds of evidence and alternatives. At the same
time, it insists that the vital utilization of these principles is entirely compatible
with the development of clear social convictions and concerted action upon those
convictions.

In short, our position supports that kind of "partiality" which is at the same
moment "defensible." Here indeed is the ultimate test of whether learning is
woven into the warp and woof of individual and group behavior—whether patterns
of belief not only are professed but consistently and fully practiced. What then, more
precisely, *is* education for "defensible partiality"?

Let us try to understand first what defensible partaility is *not*. Opposition to indoctrination follows from definition of that term. In brief, it is that method of
learning by communication which proceeds primarily in one direction (from the
"communicator" to the "communicee") for the purpose of inculcating in the mind
and behavior of the latter a firm acceptance of some one doctrine or systematic body
of beliefs—a doctrine assumed in advance by its exponents to be so supremely true,
so good, or so beautiful as to justify no need for critical, scrupulous, thoroughgoing
comparison with alternative doctrines.

It follows from this definition that most of the ways of learning which have been and are still practiced in the name of education amount in fact to plain indoctrination. For many centuries, the Church has deliberately and frankly inculcated its own doctrine as alone true and good, its chief indoctrinators being priests vested with authority to communicate its tenets to receptive minds. Today such education occurs wherever a society is under the sole domination of similarly unquestionable authority: Fascist Spain and Soviet Russia, however radically unlike otherwise, frankly indoctrinate the population in the supremacy of their respective systems. In the democracies, too, this kind of education flourishes oftener than not: inculcation of moral codes or social folklore, and especially of attitudes and programs identified with the traditional economic-political system, simply means that public schools, far more often than most of their personnel themselves realize, are under the heavy influence of the dominant ideology.

Indoctrination may occur, also, within the kind of education ostensibly most opposed to its practice. Not only do sincere devotees of academic freedom often fail to recognize the powerful ideological influences and unrational motivations working upon and molding both their own and their students' beliefs—influences generating all sorts of surreptitious rationalizations and weighted interpretations of evidence. Also, it is not difficult to point to institutions of teacher-training where the experimental-liberal viewpoint so controls the curriculum as almost totally to ignore careful, scholarly consideration of alternative viewpoints. The ironic one-sidedness of the kind of progressivist who thus considers himself the sole guardian of the "true" philosophy is perhaps matched only by the kind of positivist who smugly believes he is "true" solely to the purified canons of scientific objectivity.

The advocate of defensible partiality is, of course, far from immune to ideological and other socio-psychological forces. Nor does he seek to purge them entirely: this he thinks is impossible in any case; they are too substantial a part of all human experience. What he does aim at is to bring them under maximum democratic control, including or excluding them according to their compatibility or incompatibility with the emerging purposes and programs of the majority. Such control is possible, however, only to the extent that these forces are first analyzed and appraised by the public processes of shared experience of which he is himself part.

We must also frankly recognize that aspects of indoctrination, as defined, may be more closely approximated at some stages of education than at other stages. In the earliest years, children must absorb some facts and rules by a degree of inculcation in order to get along with any group. In high school and college, too, inculcation of evidence (the laws of natural science, for instance) or of communication (skill in writing, for instance) may also be needed temporarily. This should by no means suggest, however, that indoctrination is after all conceded: education *as a whole* is the proper frame of reference, not any part taken out of context. A school permeated with the reconstructionist philosophy will always accordingly avoid mere inculcation: whenever and wherever people learn, they should increasingly appreciate both by precept and practice that every fact, rule, or skill they acquire should eventually be judged, accepted, or rejected by themselves according to whether it contributes to their cooperatively agreed-upon values and correlative cultural designs. The rudiments of this crucial attitude can and should begin to develop in the nursery school itself.

The present theory also distinguishes between indoctrination and propaganda. The latter is defined as a "short-cut" device for influencing attitudes and consequent conduct: it attempts through colorful symbolization rich with suggestion (e.g., advertising displays, music, rhetoric) to persuade some individual or group directly and forcibly that a certain belief, practice, product, is either desirable or undesirable. Many of the meticulous arguments and much of the specific evidence that *could* be mustered are therefore deliberately omitted from effective propaganda. In this respect, although it may be a potent aid to indoctrination and shade imperceptibly into the latter, it differs in the sense that indoctrination at its best includes all possible argument and evidence at least of a sort favorable to its own or unfavorable to any contrasting doctrine. Systematic indoctrination of perennialism, for example, becomes an extremely complicated philosophic enterprise; while propaganda for perennialism is best effected through rituals and dogmas of the Church.

But propaganda is indispensable under certain conditions to other types of teaching than indoctrination. Whatever his philosophy, no instructor can avoid the need at times of taking short-cuts by omission of some of the possible evidence, some of the possible ways of communication, which would enter into a given learning situation were it to be treated as exhaustively as possible. Moreover, propaganda often reinforces a fact, problem, or value upon students much more effectively than would a coldly, neutrally analytical approach. There is no reason why learning for worthwhile ends should not be warmed with the persuasive qualities which advertisers so often exploit for deleterious ends. Much more forthrightly, however, than other philosophies (with the possible exception of perennialism), the philosophy here advocated believes that if education is to be a great cultural force in shaping of attitudes and inciting to actions it should become colorful and dramatic in the way that propaganda can be colorful and dramatic.

Let it be clearly understood that this "heresy" does not imply that propaganda and education are therefore synonymous. Education in its totality encompasses the fullest possible consideration of evidence, the most thorough effort at clear communication, and the most scrupulous respect for disagreements as well as agreements. Hence propaganda should be judged by the extent to which it is helpful while always *subordinate* to the complete process and product of democratic learning —hence also by the extent to which both students and teachers realize how and when its methods are being utilized in the school. The teacher's duty here includes two chief responsibilities: (a) to label propaganda for what it is, meanwhile giving students practice in its detection and techniques; and (b) to develop even in very young students unforgettable appreciation of the fact that they often learn rules, attitudes, beliefs, by shortcuts which, while necessary at certain times, are nevertheless deserving of additional investigation, elaboration, and experience at other times. Only thus is propaganda transformed into education proper. Only thus is a rule of health that is learned by the child genuinely relearned and incorporated into the life of the adult.

The more successfully this habit of continuous criticism and active revaluation develops in children, the less likely are they to be victimized by mere propaganda at any time. The less likely are they dualistically to separate education and propaganda in actual practice. The less likely, too, are either children or adults naively to assume that all propaganda, being "bad," should as far as possible be obliterated —an assumption not only illegitimate but thoroughly impractical either in schools or in the larger society.

It appears, then, that the viewpoint we are taking is much more sympathetic to the uses of propaganda than to indoctrination. Our opposition to the latter is fundamental for it assumes, not only that ultimate truths and values are possessed in advance by their exponent, but that neither the sometimes cumbersome and tedious process of exposure to comparative examination, nor the open construction of majority agreement, is essential to their own proven superiority. Hence by its very nature indoctrination is in sharp contrast with a philosophy of learning which holds, on the contrary, that men should build positive convictions only by public inspection of and testimony about all pertinent and available evidence, and by exhaustive consideration of alternative convictions.

Now propaganda, when it is utilized to support presumably unchallengeable, absolute doctrines, is quite as indefensible as indoctrination. At least however in certain forms, propaganda as defined is perfectly consistent also with learning in our preferred sense. In other words, as a subsidiary technique strictly governed by the principles of that theory of learning, there is no reason why the techniques and fruits of propaganda should not frequently be subjected to thoroughgoing educacational analysis and interpretation; indeed, we should make sure that they are. Thus if a colorful poster urges people to support consumer cooperatives, the plea as such may lack logic and data; it may seek to mold attitudes by direct suggestion alone; yet it may upon careful study prove wholly consistent with such logic and data.

It follows that at least one common type of propaganda, familiarly called "card-stacking"—the weighting or otherwise distorting of evidence—is under no circumstances acceptable. (Indeed, another reason for our opposition to indoctrination is that, although more elaborately, it too stacks the cards by distorting, disregarding, or underplaying antithetical views.) But propaganda which resorts merely to such devices as "name-calling" or "glittering generalities" is quite possibly opposing or favoring situations which upon exposure to evidence, communication, and agreement, fully deserve the epithet or the pleasant-sounding label, as the case may be.

A richer meaning of defensible partiality should now emerge. *What we learn is defensible simply insofar as the ends we support and the means we utilize are able to stand up against exposure to open, unrestricted criticism and comparison. What we learn is partial insofar as these ends and means still remain definite and positive to their majority advocates after the defense occurs.* If at any moment we stubbornly disregard the impact of such criticism and comparison we thereby fail to follow our own rules. We allow dogmatism or impatience to overcome our intention to accept only those truths, values, and programs reached, to the highest degree possible, according to . . . an inductive and cooperative procedure. . . . We begin to substitute indoctrination, and in all likelihood card-stacking propaganda, for learning as majority agreement.

The inference is that public education, like the culture itself, can arrive at commitments worth fighting for only as these are hammered out of the deepest and widest personal and group experiences available. To put it differently, partiality paradoxically increases in defensibility only as it is tested by the kind of impartiality provided through many-sided evidence, unrestricted communication, complete respect for criticism and minority dissent.

The teacher of our persuasion, being an important part of this community of learning, is in the long run subject to the same principles as any other member. Hence his classroom provides continuous opportunity for impartiality in study just because he and his students cannot otherwise effectively obtain majority agreements which are themselves partial. As these agreements are reached they are often put into effect in the form of policies and activities to which minorities then also submit.

It should be recognized, however, that such a teacher as we endorse already holds commitments which, unless he is sensitive to the full import of his own philosophy, may lead to an indefensible if unconscious indoctrination. To avoid this effect, it is necessary for him to distinguish between his own pattern of beliefs and those beliefs still developing among his students. It is likewise necessary that, at some point in every course of study, he be as explicit as possible both to himself and to them as to where he himself stands. By exploring and delineating the complex forces which have contributed to his own outlook; by trying to sift out his own *prejudices* (opinions and attitudes hastily, illogically, merely emotionally shaped) from his *convictions* (opinions and attitudes carefully, logically, consciously shaped); by repeatedly warning his students that even his clearest convictions are likely to be touched with predudice, as indicated possibly by the fact that they are disputed among other teachers—by these and other means, students can develop the habit of critical awareness of his own point of view. Further, as this kind of teacher encourages them to take issue with him whenever they choose to do so (to prevent counter-evidence and alternative proposals, for example, or to challenge his clarity of language), he avoids those iniquities of pontifical super-imposition which are still the rule rather than exception in public education. In these respects, he becomes more than a teacher: he becomes a democratic *leader* and *expert* in the precise sense of these terms. . . .

The two great constructive purposes which should now govern the profession of teachers follow directly. . . . They are:

1. To channel the energies of education toward the reconstruction of the economic system—a system which should be geared with the increasing socializations and public controls now developing in England, Sweden, New Zealand, and other countries; a system in which national and international planning of production and distribution replaces the chaotic planlessness of traditional "free enterprise"; a system in which the interests, wants, and needs of the consumer dominate those of the producer; a system in which natural resources, such as coal and iron ore, are owned and controlled by the people; a system in which public corporations replace monop-

olistic enterprises and privately owned "public" utilities; a system in which federal authority is synchronized with decentralized regional and community administration; a system in which social security and a guaranteed annual wage sufficient to meet scientific standards of nourishment, shelter, clothing, health, recreation, and education are universalized; a system in which the majority of the people is the sovereign determinant of every basic economic policy.

2. To channel the energies of education toward the establishment of genuine international order—an order in which national sovereignty is always subordinate to international authority in all crucial issues affecting peace and security; an order therefore in which all weapons of war (including atomic energy, first of all) and police forces are finally brought under that authority; an order in which international economic planning of trade, resources, labor standards, and social security, is practiced parallel with the best cooperative practices of individual nations; an order in which all nationalities, races, and religions receive equal rights in its democratic control; an order in which "world citizenship" thus assumes at least equal status with national citizenship.

These two great guiding principles involve a multitude of specific educational tasks to which the profession should now devote itself. Their precise delineation should involve every possible teacher, and the closest cooperation with all groups and forces which share generally in its purposes. In this statement of policy, we can only suggest what some of these tasks may be. We list them without elaboration or special concern for order of importance.

(a) There is desperate need for realistic materials regarding the economic system (the growth of corporate power is but one example), and for skill in penetrating the smokescreens of false propaganda set up by agencies of public opinion which benefit by concealment of the failures and injustices of the traditional system.

(b) There is call to develop consciousness in students, teachers, administrators, and other citizens of the meaning and content of the values and norms which govern new economic, political, and cultural purposes. The import of a potent value like "self-realization" as a criterion for measuring the effectiveness of such economic proposals as labor-management committees should be fully explored and enunciated.

(c) In aligning against an unworkable economic system and unworkable nationalism, and with a workable system and workable internationalism, there is need to develop consciousness of a distinction between the convictions already held by those who take such sides and those who do not yet do so. This is necessary in order thereby to permit development of new educational techniques which avoid indoctrination of these convictions. The task is to experiment with techniques of learning through the dynamics of group development, not by superimposing pre-judgments. Only thus can majority rule eventually become rule by an informed majority who understand what they want and how, democratically, to get what they want. The school should become a center of experimentation in attaining communities of uncoerced consensus.

(d) There is rich opportunity for extensive educational practice in building detailed social designs which come to grips with problems arising in, for example, economic planning. Intensive study of experiments and institutions already under way, such as the postal system, the consumer cooperative movement, the social security program of America and Europe, are examples. Psychological problems such as motivations and incentives; political problems such as bureaucracy and reorganization of state and federal governments; social problems such as family life and the role of women; economic problems such as the place of private property in an increasingly socialized order—these are equally important.

(e) Pressing need exists for a new conception of group-centered discipline—intellectual, moral, and social—which can be developed in schools governed by the dominant purposes of a democratic society.

(f) Contributions of arts and sciences to the erection of the new order should be examined and integrated with social studies. Community planning, the development of people's theaters and symphony orchestras, the social potentialities of science for health, home designing, communication and transportation, are but sample illustrations.

(g) The full import of the concept of "One World" and of "world citizenship" requires extended attention. Such complex problems as the retention of legitimate cultural variety by countries committed to international order should be explored, as should such issues as immigration, international educational and health standards, world-wide exchange of students and teachers. Study of the present structure of the United Nations should be supplemented by exploration of improvements needed to strengthen that structure both in regard to police power and socio-economic leadership.

(h) Equally extended attention should be paid to the unsolved problem of intercultural relations within nations. The status of minorities such as the Negro or Jew should be realistically evaluated, and the meaning of cultural equality more clearly understood and practiced.

(i) Close cooperation with educational movements of other countries, especially those working toward more or less similar objectives is imperative. . . .

What, then, is our proposal? In essence it is that *the hub of every curriculum be the study of the structure and operation of reconstructed democracy itself.* This means, not that other important areas of study are to be neglected, but that these be related to the hub as spokes are in a wheel. Let us concentrate upon the junior college (which we shall conceive as running from the present high school junior year through the present sophomore college year). During each year one central unit is devoted to one key aspect of a reorganized democracy. Each unit points toward a final unit in the last semester of the senior year where the aim is to integrate each part into a panoramic view of the whole society.

Because in every type of society the economic area is crucial to the rest, the freshman year is devoted to analysis of the systematized processes essential to the producing, consuming, and transporting phases of industrial and agricultural life. Such study must obviously remain on a comparatively simple plane, and its success can be judged in the long run by the success both of preparation on elementary levels and in the later achievements of higher levels. Nevertheless, given stimulating but by no means impossible conditions, boys and girls of about sixteen years can and should understand the elementary attributes of a system where economic planning for example, is indispensable.

Study and action proceed from key questions, such as "How would the output of publicly operated electric power be estimated so that it balances with a public demand for that power over a given time?" "How sound is the program of consumer cooperatives operated on a nation-wide basis?" "As and if private collectivities become publicly owned, how shall reimbursement to previous owners be made?" "How are salaries and wages to be equitably adjusted to varying skills and demands in the new economy?" "What limitations should be placed upon private property and wealth in a more socialized democracy?" "What reorientation is necessary toward the virtue of saving when social responsibility for old age and unemployment is largely assumed by the service state?"

In dealing with problems of this kind—problems, be it noted, which are largely neglected by typical schools—the aim always is to utilize knowledge of actual practices in America and in Europe. But while the economic unit grounds itself on evidence and the most thoughtful proposals of experts, every effort is made also to invigorate the social imaginations of students so that they themselves contribute suggestions for the consideration of fellow students and instructors.

This unit illustrates a number of further proposals in the way it cooperates with other units. We note four of these proposals.

First, in schools where the economic sphere is studied simultaneouly in a number of sections, the students of each section submit conclusions and recommendations to students of other sections for criticism or approval.

Second, their own conclusions, plus old problems and issues for which they do not find acceptable answers, or new problems and issues which they themselves raise, are pooled at the close of the year for the use of students in the following year. Thus no two years are ever identical, but rather take on a strongly inductive and evolutionary character.

Third, students of the economics unit frequently seek the assistance of second, third, or fourth year units. In considering a question like centralization, a student committee may be elected by the class to visit a unit in politics for the purpose of obtaining help. Again, an instructor or a committee from the latter may be invited to visit the economics unit. Integration of the curriculum is therefore vertical as well as horizontal.

Fourth, the spokes of the wheel (that is, the other studies being pursued by each class of students) are integrated with the hub. In the first year a course in *drawing*, let us say, supplies diagrams and blueprints for a particular plan of commodity distribution. A course in *history* concerns itself with the development of business enterprise; it notes how such development has brought both maladjustments which now demand correction, and technological achievements which must be freshly utilized. A course in *English* becomes a tool in learning how to read literature of importance to the economic unit, or in learning how to express in writing one's criticisms or interpretation of the material of that unit. As in the cooperation between sections of the same "hub" unit of one year, or between the several "hub" units of all four years, here too cooperation is constant: teachers from various "spoke" studies work with teachers of the "hub" study, often joining classes together for discussion, activity, demonstration.

The plan of next year's work, moreover, is laid out afresh at the close of each year by the entire corps of teachers, together with committees of students from the various courses. Parents are also frequently consulted. But in no case is the plan shaped so rigidly as to preclude modification during actual operation.

In implementing these important recommendations, the profession should continue to support all kinds of educational experimentation. It should continue to emphasize "learning by doing," "community schools," "the integrated curriculum," "teacher-pupil planning," and other objectives of progressivism as these now become more widely accepted.

But such objectives are now subordinate, even while indispensable to, the more encompassing objectives impelled by a world in crisis. Faced by the alternatives of economic chaos and atomic war, on the one hand, of world-wide plenty and enforceable international order, on the other hand, the teaching profession should become the clearest, most purposeful educational spokesman for the second of these alternatives.

To prove that education is *not* a mere mirror of dominant ideologies, *not* a device for bolstering outmoded economic systems and diseased nationalisms, but rather that education is a penetrating critic, dynamic leader, and imaginative re-creator which anticipates dangers *before* they crystallize into calamities, which helps simultaneously to reshape the culture of America and the world in accordance with the imperatives of this catalytic age—here is the supreme obligation of the teaching profession to the second half of our century.

Questions for Discussion

1. What reasons does Brameld give to support his conclusion that education's twin tasks are to reconstruct the economic system and establish a genuine international order? Do you agree with these reasons?
2. Assuming the validity of his goals, what pedagogical principles are implied by them? Lecturing? Team teaching? Field trips? Or are any particular principles implied at all?
3. Do you believe that the schools should have anything to do with establishing and developing a student's values? If so, what values should the school help to establish, and why? Can a school function successfully when it deliberately encourages the development of certain values in the students? What problems would this situation create?

5 Education in a Communist Society

M. I. Kalinen and G. S. Prozorow

And here is the other side of the coin, now stated in the form of the schools preserving and enhancing the values of a communist society. Kalinen holds that the values any person holds are created by the economic conditions under which he lives; the private property relationships of a bourgeois society will cause its members to believe that personal competitive endeavor is of most value while the shared ownership of property characteristic of a communist society will cause its members to value cooperative activity. In a communist society, then, the purposes of the schools are to encourage cooperative endeavor and to prepare students to contribute to the welfare of the society. How those purposes are to be achieved by the curriculum and the teacher occupy the attention of Prozorow in the last two-thirds of this selection. Notice why both work and study are said to be important in communist education, and why the correct environment, rather than a good heredity, is thought to be of central importance.

In his book, *Anti-Duhring,* Engels writes:

> . . . Men, consciously or unconsciously, derive their moral ideas in the last resort from the practical relations on which their class position is based—from the economic relations in which they carry on production and exchange. . . . Morality was always a class morality; it has either justified the domination and the interests of the ruling class, or, as soon as the oppressed class has become powerful enough, it has represented the revolt against this domination and the future interests of the oppressed.

Thus, in class society there never has been, nor can there be, education outside or above the classes.

In bourgeois society education is permeated through and through with hypocrisy, with the mercenary interests of the ruling classes; it is of a profoundly contradictory character, reflecting the antagonisms of capitalist society.

The ideal of the capitalists is to see in the workers and peasants their obedient servants bearing the burden of exploitation without a murmur. Proceeding from this, the capitalists would prefer not to foster daring and courage in the workers and peasants, would prefer not to give them any education whatsoever. For it is easier to cope with people who are ignorant and downtrodden. But you cannot win wars of conquest with such people, and they could not operate machines and machine tools without elementary knowledge. Mutual competition under conditions of technical progress, the armaments race, etc., on the one hand, and the struggle of workers and peasants to acquire an education, on the other hand, compel the bour-

Reprinted with permission of The Macmillan Company from *Soviet Educators on Soviet Education.* Copyright © by The Free Press of Glencoe, a Division of The Macmillan Company, 1964. Reprinted also by permission of Progress Publishers, Moscow.

geoisie to give the working people at least crumbs of knowledge, while wars of plunder force it to cultivate among the working masses stamina, courage and other qualities dangerous for the bourgeoisie.

No system of bourgeois education can rid itself of the contradictions.

And so, despite these contradictions which, as I have already said, are inherent in the very nature of bourgeois society, the ruling classes engage in a frantic struggle to gain control of the masses, using all means, from open suppression to subtle deception.

From the day the workingman is born and until the day he dies he is subjected in bourgeois society to the constant influence of such thoughts, sentiments and customs as are advantageous to the ruling class. This is effected through innumerable channels, sometimes in barely perceptible forms. The church, the school, art, the press, the cinema, the theatre, organizations of different kinds—all these serve as instruments for imbuing the masses with the world outlook, morals, customs, etc., of the bourgeoisie.

Take the cinema, for example. A certain bourgeois movie director has written this about American films: "Many present-day films are something in the order of a narcotic designed for people who are so tired that all they want is to sit in soft armchairs and be spoon-fed."

Such is the essence of bourgeois education.

To this system of education, which took centuries to elaborate and is designed to consolidate the position of the ruling, capitalist class and to reconcile the oppressed to their position, the Communist Party—the vanguard of the proletariat—opposes its own principles of education which are directed primarily against the domination of the bourgeoisie and in support of the dictatorship of the proletariat.

Communist education differs fundamentally from bourgeois education not only as regards its tasks, a point that is understandable without adducing proof, but also as regards methods. Communist education is bound up indissolubly with the development of political consciousness and culture in general, with the raising of the intellectual level of the masses. This is something that all Communist parties are striving to achieve.

Although the final aim of all Communist parties is one and the same, yet, inasmuch as the conditions of the working class in the Soviet Union differ from those in the capitalist countries, the education we give should correspond precisely to these specific conditions. The working class in our country is the dominant, directing force not only materially, but also spiritually.

Marx and Engels wrote:

> . . . The class that possesses the means of material production, by virtue of this also possesses the means of spiritual production. . . . The individual composing the ruling class possess, among other things, consciousness as well, and by virtue of this, think. In so far, therefore, as they rule as a class and determine the extent and scope of an epoch, it is self-evident that they do this in all its spheres, hence rule also as thinkers, as producers of ideas, and regulate the production and distribution of the ideas of their age; and that means that their ideas are the dominant ones of the epoch.

This cannot be said of the working class on the other side of the Soviet frontiers.

Communist education as we understand it is always thought of concretely. Under our conditions it has to be subordinated to the tasks facing the Party and the Soviet State. The fundamental and chief task of Communist education is to render the maximum assistance in the class struggle we are waging.

I see that you are somewhat surprised, that you want to get at the meaning of the thesis that the task is to foster in people the desire to be of the maximum assistance in the class struggle in our country, where the exploiting classes have been abolished. It seems to me this does not require any special explanation. It will be enough to remind you of the excellent reply given by Comrade Stalin to the Komsomol member Ivanov. ". . . But," wrote Comrade Stalin, "as we are not living on an island but 'in a system of states,' a considerable number of which are hostile to the Land of Socialism and create the danger of intervention and restoration, we say openly and honestly that the victory of Socialism in our country is not yet final." The events of the past year have brought practical confirmation, concrete facts to show the truth of the views set forth in Comrade Stalin's reply.

True, our class struggle has assumed forms differing from those of the class struggle beyond the bounds of the U.S.S.R. I would say that it has reached a higher level; its positive results are more effective. But, of course, it is also considerably more complicated in character.

The thesis of Marx and Engels that "the ideas of the ruling class are in every epoch the ruling ideas," in so far as it refers to the working class of the Soviet Union, places a great responsibility on us. We cannot confine ourselves to merely criticizing the bourgeois system. The main thing now is a struggle for practical achievements all along the line in political life, economics, culture, science, art, etc. It is clear that the Communist education we give should also follow the same direction.

What are the main tasks we set ourselves today in the sphere of Communist education? And, generally speaking, are these fundamentally new tasks in comparison with those set by Lenin in his speech at the Third Congress of the Komsomol twenty years ago?

Of course, the situation in the Soviet Union has changed considerably in this period. But at bottom the tasks of Communist education set by Lenin twenty years ago, retain their urgency at the present time too.

It would not be amiss if those who try to reproduce the features of Communist society in the abstract were to be reminded of these tasks more often. Such people who like to "theorize," to indulge in "profound" dreams about the specific features of the man of the future, associating Communism with some vague, bright future, impart this abstractness to Communist education as well. In my opinion, this is telling fortunes from coffee grounds, not penetrating into the future.

Comrades, one of the most important elements in the building of Communism and a mighty weapon of the working people of the U.S.S.R. in their struggle against capitalism is a high productivity of labour. Lenin said:

> In the last analysis, productivity of labour is the most important, the principal thing for the victory of the new social system. Capitalism created a productivity of labour unknown under serfdom. Capitalism can be utterly vanquished,

and will be utterly vanquished, by the fact that Socialism creates a new and much higher productivity of labour. . . . Communism is the higher productivity of labour—compared with capitalist productivity of labour—of voluntary, class-conscious, united workers employing advanced technique.

That, comrades, is what we must think and speak about, that, first and foremost, is the direction in which Communist education should be developed. It is the struggle for a high level of labour productivity. . . .

Each child is endowed by nature with some individual physiological characteristics which represent potentialities. The task of education is to create favorable conditions under which these potentialities would blossom into full development. What is being transferred by heredity is not ready-made abilities, but only the prerequisites for their development; that is, certain physiological characteristics of the organism which demand further development are transferred from parents to children in accordance with biological laws of heredity. These hereditary prerequisites may develop, but they may wilt, depending on prevailing conditions, the nature of the educational influence, and the whole system of upbringing and teaching to which a given child is exposed. Theoretically, it is possible for equally gifted children to achieve different levels of development, as well as for unequally gifted children to reach the same developmental level. This of course can be proved by many examples in real life. Everything depends on the conditions under which the children grow up, and how their abilities are fostered. Hereditary inclinations determine neither the whole process of the child's growth nor the realization of his individual potential.

Natural inclinations are mainly hidden in peculiarities of the human nervous system. But the nervous system does not remain static in its development. Conditions of life and of upbringing can reinforce or shatter the nervous system. Native abilities by no means totally determine future personality characteristics and behavior. The great Russian physiologist I. P. Pavlov wrote:

The mode of human and of animal behavior is conditioned not only by inborn native characteristics of the nervous system but also by influences which were and are exerted upon the organism during his individual existence, namely, that of continuous upbringing and education in its broadest concept.

Therefore, besides the above-mentioned characteristic of the nervous system, its very important peculiarity, that of high flexibility, is continuously apparent.

Fullest development of native abilities can be achieved only by a well-organized method of upbringing. In this process the leading role is played by specific activities. Concrete, practical work in a given field is the better way to foster growth of ability, and lack of experience may leave native potentiality undeveloped and hidden.

A. M. Gorky persistently stressed that innate ability is only a spark, which may either die out or develop into a flame. There is only one way, he says, to develop native talent: namely, through hard work and great demands upon oneself.

No matter how gifted one is, any task requires first of all effort and strength. Just as the development of a strong body is fostered by a healthy daily routine of work and rest, personal hygiene, and physical fitness, the native abilities need favorable conditions in order to blossom. What physical exercise does for the body, mental training does for the mind.

The ability of the student to study develops during the learning process. This developed capability helps the pupil to master subject matter. Realizing the close relationship, experienced teachers strive not only to furnish the pupils with knowledge but also to provide them with individual tasks which they have to fulfill independently. The method which fosters realization of potentialities is one which, as N. K. Krupskaya says, "does not provide the pupil with ready-made solutions" but forces him to think, to analyze.

Since abilities grow and strengthen during activities, it is necessary not to limit the child to a one-sided action, but to supplement his studies with physical labor. The "law of strengthening school ties with life and the further development of the national system of education in U.S.S.R." strongly supports the above premise.

The system of education wherein intellectual and physical work tasks are united and placed at the same level was discussed by Karl Marx in his *Kapital,* where he claims that "synchronizing both of them is better for the child than devoting oneself without interruption to one kind." In this way, he said, each provides a rest from the other and refreshes the pupil's strength.

This system makes the basic task of learning easier, and furnishes the pupil with useful and necessary working habits. With correct supervision, the child can acquire many good working habits appropriate for his age and school curriculum. The speed and ease with which the student will be able to absorb new material and to retain new knowledge depend largely on his aptitude in the given area. But all children, regardless of their native abilities and their development, must acquire the habit of working hard.

It is wrong to give children the impression that unsuccessful attempts indicate lack of ability; they may lose belief in their strength, and be unwilling to make further effort. It is also wrong to suggest that, without any effort on the part of the pupil, ability alone will assure him his goal. It is false to assume that gifted people can master knowledge effortlessly in a chosen field through inspiration alone. "Inspiration does not like to prompt lazy ones," said Tchaikovsky.

The prominent Soviet pedagogue and writer A. S. Makarenko believed that "while to be lazy is wicked, to be talented and lazy is horrifying." Children must be taught to work regularly and honestly to the best of their ability, and to perform not only their school assignments but also their household chores. Those who do not develop diligence during their childhood years become adolescents and adults who are fit for neither advanced study nor productive work.

Usually, knowledge that is easily acquired without being firmly imbedded is quickly forgotten. A student with great promise, who in a secondary school excelled because of his talents, may fail in an institution of higher learning because of bad study habits. It is for this reason that the school and home alike must foster a systematic approach to mental tasks, and a realization that one should depend more upon real effort and hard work than upon talent. Special abilities not only do not excuse one from work; they set additional demands. Our students must be reminded in school as well as at home of Marx's saying: "The road which leads to the glowing height of knowledge is not a comfortable one, but a hard one, and only those who are not afraid of labor manage to reach its top."

Sometimes it is said that genius or talent conquers all. This statement cannot be substantiated. Certainly, some geniuses could be named who had to overcome many difficulties before their greatness was acknowledged. However, even such people as Lomonosov and Gorky, who succeeded in developing their capacities despite unfavorable conditions, cannot serve as an example that geniuses always fulfill themselves, because many more fail to develop their creativity in an adverse environment.

The backwardness of nations which until recently were colonies is explained not by biological characteristics of "racial inequality," but by the effects of suppression. Such nations, once liberated, begin immediately to develop their economy and nurture their native culture. Many peoples of Russia, such as Karelians, Uzbekiens, Tadzhikiens, Kazakhiens, Kirghiziens, and Gashkiriens, who were not only suppressed but rendered almost extinct under tsarism, blossomed during socialism. For the first time in human history a social system was created which guaranteed to each child, regardless of his nationality, sex, and parental background, conditions favorable to the development of a well-rounded personality and the full exercise of capabilities. This is the decisive difference between a capitalist and socialist system.

The communistic re-education of the society, says the Decree dealing with the School Reorganization, "is closely tied to the upbringing of the 'new man,' who will harmoniously combine spiritual richness, morality, and physical fitness."

The task of the school and the home is to rear the children in a communistic spirit, develop in our youth a materialistic world outlook, and foster communistic ideology and behavior.

In order to clarify the decisive role upbringing plays in personality development, let us examine the limitations of heredity factors in relation to education. In the formulation of a person's view of the world, the decisive ingredients are the environment, educational goals, and the normal development of the child—not biological heredity. In case the child acquires religious or nationalistic prejudices, the only way to effect a change is to influence his consciousness; only the method of purposeful education can free a human mind from prejudice and superstition.

Heredity cannot hinder the development of such personality characteristics as honesty, truthfulness, and integrity. Each child can be brought up to live in accordance with high social ideals. The same is true with regard to work habits. Only a physical handicap can serve as an excuse for preventing mastery of relevant work.

Frequently, children become rude or nervously sick because of an unhealthy relationship between their parents and the ensuing fights and subtle conflicts that children witness in their family. When a child is surrounded by brave, lively adults who can overcome life's difficulties without undue complaint, he acquires the same characteristics. He grows up physically and mentally fit and healthy.

Pampering a child has a strongly negative effect upon his upbringing. It weakens his will power, renders him incapable of overcoming even the slightest difficulty, encourages unjustified demands toward adults in his immediate environment, and produces an egotistical and callous nature. No less negative is the effect produced by unwarranted strictness and constant threatening. When a child recognizes that the demands made on him are just, rather than designed to create fear, he will respond willingly. If, however, fear is the only operative, inevitably his effort will be paralyzed, his mental development blocked; eventually, he will turn to lies, cunning, and hypocrisy.

It is absolutely wrong to be inconsistent with a youngster, i.e., sometimes lavishing too much praise on him while at other times reprimanding or punishing him too severely. As a result of such inconsistency, the youngster grows up to be nervous, harassed, and unstable.

There are instances when single character trends are conditioned by biological causes. For example, a high degree of tension is often related to a weak physical state, resulting in the tendency to tire easily and become irritable. This condition can be ameliorated, but to achieve a change it is necessary to include pedagogical as well as medical measures. A well-balanced diet, gradual physical exercise when the child is ready, a firmly followed daily routine of work and rest, and more time in the fresh air, would offer the correct pedagogical-medical approach to diminishing or even eliminating the problem.

Clearly, then, we can conclude that heredity does not predetermine future character trends. Personality develops through the process of upbringing.

The better the educators and parents know a child, the better are the results achieved by well-organized, purposeful upbringing. Knowing a child means understanding the developmental stage he is in and recognizing his characteristics as an individual; both these elements are subjects of scientific study and research in the field of pedagogy. Parents, too, must be exposed to pedagogical findings, especially those which deal with the developmental peculiarities of different stages in the child's life. Once the general characteristics of a particular age group are understood, there is a need for a thorough study of the child (or young or older adolescent) as an individual.

Children of the same chronological age are unlike one another. There are no two identical youngsters. Just as the knowledge of the laws of nature helps one to master it, and the discovery of laws which govern the development of society enhances the possibilities of revolutionary changes, the understanding of a child creates an opportunity to influence him successfully.

All educational measures should take into consideration specific characteristics of the child; the development of his capabilities is possible only when there is a real understanding of his individuality.

Early interest evidenced by a child in a given area should not be immediately interpreted as a manifestation of his genius or exceptional talent. Not infrequently, hopeful parents, at the slightest indication of a child's interest in music or art, immediately see the boy as a future Mozart or Moussorgsky, or consider any of his paintings as good as Renoir's or Repin's. Of course, there are sometimes signs of talent in early childhood. Mozart's genius became apparent at the extremely early age of three. But this is an exception rather than a rule. Generally, children's early interests do not last long and change frequently, depending on their situation. Nevertheless, parents must pay attention to them.

Though native inclinations may appear early, lack of clearly pronounced interests during this period must not concern parents too much; abilities which later develop into talents more often are demonstrated at an older age. In an attempt to define capabilities, extreme caution and thoughtfulness should be exercised. There are too many examples of serious errors of judgment, wherein people who in their youth were considered untalented in a certain field, later contributed greatly to this given area of human endeavor. Isaac Newton in his childhood did not show any ability for studying, but this did not prevent his becoming a learned physicist.

Talents may appear at any given stage of human life, and it is never too late to begin to develop them.

Some parents complain that their children have a bad memory, which they blame upon hereditary factors: "My daughter's memory is just as bad as mine," or, "She studied and studied, thought she knew it well, but now she forgot it all, because she has such a bad memory"—says a mother using these rationalizations as excuses for her child's lack of acquired knowledge.

Obviously, the quality of people's memory varies considerably. Therefore, we can come to only one practical conclusion: One must intensify his effort to improve and develop memory through continuous practice which directs his habits toward concise thinking and efficient learning.

There are pupils who read through their home assignments only once, and believe that they have really absorbed the new material. This way of "studying" is harmful not only because it is superficial but also because it does not help to develop the memory. Students who cram a few days before finals quickly forget almost everything they have studied in this way. To retain subject matter, it is necessary to create in the cortex a definite system of associations. The more links that become developed in the process of absorbing the given material, the better remembered is the content. Mechanical memorization does not help; only clear comprehension of the text enables its mastery and the establishment of lasting associations. Automatic absorption is permissible only when the character of the material calls for it. For example, when studying foreign languages, one must often memorize words or even whole phrases; however, in a logically linked and connected text, this method only hampers and tires the memory, rather than stimulating its growth.

Like memory, attention also can be strengthened by practice. The ability to direct attention can be cultivated by deliberate training. The formation of this habit should be started at a very early age.

Holding a child's attention can be accomplished by stimulating his interest in a given subject. Parents should support and develop children's interest in learning first of all by exhibiting an interest in school and its curriculum. However, it is not possible to sustain the entire learning process solely on the basis of interest. Not all home assignments, for example, can be made to seem equally stimulating. Honor students make progress in all subject matters, even though not all subjects challenge them equally. Sheer will power, exerted during classroom sessions as well as during home study, can be of enormous help when applied to the kind of subject matter which does not inspire great natural interest.

Instead of being concerned about heredity, one should strive to instill neatness, obedience, concentration, purposefulness, strong will power, and attentiveness, through the application of correct methods of upbringing.

Thinking, which is the leading psychic process, must receive special attention not only in school but also at home. On the ability to think depends the capacity to analyze, to judge, to search for and find interrelationships, and to summarize and to generalize. The single most important aim of teaching is to develop the pupil's mental ability; and the best way to achieve this is to stimulate independent thinking. At all times, such effort should be supported and rewarded.

The thinking process begins when a need for understanding arises. The parents must try to develop the child's ability to think by stipulating systematic exercise and specific training of the brain rather than by relying upon heredity.

Will power is essential to action, especially to any undertaking which is geared to develop one's own personality, self-education, erudition, special abilities, and individual character traits. It manifests itself mostly when difficulties and hindrances have to be overcome. A strong-willed person always subordinates his wishes and desires to the moral principles by which he lives.

An individual whose fleeting desires rule his life is weak. If one is clever and talented, but without a strong will, both characteristics become quite useless. Strong will plays a decisive role in acts of heroism. Great purposefulness and a strong will are characteristic of all fighters dedicated to a cause. Unwavering determination to reach a goal is of basic significance to any task, whether the goal be a scientific task, an educational one, or the job of child rearing. Endeavors which require will power are always conscious; because of this, the development of will power in children is closely tied to the growth of consciousness, to the working out of his views of the world, his ideals, and his strivings.

A clearly formulated world outlook is one of the most important factors in developing a strong will. Lack of firm opinions and beliefs weakens the will and makes it unstable. On the other hand, it is not sufficient to influence consciousness alone. All good intentions must become accomplished deeds in order to make the will genuinely strong.

The first and basic indication of a strong will in an individual is a determination to complete each given task with persistence (a very valuable characteristic) regardless of hindrances and difficulties.

It is important that adults regularly check to be sure that children have fulfilled the duties requested of them. Often a youngster, although he understands the necessity of a given assignment, gets carried away by games or something else equally exciting and is inclined to avoid the task; but realizing that his activities will be checked by his parents, he will give up the more interesting activity in favor of the necessary one.

In the process of education, even minor incidents are significant, because the child reacts to each of them. Some parents wonder whether they should insist that the youngster put his toys in place each evening, so that he will learn order early. Developing such a habit fosters the acquisition of will power. In case the child does not want to clean up, depriving him of his toys for a time until he agrees to place them where they belong proves to be a good educational measure.

Will power develops best under the favorable conditions of collective work, when the child learns systematically to fulfill clearly defined tasks.

Older children should be instilled with a desire to train and educate themselves. An interest in spiritual growth and the development of positive character traits increases considerably during adolescence. This interest must be supported and stimulated, because in this developmental stage the method of self-improvement plays a pertinent role in the development of the whole personality.

Work education, through the systematic participation of children in socially meaningful tasks as well as in household chores, fosters their physical and mental abilities and develops characteristics which are needed and useful for study and for any future activity.

Observations of children in school and at home prove that a bad memory, weak will and short attention span usually occur in children who are excused from all physical work. They are not able to do anything independently. The laziness their parents complain about is not an inborn characteristic. It develops as a result of parents' faulty philosophy of protecting children from any demands for physical work. Work is an indispensable tool in the formation of character. Knowledge and habits play an important role in accomplishing any physical task; without them no work is possible. To work means to express oneself through action, to enrich one's intellectual horizons, and to develop one's capabilities.

One of the most important duties of parents is to condition their children to physical work. "The Decree to strengthen the ties of school with life and to further the development of the national system of education in U.S.S.R." considers it necessary to "prepare children very early for active participation in socially meaningful work. Youths of fifteen or sixteen and older must be included in all feasible socially useful work, and it is necessary for their subsequent educational experience to be closely linked with those of productive labor in the national economy."

The work education of children must begin in the family before they start school. When they are still very young, they should be taught to fulfill certain duties at home; for example, to make their own beds, clean up toys, sweep the floor, set the table, etc. In this way they will learn to be self-reliant and independent. They must learn to be responsible for the accomplishment of any tasks given to them, of short or long duration. This participation in house chores is the first very important step in work education.

The influence of the older generation upon growing children and youth stimulates their developmental process. The better the child's education, the healthier becomes his development.

Since the child's development helps to broaden his educational possibilities, a process of dialectical interrelationship takes place.

While the child learns to communicate verbally by proceeding from word repetition to talking and finally reaching an ability to differentiate between various word meanings and their complicated usage, his vocabulary becomes enlarged and his memory enriched. He goes through a process which is not only educational but also developmental.

Each generation inherits from the previous ones vast achievements in culture, art, and technique. Thanks to education and upbringing, the growing generation has an opportunity to utilize these resources in their lives and to enrich them further by new discoveries and inventions for the future descendants.

The practical conclusion from all that has been said above is that one must actively help the child's development through a purposeful education rather than by depending on his native, inherited abilities.

A correct upbringing should stimulate his positive, natural capabilities and eliminate any negative characteristics he might have inherited.

The task of Communist upbringing is to raise a well-rounded, harmoniously developed young generation. While we are striving to create a society in which each individual will utilize and realize his potentialities through productive work in his chosen field, we always emphasize the diversity which exists between individual potentialities and individual needs.

In order to prepare the generation now growing up for the demands of a Communist society which will soon become a reality, we do not rear them by methods which would eliminate the differences existing between individuals. On the contrary, we utilize means which foster the fullest development of each individual; we must satisfy more and more continuously growing variety of interests, requirements, and inclinations, as long as they are not directed against the common interests of the society.

A harmonious development means one which utilizes to their maximum all the native abilities useful to society. A child exceptionally talented in one specific area should not be forced to develop other areas of human endeavor equally well at the expense of his manifested talent. But neither should one go to the extreme of giving a talented youngster only a one-sided education. It should not be forgotten that a contemporary man cannot be considered educated without mastery of the school curriculum, which provides a basis for his future studies. In the process of acquiring knowledge the capabilities of youngsters which need special development become apparent.

The educational process is especially important to children and youth although adults also may and should be responsive to it. But educating adults is an entirely different process, since their personality is already formed, while youngsters are still engaged in the development of theirs. It is much easier to affect children, whose nervous systems are more flexible than those of grownups. The youngster, whose organism, intellect, and character are still growing, is particularly receptive to correct methods of upbringing.

Nevertheless, there are some adolescents whose behavior contradicts the established morality norms of the Soviet man. These failures are brought about not by hereditary factors, as some parents would like to believe, but by poor upbringing. The task of the Soviet family and school is to develop in youth high moral values and readiness for independence in life. The moral values are expressed not in words but in deeds. "Show your point of view not through words but through deeds," said Lenin. This means that the individual's morality is determined by his behavior.

When raising youth we must remember Lenin's statement, "The Communist up-bringing of youth should not be a sweet preaching of rules of ethics. This does not constitute an education. . . . Only through toiling together with workers in industry and in agriculture is it possible to become a real Communist. . . . All time should be found for the youth to solve a practical problem of common significance, no matter how small and simple the task might be."

In order to achieve the goals of communistic rearing of children and youth, it is necessary to provide them with practical work experience, socially meaningful, which they are ready for. "Without work and struggle," said Lenin, "theoretical knowledge acquired in Communist pamphlets is absolutely meaningless, since it continues to perpetuate the isolation of theory from practice, which composes the most repelling characteristic of the old bourgeois society." Children and youth must realize that their work brings real gain to their family or city, town or village. Otherwise the education which takes place is not Communist in spirit.

Correct upbringing is not dependent upon heredity. Children grow up as indus-trious individuals who are able to face and overcome difficulties as well as negative occurrences as an integral part of their life experience.

The decisive role which upbringing plays in the development of personality as well as the importance of practice in widening all recognized capabilities such as thinking, attention and memory, do not negate heredity completely. An examination of the whole history of humankind verifies the positive role heredity has played in human development.

When the very same irritations are elicited in certain parts of the brain during a prolonged period of time (many generations), they will definitely change the structure of the nervous tissue, and according to the laws of adjustment these changes may take hold and become hereditarily transferable. I. P. Pavlov proved that con-ditioned reflexes, being individually acquired, may change to unconditioned reflexes, which become reinforced by way of hereditary transmission.

According to the biological laws of heredity, the brain, the hand, and other organs of the human body become more developed with the passing of many genera-tions. Under the influence and stimulation of work and of social relationships, the human brain improves, as does the ability to think; and the sensory organs become perfected.

This biological part of human personality did not play a decisive role in the development of human society. The factor which differentiated the human being from the animal kingdom was work. Though man walks erect and has his hands free for toil, though his speaking ability changed his brain and he built working tools, though he earns a living and meets his social needs, still he is not completely free of animal characteristics. Frederick Engels in his book *Anti-Duhring* implies that there may be only quantitative differentiations between the degrees of bes-tiality and humanness. While it is obvious that primitive man was ruled by his ani-mal instincts subordinated to his biological nature, in time human social needs played a role which steadily grew in importance. In the process of meeting them, man changed and perfected the biological structure of his personality.

Each generation inherits, of course, the developmental level of biological personality structure which was reached by their predecessors. But human beings are not limited by it; they can progress, perfecting and enlarging their achievements in controlling nature and changing it by their action. In this process each individual also changes his own nature. By this historical course of action human society as well as the individual develops.

These changes in human nature are strengthened by way of hereditary transmission. This provides the individual with an opportunity to eliminate negative characteristics of heredity while fostering the positive ones. Therefore, parents must take care of themselves to make sure they have health, strength, and endurance. Healthy parents produce healthy children, while sick parents produce sickly children. Daily routines of work and rest, normal diet, fresh air, body hygiene and cleanliness of clothing and living quarters are all indispensable conditions for fostering the health of parents and their children. Parents who overindulge in alcoholic beverages bring great harm to their children because of the negative effect upon the whole organism. Alcoholism of parents produces hereditary aftereffects in children who often are weak not only physically but also psychologically.

And so the decisive role in the development of personality is played by purposeful education in school and at home. The task of the parents is to create such conditions of life and engage the child in those activities which will foster in him the development of a Communist world outlook, and behavior which will make him a builder of the Communist society. Every child needs education, no matter what his native abilities; without it he cannot develop his capabilities.

Differences existing among people are not the result of heredity, but of education. People often do not develop to their highest potential only because they lack favorable living conditions and correct upbringing.

In a Socialist society, where the whole environment fosters the development of the Communist world outlook, and where the efforts of the government and of society are directed toward improvement of economic living conditions as well as toward providing greater cultural and educational opportunities, the role of upbringing becomes most decisive.

Questions for Discussion

1. Do you agree that the interests of the society, whether it be communist or capitalist, should provide the principle purpose to guide the educational enterprise? Should the American school foster and preserve capitalist values just as a Russian school should foster and preserve communist values?
2. Examine the concept of motivation discussed in this selection, and evaluate its accuracy. Do Pavlov's theories of stimulus-response and the conditional reflex provide satisfactory explanations for how students learn?
3. How do you think pedagogical principles of Dewey's pragmatic education would be viewed in a communist society? What about Rousseau's ideas? Or Brameld's?

6 What Knowledge Is of Most Worth?

Herbert Spencer

Perhaps education has little to do with values, contrary to what the previous selections have argued. Perhaps the real purpose of education is to discover, validate and disseminate knowledge. This is a more traditional view of the school's purpose, and is the one which probably has guided most of your teachers, for the present lectures, textbooks, examinations, reading assignments and grades are usually good indicators of a philosophy which emphasizes the role of the teacher as a disseminator of information. What knowledge should be disseminated? Only that which is reliable and useful for self-preservation. And how can we determine which bits of knowledge have these characteristics? By paying attention to the results of scientific investigation. Do you agree with these conclusions by Herbert Spencer?

In education, then, this is the question of questions, which it is high time we discussed in some methodic way. The first in importance, though the last to be considered, is the problem—how to decide among the conflicting claims of various subjects on our attention. Before there can be a rational *curriculum,* we must settle which things it most concerns us to know; or, to use a word of Bacon's, now unfortunately obsolete—we must determine the relative values of knowledges. . . .

Doubtless the task is difficult—perhaps never to be more than approximately achieved. But, considering the vastness of the interests at stake, its difficulty is no reason for pusillanimously passing it by; but rather for devoting every energy to its mastery. And if we only proceed systematically, we may very soon get at results of no small moment.

Our first step must obviously be to classify, in the order of their importance, the leading kinds of activity which constitute human life. They may be naturally arranged into:—1. those activities which directly minister to self-preservation; 2. those activities which, by securing the necessaries of life, indirectly minister to self-preservation; 3. those activities which have for their end the rearing and discipline of offspring; 4. those activities which are involved in the maintenance of proper social and political relations; 5. those miscellaneous activities which fill up the leisure part of life, devoted to the gratification of the tastes and feelings. . . .

Happily, that all-important part of education which goes to secure direct self-preservation, is in great part already provided for. Too momentous to be left to our blundering, Nature takes it into her own hands. While yet in its nurse's arms, the infant, by hiding its face and crying at the sight of a stranger, shows the dawning instinct to attain safety by flying from that which is unknown and may be dangerous; and when it can walk, the terror it manifests if an unfamiliar dog comes near, or the screams with which it runs to its mother after any startling sight or

From the book *Essays on Education and Kindred Subjects* by Herbert Spencer. Everyman's Library Edition. Reprinted by permission of E. P. Dutton & Co., Inc., and J. M. Dent & Sons Ltd.

sound, shows this instinct further developed. Moreover, knowledge subserving direct
self-preservation is that which it is chiefly busied in acquiring from hour to hour.
How to balance its body; how to control its movements so as to avoid collisions; what
objects are hard, and will hurt if struck; what objects are heavy, and injure if they fall
on limbs; which things will bear the weight of the body, and which not; the pains inflicted by fire, by missiles, by sharp instruments—these, and various other pieces of
information needful for the avoidance of death or accident, it is ever learning. And
when, a few years later, the energies go out in running, climbing, and jumping, in
games of strength and games of skill, we see in all these actions by which the muscles
are developed, the perceptions sharpened, and the judgment quickened, a preparation for the safe conduct of the body among surrounding objects and movements;
and for meeting those greater dangers that occasionally occur in the lives of all.
Being thus, as we say, so well cared for by Nature, this fundamental education needs
comparatively little care from us. What we are chiefly called upon to see, is, that
there shall be free scope for gaining this experience and receiving this discipline—
that there shall be no such thwarting of Nature as that by which stupid school-
mistresses commonly prevent the girls in their charge from the spontaneous physical
activities they would indulge in; and so render them comparatively incapable of
taking care of themselves in circumstances of peril.

This, however, is by no means all that is comprehended in the education that
prepares for direct self-preservation. Besides guarding the body against mechanical
damage or destruction, it has to be guarded against injury from other causes—against
the disease and death that follow breaches of physiologic law. For complete living
it is necessary, not only that sudden annihilations of life shall be warded off; but
also that there shall be escaped the incapacities and the slow annihilation which
unwise habits entail. As, without health and energy, the industrial, the parental,
the social, and all other activities become more or less impossible; it is clear that this
secondary kind of direct self-preservation is only less important than the primary
kind; and that knowledge tending to secure it should rank very high.

It is true that here, too, guidance is in some measure ready supplied. By our
various physical sensations and desires, Nature has insured a tolerable conformity
to the chief requirements. Fortunately for us, want of food, great heat, extreme cold,
produce promptings too peremptory to be disregarded. And would men habitually
obey these and all like promptings when less strong, comparatively few evils would
arise. If fatigue of body or brain were in every case followed by desistance; if the
oppression produced by a close atmosphere always led to ventilation; if there were
no eating without hunger, or drinking without thirst; then would the system be but
seldom out of working order. But so profound an ignorance is there of the laws of
life, that men do not even know that their sensations are their natural guides, and
(when not rendered morbid by long-continued disobedience) their trustworthy
guides. So that though, to speak teleologically, Nature has provided efficient safeguards to health, lack of knowledge makes them in a great measure useless. . . .

Hence, knowledge which subserves direct self-preservation by preventing this loss
of health, is of primary importance. We do not contend that possession of such
knowledge would by any means wholly remedy the evil. It is clear that in our present
phase of civilisation, men's necessities often compel them to transgress. And it is

further clear that, even in the absence of such compulsion, their inclinations would frequently lead them, spite of their convictions, to sacrifice future good to present gratification. But we do contend that the right knowledge impressed in the right way would effect much; and we further contend that as the laws of health must be recognised before they can be fully conformed to, the imparting of such knowledge must precede a more rational living—come when that may. We infer that as vigorous health and its accompanying high spirits are larger elements of happiness than any other things whatever, the teaching how to maintain them is a teaching that yields in moment to no other whatever. And therefore we assert that such a course of physiology as is needful for the comprehension of its general truths, and their bearings on daily conduct, is an all-essential part of a rational education.

Strange that the assertion should need making! Stranger still that it should need defending! Yet are there not a few by whom such a proposition will be received with something approaching to derision. Men who would blush if caught saying Iphigénia instead of Iphigenía, or would resent as an insult any imputation of ignorance respecting the fabled labours of a fabled demi-god, show not the slightest shame in confessing that they do not know where the Eustachian tubes are, what are the actions of the spinal cord, what is the normal rate of pulsation, or how the lungs are inflated. While anxious that their sons should be well up in the superstitions of two thousand years ago, they care not that they should be taught anything about the structure and functions of their own bodies—nay, even wish them not to be so taught. So overwhelming is the influence of established routine! So terribly in our education does the ornamental over-ride the useful!

We need not insist on the value of that knowledge which aids indirect self-preservation by facilitating the gaining of a livelihood. This is admitted by all; and, indeed, by the mass is perhaps too exclusively regarded as the end of education. But while every one is ready to endorse the abstract proposition that instruction fitting youths for the business of life is of high importance, or even to consider it of supreme importance; yet scarcely any inquire what instruction will so fit them. It is true that reading, writing, and arithmetic are taught with an intelligent appreciation of their uses. But when we have said this we have said nearly all. While the great bulk of what else is acquired has no bearing on the industrial activities, an immensity of information that has a direct bearing on the industrial activities is entirely passed over.

For, leaving out only some very small classes, what are all men employed in? They are employed in the production, preparation, and distribution of commodities. And on what does efficiency in the production, preparation, and distribution of commodities depend? It depends on the use of methods fitted to the respective natures of these commodities; it depends on an adequate acquaintance with their physical, chemical, or vital properties, as the case may be; that is, it depends on Science. This order of knowledge which is in great part ignored in our school-courses, is the order of knowledge underlying the right performance of those processes by which civilised life is made possible. Undeniable as is this truth, there seems to be no living consciousness of it: its very familiarity makes it unregarded. To give due weight to our argument, we must, therefore, realise this truth to the reader by a rapid review of the facts.

Passing over the most abstract science, Logic, on the due guidance by which, however, the large producer or distributor depends, knowingly or unknowingly, for success in his business-forecasts, we come first to Mathematics. Of this, the most general division, dealing with number, guides all industrial activities; be they those by which processes are adjusted, or estimates framed, or commodities bought and sold, or accounts kept. No one needs to have the value of this division of abstract science insisted upon.

For the higher arts of construction, some acquaintance with the more special division of Mathematics is indispensable. The village carpenter, who lays out his work by empirical rules, equally with the builder of a Britannia Bridge, makes hourly reference to the laws of space-relations. The surveyor who measures the land purchased; the architect in designing a mansion to be built on it; the builder when laying out the foundations; the masons in cutting the stones; and the various artizans who put up the fittings; are all guided by geometrical truths. Railway-making is regulated from beginning to end by geometry: alike in the preparation of plans and sections; in staking out the line; in the mensuration of cuttings and embankments; in the designing and building of bridges, culverts, viaducts, tunnels, stations. Similarly with the harbours, docks, piers, and various engineering and architectural works that fringe the coasts and overspread the country, as well as the mines that run underneath it. And now-a-days, even the farmer, for the correct laying-out of his drains, has recourse to the level—that is, to geometrical principles.

Turn next to the Abstract-Concrete sciences. On the application of the simplest of these, Mechanics, depends the success of modern manufactures. The properties of the lever, the wheel-and-axle, etc., are recognised in every machine, and to machinery in these times we owe all production. Trace the history of the breakfast-roll. The soil out of which it came was drained with machine-made tiles; the surface was turned over by a machine; the wheat was reaped, thrashed, and winnowed by machines; by machinery it was ground and bolted; and had the flour been sent to Gosport, it might have been made into biscuits by a machine. Look round the room in which you sit. If modern, probably the bricks in its walls were machine-made; and by machinery the flooring was sawn and planed, the mantel-shelf sawn and polished, the paper-hangings made and printed. The veneer on the table, the turned legs of the chairs, the carpet, the curtains, are all products of machinery. Your clothing— plain, figured, or printed—is it not wholly woven, nay, perhaps even sewed, by machinery? And the volume you are reading—are not its leaves fabricated by one machine and covered with these words by another? Add to which that for the means of distribution over both land and sea, we are similarly indebted. And then observe that according as knowledge of mechanics is well or ill applied to these ends, comes success or failure. The engineer who miscalculates the strength of materials, builds a bridge that breaks down. The manufacturer who uses a bad machine cannot compete with another whose machine wastes less in friction and inertia. The ship-builder adhering to the old model is out-sailed by one who builds on the mechanically-justified wave-line principle. And as the ability of a nation to hold its own against other nations, depends on the skilled activity of its units, we see that on mechanical knowledge may turn the national fate.

On ascending from the divisions of Abstract-Concrete science dealing with molar forces, to those divisions of it which deal with molecular forces, we come to another vast series of applications. To this group of sciences joined with the preceding groups we owe the steam-engine, which does the work of millions of labourers. That section of physics which formulates the laws of heat, has taught us how to economise fuel in various industries; how to increase the produce of smelting furnaces by substituting the hot for the cold blast; how to ventilate mines; how to prevent explosions by using the safety-lamp; and, through the thermometer, how to regulate innumerable processes. That section which has the phenomena of light for its subject, gives eyes to the old and the myopic; aids through the microscope in detecting diseases and adulterations; and, by improved lighthouses, prevents shipwrecks. Researches in electricity and magnetism have saved innumerable lives and incalculable property through the compass; have subserved many arts by the electrotype; and now, in the telegraph, have supplied us with an agency by which for the future, mercantile transactions will be regulated and political intercourse carried on. While in the details of in-door life, from the improved kitchen-range up to the stereoscope on the drawing-room table, the applications of advanced physics underlie our comforts and gratifications.

Still more numerous are the applications of Chemistry. The bleacher, the dyer, the calico-printer, are severally occupied in processes that are well or ill done according as they do or do not conform to chemical laws. Smelting of copper, tin, zinc, lead, silver, iron, must be guided by chemistry. Sugar-refining, gas-making, soap-boiling, gunpowder-manufacture, are operations all partly chemical; as are likewise those which produce glass and porcelain. Whether the distiller's wort stops at the alcoholic fermentation or passes into the acetous, is a chemical question on which hangs his profit or loss; and the brewer, if his business is extensive, finds it pays to keep a chemist on his premises. Indeed, there is now scarcely any manufacture over some part of which chemistry does not preside. Nay, in these times even agriculture, to be profitably carried on, must have like guidance. The analysis of manures and soils; the disclosure of their respective adaptations; the use of gypsum or other substance for fixing ammonia; the utilisation of coprolites; the production of artificial manures —all these are boons of chemistry which it behoves the farmer to acquaint himself with. Be it in the lucifer match, or in disinfected sewage, or in photographs—in bread made without fermentation, or perfumes extracted from refuse, we may perceive that chemistry affects all our industries; and that, therefore, knowledge of it concerns every one who is directly or indirectly connected with our industries.

Of the Concrete sciences, we come first to Astronomy. Out of this has grown that art of navigation which has made possible the enormous foreign commerce that supports a large part of our population, while supplying us with many necessaries and most of our luxuries.

Geology, again, is a science knowledge of which greatly aids industrial success. Now that iron ores are so large a source of wealth; now that the duration of our coal-supply has become a question of great interest; now that we have a College of Mines and a Geological Survey; it is scarcely needful to enlarge on the truth that the study of the Earth's crust is important to our material welfare.

And then the science of life—Biology: does not this, too, bear fundamentally on these processes of indirect self-preservation? With what we ordinarily call manufactures, it has, indeed, little connection; but with the all-essential manufacture—that of food—it is inseparably connected. As agriculture must conform its methods to the phenomena of vegetal and animal life, it follows that the science of these phenomena is the rational basis of agriculture.

We come now to the third great division of human activities—a division for which no preparation whatever is made. Is it not an astonishing fact, that though on the treatment of offspring depend their lives or deaths, and their moral welfare or ruin; yet not one word of instruction on the treatment of offspring is ever given to those who will by and by be parents? Is it not monstrous that the fate of a new generation should be left to the chances of unreasoning custom, impulse, fancy —joined with the suggestions of ignorant nurses and the prejudiced counsel of grandmothers? If a merchant commenced business without any knowledge of arithmetic and book-keeping, we should exclaim at his folly, and look for disastrous consequences. Or if, before studying anatomy, a man set up as a surgical operator, we should wonder at his audacity and pity his patients. But that parents should begin the difficult task of rearing children, without ever having given a thought to the principles—physical, moral, or intellectual—which ought to guide them, excites neither surprise at the actors nor pity for their victims.

To tens of thousands that are killed, add hundreds of thousand that survive with feeble constitutions, and millions that grow up with constitutions not so strong as they should be; and you will have some idea of the curse inflicted on their offspring by parents ignorant of the laws of life. Do but consider for a moment that the regimen to which children are subject, is hourly telling upon them to their life-long injury or benefit; and that there are twenty ways of going wrong to one way of going right; and you will get some idea of the enormous mischief that is almost everywhere inflicted by the thoughtless, haphazard system in common use. Is it decided that a boy shall be clothed in some flimsy short dress, and be allowed to go playing about with limbs reddened by cold? The decision will tell on his whole future existence —either in illnesses; or in stunted growth; or in deficient energy; or in a maturity less vigorous than it ought to have been, and in consequent hindrances to success and happiness. Are children doomed to a monotonous dietary, or a dietary that is deficient in nutritiveness? Their ultimate physical power, and their efficiency as men and women, will inevitably be more or less diminished by it. Are they forbidden vociferous play, or (being too ill-clothed to bear exposure) are they kept indoors in cold weather? They are certain to fall below that measure of health and strength to which they would else have attained. When sons and daughters grow up sickly and feeble, parents commonly regard the event as a misfortune—as a visitation of Providence. Thinking after the prevalent chaotic fashion, they assume that these evils come without causes; or that the causes are supernatural. Nothing of the kind. In some cases the causes are doubtless inherited; but in most cases foolish regulations are the causes. Very generally, parents themselves are responsible for all this pain, this debility, this depression, this misery. They have undertaken to control the lives of their offspring from hour to hour; with cruel carelessness they have neglected to learn anything about these vital processes which they are unceasingly affecting by their commands and prohibitions; in utter ignorance of the simplest physiologic laws, they have been year by year undermining the constitutions of their children; and have so inflicted disease and premature death, not only on them but on their descendants.

Equally great are the ignorance and the consequent injury, when we turn from physical training to moral training. Consider the young mother and her nursery-legislation. But a few years ago she was at school, where her memory was crammed with words, and names, and dates, and her reflective faculties scarcely in the slightest degree exercised—where not one idea was given her respecting the methods of dealing with the opening mind of childhood; and where her discipline did not in the least fit her for thinking out methods of her own. The intervening years have been passed in practising music, in fancy-work, in novel-reading, and in party-going: no thought having yet been given to the grave responsibilities of maternity; and scarcely any of that solid intellectual culture obtained which would be some preparation for such responsibilities. And now see her with an unfolding human character committed to her charge—see her profoundly ignorant of the phenomena with which she has to deal, undertaking to do that which can be done but imperfectly even with the aid of the profoundest knowledge. She knows nothing about the nature of the emotions, their order of evolution, their functions, or where use ends and abuse begins. She is under the impression that some of the feelings are wholly bad, which is not true of any one of them; and that others are good however far they may be carried, which is also not true of any one of them. And then, ignorant as she is of the structure she has to deal with, she is equally ignorant of the effects produced on it by this or that treatment. What can be more inevitable than the disastrous results we see hourly arising? Lacking knowledge of mental phenomena, with their cause and consequences, her interference is frequently more mischievous than absolute passivity would have been. This and that kind of action, which are quite normal and beneficial, she perpetually thwarts; and so diminishes the child's happiness and profit, injures its temper and her own, and produces estrangement. Deeds which she thinks it desirable to encourage, she gets performed by threats and bribes, or by exciting a desire for applause: considering little what the inward motive may be, so long as the outward conduct conforms; and thus cultivating hypocrisy, and fear, and selfishness, in place of good feeling. While insisting on truthfulness, she constantly sets an example of untruth by threatening penalties which she does not inflict. While inculcating self-control, she hourly visits on her little ones angry scolding for acts undeserving of them. She has not the remotest idea that in the nursery, as in the world, that alone is the truly salutary discipline which visits on all conduct, good and bad, the natural consequences—the consequences, pleasurable or painful, which in the nature of things such conduct tends to bring. Being thus without theoretic guidance, and quite incapable of guiding herself by tracing the mental processes going on in her children, her rule is impulsive, inconsistent, mischievous; and would indeed be generally ruinous were it not that the overwhelming tendency of the growing mind to assume the moral type of the race usually subordinates all minor influences.

And then the culture of the intellect—is not this, too, mismanaged in a similar manner? Grant that the phenomena of intelligence conform to laws; grant that the evolution of intelligence in a child also conforms to laws; and it follows inevitably that education cannot be rightly guided without a knowledge of these laws. To suppose that you can properly regulate this process of forming and accumulating ideas, without understanding the nature of the process, is absurd. How widely, then, must teaching as it is differ from teaching as it should be; when hardly any parents, and but few tutors, know anything about psychology. As might be expected, the established system is grievously at fault, alike in matter and in manner. While the right class of facts is withheld, the wrong class is forcibly administered in the wrong way and in the wrong order. Under that common limited idea of education which confines it to knowledge gained from books, parents thrust primers into the hands of their little ones years too soon, to their great injury. Not recognising the truth that the function of books is supplementary—that they form an indirect means to knowledge when direct means fail—a means of seeing through other men what you cannot see for yourself; teachers are eager to give secondhand facts in place of firsthand facts. Not perceiving the enormous value of that spontaneous education which goes on in early years—not perceiving that a child's restless observation, instead of being ignored or checked, should be diligently ministered to, and made as accurate and complete as possible; they insist on occupying its eyes and thoughts with things that are, for the time being, incomprehensible and repugnant. Possessed by a superstition which worships the symbols of knowledge instead of the knowledge itself, they do not see that only when his acquaintance with the objects and processes of the household, the streets, and the fields, is becoming tolerably exhaustive—only then should a child be introduced to the new sources of information which books supply: and this, not only because immediate cognition is of far greater value than mediate cognition; but also, because the words contained in books can be rightly interpreted into ideas, only in proportion to the antecedent experience of things. Observe next, that this formal instruction, far too soon commenced, is carried on with but little reference to the laws of mental development. Intellectual progress is of necessity from the concrete to the abstract. But regardless of this, highly abstract studies, such as grammar, which should come quite late, are begun quite early. Political geography, dead and uninteresting to a child, and which should be an appendage of sociological studies, is commenced betimes; while physical geography, comprehensible and comparatively attractive to a child, is in great part passed over. Nearly every subject dealt with is arranged in abnormal order: definitions and rules and principles being put first, instead of being disclosed, as they are in the order of nature, through the study of cases. And then, pervading the whole, is the vicious system of rote learning—a system of sacrificing the spirit to the letter. See the results. What with perceptions unnaturally dulled by early thwarting, and a coerced attention to books—what with the mental confusion produced by teaching subjects before they can be understood, and in each of them giving generalisations before the facts of which they are the generalisations—what with making the pupil a mere passive recipient of other's ideas, and not in the least leading him to be an active inquirer or self-instructor—and what with taxing the faculties to excess; there are very few minds that become as efficient as they might be. Examinations being once passed, books are laid aside; the greater part of what has been acquired, being unorganised, soon drops out of recollection; what remains is mostly inert—the art of applying knowledge not having been cultivated; and there is but little power either of accurate observation or independent thinking. To all which add, that while much of the information gained is of relatively small value, an immense mass of information of transcendent value is entirely passed over.

Thus we find the facts to be such as might have been inferred à priori. The training of children—physical, moral, and intellectual—is dreadfully defective. And in great measure it is so because parents are devoid of that knowledge by which this training can alone be rightly guided. . . .

From the parental functions let us pass now to the functions of the citizen. We have here to inquire what knowledge fits a man for the discharge of these functions. It cannot be alleged that the need for knowledge fitting him for these functions is wholly overlooked; for our school-courses contain certain studies, which, nominally at least, bear upon political and social duties. Of these the only one that occupies a prominent place is History.

But, as already hinted, the information commonly given under this head, is almost valueless for purposes of guidance. Scarcely any of the facts set down in our school-histories, and very few of those contained in the more elaborate works written for adults, illustrate the right principles of political action. The biographies of monarchs (and our children learn little else) throw scarcely any light upon the science of society. Familiarity with court intrigues, plots, usurpations, or the like, and with all the personalities accompanying them, aids very little in elucidating the causes of national progress. We read of some squabble for power, that it led to a pitched battle; that such and such were the names of the generals and their leading subordinates; that they had each so many thousand infantry and cavalry, and so many cannon; that they arranged their forces in this and that order; that they manœuvred, attacked, and fell back in certain ways; that at this part of the day such disasters were sustained, and at that such advantages gained; that in one particular movement some leading officer fell, while in another a certain regiment was decimated; that after all the changing fortunes of the fight, the victory was gained by this or that army; and that so many were killed and wounded on each side, and so many captured by the conquerors. And now, out of the accumulated details making up the narrative, say which it is that helps you in deciding on your conduct as a citizen. Supposing even that you had diligently read, not only *The Fifteen Decisive Battles of the World,* but accounts of all other battles that history mentions; how much more judicious would your vote be at the next election? "But these are facts—interesting facts," you say. Without doubt they are facts (such, at least, as are not wholly or partially fictions); and to many they may be interesting facts. But this by no means implies that they are valuable. Factitious or morbid opinion often gives seeming value to things that have scarcely any. A tulipomaniac will not part with a choice bulb for its weight in gold. To another man an ugly piece of cracked old china seems his most desirable possession. And there are those who give high prices for the relics of celebrated murderers. Will it be contended that these tastes are any measures of value in the things that gratify them? If not, then it must be admitted that the liking felt for certain classes of historical facts is no proof of their worth; and that we must test their worth, as we test the worth of other facts, by asking to what uses they are applicable. Were some one to tell you that your neighbour's cat kittened yesterday, you would say the information was valueless. Fact though it might

be, you would call it an utterly useless fact—a fact that could in no way influence
your actions in life—a fact that would not help you in learning how to live completely. Well, apply the same test to the great mass of historical facts, and you will
get the same result. They are facts from which no conclusions can be drawn—*unor-
ganisable* facts; and therefore facts of no service in establishing principles of conduct, which is the chief use of facts. Read them, if you like, for amusement; but do
not flatter yourself they are instructive.

That which constitutes History, properly so called, is in great part omitted from
works on the subject. Only of late years have historians commenced giving us, in any
considerable quantity, the truly valuable information. As in past ages the king was
everything and the people nothing; so, in past histories the doings of the king fill the
entire picture, to which the national life forms but an obscure background. While
only now, when the welfare of nations rather than of rulers is becoming the dominant idea, are historians beginning to occupy themselves with the phenomena of
social progress. The thing it really concerns us to know is the natural history of
society. We want all facts which help us to understand how a nation has grown and
organised itself. Among these, let us of course have an account of its government;
with as little as may be of gossip about the men who officered it, and as much as
possible about the structure, principles, methods, prejudices, corruptions, etc., which
it exhibited: and let this account include not only the nature and actions of the
central government, but also those of local governments, down to their minutest
ramifications. Let us of course also have a parallel description of the ecclesiastical
government—its organisation, its conduct, its power, its relations to the State; and
accompanying this, the ceremonial, creed, and religious ideas—not only those nominally believed, but those really believed and acted upon. Let us at the same time be
informed of the control exercised by class over class, as displayed in social obser-
vances—in titles, salutations, and forms of address. Let us know, too, what were all
the other customs which regulated the popular life out of doors and in-doors: including those concerning the relations of the sexes, and the relations of parents to
children. The superstitions, also, from the more important myths down to the charms
in common use, should be indicated. Next should come a delineation of the industrial system: showing to what extent the division of labour was carried; how trades
were regulated, whether by caste, guilds, or otherwise; what was the connection between employers and employed; what were the agencies for distributing commodities; what were the means of communication; what was the circulating medium.
Accompanying all which should be given an account of the industrial arts technically
considered: stating the processes in use, and the quality of the products. Further,
the intellectual condition of the nation in its various grades should be depicted; not
only with respect to the kind and amount of education, but with respect to the
progress made in science, and the prevailing manner of thinking. The degree of
aesthetic culture, as displayed in architecture, sculpture, painting, dress, music,
poetry, and fiction, should be described. Nor should there be omitted a sketch of
the daily lives of the people—their food, their homes, and their amusements. And
lastly, to connect the whole, should be exhibited the morals, theoretical and practical, of all classes: as indicated in their laws, habits, proverbs, deeds. These facts,
given with as much brevity as consists with clearness and accuracy, should be so

grouped and arranged that they may be comprehended in their *ensemble,* and contemplated as mutually-dependent parts of one great whole. The aim should be so to present them that men may readily trace the *consensus* subsisting among them; with the view of learning what social phenomena co-exist with what other. And then the corresponding delineations of succeeding ages should be so managed as to show how each belief, institution, custom, and arrangement was modified; and how the *consensus* of preceding structures and functions was developed into the *consensus* of succeeding ones. Such alone is the kind of information respecting past times which can be of service to the citizen for the regulation of his conduct. The only history that is of practical value is what may be called Descriptive Sociology. And the highest office which the historian can discharge, is that of so narrating the lives of nations, as to furnish materials for a Comparative Sociology; and for the subsequent determination of the ultimate laws to which social phenomena conform.

But now mark, that even supposing an adequate stock of this truly valuable historical knowledge has been acquired, it is of comparatively little use without the key. And the key is to be found only in Science. In the absence of the generalisations of biology and psychology, rational interpretation of social phenomena is impossible. Only in proportion as men draw certain rude, empirical inferences respecting human nature, are they enabled to understand even the simplest facts of social life: as, for instance, the relation between supply and demand. And if the most elementary truths of sociology cannot be reached until some knowledge is obtained of how men generally think, feel, and act under given circumstances; then it is manifest that there can be nothing like a wide comprehension of sociology, unless through a competent acquaintance with man in all his faculties, bodily, and mental. Consider the matter in the abstract, and this conclusion is self-evident. Thus:— Society is made up of individuals; all that is done in society is done by the combined actions of individuals; and therefore, in individual actions only can be found the solutions of social phenomena. But the actions of individuals depend on the laws of their natures; and their actions cannot be understood until these laws are understood. These laws, however, when reduced to their simplest expressions, prove to be corollaries from the laws of body and mind in general. Hence it follows, that biology and psychology are indispensable as interpreters of sociology. Or, to state the conclusions still more simply:—all social phenomena are phenomena of life—are the most complex manifestations of life—must conform to the laws of life—and can be understood only when the laws of life are understood. Thus, then, for the regulation of this fourth division of human activities, we are, as before, dependent on Science. Of the knowledge commonly imparted in educational courses, very little is of service for guiding a man in his conduct as a citizen. Only a small part of the history he reads is of practical value; and of this small part he is not prepared to make proper use. He lacks not only the materials for, but the very conception of, descriptive sociology; and he also lacks those generalisations of the organic sciences, without which even descriptive sociology can give him but small aid.

And now we come to that remaining division of human life which includes the relaxations and amusements filling leisure hours. After considering what training best fits for self-preservation, for the obtainment of sustenance, for the discharge of parental duties, and for the regulation of social and political conduct; we have now to

consider what training best fits for the miscellaneous ends not included in these—
for the enjoyment of Nature, of Literature, and of the Fine Arts, in all their forms.
. . . To this question the answer is still the same as heretofore. Unexpected
though the assertion may be, it is nevertheless true, that the highest Art of every
kind is based on Science—that without Science there can be neither perfect production nor full appreciation. Science, in that limited acceptation current in society,
may not have been possessed by various artists of high repute; but acute observers as
such artists have been, they have always possessed a stock of those empirical generalisations which constitute science in its lowest phase; and they have habitually fallen
far below perfection, partly because their generalisations were comparatively few
and inaccurate. That science necessarily underlies the fine arts, becomes manifest,
à priori, when we remember that art-products are all more or less representative of
objective or subjective phenomena; that they can be good only in proportion as they
conform to the laws of these phenomena; and that before they can thus conform, the
artist must know what these laws are. That this *à priori* conclusion tallies with experience, we shall soon see.

Youths preparing for the practice of sculpture have to acquaint themselves with
the bones and muscles of the human frame in their distribution, attachments, and
movements. This is a portion of science; and it has been found needful to impart
it for the prevention of those many errors which sculptors who do not possess it
commit. A knowledge of mechanical principles is also requisite; and such knowledge
not being usually possessed, grave mechanical mistakes are frequently made. Take
an instance. For the stability of a figure it is needful that the perpendicular from
the centre of gravity—"the line of direction," as it is called—should fall within the
base of support; and hence it happens, that when a man assumes the attitude known
as "standing at ease," in which one leg is straightened and the other relaxed, the
line of direction falls within the foot of the straightened leg. But sculptors unfamiliar with the theory of equilibrium, not uncommonly so represent this attitude,
that the line of direction falls midway between the feet. Ignorance of the law of
momentum leads to analogous blunders: as witness the admired Discobolus, which, as
it is posed, must inevitably fall forward the moment the quoit is delivered.

In painting, the necessity for scientific information, empirical if not rational, is
still more conspicuous. What gives the grotesqueness of Chinese pictures, unless
their utter disregard of the laws of appearances—their absurd linear perspective, and
their want of aerial perspective? In what are the drawings of a child so faulty, if not
in a similar absence of truth—an absence arising, in great part, from ignorance of
the way in which the aspects of things vary with the conditions? Do but remember
the books and lectures by which students are instructed; or consider the criticisms
of Ruskin; or look at the doings of the Pre-Raffaelites; and you will see that progress
in painting implies increasing knowledge of how effects in Nature are produced.
The most diligent observation, if unaided by science, fails to preserve from error.
Every painter will endorse the assertion that unless it is known what appearances
must exist under given circumstances, they often will not be perceived; and to know
what appearances must exist, is, in so far, to understand the science of appearances.
From want of science Mr. J. Lewis, careful painter as he is, casts the shadow of a
lattice-window in sharply-defined lines upon an opposite wall; which he would not

have done, had he been familiar with the phenomena of penumbræ. From want of science, Mr. Rossetti, catching sight of a peculiar iridescence displayed by certain hairy surfaces under particular lights (an iridescence caused by the diffraction of light in passing the hairs), commits the error of showing this iridescence on surfaces and in positions where it could not occur.

To say that music, too, has need of scientific aid will cause still more surprise. Yet it may be shown that music is but an idealisation of the natural language of emotion; and that consequently, music must be good or bad according as it conforms to the laws of this natural language. The various inflections of voice which accompany feelings of different kinds and intensities, are the germs out of which music is developed. It is demonstrable that these inflections and cadences are not accidental or arbitrary; but that they are determined by certain general principles of vital action; and that their expressiveness depends on this. Whence it follows that musical phrases and the melodies built of them, can be effective only when they are in harmony with these general principles. It is difficult here properly to illustrate this position. But perhaps it will suffice to instance the swarms of worthless ballads that infest drawing-rooms, as compositions which science would forbid. They sin against science by setting to music ideas that are not emotional enough to prompt musical expression; and they also sin against science by using musical phrases that have no natural relations to the ideas expressed: even where these are emotional. They are bad because they are untrue. And to say they are untrue, is to say they are unscientific.

Even in poetry the same thing holds. Like music, poetry has its root in those natural modes of expression which accompany deep feeling. Its rhythm, its strong and numerous metaphors, its hyperboles, its violent inversions, are simply exaggerations of the traits of excited speech. To be good, therefore, poetry must pay attention to those laws of nervous action which excited speech obeys. In intensifying and combining the traits of excited speech, it must have due regard to proportion —must not use its appliances without restriction; but, where the ideas are least emotional, must use the forms of poetical expression sparingly; must use them more freely as the emotion rises; and must carry them to their greatest extent, only where the emotion reaches a climax. The entire contravention of these principles results in bombast or doggerel. The insufficient respect for them is seen in didactic poetry. And it is because they are rarely fully obeyed, that so much poetry is inartistic.

Not only is it that the artist, of whatever kind, cannot produce a truthful work without he understands the laws of the phenomena he represents; but it is that he must also understand how the minds of spectators or listeners will be affected by the several peculiarities of his work—a question in psychology. What impression any art-product generates, manifestly depends upon the mental natures of those to whom it is presented; and as all mental natures have certain characteristics in common, there must result certain corresponding general principles on which alone art-products can be successfully framed. These general principles cannot be fully understood and applied, unless the artist sees how they follow from the laws of mind. To ask whether the composition of a picture is good is really to ask how the perceptions and feelings of observers will be affected by it. To ask whether a drama is well constructed, is to ask whether its situations are so arranged as duly to consult the power of attention of an audience, and duly to avoid overtaxing any one class of feelings. Equally in arranging the leading divisions of a poem or fiction, and in combining the words of a single sentence, the goodness of the effect depends upon the skill with which the mental energies and susceptibilities of the reader are economised. Every artist, in the course of his education and after-life, accumulates a stock of maxims by which his practice is regulated. Trace such maxims to their roots, and they inevitably lead you down to psychological principles. And only when the artist understands these psychological principles and their various corollaries can he work in harmony with them. . . .

Thus to the question we set out with—What knowledge is of most worth?—the uniform reply is—Science. This is the verdict on all the counts. For direct self-preservation, or the maintenance of life and health, the all-important knowledge is—Science. For that indirect self-preservation which we call gaining a livelihood, the knowledge of greatest value is—Science. For the due discharge of parental functions, the proper guidance is to be found only in—Science. For that interpretation of national life, past and present, without which the citizen cannot rightly regulate his conduct, the indispensable key is—Science. Alike for the most perfect production and highest enjoyment of art in all its forms, the needful preparation is still—Science. And for purposes of discipline—intellectual, moral, religious—the most efficient study is, once more—Science. The question which at first seemed so perplexed, has become, in the course of our inquiry, comparatively simple. We have not to estimate the degrees of importance of different orders of human activity, and different studies as severally fitting us for them; since we find that the study of Science, in its most comprehensive meaning, is the best preparation for all these orders of activity. We have not to decide between the claims of knowledge of great though conventional value, and knowledge of less though intrinsic values; seeing that the knowledge which proves to be of most value in all other respects, is intrinsically most valuable: its worth is not dependent upon opinion, but is as fixed as is the relation of man to the surrounding world. Necessary and eternal as are its truths, all Science concerns all mankind for all time. Equally at present and in the remotest future, must it be of incalculable importance for the regulation of their conduct, that men should understand the science of life, physical, mental, and social; and that they should understand all other science as a key to the science of life.

And yet this study, immensely transcending all other in importance, is that which, in an age of boasted education, receives the least attention. While what we call civilisation could never have arisen had it not been for science, science forms scarcely an appreciable element in our so-called civilised training. Though to the progress of science we owe it, that millions find support where once there was food only for thousands; yet of these millions but a few thousands pay any respect to that which has made their existence possible. Though increasing knowledge of the properties and relations of things has not only enabled wandering tribes to grow into populous nations, but has given to the countless members of these populous nations, comforts and pleasures which their few naked ancestors never even conceived, or could have believed, yet is this kind of knowledge only now receiving a grudging recognition in our highest educational institutions. To the slowly growing acquaintance with the uniform co-existences and sequences of phenomena—to the establishment of invariable laws, we owe our emancipation from the grossest superstitions. But for science we should be still worshipping fetishes; or, with hecatombs of victims, propitiating diabolical deities. And yet this science, which, in place of the most degrading conceptions of things, has given us some insight into the grandeurs of creation, is written against in our theologies and frowned upon from our pulpits.

Paraphrasing an Eastern fable, we may say that in the family of knowledge, Science is the household drudge, who, in obscurity, hides unrecognised perfections. To her has been committed all the works; by her skill, intelligence, and devotion, have all conveniences and gratifications been obtained; and while ceaselessly ministering to the rest, she has been kept in the background, that her haughty sisters might flaunt their fripperies in the eyes of the world. The parallel holds yet further. For we are fast coming to the *dénouement,* when the positions will be changed; and while these haughty sisters sink into merited neglect, Science, proclaimed as highest alike in worth and beauty, will reign supreme.

Questions for Discussion

1. State the reasons Spencer gives for concluding that the knowledge which is of most worth is science. Do you agree?
2. Do you believe that the fine arts, humanities, even psychology and sociology, can be taught best in a scientific way?
3. One of the great values of this selection is that Spencer asks us to list our values on a priority basis. If you were to list your own priorities, would you adopt Spencer's principle, self-preservation, as the basis for making your comparisons? What other principles might you use? Or can educational values be ranked according to their degree of importance?
4. Does Spencer's selection provide you with any insight for developing the curriculum of a school program?

7 The Ascent to Wisdom

Plato

Plato was the first major thinker in the western world to write systematically and fully on the subject of education, and his influence, even today, cannot be overestimated. In this selection he describes education as the process by which a man ascends from the dark cave of ignorance into the sunlight of wisdom. He then explains the curriculum he would use to help students obtain this wisdom. He identifies gymnastics, music, arithmetic, geometry, astronomy, harmonics and dialectic as the subjects to be taught, and in his discussion of "being" he suggests the basic educational principles which underlie his curriculum. Can you identify those principles?

And now, I said, let me show in a figure how far our nature is enlightened or unenlightened:—Behold! human beings living in an underground den, which has a mouth open towards the light and reaching all along the den; here they have been from their childhood, and have their legs and necks chained so that they cannot move, and can only see before them, being prevented by the chains from turning round their heads. Above and behind them a fire is blazing at a distance, and between the fire and the prisoners there is a raised way; and you will see, if you look, a low wall built along the way, like the screen which marionette players have in front of them, over which they show the puppets.

I see.

And do you see, I said, men passing along the wall carrying all sorts of vessels, and statues and figures of animals made of wood and stone and various materials, which appear over the wall? Some of them are talking, others silent.

You have shown me a strange image, and they are strange prisoners.

Like ourselves, I replied; and they see only their own shadows, or the shadows of one another, which the fire throws on the opposite wall of the cave?

True, he said; how could they see anything but the shadows if they were never allowed to move their heads?

And of the objects which are being carried in like manner they would only see the shadows?

Yes, he said.

And if they were able to converse with one another, would they not suppose that they were naming what was actually before them?

Very true.

And suppose further that the prison had an echo which came from the other side, would they not be sure to fancy when one of the passers-by spoke that the voice which they heard came from the passing shadow?

No question, he replied.

From *The Dialogues of Plato*, translated by Benjamin Jowett, fourth edition, 1953, Vol. II. Reprinted by permission of The Clarendon Press, Oxford.

To them, I said, the truth would be literally nothing but the shadows of the images.

That is certain.

And now look again, and see what will naturally follow if the prisoners are released and disabused of their error. At first, when any of them is liberated and compelled suddenly to stand up and turn his neck round and walk and look towards the light, he will suffer sharp pains; the glare will distress him, and he will be unable to see the realities of which in his former state he had seen the shadows; and then conceive some one saying to him, that what he saw before was an illusion, but that now, when he is approaching nearer to being and his eye is turned towards more real existence, he has a clearer vision,—what will be his reply? And you may further imagine that his instructor is pointing to the objects as they pass and requiring him to name them,—will he not be perplexed? Will he not fancy that the shadows which he formerly saw are truer than the objects which are now shown to him?

Far truer.

And if he is compelled to look straight at the light, will he not have a pain in his eyes which will make him turn away to take refuge in the object of vision which he can see, and which he will conceive to be in reality clearer than the things which are now being shown to him?

True, he said.

And suppose once more, that he is reluctantly dragged up a steep and rugged ascent, and held fast until he is forced into the presence of the sun himself, is he not likely to be pained and irritated? When he approaches the light his eyes will be dazzled, and he will not be able to see anything at all of what are now called realities.

Not all in a moment, he said.

He will require to grow accustomed to the sight of the upper world. And first he will see the shadows best, next the reflections of men and other objects in the water, and then the objects themselves; then he will gaze upon the light of the moon and the stars and the spangled heaven; and he will see the sky and the stars by night better than the sun or the light of the sun by day?

Certainly.

Last of all he will be able to see the sun, and not mere reflections of him in the water, but he will see him in his own proper place, and not in another; and he will contemplate him as he is.

Certainly.

He will then proceed to argue that this is he who gives the season and the years, and is the guardian of all that is in the visible world, and in a certain way the cause of all things which he and his fellows have been accustomed to behold?

Clearly, he said, he would first see the sun and then reason about him.

And when he remembered his old habitation, and the wisdom of the den and his fellow-prisoners, do you not suppose that he would felicitate himself on the change and pity them?

Certainly, he would.

And if they were in the habit of conferring honour among themselves on those who were quickest to observe the passing shadows and to remark which of them went before, and which followed after, and which were together; and who were therefore best able to draw conclusions as to the future, do you think that he would care for such honours and glories, or envy the possessors of them? Would he not say with Homer,

> "Better to be the poor servant of a poor master,"

and to endure anything, rather than think as they do and live after their manner?

Yes, he said, I think that he would rather suffer anything than entertain these false notions and live in this miserable manner.

Imagine once more, I said, such a one coming suddenly out of the sun to be re-placed in his old situation, would he not be certain to have his eyes full of darkness?

To be sure, he said.

And if there were a contest, and he had to compete in measuring the shadows with the prisoners who had never moved out of the den, while his sight was still weak, and before his eyes had become steady (and the time which would be needed to acquire this new habit of sight might be very considerable), would he not be ridiculous? Men would say of him that up he went and down he came without his eyes; and that it was better not even to think of ascending; and if any one tried to loose another and lead him up to the light, let them only catch the offender, and they would put him to death.

No question, he said.

This entire allegory, I said, you may now append, dear Glaucon, to the previous argument; the prisonhouse is the world of sight, the light of the fire is the sun, and you will not misapprehend me if you interpret the journey upwards to be the ascent of the soul into the intellectual world according to my poor belief, which, at your desire, I have expressed—whether rightly or wrongly God knows. But, whether true or false, my opinion is that in the world of knowledge the idea of good appears last of all, and is seen only with an effort; and, when seen, is also inferred to be the universal author of all things beautiful and right, parent of light and of the lord of light in this visible world, and the immediate source of reason and truth in the in-tellectual; and that this is the power upon which he who would act rationally either in public or private life must have his eye fixed.

I agree, he said, as far as I am able to understand you.

And now shall we consider in what way such guardians will be produced, and how they are to be brought from darkness to light,—as some are said to have as-cended from the world below to the gods?

By all means, he replied.

The process, I said, is not the turning over of an oyster-shell, but the turning round of a soul passing from a day which is little better than night to the true day of being, that is, the ascent from below, which we affirm to be true philosophy?

Quite so.

And should we not inquire what sort of knowledge has the power of effecting such a change?

Certainly.

What sort of knowledge is there which would draw the soul from becoming to being? And another consideration has just occurred to me: You will remember that our young men are to be warrior athletes?

Yes, that was said.

Then this new kind of knowledge must have an additional quality?

What quality?

Usefulness in war.

Yes, if possible.

There were two parts in our former scheme of education, were there not?

Just so.

There was gymnastic which presided over the growth and decay of the body, and may therefore be regarded as having to do with generation and corruption?

Then that is not the knowledge which we are seeking to discover?

No.

But what do you say of music, what also entered to a certain extent into our former scheme?

Music, he said, as you will remember, was the counterpart of gymnastic, and trained the guardians by the influences of habit, by harmony making them harmonious, by rhythm rhythmical, but not giving them science; and the words, whether fabulous or possibly true, had kindred elements of rhythm and harmony in them. But in music there was nothing which tended to that good which you are now seeking.

You are most accurate, I said, in your recollection; in music there certainly was nothing of the kind. But what branch of knowledge is there, my dear Glaucon, which is of the desired nature; since all the useful arts were reckoned mean by us?

Undoubtedly; and yet if music and gymnastic are excluded, and the arts are also excluded, what remains?

Well, I said, there may be nothing left of our special subjects; and then we shall have to take something which is not special, but of universal application.

What may that be?

A something which all arts and sciences and intelligences use in common, and which every one first has to learn among the elements of education.

What is that?

The little matter of distinguishing one, two, and three—in a word, number and calculation:—do not all arts and sciences necessarily partake of them?

Yes.

Then the art of war partakes of them?

To be sure.

Then Palamedes, whenever he appears in tragedy, proves Agamemnon ridiculously unfit to be a general. Did you never remark how he declares that he had invented number, and had numbered the ships and set in array the ranks of the army at Troy; which implies that they had never been numbered before, and Agamemnon must be supposed literally to have been incapable of counting his own feet—how could he if he was ignorant of number? And if that is true, what sort of general must he have been?

I should say a very strange one, if this was as you say.

Can we deny that a warrior should have a knowledge of arithmetic?

Certainly he should, if he is to have the smallest understanding of military tactics, or indeed, I should rather say, if he is to be a man at all.

I should like to know whether you have the same notion which I have of this study?

What is your notion?

It appears to me to be a study of the kind which we are seeking, and which leads naturally to reflection, but never to have been rightly used; for the true use of it is simply to draw the soul towards being.

Will you explain your meaning? he said.

I mean . . . that arithmetic has a very great and elevating effect, compelling the soul to reason about abstract number, and rebelling against the introduction of visible or tangible objects into the argument. You know how steadily the masters of the art repel and ridicule any one who attempts to divide absolute unity when he is calculating, and if you divide, they multiply, taking care that one shall continue one and not become lost in fractions.

That is very true.

Now, suppose a person were to say to them: O my friends, what are these wonderful numbers about which you are reasoning, in which, as you say, there is a unity such as you demand, and each unit is equal, invariable, indivisible,—what would they answer?

They would answer, as I should conceive, that they were speaking of those numbers which can only be realised in thought.

Then you see that this knowledge may be truly called necessary, necessitating as it clearly does the use of the pure intelligence in the attainment of pure truth?

Yes; that is a marked characteristic of it.

And have you further observed, that those who have a natural talent for calculation are generally quick at every other kind of knowledge; and even the dull, if they have had an arithmetical training, although they may derive no other advantage from it, always become much quicker than they would otherwise have been.

Very true, he said.

And indeed, you will not easily find a more difficult study, and not many as difficult.

You will not.

And, for all these reasons, arithmetic is a kind of knowledge in which the best natures should be trained, and which must not be given up.

I agree.

Let this then be made one of our subjects of education. And next, shall we inquire whether the kindred science also concerns us?

You mean geometry?

Exactly so.

Clearly, he said, we are concerned with that part of geometry which relates to war; for in pitching a camp, or taking up a position, or closing or extending the lines of an army, or any other military manœuvre, whether in actual battle or on a march, it will make all the difference whether a general is or is not a geometrician.

Yes, I said, but for that purpose a very little of either geometry or calculation will be enough; the question relates rather to the greater and more advanced part of geometry—whether that tends in any degree to make more easy the vision of the idea of good; and thither, as I was saying, all things tend which compel the soul to turn her gaze towards that place, where is the full perfection of being, which she ought, by all means, to behold.

True, he said.

Then if geometry compels us to view being, it concerns us; if becoming only, it does not concern us?

Yes, that is what we assert.

Yet anybody who has the least acquaintance with geometry will not deny that such a conception of the science is in flat contradiction to the ordinary language of geo-metricians.

How so?

They have in view practice only, and are always speaking, in a narrow and ridicu-lous manner, of squaring and extending and applying and the like—they confuse the necessities of geometry with those of daily life; whereas knowledge is the real object of the whole science.

Certainly, he said.

Then must not a further admission be made?

What admission?

That the knowledge at which geometry aims is knowledge of the eternal, and not of aught perishing and transient.

That, he replied, may be readily allowed, and is true.

Then, my noble friend, geometry will draw the soul towards truth, and create the spirit of philosophy, and raise up that which is now unhappily allowed to fall down.

Nothing will be more likely to have such an effect.

Then nothing should be more sternly laid down than that the inhabitants of your fair city should by all means learn geometry. Moreover the science has indirect effects, which are not small.

Of what kind? he said.

There are the military advantages of which you spoke, I said; and in all depart-ments of knowledge, as experience proves, any one who has studied geometry is infinitely quicker of apprehension than one who has not.

Yes indeed, he said, there is an infinite difference between them.

Then shall we propose this as a second branch of knowledge which our youth will study?

Let us do so, he replied.

And suppose we make astronomy the third—what do you say?

I am strongly inclined to it, he said; the observation of the seasons and of months and years is as essential to the general as it is to the farmer or sailor.

I am amused, I said, at your fear of the world, which makes you guard against the appearance of insisting upon useless studies; and I quite admit the difficulty of believing that in every man there is an eye of the soul which, when by other pur-suits lost and dimmed, is by these purified and re-illumined; and is more precious far than ten thousand bodily eyes, for by it alone is truth seen. Now there are two classes of persons: one class of those who will agree with you and will take your words as a revelation; another class to whom they will be utterly unmeaning, and who will naturally deem them to be idle tales, for they see no sort of profit which is to be obtained from them. And therefore you had better decide at once with which of the two you are proposing to argue. You will very likely say with neither, and that your chief aim in carrying on the argument is your own improvement; at the same time you do not grudge to others any benefit which they may receive.

I think that I should prefer to carry on the argument mainly on my own behalf.

Then take a step backward, for we have gone wrong in the order of the sciences.

What was the mistake? he said.

After plane geometry, I said, we proceeded at once to solids in revolution, instead of taking solids in themselves; whereas after the second dimension the third, which is concerned with cubes and dimensions of depth, ought to have followed.

That is true, Socrates; but so little seems to be known as yet about these subjects.

Why, yes, I said, and for two reasons:—in the first place, no government patronizes them; this leads to a want of energy in the pursuit of them, and they are difficult; in the second place, students cannot learn them unless they have a director. But then a director can hardly be found, and even if he could, as matters now stand, the students, who are very conceited, would not attend to him. That, however, would be otherwise if the whole State became the director of these studies and gave honour to them; then disciples would want to come, and there would be continuous and earnest search, and discoveries would be made; since even now, disregarded as they are by the world, and maimed of their fair proportions, and although none of their votaries can tell the use of them, still these studies force their way by their natural charm, and very likely, if they had the help of the State, they would some day emerge into light.

Yes, he said, there is a remarkable charm in them. But I do not clearly understand the change in the order. First you began with a geometry of plane surfaces?

Yes, I said.

And you placed astronomy next, and then you made a step backward?

Yes, and I have delayed you by my hurry; the ludicrous state of solid geometry, which, in natural order, should have followed, made me pass over this branch and go on to astronomy, or motion of solids.

True, he said.

Then assuming that the science now omitted would come into existence if encouraged by the State, let us go on to astronomy, which will be fourth.

The right order, he replied. And now, Socrates, as you rebuked the vulgar manner in which I praised astronomy before, my praise shall be given in your own spirit. For every one, as I think, must see that astronomy compels the soul to look upwards and leads us from this world to another.

Every one but myself, I said; to every one else this may be clear, but not to me.

And what then would you say?

I should rather say that those who elevate astronomy into philosophy appear to me to make us look downwards and not upwards.

What do you mean? he asked.

You, I replied, have in your mind a truly sublime conception of our knowledge of the things above. And I dare say that if a person were to throw his head back and study the fretted ceiling, you would still think that his mind was the percipient, and not his eyes. And you are very likely right, and I may be a simpleton: but, in my opinion, that knowledge only which is of being and of the unseen can make the soul look upwards, and whether a man gapes at the heavens or blinks on the ground, seeking to learn some particular of sense, I would deny that he can learn, for nothing of that sort is matter of science; his soul is looking downwards, not upwards, whether his way to knowledge is by water or by land, whether he floats, or only lies on his back.

I acknowledge, he said, the justice of your rebuke. Still, I should like to ascertain how astronomy can be learned in any manner more conducive to that knowledge of which we are speaking?

I will tell you, I said: The starry heaven which we behold is wrought upon a visible ground, and therefore, although the fairest and most perfect of visible things, must necessarily be deemed inferior far to the true motions of absolute swiftness and absolute slowness, which are relative to each other, and carry with them that which is contained in them, in the true number and in every true figure. Now, these are to be apprehended by reason and intelligence, but not by sight.

True, he replied.

The spangled heavens should be used as a pattern and with a view to that higher knowledge; their beauty is like the beauty of figures or pictures excellently wrought by the hand of Daedalus, or some other great artist, which we may chance to behold; any geometrician who saw them would appreciate the exquisiteness of their workmanship, but he would never dream of thinking that in them he could find the true equal or the true double, or the truth of any other proportion.

No, he replied, such an idea would be ridiculous.

And will not a true astronomer have the same feeling when he looks at the movements of the stars? Will he not think that heaven and the things in heaven are framed by the Creator of them in the most perfect manner? But he will never imagine that the proportions of night and day, or of both to the month, or of the months to the year, or of the stars to these and to one another, and any other things that are material and visible can also be eternal and subject to no deviation—that would be absurd; and it is equally absurd to take so much pains in investigating their exact truth.

I quite agree, though I never thought of this before.

Then, I said, in astronomy, as in geometry, we should employ problems, and let the heavens alone if we would approach the subject in the right way and so make the natural gift of reason to be of any real use.

That, he said, is a work infinitely beyond our present astronomers.

Yes, I said; and there are many other things which must also have a similar extension given to them, if our legislation is to be of any value. But can you tell me of any other suitable study?

No, he said, not without thinking.

Motion, I said, has many forms, and not one only; two of them are obvious enough even to wits no better than ours; and there are others, as I imagine, which may be left to wiser persons.

But where are the two?

There is a second, I said, which is the counterpart of the one already named.

And what may that be?

The second, I said, would seem relatively to the ears to be what the first is to the eyes; for I conceive that as the eyes are designed to look up at the stars, so are the ears to hear harmonious motions; and these are sister sciences—as the Pythagoreans say, and we, Glaucon, agree with them?

Yes, he replied.

But this, I said, is a laborious study, and therefore we had better go and learn of them; and they will tell us whether there are any other applications of these sciences. At the same time, we must not lose sight of our own higher object.

What is that?

There is a perfection which all knowledge ought to reach, and which our pupils ought also to attain, and not to fall short of, as I was saying that they did in astronomy. For in the science of harmony, as you probably know, the same thing happens. The teachers of harmony compare the sounds and consonances which are heard only, and their labour, like that of the astronomers, is in vain.

Yes, by heaven! he said; and 'tis as good as a play to hear them talking about their condensed notes, as they call them; they put their ears close alongside of the strings like persons catching a sound from their neighbour's wall—one set of them declaring that they distinguish an intermediate note and have found the least interval which should be the unit of measurement; the others insisting that the two sounds have passed into the same—either party setting their ears before their understanding.

You mean, I said, those gentlemen who tease and torture the strings and rack them on the pegs of the instrument: I might carry on the metaphor and speak after their manner of the blows which the plectrum gives, and make accusations against the strings, both of backwardness and forwardness to sound; but this would be tedious, and therefore I will only say that these are not the men, and that I am referring to the Pythagoreans, of whom I was just now proposing to inquire about harmony. For they too are in error, like the astronomers; they investigate the numbers of the harmonies which are heard, but they never attain to problems—that is to say, they never reach the natural harmonies of number, or reflect why some numbers are harmonious and others not.

That, he said, is a thing of more than mortal knowledge.

A thing, I replied, which I would rather call useful; that is, if sought after with a view to the beautiful and good; but if pursued in any other spirit, useless.

Very true, he said.

Now, when all these studies reach the point of intercommunion and connexion with one another, and come to be considered in their mutual affinities, then, I think, but not till then, will the pursuit of them have a value for our objects; otherwise there is no profit in them.

I suspect so; but you are speaking, Socrates, of a vast work.

What do you mean? I said; the prelude of what? Do you not know that all this is but the prelude to the actual strain which we have to learn? For you surely would not regard the skilled mathematician as a dialectician?

Assuredly not, he said; I have hardly ever known a mathematician who was capable of reasoning.

But do you imagine that men who are unable to give and take a reason will have the knowledge which we require of them?

Neither can this be supposed.

And so, Glaucon, I said, we have at last arrived at the hymn of dialectic. This is that strain which is of the intellect only, but which the faculty of sight will nevertheless be found to imitate; for sight, as you may remember, was imagined by us after a while to behold the real animals and stars, and last of all the sun himself. And so with dialectic; when a person starts on the discovery of the absolute by the light of reason only, and without any assistance of sense, and perseveres until by pure intelligence he arrives at the perception of the absolute good, he at last finds himself at the end of the intellectual world, as in the case of sight at the end of the visible.

Exactly, he said.

Then this is the progress which you call dialectic?

True.

But the release of the prisoners from chains, and their translation from the shadows to the images and to the light, and the ascent from the underground den to the sun, while in his presence they are vainly trying to look on animals and plants and the light of the sun, but are able to perceive even with their weak eyes the images in the water [which are divine], and are the shadows of true existence (not shadows of images cast by a light of fire, which compared with the sun is only an image)—this power of elevating the highest principle in the soul to the contemplation of that which is best in existence, with which we may compare the raising of that faculty which is the very light of the body to the sight of that which is brightest in the material and visible world—this power is given, as I was saying, by all that study and pursuit of the arts which has been described.

I agree in what you are saying, he replied, which may be hard to believe, yet, from another point of view, is harder still to deny. This however is not a theme to be treated of in passing only, but will have to be discussed again and again. And so, whether our conclusion be true or false, let us assume all this, and proceed at once from the prelude or preamble to the chief strain, and describe that in like manner. Say, then, what is the nature and what are the divisions of dialectic, and what are the paths which lead thither; for these paths will also lead to our final rest.

Dear Glaucon, I said, you will not be able to follow me here, though I would do my best, and you should behold not an image only but the absolute truth, according to my notion. Whether what I told you would or would not have been a reality I cannot venture to say; but you would have seen something like reality; of that I am confident.

Doubtless, he replied.

But I must also remind you, that the power of dialectic alone can reveal this, and only to one who is a disciple of the previous sciences.

Of that assertion you may be as confident as of the last.

And assuredly no one will argue that there is any other method of comprehending by any regular process all true existence or of ascertaining what each thing is in its own nature; for the arts in general are concerned with the desires or opinions of men, or are cultivated with a view to production and construction, or for the preservation of such productions and constructions; and as to the mathematical sciences which, as we were saying, have some apprehension of true being—geometry and the like—they only dream about being, but never can they behold the waking reality so long as they leave the hypotheses which they use unexamined, and are unable to give an account of them. For when a man knows not his own first principle, and when the conclusion and intermediate steps are also constructed out of he knows not what, how can he imagine that such a fabric of convention can ever become science?

Impossible, he said.

Then dialectic, and dialectic alone, goes directly to the first principle and is the only science which does away with hypotheses in order to make her ground secure; the eye of the soul, which is literally buried in an outlandish slough, is by her gentle aid lifted upwards; and she uses as handmaids and helpers in the work of conversion, the sciences which we have been discussing. Custom terms them sciences, but they ought to have some other name, implying greater clearness than opinion and less clearness than science: and this, in our previous sketch, was called understanding. . . .

Dialectic, then, as you will agree, is the coping-stone of the sciences, and is set over them; no other science can be placed higher—the nature of knowledge can no further go?

I agree, he said.

Questions for Discussion

1. Does Plato say why a man would want to leave the cave of ignorance and ascend into the sunlight of wisdom? Can you say why he should? Will he be happier, or is the development of a happy person the purpose of education?

2. In what sense is the development from arithmetic to plane geometry a progression? Do astronomy, harmonics and dialetic follow the same principle?

3. Of course we have much more knowledge today than was available to Plato. Using that knowledge and Plato's educational principles, sketch the outlines of an educational program you would use for students from the ages of three to twelve. What and how would you teach them; when and how would you examine them; where and how would you house them?

4. Turn back and reread the selection from John Dewey to see whether his criticisms of "traditional education" now have any more meaning. Which man's ideas seem to you to be more persuasive?

8 The Idea of a University

John Henry Cardinal Newman

Newman believes that "the cultivation of the intellect" is the sole end of education, and that disciplining the mind to think clearly, cogently and continually is the best means to achieve that end. He contends that education should not be confused with mere experience, memorization or recreation, but rather should be identified with the ability to generalize and to understand the full implications of an idea. Moreover, he believes that most subjects, if taught properly, can achieve these purposes. Such an education, Newman says, "gives a man a clear and conscious view of his own opinions and judgments, a truth in developing them, an eloquence in expressing them, and a force in urging them."

I consider . . . that the position of our minds, as far as they are uncultivated, towards intellectual objects,—I mean of our minds, before they have been disciplined and formed by the action of our reason upon them,—is analogous to that of a blind man towards the objects of vision, at the moment when eyes are for the first time given to him by the skill of the operator. Then the multitude of things, which present themselves to the sight under a multiplicity of shapes and hues, pour in upon him from the external world all at once, and are at first nothing else but lines and colours, without mutual connection, dependence, or contrast, without order or principle, without drift or meaning, and like the wrong side of a piece of tapestry or carpet. By degrees, by the sense of touch, by reaching out the hands, by walking into this maze of colours, by turning round in it, by accepting the principle of perspective, by the various slow teaching of experience, the first information of the sight is corrected, and what was an unintelligible wilderness becomes a landscape or a scene, and is understood to consist of space, and of bodies variously located in space, with such consequences as thence necessarily follow. The knowledge is at length gained of things or objects, and of their relation to each other; and it is a kind of knowledge, as is plain, which is forced upon us all from infancy, as to the blind on their first seeing, by the testimony of our other senses, and by the very necessity of supporting life; so that even the brute animals have been gifted with the faculty of acquiring it.

Such is the case as regards material objects; and it is much the same as regards intellectual. I mean that there is a vast host of matters of all kinds, which address themselves, not to the eye, but to our mental sense; viz., all those matters of thought which, in the course of life and the intercourse of society, are brought before us, which we hear of in conversation, which we read of in books; matters political, social, ecclesiastical, literary, domestic; persons, and their doings or their writings; events, and works, and undertakings, and laws, and institutions. These make up a much

From *The Idea of a University* (New York: Longmans, Green and Company, 1947). And from the book *On the Scope and Nature of University Education* by John Henry Cardinal Newman. Everyman's Library Edition. Reprinted by permission of E. P. Dutton & Co., Inc.

more subtle and intricate world than that visible universe of which I was just now speaking. It is much more difficult in this world than in the material to separate things off from each other, and to find out how they stand related to each other, and to learn how to class them, and where to locate them respectively. Still, it is not less true that, as the various figures and forms in a landscape have each its own place, and stand in this or that direction towards each other, so all the various objects which address the intellect have severally a substance of their own, and have fixed relations each of them with everything else,—relations which our minds have no power of creating, but which we are obliged to ascertain before we have a right to boast that we really know any thing about them. Yet, when the mind looks out for the first time into this manifold spiritual world, it is just as much confused and dazzled and distracted as are the eyes of the blind when they first begin to see; and it is by a long process, and with much effort and anxiety, that we begin hardly and partially to apprehend its various contents and to put each in its proper place.

We grow up from boyhood; our minds open; we go into the world; we hear what men say, or read what they put in print; and thus a profusion of matters of all kinds is discharged upon us. Some sort of an idea we have of most of them, from hearing what others say; but it is a very vague idea, probably a very mistaken idea. Young people, especially, because they are young, colour the assemblage of persons and things which they encounter with the freshness and grace of their own springtide, look for all good from the reflection of their own hopefulness, and worship what they have created. Men of ambition, again, look upon the world as a theatre for fame and glory, and make it that magnificent scene of high enterprise and august recompence which Pindar or Cicero has delineated. Poets, too, after their wont, put their ideal interpretation upon all things, material as well as moral, and substitute the noble for the true. Here are various obvious instances, suggestive of the discipline which is imperative, if the mind is to grasp things as they are, and to discriminate substances from shadows. For I am not concerned merely with youth, ambition, or poetry, but with our mental condition generally. It is the fault of all of us, till we have duly practised our minds, to be unreal in our sentiments and crude in our judgments, and to be carried off by fancies, instead of being at the trouble of acquiring sound knowledge.

In consequence, when we hear opinions put forth on any new subject, we have no principle to guide us in balancing them; we do not know what to make of them; we turn them to and fro, and over, and back again, as if to pronounce upon them, if we could, but with no means of pronouncing. It is the same when we attempt to speak upon them: we make some random venture; or we take up the opinion of some one else, which strikes our fancy; or perhaps, with the vaguest enunciation possible of any opinion at all, we are satisfied with ourselves if we are merely able to throw off some rounded sentences, to make some pointed remarks on some other subject, or to introduce some figure of speech, or flowers of rhetoric, which, instead of being the vehicle, are the mere substitute of meaning. We wish to take a part in politics, and then nothing is open to us but to follow some person, or some party, and to learn the commonplaces and the watchwords which belong to it. We hear about landed interests, and mercantile interests, and trade, and higher and lower classes, and their rights, duties, and prerogatives; and we attempt to transmit what

we have received; and soon our minds become loaded and perplexed by the in-
cumbrance of ideas which we have not mastered and cannot use. We have some
vague idea, for instance, that constitutional government and slavery are inconsistent
with each other; that there is a connection between private judgment and democracy,
between Christianity and civilization; we attempt to find arguments in proof, and
our arguments are the most plain demonstration that we simply do not understand
the things themselves of which we are professedly treating. . . .

This is that barren mockery of knowledge which comes of attending on great
Lecturers, or of mere acquaintance with reviews, magazines, newspapers, and other
literature of the day, which, however able and valuable in itself, is not the instrument of intellectual education. If this is all the training a man has, the chance is
that, when a few years have passed over his head, and he has talked to the full, he
wearies of talking, and of the subjects on which he talked. He gives up the pursuit of
knowledge, and forgets what he knew, whatever it was; and, taking things at their
best, his mind is in no very different condition from what it was when he first began
to improve it, as he hoped, though perhaps he never thought of more than of amus-
ing himself. I say, "at the best," for perhaps he will suffer from exhaustion and a
distaste of the subjects which once pleased him; or perhaps he has suffered some real
intellectual mischief; perhaps he has contracted some serious disorder, he has admitted some taint of scepticism, which he will never get rid of.

And here we see what is meant by the poet's maxim, "A little learning is a dangerous thing." Not that knowledge, little or much, if it be real knowledge, is dangerous; but that many a man considers a mere hazy view of many things to be real
knowledge, whereas it does but mislead, just as a short-sighted man sees only so far
as to be led by his uncertain sight over the precipice.

Such, then, being true cultivation of mind, and such the literary institutions which
do not tend to it, I might proceed to show you, Gentlemen, did time admit, how, on
the other hand, that kind of instruction of which our Evening Classes are a specimen,
is especially suited to effect what they propose. Consider, for instance, what a discipline in accuracy of thought it is to have to construe a foreign language into your
own; what a still severer and more improving exercise it is to translate from your
own into a foreign language. Consider, again, what a lesson in memory and discrimination it is to get up, as it is called, any one chapter of history. Consider what a
trial of acuteness, caution, and exactness, it is to master, and still more to prove, a
number of definitions. Again, what an exercise in logic is classification, what an
exercise in logical precision it is to understand and enunciate the proof of any of the
more difficult propositions of Euclid, or to master any one of the great arguments
for Christianity so thoroughly as to bear examination upon it; or, again, to analyze
sufficiently, yet in as few words as possible, a speech, or to draw up a critique upon
a poem. And so of any other science,—chemistry, or comparative anatomy, or natural
history; it does not matter what it is, if it be really studied and mastered, as far as it
is taken up. The result is a formation of mind,—that is, a habit of order and system,
a habit of referring every accession of knowledge to what we already know, and of
adjusting the one with the other; and, moreover, as such a habit implies, the actual
acceptance and use of certain principles as centres of thought, around which our
knowledge grows and is located. Where this critical faculty exists, history is no longer

a mere story-book, or biography a romance; orators and publications of the day are no longer infallible authorities; eloquent diction is no longer a substitute for matter, nor bold statements, or lively descriptions, a substitute for proof. This is that faculty of perception in intellectual matters, which, as I have said so often, is analogous to the capacity we all have of mastering the multitude of lines and colours which pour in upon our eyes, and of deciding what every one of them is worth.

Instances such as these confirm, by the contrast, the conclusion I have already drawn from those which preceded them. That only is true enlargement of mind which is the power of viewing many things at once as one whole, of referring them severally to their true place in the universal system, of understanding their respective values, and determining their mutual dependence. Thus is that form of Universal Knowledge, of which I have on a former occasion spoken, set up in the individual intellect, and constitutes its perfection. Possessed of this real illumination, the mind never views any part of the extended subject-matter of Knowledge without recollecting that it is but a part, or without the associations which spring from this recollection. It makes everything in some sort lead to everything else; it would communicate the image of the whole to every separate portion, till that whole becomes in imagination like a spirit, everywhere pervading and penetrating its component parts, and giving them one definite meaning. Just as our bodily organs, when mentioned, recall their function in the body, as the word "creation" suggests the Creator, and "subjects" a sovereign, so, in the mind of the Philosopher, as we are abstractedly conceiving of him, the elements of the physical and moral world, sciences, arts, pursuits, ranks, offices, events, opinions, individualities, are all viewed as one, with correlative functions, and as gradually by successive combinations converging, one and all, to the true centre.

To have even a portion of this illuminative reason and true philosophy is the highest state to which nature can aspire, in the way of intellect; it puts the mind above the influences of chance and necessity, above anxiety, suspense, tumult, and superstition, which are the portion of the many. Men, whose minds are possessed with some one object, take exaggerated views of its importance, are feverish in the pursuit of it, make it the measure of things which are utterly foreign to it, and are startled and despond if it happens to fail them. They are ever in alarm or in transport. Those on the other hand who have no object or principle whatever to hold by, lose their way, every step they take. They are thrown out, and do not know what to think or say, at every fresh juncture; they have no view of persons, or occurrences, or facts, which come suddenly upon them, and they hang upon the opinion of others, for want of internal resources. But the intellect, which has been disciplined to the perfection of its powers, which knows, and thinks while it knows, which has learned to leaven the dense mass of facts and events with the elastic force of reason, such an intellect cannot be partial, cannot be exclusive, cannot be impetuous, cannot be at a loss, cannot but be patient, collected, and majestically calm, because it discerns the end in every beginning, the origin in every end, the law in every interruption, the limit in each delay; because it ever knows where it stands, and how its path lies from one point to another. . . .

And now, if I may take for granted that the true and adequate end of intellectual training and of a University is not Learning or Acquirement, but rather, is Thought or Reason exercised upon Knowledge, or what may be called Philosophy, I shall be in a position to explain the various mistakes which at the present day beset the subject of University Education.

I say then, if we would improve the intellect, first of all, we must ascend: we cannot gain real knowledge on a level; we must generalise, we must reduce to method, we must have a grasp of principles, and group and shape our acquisitions by them. It matters not whether our field of operation be wide or limited; in every case, to command it, is to mount above it. Who has not felt the irritation of mind and impatience created by a deep, rich country, visited for the first time, with winding lanes, and high hedges, and green steeps, and tangled woods, and everything smiling indeed, but in a maze? The same feeling comes upon us in a strange city, when we have no map of its streets. Hence you hear of practised travellers, when they first come into a place, mounting some high hill or church tower, by way of reconnoitring its neighbourhood. In like manner you must be above your knowledge, gentlemen, not under it, or it will oppress you; and the more you have of it the greater will be the load. . . .

Nor indeed am I supposing that there is any great danger, at least in this day, of over-education; the danger is on the other side. I will tell you, gentlemen, what has been the practical error of the last twenty years—not to load the memory of the student with a mass of undigested knowledge, but to attempt so much that nothing has been really effected, to teach so many things, that nothing has properly been learned at all. It has been the error of distracting and enfeebling the mind by an unmeaning profusion of subjects; of implying that a smattering in a dozen branches of study was not shallowness, which it really is, but enlargement; of considering an acquaintance with the learned names of things and persons, and the possession of clever duodecimos, and attendance on eloquent lecturers, and membership with scientific institutions, and the sight of the experiments of a platform and the specimens of a museum, that all this was not dissipation of mind, but progress. All things now are to be learned at once, not first one thing, then another, not one well but many badly. Learning is to be without exertion, without attention, without toil; without grounding, without advance, without finishing. There is to be nothing individual in it; and this, forsooth, is the wonder of the age. What the steam-engine does with matter, the printing-press is to do with mind; it is to act mechanically, and the population is to be passively, almost unconsciously enlightened, by the mere multiplication and dissemination of volumes. Whether it be the schoolboy, or the schoolgirl, or the youth at college, or the mechanic in the town, or the politician in the senate, all have been the victims in one way or other of this most preposterous and pernicious of delusions. Wise men have lifted up their voices in vain; and at length, lest their own institutions should be outshone and should disappear in the folly of the hour, they have been obliged, as far as was conscientiously possible, to humour a spirit which they could not withstand, and make temporising concessions at which they could not but inwardly smile.

Now I must guard, gentlemen, against any possible misconception of my meaning. Let me frankly declare then, that I have no fear at all of the education of the people: the more education they have the better, so that it is really education. Next, as to the cheap publication of scientific and literary works, which is now in vogue, I consider it a great advantage, convenience, and gain; that is, to those to whom education has given a capacity for using them. Further, I consider such innocent recreations as science and literature are able to furnish will be a very fit occupation of the thoughts and the leisure of young persons, and may be made the means of keeping them from bad employments and bad companions. Moreover, as to that superficial acquaintance with chemistry, and geology, and astronomy, and political economy, and modern history, and biography, and other branches of knowledge, which periodical literature and occasional lectures and scientific institutions diffuse through the community, I think it a graceful accomplishment, and a suitable, nay, in this day a necessary accomplishment, in the case of educated men. Nor, lastly, am I disparaging or discouraging the thorough acquisition of any one of these studies, or denying that, as far as it goes, such thorough acquisition is a real education of the mind. All I say is, call things by their right names, and do not confuse together ideas which are essentially different. A thorough knowledge of one science and a superficial acquaintance with many, are not the same thing; a smattering of a hundred things or a memory for detail, is not a philosophical or comprehensive view. Recreations are not education; accomplishments are not education. Do not say, the people must be educated, when, after all, you only mean amused, refreshed, soothed, put into good spirits and good humour, or kept from vicious excesses. I do not say that such amusements, such occupations of mind, are not a great gain; but they are not education. You may as well call drawing and fencing education, as a general knowledge of botany or conchology. Stuffing birds or playing stringed instruments is an elegant pastime, and a resource to the idle, but it is not education; it does not form or cultivate the intellect. Education is a high word; it is the preparation for knowledge, and it is the imparting of knowledge in proportion to that preparation. We require intellectual eyes to know withal, as bodily eyes for sight. We need both objects and organs intellectual; we cannot gain them without setting about it; we cannot gain them in our sleep or by haphazard. The best telescope does not dispense with eyes; the printing-press or the lecture room will assist us greatly, but we must be true to ourselves, we must be parties in the work. A University is, according to the usual designation, an Alma Mater, knowing her children one by one, not a foundry, or a mint, or a treadmill.

But I must bring these extracts to an end. To-day I have confined myself to saying that the training of the intellect, which is best for the individual himself, best enables him to discharge his duties to society. The Philosopher, indeed, and the man of the world differ in their very notion, but the methods by which they are respectively formed are pretty much the same. The Philosopher has the same command of matters of thought, which the true citizen and gentleman has of matters of business and conduct. If then a practical end must be assigned to a University course, I say it is that of training good members of society. Its art is the art of social life, and its end is fitness for the world. It neither confines its views to particular professions on the one hand, nor creates heroes or inspires genius on the other. Works indeed of genius fall under no art; heroic minds come under no rule; a University is not a birthplace of poets or of immortal authors, of founders of schools, leaders of colonies, or conquerors of nations. It does not promise a generation of Aristotles or Newtons, of Napoleons or Washingtons, of Raphaels or Shakespeares, though such miracles of nature it has before now contained within its precincts. Nor is it content on the other hand with forming the critic or the experimentalist, the economist or the engineer, though such too it includes within its scope. But a University training is the great ordinary means to a great but ordinary end; it aims at raising the intellectual tone of society, at cultivating the public mind, at purifying the national taste, at supplying true principles to popular enthusiasm and fixed aims to popular aspiration, at giving enlargement and sobriety to the ideas of the age, at facilitating the exercise of political power, and refining the intercourse of private life. It is the education which gives a man a clear conscious view of his own opinions and judgments, a truth in developing them, an eloquence in expressing them, and a force in urging them. It teaches him to see things as they are, to go right to the point, to disentangle a skein of thought, to detect what is sophistical, and to discard what is irrelevant. It prepares him to fill any post with credit, and to master any subject with facility. It shows him how to accommodate himself to others, how to throw himself into their state of mind, how to bring before them his own, how to influence them, how to come to an understanding with them, how to bear with them. He is at home in any society, he has common ground with every class; he knows when to speak and when to be silent; he is able to converse, he is able to listen; he can ask a question pertinently, and gain a lesson seasonably, when he has nothing to impart himself; he is ever ready, yet never in the way; he is a pleasant companion, and a comrade you can depend upon; he knows when to be serious and when to trifle, and he has a sure tact which enables him to trifle with gracefulness and to be serious with effect. He has the repose of a mind which lives in itself, while it lives in the world, and which has resources for its happiness at home when it cannot go abroad. He has a gift which serves him in public, and supports him in retirement, without which good fortune is but vulgar, and with which failure and disappointment have a charm. The art which tends to make a man all this, is in the object which it pursues as useful as the art of wealth or the art of health, though it is less susceptible of method, and less tangible, less certain, less complete in its result.

Questions for Discussion

1. Do you agree that an educated man is one who can "see things as they are, can go right to the point, can disentangle a skein of thought, can detect what is sophistical and can discard what is irrelevant?" Do you think Rousseau would agree?
2. Can the mind be disciplined? How?
3. Do you see any elements of Spencer's and Newman's educational ideas in your own learning situation? Be specific. Do you like what you see?

9 The Meaning of a Liberal Education

Everett Dean Martin

In one sense, this selection is a continuation of the previous one, for like Newman, Martin holds that "one becomes an educated person by virtue of patient study, quiet meditation, intellectual courage, and a life devoted to the discovery and service of truth." Martin, too, wants to reject the notion that education should be identified with training or propaganda, with professional competence or social advantage, but unlike Newman, who values this kind of education because it enables man to see life clearly and see it whole, Martin defends liberal education as the best means for individual self-expression and fulfillment. And this view sounds remarkably like Rousseau's. Has our study of various theories about education come full circle, then, or are there significant differences between Rousseau and Martin?

In a sense no living person is yet educated, for the learning process is never completed. But there must come a time when the process results in some differences in behavior. Often these differences seem to be small and irrelevant, amounting merely to added social grace or more correct use of language. Something more than this must differentiate the educated from the uneducated or so much human energy would not be expended in the effort to get education.

When we inquire what the difference is, we find there is much confusion. In the process of education knowledge is acquired. Many a person's education consists of what he has learned. May one possess much knowledge or information and remain uneducated? I know a physician who has great skill and wide professional information, yet he is essentially vulgar in his tastes and enjoyments and bigoted in his human relationships, and his judgments concerning most things are narrow and hasty and are determined largely by passion and prejudice. You feel that his learning has never become integrated with his personality. It is a property annexed to his estate over which he is an absentee landlord. It has made no changes in his general habits of thought and behavior.

There are people whom no one would think educated, who yet have an astounding amount of information. They know all about race horses, or bridge, or baseball scores, or stocks and bonds. Many have a knowledge of such things which may be greater both in range and accuracy than that which some professional scholars have of their special subjects.

Shall we say then that some kinds of knowledge have educational value and that others have not? But why should not all knowledge be equally education? Is there a psychological reason for the alleged difference or is the exclusion of some kinds of knowledge the result merely of a conventional attitude? Our discussion of education resolves itself into a philosophical problem.

The issue of practical education versus the so-called cultural comes up whenever people are interested in the subject. Partisans of the latter type of learning are inclined to look down upon the former. They say it is not education but only skill and efficiency. They hold that education is scholarship and properly has to do with such subjects as the classics, the humanities, philosophy, etc., which discipline the mind and enoble the spirit. This is the traditional view.

Those who take the opposite view ask what earthly purpose can useless and sequestered learning serve? They are suspicious of education for "refinement" or the "genteel tradition." Is it not the aim of the pursuit of knowledge to enable one to do something, to attain mastery, to equip the mind to function well in an environment which demands activity of us all? Is not anything well learned culture? An excellent statement of this point of view can be found in Huxley's lectures on education.

There has been much discussion of this question in the universities and colleges. There are those who deplore the decline of interest in the classics and philosophy. They say that institutions of higher learning are becoming mere "intellectual cafeterias," that the change from classical education to an elective system embracing all sorts of vocational courses is a distinct loss, inasmuch as the knowledge so acquired lacks coordination and balance, while specialization crowds out the general and cultural subjects that form the foundation of education.

On the other hand, why should not a University teach anything that people wish to know? There was once resistance to including the sciences, chemistry and physics and biology. The liberalizing effect and cultural value of these subjects is now recognized, and their usefulness is a social gain. Then why not domestic science, agriculture, mechanics, business methods? What is wrong with the schools of business at Harvard and Columbia?

A similar issue exists in secondary education. It is often said that high schools pay too much regard to college entrance requirements, since only a small portion of graduates expect to continue their education. The students have gained only a most superficial introduction to the classics and have learned nothing practical. Schools of trade, commerce, and of technology are increasing in number and the movement for such training is guided by principles of education very different from those of the classical tradition. . . .

Hence in all phases of education, this issue is debated. The issue is inevitable in a time like the present, with a classical tradition surviving in an industrial civilization. Have we any need in the modern world of cultural traditions which have their origin in antiquity? Should we or could we dispense with all educational values except those which are coterminous with the present industrial situation?

Wherever such an issue arises, I have learned to suspect both sides. As a rule both are based upon a common presupposition which is an error. Here the presupposition is that the important factor in education is the question what is to be taught, rather than the spirit of learning itself. Education is conceived of as knowledge acquired. Attention is fixed not on the learning process through which an individual becomes reoriented to his world, but upon the end result, something fixed and done, a certain amount of information stored up. Is this what we mean by learning? Is it receiving and memorizing a given something either cultural or practical? Or is it an adventure in any kind of truth seeking which changes the quality of one's future experience and enables one to behave not merely efficiently but wisely, with a broad view and a sympathetic understanding of the many ways in which men have striven to create meaning and value out of the possibilities of human life? If this last is correct, the real question is not what shall be learned but how and why and to what end. Is learning a venture in spiritual freedom that is humanism, or is it a routine process of animal training? Both cultural and practical knowledge may be reduced to animal training—and they generally are. It is there that the issue between them arises.

To my mind, an educated person is not merely one who can do something, whether it is giving a lecture on the poetry of Horace, running a train, trying a lawsuit, or repairing the plumbing. He is also one who knows the significance of what he does, and he is one who cannot and will not do certain things. He has acquired a set of values. He has a "yes" and a "no," and they are his own. He knows why he behaves as he does. He has learned what to prefer, for he has lived in the presence of things that are preferable. I do not mean that he is merely trained in the conventions of polite society or the conformities of crowd morality. He will doubtless depart from both in many things. Whether he conforms or not, he has learned enough about human life on this planet to see his behavior in the light of a body of experience and the relation of his actions to situations as a whole. Such a person is acquiring a liberal education and it makes little difference whether he has been trained in philosophy or mechanics. He is being transformed from an automaton into a thinking being.

Much contemporary educational philosophy is openly and avowedly a technique of animal training; so much so that it quite properly borrows its pedagogical principles from animal psychology. It would be difficult to over estimate the importance of animal experimentation for modern theories of education. Schools of education are deeply interested in the psychology of the learning process. Education is learning, and learning is habit formulation. Habits are the acquired modes of response of men and animals. They may be organized in the nervous tissue by any environmental factors which "condition" certain reflexes; that is, chain certain responses to given stimuli. It is possible for an animal experimentor or an educator of children to organize the environmental situation in such a manner that definite systems of desired responses may be regularly obtained whenever a stimulus of a certain kind is given. A simple and well-known experiment which will serve to explain what we mean by the conditioned reflex is that of Pavlov. A hungry dog when shown meat secretes saliva. At the time the dog sees the meat a bell is rung. This is repeated a number of times until the dog will secrete saliva at the sound of the bell, without the presence of the meat stimulus. The saliva response, induced by the bell stimulus, is the conditioned reflex.

It is said that all learning takes place after this fashion. An animal, a cat, may be placed in a cage, the door being so arranged that escape is possible only when the cat strikes a certain latch. After a period during which the cat makes all sorts of frantic random movements, the successful movement finally occurs and the cat escapes. The experiment is repeated and perhaps the period of futile activity will not be so long as at first. After a number of trials the cat will give up the random movements and at once unlock the door. The gradual shortening of the interval of time required for the desired response may be plotted. It is then called the animal's "learning curve."

Such curves may also be made of human learning processes. It is said that there is no essential difference between this animal learning and our own learning whether it be to swim or play tennis, or to memorize a poem, or solve a problem in algebra, or to master the technique of a profession. One's education thus consists wholly of one's organized systems of responses, or habit patterns. We speak of education as the development of personality. But from this point of view personality is nothing but the sum total of an individual's conditioned reflexes:—that is, it is merely the manner in which the organism has been taught to work. One eminent Behaviorist among the psychologists compares personality to the running of a gas engine.

I will not enter upon a psychological discussion of this view of education, except to say that the method of animal training which is taken for granted is open to serious criticism. The theory proceeds on the assumption that *insight into the situation* is not necessary to learning. The cat in the cage hits upon the successful gesture as a matter of pure chance. After a number of experiments, each said to place the animal in an identical situation, the successful action becomes "over determined," and fixed as a habit. It is doubtful whether such training is learning at all. The animal—and conceivably the human being—need never take in the situation. The successful art, the more this learning process is perfected, degenerates into a mere gesture, related to the event in a purely external and arbitrary manner. It is difficult to see how educational methods guided by such a theory could do much to train the student in habits of independent judgment. . . .

It seems to me that the animal training theory rests upon two presuppositions, both of which are wrong. The first is that the mind consists of what it has learned, that is, that it is the product of environment. This is really not a psychological doctrine, but a metaphysical assumption. It is the mechanist theory; an idea which works well as scientific method, but which leads to false conclusions when taken as a description of ultimate reality.

The second presupposition is a by-product of present day industrial democracy. It is that education is a means to efficient service, with its rewards, getting on, general prosperity, etc. But is industry the end and aim of our existence? It is said that man if he is to be happy must be able to express himself in his work. I would not dispute this statement, but it is important to consider what it is that finds expression in one's work. If work, in addition to being the means to some material end or bodily good, is also to be a form of self-expression, then the point of interest is the kind of selfhood, or quality of experienced expressed. Then work exists for education, not education for work.

Something is possible to mankind, which transcends work and by which work itself is valued. As mere craftsmen we lose the sense of what good workmanship is and become the blind slaves of necessity or of desire the moment that education ceases to be the goal of labor. I do not mean merely that we learn by doing. That is the way animals learn and it is all they learn. By repeated performance an individual learns how to do a task, but he does not thereby learn what to do, nor why it is done. Education has to do with insight, with valueing, with understanding, with the development of the power of discrimination, the ability to make choice amongst the possibilities of experience and to think and act in ways that distinguish men from animals and higher men from lower. The ancients thought of education as the attainment of the virtues, wisdom, courage, temperance, justice. It is the pursuit of that knowledge which gives self-mastery. It is an interest which is never exhausted, but grows always broader and richer. It consists not in learning tricks but in developing ourselves. It is a victory won in some secret chamber of the mind which gradually transforms the whole personality and reveals itself as an indefinable quality in every word and act. It is a spiritual awakening; and if this awakening does not come, a person is not being educated however much he knows. I think it is the inability to win this psychological victory, or the disinclination to make the effort necessary to it, that accounts for the fact that some people cannot be educated. Though the change in the quality of the personality is indefinable, it is a very concrete fact in human life. Its presence is evident in the work of writers as different otherwise as Sir Thomas More, Galsworthy, Anatole France, Jonathan Edwards, Henry Adams, etc. There is a quality of the educated mind which may best be described as a kind of sincerity, and conversely the outstanding trait of ignorance is that of clever insincerity. The pathetic thing about the wrongly educated,—those who are trained merely to produce an effect, or get results, is that in the deeper human relationships they seldom know what sincerity is. Education is the antithesis of vulgarity.

Directly and immediately, it is useless. It is a kind of living which is of value for its own sake, a personal achievement which possesses intrinsic worth. It is not *for* anything. To subject it to an ulterior end—citizenship, efficiency, the economic emancipation of the working class, increased income; or to educate people for "character," or to perpetuate a religious faith, or any other purpose however good, is to make education a means to something quite irrelevant. Such misuse shows that people are not interested in their education but in something else. Education, the development of people, is not a means, it is itself the true end of civilization.

While education is not *for* anything, indirectly it improves everything that people do. Make education the aim and meaning of living, and all becomes different. Experience has a new center of gravity. Facts fall into new and more significant perspective. Objects, distinctions, relationships, qualities, are seen which before passed unnoticed. And as personality does not exist in a vacuum but in the relationships established between organism and environment, no improvement of it can fail to make itself felt in the quality of one's work. Animal training may give one the means to make a living; liberal education gives living a meaning.

Whoever is concerned about his education should be on his guard against propaganda. He who assists in the education of another should be doubly cautious. The temptation to convert people to our own particular cause, movement or belief is almost irrestible. An epidemic itch for manipulating the public has infected the whole population. Perhaps never was the business of "selling" ideas and interests of all sorts so common a practice or so cleverly done. Press agents, publicity experts, advertisers and propagandists have become a pest. Much of the news is "treated" for interests which may or may not be disclosed. Militarists, pacifists, prohibitionists,

birth controlists, social workers, business interests, anti-vivisectionists, radicals, reac
tionaries and all kinds of reformers insinuate themselves everywhere like crawling
insects. Every legislative body is over-run with lobbyists. Every government, our own
included, fights with propaganda as deadly as poison gas. Churches have reduced
even the spreading of the gospel to the level of advertising. And to judge by the
popularity of one of the vulgarest books ever written about the founder of Christianity, a large number of churchmen are happy to believe that Jesus Christ was
the world's greatest salesman and business executive!

It ought not to be necessary to say that propaganda is not education. But the confusion of the two is common. It is often very difficult to enlist the interest of people
even in their own education if the propagandist motive is left out of it. I find that
our students are often at first perplexed. They ask me, "What party or creed or
social movement do you represent? What are you trying to convert us to?" I have
even been asked why I lecture at all, if it is not my purpose to tell students what
they should think and do. The idea of a course of study as an adventure in truth-
seeking, an investigation deliberately planned without made-in-advance conclusions
or ulterior aims, is difficult for many minds. If no partisan motive is apparent, students often suspect that there must be some dark and secret conspiracy. People like
to have their instructors labeled and tagged. Otherwise they feel that they are
not being given anything. They prefer to be told what to think. . . .

Although the educator and the propagandist are both concerned with the dissemination of information, they have nothing else in common. They use contrary
methods and they strive for opposite goals. The propagandist is interested in *what*
people think; the educator in *how* they think. The propagandist has a definite aim.
He strives to convert, to sell, to secure assent, to prove a case, to support one side
of an issue. He is striving for an *effect*. He wishes people to come to a conclusion;
to accept his case and close their minds and act. The educator strives for the open
mind. He has no case to prove, which may not later be reversed. He is willing to
reconsider, to be experimental, to hold his conclusions tentatively. The result for
which he strives is a type of student who will not jump at the propagandist's hasty
conclusions or be taken in by his catch-words. To the one "learning" is passively
accepting something; criticism of the matter offered is not encouraged. To the other,
learning comes by examining. The propagandist need have no respect for the personalities of those he manipulates. The educator must respect his student, since the
development of personality is his aim. In the end the question is whether people are
to be *used* for purposes other than their own. This is the sole object of the propagandist; its successful achievement is the defeat of the educator.

Even in the service of a good cause, propaganda makes for superficiality in both
him who gives and him who receives it. The convert has seen the light. He is on
the right side. He need have no more doubts or hesitation. Curiosity and further
speculation are no longer necessary. Reasoning henceforth can become special
pleading—mere rationalization, an array of clever plausibilities designed to
strengthen the faith and protect the devotee against the danger that he may change
his mind. He now becomes a propagandist himself, a lay preacher as it were, whose
mission in life is to convert and uplift others. He begins to harp on one string. In
his eagerness to convince he resorts to the obvious, the thing said for effect. He is

more concerned with the force of his arguments than with the accuracy of his statements. He is so busy with the general good that he neglects to purify himself. With unwashed hands he breaks his bread and serves it to his neighbors. I have seldom seen a person who has spent years making converts, who has not lost in intellectual integrity. Emerson noted this trait in the abolitionists of his day. It is a quality which world menders of all types have in common. Sooner or later the passion to convert, like any other passion overindulged, warps the whole personality. The propagandist becomes intemperate. He loses something in delicacy and sense of humor. There is in his manner a mixture of emotion and coercion and a kind of slyness. Finally from much repetition of stock phrases the great cause itself becomes hackneyed and professionalized. Most of the messages which men would carry to the masses slip through the propagandists' fingers and dribble out before they arrive at their destination.

I have tried to make clear the differences between propaganda and education. If I am correct, it follows that whenever the educator becomes a propagandist he gives up his proper function. I do not mean that a school teacher should not advocate political change or any other reform he chooses. He is a citizen as well as a teacher, and has the right to express his convictions, however unpopular they may be. But it is not as a teacher that he does so. Ordinarily the public insists that there are certain views that he may not express either in or outside his classroom. At the same time he is required to be the advocate of popular moral, religious and political prejudices, however erroneous he knows them to be. Public education suffers much from this lack of freedom, for it operates to keep independent minds out of the teaching profession. Unless any subject may be presented and every relevant fact discussed without fear or favor, the instruction offered students is a cheat.

It is however in the process of teaching itself that the spirit of the propagandist may supplant that of the educator. It is much easier to appeal to authority than to experiment, to command assent than to awaken curiosity, to tell the student what he must believe than to wait for the maturing of his judgment.

The motives which lead people to seek college education divide the students into three types. First there are the few who love learning. The spirit which once caused groups of young men to follow Abelard or Erasmus still brings an occasional youth to college. Such students may need guidance, advice and the fellowship of mature scholars. It is not necessary to force them to study, or offer them "snap courses," or cram them for examination. Much of the procedure and regulation—the regimentation common in institutions of learning—is unnecessary and sometimes harmful to them. Most of them would become educated persons even if they never saw a college class-room.

A second type of student attends college and university in large numbers. The motive is preparation for a professional career. Many of the best students belong to this type. Whether in addition to their professional training they ever gain a liberal education—we have seen that the two are not necessarily the same—will depend largely upon what they do after they get their degrees. If they then have an interest in educating themselves, their technical training ought to be an advantage, for most of them have learned how to study. But so much purely technical knowledge must be drilled into a man's head that the student who is preparing for a degree in engineering, law, medicine or scientific research has very little time for anything else. Many of the most successful physicians, engineers and scientists need adult education quite as much as do ordinary working men.

The third type, the majority of undergraduate students, are for the most part pleasant young men and women of the upper middle class. Their parents are "putting them through college" because it is the expected thing to do. A man wishes to give his children every advantage. While a bachelor's degree is not exactly a social necessity, there are many who would have something like an inferiority complex without it. I knew one family in New York City who almost went into mourning when the only son failed in his Harvard entrance examinations. Students of this type enjoy four happy years, largely at public expense, with other young people of their own age in an environment designed to keep them out of mischief. I have no doubt this grown-up kindergarten life is good for them; most of them seem to appreciate it. In later years they remain enthusiastically loyal to Alma Mater, coming back to football games and class reunions and contributing to the support of the college. As alumni their influence is not always on the side of progress in education, but perhaps they make up for this failure in other ways.

I am prepared, moreover, to say that the existence of hundreds of centers filled with such care-free young people may be a good thing for the country. They keep alive a tradition of good cheer and of man's right to happiness in a country that is otherwise sordidly commercial. . . .

But while all this may be good for the country, it is not very good for the colleges. It is bad for the morale of any institution to sail under false colors, and colleges are popularly supposed to be educational institutions. The college faculties themselves must to some extent share this popular delusion, or else they would not permit the public to go on believing it. The attempt to live up to this erroneous idea puts everybody under a strain, students and faculty alike, and is the one unpleasant thing about college life. Instructors are forever annoying the students, trying to get some work out of them. . . .

What the average student gets from college, then, is an opportunity to complete his adolescence in an interesting and healthy environment, the experience of being away from home and on his own, and fraternity and club life—pleasant in itself—in which friendships are formed that last through life and are often useful business connections in after years. There is also athletics, through which the student may develop his muscles, gain the desirable moral quality of good sportsmanship, and satisfy any ambition he may have to become a college hero. One always becomes famous in college outside the class-room, never in it. Incidentally, if a student is naturally clever at picking up bits of information with a minimum of reading, he gains a bowing acquaintance with about as much knowledge as should be the possession of one with a fair secondary education. Finally, he forms certain habits and acquires certain manners and tastes which mould him to the type of the average college graduate, and goes out in the world to take his place in the social and business circles of his home town, where, if he should ever mention Aristotle, people would think he was crazy.

The college graduate can play a good game of tennis, wear his clothes well, talk

about the latest novel, walk across a room with grace and dignity, and share the
club opinions of his set, and there is nothing offensive in his table manners. I do
not mean to underrate these accomplishments. The person who does not have them,
however great his achievement in scholarship, is a boor, too lacking in sensitiveness
to assimilate the knowledge he has stored in his head. But these are accomplishments
that should be learned at home, as a matter of course; colleges ought not to be
necessary for training of this sort.

Wherein the education of the average college graduate fails of its true ends is seen
in what might be called the deeper things of the spirit. No profound intellectual
passion has been awakened, no habit of independent judgment formed. The college
man shares the usual popular prejudices of his community. He runs with the crowd
after the hero of the hour, and shows the same lack of discrimination as do the
uneducated. He votes the same party ticket, is intolerant along with his neighbors,
and puts the same value on material success as do the illiterate. His education has
made very little difference in his religious beliefs, his social philosophy, his ethical
values, or his general outlook on the world. Like all opinionated and half-educated
people, he jumps to hasty conclusions, believes what others believe, does things
because others do them, worships the past, idealizes the present.

In contrast with this, let me quote a passage from John Stuart Mill. The author
meant it to be a description of the scientist. It stands as a suggestion of what a
liberally educated mind should be.

> To question all things;—never to turn away from any difficulty; to accept
> no doctrine either from ourselves or from other people without a rigid scrutiny
> by negative criticism; letting no fallacy, or incoherence, or confusion of
> thought, step by unperceived; above all, to insist upon having the meaning of
> a word clearly understood before using it, and the meaning of a proposition
> before assenting to it;—these are the lessons we learn "from workers in Sci-
> ence." With all this vigorous management of the negative element, they inspire
> no scepticism about the reality of truth or indifference to its pursuit. The
> noblest enthusiasm, both for the search after truth and for applying it to its
> highest uses, pervades those writers.

When all is said, the ignorance and folly of men are things that institutions cannot cure. Each must discover the path of wisdom for himself. One does not "get" an
education anywhere. One becomes an educated person by virtue of patient study,
quiet meditation, intellectual courage, and a life devoted to the discovery and
service of truth.

Common men cherish their naïve faiths and ask no questions. They imagine that
education is simply greater information of the same sort which they also possess in
some measure, and that it is the part of wisdom to establish the reality of their
shadows. They resent a wisdom which is different from their own and unsettles belief. He who acquires information without the will to doubt is a common man and
his kind understand him. Hence men tend to display their information and conceal
their education. However much a man may know, so long as he does not become
re-oriented, the crowd does not suspect him, but admires his learning. He is like a
former Mayor of New York in his high hat at the head of the Policeman's Parade.

The multitude used to stand with their mouths open gazing at him. Each in imagination saw in the exalted figure himself risen to a place of honor and success. So it is with the "brainy man." The "lightening calculator" or the man who can recite from memory the population statistics of the cities of the United States is a museum wonder. But when it was announced in a New York theater that only twelve men could understand Einstein's theory of relativity, I am told that the crowd hissed.

Information is a kind of skill. Everyone can possess this skill to the extent he chooses, and people do not resent an exhibition of unusual skill of such a nature. In America most men and boys have some measure of skill at the game of baseball, so this game is the popular national form of sport. The skillful professional ball-player is simply one of the common boyhood ideals realized. He differs from the spectators of the game in degree, but not in kind. He plays the same game they all played, and is the same sort of person they all were as boys—only more so. So with most kinds of information, the amount one may acquire makes only a quantitative difference, not a difference in kind. But as a man becomes educated he discovers that he is playing a new game; he is becoming a different kind of person, with different likes and dislikes, different interests, different ideals and faiths, and such beliefs as he has he holds differently.

What the multitude most fears in education is the danger that the crowd faith will be lost in the process. This fear is often justified. Old beliefs will be lost and they should be. The fear appears in consciousness as solicitude for the spiritual welfare of the person being educated. It is really anxiety over the menace of education to herd living and thinking. It is the function of education to lure the individual out of the pack and give him opportunity to know his own mind, a thing he can never do so long as he runs and barks and bites along with all the rest. To return to Plato's figure, every person who climbs out of the cave not only loses his own faith in the reality of shadows but weakens the faith of those who remain behind. Cave men make strenuous efforts to resist education. Their common practice is to maintain their own systems of pseudo education in which no one is permitted to turn his eyes away from the wall.

Again, education has been likened to leaven. When it is honest it is very much like yeast. Before the culture is introduced the solution of ideas is in equilibrium. The mind has simply accepted what was poured into it by parents, teachers, priests, and politicians. In the solution there is reflected a compact, "still," neatly ordered little system of knowledge. "God's in his heaven, all's right with the world." Duty is clear, all is conventionally arranged, truth is eternal and logic can prove it. Human rights are decreed by the founders of the republic. The course of destiny is disclosed to reason and faith and the promise sealed in divine revelation. At this stage, most minds are carefully sealed up or a prophylactic is stirred in, for if those sugary solutions are exposed to a live spiritual culture they begin to "work." Then they are spoiled for certain purposes. With the fermentation there is sometimes foam and gas; but a chemical change is taking place, brewing a mind with a "kick" in it. It is interesting that bread and wine and education are all made by a similar process; hence an educational Volsteadism has often been enforced so that many of the best minds have had to be "home brewed."

Professor Dewey somewhere speaks of education as freeing the mind of "bunk." It is a large task. No one wholly succeeds. I neved saw a completely "debunked" individual. Strive as we may to eradicate it, there is always in our thinking an amount of error, of wish-fancy accepted as objective fact, of exaggeration, special pleading, self-justification. Many of our beliefs are not founded in reason at all, but are demanded by some unconscious and repressed impulse in our nature. Men make a virtue of their faith when in fact they are *victims* of it; they can no more help believing certain things than a neurotic can stop a compulsive habit.

It is said that it is easy to doubt and that to believe is an accomplishment. It is not so. It is easier to believe than to doubt. The things we must train ourselves to doubt are as a rule just the things we wish to believe. It is children and savages and the illiterate who have the most implicit faith. It is said that unbelief is sin. This is not so; it is nobler to doubt than to believe, for to doubt is often to take sides with fact against oneself. Nietzsche said that this trait is characteristic of "higher men." It was Huxley, as I remember it, who considered that man could in nothing fall so low as when he deliberately took refuge in the absurd. Even with a rationalist like Huxley doubt is not merely a function of the intellect. Under certain circumstances it is a moral necessity.

The pursuit of knowledge is not the same, however, as scrupulous avoidance of error. He who strives to do his own thinking must accept responsibility for himself. He must expect that he will make mistakes. He may end in total failure. He must take his chances and be willing to pay the cost of his adventure. I know professional scholars who are so afraid they may write or say something which their colleagues will show to be wrong that they never express an opinion of their own or commit themselves to any down-right statement. Such equivocation and qualifying—playing safe—is not what I mean by doubt. I do not mean merely that one should be always on guard against the possibility of error, but that one should learn to hold all one's beliefs with a half-amused lightheartedness. Most minds are loaded down with the seriousness of their convictions. Solemnity in the presence of our eternal verities is awkwardness, and makes us always a little ridiculous, giving us the appearance of one about to shake hands with the President. Why not enjoy the humor of the situation? Our great truths may all the while be "spoofing" us. It will do no harm to give them a sly wink now and then.

Crowd men have no sense of humor. It is very difficult to educate solemn and opinionated people. Like Omar, they always come out by that same door wherein they went. I have known students to complete a course of study having learned nothing, because of their disinclination to consider any fact which might cause them to surrender some belief about religion or economic theory with which they entered. Whoever leaves an institution of learning with the same general outlook on life that he had when he first came might better have employed his time otherwise. He is not a student; he is a church-member.

Education may not end in doubt, but it ends when a man stops doubting. But why speak of the end of a process that should continue through life? As I see it, the process is more often discontinued at the point of some fictitious certainty than in any moment of doubt. Doubt, the willingness to admit that conjecture is subject to revision, is a spur to learning. The recognition that our truths are not copies of eternal realities but are human creations designed to meet human needs, puts one in a teachable frame of mind. And the discovery that thinking may be creative makes intellectual activity interesting. Much has been written by indoctrinators about the wretchedness of the dogmatic sceptic. I wonder how these writers, themselves so innocent of doubt, know so much about him. I have never found such a man. I do not believe he ever existed. There are writers who question things that most men do not even know exist, compared with whom professional "freethinkers" are often naïve. But such writers are often gentle and cheerful spirits whose minds are not at all paralyzed by doubt, but are active, subtle, stimulating.

Humanity during the course of civilization has fixed certain habits, made certain discoveries, constructed certain systems of ordered knowledge by emphasizing the relevant and significant. There is little likelihood that the whole structure will come tumbling about our heads because somebody examines into its nature. In fact the highest achievement of civilization would appear to be a mind capable of understanding our human ways of thinking for what they are. But if our learning should cause us to abandon all our consoling beliefs and ideals and pet theories; if it should reveal human folly in our every great cause, and futility in our every scheme of social reconstruction, even then we cannot for such reasons shirk the task of educating ourselves. There would remain for each of us the ideal of what an educated mind might become; no knowledge could take from us the ideals of courage, of preserving our integrity, of standing undaunted before the challenge to our spirit.

Questions for Discussion

1. How would you teach a class in American government using the education principles advocated in this selection?
2. Is the type of liberal education Martin advocates an aid or a hindrance for professional education? Could a society exist—or make any progress—if everyone were educated according to the principles advocated in this selection?
3. Would Martin's ideas imply any particular pedagogical arrangements, i.e., lectures or discussions; objective or essay examinations; circular or row seating arrangements?
4. Are there any fundamental differences—in either the purposes proposed or the methods advocated—between Rousseau and Martin? Could they both be considered as exponents of liberal education?

10 Metaphors for the University

Charles H. Monson, Jr.

This selection should be fun. It encourages you to use your imagination when thinking about what a school is. Is a school like a dispensing machine, handing out so many goodies for each dollar you put in? Is it like a zoo where you can watch exotic creatures perform? Is it like a cave where you can explore the unknown continually? Or is a school more like a search-light or a cafeteria or a hospital? Or is a school like a service station or a subway or a city? Or, perhaps, like an egg-candling machine? Or, to be current, perhaps, it is like a battlefield. Think of all the elements which are a necessary part of a school: teachers, students, classroom, resource ma-terials, etc., then pick your metaphor and apply each of these elements to the corresponding parts of that metaphor. Not only should you have fun when discovering the implications of some metaphors, but you should gain some new insights into your own views on the purposes of the edu-cation enterprise.

Every writer knows that metaphors illustrate conclusions and sharpen distinctions in a way not possible with abstract words, and writers in educational philosophy have used metaphors in rich and wildly diverse ways. From the time when Plato contended that education is a means for escaping from the cave, to the present, when Kerr asserts that a university is a bargaining table, writers have likened the educational process to many other aspects of experience.

Cardinal Newman, for instance, insists that a university is neither a mint in which semifinished material is stamped in a common mold nor a treadmill where students perform the same tasks endlessly and uselessly; it is, rather, an old mother, an *alma mater*, who nurtures her children. Whitehead contends that students are not trunks to be filled with ideas; that universities are regiments, not rabble; and that educa-tion is the process of a body assimilating new material and growing, often in un-expected ways. Ortega y Gasset asserts that a university is a path leading people through the tangled and confused jungle in which men are lost, and that it is a spirit of adventure rather than a body of knowledge, and so is not a machine. Hutchins believes a school should be viewed as an active monastery rather than the service station it has become.

Clark Kerr, who is fast becoming the master metaphor-maker, suggests that a university is a city composed of anonymous citizens with diverse interests, an egg-candling machine where ideas are examined, a factory for producing knowledge, and a bargaining table where conflicts are adjudicated. Zacharias thinks that most univer-sities are mazes where students are trying to find a way out rather than trees where

Reprinted from *The Educational Record*, Winter, 1967. Washington, D. C.: The American Council on Education.

they can explore new branches of knowledge; Hofstadter takes a similar view, arguing that universities should be springboards rather than hurdles. Dickens compares teachers to jugs and students to well-ordered juglets into which knowledge is poured. Hardy contends that a school is a work of art or a chamber orchestra. Becker believes it is a baseball team where the president, interestingly, is an umpire, not a manager. Ulich compares a university to a theater.

Barzun says today's university is a cookie cutter, carelessly handled, while Russell says it is a mold. Martin compares education to the leavening in bread. Hook says it is an antiseptic. Carmichael asserts it is a hospital for curing society's ills, but Weiss thinks it is a marketplace where able individuals display their intellectual wares. Van Doren describes society as a jungle and education as a searchlight and as a fire. Wallis contends that a school is a beehive, each member of the community industriously serving the interests of the whole, and that it should not be a refuge for exotic migratory birds.

Many writers have described the university as a business that produces goods to be purchased, but none more colorfully—or more scathingly—than Veblen, who identifies the curriculum with a department store, the professors with the drillmasters, and the president as the "captain of erudition." Dewey contends a school is a large home, and Rickover laments that the school has become a private preserve with "no trespassing" signs posted everywhere. However, seldom does anyone now use Beadle's metaphor of the extinct dinosaur that failed to adjust to its new environment.

The richness and range of these metaphors is perhaps surprising. But anyone who has ventured into the labyrinths of educational philosophy knows that this diversity simply reflects the diversity of educational aims: Schools do provide the services of a department store, the guidance of a searchlight, the cures of a hospital, and the security of a mother.

New Metaphors for Old

Yet a metaphor can be more than illustrative, more than a vividly memorable conclusion. It can be educational, too, for a fully developed metaphor clarifies the implications of an idea, often in unexpected, even delightful, ways. Thus, if a university is an egg-candling machine, then professors are the egg-candlers and, depending on one's educational philosophy, students must be either the cartons into which the candled eggs are put or—I hesitate to say it—the chickens who lay the eggs to be candled. Or, if a university is a chamber orchestra where different instruments produce harmonious sounds, then the conductor must be the president waving his arms enthusiastically, the first-chair men must be the deans keeping their charges in harmony, the audience must be the students applauding on cue, and the discordant rehearsal must be a general faculty meeting!

With the possible exception of Veblen, no writer has used metaphors in this educational sense. Yet trying to match the elements of a metaphor with its educational counterparts can provide, at once, a test of the metaphor's accuracy and a fresh perspective from which to view the educational enterprise. Since the implications of an idea are always as interesting as, and frequently more important than, the idea itself, a fully developed metaphor can give new insight into the nature of a university, or of any other educational institution. It can, but does it? That is the thesis this paper examines.

The Dispensing Machine

Many of the preceding metaphors were based on the idea that a university has a service function. Thus it was described as a department store, a service station, a factory, a hospital and, we might add, it can be called a cafeteria, a market, a government agency. Moreover, most universities were established with a service motive in mind: John Harvard, for instance, bequeathed his library "dreading to leave an illiterate ministry to the churches when our present ministers shall lie in the dust," and Ezra Cornell gave his land and Western Union stock to "found an institution in which any person can find instruction in any subject."

To say a university has a service function is to assert both that there is an institution that has resources to offer and that there is a public who will purchase them. An appropriate unused metaphor, therefore, would seem to be that the university is a dispensing machine.

There are many publics, each with its own needs and interests, who patronize this dispensing machine. Those students who already know that they want to be lab technicians or librarians or whatever drop their coins, marked "tuition," into the slots over the windows marked "Technical Education," "Library Science," and so forth. Others, not quite so sure, are sent to the window marked "General Education," where they sample indiscriminately, hoping to find some nourishing and tasty commodity. But very soon most students discover that quality control of the products has been poor, that some slots always produce healthful goods while others, deservedly, have a poor reputation. Indeed, even the same window can produce a wide variance in quality, a fact that prompts some of the more imaginative purchasers to look for hidden doors in the machine so they can refine the selection process and thus obtain goods of consistently high quality.

But students are not the only customers of this dispensing machine. Those concerned with the nation's security visit regularly those windows marked "Engineering," "Physics," and "Chemistry." They drop coins marked "research funds" into the machine, and while the packaging of the product is nondescript, the contents usually are good indeed. Sometimes the machine ejects a small card reading "Inconclusive results" or "Found a new problem," and, in small letters on the other side, "Want to try again?" but most purchasers go away smiling.

Still others come to the machine, their hands heavy with coins marked "consultant fees." Some of these buyers are public school administrators, others are businessmen, still others are the operators of other vending machines, but all come to the university because they believe its resources can help them solve their own problems. Sometimes a purchaser has to wait in line for a particular product and, more frequently than he hopes, he discovers that all his product has to offer was written on the advertising wrapper that he saw long ago. But, as a whole, the resources purchased with consultant coins are useful, and are a deductible expense besides.

Before anyone will come to the coin slots and windows, however, the dispensing machine must be located in an attractive atmosphere. Those machines surrounded by arching oaks with ivy growing up the sides are most inviting, although operators have discovered that a nearby entertainment stadium where boys run and girls cavort on the grass is a definite asset.

Most importantly, the windows themselves must be attractive. This is not too difficult for some, such as Engineering or Chemistry or Mathematics, where long lines of purchasers are always waiting with tuition, research, or consultant coins in hand. Others, such as Marketing and Psychology, have learned to package their products attractively. Others, such as Literature and History, are tantalizing but provide little nourishment. Every dispensing machine operator knows he must give special attention to the window marked "Teacher Education" to overcome its shoddy reputation. Some customers view with nostalgia, and perhaps remorse, those windows marked "Philosophy" and "Classics," seldom used, once proud and shining, now tarnished and dusty. (An alert observer will notice that a Semantics sign continually slips in over the Philosophy label. No such changeable label is apparent in the Classics window.) Indeed, none of the Humanities windows have long lines of customers; their slots for research and consultant coins are rusted and overgrown with ivy. The president, of course, must do what he can to improve their appearance, but then he must not neglect his major customers, and, thank goodness, Humanities machines cost so little to operate and service!

In contrast to the smooth and orderly exterior the machine presents to its customers, its interior is infinitely complex. Intricate channels of authority lead to disused windows, slots are clogged with research coins, products dispute over their relative worth, there are arguments about the division of receipts, and always discussion and disagreement. A brave operator may try to straighten out the circuits and reconcile the differences, but most—resting content in the conviction that as long as the books balance and students graduate, they must be doing a good job—prefer to hire a deputy operator, called the vice-president, to keep the machine from blowing up. (Soon the vice-president will weary and so hire an associate and he, in time, an assistant, and so on, as Parkinson said. All the while, a good secretary is irreplaceable.)

So, if a university is thought of as a dispensing machine, the outside publics should be thought of as customers purchasing a product which the faculty members have to sell. Teaching is a commodity valued for its usefulness, and research is done because it can be funded. But organizationally, the crucial person is the president, the dispensing-machine operator. He does not need to know how a product is produced or whether the need it satisfies should be satisfied, or even what the need is. But he must be aware of the interests of his many publics, and he must know whether they pay a fair price for the goods they receive. He must keep his machine well stocked with interesting and useful products, recruit able young helpers, open new windows as new interests develop, and occasionally close out those products that don't sell. He must be sensitive to complaints from his customers and cautious with his finances, and he must make the public aware of his machine and its advantages over competing machines. If he can do all this, he can look proudly at the arch leading to his academic dispensing machine, knowing that his university proudly fulfills its purpose: "Servamus Te."

The Zoo

The primary metaphor in Clark Kerr's provocative *The Uses of the University*—
one which arises from his emphasis on the multidimensional aspects of the modern
university and on the need for a president to mediate between the claims of research
and teaching, scientist and humanist, public and scholar, student and faculty—is the
bargaining table. But he also uses the metaphor of a city: Some citizens are lost,
others are searching, a few have found a modicum of security, and all live together
in an incredibly complex environment where knowledge has become so fractionalized
that the inhabitants of the city have little in common with each other. This description suggests still another metaphor: namely, that the university is a collection of
unique and interesting creatures, as is a zoo.

Others, too, have suggested this image. Cardinal Newman described the university
as "an assemblage of learned men, zealous for their own sciences and rivals of each
other." Veblen thought of university presidents as "captains of erudition," endlessly
trying to standardize the diversity of their institution. Wallis contends that a university is a haven for exotic migratory birds. And epigrammatically, a professor has been
defined as a man who thinks otherwise, a president as one who tries to stay out of
bear traps.

If a university is thought of as a zoo, then the center of interest is the exhibits,
the professors, rather than the head keeper, the president. In this zoo, specimens from
far and near are brought together to have their uniqueness observed by curious spectators. Some specimens burrow into the ground to discover its secrets while others
contemplate the mystery of the heavens or investigate the nature of the trees or the
earth or the other specimens or, sometimes, the spectators. A few preen themselves
all day, admiring their own beauty while deprecating the others' deficiencies, and
some constantly make loud noises, prompting the spectators to say: "I'm glad he is
caged in here where he can do no harm." Each specimen is proud of his uniqueness
and displays it colorfully at least once a year, usually in June.

Spectators pay an admission fee to listen to these specimens talk about their observations and themselves. Sometimes the spectators find that the conversation is in
an alien tongue and so consider it very erudite, and at other times the words are so
wise that they try to reward the specimen with some extra payment, a practice discouraged by the zookeeper. They notice, also, that each creature has a den to which
he can retire when he wearies of examining trees, contemplating mysteries, or discoursing learnedly. In this den he can record and analyze, classify and cogitate, issuing forth from time to time to check his observations, make a learned pronounce-
ment, or initiate a new project, all of which is wonderfully interesting to watch, even
if barely understandable.

An observant spectator will soon notice that each exhibit is happiest when with his
own kind, buffalo with buffalo, economist with economist. Each speaks a language
the other understands, thereby making for an in-group camaraderie broken only occasionally by Young Turks challenging The Establishment. This is not to say that
every cage is peacefully harmonious, for the discussions frequently erupt in an over-
flow of noise and a show of anger, and sometimes a member of the group must be

isolated until his distemper recedes. Better occasional internecine fights, though, than putting all the exhibits in one cage, where a ferocious empirical physicist could devour a moralizing philosopher with barely a touch of indigestion.

Yet conflict is inherent in diversity, so a good zookeeper must always be alert to keep his exhibits contented and well fed, thereby encouraging each to exhibit his own uniqueness to the spectators. Yes, bars and cages are the answer, arbitrarily limiting each species to his own department and thereby encouraging each to do that which he can do best. But different species like to mate, and before long the zookeeper has to build a connecting passageway between Physics and Biology and label the central area "Biophysics," or one connecting Sociology, Psychology, and Anthropology to be labeled "Institute for the Behavioral Sciences." These new passageways clutter the institution's blueprints horribly and sometimes raise questions about who is to feed these hybrids. But they quickly attract their share of followers, particularly if the keeper announces loudly and frequently: "New Addition: The Most Recent Specimen in Captivity."

Moreover, certain disciplines refuse to stay caged. The historian, for instance, insists that every other specimen belongs in his cage, and so does the anthropologist. The philosopher burrows assiduously to show that the foundations of every other cage are only offshoots of his own. So the discrete cages give way to conglomerates, and those who contemplate mysteries are thrown in with those who study trees or spectators. The explosiveness of this situation is heightened by a few unwashed spectators who, feeling no obligation to the institution, climb fences, make speeches, and shake the cages.

But most spectators are content to observe, taking notes on what they see and hear. Sometimes they ask questions of the specimens but usually find the answers of their peers more understandable. They pass from cage to cage gathering data, savoring an occasional insight, accumulating credit hours. Finally, they discover they have visited cages long enough and must go out into the real world. Some leave gladly, thinking they have wasted their time and money; others reluctantly, wishing to see exhibits they know they have missed; others not at all, eagerly trying to find an empty cage where they, too, can spend their lives investigating and contemplating.

So if a university is a zoo, students really are spectators and professors really are performing animals. Teaching is self-fulfillment; learning is observation. Research is to be equated with the development of each species' uniqueness, and it is done for personal reasons, not because it is funded. The chief zookeeper, the president, is important but unobserved. He must make certain his exhibits are lively, interesting, and informative, and he must keep them from fighting each other, especially during visiting hours. He must charge the spectators enough to feed his exhibits and maintain the grounds; he must also keep the visitors out of the cages, encouraging them to see rather than be. And he must do all this within the rules established by his board, very nice men who know absolutely nothing about running a zoo. But the exotic exhibits are what visitors come to see; their uniqueness is what the university is all about.

Mammoth Cave

Whether the university is thought of as a dispensing machine or a zoo, both meta-phors assume that a university provides resources to be used, as from a machine, or to be admired, as in a zoo. But this assumption does not fit the dominant emphasis in Western higher education. Traditionally, writers on educational philosophy have emphasized the search rather than the answer, the exploration rather than the utility of knowledge. To be sure, knowledge may be nourishing and professors entertaining, but a university is thought of as that unique institution in which students can join with their faculty mentors to explore the unknown.

This liberal arts tradition has its psychological origins in man's curiosity about the world and its metaphorical origins in Plato's account of the educated man's ascent out of the cave into the sunlight. Its echoes are to be found in Henry Tappan's belief that a university is a light, in Ortega y Gasset's reference to a path leading through a dangerous forest, in Newman's *alma mater*, in Hutchins's Utopia, in Adler's intelligent farmer, and in many other images. But seldom has this ideal been stated more cogently than in the Robbins report on British higher education.

> It is the essence of higher education that it introduces students to a world of intellectual responsibility and intellectual discovery in which they are to play their part. They have to be taught techniques and methods to acquire a corpus of relevant knowledge; but more important, they have to be inspired to learn to work. Here an ounce of example is worth a pound of exhortation.[1]

But in today's world, Plato's image is too simple. Large numbers of people, not just a few, are prisoners in the cave, and some of them already are conscious of their ig-norance. Most guides know only a part of the cave, some know only the general direction in which to go, and others are lost, too. The cave has many openings to Truth, not one, and the obstacles to be overcome include not only ignorance and apathy but also discouragement and complexity. Guides must be connected with each other, for exploration today is a group, not an individual, activity. Moreover, some guides don't want to leave the cave; they want to explore it.

Despite these limitations, however, the metaphor is still applicable, for exploring the unknown is thought by many to be central to a university's purpose. Perhaps Plato's cave was too small; perhaps he should have been exploring Mammoth Cave.

Mammoth Cave has many rooms, some known and well lighted, others—perhaps a majority, possibly an infinite number—unknown and shrouded in darkness. Guides have chosen different rooms to become intimately familiar with and are hired to lead visitors through the cave, explaining its nature and beauty. Most of the visitors are young and, although more knowledgeable than Plato's prisoners, still largely prisoners of their own ignorance. Like Mark Twain, they are ashamed, at eighteen, of their parents' ignorance; and they come to a university expecting to earn an additional $200,000 in their lifetime. A wise guide will begin with this recognition and so initially lead his charges into rooms well lighted and ventilated, all the while

[1] Committee on Higher Education, *Higher Education: Report of the Committee Appointed by the Prime Minister under the Chairmanship of Lord Robbins,* Cmnd. 2154 (London: Her Majesty's Stationery Office, 1963), p. 181.

helping them to realize that their wisdom is not theirs alone. In time, however, he must plunge them into the unknown. For many, this will be a perilous experience as they feel the certainty of their beliefs give way beneath their feet. Some spelunkers will close their eyes against the danger, holding tenaciously to their guide, hoping that he will return them to their former location without forcing them to grapple with the unknown. Once the terrifying experience is over, these students will stay in the well-lighted corridors, watching Mickey Mouse movies and consuming the products of the dispensing machines.

But those students who press on soon begin to witness sights they have never imagined before: huge pools of literature into which they can plunge; stalagmites, large and small, to be climbed; caverns filled with echoes waiting to be interpreted; and always side labyrinths to be explored. The rush of an underground river continually reminds them of what remains to be discovered, but every so often they glimpse an opening to the sunlight, although most truth is seen as through a glass darkly.

The observant spelunker will notice how certain guides seem to know certain portions of a cavern well: they may climb the Dryden pinnacle for days, exploring each nook and crevasse, the guide's flashlight illuminating the most interesting features. Some students will wonder why their guides dally to argue that an object cannot be seen as well from one point of view as from another, but then, they conclude, those who spend all their time in the caves can hardly be expected to have a balanced judgment. Students will soon learn which guides follow much-worn paths, uninterestedly reading from well-thumbed notes, and which try different routes each time, admonishing their fellow explorers: "Watch your step, the footing is dangerous here," or "Try that opening; let's see what happens."

Some guides inspire their students to surmount the huge landslides or traverse the deep crevasses blocking the path to Truth. Other guides take notes on their groups' reactions to the mazes. Many would prefer to explore their caverns alone, without the distraction of students' questions. Always the guides like to talk to each other about their respective caverns, comparing their features and the degree to which they have been explored. Some claim a superior beauty and value for their own, a claim sure to be hotly disputed by others and set aside only when the intercom announces: "Committee on cave beautification will meet at 4:00 P.M."

The guides view such announcements with some resignation but with more irritation, for they know the real work in the cave is done by the explorers, not by those who control the intercom. To be sure, the guide must have rope and lights and food, and these, as well as his freedom from outside interferences, must be guaranteed by the chief guide. But the purpose of the university is to explore the unknown, a task only working guides can perform, so when a guide becomes an administrator, with reports to make, the other guides think he had betrayed his calling, selling his integrity for the power of an intercom set.

The chief guide, however, views himself in a different light. Not only does he supply the lights and food and rope (with the occasional hope that some guides will hang themselves), but also he keeps in constant contact with each cavern to discover where reinforcements are needed most. Some caverns are swamped with visitors, others have likely areas for exploration, still others need more informed guides; and someone, namely the chief guide, must make these judgments. Moreover, Mammoth Cave must be advertised, tickets must be sold, parents must be reassured, records must be kept, new guides must be hired, old ropes must be replaced, and, most importantly, the conditions for exploration must be maintained: enough fresh air and light for free discussion, and lots of coffee.

The university president as chief guide, then, must establish and maintain the conditions which will enable others to explore the unknown. He must fend off those low-minded utilitarians who want to consume the university's products, and yet he must make the cave sufficiently attractive that people do not spend all their money at the vending machines. He must help his guides explore the caverns without seeming to interfere with the explorations. He must placate irate fathers whose money has educated a son to believe, unlike Mark Twain at twenty-two, that all fathers are stupid. And he must find the means to buy new rope and supplies for those young spelunkers who become so excited by their studies that they continue exploring the cave more minutely, quietly entering academia as one of the guides.

As the Metaphor Is Bent . . .

Metaphors can not only illustrate and clarify but also relate means to ends, for the existence of a university implies an organization and that implies a leader, and he requires training. But the training he receives will depend on what he and his teachers think a university is, on which metaphor seems to them most appropriate.

Thus, if a university is thought to be an institution that sells knowledge, a potential president will learn to think that the most important questions he must ask himself are: "Is the product selling?" "Do the books balance?" "What do my publics want?" Also, he must learn how to establish a line organization holding each subordinate strictly responsible for his sphere of influence, and he will treat his faculty as a commodity whose value depends on their ability to satisfy. (Tenure rules and personal compassion may complicate the matter.) He will think of students as consumers who enter the outside world once their immediate needs have been satisfied, but who, as alumni, may realize they received more than they paid for and so become benefactors. Disturbances such as student protests and faculty unrest will be viewed with the same alarm as would a balky machine, the trouble to be diagnosed and remedied by those responsible. And he must learn that the budget always is of central importance, for it tells what is well accepted. An aspiring college president, then, should be trained in the principles of business administration, since a good administrator can manage any machine, whether it dispenses candy or knowledge.

Quite a different set of qualities is necessary if one views the university as a zoo. As zookeeper the president's talents must be turned both inward, to make certain each exhibit develops his own uniqueness, and outward, to provide the conditions for others to observe. He thus must learn to view his faculty, not as commodities, but as unusual and interesting people, and to view students not as buyers, but as spectators who come to observe, listen, and learn. A new president must learn that as alumni, students never repay a debt with their contributions; rather, they donate to the Institute to Preserve Uniqueness. A president must develop an abiding sensitivity to and respect for uniqueness; he must cultivate an ability to have each party to a dispute feel satisfied, especially when he has received only part of his due. He must know about motivation and interpersonal relationships, and in doing so, he discovers that the conference table, not the budget, is the critical point in the institution. Hence, a potential university president must develop the talents of the preserver, innovator, and mediator, for his task is more psychological than managerial.

More than the other two, the chief guide at Mammoth Cave must have a deep commitment to the educative process itself, since his role is to supply his faculty and students with the means for exploring the unknown. Accordingly, he does not view his faculty as expendable commodities or interesting oddities; rather, they are of central importance; indeed, they are at the heart of the university. He views students not as spectators but as participants. And he views his alumni as those who will now pay the adult price of admission. Knowledge of a budget is necessary but quite secondary; mediating techniques are helpful but used infrequently in a good school. The best president, then, will be one who already has experienced the delights of solitary search and so knows the conditions necessary for its success. He is a person who will accept the role of administrator, not because of interest or gain, but because of his obligation to the institution, and he will eagerly await the time when he can return to his own particular cavern.

A university administrator's training, therefore, could be that of a businessman, a mediator, or a faculty member, depending on which metaphor is thought to be most important. But more than that, the kind of training he receives will determine, in large part, the type of institution he administers. If he has been taught that the budget is the crucial part of the university, he will tend to view his students as customers and his faculty as commodities. If he thinks faculty support is the critical item, he may tend to neglect his public relations. Which will be his top priorities? finances or the classroom? the university's publics or the faculty's needs? The way an administrator answers these questions will depend on what he thinks his institution is, and what he thinks it is, in turn, will help to determine what it becomes.

So metaphors can be interesting and instructive and also a force for shaping the future, for as a man thinks, so will his institution become. Or is it that as the twig is bent, so will the tree grow? Or, perhaps, as the machine is patronized, so will it be refilled?

Questions for Discussion

1. All right, try on these metaphors for educational size. A school is like a (a) cafeteria, (b) hospital, (c) searchlight, (d) battlefield, (e) playground, (f) service station, and (g) bargaining table.
2. Try describing some of the earlier selections in terms of the metaphors they might use. Do you happen to remember that Dewey thought of the school as an ideal home and that Prozorow thought of learning on the stimulus-response model? What metaphors would fit Rousseau's Emile? Or Martin's liberal education? How imaginative are you?
3. Which of these many metaphors, if any, seem to you to come closest to describing the essential nature of a school? What does this tell you about your own views on the ends and means of education?

Epilogue: What's New in the Old?

Rousseau, Dewey and Newman are names familiar to everyone who studies man's past thinking about the purposes of education; they are important in any study of the traditional philosophy of education. They are important because each presents a coherent statement of what education is all about, as well as a plan for achieving those purposes. Rousseau, for instance, asserts that the purpose of education is to encourage each child to develop his own capacities, and he also concludes that the teacher's sole task is to maintain the condition of freedom which will allow each child to do so. Newman insists that an educated man is one who knows how and when to generalize from incomplete data, and he also describes a curriculum and teaching methods which will enable a teacher to help discipline the minds of his students. And if the purpose of education is to help students become intelligent problem-solvers, as Dewey says, then the school's facilities and curriculum should be arranged so the students will encounter genuine problems and have experience in discerning relevant facts and proposing alternative hypotheses for solving these problems. These men, then, are important because they present a consistent and comprehensive account of possible ends and means of education.

But these are not the only men important in traditional educational philosophy. Other ideas presented in Part I are equally influential and important, even though their authors might be less familiar. How many educators—and citizens—believe that the school's major function is to develop in students an appreciation for the society's history and institutions, and thus preserve the society's values and beliefs? The communists, Kalinen and Prozorow, hold this view in regard to communist education, and is there any reason why the same argument could not be made for the educational system in a capitalist society? Or, should the schools become the leading edge for reforming outmoded economic and political institutions, as Brameld—and the Students for a Democratic Society—contend? Martin contends that education should liberate the mind from prejudice and propaganda, and thus asserts the liberal arts' tradition so central in the history of western civilization. Spencer argues that all reliable knowledge is gained only by the use of scientific method. Is that such an unusual idea? These writers are not saying the same things, for the fact is that they—and people generally—have quite different notions as to what is the purpose of education. Even a casual, but certainly an extended, examination of the metaphors writers on education use should indicate this conclusion quite clearly.

At first glance, this conclusion might be disconcerting to you, for if concerned and thoughtful men such as these cannot agree on the purpose of education then who are you to even try? And yet try you must, if you ever are to enter a classroom as a teacher; and try you do, as you evaluate the individual classes and educational program in which you are now engaged. The fact is that you cannot teach and you cannot evaluate what you are taught unless you have some notion of why you are teaching and what you hope to be learning. But perhaps that is to say the obvious: a theory about education is an inherent part of any educational enterprise.

On reflection, however, this diversity of purposes should not be so disconcerting.

It helps to explain, and to justify, a pluralistic society. It helps us to understand why so much is expected of an educational system, and why it can be the subject of such intense criticism—usually by those who hold a different educational philosophy. It explains why different teachers approach the same subject matter in different ways—so different, in fact, as to suggest the subject matter is not really the same. Most importantly, this diversity of ends encourages us to consider the possibility that there is no single purpose for education, but that the purposes proposed are directly related to the subject matter being taught, the personality of the person doing the teaching, and the capacities and interest of those who are learning.

Thus, it could be argued that Rousseau's theory of the child's need for free development is correct when applied to small children but that Newman's advocacy of the disciplined mind is what ought to guide the teacher of secondary school students. Or, that all scientific subjects should be taught according to Spencer's theory while Martin's notions on liberal education ought to guide the efforts of all those who teach the humanities. Different subjects, then, might elicit different purposes, and different types of students might suggest different styles of teaching.

Thus, the kind of purpose and the type of student, the teaching technique and the kind of subject matter, the availability of outside resources and the students' own level of comprehension, the teacher's present personality and the students' past achievement; all of these, and many other factors, too, must enter into any discussion of the educational process.

Moreover, as our authors recognize, certain purposes imply certain techniques. The appropriate method for teaching a subject grows out of the purposes proposed by the teacher. Rousseau does not advocate that a teacher lecture to Emile; rather, he believes that the teacher must have a different conception of his role. Spencer does not suggest that a free-flowing discussion is the best means for disseminating the knowledge gained by science. Nor does Kalinen advocate critical problem-solving as the best means for developing an appreciation of his society's beliefs and values. No, certain methods are appropriate to achieve certain purposes, and none of these writers suggests that these methods will bring about the ends they desire. One of the major tasks facing anyone who is seriously interested in the educational process, then, is that of clearly relating means to ends, discovering which techniques are most appropriate for achieving stated purposes.

At this stage in your thinking about the educational enterprise, you do not need to decide which means are appropriate to which ends; whether lecturing and objective tests are more appropriate means for developing an appreciation of the society's values than small group discussions and essay examinations. Indeed, you do not even need to accept the hypothesis on which this book is based; namely, that a statement of purpose implies something about the teaching techniques, type of student, and type of subject matter which are involved in the teaching and learning process. But, you do need to understand the ends-means relationships proposed by the authors in Part I.

Rousseau clearly does not want his "teacher" to be a lecturer. Well, what does Rousseau want his teacher to do? Do you know? Dewey clearly does not believe that objective tests are the correct way to evaluate a student's performance—or does he? What does Martin say about the importance of students studying an established curriculum? Do you remember—or did you ever know? And what should students study, and how, in order to change the society, as Brameld suggests?

Can you answer these questions about Rousseau and Dewey, Martin and Brameld? And could you answer the same kind of questions for Newman and Spencer, Plato and Kalinen? How would you teach and test students if your school were like a dispensing machine, or like a zoo? If you can answer these questions, then your reading has been thoughtful as well as diligent. But if you can't, now is the time for you to review the material, and to find your authors' answers to each of the following questions: What is the purpose of education? What is the role of the teacher? What subjects should be taught, and how? What does a test test, and why should that material be tested? When does a student learn, and why should he learn? Is lecturing, discussing or problem-solving the best means for teaching? Will the stated means necessarily—or even probably—bring about the stated purposes?

It is important for you to have the answer to these questions clearly in mind now, for then you will understand the substance—and some of the justification— for the dominant theories about the educational process which have found acceptance in the world today. Not only should this help you to begin to clarify your own thinking on the ends and means of education, but it should provide you with a foundation for approaching the readings in Part II. For there you will be reading and thinking with writers whose criticism of the present educational system(s) range from contemptuous to vitriolic.

Not only should you hear what they say, but you should evaluate what you hear as well. This can be done best if you already have some knowledge of what thoughtful men have said about the educational process, for then you can determine whether the critics of today's educational enterprise point the way to new theories of education, and new means, or whether they merely repeat, perhaps in more colorful language, some of the ends and means already explored in the more traditional views. Moreover, do these critics propose means for achieving the ends they propose —or, are they even clear about their own ends, or their means? What can we learn about lecturing and testing, curriculum building and student motivation, subject matter and teaching techniques from these critics, and how is that knowledge similar to and different from the views expressed in these traditional philosophies of education? Keep these questions uppermost in your mind while reading Part II; otherwise, you may experience only shock.

What's new in the old? First, clear, cogent and comprehensive statements of the theories of education which people accept today. Second, a recognition of the interrelationships between ends and means. Above all, some answers to the perennial questions of the educational enterprise: What is meaningful learning? When does a teacher teach? What subjects should be taught and how? What should be tested, and why? The authors you have just read have given their answers to these questions, but which, if any, of these answers is right, I mean *really* right? You may still have a little more thinking to do on the subject.

Part Two
Some Critical Contemporary Perspectives

Prologue: Revolution in Education

If history will recall young people from the 1950's as the Silent Generation surely it will call the youth of the 1960's the Revolutionary Generation. On all sides, the young people of this decade are calling for change, not gradual or halting or halfway change, but significant and radical change in the institutions which comprise our society, now, and to dramatize their demands they have conducted sit-ins, lie-ins, talk-ins, and lock-outs. They have overflowed drugstores, telephone exchanges, presidents' offices and computer centers. They have argued, cajoled, demanded, demonstrated and fought. And for what? To bring about fundamental changes in our society; to create a revolution, hopefully by peaceful means.

There is no doubt that some of this decade's revolutionaries are simply angry young men striking out at the system in whatever way they can, but many others are dedicated, serious and intelligent young men and women who believe that the achievements of today's institutions do not begin to approach their ideal of what institutions ought to do, and that they know how to bring about a closer approximation. These three, an ideal, a perception of the present, and a method for effecting change, are essential elements in all revolutionary thinking, and could provide an intellectual framework to use when thinking about what you read in Part II.

But you will quickly discover that these writers, all of whom are advocating fundamental changes in some or all parts of the educational enterprise, have thought out their revolutionary programs in varying degrees. Some have only an anger or a contempt for the present system; others, only a vision; still others, a vision, a criticism and a proposal. Accordingly, you should try to determine what each author says, if anything, about three distinct questions. First, what are the characteristics of the present educational system, and why are they wrong? Second, what should the system be like, and why? Finally, how should we move from the ugly present to the shining future? Most of your authors have a perception and a criticism of the present, but many have no account of either the ideal or the implementing mechanisms; here is where your reading from Part I might prove useful, for there the emphasis was on the ends and means of education.

As you read Holt's account of how children fail, then, ask yourself what type of educational system he is describing and why he thinks it is wrong, then see if you can infer what ideal he would like, and how it can be achieved. If you find his account incomplete, you might try adding Rousseau's or Plato's or Martin's educational ideas to Holt's statement to determine whether there is a match at the particularly crucial joints—the places where testing, curriculum, teaching methods and the assumptions regarding what constitutes learning come together—and whether the completed structure can present an aesthetically and educationally unified whole, or just a grotesque monstrosity. Try this same procedure for each selection, reading for what the author both does and does not say, supplementing with relevant and appropriate theories from Part I to make the incomplete statements into coherent educational philosophies.

You should make these additions because revolutionaries, whether political, social or educational, are notoriously long on criticism and short on constructive ideas. That is because they are concerned with changing the present, not managing the future. But should the present be changed? Are the criticisms really justified, and are they of sufficient importance to warrant a fundamental change in our present institutions? Is this revolution really necessary? Undoubtedly you already have some visceral feelings on that question; you cannot live through the times of the Revolutionary Generation without drawing some conclusions. But as you read these selections, try to let your mind rather than your feelings do the reading. What does the writer say? How accurate and perceptive is his analysis? How cogent is his argument? What reasons does he offer to suggest his conclusions? Read these selections thoughtfully, for in the process you will soon discover whether you too are a revolutionary!

11   How Children Fail

John Holt

Many educators, including some very good teachers, have found Holt's book profoundly disturbing, for they have recognized in his descriptions elements in our present educational system which encourage students to drop out, mentally and physically, or to seek after trivial goals. But you need to read carefully to discover what kind of "failure" Holt is describing, and precisely how the system allows, nay, encourages *this failure. You might also keep a list of the many techniques he describes by which teachers encourage children to fail. The completed list might be useful to you for years to come.*

February 18, 1958

Intelligence is a mystery. We hear it said that most people never develop more than a very small part of their latent intellectual capacity. Probably not; but *why* not? Most of us have our engines running at about ten percent of their power. Why no more? And how do some people manage to keep revved up to twenty percent or thirty percent of their full power—or even more?

What turns the power off, or keeps it from ever being turned on?

During these past four years at the Colorado Rocky Mountain School my nose has been rubbed in the problem. When I started, I thought that some people were just born smarter than others and that not much could be done about it. This seems to be the official line of most of the psychologists. It isn't hard to believe, if all your contacts with students are in the classroom or the psychological testing room. But if you live at a small school, seeing students in class, in the dorms, in their private lives, at their recreations, sports, and manual work, you can't escape the conclusion that some people are much smarter part of the time than they are at other times. Why? Why should a boy or girl, who under some circumstances is witty, observant, imaginative, analytical, in a word, *intelligent,* come into the classroom and, as if by magic, turn into a complete dolt?

The worst student we had, the worst I have ever encountered, was in his life outside the classroom, as mature, intelligent, and interesting a student as anyone at the school. What went wrong? Experts muttered to his parents about brain damage—a handy way to end a mystery that you can't explain otherwise. Somewhere along the line, his intelligence became disconnected from his schooling. Where? Why?

This past year I had some terrible students. I failed more kids, mostly in French and Algebra, than did all the rest of the teachers in the school together. I did my best to get them through, goodness knows. Before every test we had a big cram session of practice work, politely known as "review." When they failed the exam, we had post-mortems, then more review, then a make-up test (always easier than the first), which they almost always failed again.

I thought I knew how to deal with the problem: make the work interesting and the classroom a lively and enthusiastic place. It was, too, some of the time at least; many of these failing students actually liked my classes. Overcome children's fear of saying what they don't understand, and keep explaining until they do understand. Keep a steady and resolute pressure on them. These things I did. Result? The good students stayed good, and some may have got better; but the bad students stayed bad, and some of them seemed to get worse. If they were failing in November they were still failing in June. There must be a better answer. Maybe we can prevent kids from becoming chronic failers in the first place.

February 24, 1958

Observing in Bill Hull's Class

In today's work period three or four people came up to you for help. All were stuck on that second math problem. None of them had made any effort to listen when you were explaining it at the board. I had been watching George, who had busied himself during the explanation by trying, with a pencil, to ream and countersink a hole in the side of his desk, all the while you were talking. He indignantly denied this. I showed him the hole, which silenced him. Gerald was in dreamland; so for the most part was Nancy, though she made a good recovery when asked a question. Unusual for her. Don listened about half the time, Laura about the same. Martha amused herself by turning her hand into an animal and having it crawl around her desk.

Watching older kids study, or try to study, I saw after a while that they were not sufficiently self-aware to know when their minds had wandered off the subject. When, by speaking his name, I called a daydreamer back to earth, he was always startled, not because he had thought I wouldn't notice that he had stopped studying, but because *he* hadn't noticed.

Except by inflicting real pain on myself, I am never able to stay awake when a certain kind of sleepiness comes over me. The mind plays funny tricks at such times. I remember my own school experience of falling asleep in class while listening to the teacher's voice. I used to find that the "watchman" part of my mind that was saying, "Keep awake, you fool!" would wake me when the teacher's voice began to fade. But the part of my mind that wanted or needed sleep was not so easily beaten. It used to (and still does) counterfeit a voice, so that as I fall asleep an imaginary voice continued to sound in my head, long enough to fool me until the watchman no longer had the power to awaken me. The watchman learned, in turn, that this counterfeit voice was liable to be talking about something different, or pure nonsense, and thus learned to recognize it as counterfeit. Many times, I have dozed off with a voice sounding inside my head, only to have the watchman say, "Hey! Wake up! That voice is a phoney!"

Most of us have very imperfect control over our attention. Our minds slip away from duty before we realize that they are gone. Part of being a good student is learning to be aware of the state of one's own mind and the degree of one's own understanding. The good student may be one who often says that he does not understand, simply because he keeps a constant check on his understanding. The poor student, who does not, so to speak, watch himself trying to understand, does not know most of the time whether he understands or not. Thus the problem is not to get students to ask us what they don't know; the problem is to make them aware of the difference between what they know and what they don't.

All this makes me think of Herb. I saw the other day why his words so often run off the paper. When he is copying a word, he copies about two letters at a time. I doubt whether he looks beyond them, or that he could tell you, in the middle of a word, what the whole word was. He has no idea, when he begins to copy a word, how long the word is going to be, or how much room it may take up.

May 10, 1958

Children are often quite frank about the strategies they use to get answers out of a teacher. I once observed a class in which the teacher was testing her students on parts of speech. On the blackboard she had three columns, headed Noun, Adjective, and Verb. As she gave each word, she called on a child and asked in which column the word belonged.

Like most teachers, she hadn't thought enough about what she was doing to realize, first, that many of the words given could fit into more than one column; and secondly, that it is often the way a word is used that determines what part of speech it is.

There was a good deal of the tried-and-true strategy of *guess-and-look,* in which you start to say a word, all the while scrutinizing the teacher's face to see whether you are on the right track or not. With most teachers, no further strategies are needed. This one was more poker-faced than most, so *guess-and-look* wasn't working very well. Still, the percentage of hits was remarkably high, especially since it was clear to me from the way the children were talking and acting that they hadn't a notion of what Nouns, Adjectives, and Verbs were. Finally one child said, "Miss —, you shouldn't point to the answer each time." The teacher was surprised, and asked what she meant. The child said, "Well, you don't exactly *point,* but you kind of stand next to the answer." This was no clearer, since the teacher had been standing still. But after a while, as the class went on, I thought I saw what the girl meant. Since the teacher wrote each word down in its proper column, she was, in a way, getting herself ready to write, pointing herself at the place where she would soon be writing. From the angle of her body to the blackboard the children picked up a subtle clue to the correct answer.

This was not all. At the end of every third word, her three columns came out even, that is, there were an equal number of nouns, adjectives, and verbs. This meant that when she started off a new row, you had one chance in three of getting the right answer by a blind guess; but for the next word, you had one chance in two, and the last word was a dead giveaway to the lucky student who was asked it. Hardly any missed this opportunity; in fact, they answered so quickly that the teacher (brighter than most) caught on to their system and began keeping her columns uneven, making the strategist's job a bit harder.

In the midst of all this, there came a vivid example of the kind of thing we say in school that makes no sense, that only bewilders and confuses the thoughtful child who tries to make sense out of it. The teacher, whose specialty, by the way, was English, had told these children that a verb is a word of action—which is not always true. One of the words she asked was "dream." She was thinking of the noun, and apparently did not remember that "dream" can as easily be a verb. One little boy, making a pure guess, said it was a verb. Here the teacher, to be helpful, contributed one of those "explanations" that are so much more hindrance than help. She said, "But a verb has to have action; can you give me a sentence, using 'dream,' that has action?" The child thought a bit, and said, "I had a dream about the Trojan War." Now it's pretty hard to get much more action than that. But the teacher told him he was wrong, and he sat silent, with an utterly baffled and frightened expression on his face. She was so busy thinking about what she wanted him to say, she was so obsessed with that *right answer* hidden in her mind, that she could not think about what he was really saying and thinking, could not see that his reasoning was logical and correct, and that the mistake was not his, but hers.

At one of our leading prep schools I saw, the other day, an example of the way in which a teacher may not know what is going on in his own class.

This was a math class. The teacher, an experienced man, was doing the day's assignment on the blackboard. His way of keeping attention was to ask various members of the class, as he did each step, "Is that right?" It was a dull class, and I found it hard to keep my mind on it. It seemed to me that most students in the class had their minds elsewhere, with a mental sentry posted to alert them when their names were called. As each name was called, the boy who was asked if something or other was right answered "Yes." The class droned on. In time my mind slipped away altogether, I don't know for how long. Suddenly something snapped me to attention. I looked at the teacher. Every boy in the class was looking at him, too. The boy who had been asked if what had just been written was right, was carefully looking at the blackboard. After a moment he said, "No, sir, that isn't right, it ought to be so-and-so." The teacher chuckled appreciatively and said, "You're right, it should be." He made the change, and the class and I settled back into our private thoughts for the rest of the period.

After the boys had left, I thanked the teacher for letting me visit. He said, "You notice I threw them a little curve ball there. I do that every now and then. Keeps them on their toes." I said something in agreement. It didn't seem the time or place to tell him that when he threw his little curve ball the expression in his voice changed enough so that it warned, not only the boys, but also a complete stranger, that something was coming up and that attention had better be paid.

July 25, 1958

Observing in Bill Hull's Class:

Of all I saw and learned this past half-year, one thing stands out. What goes on in class is not what teachers think—certainly not what I had always thought. For years now I have worked with a picture in mind of what my class was like. This reality, which I felt I knew, was partly physical, partly mental or spiritual. In other words, I thought I knew, in general, what the students were doing, and also what they were thinking and feeling. I see now that my picture of reality was almost wholly false. Why didn't I see this before?

Sitting at the side of the room, watching these kids, not so much to check up on them as to find out what they were like and how they differed from the teen-agers I have worked with and know, I slowly became aware of something. You can't find out what a child does in class by looking at him only when he is called on. You have to watch him for long stretches of time without his knowing it.

During many of the recitation classes, when the class supposedly is working as a unit, most of the children paid very little attention to what was going on. Those who most needed to pay attention, usually paid the least. The kids who knew the answer to whatever question you were asking wanted to make sure that you knew they knew, so their hands were always waving. Also, knowing the right answer, they were in a position to enjoy to the full the ridiculous answers that might be given by their less fortunate colleagues. But, as in all classes, these able students are a minority. What of the unsuccessful majority? Their attention depended on what was going on in class. Any raising of the emotional temperature made them prick up their ears. If an argument was going on, or someone was in trouble, or someone was being laughed at for a foolish answer, they took notice. Or, if you were explaining to a slow student something so simple that all the rest knew it, they would wave their arms and give agonized, half-suppressed cries of "O-o-o-o-oh! O-o-o-o-oh!" But most of the time, when explaining, questioning, or discussing was going on, the majority of children paid little attention or none at all. Some daydreamed, and no amount of calling them back to earth with a crash, much as it amused everyone else, could break them of the habit. Others wrote and passed notes, or whispered, or held conversations in sign language, or made doodles or pictures on their papers or desks, or fiddled with objects.

There doesn't seem to be much a teacher can do about this, if he is really teaching and not just keeping everyone quiet and busy. A teacher in class is like a man in the woods at night with a powerful flashlight in his hand. Wherever he turns his light, the creatures on whom it shines are aware of it, and do not behave as they do in the dark. Thus the mere fact of his watching their behavior changes it into something very different. Shine where he will, he can never know very much of the night life of the woods.

So, in class, the teacher can turn the spotlight of his attention, now on this child, now on that, now on them all; but the children know when his attention is on them, and do not act at all as they do when it is elsewhere. A teacher who is really thinking about what a particular child is doing or asking, or about what he, himself, is trying to explain, will not be able to know what all the rest of the class is doing. And if he does notice that other children are doing what they should not, and tells them to stop, they know they have only to wait until he gets back, as he must, to his real job. Classroom observers don't seem to see much of this. Why not? Some of them do not stay with a class long enough for the children to begin to act naturally in their presence. But even those who are with a class for a long time make the mistake of watching the teacher too much and the children too little. Student teachers in training spend long periods of time in one classroom, but they think

they are in there to learn *How To Teach,* to pick up the tricks of child management from watching a *Master At Work.* Their concern is with manipulating and
controlling children rather than understanding them. So they watch the teacher, see
only what the teacher sees, and thus lose most of what could be a valuable experience.

There should be more situations in which two experienced teachers share the
same class, teaching and observing the same group of kids, thinking, and talking to
each other, about what they see and hear. Schools can't afford to support this; they
can barely pay the one teacher in each class. I should think foundations might be
willing to support this kind of work. They seem ready at the drop of a hat to spend
millions of dollars on grandiose projects which produce, in the main, only publicity
and doctoral dissertations. Perhaps they feel that to have two teachers learn a great
deal more about children than they knew before is not worth spending money on.
If so, I think they're wrong. When I think what this year's experience has revealed
about children's work, behavior, and thought, what avenues of exploration and
speculation it has opened up, I can only wonder what extraordinary discoveries
about learning might be made if other teachers in other places could work in this
way.

July 27, 1958

It has become clear over the year that these children see school almost entirely
in terms of the day-to-day and hour-to-hour tasks that we impose on them. This is not
at all the way the teacher thinks of it. The conscientious teacher thinks of himself
as taking his students (at least part way) on a journey to some glorious destination,
well worth the pains of the trip. If he teaches history, he thinks how interesting, how
exciting, how useful it is to know history, and how fortunate his students will be
when they begin to share his knowledge. If he teaches French, he thinks of the
glories of French literature, or the beauty of spoken French, or the delights of
French cooking, and how he is helping to make these joys available to his students.
And so for all subjects.

Thus teachers feel, as I once did, that their interests and their students' are fundamentally the same. I used to feel that I was guiding and helping my students on a
journey that they wanted to take but could not take without my help. I knew the
way looked hard, but I assumed they could see the goal almost as clearly as I and
that they were almost as eager to reach it. It seemed very important to give students
this feeling of being on a journey to a worthwhile destination. I see now that most
of my talk to this end was wasted breath. Maybe *I* thought the students were in
my class because they were eager to learn what I was trying to teach, but they knew
better. They were in school because they had to be, and in my class either because
they had to be, or because otherwise they would have had to be in another class,
which might be even worse.

Children in school are like children at the doctor's. He can talk himself blue in
the face about how much good his medicine is going to do them; all they think of
is how much it will hurt or how bad it will taste. Given their own way, they would
have none of it.

So the valiant and resolute band of travelers I thought I was leading toward a much-hoped-for destination turned out instead to be more like convicts in a chain gang, forced under threat of punishment to move along a rough path leading nobody knew where and down which they could see hardly more than a few steps ahead. School feels like this to children: it is a place where *they* make you go and where *they* tell you to do things and where *they* try to make your life unpleasant if you don't do them or don't do them right.

For children, the central business of school is not learning, whatever this vague word means; it is getting these daily tasks done, or at least out of the way, with a minimum of effort and unpleasantness. Each task is an end in itself. The children don't care how they dispose of it. If they can get it out of the way by doing it, they will do it; if experience has taught them that this does not work very well, they will turn to other means, illegitimate means, that wholly defeat whatever purpose the task-giver may have had in mind.

They are very good at this, at getting other people to do their tasks for them. I remember the day not long ago when Ruth opened my eyes. We had been doing math, and I was pleased with myself because, instead of telling her answers and showing her how to do problems, I was "making her think" by asking her questions. It was slow work. Question after question met only silence. She said nothing, did nothing, just sat and looked at me through those glasses, and waited. Each time, I had to think of a question easier and more pointed than the last, until I finally found one so easy that she would feel safe in answering it. So we inched our way along until suddenly, looking at her as I waited for an answer to a question, I saw with a start that she was not at all puzzled by what I had asked her. In fact, she was not even thinking about it. She was coolly appraising me, weighing my patience, waiting for that next, sure-to-be-easier question. I thought, "I've been had!" The girl had learned how to make me do her work for her, just as she had learned to make all her previous teachers do the same thing. If I wouldn't tell her the answers, very well, she would just let me question her right up to them.

Schools and teachers seem generally to be as blind to children's strategies as I was. Otherwise, they would teach their courses and assign their tasks so that students who really thought about the meaning of the subject would have the best chance of succeeding, while those who tried to do the tasks by illegitimate means, without thinking or understanding, would be foiled. But the reverse seems to be the case. Schools give every encouragement to *producers*, the kids whose idea is to get "right answers" by any and all means. In a system that runs on "right answers," they can hardly help it. And these schools are often very discouraging places for *thinkers*.

Until recently it had not occurred to me that poor students thought differently about their work than good students; I assumed they thought the same way, only less skillfully. Now it begins to look as if the expectation and fear of failure, if strong enough, may lead children to act and think in a special way, to adopt strategies different from those of more confident children. Emily is a good example. She is emotionally as well as intellectually incapable of checking her work, of comparing her ideas against reality, of making any kind of judgment about the value of her thoughts. She makes me think of an animal fleeing danger—go like the wind, don't look back, remember where that danger was, and stay away from it as far as you can. Are there many other children who react to their fears in this way?

March 27, 1958

We agree that all children need to succeed; but do we mean the same thing? My own feeling is that success should not be quick or easy, and should not come all the time. Success implies overcoming an obstacle, including, perhaps, the thought in our minds that we might not succeed. It is turning, "I can't" into "I can, and I did."

We ought also to learn, beginning early, that we don't always succeed. A good batting average in baseball is .300; a good batting average in life is a great deal lower than that. Life holds many more defeats than victories for all of us. Shouldn't we get used to this early? We should learn, too, to aim higher than we think we can hit. "A man's reach should exceed his grasp, or what's a Heaven for?" What we fail to do today, we, or someone, may do tomorrow. Our failure may pave the way for someone else's success.

Of course we should protect a child, if we can, from a diet of unbroken failure. More to the point, perhaps, we should see that failure is honorable and constructive, rather than humiliating. Perhaps we need a semantic distinction here, between nonsuccess and failure.

It is tempting to think that we can arrange the work of unsuccessful students so that they think they are succeeding most of the time. But how can we keep secret from a child what other children of his own age, in his own or other schools, are doing? What some of these kids need is the experience of doing something really well—so well that they know themselves, without having to be told, that they have done it well. Maybe this means that someone must supply them, from outside, with the concentration and resolution they lack.

December 3, 1958

The other day I decided to talk to the other section about what happens when you don't understand what is going on. We had been chatting about something or other, and everyone seemed in a relaxed frame of mind, so I said, "You know, there's something I'm curious about, and I wonder if you'd tell me." They said, "What?" I said, "What do you think, what goes through your mind, when the teacher asks you a question and you don't know the answer?"

It was a bombshell. Instantly a paralyzed silence fell on the room. Everyone stared at me with what I have learned to recognize as a tense expression. For a long time there wasn't a sound. Finally Ben, who is bolder than most, broke the tension, and also answered my question, by saying in a loud voice, "Gulp!"

He spoke for everyone. They all began to clamor, and all said the same thing, that when the teacher asked them a question and they didn't know the answer they were scared half to death. I was flabbergasted—to find this in a school which people think of as progressive; which does its best not to put pressure on little children; which does not give marks in the lower grades; which tries to keep children from feeling that they're in some kind of race.

I asked them why they felt gulpish. They said they were afraid of failing, afraid of being kept back, afraid of being called stupid, afraid of feeling themselves stupid.

Stupid. Why is it such a deadly insult to these children, almost the worst thing they can think of to call each other? Where do they learn this?

Even in the kindest and gentlest of schools, children are afraid, many of them a great deal of the time, some of them almost all the time. This is a hard fact of life to deal with. What can we do about it?

June 16, 1959

A year ago I was wondering how a child's fears might influence his strategies. This year's work has told me. The strategies of most of these kids have been consistently self-centered, self-protective, aimed above all else at avoiding trouble, embarrassment, punishment, disapproval, or loss of status. This is particularly true of the ones who have had a tough time in school. When they get a problem, I can read their thoughts on their faces, I can almost hear them, "Am I going to get this right? Probably not; what'll happen to me when I get it wrong? Will the teacher get mad? Will the other kids laugh at me? Will my mother and father hear about it? Will they keep me back this year? Why am I so dumb?" And so on.

Even in the room periods, where I did all I could to make the work non-threatening, I was continually amazed and appalled to see the children hedging their bets, covering their losses in advance, trying to fix things so that whatever happened they could feel they had been right, or if wrong, no more wrong than anyone else. "I think it will sort of balance." They are fence-straddlers, afraid ever to commit themselves—and at the age of ten. Playing games like Twenty Questions, which one might have expected them to play for fun, many of them were concerned only to put up a good front, to look as if they knew what they were doing, whether they did or not.

These self-limiting and self-defeating strategies are dictated, above all else, by fear. For many years I have been asking myself why intelligent children act unintelligently at school. The simple answer is, "Because they're scared." I used to suspect that children's defeatism had something to do with their bad work in school, but I thought I could clear it away with hearty cries of "Onward! You can do it!" What I now see for the first time is the mechanism by which fear destroys intelligence, the way it affects a child's whole way of looking at, thinking about, and dealing with life. So we have two problems, not one: to stop children from being afraid, and then to break them of the bad thinking habits into which their fears have driven them.

What is most surprising of all is how much fear there is in school. Why is so little said about it? Perhaps most people do not recognize fear in children when they see it. They can read the grossest signs of fear; they know what the trouble is when a child clings howling to his mother; but the subtler signs of fear escape them. It is these signs, in children's faces, voices, and gestures, in their movements and ways of working, that tell me plainly that most children in school are scared most of the time, many of them very scared. Like good soldiers, they control their fears, live with them, and adjust themselves to them. But the trouble is, and here is a vital difference between school and war, that the adjustments children make to their fears are almost wholly bad, destructive of their intelligence and capacity. The scared fighter may be the best fighter, but the scared learner is always a poor learner.

March 21, 1961

Today Andy had a long, tough session with me. He finally solved the problem I had given him. But I can't help wondering what he learned. Not much; he certainly didn't gain any insight into the property of multiplication in which I was interested. All that he had to show for his time was the memory of a long and painful experience, full of failure, frustration, anxiety, and tension. He did not even feel satisfaction when he had done the problem correctly, only relief at not having to think about it any more.

He is not stupid. In spite of his nervousness and anxiety, he is curious about some things, bright, enthusiastic, perceptive, and in his writing highly imaginative. But he is, literally, scared out of his wits. He cannot learn math because his mind moves so slowly from one thought to another that the connections between them are lost. His memory does not hold what he learns, above all else because he won't trust it. Every day he must figure out, all over again, that $9 + 7 = 16$, because how can he be sure that it has not changed, or that he has not made another in an endless series of mistakes? How can you trust any of your own thoughts when so many of them have proved to be wrong?

I can see no kind of life for him unless he can break out of the circle of failure, discouragement, and fear in which he is trapped. But I can't see how he is going to break out. Worst of all, I'm not sure that we, his elders, really want him to break out. It is no accident that this boy is afraid. We have made him afraid, consciously, deliberately, so that we might more easily control his behavior and get him to do whatever we wanted him to do.

I am horrified to realize how much I myself use fear and anxiety as instruments of control. I think, or at least hope, that the kids in my class are somewhat more free of fear than they have been in previous classes, or than most children are in most classes. I try to use a minimum of controls and pressures. Still, the work must be done—mustn't it?—and there must be some limits to what they can be allowed to do in class, and the methods I use for getting the work done and controlling the behavior rest ultimately on fear, fear of getting in wrong with me, or the school, or their parents.

Here is Andy, whose fears make him almost incapable of most kinds of constructive thinking and working. On the one hand, I try to dissipate those fears. But on the other, I have to do something to get him to do the work he so hates doing. What I do boils down to a series of penalties, which are effective in exactly the proportion that they rouse the kind of fears that I have been trying to dispel. Also, when children feel a little relieved of the yoke of anxiety that they are so used to bearing, they behave just like other people freed from yokes, like prisoners released, like victors in a revolution, like small-town businessmen on American Legion conventions. They cut up; they get bold and sassy; they may for a while try to give a hard time to those adults who for so long have been giving them a hard time. So, to keep him in his place, to please the school and his parents, I have to make him fearful again. The freedom from fear that I try to give with one hand I almost instantly take away with the other.

What sense does this make?

June 15, 1959

Kids in school seem to use a fairly consistent strategy. Even the good students use it much of the time; the bad students use it all the time; and everyone uses it when they feel under pressure. One way of describing this strategy is to say that it is answer-centered rather than problem-centered. The difference can best be seen by comparing the way in which the two kinds of people deal with a problem.

The problem-centered person sees a problem as a statement about a situation, from which something has been left out. In other words, there is in this situation a relationship or consequence that has not been stated and that must be found. He attacks the problem by thinking about the situation, by trying to create it whole in his mind. When he sees it whole, he knows which part has been left out, and the answer comes almost by itself. The answer to any problem, school problem, is in the problem, only momentarily hidden from view. Finding it is like finding a missing piece in a jigsaw puzzle. If you look at the empty space in the puzzle, you know the shape of the piece that must fill it.

But most children in school are answer-centered rather than problem-centered. They see a problem as a kind of announcement that, far off in some mysterious Answerland, there is an answer, which they are supposed to go out and find. Some children begin right away to try to pry this answer out of the mind of the teacher. Little children are good at this. They know, especially if they are cute-looking, that if they look baffled or frightened enough, teacher will usually tell them what they need to know. This is called "helping them." Bolder children are ready to sally forth into Answerland in a kind of treasure hunt for the answer. For them, the problem is an answer-getting recipe, a set of hints or clues telling them what to do, like instructions for finding buried pirate treasure—go to the big oak, walk a hundred paces in line with the top of the church steeple, etc. These *producers* think, "Let's see, what did I do last time I had a problem like this?" If they remember their recipes, and don't mix them up, they may be good at the answer-hunting game, and the answers they bring home may often be right ones.

Take the problem, "Anne is three years older than Mary, and their ages add up to 21. How old is each?" The problem-centered person tries to make these girls real in his mind. Are they grown up? No; their ages will add up to too much. They have to be about 10. All but a few of the possible Annes and Marys disappear, and the correct pair looms up larger and larger, until there they are, aged 9 and 12.

The problem-centered person may use a formula. He might see very quickly that Ann's and Mary's ages added up to twice Mary's age, plus three. He might even write down something like $A + M = 21$; $M + M + 3 = 21$; $2M = 18$; so $M = 9$ and $A = 12$. But the point is that he would get this formula, this problem-solving process, *out of the problem itself*, not out of his memory.

The answer-centered person, on the other hand, the skilled one, not the coaxer of teachers or the reader of teachers' minds, think, "Now let me see, how are we supposed to do this kind of problem? When did I have one like it? Oh yes, I remember, you write down something about their ages, let's see, let x equal Mary's age, then we have to let Ann's age be something, I guess $x + 3$, then what do we do, add them together, maybe, yes, that's right, $x + x + 3 = 21$, then we have to transpose the 3, how do we do that, subtract from both sides . . ." and so on until he gets an answer which he takes to the teacher and says, "Is this right?" But this answer was *elsewhere,* not in the problem, and the answer-getting process had to be dredged up out of blind memory.

Practically everything we do in school tends to make children answer-centered. In the first place, right answers pay off. Schools are a kind of temple of worship for "right answers," and the way to get ahead is to lay plenty of them on the altar. In the second place, the chances are good that teachers themselves are answer-centered, certainly in mathematics, but by no means only there. What they do, they do because this is what they were or are told to do, or what the book says to do, or what they have always done. In the third place, even those teachers who are not themselves answer-centered will probably not see, as for many years I did not, the distinction between problem-centeredness and answer-centeredness, far less understand its importance. Thus their ways of teaching children, and, above all, the sheer volume of work they give them, will force the children into answer-directed strategies, if only because there isn't time for anything else. I have noticed many times that when the workload of the class is light, kids are willing to do some thinking, to take time to figure things out; when the workload is heavy, the "I-don't-get-it" begins to sound, the thinking stops, they expect us to show them everything. Thus one ironical consequence of the drive for so-called higher standards in schools is that the children are too busy to think.

The other day I was working with a sixteen-year-old boy who was having trouble with first-year physics. I asked him to do one of the problems in his book. Immediately he began to write on his paper, "Given": then, under it, "To Find": and under that, "Use." He began to fill in these spaces with a hash of letters and figures. I said, "Whoa, hold on, you don't even know what the problem is about, at least think about it before you start writing down a mess of stuff." He said, "But our teacher tells us we have to do all our problems this way." So there we are. No doubt this teacher would say that he wants his students to think about problems, and that he prescribed this form so that they would think. But what he has not seen, and probably never will see, is that his means to the end of clearer thinking has become an end in itself, just part of the ritual mumbo-jumbo you have to go through on your answer-hunt.

When kids are in a situation where they are not under pressure to come up with a right answer, far less do it quickly, they can do amazing things. Last fall, about November, I gave the afternoon section some problems. I said, "You have never seen problems like these, you don't know how to do them, and I don't care whether you get them right or not. I just want to see how you go about trying to do them." The problems were basically simple algebra problems, like the one about Anne and Mary, or a certain number of nickels and dimes adding up to 85 cents—the kind of problem that many first-year algebra students find so difficult. These fifth graders tore into them with imagination, resourcefulness, and common sense—in a word, intelligently. They solved them in many ways, including some I hadn't thought of. But it was about that time that the school began to worry about my going too slowly. Soon I was told to speed up the pace, which I am ashamed to say I did, and the children lapsed right back into their old strategies. Probably for keeps.

June 20, 1960

How can we tell whether children understand something or not? When I was a student, I generally knew when I understood and when I didn't. This had nothing to do with marks; in the last math course I took in college I got a respectable grade, but by the end of the year I realized I didn't have the faintest idea of what the course was about. In Colorado, I assumed for a long time that my students knew when they did, or did not, understand something. I was always urging them to tell me when they did not understand, so that with one of my clever "explanations" I could clear up everything. But they never would tell me. I came to know by painful experience that not a child in a hundred knows whether or not he understands something, much less, if he does not, why he does not. The child who knows, we don't have to worry about; he will be an A student. How do we find out when, and what, the others don't understand?

What first comes to mind is some external test. But what kind? By now I have many times seen children crank out right answers to problems without the faintest idea of what they were doing. They are blind recipe-followers. Some can even parrot back my explanations, but again without knowing what they mean. On the other hand, there are many children who are so paralyzed by their fear of tests that they can't show what they do know, while others who understand clearly what they are doing get confused and scared when they try to put it into words.

Part of the answer to the problem may be to give children the kind of tests I used this year, in which there was a mixture of problems. These tend to throw the automatic answer-finding machinery out of gear and to make them do some thinking about what they are doing. It may help, too, to give problems in a form new to them. But what do we do when the result of such tests is to show that hardly any of our pupils understand anything of what we have been trying to teach them during the year?

It may help to have in our minds a picture of what we mean by understanding. I feel I understand something if and when I can do some, at least, of the following: (1) state it in my own words; (2) give examples of it; (3) recognize it in various guises and circumstances; (4) see connections between it and other facts or ideas; (5) make use of it in various ways; (6) foresee some of its consequences; (7) state its opposite or converse. This list is only a beginning; but it may help us in the future to find out what our students really know as opposed to what they can give the appearance of knowing, their *real learning* as opposed to their *apparent learning*.

There are many, of course, who say that this distinction does not exist. It's their handy way of solving the knotty problem of understanding; just say there is no such thing. Apparently this view is currently in fashion among psychologists. According to many of them, if you can say that $7 \times 8 = 56$, you know all there is to know about that particular fact, and you know as much about it as anyone else who can say it.

The mathematician, the third grader, and, presumably, a well-trained parrot, would all have an equal and identical understanding of this fact. The only difference between the mathematician and the child is that the mathematician carries around in his head many more such facts. So to make children into mathematicians all we have to do is train them, condition them, until they can say many such facts. Teach them to say everything that Einstein knew, and hey, presto! another Einstein!

It's amazing what nonsense people will believe.

Of course, this notion fits neatly into behaviorism, which is also still very much in fashion, despite all it cannot explain. It is also comforting to teachers, who have felt all along that their job is to drop, or push, one at a time, little bits of information into those largely empty minds that are moving slowly before them down the academic assembly line. And finally, it has set into motion the apparently endless gravy train of programed instruction and machine teaching, onto which everyone and his brother seem to be happily clambering.

But pieces of information like $7 \times 8 = 56$ are not isolated facts. They are parts of the landscape, the territory of numbers, and that person knows them best who sees most clearly how they fit into the landscape and all the other parts of it. The mathematician knows, among many other things, that $7 \times 8 = 56$ is an illustration of the fact that products of even integers are even; that 7×8 is the same as 14×4 or 28×2 or 56×1; that only these pairs of positive integers will give 56 as a product; that 7×8 is $(8 \times 8) - 8$, or $(7 \times 7) + 7$, or $(15 \times 4) - 4$; and so on. He also knows that $7 \times 8 = 56$ is a way of expressing in symbols a relationship that may take many forms in the world of real objects; thus he knows that a rectangle 8 units long and 7 units wide will have an area of 56 square units. But the child who has learned to say like a parrot, "Seven times eight is fifty-six" knows nothing of its relation either to the real world or to the world of numbers. He has nothing but blind memory to help him. When memory fails, he is perfectly capable of saying that $7 \times 8 = 23$, or that 7×8 is smaller than 7×5, or larger than 7×10. Even when he knows 7×8, he may not know 8×7, he may say it is something quite different. And when he remembers 7×8, he cannot use it. Given a rectangle of 7 cm. $\times$ 8 cm., and asked how many 1 sq. cm. pieces he would need to cover it, he will over and over again cover the rectangle with square pieces and laboriously count them up, never seeing any connection between his answer and the multiplication tables he has memorized.

Knowledge, learning, understanding, are not linear. They are not little bits of facts lined up in rows or piled up one on top of another. A field of knowledge, whether it be math, English, history, science, music, or whatever, is a territory, and knowing it is not just a matter of knowing all the items in the territory, but of knowing how they relate to, compare with, and fit in with each other. It is the difference between being able to say that a room in your house has so many tables, so many chairs, so many lamps, and being able to close your eyes and see that this chair goes here and that table there. It is the difference between knowing the names of all the streets in a city and being able to get from any place, by any desired route, to any other place.

Why do we talk and write about the world and our knowledge of it as if they were linear? Because that is the nature of talk. Words come out in single file, one at a time; there's no other way to talk or write. So, in order to talk about it, we cut the real, undivided world into little pieces, and make these into strings of talk, like beads on a necklace. But we must not be fooled; these strings of talk are not what the world is like. Our learning is not real, not complete, not accurate, above all not useful, unless we take these word strings and somehow convert them in our minds into a likeness of the world, a working mental model of the universe as we know it. Only when we have made such a model, and when there is at least a rough correspondence between that model and reality, can it be said of us that we have learned something.

What happens in school is that children take in these word strings and store them, undigested, in their minds, so that they can spit them back out on demand. But these words do not change anything, fit with anything, relate to anything. They are as empty of meaning as parrot-speech is to a parrot. How can we make school a place where real learning goes on, and not just word swallowing?

February 27, 1958

A few days ago Nell came up to the desk, and looking at me steadily and without speaking, as usual, put on the desk her ink copy of the latest composition. Our rule is that on the ink copy there must be no more than three mistakes per page, or the page must be copied again. I checked her paper, and on the first page found five mistakes. I showed them to her, and told her, as gently as I could, that she had to copy it again, and urged her to be more careful—typical teacher's advice. She looked at me, heaved a sigh, and went back to her desk. She is left-handed, and doesn't manage a pen very well. I could see her frowning with concentration as she worked and struggled. Back she came after a while with the second copy. This time the first page had seven mistakes, and the hand-writing was noticeably worse. I told her to copy it again. Another bigger sigh, and she went back to her desk. In time the third copy arrived, looking much worse than the second, and with even more mistakes.

At that point Bill Hull asked me a question, one I should have asked myself, one we ought all to keep asking ourselves: "Where are you trying to get, and are you getting there?"

The question sticks like a burr. In schools—but where isn't it so?—we so easily fall into the same trap: the means to an end becomes an end in itself. I had on my hands this three-mistake rule meant to serve the ends of careful work and neat compositions. By applying it rigidly was I getting more careful work and neater compositions? No; I was getting a child who was so worried about having to recopy her paper that she could not concentrate on doing it, and hence did it worse and worse, and would probably do the next papers badly as well.

We need to ask more often of everything we do in school, "Where are we trying to get, and is this thing we are doing helping us to get there?" Do we do something because we want to help the children and can see that what we are doing is helping them? Or do we do it because it is inexpensive or convenient for school, teachers, administrators? Or because everyone else does it? We must beware of making a virtue of necessity, and cooking up high-sounding educational reasons for doing what is done really for reasons of administrative economy or convenience. The still greater danger is that, having started to do something for good enough reasons, we may go on doing it stubbornly and blindly, as I did that day, unable or unwilling to see that we are doing more harm than good. . . .

There must be a way to educate young children so that the great human qualities that we know are in them may be developed. But we'll never do it as long as we are obsessed with tests. At faculty meetings we talk about how to reward the *thinkers* in our classes. Who is kidding whom? No amount of rewards and satisfactions obtained in the small group thinking sessions will make up to Monica for what she felt today, faced by a final test that she knew she couldn't do and was going to fail. Pleasant experiences don't make up for painful ones. No child, once painfully burned, would agree to be burned again, however enticing the reward. For all our talk and good intentions, there is much more stick than carrot in school, and while this remains so, children are going to adopt a strategy aimed above all else at staying out of trouble. How can we foster a joyous, alert, whole-hearted participation in life, if we build all our schooling around the holiness of getting "right answers"?

March 8, 1960

The other day a lady said for me, better than I ever could have said it for myself, just what is wrong with the whole school setup. During this past vacation I visited a school that was still in session. It has the reputation of being very "good" and "tough." The headmistress, who was very nice, asked me where I had taught. When I told her, she said with false humility, "I'm afraid you'll find us very old-fashioned." But she made me welcome, and particularly urged me to visit the arithmetic class of her fourth-grade teacher, who had been there for many years and was generally felt to be a jewel among teachers and the pride of the school. I went. Soon after I arrived the class began. The children had done some multiplication problems and, in turn, were reading answers from their marked papers. All went smoothly until, right after a child had read his answer, another child raised his hand. "What is it, Jimmy?" the teacher asked, with just the faintest hint in her voice that this interruption could not be really necessary. "Well, I didn't get that answer," said Jimmy, "I got . . ." but before he could say more, the teacher said, "Now, Jimmy, I'm sure we don't want to hear any *wrong* answers." And that was the last word out of Jimmy.

This woman is far ahead of most teachers in intelligence, education, and experience. She is articulate, cultivated, has had a good schooling, and is married to a college professor. And in the twenty years or more that she has been teaching it has apparently never occurred to her that it might be worth taking a moment now and then to hear these unsuccessful Jimmies talk about their wrong answers, on the chance that from their talk she might learn something about their thinking and what was making the answers come out wrong. What makes everyone call her such a good teacher? I suppose it is the ability to manage children effortlessly, which she does. And for all I know, even the Jimmies may think she is a good teacher; it would never occur to them that it was this nice lady's fault that they couldn't understand arithmetic; no, it must be their own fault, for being so stupid.

Questions for Discussion

1. Did you make that list of surefire techniques for causing failure in your students? Look at your own educational experience to determine which, if any, of them are being used on you by your present teachers? Are they aware they are using these techniques?
2. This selection is critical. Could you develop a list of constructive comments which will help children to succeed? You can check the adequacy of your list by now looking at Holt's recent book, *How Children Learn*.
3. Is there a theory of educational ends and means presupposed by Holt's comments? Is it like the theory expressed by any of the writers in the first section of this book? Be specific.

12   Education and the Cult of Efficiency

Raymond Callahan

As a teacher you will be most aware of your classroom and your students, at least initially. But you also will learn that there is another factor which influences your teaching: the administration. Reports, formulas, papers, meetings, memos, and reminders will occupy your desk and your attention. Why is this so—and does administrative detail enhance the educational enterprise?

This selection traces a bit of educational history, that period in the first two decades of this century when business methods were applied to the schools' operations. Callahan describes the rationale which motivated that development and some of the implications which followed for cost accounting, class size and faculty load. He concludes that in the age of efficiency "the education of children is bound to suffer." Do you know enough about how schools operate to be able to determine whether his conclusion is accurate?

In the total story of the response by the educators to society's criticism and pressure in the first two decades of the twentieth century, perhaps the most important and, in consequences, the most far-reaching aspect was the change that occurred in the nature of the superintendency. Because of the nature of their position in the schools and of their vulnerability to public opinion and pressure, it was the superintendents who interpreted and applied scientific management, as well as other business methods, to education. One result was that by 1925 the position had more of the characteristics of a managerial job in business or industry than it did of an educational one in the schools. This was reflected both in the superintendents' work and in the nature of the work in administration being offered in the universities.

The transition of the superintendent of schools from an educator to a business manager, although most rapid between 1911 and 1918, was already going on at the turn of the century. At that time many educational administrators were quite conservative and tended to identify themselves with business leaders. The strengthening of these tendencies paralleled the year-by-year ascendency of the businessmen to a position of dominance in American society. Temporarily deterred by the criticism of the muckrakers, the business groups recovered their prestige after 1909 and, assisted by the sensational debut of the efficiency expert and the subsequent miracles expected through the application of efficiency principles, and by the equally impressive achievements of the Ford Motor Company, they moved steadily to the peak of their power and influence in the twenties. Interestingly, although these great successes were in the main based upon advances in technology, in the educational litera-

From *Education and the Cult of Efficiency* by Raymond Callahan (Chicago: University of Chicago Press, 1962). Reprinted by permission of The University of Chicago Press and the author.

ture at least, credit was generally given to businessmen and to "modern business methods."

Another factor which contributed to the tendency of administrators to think in business terms was the sheer size and magnitude of the school systems, especially in the large cities, which made the organizational and administrative aspects of the educational work seem—on a superficial basis, at least—comparable to those aspects of large industry which, it was claimed, were being handled so efficiently by businessmen. In these huge systems there was no question but that the administrative detail work was considerable. It was also certain that the financial aspects of the superintendents' job, involving as it did large sums of money, required that careful attention be given to expenditures.

In addition to the increasing difficulty and complexity of the administration of the large school systems, administrators had to contend with the interference of school boards in the administrative and often in the educational functions of the school. These had resulted in a general feeling of discontent and, frequently, in outspoken criticism by educators of the administration of the schools. Typical of such criticism was the statement by Andrew S. Draper, president of the University of Illinois, and later commissioner of education in New York: "It must be said that there has been much dissatisfaction with the way school affairs have been managed in the larger cities. . . . There have been many and serious complaints of the misuse of funds, of neglect of property, of the appointment of unfit teachers, and of general incapacity, or worse, on the part of the boards. . . . It would not be true to say that the business of the schools has suffered as seriously as municipal business, but it certainly has been managed badly enough." To correct this condition Draper recommended that the school board be reduced in size, be appointed rather than elected, and be removed from partisan or municipal politics, and that it limit itself to legislative, as opposed to executive, functions. He also advocated the separation of the administration into two independent departments, one to manage the business interests and the other to supervise instruction.

There is no question that at the turn of the century new and large problems existed in educational administration—problems that to some extent at least, were comparable to other problems of municipal government at that time. And during the Progressive era the solution to these problems paralleled the solution to other problems of city government, which . . . frequently entailed introducing business-like procedures and often businessmen themselves into government. Thus, as the years passed, the school boards were reduced in size and were increasingly dominated by businessmen. By 1917, Professor Scott Nearing found in a study of the composition of school boards in 104 large cities that, of the total of 967 board members, 433 were businessmen, 333 were professional men, 87 were workers, and many of the remainder were either retired businessmen or the wives of businessmen.

Many school administrators believed, and frequently asserted, that manufacturers, merchants, and bankers made the best school board members. This viewpoint was presented in an important book on educational administration in 1904 by William Estabrook Chancellor, superintendent of schools in Paterson, New Jersey. At the top of his list of those who were best qualified Chancellor placed manufacturers. "These men," he said, were "accustomed to dealing with large bodies of men and with important business interests." Second on his list were merchants, contractors, bankers, and "other men of large affairs." These men were qualified, he said, because "a board of education controls a business and deals with the business side of education." Among those whom Chancellor thought did *not* make good board members were inexperienced young men, unsuccessful men, politicians, newspaper men, men in subordinate business positions, and women.

The same view was expressed by Superintendent L. N. Hines, speaking before the National Education Association in 1911 on the subject "The Ideal School Board from the Superintendent's Point of View." Hines believed that board membership "should be confined to wide-awake, sane, progressive, business and professional men who have business ideas. . . ." And he stated that a superintendent who had such a board could "count himself fortunate above all things." On the other hand, he said there was no room for cranks or extremists, women were not fitted to deal with the problems, and "politicians of a low sort, saloon-keepers, and kindred spirits have no place on school boards."

These ideas were reinforced and spread throughout educational administration in 1916 by Ellwood P. Cubberley in his widely used textbook, *Public School Administration.* His words are interesting not only because they show a heavy borrowing from Chancellor and Hines, but also because they are not so much a statement of fact as they are a projection of things as Cubberley would have liked them to be. Concerning the individuals who made the best school board members he wrote:

> Men who are successful in the handling of large business undertakings—manufacturers, merchants, bankers, contractors, and professional men of large practice—would perhaps come first. Such men are accustomed to handling business rapidly; are usually wide awake, sane, and progressive; are not afraid to spend money intelligently; are in the habit of depending upon experts for advice, and for the execution of administrative details; and have the tact and perseverance necessary to get the most efficient service out of everybody from superintendent down.

Those who did not make good board members were: "Inexperienced young men, unsuccessful men, old men who have retired from business, politicians, saloon-keepers, uneducated or relatively ignorant men, men in minor business positions, and women. . . ."

The evidence indicates that these educators got what they wanted and school board positions were occupied largely by businessmen. As a result, administrators did achieve more job security, but they had to behave and operate the school in a businesslike way to do so.

In addition to the influence of businessmen on school boards, and to the continuous pressure for efficiency and economy from the popular journals, outside businessmen and educators themselves prodded administrators into conceiving of education as a business enterprise. Thus a school board member from Huron, Ohio, wrote in October, 1911, that "a board of education is only a board of directors; the taxpayers, the stockholders. The superintendent is a sales manager; the teachers salesmen." In 1915 a businessman speaking before the Department of Superintendence of the N.E.A. told his audience, "It is proper to say that the schools are like factories turning out graduates, which, in turn, became employees of the business houses and may be considered the raw material of business."

Although educational discussion and educational writing, particularly that pertaining to administration, was saturated by business and industrial terminology and analogies, indicating that many administrators used them, perhaps the individual who did the most to contribute to the conception of education as a business and of the school as a factory was Cubberley. This was not because he believed more deeply in this conception or carried it further than many others, but because his writing was so widely read in the profession. His *Public School Administration*, while showing that the author had a deep concern for and dedication to public education, is filled with business-industrial analogies. For example, at one point he wrote,

> Our schools are, in a sense, factories in which the raw products (children) are to be shaped and fashioned into products to meet the various demands of life. The specifications for manufacturing come from the demands of the twentieth-century civilization, and it is the business of the school to build its pupils to the specifications laid down. This demands good tools, specialized machinery, continuous measurement of production to see if it is according to specifications, the elimination of waste in manufacture, and a large variety in the output.

This same theme with similar language was repeated in his history of American education, a book which was originally published in 1919 and which sold some 100,000 copies by 1941....

Demonstrating Efficiency Through Records and Reports

Schoolmen had been criticized for not keeping adequate records and for not providing adequate reports as early as 1909 by Leonard Ayres in his study on retardation in the schools. In his book Ayres had told educators that large corporations regarded their records of the manufacturing process as their most valuable asset.

> If the directors of large corporations have found through experience that it pays to know what happened to a stove or a shoe in the process of manufacture, who worked on it, how long it took to complete it, and, if it is in any way deficient, at whose door the responsibility lies, is it not much more the duty of those in charge of training citizens to be able to find out what happened in the course of the education given, when the child entered, how long he spent in each grade, where he progressed slowly and where rapidly, and, if he left school before completing the course, when and why? ...

Administrators responded quickly to the demands for records and in May, 1912, Ayres reported that, whereas in 1909 the number of cities having systems of individual record cards for keeping the school histories of their children was only 29, by 1912 "a uniform system for this purpose" had been adopted by 216. "Those cities," said Ayres approvingly, "intend to judge processes by results." And they responded even more quickly in adopting more elaborate, detailed, and uniform accounting records. Ayres stated that between May, 1911 (when Taylor's last article appeared in the *American Magazine*), and May, 1912, the number of school systems using such

records increased from 15 to 418. Commenting on this tremendous increase, George
Strayer pointed out that it meant an "increased addition to the business aspect of
school administration."

Strayer also testified in 1913 that the increased attention to records and reports
as well as other aspects of educational cost accounting resulted from public pressure. He wrote:

> The development of adequate school records and significant school reports
> may be traced on the one hand to the growth of the profession of education,
> and on the other to the demand which the public is now making for complete
> information concerning public enterprises. . . .
>
> During the past five years there has been much discussion concerning the
> efficiency of those charged with the control of various city departments, budget
> exhibits and surveys. Our schools have come in for their share of these investi-
> gations. There has developed a demand for adequate records and reports, for
> the standardization of supplies and for definite units of cost for various educa-
> tion activities.

The reasons for the energetic demand for uniform accounting records are not hard
to find. With this system, as Ayres pointed out, school systems could be compared for
their relative cost efficiency. Obviously, leaders in the community and school board
members would want a system that would enable them to compare their schools with
those of other communities. As for the superintendents, they probably had no real
choice in the matter but undoubtedly welcomed the system, as they welcomed the
school survey, as a means of proving their operating efficiency, or, if they were found
to be relatively inefficient, as a means of knowing exactly what to do to make their
system compare favorably with the most efficient. With this arrangement, however,
each system had to be brought in line with the most efficient—efficient, that is, in
terms of costs. Thus if one school superintendent eliminated the teaching of Greek,
or increased the size of his classes, or increased the load of his teachers and reduced
expenditures thereby, other superintendents would be under pressure to do the
same. . . .

Educational Cost Accounting

A second major kind of activity engaged in by administrators and one which illustrated the extent of the infiltration of business values into education was the
application of cost analysis and accounting to the work of the schools. In these
efforts the objective was to determine the costs of instruction and to establish a
"standard" cost for the purpose of cutting costs and of demonstrating efficiency. For
the most part the cost accounting was directed toward the high schools because they
were more expensive, especially in the junior and senior years, than the elementary
schools.

That a detailed financial cost accounting of the instructional work of the public
schools would have been demanded by an economy-minded society seems natural
enough. What was surprising was the eager way some administrators embraced and
fostered the notion that educators were servants of the taxpayers and not only had to

acquiesce meekly but also had to attempt to meet enthusiastically the demands made upon them by the public. One such administrator was William McAndrew, principal of the Washington Irving High School in New York City. In November, 1911, Mc-Andrew wrote a statement on "Success in School" which was published in the *School Review*. Educators were told that the schools suffered from the lack of competition among teachers as well as from the reluctance of schoolmen to accept the business criteria. "We are accustomed," said McAndrew, "to regard ourselves as above business and incapable of measurement by dollars and cents, yet the past ten years have made it more clear that one of the best things that can happen to us is the realization that education is public business and that a dollar-and-cents measurement is inevitable. It is the duty of the principal to give to the city returns for this investment."

But the real leaders in educational cost accounting were the two men who had led the movement to apply scientific management to education—Frank E. Spaulding and Franklin Bobbitt. It will be recalled that Spaulding's application of Taylor's system resulted in a cost analysis. His contribution had been the introduction of the dollar as the criterion for judging the relative value of the various school subjects. Characteristically, he had abandoned the attempt to attain a social-philosophical judgment in favor of a concrete, practical, financial one. He didn't know, he said, whether music was more valuable than Greek, but Greek was more expensive and so from a financial standpoint it was less valuable. Bobbitt, concerned about developing standards and impressed with Spaulding's work, turned his talent to applying Spaulding's standard—the financial standard—to the work of the secondary schools. Spaulding's advice was followed, and a number of studies were made of the cost of instruction. One of these was a study of nineteen high schools in the Chicago area in 1913 and in 1914 by Robert Charles Harris, who was a student of Bobbitt's. An account of the work was published in the *School Review* (of which Bobbitt was an editor) in June, 1914. Harris collected his data by means of a questionnaire and used the "cost per year-minute" as the basic unit since, he said, it was a much "fairer unit than the cost per pupil, because it takes into account the time that is distributed to each pupil." His procedure was to determine the cost per pupil and divide this by the year-minutes of each teacher (a teacher with 5 weekly periods of 40 minutes each during the school year had 200 year-minutes) which gave him the cost per year-minute. His findings, which were presented in tables and charts, showed great differences in the cost of instruction among the high schools. After presenting his findings Harris made recommendations which would enable the schools with high year-minute costs to economize. For example, he indicated what changes he would make in one of the high schools which was paying "329 per cent above the average for Foreign Language." "Suppose the salary remains the same, $1,460. Let the teacher have five periods per day instead of 3.5. Let the size of the class be 25 instead of 12.8. Let the term be 40 weeks instead of 34. Then we shall have: salary, $1,460; number of pupils per teacher, 125; teaching time of teacher, 200 year-minutes. From these figures the cost-per-year-minutes is 5.84 cents as compared with 27.31 cents in the present case. The average for all the schools in Foreign Language is 6.37."

Harris had other recommendations for reorganizing the work of the schools. One of these was "in such subjects as History and Civics, English, Science, Manual Training, and Domestic Science, pupils of different years can be instructed in one class.

Here again the saving is above one-half." And he had a plan to standardize the cost regardless of the size of the class. Under his arrangement "a class of 10 pupils ought not to be entitled to more than 20 minutes of recitation, if the standard for the size of the class is 25 pupils and the length of the recitation period is 40 minutes. Another plan is to have such a small class recite every other day, covering double work for the one recitation. Either of these plans would reduce the cost per year-minute for that subject approximately one half." In addition Harris worked out an equation for "cost efficiency" which provided a standard formula for the amount of time and the number of pupils a teacher should instruct per day.

At about the same time that Harris' study was published, an article written by a leading educator appeared in the *American School Board Journal* supporting Spaulding's educational cost accounting. The educator was W. S. Deffenbaugh, chief of the Division of School Administration in the U.S. Bureau of Education. He stated that before administration could be efficient such problems as "what instruction to buy; how much and in what subjects; how many daily recitations a high school should conduct; and how many hours a high school pupil should carry" had to be solved. He pointed out that in a high school with 600 students, $3,000 a year could be saved by increasing the class size from 25 to 30 students because three fewer teachers would be needed, and he cited Spaulding's work at Newton in which $4,000 per year had been saved by reducing the recitations. Then he asked "what would be the educational loss if a high school teacher instructs six classes a day instead of five? What will be the financial gain?" Significantly, he did not discuss what the educational loss would be but he did point out the financial gain. Before educational administration could be efficient, he warned, "each superintendent must make a study of the problems I have just mentioned."

The following year, 1915, Bobbitt made his contribution to cost accounting by publishing the results of a study he had made of costs in twenty-five high schools in seven states. His purpose was to "present a *method* of finding standards of practice and comparing individual schools with such standards." He began his analysis with a lengthy statement in which he indicated how the problem was being handled effectively in industrial management:

> Accurate cost-accounting lies at the foundations of all successful business management. In railroad administration, for example, it is known that under normal conditions locomotive repair-cost should average about six cents per mile-run; lubricating oils should cost about eighteen cents per hundred miles for passenger locomotives, and about twenty-five cents for freight locomotives; and so on for each item involved in the entire management. With these cost-standards at hand, derived from wide general practice, if a railroad manager finds at the end of the year that locomotive repairs average fifteen cents per mile run, then it is quite evident upon the surface that something is wrong somewhere. . . .

The same procedure could be applied to education if "standard unit-costs" were developed for the various school expenditures. If, he argued, educators knew

> . . . that satisfactory instruction in high school English can be had for fifty dollars per thousand student-hours, and that this price represented the norm of practice, then those responsible for high-school management have a standard

of judgment that can be used for measuring the efficiency of their practices. If instruction in this subject is costing them $75 per 1,000 student-hours, and they are aiming at results of only the usual sort, it is evident that they are wasting money, and that administrative adjustments need to be made.

In his study the cost unit was the student hour (the instruction of one student for sixty minutes) and he determined the "cost per 1,000 student-hours" in mathematics, Latin, English, history, science, modern languages, commercial studies, household occupations, shop work, agriculture, music, and normal training. With each subject at each school he figured the cost per 1,000 student hours, and then the median cost among the twenty-five schools. Then he used the cost of the seventh most expensive school as one end of the scale and the cost of the seventh least expensive as the other to form what he called a "zone of safety."

He presented this explanation of his system, which indicated how his standard costs had been derived:

> Fifty-nine dollars paid in Rockford is the median price paid for algebra and geometry. There is no reason to think that the results obtained in Rockford are in any degree inferior to those obtained in the dozen cities paying a higher price. Fifty-nine dollars for mathematics represents the consensus of practice and is a *safe* standard of judgment for high schools.
>
> Such a standard of practice is too rigid for universal application. The diversity represented by the middle half of the cities is probably normal. The standard of practice should probably be so formulated as to permit the flexibility of practice found in this middle 50 per cent of the cities. We can say, therefore, that between $52 and $74 is a safe standard price for high-school mathematics. This is what we call the "zone of safety."

The same procedure was followed with regard to Latin instruction. He found that the cost ranged from $244 per 1,000 student hours in Maple Lake, Minnesota, to $46 in Greensburg, Indiana; his median was $71 in Dekalb, Illinois; while his zone of safety was from $92 to $54. This was 20 percent higher than the "price" for mathematics and this bothered him. The difference in price, he said, could not be "due to the greater value of the subject, to any diminished supply of the commodity, or to higher salaries paid to the teachers. It is simply due to administrative maladjustments in the teaching-hours per week." As a result he departed from his statistical procedure and gave his readers some insight into the thinking of the educational business manager, as well as a lesson in market place psychology:

> It is interesting to observe the highly extravagant price paid by certain villages that really can least afford such wastefulness. Maple Lake is probably getting no more results for each 1,000 student-hours than is Dekalb at one-third the cost or Rockford at one-fifth of the cost. Practical men, before buying wheat, or cotton, or railroad stocks, examine into market conditions and pay something in the neighborhood of current market prices. These figures appear to indicate that the same practical school-board members, when they are investing the people's money in a supposedly necessary community commodity, are, certain of them, paying prices very greatly in excess of current market prices as represented by the standards of practice in those cities that lie within the "zone of safety." It probably is sufficiently extravagant to pay even the price of $90 for

its Latin, when the median city is getting it done for $71. When the same city is getting its mathematics for $59 and its English for $51, it is more than probable that the upper limit of our middle zone in this case represents wasteful extravagance; and that it is the lower portion of the middle zone that more nearly represents safety.

In order to standardize the costs Bobbitt advocated increasing the size of classes which were below average and reducing those which were above average, and the same procedure was suggested with regard to the working hours of teachers and to teachers' salaries. When this had been done, the administrators would have a basis for judging (as the railroad manager had) whether his enterprise was being operated efficiently. And by using this system of cost accounting continuously he would have a means "of diagnosing the situation and locating irregularities of management." . . .

The Educational Balance Sheet and Child Accounting

It will be recalled that Ayres brought the problem of retardation and elimination to the attention of the country through his book *Laggards in Our Schools.* The report was significant because it accused educators of gross waste in handling public funds and this accusation was more effective because Ayres claimed his study to be (and it had the outward appearance of being) "scientific." In the years that followed, Ayres continued to investigate and to publish his findings on the problem under the impressive auspices of the Russell Sage Foundation. At the same time other educators joined in the work, contributing numerous articles and speeches that kept the problem before the profession and an efficiency-conscious public. Most often these men presented the problem in terms of economy and efficiency with the result that school systems were judged wasteful and inefficient on the basis of the number of children who dropped out before completing the eighth grade or were "retarded," without regard to the social or economic or educational factors responsible for the situation.

A few months after Ayres's book appeared, the superintendent of schools in Cleveland, William Elson, together with one of his assistants, wrote an article in which they repeated Ayres's demand for better records and reports, and his criteria for efficiency. Educators were told that the school system was "most efficient" which had "the smallest per cent of withdrawals." The following year, through an unfavorable comparison with industrial management, administrators were criticized by another educator for allowing drop-outs. They were told that the number of drop-outs was "a sheer loss of an astoundingly large per cent of the raw material during the process of production, any private manufacturing industry that should, because of operating methods lose or cast aside from its unfinished product one-tenth of what is lost through the maladministration of our school system would be forced into voluntary or involuntary bankruptcy in an incredibly short time—and it ought so to be."

In the spring of 1911 under the sponsorship of the Russell Sage Foundation, Ayres conducted another major study of retardation and elimination, involving 206,495 children in elementary schools. He received the co-operation of superintendents from twenty-nine cities. In January, 1912, when public demands for economy were growing stronger, an account of the study written by Ayres was published in the *American School Board Journal* with the significant title "The Money Cost of Repetition Versus the Money Saving through Acceleration." Ayres stated that many studies of retardation and elimination had been made in the "past few years," but he said these studies were open to criticism because, while they computed the cost to the school of the repeaters, they did not take account of the "children who make rapid progress and thus counterbalance part of this added expense." He presented his solution for the problem and indicated how the educational balance sheet would operate: "Now it is evident that if the number of years lost by slow children in a school system were equalled by the number of years gained by those making rapid progress, the money expenditure would be just the same as though every child were regularly promoted every year."

According to Ayres the results of the study showed that while there were a few cities where the years lost by slow pupils were "nearly counterbalanced by those gained by the rapid ones" most were out of balance and in some cities the number of years lost was "from twenty to thirty times as great as the number gained." This indicated, he said, that most school programs were adjusted to the bright child rather than the average pupil. A well-adjusted school system would be one in which the number of double promotions balanced the number of failures so that from a financial standpoint the books would be in balance. Ayres cited Danville, Illinois, as a school system that was poorly adjusted in this respect and he pointed out that this cost the citizens $20,660. For all the cities he found that the "maladjustment" involved "an increase in school expense amounting to about 11 per cent" and the "annual money cost to the taxpayers" was about $45,543.

Undoubtedly the quick and easy manner by which such an efficiency test could be applied, plus the substantial saving which it was possible to achieve made Ayres's system seem attractive enough to superintendents and school board members. As if these factors were not sufficient, the editor of the *American School Board Journal* threw his weight behind the plans by endorsing the reports and suggesting that they would be "well worth the study of every school board member." . . .

In May, 1913, another of his articles, this one on "The Effect of Promotion Rates on School Efficiency," was also published in the *American School Board Journal*. In this article he was able to report that the number of students promoted had increased from 84 out of 100 in 1908 to 88 out of 100 in 1913 in the elementary schools of sixteen large cities. And he added that there was "abundant evidence that a similar general increase in promotion rates is taking place throughout the country." His purpose was to encourage this progress, and he did it as he had done earlier, by using business or industrial analogies and by evaluating the results in terms of dollars and cents. Then he illustrated what he means by actually translating the results of increasing promotion rates into financial terms with the following statement—a statement, by the way, which was reprinted and endorsed by Bobbitt in an editorial in the *Elementary School Journal* in September.

> The importance of small changes in promotion rates may be best illustrated by figuring the results of a change of one per cent, for example from 80 per cent to 81 per cent, in the promotion rate in the elementary schools of a small city. Let us suppose that 1,000 children enter the elementary schools each year, the annual per capita cost for schooling is $40, and the buildings, ground, and equipment have a value of $200 per child.

Under these conditions, the change in the promotion rate from 80 per cent to 81 per cent will have the following results: The time saved by each 1,000 children if they complete the elementary course will amount to 130 years of schooling which means a saving of $5,200 annually. The plant required to accommodate the children will be decreased by about $25,600 worth, and the salaries of four teachers will be saved. The number of failures among the 1,000 children during eight years of school life will be reduced by 70, while the number of children failing during that period will be lessened by 19. The number of over-age children in the grades will be reduced by 220. These figures strikingly illustrate the importance of even the smallest changes in promotion rates.

With this economic motivation to promote students, plus the practice of rating the efficiency of teachers on the basis of promotions, it is clear that two potent forces were at work which contributed to the practice of passing students regardless of educational considerations.

In February, 1912, Superintendent Elson of Cleveland in a speech before the Department of Superintendence indicated that Ayres's ideas had been accepted and that his system was being applied in Cleveland. He stated that between one-tenth and one-eighth of all the money spent on public education was spent on repeaters, and he added that "when the school is tested for efficiency by its ability to carry children through its course on time it shows great waste." This condition was being corrected in Cleveland through the use of double promotions. With this arrangement, he said, "A school system thus becomes its own clearinghouse, is made to check itself, and certain bad effects of repetition and retardation are neutralized. In this way the money cost of the 'repeater' is offset by the acceleration of the stronger pupils." The result was that "the school system practically checked its own losses and created a balance sheet, the number of children who lost time being equalled by the number who gained time."

In the years that followed superintendents were engaged in applying the procedures worked out by Ayres and Elson. One superintendent from Johnstown, Pa. reported that in his school system more than nine hundred pupils had had double promotions in 1916–17 and that, as a result, $16,092 has been saved. Another, H. O. Dietrich of Kane, Pennsylvania, reported his activity in detail in an article called "The Schools' Responsibility towards Child Accounting," published in the *American School Board Journal* in October, 1917. Dietrich began by informing his readers that "any corporation that does not at times make a survey of its business, the efficiency of its men, the methods of administration, etc., will soon be running at a loss, and this is just as true of our school systems as of corporations." Then he reported on the balance sheet in Kane, which he presented in terms of years instead of dollars, as follows:

Total normal years of schooling	4982
Years lost by slow pupils	604
	5586
Years gained by rapid pupils	−239
Years actually required by all pupils	5347
	−4982
Excess over normal years	365

So we see that these children have spent 365 years more time in school than they should have. For every year gained there were three years lost. . . .

Binding Education in Red Tape

In the effort to demonstrate efficiency through the adoption of business methods, by far the greatest amount of energy was spent on keeping track of the mechanical-financial aspects of education—such as ordering supplies, making out time sheets and payrolls, and caring for the maintenance of buildings and equipment. The first step in this process was to produce the accounting forms which would be necessary.

The standard work on this problem (which was generally referred to by administrators or cited by them as having made possible "scientific school accounting") was a doctoral thesis written by J. Howard Hutchinson at Teachers College, Columbia University, under the direction of George D. Strayer. Hutchinson drew his inspiration for the study from the memorable 1913 meeting of the Department of Superintendence at which Spaulding had delivered his influential address on scientific management. From the discussions at this meeting he realized "that the magic word efficiency that is causing such a revolution in industry is beginning to work in education." But efficiency in industry was based upon "complete knowledge," and he stated that it was shown by the discussion at the meeting "that administrative officers have not yet demanded and obtained knowledge sufficient to enable their school systems to work at anything like high efficiency. . . ." Before complete data could be provided, an accounting system complete with forms and requisition sheets had to be developed. His mission was to create such a system and urge its adoption by administrators.

In discussing the function and importance of school accounting, Hutchinson provided evidence that it fitted into the pattern of the other steps taken by administrators. It would serve as a defense against criticism. He indicated this when, after citing an example of inadequate accounting being carried out in one school system, he said, "Suppose an inquisitive citizen, jealous of his wealth, should ask, 'How much was that per pupil?' 'How does that compare with the cost per pupil a year before?' No information could be given him. Indeed no information at all is given of the amount of service purchased for the expenditures and of the cost per unit of that service." He pointed out that Spaulding had shown that this situation would have been unthinkable in industry. He told administrators that producing shoes without regard to cost was "the first step in bankruptcy proceeding," and he warned them that in the future the "administration of education without regard to cost will be sufficient evidence of inefficiency of administrative officers."

During his investigation Hutchinson visited and studied the accounting procedures in 38 cities. He found that in 18 of these cities the data were either inadequate or unavailable, and so he used the material from only 20 cities. After examining the financial statements of the school boards and of the superintendents in these cities, he found them to be so full of defects that they were worthless for his purpose. Administrators were not devoting enough time to the financial side of education. He was particularly irritated by one superintendent who told him that he (the superintendent) was employed to see that children were educated, not to look after the money; that was the treasurer's job.

Since the accounting procedures and mechanisms were found to be inadequate Hutchinson devoted the last third of his study to an explanation of a system of accounting designed to remedy the situation. He acknowledged that he had borrowed ideas from some of the cities he had visited, from manufacturing concerns, and from manuals on accounting, and he claimed that he had recommended nothing that had not been used in principle in public or industrial accounting. He suggested that at the outset in some school systems the installation of his system might require an additional expenditure of $1800 for a clerk and assistant, but he assured his readers that this sum would be repaid many times through the saving that would be achieved.

In his system of accounting each step was, he said, designed to accomplish one or more of these three purposes:

1. To provide for each transaction an original document that will contain a complete history of the transaction from its beginning to its completion, including the giving of personal responsibility for each step taken, and will serve as the best evidence obtainable to protect the city in any action that might be taken as a result of the transaction.

2. To make it possible for those in authority to account for funds appropriated for school purposes.

3. To furnish the administrative officers such information as will enable them to decide whether every service is performed at the lowest cost compatible with maximum efficiency.

Then he listed the forms that would be required: Requisition for supplies; work requisition; purchase order; purchase order voucher; payroll for elementary schools; principal's time sheet; and so on through 22 special forms for every possible expenditure. The remainder of the study consisted of a description, together with some explanation, of each of the forms. Hutchinson prefaced this material with a short statement on the time-saving benefits of using these forms and then described the procedure for ordering supplies:

The teacher, using two sheets of carbon paper, enters on the three copies the number of the grade, the name of the school, the latest date on which she wishes the goods delivered, the description of the articles desired, the quantity she has on hand, the quantity she desires, and signs her name with date showing when she makes out the requisition. The three copies are forwarded to the principal. The principal examines the requisition, and using two sheets of carbon signs the copies to show that he approves the requisition, giving the date of his approval. He keeps the triplicate copy on file. The original and duplicate copies are sent to the secretary, who should examine the requisition to see whether the quantity on hand warrants the issue of the goods, whether the quantity on hand is what it should be according to the ledger sheet of the grade. *If, after examination, he believes the goods or any part of them should be delivered, the secretary enters in the column "Ordered Delivered" the quantity of each article that he will allow.* His signature with the date shows that he so orders the storekeeper. The use of a carbon sheet has entered the same information upon the duplicate copy. . . .

The storekeeper takes from the storeroom the goods ordered, on the store's tag deducts the quantity to be issued, entering also the date, and delivers the goods to the room on or before the date given in the requisition. He has the teacher check the items to show they have been delivered. She also signs her name to the form and writes the date to show that the goods checked have been received on the date given. The one delivering the goods also puts his signature on the sheet and the date of delivery. At this time the principal being notified of the receipt of goods checks the delivery on his copy and enters the date. . . .

The same form of requisition may be used by the principal in requesting goods for his office or for the school as a whole. The operations to be performed will be the same, except that the secretary will enter the cost on the proper school ledger sheet under "Administration," "Supplies."

The requisition used by janitors is the same as that for teachers, except for the substitution of the word janitor for teacher, and the omission of the number of the grade. The procedure to be followed is the same as that for a principal's requisition; i.e., the charge is made against the proper school in the ledger under "Operation," "Janitorial Supplies," or other object. . . .

Although education is not a business and the schools are not factories, no reasonable man can deny the advisability of applying certain business practices where they are appropriate to the work of the schools. But they are a means to an end—the end being to provide the best possible education for our children. When efficiency and economy are sought as ends in themselves, as they were in education in the age of efficiency (and are in too many communities in 1962), the education of children is bound to suffer. The same thing is true regarding certain business values. A concern about the wise expenditure of funds and the avoidance of waste is as desirable in education as it is in business. But a "wise" expenditure of funds depends on the outcomes which are expected or, in business terms, the quality of the product desired. Cutting costs and producing an inferior "product" is not efficient in business or education. True efficiency in either case is achieved by producing a product of the quality desired or developing a well-educated individual at minimum cost. It is clear that what administrators sought, after 1911, was not efficiency but *economy plus the appearance of efficiency.* They did this partly because the public was primarily interested in economy and partly because they were unable or unwilling to make the complex and difficult decisions on the kind and quality of education they believed young Americans needed, and then accomplish the equally difficult task of determining the means (including the cost) which would be required. A few administrators such as Ben Blewett of St. Louis saw that efficiency had to be related to the aims of education and some others, including Cubberley, pointed out occasionally that a cheap school might be a very inefficient school but that was as far as it went.

Undoubtedly the "efficiency" measures helped school administrators to defend themselves and to keep their jobs in a business-dominated, efficiency-conscious society, but the price the nation has paid has been high. Not only were our educational leaders devoting their time and energy to matters that are incidental to the real purpose of the schools, but our teachers were forced to spend countless hours on meaningless clerical work—hours that should have been devoted to teaching and learning. And, unfortunately, much of this clerical work has survived down to the present time. This is so partly because administrators who were trained as bookkeepers in their graduate work in the twenties and thirties are still in key positions in our schools. It is also due to the adoption by teachers of some aspects of the business-managerial role in their classrooms. Just as administrators adopted this posture to please a business society and especially school boards dominated by businessmen, so teachers learned how to behave to please business-oriented administrators.

Questions for Discussion

1. Why does Callahan say that the education of children suffers when cost accounting procedures are applied to the educational enterprise? Could schools be operated without those procedures? Should a concern for cost accounting be an integral part of any educational philosophy?
2. How did you react to Harris's account of the cost per year-minute given on pp. 161–162?
3. What values, if any, do administrators contribute to a school?

13 Education Through Play

A. S. Neill

How do you react to a teacher who says: (1) "To the children, I am no authority. . . . I am their equal." (2) "Most of the schoolwork that adolescents do is simply a waste of time." (3) "The educational benefit of practical civics cannot be overemphasized." (4) "Children's interests are immediate, and the future does not exist for them." (5) "I have never yet seen a lazy child." (6) "Children should be allowed to play all the time, if they wish to." (7) "We should give a child freedom, and so refuse to teach him religion, or politics, or class consciousness."

An H.M.I. said to me: "What would you teach if there were no G.C.E. exams?" I could not think of an answer, possibly because when one has been conditioned from infancy to accept school subjects as education, no one is free enough to answer.

That the products of schools are much more interested in things outside the school system . . . football pools, cheap press, television, sex, games . . . than they are in all the subjects we teach suggests that our schools are never adapted to the life outside. This is primarily due to the fact that emotion is of infinitely more moment than is intellect; the above mentioned post-school interests are emotional ones, whereas G.C.E. subjects are all head subjects. We see the same result of this unbalance in books like *Blackboard Jungle* in the U.S.A. and *The Young Devils* at home. This raising of the leaving has too often meant adolescents having to continue sitting at desks saying what has no appeal to their minds or senses. It is just nonsense to say that our schools give children culture . . . the sales of our most sensational newspapers prove this point . . . education precedes a national interest in the inferior and unessential.

La Plume de . . .

Cultures! Thousands of our pupils learn French up to G.C.E. standard. Few ever will go to France, few will ever read French books; in two years most of what they learnt has gone. So with other subjects. Math! What passer of the O level exams could do a quadratic equation five years later? English! What proportion of G.C.E. passers read whodunnits instead of the cultural reading their grammar schools taught them . . . Lamb's Essays, Shakespeare, Milton, Coleridge? Geography! How do we apply what we learn after we leave school? When ever I go to Scotland I cannot get rid of the notion that I am going uphill: the wall map had Scotland at the top. The only geography we use is of the place-on-the-map variety and that vaguely to be sure. How many of us know exactly where these places are . . .

From "Why Have Exams?" and "Each His Own Dramatist," by A. S. Neill, *The Times Educational Supplement*, May 8, 1959, and December 2, 1960. Reprinted by permission of *The Times* of London.

Thursday Island, Vermont, Salzburg? Post-school life does not concern itself with the exports of Brazil or the climate of Timbuctu.

What to Teach

I feel like replying to the H.M.I. by saying: "I'd scrap the lot," but then would have the painful task of saying what my school would teach. Painful because it is so difficult to assess change of values. In my youth a university education was the criterion of an educated man; the scholar with his Latin and Greek and philosophy was the man to respect and emulate. To-day that is not so. The standard has altered, mainly because of the great and rapid advance in mechanical theory and practice. In terms of utility to-day the expert who can make or even repair a television set is of more importance than an M.A. who has specialized in—say—English, for the M.A. can only teach in a small circle while the other man can do in a large one. We see the same in music. Whatever a school may do to give pupils a love for classical music, the fact remains that (I am guessing here) the records of the rock 'n' roll singers far exceed in volume and sale those of all the classics lumped together.

Given freedom from examinations I should aim at catching the children's interests and following them. Rock 'n' roll? Good, the music of the school would start with Elvis Presley and Tommy Steele. Reading would be all the whodunnits the school could procure. I should reverse the process by which the school begins with Addison and goes on to the post-graduate *News of the World*, feeling uneasily that my pupils' daily perusal of the *News of the World* might not automatically lead later to the reading of Addison.

But perhaps I should teach nothing at all on the ground that you cannot teach anything of importance. I know of no school that has been free enough to follow in its teaching the dictates of child nature; every school is to some extent divorced from outside life and interest; that follows the pre-psychology period that treated children as small adults. Adults must work and therefore children must be taught to work. Since the importance of play in a child's life has been recognized no fundamental alteration has been made to the timetable. I can fantasy a non-exam school which would be a large playground . . . not playing fields which are not really play at all. Play with books and tools and music and dance and—in Utopia—play with love. I doubt if the adage that tells that the hard way forms character has any validity in psychology. I see rock 'n' roll as a flight from the hard way of schooling with its insane demand for homework, yet to be honest I do not think that is the whole truth for my pupils who are as free as can be in a school to-day love rock 'n' roll records, but to be honest again they do not seem to carry on the interest into the later teen age. Nor are my own pupils free from the G.C.E. obstacle to real education.

Forming Character

I ask: What does it matter what we teach? The only importance in education lies in character formation, and here many a teacher will agree. But not many will agree that character formation must come from inside. No study will form a good character. Indeed character is seldom mentioned by teachers; the cry to-day is not for better science, better science in an era in which knowing has run far ahead of emotion, and science has almost become synonymous with keeping up with the Joneseskis.

This insistence on the importance of playhood may sound mad to many a teacher. Maybe it is mad, but it is at least a tentative suggestion for coping with a most dangerous situation, that of a sick world whose values have little or nothing to do with schooling, and I do not mean Britain alone; the news of anti-social rebellious youth in Sweden, America, Russia shows that schooling is failing in many lands. Personally I think that conscious or more probably unconscious fear is at the bottom of youth's revolt. . . . Let us eat, drink, and be merry, for to-morrow we die. Sex repression is not enough to account for it; we had sex repression long before the H-bomb appeared and it did not seem to go so far as flick knives and cycle chains.

Revolt Against School

The question is this: Is youth rebelling because of its education or in spite of it? I suggest the former. I question if a lessonless school would produce any anti-social, any criminal products; I feel sure that most hateful coshings and stabbings are the result of unlived-out play, but again that cannot be the whole truth, for children of the upper and middle classes are not usually teddy boys. I am not wise enough to pose as an authority, but in the days when I had to deal with many anti-social adolescents, I saw most of them go out cured, not by lessons, not by my analyses, but cured because they had freedom to live out their playhood, cured because allowed to be themselves. And of moment, cured because relieved of guilt about sex. An odd thought to end up with: When any madman or fool of a statesman can press the button that could kill us all, why does such a small thing as sex retain its Victorian significance? Until the guilt complex of youth is relieved all or nearly all of our school subject teaching will remain useless and a matter of indifference to the young.

I first began to experiment with spontaneous acting when I had my school in Germany in 1922. I very much doubt that I invented the idea. Since that time I have had many a pleasant hour with children. The idea is quite simple; the teacher gives a skeleton plot. . . . You are a father: you are a mother: you are a son who has been expelled from school for stealing: carry on. To give more than the skeleton is to curb all invention and imagination.

You begin with easy situations not requiring speech. Don an overcoat, pick flowers, load and wheel a barrow, be a blind man crossing the street. Try to pass a vicious chained dog. One girl of 10 solved the problem by patting its head, saying: "So you missed your walk today, Hector?" A teacher can think of scores of ideas. I find that children very seldom have an idea that can be carried out well.

The next and last step is to introduce dialogue. Ask a policeman the way to the station. Often a child acts a foreigner in this case. Two wives gossiping over the garden fence. Take a hasty meal at a railway restaurant in dread that your train will depart. Rob a safe and the householder walks in. This one draws some ingenious defences. . . . "Ah, there you are, sir. My firm is sorry it could not send a man to repair your safe until now. . . ." "I must have got into the wrong house. Your safe is exactly like mine."

No Love Scenes

Children will not attempt any acting that deals with love or death. Almost always they make the story a comedy, but there is one story they never try to make comic: Gangster has been framed and has done five years hard. He goes to shoot his framer, Spike. It takes him some time to realize that Spike is blind, blinded by the bank safe explosion that sent the other to gaol. Not once has a child shot Spike. Generally, as I say, they want comedy. A funeral on a windy day. The parson's tall hat on the brink of the grave moves in the wind. Will it fall in? This affords a fine chance for factual expression.

Telephone conversations when one has got the wrong number appeal to the more imaginative ones. Mrs. Brown rings the butcher and gets the doctor.

"I think of liver today."

"Oh, what symptoms? Pain in the right side?"

The best dialogue I had was during the war. Situation: you are a young lady with toothache and you go out to find a dentist, but owing to the blackout you get into the office of the undertaker. Carry on.

She (13) enters looking very miserable. He (13) says: "Well, madam, what can I do for you?"

"This is terrible."

"I know, madam, these sufferings are difficult to bear. Tell me about it."

"I think it's decaying."

"Good Lord, how long have you had it?"

"About a month."

"But this is absurd. Haven't you done anything about it?"

"I tried stuffing it with cotton-wool."

"But, madam, you must have it removed."

"I refuse to have it removed unless you promise to give me a gold plate."

"Sorry, madam, but we only make brass plates."

"But it will go all verdigris!"

"That, madam, won't matter. No one will see it."

But I grant that the usual dialogue does not come up to that standard.

I find that shy pupils who do not volunteer to act a part alone will often take part in a group situation. I am an immigration officer at Harwich. Here I confess I have to lead in questioning the arrivals. I am a businessman and advertise for an amanuensis, a word very few children ever heard of. I ask a girl what she knows about amanuensis; she replies: "I breed them." Another tells of her skill in dealing with hands and nails. Again I am Sam Goldwyn seeking a film star and giving tests in acting. Take a cold bath in January brings forth some good action. Let a savage find an alarm clock in the sand. Sell quack medicines, dogs, wooden legs . . . anything. The situations in spontaneous acting are infinite in number.

Oddly enough some children who can learn a part and act well in a written play are hopeless in spontaneous acting. Years ago we had a London group of players down for a summer school. They gave us a party the night before they broke up, entertaining us with turns and sketches. They ran out of material and I suggested spontaneous acting. I said to the teacher: "Be St. Peter at the Golden Gate and let them try to get in." "Splendid!" he said, and told his company. They all rejected the idea with alarm. Since then I fancy that the training of actors and actresses has been influenced by the views of Stanislawski and that training in spontaneous acting enters into every acting school. The teacher should be a bit of an actor himself, but if he is dignified his attitude will inhibit the spontaneity of his class. Only a human guy can encourage human acting.

Bringing Them Out

What is the good of it all? The motive is not to make professional actors and actresses; it is merely to bring out any originality a child has, to let him gain self-confidence in expressing himself, to give him enjoyment. Only a minority of children take part in the acting, but the others seem to get as much fun out of watching as the performers get out of acting.

I end by giving a situation that appeals to most young actors. Father says: "Mrs. Brown is coming to tea this afternoon. You all know that her husband was hanged last month. For heaven's sake think twice before you speak to her."

Of course the M. Hulot of the family welcomes her with a request to partake of a "drop" of something. The youngest son asks her to watch his skill with a rope when he lassoes the cat. A daughter asks her if she likes swing music. It is all good clean fun. In a long experience of child actors I have seldom if ever seen one use the cheap method of the music halls to get a laugh by pornographic *double entendre*.

The method can easily be carried out in state schools, and in fact some teachers use it. But I cannot think of there being much success when the teacher is a disciplinarian, a feared person, a person apart. If a teacher cannot make a fool of himself, cannot laugh at himself, he should stick to producing *A Midsummer Night's Dream* . . . a play I find beyond the grasp of most children. The bright girl mentioned in the toothache story was Puck when our English master produced the play. She acted badly. I asked her why. "Because I didn't understand the words." Personally I think that Shakespeare should not be acted by children. In Summerhill they write their own plays, and long ago I wrote that I would rather see a child write a bad limerick than be able to recite the whole of *Paradise Lost*.

Questions for Discussion

1. Describe the theory of learning which is assumed by this account. What is the role of the teacher? How are students evaluated, or are they? Would texts be used in such a learning situation?
2. Do you believe that men and women who are given so much freedom as students would be able to become productive and contributing members of a society?
3. Are you attracted to the sort of school Neill sees as ideal? Read his book *Summerhill* and see if you are still attracted.

14   Imperative Issues in Urban Education

Donald H. Smith

The next three selections deal with a problem of growing national concern: the education of students from minority groups. Should students who come from a different culture, who have different aspirations and skills, different motivations and even language backgrounds, be given the same type of education as that given to students of the white majority? If they should, how can this transformation be effected most easily? If not, then what kind of educational system would be best? In this article, Smith calls attention to five imperatives which must occur if urban education is even to begin to reach its goals. Note his imperatives carefully, making certain you understand why they are imperatives, not just nice things to do.

The great American Dream of free public education for all children to the upper limits of their potential has never materialized. And for the disadvantaged minorities: Negroes, Mexicans, Puerto Ricans, Amerindians, and poor Southern whites, American public education has been pitifully ineffectual. Judged by almost any critical factor, number of dropouts, level of achievement, number of college entrants, type and duration of employment, and lifestyle, the schools have failed the dispossessed minority pupils.

Two recent works, *Our Children Are Dying* by Nat Hentoff and *Death at an Early Age* by Jonathan Kozol, attest to the shocking and inhumane waste of Negro pupils in the New York and Boston public schools, respectively. The picture in Chicago, Los Angeles and our other large cities is no less bleak. So distressing is the plight of poor kids in our schools that Edgar Friedenberg was compelled to write for *Saturday Review* an article entitled "Requiem for the Urban School." Friedenberg concludes that:

> Improvement in the urban schools will come when—and only when—the residents whose children attend those schools demand and get enough political power either to destroy and replace the present school bureaucracy or to impress upon it that they can no longer be patronized.[1]

The schools have failed and their and society's agents, the teachers, have failed and those who have trained the teachers have also failed. Only if we can recognize the magnitude of our failure and its price, hungry, angry, bitter citizens whose lowly state threatens the security of all, can we then begin to reverse the tide.

Too often so-called experts on the disadvantaged child—and disadvantaged means Negro to most of them—place the burden of education on the shoulders of the

[1] Edgar Friedenberg, "Requiem for the Urban School," *Saturday Review,* November 18, 1967.

From *Teacher Education: Issues and Innovations,* pp. 49–68. The American Association of Colleges for Teacher Education, 21st Yearbook, 1968.

children and their parents. Since it is well known that most disadvantaged children come from homes that are economically and educationally deprived, it is presumed that however dedicated and talented the teacher may be the cause is hopeless—witness *Up the Down Staircase*. Only a super god, Phi Beta Kappa—perhaps "Sir Poitier"—can teach the unteachable.

Such mushy thinking has gotten us in the fix we're in now: the collapse of the urban school.

I reject the thesis that the fault lies within the ghetto; and neither does it lie within the stars. *The fault lies within the larger society that fails to acknowledge the existence of black people, and subsequently trains teachers and constructs curricula and materials for a presumably monolithic white middle-class society.*

Teachers have failed because, for the most part, they don't know anything about, care little about and have not been trained to teach their black and brown pupils.

These children are no longer only a part of, but have in fact *become* the urban school population. Negro pupils are in the majority in twelve of our largest cities and are better than forty per cent of the population in at least five other large cities. Add to this total the Mexicans and the Puerto Ricans, and the revelation is that the white child is the urban minority. The new teacher training curricula are going to have to face up squarely to this hard racial fact and to other hard facts if we are to save the one institution that has within it the potential to save our nation.

These are critical times, times when men young and old, liberal and conservative, black and white must talk and must listen.

Let us consider together five imperative issues in urban education. Certainly these are not the only significant issues, but I make no effort to touch all bases.

Imperative Number One is *the need to change the attitudes and expectations of teachers of disadvantaged youth.*

A number of years ago when I was a guidance counselor in an inner city high school I suggested to the valedictorian that he apply to Harvard. Inner city admissions to the Ivy League are few—male valedictorians at inner-city high schools are also few. Yet even though he had achieved the distinction of leading his class in scholarship, this Negro youngster could not conceive of his applying to Harvard. The idea was even more implausible to the white scholarship counselor at the high school, who did everything to discourage the boy. True, he was a brilliant student in math and science but surely his college board scores in the language arts were too low for him to consider a first-rate university.

The combination of the student's poor self-image and its reinforcement by his white counselor were difficult to overcome, but after much persistence and pressure, I finally succeeded in getting our valedictorian to apply. The April rejection slip he received seemed to indicate that he and the scholarship counselor were right. But on the day the rejection notice came, I received a call from Harvard's Director of Admissions. He had detected something about my letter of recommendation that indicated my understanding of this boy. The Harvard official went on to explain that in spite of his low language scores, and in spite of this year's rejection, he was the kind of boy that Harvard wanted. Would he consider enrolling in an Eastern prep school for a year? Perhaps a scholarship could be arranged. If not, Harvard would be his anonymous benefactor. This young man did attend that prep school for a year and he graduated from Harvard last June. Last summer he worked as a teacher of hard-core dropouts, and now he is back at Harvard, in law school.

I have talked to teachers and children in Harlem, in Watts, in Alabama, and Georgia and Mississippi and in many other parts of the nation, and while I have found some superior teaching in almost every school I've visited, I have generally been appalled by the pervasive discouragement and low levels of expectation which are held by most teachers for poor children, particularly black ones.

A few decades ago a brilliant young boy attended an East Lansing, Michigan, high school, the only Negro in his class. In his autobiography he wrote about his English teacher who would daily give words of encouragement to the class, urging them to go on to college, to make something of themselves. One day the boy confided to his teacher that he, too, had been inspired and that he hoped some day to become a lawyer. The boy was crushed when his teacher advised him to forget the law and become a plumber or carpenter. Circumstances determined that this boy would not finish high school and, hence, enter any profession. But one can only wonder what contribution he might have made to all Americans had Malcolm "X" been encouraged to realize his dreams. Perhaps he might have lived to be appointed to the Supreme Court.

Of great irony was the teacher's advice to become a plumber or a carpenter, when the reality is that it is easier for a Negro lad to get into law school than into plumbers' or carpenters' unions.

It is a moot point whether teachers and counselors discourage black children because of bigotry or out of some misguided paternalism, which is itself a form of racism. But as long as school personnel continue to have dual punishment and reward systems, and dual levels of expectation, they will continue to maim poor children psychologically and deprive them of their opportunity to enter and flourish in the mainstream of a land of plenty.

Unfortunately, it is not only in the area of college and vocational guidance that teacher attitudes and expectations hurt children, but also right within the instructional setting the behavior of teachers can mediate the achievement of pupils.

Worthy of our consideration is the very important research of Robert Rosenthal and Lenore Jacobson[2] which clearly indicates the critical relationship between teacher expectations and pupil achievement. Rosenthal and Jacobson found that experimenters working with rats which they had been led to believe were dull had little success in teaching them, but working with rats which were allegedly bright, they had significant success. Rosenthal and Jacobson concluded that:

> Regardless of whether the rat's task was to learn a maze or the appropriate responses in a Skinner box, the results were the same. Rats who were believed by their experimenters to be brighter showed learning which was significantly superior to the learning by rats whose experimenters believed them to be dull.

[2] Robert Rosenthal and Lenore Jacobson, "Self-Fulfilling Prophecies in the Classroom; Teachers' Expectations as Unintended Determinants of Pupils' Intellectual Competence," a paper presented at the American Psychological Association, Washington, D.C., September, 1967.

But rats are not children, so Rosenthal and Jacobson moved their experiment into a school of the South San Francisco Unified School District. They administered to all of the children of the Oak School a test which they called the "Harvard Test of Inflected Acquisition," actually a standardized intelligence test, generally non-verbal, the Flanagan Tests of General Ability.

Based not upon test results, but upon a random selection, twenty per cent of the children in each classroom were "identified" to their teachers as pupils whose test results indicated they were intellectual bloomers who would undergo significant learning spurts during that year. Once again the Mertonian self-fulfilling prophecy was confirmed: Children designated as spurters did show greater intellectual gains than children not so designated. This was true of children of high intellectual ability as well as children of lower ability. Because their teachers had been conned into believing that some children were going to bloom, their own behavior toward and perceptions of those children served as mediating factors that helped to make the learning spurts possible.

If we are going to begin to put an end to the human waste in our schools then imperative number one is to change teachers' perceptions of and consequent behavior toward pupils they have formerly believed are racially and intellectually inferior. And this imperative leads to imperative number two.

Imperative Number Two is *the need for drastic changes in the training of teachers*. Teachers are frightened and frustrated as they attempt each day to confront what is for most of them the urban ordeal. My own experience as a new teacher was common to the experiences of many teachers. The educational training that I had received as an undergraduate, and even later as a graduate student, was in no way related to the problems I encountered in the schools and to the needs of my pupils. For the most part—and surely there are a few notable exceptions—teacher training for urban schools has been and is irrelevant. Except for rare instances, it has not begun to address itself to the kinds of information and experiences young people need to develop appropriate attitudes to teach successfully in the ghetto.

No engineering school in the country would attempt to teach its students to build bridges without first attempting to teach the concept of what a bridge is and such factors as how bridges differ in structure and purpose. Further, the would-be bridge builder would have to know something about soil dynamics, the nature of the neighborhood, to determine whether or not or how his structure could be supported at the desired location.

No medical school would attempt to teach surgery or dermatology without first teaching the anatomy of the whole body and the functions of various organs.

Yet schools of education send their products into Spanish Harlem or Lawndale or Watts with no knowledge of the nature of the children, no knowledge of the neighborhood and the community residents, and no appreciation for the culture of those communities. It is amazing that any excellent teaching occurs. When it does it is as a result of on-the-job training come by through a rat in the maze, hit and miss procedure. Schools of education must cease attempting to prepare teachers for a monolithic white school which does not exist in the heart of the interior, if it exists anywhere.

The proper study for inner-city teachers is the inner city. To teach Negro, Mexican, Puerto Rican, Amerindian, and poor Southern white children, a teacher will have to be taught, herself, the history and culture of Negroes, Spanish-speaking, American Indians and Southern white migrant children. Teachers must be taught the anthro-sociopsychological factors related to poverty, racism, and oppression. And they will need to know the idiom of the black ghettos and the Southern mountains, and the Spanish of El Barrio. Further, teachers in training should, early in their undergraduate years, be exposed to a variety of experiences which will help them to understand the lifestyle and coping mechanisms imposed by social and economic exclusion.

Hopefully, through early contacts with children of poverty and through formal study of their history and culture, teacher cadets will learn not only about the needs of the children and their communities, but also they will gain insights into themselves, their stereotypes and biases and into how their behavior affects the lives of children entrusted to them.

Just how we convince colleges and universities to re-order their teacher-training curricula and practices is difficult to know. Even if a significant number of the great teacher-producing institutions were to decide tomorrow to bring their training programs into consonance with pressing urban needs, they would be hard-put, indeed, to get their faculties to step to a new drummer or to acquire faculty with the new visions. Perhaps it is just this type of dilemma which has induced the U.S. Office of Education to initiate the Triple T Project (Training the Teachers of Teachers).

At the Center for Inner City Studies we don't pretend that we have all the religion, but we are attempting, on the graduate level, to provide the kind of urban immersion that I am advocating. A few of our recent graduates have already been hired by Teacher Corps and universities to give some direction.

Imperative Number Two urges radical change in the training of teachers and other school personnel to satisfy both the needs of the children and of the teachers themselves.

The Third Imperative is *the need for curriculum change within the schools*. Many researchers have documented the psychic damage which racism has done to young Negro children. Exposed to a society which postulates and which reinforces an image of inferiority through the mass media and through the assignment of a second-class lifestyle to black people, little children of color and older ones doubt themselves, and frequently reject themselves and others like them. School curriculum will have to be restructured to be responsive to the affective as well as the cognitive needs of disadvantaged pupils.

Curriculum is defined here as any experiences which help children to learn and which help pupils to develop qualities of self-actualization.

Courses will have to be instituted into public school curricula which will re-order reality for black children, and for that matter, white children, too. Black and Spanish-speaking children must be taught their heritage, and they must be encouraged to take great pride in that heritage. I will leave to the historians whether, for example, Afro-American history ought to be taught separately or as a part of the general American history, from which it is presently absent. My concern is that all children be informed that the miraculous achievements of Dr. Christiaan Barnard were, in some measure, made possible by the work of a black man, Dr. Daniel Hale Williams who in 1893 performed the first successful heart surgery in America. A single achievement, however great, would not be so significant in the history of civilization which has witnessed many great achievements. But what is significant, however, is that black people have made countless contributions to mankind, which have been deliberately omitted from world and American history. If black people really knew the truth about themselves and their magnificent accomplishments, they would soon discontinue the self-abnegation which has characterized the black experience in America.

But black and other exploited poor need more than their history. Self-acceptance and racial pride are important affective development. But what of cognitions? Black people will need specific weapons to fight back against oppression and exploitation. They need economics and they need politics. Who controls the ghetto? Why are rents disproportionately higher in the black belt? Why are food prices higher and meat inferior at white-owned black stores than at white-owned white stores? Why do drugstores in the ghetto charge more, sometimes 100 percent more for medicines? And what about auto dealers? Why do the poor pay more? Why do the black poor pay the most? How can poor people develop and martial economic and political forces to control their own destinies? These and others are the burning questions for which curriculum and instruction must provide some answers.

For example, mathematics can be taught in terms of budgets, interest rates, insurance payments and the like. The sciences can be taught with respect to the ghetto's needs: the biology of reproduction, the chemistry of foods and medicines and so on.

Language arts and social studies should also serve the community's culture and its needs. In this regard James Baldwin, Martin Luther King, and Malcolm "X" are more important than Shakespeare and Melville. Charles Drew, the discoverer of blood plasma is more important to black people than Enrico Fermi. And the biography of Frederick Douglass is more significant than the biography of George Washington. I am not suggesting that a sonnet of Shelley should never find its way into the black school, or that the discoveries of Steinmetz and Edison are not important for all science students, but I am clearly and strongly advocating that the genuine accomplishments of distinguished black men are of greater importance to the intellectual development of black children.

Schools must stop preparing Afro-Americans for menial jobs and minor roles in the social order. The task of curriculum and instruction in the black community is to prepare black pupils to celebrate themselves and to help them discover the wherewithal and the methodology to begin to enjoy the fruits of an affluent nation, heretofore available only to whites and a few hand-picked blacks.

Imperative Number Four is *the need to change controls in the urban schools.* The subject of control has become a topic of concern in many quarters. For instance, the Coleman Report of *Equality of Educational Opportunity* talks about a sense of control as one of the important variables that determine Negro achievement.[3] The

[3] *Equality of Educational Opportunity*, U.S. Government Printing Office, Washington, D.C., 1966.

Coleman Report postulates that a Negro pupil's sense of control is heightened as the proportion of white pupils in his environment is increased. Increasing the control factor, Coleman and associates contend, increases achievement. Yet, the same Coleman Report also claims that while achievement increases in the integrated school, the self-concept of Negro pupils is diminished.[4] More attention to this in a moment.

Other voices than Coleman's are speaking of control, *actual* rather than a *sense* of control. Black people all over America are demanding that they be self-determining by controlling all factors in the ghetto: the economy, the politics, the schools, everything.

Returning to the Coleman Report, I am not surprised that young black children feel a sense of diminished self-esteem in integrated schools. Picture yourself being bussed across town to the white school. Obviously your school wasn't good enough for you to learn there, or for white children to come and join you. So for your own good you had to be herded off on buses to the good school. Once there you might have to wade through jeering pickets to reach the building. Or if not that, then you encounter hostile teachers, some overtly, some subtly so. Most white students will ignore you, a few well-meaning ones will patronize you. Under such circumstances I find highly questionable Professor Coleman's assertion that black pupils do, indeed, achieve more because of a newly acquired sense of control. I would assert that a more logical explanation for increased achievement is a combination of the following:

(1) The schools to which the black pupils were bussed are middle-class white schools where there is considerable academic press. White middle-class parents demand that teachers teach. They accept no nonsense about missing library books and cognitive deficits.

(2) Faculties in those schools are stable. They are permanent rather than substitutes. Children in those schools expect and have continuity. They have the same teachers every day, unlike children in the ghetto who may have as many as ten or more teachers in a single term.

(3) Negro pupils learn because of the above factors and because the teachers expect their pupils to learn, and teach accordingly. I cannot understand how Negroes could feel a greater sense of control when, as even Professor Coleman reveals, their self-esteem is lessened in the white school.

Because the control factor is alleged to be critical, and I believe that it is, let us look at the matter of control in terms of the ghetto school. It is hardly conceivable that any but a few children could feel a sense of control in the black school where the principal is white, the assistant principal and the counselors are white, the school engineer is white, the window washers are white and if the windows get broken the glaziers are white. And so is the superintendent of schools, even in Washington, D.C. It is virtually impossible for black pupils or black teachers to feel a sense of potency when from the top of the school system right to the boiler room, they are administered, supervised and manipulated by white people. This pattern of white domi-

---

[4] *Ibid.,* p. 323.

nance of black welfare and black interests is omnipresent and pervasive in all areas of the black existence.

Of special interest is the finding of the Report, *Racial Isolation in the Public Schools,* that no known compensatory education program has been successful in increasing the achievement of Negro pupils.[5] Assess that finding against the fact that at a recent national meeting of all the State ESEA Title I Directors, there was not a single Negro in the group. Further, at a recent meeting held in Washington, which was comprised of over six hundred NDEA and Experienced Teacher Fellowship Program directors there were not more than twenty-five Negroes among the six hundred. It is little wonder that compensatory programs designed and administered by white people conducted in black schools run by white people have yielded few positive results for black children.

Carrying the analysis a step further, one is hard-pressed to find black and brown decision makers in the U.S. Office of Education, which commissions, approves, and dispenses funds for these programs.

I am sure there are hundreds of reasons why white people are in complete control of the education of twenty-two or more million blacks. These reasons range from arguments of longevity, color-blindness, professional territoriality, and "Divine Right of Kings," to the simple equation: "We've got you outnumbered."

It would be futile for me to enumerate and attempt to answer all of these questions. I would simply submit that there are a few reasons which are superordinate and are more compelling reasons why substantial changes must be made in this self-defeating structure.

First, the urban schools are in shambles as black students are struggling and fighting to live. They are being cheated and they know it, but they have no sense of control and no socially approved means of self-determination. Therefore some of them find other sources of potency, other ways to confront a dehumanizing, oppressive system: hurling bottled fire, smashing windows, stealing cars, looting.

I would prefer and I think you would prefer to have these angry, abused young people find their power and their self-esteem by flexing their muscles and developing their manhood in the determination and direction of their own destinies. Through their own black symbols of authority, real ones, not white-appointed Uncle Toms, they will have available more positive channels for self-actualization.

Second, white people have already demonstrated their inadequacy or their unwillingness to provide quality education for black people. Joseph Alsop has written that if the worst racist in America set out to design a structure which would keep the Negro enchained, he could do no better than to use the present public educational system.[6]

Third, as evidenced by the two-year controversy at IS 201, black people are becoming determined that they will run their own schools, and they are determined that teachers and administrators will be held accountable to black communities. As

[5] *Racial Isolation in the Public Schools,* U.S. Commission on Civil Rights. U.S. Government Printing Office, Washington, D.C., 1967, chapter IV.

[6] Joseph Alsop, "No More Nonsense About Ghetto Education!" *New Republic,* July 22, 1967.

black communities stiffen, fewer and fewer white people will be permitted to have authoritative positions in those communities.

Therefore, it is my contention that the survival of the urban schools is dependent upon the willingness of the educational establishment to change the control factors in all aspects of urban education, from the U.S. Office of Education right down to the pre-schools. Enlightened self-interest would seem to dictate this.

The Fifth and final Imperative is *the upgrading of the black schools.* Even if integration were a desirable goal, though a growing number of black people believe it is not, its achievement does not seem likely in the immediate future. The masses of black children cannot wait until the millennium for their equal educational opportunities. We must, therefore, make it possible for quality education to take place in the black school.

Yet, if the teachers who work in the black school, the children who attend it and the community perceive it as an inferior school, then it is, in fact, an inferior school.

We must change the black school's ethos. This can be done by staffing it with teachers who have been trained to understand and respect black and brown people; by administering it with black and brown people who are accountable to the pupils and their community; and by re-ordering curriculum and instruction to meet the real not imaginary needs of the pupils. Finally, though I have not listed adequate financing as an imperative, it nonetheless is. However, I have limited my discussion to those factors which do not involve substantial additional expenditures, but which call instead for changes in attitudes, assumptions and structures. Unquestionably, the demands that Negroes are placing upon society for changes in all institutions, particularly the schools, can result in all Americans being the beneficiaries.

If, somehow, we can sense the urgency of abandoning a public school that never worked; if we can change curriculum and materials so radically that all children can identify with the curriculum because it is relevant to their needs; if we can train teachers to understand and love most of their children—irrespective of race or class, if we can change the symbols of control, then perhaps there is some hope for the American school.

If we cannot bring about these changes which beg to be made, there is little hope for the schools or for the nation.

Questions for Discussion

1. List the five imperatives Smith mentions. Do some seem more imperative than others? Are all imperative?
2. Does Smith mention any specific ideas for teaching students in the urban schools? Would any of these ideas be applicable to other classrooms?
3. Can you describe what you would do if you were teaching in a classroom composed entirely of students from minority groups?
4. Would you rather put more money, time and energy, perhaps twice as much, into developing the school system for students from minority groups or put that time, energy and money into the schools for the white majority, granting that both are important? What does your answer say about your own values?

15 Our Children Are Dying

Nat Hentoff

The second selection dealing with the education of students from minority groups describes the efforts of a principal in Harlem, Dr. Elliott Shapiro, to keep his children from dying in intellect and aspiration. Notice how he works at his goal, and see if you can identify some educational principles which guide his activities.

During recent years of looking into the New York City public school system in what are euphemistically known as "disadvantaged" neighborhoods, I have listened to vehement condemnations of many schools by parents, civil rights activists, and unaffiliated but concerned adults in the community. The complaints most frequently focus on teachers who appear to be convinced that Negro and Puerto Rican students have limited capacities for learning and on principals who have insulated themselves from the children—and the neighborhood. But in visits to Central Harlem, I've noted that these indictments invariably except one elementary school and its principal—P.S. 119 and Dr. Elliott Shapiro. Mrs. Thelma Johnson, for instance, a former official of the Harlem Parents Committee, regards Shapiro as being "beyond category." In Harlem, she says, "we either get principals who consider their work as just a job, a certain number of hours to be filled, or occasionally we get a liberal. The liberal feels he must help the heathen, but since he does indeed see the children as heathen, his attitude precludes his being of any help. Elliott sees them as children, and he has a strong sense of the importance—and individuality—of each one of them." In November 1964, for another example of the community's feeling about Shapiro, a testimonal dinner was held for the principal by a neighborhood association—the Community League of West 159th Street—in conjunction with the staff of P.S. 119 and the parents of its pupils. Among the tributes to Dr. Shapiro was an appraisal by Ralph Edwards, a slight, taut Negro teacher at the school: "His concerns are not empathic in the clinical sense which treats each separate instance of suffering with the same 'detached' sympathy, emphasizing interest rather than involvement. No, Elliott Shapiro learned a long time ago that we are all in trouble, himself included. He finds it impossible to be detached from a condition in which he is so inextricably involved."

Curious, in the spring of 1965 I began a series of visits to the school and the involved principal. The most immediate mark of the neighborhood's poverty is its idle men. In midmorning, men stand, like statues, in front of storefronts on Eighth Avenue and on the stoops of decayed brownstones along 133rd Street, where the school is located, off Eighth Avenue. Most of the men stand alone. P.S. 119, built in 1899, is bleak and forbidding. A massive five-story structure, with its cornices and towers it is medieval in appearance. Whatever their original color may have been, its bricks have weathered into a sickly beige. The only relief from the gloom are bright patches of color from children's drawings in the windows. When I started my visits, next to P.S. 119, its replacement was under construction, and in February 1966, P.S. 119 yielded to P.S. 92.

On the ground floor of P.S. 119, a sign pointed to the principal's office on the floor above. At the head of the staircase, on the wall to the right, were pictures in color of Nigerian political leaders; circus cutouts in orange construction paper; and a display, titled WHAT WOULD YOU LIKE TO BE?, with pictures and descriptions of various professions (Organic Chemist, Histologist, Satellite Tracker, Medical Social Worker, Radar System Designer). On the opposite wall were pictures of Phillis Wheatley, Booker T. Washington, Martin Luther King, Sidney Poitier, and Constance Baker Motley. Beneath each was an essay on the luminary by one of the students. Next to that exhibit a poster announced a BOOK FAIR FOR CHILDREN AND ADULTS sponsored by the Parents' Association of P.S. 119.

The office, I note, is distinctly different from principals' offices in most other elementary schools I've visited. Instead of the customary unsmiling, impersonal attitude of the secretaries, the office personnel seem to erect no barriers of not-to-be-questioned authority between themselvs and the children who come in and out bearing messages or wanting to see the principal. Busy but relaxed, the secretaries talk to, rather than at, the children. At the back of the room, on the left, is Dr. Shapiro's small private office. Its door is almost always open. In his mid-fifties, six feet tall but slightly stooped, gray-haired, Shapiro has the face of a watchful but gentle eagle. He is soft-spoken and often wry. "It's like a medieval castle, isn't it?" He points to the battlements outside his window. "When it rains and the yard gets flooded, all you need is a drawbridge."

As Shapiro began to walk out of his office into the outer room, a wiry eight-year-old girl in a white sweater and flowered skirt walked by the secretaries and stopped him. He leaned down to listen. "Dr. Shapiro, do you know where they put the books you can buy from the book fair? I wrote down the one I want." He took a slip of paper from her and read it. "You're a little bit late, Debbie, but I'll try to save one for you. I think we have some of those left." "I don't have any money, but I'll have it later." Shapiro nodded and she waved good-by. "Thank you for coming," he said.

There are eleven hundred children in the school in classes from pre-kindergarten through the sixth grade. The area served is from 129th Street north to 134th Street and from St. Nicholas Avenue east to Seventh Avenue. It is what social workers call a high delinquency neighborhood. About thirty-five percent of its families are on welfare and the rest have low-income jobs. "The level of family income," Shapiro says, "is from forty to seventy dollars a week. Almost all the parents earn so little that their children qualify for free lunch." (Later I discovered that some of the parents too come in for free lunch.)

"As for housing," Shapiro continued, "our *middle*-income housing is the low-income St. Nicholas housing project. They send us about three hundred and fifty children. The housing conditions for many others are very bad. Across the street a house built for eight families has forty-five. Next door there are two houses with serious heating problems. Two winters ago, I spent hours trying to track down the owner, and finally I told the man who said he was only the agent that if heat weren't provided, there'd be a picket line of teachers and me. There was heat for the rest of the winter. The next year there was no heat again and we couldn't even find the agent. Finally the city took it over as a public nuisance. Another time for another building, we found someone in the Mayor's office who was vulnerable to picketing and he arranged for the city to take that one over. Nonetheless, the furnace remained broken, and it took us fifteen days of constant pressure to get it fixed. People talk about the 'apathy' of the people here. Well, all of us middle-class 're-spectable' forces, including a neighborhood priest, couldn't get any action for *fifteen days* in the dead of winter with people sick in the building. How do you expect poor people to have confidence *they* can get anything done?"

I mentioned my surprise that a principal would get himself involved in neighborhood housing problems. "Our school," Shapiro answered, "has to have an organic relationship with the community. If the staff tries to take action, that indicates to the community that there *is* hope. *Then* the parents come alive; and in any case, what happens in the street affects our children. Education that stops at three in the afternoon is mis-education."

About ninety-six per cent of the children, Shapiro continued, are Negro. The rest are Puerto Rican, along with a few Chinese children. "We haven't had a white child since 1958." The average class size is 28.3, a little lower than the city average for elementary schools, which is 30.5. "But it's still far too large for our purposes," Shapiro emphasized. "There should be one adult to twelve children, and never more than one to twenty-two. For certain children, one adult for three is right. For some, one for one. And I can think of cases where two adults for one child is the proper ratio."

The little girl in the flowered skirt was back. She gave Shapiro an envelope. "The money's in there." He took it. "When you leave money with someone, Debbie, you should ask for a receipt." "Uh-huh." Shapiro made out a receipt and gave it to her. She put it in her pocket, giggled, and walked away. "Don't lose it," Shapiro said after her.

I observed that the child hadn't been at all constrained about interrupting while Shapiro was talking with an adult. "Oh," he said, "we encourage interruptions. Many of our children are not in real communication with adults. So we have to bring adults into their lives, adults they can depend on and feel at ease with. Coming from large families, often with working mothers and no fathers, our children lose their childhood too early. They become self-reliant, in one sense, too soon. When they're seven or eight, they're as self-reliant as a middle-class young adult. But a dependency relationship with an adult is necessary for children. They should have a long childhood because there's so much to learn. And the school has to be the place where they can be children—a specially created world in which small events are important and in which they can discuss those events with an adult they trust. That's why I keep coming back to the need for smaller classes.

"These interruptions," he continued, "often consist of complaints. The fact that the children have someone—an adult—who listens means that they don't have to be quite so self-reliant, they don't have to take the law into their hands. It means that they can remain children."

We walked into the hall and a gaggle of children rushed by. "They look lively, don't they?" said Shapiro. "And they're very charming. But our children are dying. The way they look conceals the fact that they're dying. It's not like being killed by a car. There's no blood on them, and because there is no visible injury, nobody in the middle class is aghast at the sight. Nobody gets really involved. Let me give you an example of what I mean. Fourteen years ago, two years before I came here, of one hundred and twenty-two children in the sixth grade, only three were reading at grade level. That means one hundred and nineteen children had been separated very effectively from society. They're now twenty-five or twenty-six years old. What kinds of jobs do you think they have? I don't know for sure, but I can make an informed guess. That year one hundred and nineteen children died. And thousands and thousands of other children in this city have been dying because their brain cells have never been fully brought to life. But the white middle class doesn't *see* this. Living in a ghetto, the children are out of sight and out of conscience." . . .

I asked about the current emphasis on preschool training, such as the Head Start program that has been sponsored by the Federal government. "It's important," Shapiro began, "but it's hardly the whole answer. The lives of our children get worse as they grow older, primarily because the lives of their parents get worse. As our children age, when something unusual happens, it's usually something bad. And simultaneously their responsibilities increase. They have more younger siblings to take care of, and their mothers are forced to become more distant as *their* problems and number of children increase. That's why we have to build more and more of an inner protection against the worsening of their lives as they become older. In the kindergarten and the first grade, for instance, there are more children of unbroken families than in the fifth or sixth grades. It gets harder and harder for the fathers to find employment that will bring in enough money and that will also keep their egos intact. And as fathers, precisely because they have self-respect, can no longer fulfill their ego ideals, they begin to disappear. I remember that during the Depression we didn't know what to do with ourselves. But the Negro male in a neighborhood like this is in a permanent Depression much worse than that of the 1930s.

"Therefore, a Project Head Start by itself is not enough. The whole system has to be radically improved. Moreover, the emphasis on the need for preschool educational experience often leads to the assumption that nearly all our children begin school badly damaged. Well, four years ago, we decided to compare a group of children from three schools in poor neighborhoods—one of them P.S. 119—and three schools from middle-class sections. We tested kindergarten children and first-graders who had not gone to kindergarten; and we tested them in their first weeks in class, before they had become contaminated by schooling. We expected great disparity between the Harlem children and the others. Actually, while twenty-five per cent of our children were severely deprived, the other seventy-five per cent were much closer to middle-class norms in terms of knowledge and in terms of their apperceptive abilities than most people had given them credit for. It is *after* the first grade that the disparities between our children and those of the middle class start showing up."

A few mornings later, I was at P.S. 119 a little after nine for an assembly on the fourth floor. As I walked in, I noticed Shapiro standing at the back of the auditorium. At the front, a buxom woman, Mrs. Bonnie Taylor, announced that the assembly was being dedicated to Dr. Shapiro. He winced. Eleven girls stood and sang in unison:

"Oh he is the bravest
Oh he is the greatest
We'll fight before we switch!"

"Talk about brainwashing," Shapiro mumbled, slumped in a back row seat. The children performed—some singing, others reciting. From time to time Shapiro looked around the room. At one point he said softly, "You see that plumpish girl with the brown blouse in the center of the back row? We may lose her, I'm afraid. Her mother is known in the area as a quasi-prostitute, and the other kids used to tease her unmercifully. She'd react with various kinds of aggression and was very difficult to handle. Then I put her in Mrs. Taylor's class. It's an unusual class in that it includes children from the second to the sixth grades who need extra support—who need to be able to believe that an adult cares enough about them to protect them. When they're strong enough, they leave her room to go into their regular grade classes. Mrs. Taylor has forbidden the children in her room to tease that girl, but the child has other problems too. I don't know how long we'll be able to hold her.

"I started that class," Shapiro continued in a whisper, "in 1954. So far as I know, only a few principals in other schools have since tried similar projects. For eight years, we also had a second-grade class for children who had been severely rejected by their parents or whose home situation was especially catastrophic in other ways. These were kids who had to be softened up by close contact, often physical contact."

"You mean," I said, "mothering them? Holding them?" I added that I asked because, in passing a classroom that morning, I had seen a young teacher, whom I later found out to be Lawrence Greenfield, with his arms around a boy. The boy's face was on Greenfield's chest, and Greenfield was patting him gently on the back.

"Yes," Shapiro answered. "In fact, Greenfield had that second-grade class for a couple of years. But I found that teachers couldn't take the strain for more than a year or two, and two years ago I discontinued it because I didn't have a teacher for it at the time. But Mrs. Taylor seems indestructible. She has the kind of bull strength of a King Canute ordering the waves to go back. The most aggressive children soon learn they can't act out against her, and they also learn that she'll protect them against the aggression of others. She visits the homes and makes the relatively few mothers who reject their children toe the line too and support the children. Usually she starts out with a class of about ten, but it increases as the year goes on. Right now she has forty. In addition she comes in very early to be in charge of the yard and she works in the after-school center."

Mrs. Taylor asked Dr. Shapiro to say a few words. He rose, his stoop more pronounced than usual, went to the front of the room, looked at the children, and said, "I'm very moved by this unexpected treat. I've had very few assembly programs

dedicated to me, and I think it's more than I deserve. Thank you very much." He
returned to his back-row seat. "Oh, well," he smiled, "I didn't realize until just now
that today is April Fool's Day."

A thin, alert girl with pigtails and blue-tinted glasses began to conduct an instrumental ensemble. "That's Doreen. She looks charming, doesn't she?" said Shapiro.
"She has very severe problems of aggression. She's in Mrs. Taylor's class too."

I wondered how Shapiro was able to know so many of the children by name and
condition. "I'm not doing as well as I used to," he answered. "A school isn't worth
much unless the principal knows every child by name, but I'm falling behind."

A teacher walked by and Shapiro identified him as Richard Stephenson, a fifth-
grade teacher. A brisk man in his early thirties, Stephenson had found out about
P.S. 119 a couple of years before, while engaged in a remedial reading project for
Negro children in Prince Edward County, Virginia. He had come to see Shapiro
and had been hired.

"He's a very resourceful teacher," Shapiro observed. "He uses all kinds of teaching
methods. Montessori, role playing—anything that seems to work. When he started
with his present class, they were below the national average in reading, but they've
been moving up. He's had them putting together a computer, for example. That
stimulated them to read better because they wouldn't have been able to assemble it
without understanding the instructions. He also makes considerable use of volunteer helpers among the mothers. That project started with his belief mothers should
visit the class whenever they felt like it. More and more did, and some stayed to
help. He visits the homes, sends messages, and is quick to give publicity to the
parents who encourage the children to do their homework conscientiously. He cites
them in a class paper the children put out. The way the children got the computer
kit was by selling cookies. From the proceeds of that they bought stock in a bowling
ball company. When the stock went up, they sold it and bought the kit." . . .

In an hour, Shapiro told me, there was to be a meeting of the school's parents'
association in the teachers' room. I mentioned that Mrs. LaBeet had told me the
P.S. 119 Parents' Association was an aggressive one, although one of the sterotypes
about schools in neighborhoods of the poor is that it's difficult to get parents involved in such groups.

"Well"—Shapiro leaned back—"for a long time it was difficult here too. The
parents didn't trust us and they had good reason not to. One of the problems with
parents in this kind of neighborhood is supposed to be that they're nonverbal. But
they often have very good reasons for not saying much to school administrators.
They're thinking, 'Why don't the children have readers to take home and why don't
they have more of other things too?' But often the parents don't ask, because they
sense the principal is loyal to the system and not to the children, and they figure
'What's the use? He's not going to do anything to change the system.' So it's an act
of intelligence on their part to refuse to enter into what would be a phony dialogue.

"Here the parents were slow to accept that we were talking honestly about the
deficiencies of the school. We told them that what we were doing was much im-
paired because we didn't have the resources to do very much. That kind of admission
was something new in their experience. We admitted, for example, that we didn't
have enough books, and finally we got the parents to write to the Board and ask

for more. Between their efforts and ours we did get more, and then we discovered
that many of the same parents who had seemed inarticulate were very verbal and
quite sophisticated. We began with only ten parents coming to meetings, but eventually we were getting seven hundred and fifty at important meetings. The other
day the room was so full that I, one of the speakers, had to stand in the hall.

"However, there's always a residue of criticism of our school. When I first came,
I began to relax the discipline in the school—in the narrow sense of that word—
and there were parents who interpreted that action as indicating I was just another
white man who didn't care about their children. If I cared, I'd discipline them more.
I think we've proved we do care, but there are still parents who feel our discipline
isn't strong enough. They go off to work and are worried about their children being
alone. So the threat of severe corporal punishment if the child misbehaves is always
in the air, almost like a wireless between the parent and the child. They want us to
'protect' the child in the same way they do. I keep telling them it would actually
be easier for us to use strong discipline—in that narrow sense—but that our staff
tries to develop the children's liveliness. Being 'good' in a rigid sense gets in the
way of learning. The child begins to give the teacher only what the teacher wants
and loses his appetite for learning, his curiosity, and part of his identity.

"We're trying to help them develop an *inner* discipline. A child must have enough
energy left in him to remain courageous. By that I mean the ability to question
rather than always saying, 'Yes, sir,' and 'No, sir.' I think it's good that many of
our children are able to question the wisdom of the adults in this building. It's particularly important for Negro children. They've been taught it's safe to be respectful.
We want them to understand that they're citizens and they *can* question. That is,
they're citizens except for one right—the right not to go to school. It's a very important right, and since we've taken it away from them, it's our responsibility to
make the school as interesting as possible. You know, at Junior High School 136,
where many of our children go when they leave here, our kids are considered outstanding in behavior in that they're not hostile to the teachers. Being able to question them, they can respect and trust them.

"The children in Mr. Marcus's fifth-grade class, incidentally," Shapiro said with
evident satisfaction, "have been doing some important questioning. They analyzed
a sizable number of social studies textbooks and they found every one to be wanting.
Then they wrote letters to the publishers and to some of the people in the school
system pointing out that certain matters of opinion were being treated as facts. The
statement in one book, for example, that on the whole, the slaves were happy on
the plantations. The children got many replies, and not being satisfied with some
of them, they wrote again."

I asked Shapiro what the reaction had been from on high in the school system.

He smiled. "There were inquiries. Nothing was said that was an outright condemnation, but implicit in the questions was: 'How could you let this happen?'
Among the inquiries were: 'What kinds of lessons are being given in that social
studies class? Was the teacher biased? Did you discuss this project with the children?
Perhaps there were better textbooks in the catalogue that were not analyzed?'
Those are the kinds of questions that keep teachers passive. My answer was that at
this point there is no social studies textbook which treats the Negro fairly, and that

the children's questions were a true culmination of their research and were an excellent learning experience.

"Another residue of criticism from the parents," Shapiro continued, "is that the
children aren't achieving well enough. It's obvious to some parents of sixth-grade
children, for instance, that their kids are not reading at sixth-grade level. Some say,
'Why don't you hold the child back?' We do hold some back, but we don't have the
facilities to do much good if we were to keep a lot of them back. And we do have
Reading Improvement Teachers who take small groups out of the classroom for
remedial reading work and who also work with teachers inside the classroom by
concentrating on a particular group and leaving the teacher free to focus on the
rest of the class. We do more of that than most schools. But we don't have enough
teachers and small enough classes to do all that has to be done. The parents have
a very real grievance. Two-thirds of our children in the sixth grade are not reading
at grade level. That's better than ninety-nine per cent when I came, but it's hardly
a triumph. If every teacher in the school were superior, we'd be able to reduce that
proportion to one-third—even with big classes. But the human race being what it
is, it's impossible to get that many superior teachers, just as it's impossible to find
that many superior doctors, psychiatrists, and engineers. Therefore, we have to make
conditions for teaching so good that the average teacher can become effective. If the
context for teaching is superior, the average teacher will do as well as a superior
teacher would have done in a bad setting."

The incident of the rat and the parents' boycott did not make Dr. Shapiro's relationship with his superiors any warmer than it had been. One morning I asked him to
estimate his status at 110 Livingston Street in Brooklyn, the Board's headquarters. "I
would say," he said drily, "that for a long period, it has been recognized that my
opinions are often different from those of the Board of Education, some headquarters
personnel, and the Council of Supervisory Associations, to which most of the other
principals belong. I have regard for the Board of Education, but it has never fully
recognized that it ought to be functioning as the representative of the children. All
children, but most particularly poor children who have the fewest representatives to
power. The Board should make strong, continual statements about the urgent need
for money and services. They should organize their energies in much more dramatic
ways. So far the Board has represented education in a taxpayers' style. Instead they
ought to keep haranguing the city to the point at which a real exploration takes
place of how to get the essential funds. A change in the tax structure, for one way.
Taxation from real estate now accounts for a much smaller proportion of city
revenues than ever before in history. They have to carry the fight to the State and
Federal governments, not just petition. Sure, there'd be some complaints from parts
of the citizenry, but it's useful to get those complaints out in the open. And the
middle class as a whole would not really oppose this kind of push. The middle is
always passive. Alienated from its own beliefs, it doesn't know it has beliefs until
things are stirred up. We have to make education *the* basic industry in this city.

"Specifically," Shapiro said, "if we could extend the school budget by some four
hundred million dollars a year—and that's not much—we could reduce class size
significantly. Oh, it's a sizable sum, but consider it in the context of a municipal

budget that is over *four billion dollars* a year! For only sixty million dollars a year, we could make every elementary school—and perhaps the junior high schools too—in Harlem, the South Bronx, Jamaica, and Bedford-Stuyvesant a qualitatively effective school. In Harlem, it would take six to seven million dollars more a year to make the twenty elementary and junior high schools into qualitatively effective schools. It certainly can't be impossible to get that kind of money."

I mentioned to Shapiro that on the previous Sunday I had heard an assistant superintendent of schools, in a speech to Harlem parents on radio station WLIB, say that "Educationally, we have nothing to be ashamed of here in Harlem."

"It was an honest opinion," Shapiro said, "and it's shared by many people in the system. They mean that they're doing about the best they can with the present resources. But they fail to recognize that resources are not so limited as they have taken them to be. We ought to be ashamed—I mean those of us in the school system—that we have not been leaders for dramatic improvements and that we do participate in a process in which two-thirds—or maybe three-fourths—of the children are being so badly undereducated that we're giving them a lifetime of unemployment.

"Let me give you another example of how all of us have been dropouts as educators," Shapiro went on. "For years, we gave children in neighborhoods like this reading tests—geared to the experiences of middle-class children—and we used those tests as indices of the children's intelligence quotients. The result was a self-fulfilling prophecy. The children, the theory ran, were reading poorly because they were stupid. Consider the insensitivity of the educators in charge. We were torturing the kids with those tests and we were tormenting the teachers as well. Yet no group of principals or of headquarters personnel criticized that technique of demeaning the children. Of course, we had a kind of vested interest in not complaining about the way we were testing them. If you accept the premise that these children have low I.Q.s, according to the national average, our own woeful inefficiency doesn't come out. Only in the past couple of years, as a result of pressure from the civil rights movement, have we stopped giving those standardized, middle-class-biased I.Q. tests. Now we're giving them achievement tests in various subject areas. They too remain middle-class-biased, but at least they're used to judge the child's achievement level rather than as an index of his native endowment of intelligence.

"Why do we have tests?" Shapiro answered his question: "Primarily because we don't have enough personnel. If we had enough personnel, we'd have sufficient understanding of each child in depth and we'd see the test results as they really are—embryonic in a very rudimentary sense." I asked Dr. Shapiro's reaction to a recent statement by Harold Taylor, a former president of Sarah Lawrence College: "We have more tests than we can use now. We test for the wrong things . . . standardized testing paralyzes thinking. Let's throw all the tests out, abolish them, and concentrate on teaching."

Shapiro nodded approvingly. "But," he added, "if we do give tests, let's give them on a one-to-one basis. One child to each tester. That way the test would involve real communication between the tester and the child. If a test is being given to a group of thirty, how can one tester know which children are daydreaming that morning and which didn't have any breakfast?

"There's so much more that can be done besides radically revising testing procedures and getting smaller classes. Take this neighborhood. It's poor. Stores go out
of business, leaving many vacant storefronts—some with backyards—that could be
used as classrooms. From 110th to 145th Streets and between Seventh and Eighth
Avenues, there are the equivalent of forty to fifty potential classrooms. Why not
use them primarily for young children—with the backyards as schoolyards, and with
libraries interspersed here and there? The libraries could be for parents as well as
children and could be open until eight or nine in the evening. We would be coming right into the heart of the community, creating the kind of reciprocal relationship between the community and the schools that you don't find anywhere in this
city—or in the country. We'd be on constant display, and people would be welcome
to come in and see what we're doing. And if they wanted to, they could help as
parent aides. The plan would take care of classroom shortages and would represent
real decentralization. It could be a stimulus toward the creation of a new society. But
we couldn't have an adult-to-pupil ratio of one to twenty-eight in those storefront
schools. That way it couldn't be made interesting enough so that the kids would be
eager to come. The classes would have to be quite small.

"I've proposed this idea to the Board, with the estimate that it would take $4,000
to transform each vacant store into a classroom. The Board's estimate was $10,000,
but even $10,000 isn't that much money when you consider that the average class-
room in a regular school costs more than $60,000 to construct."

I mentioned that Shapiro had yet to talk about ways to integrate the schools. "To
begin with," he said, "the storefront classrooms could increase the possibilities of integration. As you spread out along the avenues, you would break through district
lines and move into neighborhoods that would allow for different racial balances
in those classrooms. There are other ways too. Often segregation is on an economic
basis. Segregation of black and white is more obvious in appearance, but look at
what we have in Harlem. Increasingly fewer middle-class parents—those, for instance,
in Lenox Terrace or the Riverton Houses—send their children to public schools.
Take P.S. 197. It's in a largely middle-class Negro community, and its teachers are
the equivalent of those in the private schools, but hardly any of those middle-class
parents send their children there. We—I mean teachers—have to begin by leafleting
and by approaching these parents and other middle-class parents, both Negro and
white, in other ways, to make an issue of this. Of course, simultaneously, the public
schools in Harlem have to be made much more effective. At present, it may be that
a middle-class child, Negro or white, isn't sufficiently challenged in a class of thirty
made up largely of kids at lower levels of achievement. But in a class of twelve or
fifteen, children coming from different backgrounds would have a lot to offer each
other. Certainly if the class size at P.S. 197 were around ten, those middle-class
parents would send their children there. . . ."

As we talked further about integrating the schools, we moved out of Shapiro's
office because it was time for him to put a dime in the parking meter.

For the new school year, it had been necessary for Shapiro to hire several new
teachers, and when we were back in his office, I asked him what his criteria were.
"Well, if I can see an applicant on the job first as a student teacher, I can perhaps

tell something about her capacities, but I've made mistakes even then. One thing I look for is whether they have a feeling, a liking for children. And whether they have the ability to identify with the needs of the children and of the parents. Are they likely to become self-righteous and recriminatory about parents who, for various reasons, can't or won't come to school often? Then, when I locate a man, I'm apt to be biased in his favor because our children—and for that matter, children in all elementary schools—need more men teachers. Young children are mostly in contact with mothers or substitute mothers, but young girls and boys need to be able to relate to an adult male. Boys, obviously in order to get encouragement to develop ego models; and girls, so that they can more easily accept their essential feminine worth.

"One problem is you may find a teacher—male or female—who appears to have many excellent qualities, and yet that very teacher may do worse in her first year than mediocre colleagues. It's the class size. The best teachers are apt to be those most reluctant to set up routines—ways of passing out paper, raising a hand for recognition to speak or leave the room or go to the wardrobe. They're reluctant because they'd prefer a more human, spontaneous atmosphere in the classroom. But if the class is large, they have to develop routines because they're so outnumbered. They have to show they can control the class. And in the process, their humanity is attenuated. In order to survive, they have to go against their better nature. They're trapped, even as I'm trapped by having to permit more rules in the school than I'd like. And so, when classes are too large, even in the warmest teacher something is lost. As the years go on, moreover, if the classes *remain* large, more and more is lost."

I wondered what he thought of the teacher-training programs in the colleges. "They're not useless, and it's probably better to have them than not, but too often they're given by professors who have had very little experience in large urban school systems. They're not only, by and large, too theoretical, but they're unreal insofar as our kind of school is concerned. For one thing, the professors tend to develop methods and practices that pertain to middle-class suburban school systems, where the class sizes are small. Or, when purportedly dealing with the big city schools, professors often underrate the many poor children who attend those schools. At the same time, they overestimate the help young teachers receive when they break into the public school system. As a result, new teachers become quite discouraged when that degree of assistance isn't forthcoming.

"As for what should be emphasized, I don't like to see someone who's been entirely an education major. The teacher ought to have a major interest in at least one other subject—social studies or math or English—and a good liberal arts background, in general. Also, at one point or another—in the senior year or after graduation—the prospective teacher should become involved in an intensified internship program, much like a medical internship. I mean working in a public school and attending workshops held in that school. Workshops based on a critical evaluation of what they've participated in and perceived in the classrooms, the corridors, the school-yards, and at parents' meetings. And there ought to be another workshop on how the teacher can become a citizen of the school and of the community.

"That," said Shapiro forcefully, "is why I'd especially like to see teacher-training programs oriented toward trade unionism. In New York City, the United Federation of Teachers is providing a structure of support so that the teacher *can* be lively, energetic, and inventive without fear of reprisals. Now 'lively' is a tricky word in some cases. I've said that our children are lively, and they are; but sometimes what seems to be liveliness may be a galvanic response after the rest of the body has been killed. It may be an irritability left over after the rest of the body has died. But let us grant the essential liveliness of our children. How does a teacher make the most of that liveliness, and how can he best avoid dampening it?

"Suppose, for example, in a social science lesson, the teacher is talking about this being a democratic society. And a kid says, 'Teach, we have no heat at home. What do we do in this democratic society to get heat?' If the teacher doesn't formulate some plan in which the children can participate—picketing or other ways that might change the situation—the children won't buy the lesson. In New York, because of the U.F.T., teachers *can* work out that sort of plan. They can capitalize on the real liveliness in the children and they can extend irritability into liveliness. Almost nowhere else in the country can a teacher do this. But so far, hardly any New York teachers *know* the scope of the possibilities in this direction. They don't have a full enough sense of their own strength through the grievance machinery that's been set up.

"Previously, if a teacher in the system had advocated, let us say, a rent strike, the principal could forbid it. And most would have forbidden it on the ground that a rent strike is not proper activity for a teacher. If the teacher had gone ahead, he would have been found guilty of insubordination or of conduct unbecoming a teacher. So, under those circumstances, it was more than an existential act for a teacher to follow through. It was a reckless act. Now teachers *can* follow through, but the U.F.T. leadership is failing in its responsibility to make its members aware of the extent of this breakthrough.

"What I'm driving at is that when some educational theorists call for teachers to nurture the liveliness of slum kids, they must also recognize that once the liveliness *is* aroused, it cannot always be contained in a classroom. But since teachers outside New York City cannot go beyond the classroom, they'd be betraying the children in an example like the one I cited of *telling* them this is a democratic society but not showing them how to *make* it democratic for *them*. There would be no way for the children to *experience* that democracy in action. That's why, when I was asked recently at a meeting of educators whether I thought a teacher should first encourage the liveliness of his children or should first join the U.F.T., I said unhesitatingly that he should start by joining the U.F.T. Then, when he does nurture that liveliness—and is inevitably tested by the kids to take some kind of action inside the school or out—he's able to prove he's for real.

"You see, with this kind of protection from their union, teachers could be so important in advising, participating in, and stirring up community action. Not only about education, but about neighborhood rehabilitation and other problems that directly concern the children as well as their parents. Think of masses of teachers marching with parents and with other people in the community! That's an important new role for teachers to play—instead of being dropouts, as teachers and as human beings.

I dropped in to see Miss Carmen Jones. The assistant principal was in her office, looking glumly at a sheaf of achievement scores. "I'm always dismayed," she said, "that some of our children do so poorly on tests. I go into classes and see children who are so bright and knowledgeable, who express themselves so freely. But often none of those qualities are reflected in their test scores. I don't know why. If I did, I'd do something about it. Sure, the scores show that we're doing a little better, but the scores are not good enough for the time and effort we put in. Part of it, I'm convinced, is that, even though we no longer have the group intelligence tests, there's a middle-class bias in the language used for the achievement tests. Much of the terminology is simply outside our children's experience. Look." She showed me a page of questions in a third-grade vocabulary test. "Trout. These kids don't know about trout. Their mothers buy porgies. And their fathers certainly don't go fishing. Well, we're going to have to give the children more practice in the types of tests they have to take." . . .

The conversation with Miss Jones reminded me of a talk I'd had during the summer with a woman who has long been active in organizations committed to greater integration in the New York City public school system and to radical improvement in the education of all slum children. She has been a frequent visitor to P.S. 119 and is an admirer of Dr. Shapiro. "But there's still something wrong there," she had told me. "Those kids are not scoring as high as they should in the tests. It may be that all the understanding they get in that school, while it does help them develop a better self-image, doesn't help them to achieve. Shapiro and his teachers are certainly compassionate, but the children's parents are *ambitious* for their kids. Shapiro is like from another world. He has the kind of values all of us ought to have. But when they leave the school, those kids aren't going into his kind of world. They're going into a world that's increasingly competitive, and increasingly cybernated as well. Maybe it damages a kid to push him, but I keep wondering whether Shapiro isn't damaging them in another way. Are his kids going to have enough competitive drive to do more than survive?"

Later in the day, while we were walking again to the parking meter, I told Shapiro what the woman had said. "I agree with her," he began, "at least on the point that our children do not achieve enough. We're far behind. But as for the style of our school, just because they are going to have to be in a cybernated world, it's imperative that children remain human beings. In that respect, it's vital, for example, for children of all kinds of backgrounds to be in small enough classes so that they can have close and pleasurable relationships with adults. All of us are becoming more and more like I.B.M. machines in an increasingly organized and rationalized society, and all children ought to have the experience of real human contact, so they'll remember later on that human contact is both possible and pleasurable. And our children, of course, need that most of all.

"Getting back to achievement, you have to remember that our children are among the poorest of the poor. But they are achieving more, as a group, than children used to achieve here in the past. And again, part of the measure of their achievement is lost, because in the fourth grade we send out our best achievers to I.G.C. classes. The children, moreover, are also achieving the courage of their convictions. The very fact that Mr. Marcus' fifth-graders were able to write critically to publishers and to superintendents about the inadequacies of social studies textbooks is an indication they may have the spirit to contend with what lies ahead. It's most important to nurture that kind of spirit. Our children are Negro, and as young Negro adults, they'll have more than their proper share of responsibilty for making the human race live like human beings."

Shapiro was silent for a minute or two. "However, there is disturbing validity in the criticism about underachievement, and it pertains to every school that is seriously understaffed." I asked Shapiro about an observation by one of the parents that at P.S. 119, it was the middle group—rather than the best and the worst of achievers—which was often overlooked. He nodded. "Around 1955," he said, "I became aware of the fact that no child in the school at the time was going to make it to college. It seemed to me that we therefore had to put a sizable amount of the resources we had into working with those children who seemed to be the most likely achievers. And since those resources were so slight, we had very little left over. Now, barring not too catastrophic circumstances in junior high school, in high school, in their lives, and in the community, twenty per cent of our children have a good chance to reach college. That's a great improvement, but the degree of our deprivation can be measured by the fact that sixty per cent of *all* children in the country are now reaching college.

"What of the others here? While we were focusing a great deal of energy and resources on the better achievers, we were also trying to make the entire school a place more favorable for, as it were, human contact—a freer place in which to teach and in which to be a child. Gradually, we were able thereby to develop a relatively stable staff, so that the middle range of children also would have a sequence of teachers who were relatively more experienced than those the children used to have here. And there has been some degree of improvement in the achievement of the middle children. But the fact remains that, after we get past the best achievers, there is a precipitous drop. We have a very long way to go. And we need a great deal of help."

Questions for Discussion

1. Specifically, what does Shapiro do to try to keep his children from dying?
2. Do you believe that a school principal—or teacher—should be actively involved in helping correct the home life and living conditions of his students?
3. Are you attracted to the idea of the storefront schools? What about analyzing social science textbooks as the subject for studying the social sciences? And do you agree with his comments on the teacher-training programs in colleges?

16 Teaching the Disadvantaged

Joseph Loretan and Shelley Umans

Finally, we come to the teacher in a classroom of disadvantaged students. How will he teach language and communication skills? Social studies? Vocational training? Physical sciences? Art? The authors describe some of the research conclusions on these topics, and apply them to the classroom situation. As you read, note not only the specific suggestions which are made, but try to discern the underlying theory of the ends and means of education which is assumed by these authors.

The youngster from the disadvantaged home is half a reality, half a myth. The reality of him startles us because it is unpleasant and with us all the time—in the subways, on the streets, on the unemployment lines, in the newspapers, and in the so-called difficult schools. This reality affects our emotions, our physical safety, and our taxes.

The myth, on the other hand, does not startle us. It is something we unthinkingly accept. We speak of this mythical youngster as being of a "different breed"; we say that his intellectual capacity is below par, and, therefore, his school experience should be curtailed; we term his educational needs "basic" and so decide that his curriculum must be simplified and repetitive; we call him "culturally different" and spend our time (and his) teaching him to conform.

Let us, however, look at this child, not through our reaction to him, but through a study of his intellectual and emotional anatomy. When we speak of the deprived child, we speak of all nationalities and races—Puerto Ricans, Mexicans, Negroes, and whites—whether born in rural areas, small towns, or cities. The designation of "deprived" should not be equated with membership in any ethnic group, but should be defined in terms of characteristics of the individual and/or his environment. Furthermore, not all such youngsters will exhibit all the symptoms of the "deprivation syndrome"; in some such children, all these may be absent. What will be described here are those characteristics that are found with sufficient frequency in this population to be given primary consideration.

Who Is the Disadvantaged Child?

The child whom we designate as "deprived" or "disadvantaged" differs from the "undeprived" or "advantaged" in language development, self-concept, and social skills, as well as in attitude toward schooling and society. He has fewer interests than the middle-class child. His form of communication, unlike that of other children entering school, tends to consist mostly of gestures, sounds (nonwords), and local words. Just as he has inadequate linguistic skills of expression, so has he in-

Reprinted with the permission of the publisher from Joseph Loretan and Shelley Umans' *Teaching the Disadvantaged* (New York: Teachers College Press), © 1966, Teachers College, Columbia University.

adequate receptive skills. He does not hear sounds as we pronounce them. He tends to "close out" many noises around him (including the teacher's voice). When he does hear us, our words do not necessarily mean to him what they mean to us. He does not feel the need to communicate through language. In fact, language—like schooling—is for others, not him. Perhaps the most serious characteristic of the deprived child is his feeling of inadequacy. He devalues himself. He comes into school feeling that accomplishment and success are impossible for him. This suspicion, of course, is quickly confirmed, not only by academic failure, which he experiences almost from the day he enters school, but also by his recognition that he lacks the social skills demanded by the middle-class teacher: manner of dress, mode of response, respect for authority. If, in class, he finds himself among children from the dominant culture, his feeling of being different is reinforced—their ways are "acceptable"; his are not.

The disadvantaged youngster has experienced no logical pattern in life; things just happen. He lives *now*, not in the future. He has had little or no experience in setting and proceeding toward goals and in evaluating or reviewing past actions as to whether or not they were "worth it." When the disadvantaged youngster acts, it is usually in response to an immediate stimulus; there is little room in his scheme for second thoughts, meditation, or planning.

Sidney Kingsley's play, *Dead End,* produced in 1936, described what we now refer to as the disadvantaged, although he viewed them as a geographical phenomenon— "have-nots" who were living in a district surrounded by "haves." Today we view these children in another dimension. The "dead end" applies, not only to their physical environment, but to their intellectual environment as well. Because enlarging experiences are missing from their lives, their intellectual world is restricted to the apparent; their experiences are action experiences; a task accomplished is self-fulfilling and seldom opens up other fields of investigation. These youngsters may realistically be referred to as "limited," but limited in scope, not in intellect. The world is not open to them.

Children from disadvantaged homes are not motivated to learn. Schooling has not "paid off" for their kind. They see little value in spending time in school. Perhaps their most perplexing problem in this completely alien world of education is finding their role: Who am I? Am I really different? Will I always be like this? Is it wrong to be like this? Am I guilty? This searching for self is subconscious, rarely verbalized. On the contrary, the disadvantaged child often gives the impression of not caring. All his behavior, however, points to the conclusion that he is searching for an answer, for an identity.

The problems of this youngster become aggravated as he proceeds through school. Although the "deprivation syndrome" is generally recognized by teachers and school people, little has been done to accommodate school experience to the needs of this child. As early as the first grade, he is grouped homogeneously because he is lowest on the scale of readiness to learn. By the time he enters second grade, he has fallen behind the rest of the class—he has become a misfit. At this point, it is justifiable to ask whether the objective of education is to fit the youngster into the school at any cost, or to bring the school into harmony with the child. (Does "child-centered" school really mean "conforming-child-centered" school?) The cycle of defeat starts almost immediately. Instead of overcoming, or at least compensating for, cultural limitations, the school reinforces negative feelings and now adds educational deprivation to cultural deprivation.

The problem of the disadvantaged child is not new to educators. However, in considering children with cultural and educational problems, we appear to have spent most of our time and energy classifying them, describing their characteristics, seeking to isolate the causes of deprivation, and warning society of the consequences if nothing is done. Yet, in terms of actually improving the curriculum for these children, we have done little except to intellectualize the problem. A recent cartoon in a New York newspaper depicts an impoverished sage who aptly expresses this point of view:

I used to think I was poor.
Then they told me I wasn't poor, I was NEEDY.
Then they told me it was self-defeating to think of myself as needy, I was DEPRIVED.
Then they told me deprived was a bad image, I was UNDERPRIVILEGED.
Then they told me underprivileged was overused, I was DISADVANTAGED.
I still don't have a dime.
But I have a GREAT vocabulary.[1]

Is this what we have been doing—creating a vocabulary, a jargon, a cult, but producing disadvantaged adults to replace disadvantaged children?

The authors of this book predicate their thesis upon two basic assumptions: (1) Despite the negative approach to school and school learnings, children from disadvantaged homes have intellectual capacities far greater than is commonly believed. (2) The school, operating on the assumption stated above, and constructing curricula based upon the new developments in the behavioral sciences, can—to a great extent—counteract the effects of cultural deprivation.

The Intellectual Capacities of Children from Disadvantaged Homes

So long as it was assumed that intelligence was fixed, and was a consequence of the genes, we wrongly accepted the intellectual inferiority of children who tested below normal. We found, by apparent coincidence, that these same youngsters came from backgrounds of economic and educational deprivation. Again we were misled; since a disproportionate number of the children in economically and educationally deprived areas were Negro, it was assumed, at least by some, that there were inherent racial differences accounting for differences in the capacity to learn. However, this theory has been refuted by almost all scientific opinion. The UNESCO international committee of sociologists, anthropologists, psychologists, and geneticists said in its report:

It is now generally recognized that intelligence tests do not themselves enable us to differentiate safely between what is due to innate capacity and what is the result of environmental influences, training and education. . . . In short, given similar degrees of cultural opportunity to realize their potentialities, the average achievement of the members of each ethnic group is about the same.[2]

[1] Jules Feiffer, *The New York Post* (February 17, 1965), p. 41.
[2] UNESCO, *The Rau Concept: Results of an Inquiry.* (Paris: UNESCO, 1952), p. 100.

A similar conclusion was reached by the American Association for the Advancement of Science Committee on Science in the Promotion of Human Welfare.[3]

What is now being seriously questioned is the use of our basic intelligence indicators, the IQ test. There is sufficient cumulative research to prove that there are significant differences in intelligence score distribution between children who live in depressed areas and those who do not, and that cultural differences *do* affect IQ scores to the extent that such scores have low predictive validity when used for cross-cultural comparisons.

The Journal of Social Issues (April 1964) offers one of the most direct presentations of current evidences of the effects of culture on the educational aspirations and achievements of U.S. Negroes. As a Supplement, the *Journal* reports the findings of the Work Group for the Psychological Study of Social Issues (Division 9 of the American Psychological Association). The committee concludes flatly that social deprivation challenges the validity of tests. In part, it explains that national norms do not allow for adequate differentiation at the lower end of aptitude or ability scales.[4] In discussing predictive validity, the committee states:

> For example, no inequity is necessarily involved if a culturally disadvantaged child is simply reported to have an IQ of 84 and a percentile rank of 16 on national norms for a certain intelligence test. However, if this is interpreted as meaning that a child ranks as well as or will rank no higher in learning ability than does a middle-class, native born child of the same IQ, the interpretation might well be erroneous.[5]

Deutsch and Brown conclude on the basis of their studies:

> The present data on family cohesion and pre-school experience represent two possible environmental modifiers of intelligence test performance that would seem to account for a portion of differences found between ethnic, class or experiential groups.[6]

Interpretation of test scores is perhaps the greatest danger in testing. If an individual's score is to be used to describe his standing among a *specified norm group,* the fact that a child has had a minority group background is not important. It is when *prediction* enters the picture that background becomes important.

Back in 1900, before he had turned most of his attention to psychometrics, Binet concerned himself with the educability of intelligence, taking five or six aspects of intelligence that he thought could be trained. He organized classes to prove that "mental orthopedics" could be used to improve the ability to memorize, reason, and perceive. Working among the poor in Paris, he suggested that learning and environment interacted and that with a richer environment one's mental abilities could be improved. He wrote:

[3] Editorial, *Science,* 142, No. 3592 (November 1, 1963), pp. 558–561.

[4] Work Group for the Psychological Study of Social Issues, "Guidelines for Testing Minority Group Children," *The Journal of Social Issues* (Supplement), 20, No. 2 (April 1964), p. 133.

[5] *Ibid.,* p. 134.

[6] Martin Deutsch and Bert Brown, "Social Influences in Negro-White Intelligence Differences," *The Journal of Social Issues,* 20, No. 2 (April 1964), p. 34.

A child's mind is like a field for which an expert farmer has advised a change in the method of cultivation, with the result that in place of desert we now have a harvest. It is in this particular sense, the one which is significant, that we say that the intelligence of children may be increased. One increases that which constitutes the intelligence of a school child, namely, the capacity to learn to improve with instruction.[7]

Yet, in the years to come, Binet's hypothesis was largely neglected. Training of mental abilities was not considered possible. Some of the experimental work of Thorndike and others was used as proof that attempts to "improve the mind" in a general way through a study of specific discipline was useless. The presumption that genetic factors weighed heavily in intelligence also discouraged attempts at intellectual training. Now these concepts are being modified through the research of Bruner, Piaget, Guilford, and others. IQ is no longer considered "constant," nor is it deemed to measure all aspects of intelligence. We now realize the enormous effect of deprivation on learning. More and more the evidence is piling up that grinding poverty, because of its detrimental physical effect on the mother and its concomitant stunting of stimulation in the growing child, is a powerful factor in causing the educational retardation of the children of the poor. . . .

A Curriculum to Counteract Cultural Deprivation

In looking at the curricula developed in the universities and school systems over the last ten years, several factors become evident: (1) They are generally based on the newer findings of the behavioral scientists regarding how children learn; (2) they are developmental; and (3) their content is current, sophisticated, and challenging.

However, almost all curriculum innovations developed in the 1950's and early 1960's were directed toward the gifted youngster. From Harvard to Berkeley, the bright child was the chief object of experimentation. On the basis of his reactions, curriculum experiences were planned and tried. At about the same time, however, scientific inquisitiveness led the developers of these new programs to take their curricula into the inner city and to the Appalachia-like rural districts. They knew their new curricula could be successful with the "haves"; they wanted to know the effect on the "have-nots." What they found was what they had suspected. These youngsters did not, of course, move as fast or as far as the gifted children for whom the curricula were developed, but they did become interested, stimulated, and intellectually restless. In most cases, attendance improved and teachers became more interested in teaching.

What are the elements in the newer curricula that "stir" the disadvantaged youngster? The literature and courses of study concerning disadvantaged children are filled with such statements as: "He needs less," "The curriculum must be simplified," and "We must stress the basic skills." These sentiments are usually reflected in the curriculum. The programs are bland, watered down, and lacking in content. Yet the disadvantaged youngster needs just the opposite of a bland, dull curriculum.

[7] Alfred Binet, *Les Idées Modernes sur les Enfants* (Paris: Ernest Flamarion, 199), pp. 54–55, cited in G. D. Stoddard, "The IQ, Its Ups and Downs," *Educational Record*, 20 (1939), pp. 44–57.

He is the one who lives for today, who settles his problems as they come, who seldom plans. He is the one who needs stimulation, motivation, challenging content. He needs exposure, not enclosure. . . .

[In addition,] given the minimal language facility of disadvantaged children versus the heavy emphasis, in the first few grades, on verbalization, how can they avoid frustration and failure? Piaget has demonstrated that children can handle problems intuitively. He calls for teaching techniques in which children can work on problems without giving verbal explanations. Bruner says that children, during this operational stage from seven to eleven, are capable of grasping many of the basic ideas of mathematics, science, humanities, and social science. Bruner defines this capability as "a means of getting data about the real world into the mind and then transferring them so that they can be organized and used selectively in the solution of a problem."[8] Gallagher says:

> The apparent mistake of past generations of teachers was to assume that the child had to be able to present a formal structure of thought (for example, the formulation of a proof for a geometric theorem) in order to demonstrate his grasp of the concept. The child in the stage of concrete operations cannot give a formal organization of complex theoretical ideas, but he *can* solve many problems depending upon such ideas.[9]

We make the error of assuming that the child must *verbalize* the answer in order to show he has learned it. At this stage the youngster cannot formulate theoretical ideas, but he can *solve* problems that depend on these ideas.

Many of the programs described in this book do not demand verbal responses; neither do they reject them, if the child wishes to state the concept. The youngster has the learning experience as often as is necessary and may solve the problem in his own mind. The theory, or generalization, can take its time. It may not be until the second grade, or even later, in the elementary school that he formulates the theory. Not requiring verbal responses, however, does not mean that these children do not need help in language development. It merely means that formal verbalizing is not necessary to prove that learning has taken place and that children should not be "pressed" into formulating answers.

It is important, of course, that children from disadvantaged homes be given language experiences as early as they are psychologically ready for them. Deutsch[10] indicates that class differences in perceptual abilities and general environmental orientation decrease with age, while language differences tend to increase. Compensatory programs in language, offering these students experiences in syntactical forms in written and oral language, rather than emphasis on grammatical forms,

[8] Jerome S. Bruner, *The Process of Education* (Cambridge, Mass.: Harvard University Press, 1960), p. 35.

[9] James J. Gallagher, "Productive Thinking," in Martin L. Hoffman and Lois Wladis Hoffman (Eds.), *Review of Child Development Research*, Vol. 1 (New York: Russell Sage Foundation, 1964), p. 356.

[10] Martin Deutsch, "The Disadvantaged Child and the Learning Process," in A. Harry Passow (Ed.), *Education in Depressed Areas* (New York: Teachers College Press, Teachers College, Columbia University, 1963), pp. 163–179.

are not only advisable for language development but important in minimizing language differences as children get older.

In the general area of language development, one might also question the place of reading in the hierarchy of communication. Times have changed, and the media of communication have multiplied. Since the advent of the printing press, books have been the principal repository of man's heritage—intellectual, cultural, and social. "Book learning" was synonymous with education. Today there are other media and repositories of communication, such as radio, films, television, and teaching machines. The average man can function in society as a social being, a wage earner, and a citizen with far less reading ability than in the past.

We do not suggest that man could not improve himself if he had more competency in reading, but nevertheless he can still function adequately on a less verbal level. Marshall McLuhan says:

> In the electronic age which succeeds the typographic and mechanical ear of the past five hundred years, we encounter new shapes and structures of human interdependence and of expression which are "oral" in form even when the components of the situation may be non-verbal.[11]

Should we not then re-examine the value of giving priority to reading instruction and consider, instead, rearranging the order of communication skills and reading's primary position? This proposal might be considered for all children, but it should be given special consideration for the disadvantaged youngster in whom prereading skills are almost completely lacking upon entrance into school. This child does have other communication skills. For example, the slum child has a highly selective hearing instrument by the time he enters school. He is able to close out sound at will, and he can select, therefore, what he wishes to hear and what he does not. He will usually make his choice, not on an intellectual basis, but on subjective bases, depending upon who is talking or whether he feels like listening at all. When he enters school, he often closes out the teacher and other sounds relating to schooling, electing to listen to sounds that do little for his education. Deutsch, in his experiments with slum children in New York City, bases part of his program on "selected listening." Once the youngster learns to tune in, instead of close out, the school sounds, he has a communication skill that is invaluable for learning.

Another communication skill seen in children from disadvantaged neighborhoods is the use of gesture to convey meaning. They have always used their bodies and their hands to express themselves, probably more so than verbally communicative children. The linguists tell us that bodily movements, as well as the stressing of words and syllables, give meaning. Why not encourage this skill and combine it with listening and speaking, so that communication becomes easier and more interesting? . . .

A strong argument can be made for giving the disadvantaged child an earlier start. John Fischer compares present-day schooling to a race in which the disadvantaged start twenty feet behind the others. Perhaps an earlier start can help

[11] Marshall McLuhan, *The Gutenberg Galaxy: The Making of Typographic Man* (Toronto: University of Toronto Press, 1962), p. 3.

compensate for the experiences denied this child in his home environment and help diminish the twenty-foot "handicap."

Until the middle 1950's, the theory persisted that children should not have their infancy spoiled by having to start school too early. The theories of Washburn and his contemporaries persisted: The very young child was just not ready for school. In the face of later research, however, a new attitude began to emerge. Bloom,[12] in describing general intelligence and using the absolute scales of intellectual development formulated by Thorndike, Thuston, and Heines, suggests that 50 per cent of development takes place between conception and age four, 30 per cent between ages four and eight, and 20 per cent between eight and seventeen. Bloom does not subscribe to the thesis that intelligence is a physical or neurological growth function analogous to height growth and that it must have a definite terminal growth point; however, he maintains that intelligence, as presently measured, does reach a plateau in the period ages of ten to seventeen, after which further growth and development are likely only if encouraged by powerful forces in the environment.

If, as according to the above view, as much development takes place in the first four years of life as in the next thirteen, then any years lost in a poor environment are almost irretrievable. It is impossible to emphasize too heavily the importance of the first few years of elementary school, as well as of the preschool period, in the development of learning patterns and general achievement. Failure to develop learning patterns in these years may lead to failure throughout the student's school career. Bloom, in another study,[13] further breaks down the figures and estimates that 17 per cent of intellectual growth takes place between the ages of four and six. If this is the case, then it is reasonable to assume that schooling during these years can have far-reaching effects in a child's learning patterns.

These studies also raise questions as to the value of remedial programs. If 80 per cent of one's intellectual development takes place before the age of eight, how much can be accomplished by remediation, or unlearning and relearning, after that age? The country is spending millions of dollars on dropout and "last-chance" programs; however, what little evaluation we have done on these programs tells us that few are "saved," and even those who do stay on in school have marginal existences there—the slightest upset drives them out of school. The implications of early intellectual development, coupled with the apparent lack of success of salvage programs, support the basic hypothesis that a curriculum based on learning theory appropriate to the disadvantaged child, and starting at least two years before the traditional schooling, can compensate for much of the deprivation experienced by these youngsters.

A word of caution should be expressed, however, as to the evaluation of preschool programs. Just as the dropout programs have not been adequately scrutinized, so is there a danger that preschool programs will be adopted emotionally, without proper field testing. Although we have theoretical bases for establishing preschool

[12] Benjamin S. Bloom, *Stability and Change in Human Characteristics* (New York: Wiley, 1964), p. 68.
[13] *Ibid.*, p. 110.

education, we have very few longitudinal studies of present projects to show the results of preschool education. This lack of research may be due to the newness of the programs. It is hoped, however, that educators will not forget to build such evaluation studies into the programs at their onset.

Value Conflicts Between the Haves and the Have-nots

Changing concepts of "moral conduct," "sets of values," or "good behavior"— whatever term one uses—have given rise to many questions regarding social relationships. Morality has generally been regarded as conscience, as a set of culture rules of social action which have been internalized by the individuals. Moral development has been conceived of as the increase of such internalization of basic cultural rules.[14]

When communities were separate and remote, they were entities unto themselves. A value system evolved, and all those who lived in the community were expected to adhere to it. But, as the members of communities increased, people spilled over the boundaries, and the law of one community sometimes clashed with the law of the neighboring community. The United States is moving increasingly toward the establishment of common values. However, when we examine these common values, we find they do not apply to disadvantaged groups. These people have not become acculturated; they guard their identity and live in a culture as different from the standard culture as their speech is from standard speech.

To begin with, children from disadvantaged cultures usually have different codes of behavior. Their values are weighted differently because of their experiences. It is at school that the first confrontation with another culture takes place. Havighurst and Taba describe the basic character traits of our cultural ideal as honesty, loyalty, responsibility, moral courage, and friendliness. With the exception of friendliness, all these traits require adhering to cultural norms of action. The problem for the school, therefore, is to build a bridge to help these children understand the cultural norms of the school.

There are those who argue for *adherence* to the prevailing cultural norms, while others maintain that the school should adapt the culture norms to the community culture. Whichever view one takes, the norms, or standards, should be those that provide for mutual respect among all people.

There are also those who argue that values can only be taught by the home and the church. This is questionable since no institution has been found to be the infallible impregnator of values. Perhaps each can attempt inculcation in its own way, but the role of the school cannot be underestimated.

Piaget believes that the cognitive limitation in the child from age three to eight leads him to confuse moral rules with physical laws and to view laws as fixed external things, rather than as the instruments of human purposes and values.[15] Sears,

---

[14] Lawrence Kohlberg, "Development of Moral Character and Moral Ideal," in Harold W. Stevenson (Ed.), *Child Psychology*, Sixty-second Year-book of the National Society for the Study of Education, Vol. I (Chicago: University of Chicago Press, 1963), p. 384.

[15] Jean Piaget, *The Moral Judgment of the Child* (Glencoe, Ill.: The Free Press, 1948).

Maccoby, and Levin place the age in which conscience is determined as approximately in the first six to ten years.[16]

If as according to Piaget, the preschool years have little effect in shaping moral values, and if the six-to-ten period is as important as Sears and others claim, then it is incumbent upon the custodians of the child during those years to help him develop an inner moral structure. This is particularly important to the disadvantaged child who may not live by the normal code of the school society.

The problem arises as to how this is done. How does one instill a code of ethics? Can it be achieved through a direct method of moral persuasion, of setting down rules to live by and taboos to avoid? To what extent can one's behavior be shaped by dogma? The research of Hartsharne and May, for example, found no relationship between behavioral tests of honesty or service, and exposure to Sunday school or to the Boy Scout code. In fact, Rau,[17] as recently as 1964, found no positive or consistent relationship between training in good habits and the measure of a child's obedience.

Without completely rejecting the fact that rules or laws may in and of themselves have value to some children, how can one provide other avenues for formulating values? The curriculum thus far has been untapped in this area. Although we have always declared that the purpose of education is to create the better man, there are two questions we have not been able to answer specifically: (1) What do we mean by a better man—is he rigidly "moral," or is he flexible and adaptable? (2) How do we go about creating this man? Values and moral judgments can be taught as part of the curriculum, not in the sense of the "model" or the reprimand, but by introducing through the disciplines the content from which one can evolve values. By introducing into the elementary school and secondary school curricula the study of such areas as political science, sociology, history, psychology, anthropology, the law, economics, government, the family, the work order, the human mechanism, and the interrelationships of man, one can present situations that cause children to make value judgments.

For example, in anthropology, the study of other cultures can lead a student to understand that there are ways other than his own which are compatible with human needs and dignity. He might then be able to re-examine his own culture with a certain objectivity and with a view toward considering his own conduct and the institutions of his own society. If he could understand that each culture has its values and that such values make sense, the youngster from the disadvantaged area might not be as hostile to the values of the school culture. The study of civil rights and civil responsibilities, of the making of revolutions, and of political upheaval and its causes can all lead children to discuss reasons for actions and outcomes. Perhaps he can then see the need for certain values and internalize these values so that he controls and applies them, not because they are "right," but because he understands and accepts them.

At no time should one underestimate the contribution of the teacher. A thorough-

[16] R. R. Sears, E. E. Maccoby, and H. Levin, *Patterns of Child Rearing* (Evanston, Ill.: Row, Peterson, 1957), p. 367.
[17] L. Rau, "Conscience and Identification," in R. R. Sears, L. Rau, and R. Alpert (Eds.), *Identification and Child Rearing* (Stanford, Calif.: Stanford University Press, in press).

going "moralist" may antagonize the child by building up an unwholesome sense of guilt, but a teacher with a conscientious interest in stimulating moral development may, through subject matter, provide a valuable supplement to concrete experience.

A New Look at Guidance

Instilling in youngsters an understanding of values and moral conduct is, or should be, closely allied to that part of the school program known as "guidance." In reviewing school budgets in areas where large numbers of children come from disadvantaged homes, we find that one of the largest allocations of funds is for "guidance." It is interesting to note that children who come into school with what the school terms academic ability are given a rich program of academic subjects. On the other hand, children who come into school with less academic ability are given fewer academic experiences and more "guidance."

In a study published by the Russell Sage Foundation,[18] involving four hundred post-delinquent fourteen-year-old girls who had entered a central Manhattan vocational high school six years earlier, it was found that individual counseling by itself was ineffective in improving their school behavior or in reducing the number of dropouts.

Again we must question the method. Can we change school behavior of a child from a disadvantaged environment by motivating him to learn through an understanding of his problems, which is the general goal of guidance programs? Or, are there other methods of creating motivation and change in school behavior? Ausubel, in discussing intrinsic motivation, suggests that, although culturally deprived children typically manifest little motivation to learn, we may discover a more effective method of developing intrinsic motivation by focusing on the cognitive rather than the motivational aspects of learning, the idea being, that successful educational achievement may develop "retroactively" motivation that was not previously in evidence. Ausubel continues: "Frequently, the best way of motivating an unmotivated pupil is to ignore his motivationless state and to concentrate on teaching him as effectively as possible."[19] Furthermore, success through achievement is perhaps the longest but most effective way of fostering an improved self-concept, of helping children overcome their tendency to devaluate themselves as scholars or students.

It is suggested by the authors, therefore, that the cycle be reversed and that more time be given to academic endeavors and less time to guidance, that children be given the opportunity to learn and achieve through learning, and in that way become motivated toward schooling. In addition to improving his self-image by proving that he *can* achieve, the child also learns to understand himself and his problems through a study of the subject disciplines. The English language, the social sciences, and the physical sciences help children, through the study of man, his origin, his psyche, his social environments, his means of communicating, and his physical and social abilities and limitations, to gain a better understanding of themselves.

[18] Russell Sage Foundation, *Girls and Vocational High* (New York, Author, 1965).
[19] David P. Ausubel, "How Reversible Are the Cognitive and Motivational Effects of Cultural Deprivation?", paper read at the Conference on Teaching the Culturally Deprived Child, Buffalo, N.Y., March 28–30, 1963 (mimeographed).

Through an understanding of one's self and one's place in society and school, it is possible to develop a "built-in" self-guidance. . . .

We must also look at the whole spectrum of vocational education. We must ask ourselves whether we may not be mistaken in assuming that children from disadvantaged homes, in order to be successful, must be relegated to vocational education. Indeed, if this is the case, how are we to account for the high rate of unemployment among the disadvantaged? A more important and basic question must be raised: What are the elements of learning that are vital to becoming a successful worker in the working society?

To begin with, children need a knowledge of the work process: What does it mean? What is its structure? Students can be introduced into the work process through the social sciences—anthropology, sociology, and psychology. They can learn how people have used work as a means of bettering themselves through the centuries and discover how to achieve personal satisfaction from doing a job well. Technology must not be regarded as something divorced from the essence of humanity. Technology is inseparable from men and communities. When the Peace Corps builds a road in tropical Africa, that road is more than an exercise in civil engineering. It is a major experiment in social anthropology, for it effects the primitive, up-country villages and acts as a communication link which will stimulate the acculturation of these people to modern Western society. Nearly every technical activity has social consequenses; technology is of humanistic interest, not only because it is a product of the human mind, but also because it affects the course of human and social development.[20]

As noted by President Johnson's recent Panel of Consultants on Vocational Education, the worker of tomorrow will need a *sound general education* which will give him the knowledge, the skill and flexibility he needs to learn new techniques and adapt himself to new jobs. He will need even more mathematics and science than he has now. Should we not, then, plan a curriculum that offers mathematics and the physical and social sciences, rather than vocational subjects that often are obsolete by the time the student finishes the semester? With this general education as a foundation, a child can move on *with understanding* to the more complicated studies of the sciences and mathematics and, hopefully, receive a better training for future vocations.

Therefore, although not rejecting completely the need for some specifics in vocational preparation, the present authors propose that emphasis be placed on academic subjects as preparation for work experiences.

School Language as a Second Language

A youngster coming to school with a highly developed language of a kind that is not acceptable in the school culture suffers from another form of verbal inadequacy. Many situations arise where the teacher and the student *never* make contact. The situation is similar to that of a Spaniard and a Portuguese talking to each other,

[20] Melvin Kranzberg, "Technology and Culture: Dimensions for Exploration," *The Journal of Industrial Arts Education*, 23, No. 5 (May–June 1964), p. 25.

with neither one quite knowing the other's language. There is, of course, a certain similarity between the languages, and now and then meaning does come through, but comprehension is not frequent or precise enough to lead to fruitful communication.

In looking at language deprivation, we must also think of the union of concepts and languages. As O'Shea pointed out more than fifty years ago, "a man is effective linguistically in those situations, and those only, in which he has often been placed, and in reaction upon which he has been constantly urged, by force of circumstances, to express himself readily and to the point."[21] Children from deprived homes may not have the experiences that give meaning to "school vocabulary." This does not necessarily mean that they may not have achieved a highly developed vocabulary from their own experiences; but this vocabulary is simply not the same as the school's. As one youngster said, with tears in his eyes, to a teacher who repeatedly asked him to talk about a subject completely foreign to him, "Ask me to talk about what I talk about."

Some of the newer approaches to language study take into consideration the factors of lack of opportunity to use language, the use of a different kind of language, and the lack of experiences in the school language. One might classify these approaches or curricula under the heading of compensatory education, since their purpose is to offer the disadvantaged youngster a counterbalance to the language facility of his advantaged peers.

The traditional method for establishing communication with a verbally limited child is to teach the child to imitate the teacher's speech. In effect, her speech becomes the model. This could be described as "direct transfer" from dialect to standard speech.

A second approach, suggested by modern linguists, is that, instead of making the child parrot the teacher's speech, the teacher might try to become facile in using the child's language, thus creating a bridge for communication with the child. The teacher, by communicating on the child's own terms, can gradually lead him into the more acceptable regional speech pattern.

There are two sound reasons for accepting the child's speech "as is" during his early language education. First, it gives the youngster the advantage of bringing something of his home and neighborhood environment into the school. If we begin setting up models of behavior—in speech or in any other activity—on the very first day the child enters school, we are, in effect, saying to him: "Reject the things you bring with you from your home; they are not desirable. Learn to do things our way." This, of course, is never verbalized, either by teachers or by curriculum guides, but the rejection is implicit in much that is done.

The second reason is that a child does not *need* to change his speech pattern in order to learn how to read. Standard, printed English is the same, whether one speaks the dialect of the North, of the South, of New England, or of the West. People speaking all the dialects of the immigrants to the cities learn to read the same printed words. Therefore, the argument that retraining of speech patterns is needed in order to teach reading is not based upon fact. Donald Lloyd, in study-

[21] M. V. O'Shea, *Linguistic Development and Education* (New York: Macmillan, 1907), pp. 234–235.

ing subcultural patterns affecting language, asks that we let these children "in on literacy," that a successful language arts program should, for these children, begin

> . . . where they are in language, wherever they are. It rests on the rich and viable culture that almost any child carries within him to school, and it respects that culture. It relates the children's actual language to the printed page, and it lets the reading child talk the way his parents talk instead of "sounding out words" painfully, one by one, tonelessly, with strange and difficult sounds.[22]

A third approach is that of Raven I. McDavid, Jr., of the University of Chicago, who is also associate director of the Dialect Atlas of the United States. He suggests that inner city children, who come to school with a dialect of the language, be taught standard English as a *second language,* side by side with the dialect.[23]

The one objective, however, agreed upon by all—the proponents of standard models, the defenders of regional or local patterns, and the advocates of letting the child become bilingual within his own language—is that the youngster, in time, should be able to use the standard speech pattern. The difference lies in how this objective is to be reached. Those who believe in "emulating a model" introduce the model concurrently with the school experience. Those who believe in the teacher's adopting local speech patterns to bridge the gap, introduce acceptable speech patterns after the relationship has been established and the youngster feels secure in the school surroundings.

Whatever the approach—the standard English model, the acceptance of the dialect, or English as a second language—it is hoped that eventually the youngster will take on the acceptable speech pattern and, in McDavid's words, "the child is thus introduced to the values of the dominant culture."[24] If the school is to be effective, and if these youngsters are not to be discharged into the ever-larger group of unskilled unemployables, then meaningful, expressive, and receptive language training must become a conscious part of curriculum organization. Inability to speak and understand standard English can make social mobility in our society almost impossible.

Pre-Kindergarten Language Training

Most of the language programs for children from disadvantaged homes are started as early as it is possible to reach both child and parent. Israel, facing a similar problem in acculturation of the oriental Jews, established pre-kindergarten schools several years ago. The Israeli program is more far-reaching than most, as it begins on the prenatal level; social workers visit *future* parents to discuss with them the importance of playing with, talking to, and singing to the newborn baby. The social workers supply records, books to read, and songs to sing; toys are loaned to the family by the government until the youngster is ready to enter nursery school. The

22 Donald J. Lloyd, "Sub-Cultural Patterns Which Affect Language and Reading Development," in *Language, Linguistics, and School Programs* (Champaign, Ill.: National Council of Teachers of English, 1963), p. 54.
23 Raven I. McDavid, Jr., "Dialectology and the Teaching of Reading," *The Reading Teacher*, 18, No. 9 (December 1964), p. 206.
24 *Ibid.*, p. 206.

Israelis are convinced that anyone, given the proper preparatory background and subsequent appropriate instruction, can be taught to function in an educated society.

Pre-kindergarten programs are emerging in the United States: Pennsylvania's Environment Enrichment Program; programs in Racine, Wisconsin, Dayton, Ohio, and White Plains, New York, the Texas program for Mexican-American children; and several programs in New York City. These, among others, have all been pio-neers in establishing programs for pre-kindergarteners.

Most of the new preschool and primary-school language programs are based upon structural linguistics. The young child learns his language through imitation. By presenting common language patterns and having the child repeat and manipulate them, the teacher instills in him the concept of the sentences. No matter how de-pressed the background of children, they can all learn to speak *simple* sentences. These sentences fall into four common language patterns:

1. noun + verb   The man came.
2. noun + verb + noun   The man bought a book.
3. noun + linking verb + adjective   The man is good.
4. noun + linking verb + noun   The man is my friend.

The important column is the one on the right. These basic sentences can be ma-nipulated and repeated with other words. The idea is to help the youngster, by practicing, to see similarities and differences in the sentences and eventually to adopt these into his own language pattern.

In such presentations as the one described above, timing is an important factor. If the child is introduced too early to the accepted language pattern, the student-school relationship may be destroyed. Gradual presentation of the desired language patterns can be far more effective than if such presentation is made at the outset of the school experience.

The Philadelphia Public Schools' language program urges children to "play" with words in patterns. Jingles, simple poems, and nonsense poems are used. Gradually, the youngster achieves an awareness, not only of sentence forms and manipulability, but of sounds and of the fact that letters represent sounds. Most linguists suggest teaching, first, words of "orthodox" spellings, such as: hat, fat, cat; cat, cap, cab; cat, cot, cut. After listening to the teacher and saying the words themselves, children should be encouraged to discuss the words and to find additional words they can bring into the pattern by substituting either individual vowels or consonants. In this way children begin to realize that every word is not completely different from every other word, but, rather, that there *is* order and system to English. This is where the "old grammar" and the "new grammar" (linguistics) differ. The old grammar emphasized words in a linear sequence; the new grammar emphasizes re-lationship. Words are related to each other by common sounds and by their effect upon each other. Sentences form a hierarchy of construction within construction on different levels.

Linguistics, however, sheds light on only one facet of instruction: that of a rela-tionship of sounds and structure. The fact that the child learns most readily those words relating to concrete experiences makes it important that he be given more than just oral practice with words and sentence combinations. As a starting point, children from disadvantaged homes should work within content that is familiar to them, content that is real, observable, and interesting. Illustrations in books should be realistic. A mother should look like *their* mothers, a home like *their* homes, a neighborhood like *their* neighborhood. The disadvantaged child often comes from an integrated community, even if his immediate neighborhood is not integrated. Therefore, pictures of people in books and magazines and charts should show a *pluralistic society* in which the child can picture himself. Children in this group should have as many sensory experiences with letters and words as possible: alphabet letters that have texture, words in color, and opportunity to see words, feel words, hear words, and build words.

One current effort is the Enrichment Program of the Institute for Developmental Studies. In his work with young children from disadvantaged homes, Deutsch[25] stresses the verbal and perceptual skills needed for all types of communication. Many of these children come from homes where things are seldom referred to by name; a chair, a table, or a lamp is pointed at, but not identified. Deutsch stresses labeling in his approach, getting across the idea that everything has a name, a name to be seen and a name to be used. In training the child to offer oral responses, the teacher first discourages pointing and "partial" language. Once the oral response is given, the teacher encourages the child to play with the word, or with a word like it, in a phrase, a sentence, or a jingle. Deutsch combines the learning of concepts with perception and linguistics.

Another aspect of this program is combating the disadvantaged child's habit of closing out school sounds. Deutsch has developed a series of tapes in which background noise is used to mask an important sound; the volume of the background noise is gradually stepped up to sharpen the youngster's sense of discrimination. With practice, the child learns to identify the important sound and trains himself to listen to it regardless of the volume of external noises.

In the Wilmington, Delaware, Three-Year Experimental Project on Schools in Changing Neighborhoods, the focus is on developing language skills through planned experience units which will help children grow in human relations sensitivities, skills, knowledge, and information. One of the media through which these units are taught is that of role playing, aloud or in pantomime. The purpose of this is to give children the opportunity to express themselves as *other* people do, through gestures, words, or a combination of both. Any child will often find the role of another person easier and more fun to deal with than his own role in life. This is especially true for children from disadvantaged backgrounds, who are sensitive as to the color of their skin, their clothes, their lack of identity. Role playing gives them a ready-made, "safe" identity, one they may choose for themselves, and yet it also opens doors into other people's lives and into their own. Role playing has many variations; "foreign characters," "real people," or even inanimate objects such as trees, clouds, and mountains. Classroom situations are rich in real character possibilities. . . .

[25] Martin Deutsch, "The Role of Social Class in Language Development and Cognition," *American Journal of Orthopsychiatry* (January 1965), pp. 78–88.

The value of this type of experience depends very much on the questions pro-posed by the teacher. Some questions suggested in the Wilmington Project are:

What motives did each person have for acting as he did?

How does each of the characters feel about the others?

What attitudes or actions of either of the characters would make you want him for a friend?

Do you think either of the characters would want the other for a friend? What actions caused this to be true?

Do you think other children would like the attitude of either of the characters? What made them feel this way?

How could each of the characters have acted differently?

If either of the characters had acted differently, in what way do you think the other character would have acted?[26]

Role-playing experiences of the Wilmington type not only allow for discussion and oral exchange, but make it possible for children to express themselves physically while acting out the problem; the children can build on what might be, for them, a successful means of expression (physical), at the same time that language is subtly introduced through the dialogue. . . .

Perhaps the most structured approach to the teaching of language is that of Omar K. Moore. He has reported, in a number of studies, successful experience in teach-ing children from culturally different and educationally deprived homes. Like Deutsch, Moore believes in starting early, but his approach is different in that he uses reading as a "self contained" method. Whereas Deutsch develops language through concept and perception formation, Moore uses the typewriter to develop language. The "talking typewriter," developed by the Thomas Edison Research Laboratories, teaches reading by programing the machine. After allowing the child to press the keys at random for a while, the program gradually becomes more struc-tured. As the child strikes a key, the letter appears on a sheet of paper in the type-writer and is spoken by a recorded voice. After two or three sessions, the recorded voice assumes more authority; instead of repeating letters as they are struck, the voice starts to dictate them to the pupil. At this point, all keys on the typewriter lock except for the demanded letter, so the child has no choice but to strike the correct letter. In the next step, the recorded voice dictates whole words and, gradually, sen-tences. The learner is expected to respond by typing the words and the sentences on the machine. Another feature of this approach is that the typewriter keys are coded in eight colors and the child's fingernails are painted in corresponding colors; thus, the child learns touch-typing while he learns to read.

There may be several reasons for the success of this approach with the disadvan-taged youngster: first, the tactile or physical attraction to the child of using a ma-chine; second, the opportunity the child has to see, listen, touch, and speak, all at almost the same time; third, the sequential teaching by means of small, discrete steps, in which the child moves on only after he has responded with the correct

[26] Questions adapted from the unpublished edition of the Wilmington, Delaware, Three-Year Experimental Project on Schools in Changing Neighborhoods, "An Adventure in Human Relations."

answer. Moore's program includes another advantage—one found in all self-teaching devices—for children who do not respond well in public: errors and corrections may be made without public censure. (This is what Deutsch means when he suggests automated devices for children from "unacceptable cultures.") Moore's program deserves careful watching, as it seems to contain certain elements that are successful with children from almost all types of backgrounds.

History and the Social Sciences

The social sciences deal with man as a dynamic, creative person, not as a helpless pawn of blind forces. As an intellectual, social, and ethical being, man exercises initiative and imagination in his relations with other persons. The social sciences help describe man and his relationships to other men and to his environment. They enable us, on the basis of past behavior, to draw inferences as to present and future conduct.

For the disadvantaged child—unaware of the sweep of history—living amid lethargy, hopelessness, and defeat—the knowledge that people like himself have in past centuries broken through barriers of deprivation far worse than his can make a tremendous impression. What are some of the guidelines particularly appropriate for teaching social sciences to deprived children? Studies of slum children indicate that they are weak in communication abilities, in abstract thinking, and in logic. In younger children these weaknesses take the form of a limited vocabulary; in older ones, they are evidenced in a lack of ability to understand general ideas or conclusions. These students are handicapped by an inability to recognize the application of generalizations to new situations.

Skilled instruction and exposure of children to a variety of materials, experiences, and value systems should result in what Bruner refers to as "discovery." The student learns how to ferret things out for himself, how to draw his own generalizations. This is the great highway to learning. On this road teachers talk less and learners achieve more.

Questions for Discussion

1. How do you react to the idea of teaching English as a foreign language to these small American children, the teacher speaking in their language initially?
2. How are values taught to these children? Do you think that a school should be involved in teaching values? Is it? If so, what kind of values are taught? Should these specific values be taught?
3. After reading these three articles, how do you feel? Depressed? Overwhelmed? Challenged? Unsettled? As you reflect on your feelings, what do you learn about your own theory of education? Has this introduction of material concerning the education of students from minority groups given you any clearer insight into your own beliefs?

17 The Port Huron Statement

Students for a Democratic Society

*One of the foremost groups involved in attempts to modify the structure of
schools and society has been the Students for a Democratic Society, and
this selection is a portion of the first statement of principles they adopted.
They consider the role of the school within the wider context of human
life, and they deplore the apathy, bureaucracy and malaise created by those
schools. This first of four articles dealing with the contemporary college
scene might give you some basis for thinking about your own learning
environment.*

Introduction: Agenda for a Generation

We are people of this generation, bred in at least modest comfort, housed
now in universities, looking uncomfortably to the world we inherit.

When we were kids the United States was the wealthiest and strongest country in
the world; the only one with the atom bomb, the least scarred by modern war, an
initiator of the United Nations that we thought would distribute Western influence
throughout the world. Freedom and equality for each individual, government of, by,
and for the people—these American values we found good, principles by which we
could live as men. Many of us began maturing in complacency.

As we grew, however, our comfort was penetrated by events too troubling to
dismiss. First, the permeating and victimizing fact of human degradation, symbolized by the Southern struggle against racial bigotry, compelled most of us from
silence to activism. Second, the enclosing fact of the Cold War, symbolized by the
presence of the Bomb, brought awareness that we ourselves, and our friends, and
millions of abstract "others" we knew more directly because of our common peril,
might die at any time. We might deliberately ignore, or avoid, or fail to feel all
other human problems, but not these two, for these were too immediate and crushing in their impact, too challenging in the demand that we as individuals take the
responsibility for encounter and resolution.

While these and other problems either directly oppressed us or rankled our con-
sciences and became our own subjective concerns, we began to see complicated and
disturbing paradoxes in our surrounding America. The declaration "all men are
created equal . . ." rang hollow before the facts of Negro life in the South and the
big cities of the North. The proclaimed peaceful intentions of the United States
contradicted its economic and military investments in the Cold War status quo.

We witnessed, and continue to witness, other paradoxes. With nuclear energy
whole cities can easily be powered, yet the dominant nation-states seem more likely
to unleash destruction greater than that incurred in all wars of human history. Although our own technology is destroying old and creating new forms of social

organization, men still tolerate meaningless work and idleness. While two-thirds of mankind suffers undernourishment, our own upper classes revel amidst superfluous abundance. Although world population is expected to double in forty years, the nations still tolerate anarchy as a major principle of international conduct and un-controlled exploitation governs the sapping of the earth's physical resources. Al-though mankind desperately needs revolutionary leadership, America rests in na-tional stalemate, its goals ambiguous and tradition-bound instead of informed and clear, its democratic system apathetic and manipulated rather than "of, by, and for the people."

Not only did tarnish appear on our image of American virtue, not only did dis-illusion occur when the hypocrisy of American ideals was discovered, but we began to sense that what we had originally seen as the American Golden Age was actually the decline of an era. The worldwide outbreak of revolution against colonialism and imperialism, the entrenchment of totalitarian states, the menace of war, over-population, international disorder, supertechnology—these trends were testing the tenacity of our own commitment to democracy and freedom and our abilities to visualize their application to a world in upheaval.

Our work is guided by the sense that we may be the last generation in the experi-ment with living. But we are a minority—the vast majority of our people regard the temporary equilibriums of our society and world as eternally functional parts. In this is perhaps the outstanding paradox: we ourselves are imbued with urgency, yet the message of our society is that there is no viable alternative to the present. Beneath the reassuring tones of the politicians, beneath the common opinion that America will "muddle through," beneath the stagnation of those who have closed their minds to the future, is the pervading feeling that there simply are no alterna-tives, that our times have witnessed the exhaustion not only of Utopias, but of any new departures as well. Feeling the press of complexity upon the emptiness of life, people are fearful of the thought that at any moment things might be thrust out of control. They fear change itself, since change might smash whatever invisible frame-work seems to hold back chaos for them now. For most Americans, all crusades are suspect, threatening. The fact that each individual sees apathy in his fellows per-petuates the common reluctance to organize for change. The dominant institutions are complex enough to blunt the minds of their potential critics, and entrenched enough to swiftly dissipate or entirely repel the energies of protest and reform, thus limiting human expectancies. Then, too, we are a materially improved society, and by our own improvements we seem to have weakened the case for further change.

Some would have us believe that Americans feel contentment amidst prosperity—but might it not better be called a glaze above deeply felt anxieties about their role in the new world? And if these anxieties produce a developed indifference to human affairs, do they not as well produce a yearning to believe there *is* an alterna-tive to the present, that something *can* be done to change circumstances in the school, the workplaces, the bureaucracies, the government? It is to this latter yearn-ing, at once the spark and engine of change, that we direct our present appeal. The search for truly democratic alternatives to the present, and a commitment to social experimentation with them, is a worthy and fulfilling human enterprise, one which moves us and, we hope, others today. On such a basis do we offer this document of our convictions and analysis: as an effort in understanding and changing the conditions of humanity in the late twentieth century, an effort rooted in the ancient, still unfulfilled conception of man attaining determining influence over his circumstances of life.

Values

Making values explicit—an initial task in establishing alternatives—is an activity that has been devalued and corrupted. The conventional moral terms of the age, the politician moralities—"free world," "people's democracies"—reflect realities poorly, if at all, and seem to function more as ruling myths than as descriptive principles. But neither has our experience in the universities brought us moral enlightenment. Our professors and administrators sacrifice controversy to public relations; their curriculums change more slowly than the living events of the world; their skills and silence are purchased by investors in the arms race; passion is called unscholastic. The questions we might want raised—what is really important? can we live in a different and better way? if we wanted to change society, how would we do it?—are not thought to be questions of a "fruitful, empirical nature," and thus are brushed aside.

Unlike youth in other countries we are used to moral leadership being exercised and moral dimensions being clarified by our elders. But today, for us, not even the liberal and socialist preachments of the past seem adequate to the forms of the present. Consider the old slogans: Capitalism Cannot Reform Itself, United Front Against Fascism, General Strike, All Out on May Day. Or, more recently, No Cooperation with Commies and Fellow Travelers, Ideologies are Exhausted, Bipartisanship, No Utopias. These are incomplete, and there are few new prophets. It has been said that our liberal and socialist predecessors were plagued by vision without program, while our own generation is plagued by program without vision. All around us there is astute grasp of method, technique—the committee, the *ad hoc* group, the lobbyist, the hard and soft sell, the make, the projected image—but, if pressed critically, such expertise is incompetent to explain its implicit ideals. It is highly fashionable to identify oneself by old categories, or by naming a respected political figure, or by explaining "how we would vote" on various issues.

Theoretic chaos has replaced the idealistic thinking of old—and, unable to reconstitute theoretic order, men have condemned idealism itself. Doubt has replaced hopefulness—and men act out a defeatism that is labeled realistic. The decline of utopia and hope is in fact one of the defining features of social life today. The reasons are various: the dreams of the older left were perverted by Stalinism and never recreated; the congressional stalemate makes men narrow their view of the possible; the specialization of human activity leaves little room for sweeping thought; the horrors of the twentieth century, symbolized in the gas ovens and concentration camps and atom bombs, have blasted hopefulness. To be idealistic is to be considered apocalyptic, deluded. To have no serious aspirations, on the contrary, is to be "tough-minded."

In suggesting social goals and values, therefore, we are aware of entering a sphere of some disrepute. Perhaps matured by the past, we have no sure formulas, no closed

theories—but that does not mean values are beyond discussion and tentative determination. A first task of any social movement is to convince people that the search
for orienting theories and the creation of human values is complex but worthwhile.
We are aware that to avoid platitudes we must analyze the concrete conditions of
social order. But to direct such an analysis we must use the guideposts of basic principles. Our own social values involve conceptions of human beings, human relationships, and social systems.

We regard *men* as infinitely precious and possessed of unfulfilled capacities for
reason, freedom, and love. In affirming these principles we are aware of countering
perhaps the dominant conceptions of man in the twentieth century: that he is a
thing to be manipulated, and that he is inherently incapable of directing his own
affairs. We oppose the depersonalization that reduces human beings to the status of
things—if anything, the brutalities of the twentieth century teach that means and
ends are intimately related, that vague appeals to "posterity" cannot justify the
mutilations of the present. We oppose, too, the doctrine of human incompetence
because it rests essentially on the modern fact that men have been "competently"
manipulated into incompetence—we see little reason why men cannot meet with increasing skill the complexities and responsibilities of their situation, if society is
organized not for minority, but for majority, participation in decision-making.

Men have unrealized potential for self-cultivation, self-direction, self-understanding, and creativity. It is this potential that we regard as crucial and to which we
appeal, not to the human potentiality for violence, unreason, and submission to
authority. The goal of man and society should be human independence: a concern
not with image of popularity but with finding a meaning in life that is personally
authentic; a quality of mind not compulsively driven by a sense of powerlessness,
nor one which unthinkingly adopts status values, nor one which represses all threats
to its habits, but one which has full, spontaneous access to present and past experiences, one which easily unites the fragmented parts of personal history, one
which openly faces problems which are troubling and unresolved; one with an
intuitive awareness of possibilities, an active sense of curiosity, an ability and willingness to learn.

This kind of independence does not mean egotistic individualism—the object is
not to have one's way so much as it is to have a way that is one's own. Nor do we
deify man—we merely have faith in his potential.

Human relationships should involve fraternity and honesty. Human interdependence is contemporary fact; human brotherhood must be willed, however, as a
condition of future survival and as the most appropriate form of social relations.
Personal links between man and man are needed, especially to go beyond the
partial and fragmentary bonds of function that bind men only as worker to worker,
employer to employee, teacher to student, American to Russian.

Loneliness, estrangement, isolation describe the vast distance between man and
man today. These dominant tendencies cannot be overcome by better personnel management, nor by improved gadgets, but only when a love of man overcomes the
idolatrous worship of things by man. As the individualism we affirm is not egoism,
the selflessness we affirm is not self-elimination. On the contrary, we believe in
generosity of a kind that imprints one's unique individual qualities in the relation

to other men, and to all human activity. Further, to dislike isolation is not to favor the abolition of privacy; the latter differs from isolation in that it occurs or is abol ished according to individual will.

We would replace power rooted in possession, privilege, or circumstance by power and uniqueness rooted in love, reflectiveness, reason, and creativity. As a *social system* we seek the establishment of a democracy of individual participation, governed by two central aims: that the individual share in those social decisions determining the quality and direction of his life; that society be organized to encourage independence in men and provide the media for their common participation.

In a participatory democracy, the political life would be based in several root principles:

that decision-making of basic social consequence be carried on by public groupings;

that politics be seen positively, as the art of collectively creating an acceptable pattern of social relations;

that politics has the function of bringing people out of isolation and into community, thus being a necessary, though not sufficient, means of finding meaning in personal life;

that the political order should serve to clarify problems in a way instrumental to their solution; it should provide outlets for the expression of personal griev ance and aspiration; opposing views should be organized so as to illuminate choices and facilitate the attainment of goals; channels should be commonly available to relate men to knowledge and to power so that private problems— from bad recreation facilities to personal alienation—are formulated as general issues.

The economic sphere would have as its basis the principles:

that work should involve incentives worthier than money or survival. It should be educative, not stultifying; creative, not mechanical; self-directed, not manipulated, encouraging independence, a respect for others, a sense of dignity and a willingness to accept social responsibility, since it is this experience that has crucial influence on habits, perceptions and individual ethics;

that the economic experience is so personally decisive that the individual must share in its full determination;

that the economy itself is of such social importance that its major resources and means of production should be open to democratic participation and sub ject to democratic social regulation.

Like the political and economic ones, major social institutions—cultural, educational, rehabilitative, and others—should be generally organized with the well-being and dignity of man as the essential measure of success.

In social change or interchange, we find violence to be abhorrent because it re quires generally the transformation of the target, be it a human being or a community of people, into a depersonalized object of hate. It is imperative that the means of violence be abolished and the institutions—local, national, international— that encourage nonviolence as a condition of conflict be developed.

These are our central values, in skeletal form. It remains vital to understand their denial or attainment in the context of the modern world.

The Students

In the last few years, thousands of American students demonstrated that they at least felt the urgency of the times. They moved actively and directly against racial injustices, the threat of war, violations of individual rights of conscience and, less frequently, against economic manipulation. They succeeded in restoring a small measure of controversy to the campuses after the stillness of the McCarthy period. They succeeded, too, in gaining some concessions from the people and institutions they opposed, especially in the fight against racial bigotry.

The significance of these scattered movements lies not in their success or failure in gaining objectives—at least not yet. Nor does the significance lie in the intellectual "competence" or "maturity" of the students involved—as some pedantic elders allege. The significance is in the fact the students are breaking the crust of apathy and overcoming the inner alienation that remain the defining characteristics of American college life.

If student movements for change are still rarities on the campus scene, what is commonplace there? The real campus, the familiar campus, is a place of private people, engaged in their notorious "inner emigration." It is a place of commitment to business-as-usual, getting ahead, playing it cool. It is a place of mass affirmation of the Twist, but mass reluctance toward the controversial public stance. Rules are accepted as "inevitable," bureaucracy as "just circumstances," irrelevance as "scholarship," selflessness as "martyrdom," politics as "just another way to make people, and an unprofitable one, too."

Almost no students value activity as citizens. Passive in public, they are hardly more idealistic in arranging their private lives: Gallup concludes they will settle for "low success, and won't risk high failure." There is not much willingness to take risks (not even in business), no setting of dangerous goals, no real conception of personal identity except one manufactured in the image of others, no real urge for personal fulfillment except to be almost as successful as the very successful people. Attention is being paid to social status (the quality of shirt collars, meeting people, getting wives or husbands, making solid contacts for later on); much, too, is paid to academic status (grades, honors, the med school rat race). But neglected generally is real intellectual status, the personal cultivation of the mind.

"Students don't even give a damn about the apathy," one has said. Apathy toward apathy begets a privately constructed universe, a place of systematic study schedules, two nights each week for beer, a girl or two, and early marriage; a framework infused with personality, warmth, and under control, no matter how unsatisfying otherwise.

Under these conditions university life loses all relevance to some. Four hundred thousand of our classmates leave college every year.

But apathy is not simply an attitude; it is a product of social institutions, and of the structure and organization of higher education itself. The extracurricular life is ordered according to *in loco parentis* theory, which ratifies the administration as the moral guardian of the young.

The accompanying "let's pretend" theory of student extracurricular affairs validates student government as a training center for those who want to spend their lives in political pretense, and discourages initiative from the more articulate, honest, and sensitive students. The bounds and style of controversy are delimited before controversy begins. The university "prepares" the student for "citizenship" through perpetual rehearsals and, usually, through emasculation of what creative spirit there is in the individual.

The academic life contains reinforcing counterparts to the way in which extracurricular life is organized. The academic world is founded on a teacher-student relation analogous to the parent-child relation which characterizes *in loco parentis*. Further, academia includes a radical separation of the student from the material of study. That which is studied, the social reality, is "objectified" to sterility, dividing the student from life—just as he is restrained in active involvement by the deans controlling student government. The specialization of function and knowledge, admittedly necessary to our complex technological and social structure, has produced an exaggerated compartmentalization of study and understanding. This has contributed to an overly parochial view, by faculty, of the role of its research and scholarship, to a discontinuous and truncated understanding, by students, of the surrounding social order; and to a loss of personal attachment, by nearly all, to the worth of study as a humanistic enterprise.

There is, finally, the cumbersome academic bureaucracy extending throughout the academic as well as the extracurricular structures, contributing to the sense of outer complexity and inner powerlessness that transforms the honest searching of many students to a ratification of convention and, worse, to a numbness to present and future catastrophes. The size and financing systems of the university enhance the permanent trusteeship of the administrative bureaucracy, their power leading to a shift within the university toward the value standard of business and the administrative mentality. Huge foundations and other private financial interests shape the under-financed colleges and universities, not only making them more commercial, but less disposed to diagnose society critically, less open to dissent. Many social and physical scientists, neglecting the liberating heritage of higher learning, develop "human relations" or "morale-producing" techniques for the corporate economy, while others exercise their intellectual skills to accelerate the arms race. . . .

There are no convincing apologies for the contemporary malaise. While the world tumbles toward the final war, while men in other nations are trying desperately to alter events, while the very future qua future is uncertain—America is without community, impulse, without the inner momentum necessary for an age when societies cannot successfully perpetuate themselves by their military weapons, when democracy must be viable because of the quality of life, not its quantity of rockets.

The apathy here is, first, *subjective*—the felt powerlessness of ordinary people, the resignation before the enormity of events. But subjective apathy is encouraged by the *objective* American situation—the actual structural separation of people from power, from relevant knowledge, from pinnacles of decision-making. Just as the university influences the student way of life, so do major social institutions create the circumstances in which the isolated citizen will try hopelessly to understand his world and himself.

The very isolation of the individual—from power and community and ability to aspire—means the rise of a democracy without publics. With the great mass of peo-

ple structurally remote and psychologically hesitant with respect to democratic institutions, those institutions themselves attenuate and become, in the fashion of the
vicious circle, progressively less accessible to those few who aspire to serious participation in social affairs. The vital democratic connection between community and
leadership, between the mass and the several elites, has been so wrenched and perverted that disastrous policies go unchallenged time and again.

Politics Without Publics

The American political system is not the democratic model of which its glorifiers
speak. In actuality it frustrates democracy by confusing the individual citizen, para-
lyzing policy discussion, and consolidating the irresponsible power of military and
business interests.

A crucial feature of the political apparatus in America is that greater differences
are harbored within each major party than the differences existing between them.
Instead of two parties presenting distinctive and significant differences of approach,
what dominates the system is a natural interlocking of Democrats from Southern
states with the more conservative elements of the Republican Party. This arrangement of forces is blessed by the seniority system of Congress which guarantees Congressional committee domination by conservatives—ten of seventeen committees in
the Senate and thirteen of twenty-one in the House of Representatives are chaired
currently by Dixiecrats.

The party overlap, however, is not the only structural antagonist of democracy in
politics. First, the localized nature of the party system does not encourage discussion
of national and international issues: thus problems are not raised by and for people,
and political representatives usually are unfettered from any responsibilities to the
general public except those regarding parochial matters. Second, whole constituen
cies are divested of the full political power they might have: many Negroes in the
South are prevented from voting, migrant workers are disenfranchised by various
residence requirements, some urban and suburban dwellers are victimized by gerry-
mandering, and poor people are too often without the power to obtain political
representation. Third, the focus of political attention is significantly distorted by
the enormous lobby force, composed predominantly of business interests, spending
hundreds of millions each year in an attempt to conform facts about productivity,
agriculture, defense, and social services, to the wants of private economic groupings.

What emerges from the party contradiction and insulation of privately held
power is the organized political stalemate: calcification dominates flexibility as the
principle of parliamentary organization, frustration is the expectancy of legislators
intending liberal reform, and Congress becomes less and less central to national
decision-making, especially in the area of foreign policy. In this context, confusion
and blurring is built into the formulation of issues, long-range priorities are not
discussed in the rational manner needed for policy-making, the politics of personality and "image" become a more important mechanism than the construction
of issues in a way that affords each voter a challenging and real option. The American voter is buffeted from all directions by pseudo-problems, by the structurally initi-
ated sense that nothing political is subject to human mastery. Worried by his mun-

dane problems which never get solved, but constrained by the common belief that politics is an agonizingly slow accommodation of views, he quits all pretense of bothering.

A most alarming fact is that few, if any, politicians are calling for changes in these conditions. Only a handful even are calling on the President to "live up to" platform pledges; no one is demanding structural changes, such as the shuttling of Southern Democrats out of the Democratic Party. Rather than protesting the state of politics, most politicians are reinforcing and aggravating that state. While in practice they rig public opinion to suit their own interests, in word and ritual they enshrine "the sovereign public" and call for more and more letters. Their speeches and campaign actions are banal, based on a degrading conception of what people want to hear. They respond not to dialogue, but to pressure: and knowing this, the ordinary citizen sees even greater inclination to shun the political sphere. The politician is usually a trumpeter to "citizenship" and "service to the nation," but since he is unwilling to seriously rearrange power relationships, his trumpetings only increase apathy by creating no outlets. Much of the time the call to "service" is justified not in idealistic terms, but in the crasser terms of "defending the free world from Communism"—thus making future idealistic impulses harder to justify in anything but Cold War terms.

In such a setting of status quo politics, where most if not all government activity is rationalized in Cold War anti-Communist terms, it is somewhat natural that discontented, super-patriotic groups would emerge through political channels and explain their ultra-conservatism as the best means of Victory over Communism. They have become a politically influential force within the Republican Party, at a national level through Senator Goldwater, and at a local level through their important social and economic roles. Their political views are defined generally as the opposite of the supposed views of Communists: complete individual freedom in the economic sphere, non-participation by the government in the machinery of production. But actually "anti-Communism" becomes an umbrella by which to protest liberalism, internationalism, welfareism, the active civil rights and labor movements. It is to the disgrace of the United States that such a movement should become a prominent kind of public participation in the modern world—but, ironically, it is somewhat to the interests of the United States that such a movement should be a public constituency pointed toward realignment of the political parties, demanding a conservative Republican Party in the South and an exclusion of the "leftist" elements of the national GOP. . . .

Questions for Discussion

1. How do the physical and educational requirements of a school cause students to be apathetic, indeed, to be apathetic towards their own apathy?
2. Do you believe that students should be active in planning the curriculum, establishing the requirements and hiring the professors who will be teaching the courses they take? What positive values would result from these involvements? What problems are created? If you were able to be active in this sense, what would you want to do with your opportunity? Or do you shrink from the responsibility?
3. What is a revolution? Should we have revolutions in our schools? In our society?

18   A Letter to Undergraduates

Brad Cleaveland

The language is getting a little rougher, the arguments more militant, and the proposals more revolutionary. Here, a student at Berkeley addresses undergraduates telling them they should do "nothing less than begin an open, fierce and thoroughgoing rebellion on this campus." As you read, try to discern whether Cleaveland gives any reasons to support this conclusion or whether this is merely the expression of an angry young man.

THERE IS NO BLUEPRINT FOR AN EDUCATIONAL REVOLUTION!!!

It was like this: on the one hand there was substantial agreement that the University stamps out consciousness like a super-madison-avenue-machine; on the other, people saying, "So what?" or "Bring me a detailed and exhaustive plan." *But there is no plan for kicking twenty thousand people IN THEIR ASSES!* No plan will stop excessive greed, timidity, and selling out. At best the University is a pathway to the club of "tough-minded-liberal-realists" in America, who sit in comfortable armchairs talking radical while clutching hysterically at respectability in a world explosive with revolution. At worst the University destroys your desires to see reality, and to suffer reality with optimism, at the time when you most need to learn that painful art. In between those two poles is mostly garbage: Bus Ad; PhD candidates "on the make"; departmental enclaves of "clever and brilliant" students who will become hack critics; and thousands of trainees for high-class trades which will become obsolete in ten years.

Dear undergraduate, let me make this crystal clear for you. There is a contrast which exists on this campus between the common (and sometimes beautiful) illusions which we have all had, and what actually happens! . . . a gap which seems to be reaching catastrophic proportions. I will offer two sets of utterly obvious facts to show you that a violent contrast does exist; and that the University is a grotesque perversion of the conditions necessary for your freedom to learn reality and to suffer it with optimism. The first set of facts is your Charter Day Ceremony, the second is the essentials of your undergraduate routine—a grotesque perversion of your freedom to learn.

YOUR UNDERGRADUATE ROUTINE

. . . your routine is comprised of a systematic psychological and spiritual brutality inflicted by a faculty of "well-meaning and nice" men who have decided that your situation is hopeless when it comes to actually participating in serious learning. As an undergraduate you receive a four-year-long series of sharp staccatos: eight semesters, forty courses, one hundred twenty or more units, fifteen hundred to two

From Volume II, No. 1 of the *SLATE Supplement to the General Catalog,* an independent publication of the students of the University of California at Berkeley. Copyright 1965.

thousand impersonal lectures, and over three hundred oversized "discussion" meetings. Approaching what is normally associated with learning; reading, writing, and exams, your situation becomes absurd. Over a period of four years you receive close to fifty bibliographies, ranging in length from one to eight pages, you are examined on more than one hundred occasions, and you are expected to write forty to seventy-five papers. As you well know, reading means "getting into" hundreds of books, many of which are secondary sources, in a superficial manner. You must cheat to keep up. If you don't cheat you are forced to perform without time to think in depth, and consequently you must hand in papers and exams which are almost as shameful as the ones you've cheated on. You repeat to yourselves over and over as an undergraduate that "It doesn't make any difference . . . it's the grade that counts," . . . a threadbare and worn phrase (if you are lucky enough to make it to the third or fourth year); used as commonly as your word "regurgitation" in place of "exam." You know the measure of truth in those bits of slang: it *is* nauseous . . . you almost *do* "puke up your work" to professors. I personally have known students who have gotten physically sick by merely reflecting upon their routine. In the sciences and technical fields your courses are bluntly and destructively rigorous. . . . you become impatient with "that social sciences and humanities crap." How did you get to be such puppets? You perform. But when do you think? Dutifully and obediently you follow, as a herd of grade-worshiping sheep. If you are strong at all, you do this with some sense of shame, or if you are weak, you do it with a studied cynicism . . . as jaded youth with parched imaginations that go no further than oak-panelled rooms at the end of the line . . . BUT WHETHER YOU ARE STRONG OR WEAK YOU PERFORM LIKE TRAINED SEALS, AND LIKE SHEEP YOU FOLLOW . . . WITH THE THOROUGHBRED PHI BETA KAPPA SHEEP LEADING YOU!! up the golden stairway to the omnipotent A, to the Happy Consciousness, to success, and a very parochial mind. This is the core of your dutiful daily lives, and your homage to respectability. Reluctantly, or otherwise, you permit it to be applied by administrators who use computers on you as much because they are afraid of personal contact with you as for the reason that they wish to keep the assembly line moving efficiently. You permit professors to extract your performance by the coercion of grades. Why do you permit this apostasy of learning . . . a process which prevents you from extending your thought beyond a shallow dilettantism?

IF THE FACTS OF YOUR UNDERGRADUATE EXISTENCE WERE SOLELY DETERMINED BY THE "COURSE/GRADE/UNIT SYSTEM," YOUR "INCIPIENT REVOLT," TO WHICH PRESIDENT KERR HIMSELF IRRESPONSIBLY ALLUDED IN THE GODKIN LECTURES, WOULD PROBABLY HAVE ALREADY OCCURRED.

The reason why you permit, dear undergraduate, your minds to be abused, is because you are given a magnificent bread and circus. What a pain reliever! . . . these "extracurricular" activities. Coming to you from your ASUC student "government," other special bureaucracies such as the Committee on Arts and Lectures, and added to by more intellectual offerings from departmental and special grants lecture series, comes a semesterly tidal wave of exciting and highly intense stimuli which dazzles you away from the fact that you are obstructed from learning, or even questioning whether you should be learning while you are here. This bread and circus assures you that the world is really *not* in the midst of anything so serious as *revolution,* much less within your own sacred borders!! From the powerfully entertaining to the scholastically intellectual you get films, debates, art exhibits, athletics, drama, "spirit" groups, recreations, seductions of hundreds of social groups; this pyrotechnical explosion of *Kultur* is something terribly "other directed"; happily away from your puppet-like performance in the course/grade/unit procedural core. Your attention is diverted away from your treadmill to the candied goodness of the bread and circus. Hopefully, when you get your bachelor's degree, you will step up to higher plateaus where many kinds of "success" await you. You are blinded to the fact that you are really getting something of terrible importance while you are here:

TRAINING IN THE CAPACITY FOR UNQUESTIONING OBEDIENCE TO A COMPLEX FLOOD OF TRIVIAL BUREAUCRATIC RULES. IN THE NAME OF HUMAN LEARNING YOU ACQUIRE THE CAPACITY TO BE DOCILE IN THE FACE OF RULES. WHILE YOU ARE TRAINING, THE RULES WHICH TELL YOU HOW TO GO ABOUT YOUR TRAINING ARE DISPLACING YOUR FREEDOM TO THINK. . . . SKILL AND OBEDIENCE ARE WHAT YOU ACQUIRE.

Aren't you the least bit aware that such a capacity is not only necessary for life in America's giant public and private corporations, but that it is also a first-class ticket to a traditional form of statehood under the designation of tyranny? No matter how well trimmed you keep your grassy lawns in suburbia after you get your bachelor's degree, your moral and spiritual servitude will not be reduced. If you have attended a Charter Day Ceremony, and can recall the feelings you had, you might feel the temptation to say that it is this indictment which is grotesque, and *not* the University . . . but *you* are the University . . . it is *your* life I have described in its essentials.

Has it ever occurred to you, dear undergraduate, that human learning is a painful and exhilarating process which comes from asking the kinds of questions which *YOU* would like to ask: "WHY AM I IN THE UNIVERSITY? WHAT IS KNOWLEDGE? WHAT IS EXTREMISM, AFTER ALL, AND HOW DOES POLITICAL EXTREMISM AFFECT ME? In your present situation, if you *insisted* on . . . now listen . . . if you *insisted* on the freedom to spend large amounts of time in a single-minded devotion to pursuing such questions, you would soon begin to feel rather out of it . . . you would be a kook. Any question of a fundamental, or a general character; or any question which hits you personally in a deep way, can only be considered naïve and stupid. Can you conceive of taking any such question and studying, talking, and reading about it for an entire semester—free of any other requirement—or for an entire year, or even more time? Without interference, but only earnest guidance from "teachers"? Or is it that you must always attend to that "other" paper, the "midterm next week," or the "reading in another course"? Or is it that you do this half the time and say to hell with it the rest of the time: go to an art film, or to Strawberry Canyon, or to an exciting lecture for a one-night stand on the topic of Western Civilization?

Dear undergraduate, you *know* what really happens to you. You almost don't have to be told. It is as though the BENEFACTORS OF THE FRUITS OF LEARNING said to you, "Here, take this beautiful piece of fruit . . . ," and you do, and you try a bite, when "STOP!!," you are being offered another piece of fruit, another, and then another. At the same time, before you really begin to taste and speculate about the taste of any one piece of fruit, your FRUIT BENEFACTORS, and FRUIT BENEFACTORS' ASSISTANTS, are demanding that you describe in detail the intricate beauty of each piece; they become impatient if you do not describe the fruit "properly," and they penalize you for thoughtful slowness by calling it stupidity, and by lowering your respectability rating. Most of you learn to hate the fruits of learning. But there are a few of you—the "clever and brilliant"—(preferably transfers from the Ivy League), who learn in a terrific quickness, to take quick little bites from the large and beautiful fruits and then furiously hurl them as far away as possible. You clever ones learn to devour the small fruits of skill and training; those fruits are your "security insurance" in life, or perhaps you think they will lead you later to an XK-E and sexy-intelligent-wife-in-silk-dress. You perform your tricks well: smiling up at your benefactors and saying "delicious . . . excellent!"

DEAR UNDERGRADUATES!!

I am no longer interested in cajoling you, arguing with you, or describing to you something you already know. What I am about to say to you at this point concerns you more directly. I will entreat you to furiously throw your comforting feelings of duty and responsibility for this institution to the winds and act on your situation. This institution, affectionately called "Cal" by many of you, or, as the *Daily Cal* might put it, "the Big U," does not deserve a response of loyalty and allegiance from you. There is only one proper response to Berkeley from undergraduates: that you *organize and split this campus wide open!*

FROM THIS POINT ON, DO NOT MISUNDERSTAND ME. MY INTENTION IS TO CONVINCE YOU THAT YOU DO NOTHING LESS THAN BEGIN AN OPEN, FIERCE, AND THOROUGH-GOING REBELLION ON THIS CAMPUS.

I would like to briefly explain to you now why such a course of action is necessary, and how, if such a revolt were conducted with unrelenting toughness and courage, it could spread to other campuses across the country and cause a fundamental change in your own futures.

I have used the phrase "world-in-revolution" several times to this point. I would like to say to you now that most of you are incompetent to deal with that phrase. It is a phrase which betrays a distinct view of reality . . . a view of reality out of which might grow an effective "opposition" in the present American scene where the only opposition seems to be crystallizing along reactionary lines. "World-in-revolution" is a phrase . . . a view of reality which contains a large measure of truth, one which is certainly debatable. BUT IT IS NOT DEBATED BY *YOU*. The catastrophic gap between the incubator world of your Multiversity, and the world of reality is represented by your ignorance of what "world-in-revolution" means. The University teaches you to bury your heads in the sand, trembling in ignorance of the American black revolution for Civil Rights, the impending revolution in Automation, and likewise in ignorance of political revolutions, which, like thunderclapping salvos, explode the world over. The Multiversity is the slickest appeal ever made for you to fortify your organization man mentalities, for you to lead privatized lives in which it is a virtue for you to go greedily "on the make." In urging you to rebellion, I have action in mind, not further understanding. What more is there to understand when you can so easily discover that a Peace Corpsman who left Cal is now living in Nigeria in a separate small house with the conveniences of suburban America, plus two houseboys, and that a young girl Civil Rights worker from the Bay Area who goes to Mississippi lives in abject poverty with a family of eleven black American citizens, in a shack with no running water, with lice, with rats, and in constant fear for her life?

In this Multiversity, you will not learn so much as a cursory meaning of what a world-in-revolution means to you. You will not learn the utterly profound fact of what a revolution is:

THAT A REVOLUTION COMES ABOUT WHEN ENORMOUS NUMBERS OF FELLOW HUMAN BEINGS ARE OPPRESSED TO POINTS FAR BEYOND WHAT WE BLANDLY LABEL AN "IN-TOLERABLE SET OF CONDITIONS."

Nor will you learn that to be a counter-revolutionary is to go about the business of slaughtering enormous numbers of human beings whose inflamed spirits and starved stomachs force them to cry out for the freedoms which you spit upon in your apathy.

AND YOU WILL LEARN MOST OF ALL NOT TO ENTERTAIN SO MUCH AS THE POSSIBILITY THAT AMERICAN FOREIGN POLICY IN KOREA AND SOUTH VIETNAM ARE PRECISELY COUNTER-REVOLUTIONARY . . . THAT THE AMERICAN NATION IS INVOLVED IN DESTROY-ING POPULAR NATIONAL REVOLUTIONS, AND APPEARS TO BE GETTING ITSELF LOCKED MORE AND MORE IN THAT SUICIDAL AND INHUMANE POLICY.

You will learn not to entertain such thoughts, even though such statements have been made on the floor of the U.S. Senate (by Wayne Morse, U.S. Senator from Oregon), where nobody seems to have taken these fantastic charges seriously. And you will learn not to react when you hear other Americans say "After all, God's on our side, we're savin' those illiterate savages from the Commies, even if we gotta mu-tilate 'em to do it, Goddamit!!"

You will not learn that, at home, here in the good ole U.S.A., in the Civil Rights Revolution which is now going on, the phrase "white backlash" is the simplest way to say "the bigotry of the majority"; that "white backlash" is a counter-revolutionary phrase, used by "scholars," so-called liberals, advocated by conservatives, or used by anyone else who adopts the hideous posture of "studying," or analyzing the "prob-lem" of the black man in America. Nor will you learn that the real meaning of "white backlash" is "Don't bug me nigger . . . you're buggin' me with that civil disobedience . . . now stop that or we'll show you who has the tear gas, cattle prods, and shotguns!!" . . .

Regarding the radicals, those who are now going to jail in the Civil Rights Revo-lution: they are beginning to learn what the world-in-revolution means. I would make only one irreverent comment to them. They shouldn't bitch because the whole campus doesn't go to jail with them: because they are the real leaders on the campus, and yet while *on the campus* they too become sheep. They take the flunkings of professors, who penalize them for attending a San Francisco court rather than a

Berkeley class; the same professors who donate money to the Civil Rights fight as long as it stays three thousand miles away in the South.

The only large group of students I personally respect, other than the Freedom Fighters, are the dropouts. Ignominious lot! What a fate . . . that one would be forced to give up that little registration card with respectability written all over it! This "Hidden Community" of unseemly hangers-on in Berkeley now numbers in the thousands. Those most bugged by this "element" are the ASUC types. They screech, "You can't even tell them from students sometimes (although some are very dirty) . . . and they're using *our* student union!" If they have flunked out (or dropped out) of the University how can they deserve respect? Well . . . if I thought it was a virtue to perform like sheep I wouldn't be urging revolt. The fact is that these students are the real ones. Many have had the guts to cut their social umbilical cords, become genuinely *free,* and to begin coughing up their own mistakes. They don't take the fatal step which the Cowell Psychiatric Clinic calls "regressive": which means to go back to Mama, or, God forbid, to a Junior College. They face life in its own terms, and many do something rather shocking around Berkeley: they learn to read a book. And I might add that many of them are also Freedom Fighters. (Incidentally, do you know the latest figures? According to Cowell, close to 50 percent of those of you who are graced with the mantle of "Freshman at Cal" are eliminated by the end of the third year.)

Are you aware that the most salient characteristic of the "Multiversity" is massive production of specialized excellence? SPECIALIZED EXCELLENCE. It will be some time before machines will displace the super-trades; thus massive training centers are necessary. But why do we insist upon calling them educational centers rather than training centers?

THE MULTIVERSITY IS NOT AN EDUCATIONAL CENTER, BUT A HIGHLY EFFICIENT IN-DUSTRY: IT PRODUCES BOMBS, OTHER WAR MACHINES, A FEW TOKEN "PEACEFUL" MACHINES, AND ENORMOUS NUMBERS OF SAFE, HIGHLY SKILLED, AND RESPECTABLE AUTOMATONS TO MEET THE IMMEDIATE NEEDS OF BUSINESS AND GOVERNMENT.

We all know that this is necessary to some extent for the maintenance of "American know-how"; otherwise the system would collapse and anarchy would reign, etc. But the forbidden fruit is to ask the devasting questions WHY? WHY *ONLY KNOW-HOW?* Or is it that we wish to produce the largest population ever known to man of highly skilled idiots? We may safely say that graduate schools should perform the function of training for specialized excellence . . . but even then not exclusively. And if you recall, we are discussing the matter of undergraduate freedom to learn. What has occurred when undergraduate education is eradicated; whether it be for the excuse of "too many students," or "exploding knowledge," or in the name of political expedience during the "Cold War"?

WHEN THIS OCCURS IN PUBLIC UNIVERSITIES, THE RESULT IS ABANDONMENT OF THE AMERICAN DEMOCRATIC EXPERIMENT IN WHICH THE RADICAL PROPOSITION OF EDU-CATION FOR ALL IS THE CENTRAL AXIOM. . . .

Dear undergraduate, there is perhaps no other set of questions, in the political realm, of greater importance for you. Let us return for a moment to the matter of who is responsible for your freedom to learn. As I said, . . . the Regents have delegated power and responsibility to the Academic Senates of the eight campuses. Let us just call the Academic Senate the "Faculty," which is the automatic membership of the Senate. At any rate, there is something terribly wrong here. If we assume that the faculty is incompetent to effect the necessary changes, then it would seem of the greatest urgency that the Regents themselves do something to correct the situation. If the Regents do not act, then we must conclude that they are (1) satisfied; or (2) incompetent; or (3) both. Two things are certain: (1) as corporate men of power, the Regents are getting precisely what they most desire—enormous numbers of highly skilled graduates to fill the corporate structure and to keep it running smoothly; (2) IT IS DEBATABLE, from their own point of view, whether the Regents would find it practical to "educate" these skilled people as well as to *train* them. Why? To put the answer very crudely: the Regents, who run private corporations, just as the politicians who run public corporations, desire highly skilled, but politically and economically *dumb* "personnel." The politicians have, of course, even made laws to that effect . . . in the form of such legislation as the Hatch Act, which forbids partisan politics in government bureaucracies. Consequently, if the faculty refuses to face the problem of educating undergraduates, but instead is encouraged, and agrees, to make only piecemeal reform which only slightly lessens pressures in some areas while making them more severe in other areas, the Regents might be said to be very happy with such a course of action . . . in fact that is what they are doing. The course/grade/unit system will probably be "adjusted," and the bread and circus will become more intense and dazzling: note the priority in the University building program . . . first you build the Student Union complex, then an auditorium which will be the "largest this side of the Mississippi," and "sometime in the future" will come an undergraduate library. But why do private and public corporate men act this way?

FROM TIME IMMEMORIAL, MEN OF POWER HAVE CONSIDERED IT WISE TO KEEP THEIR CONSTITUENTS AT A LEVEL OF IGNORANCE WHEREBY THE PROCESS OF RULING THEM IS MOST EASILY ACCOMPLISHED.

Or are we to entertain the possibility that the Regents have upset the applecart of history? Have they become revolutionaries? It is true that they recently removed the ban on Communist speakers on campus. Of course, they resisted for fifteen years . . . since the McCarthy era. And during the McCarthy era they were able to force the Academic Senate into adopting a loyalty oath. If you can forgive the faculty of a university for *that*, you can forgive them for anything. Many professors did not forgive the Senate, however, and resigned. The spine of this faculty, close to forty professors, left in disgust; left scars behind which will never heal. Moreover, what the hell difference does it make whether you hear a Communist every year or so. Most of you would laugh at him . . . like laughing at a movement which involves the entire world! If any one of you wisely decided to study a Communist speaker's proposals, to think about them, to read about them seriously, you not only would find it *impossible from the standpoint of time,* but you would also be considered a heretic by your fellow "students." It is probably accurate to say that the removal of the speaker ban on Communists was a great contribution on the symbolic level . . . like a Charter Day Ceremony. Politically, it was very wise.

Speaking of politics, what relation exists between University and the U.S. Government? Aside from providing trained personnel for public corporations (agencies, bureaus, etc.) as in private ones, is there as direct a relation between the University and Government as between the University and the Regents? Yes, it seems that the University, or shall we call a spade a spade—the Regents—it seems that the Regents are snuggled up pretty tightly to the seats of power in Washington (though it is difficult to tell who-hugs-who the hardest in Washington) :

> Item—from the *Cal Reporter,* May 13, 1963: According to the Financial Report of 1961–62, the U.S. Government spent about 227 millions on Special Projects. These included 190 millions for Lawrence Radiation Laboratory (U.C.), 76 millions for Los Alamos Radiation Lab (U.C.). The income for the entire University (eight campuses) excluding these special projects was 250 millions.

Let us summarize for a moment. Your learning opportunities are limited to "getting ahead," or acquiring a skill to do so. You are obstructed from the realities of the twentieth-century world-in-revolution. You are left with the conclusion that the Regents are conducting a major love affair with the U.S. Government, both of whom are not particular anxious to see you "get smart" for fear that you might become radical student politicos. In conducting this love affair with the Government, the Regents have left the matter of "educating" the infant-undergraduate to the adolescent faculty, knowing that they cannot do the job properly. The major implication in all of this is that if you wish to remain infants then you can . . . but if you wish to deny your infantile character then you must realize that you can't talk to your adolescent babysitters, the faculty, about your corrupt daddies, the Regents. The reason is simple: the babysitters are afraid of their daddies. No . . . if you really want to do something, then you must stand up straight, like the young men and women you really are, and begin to SPEAK what you feel, to speak loudly, strongly, and to say your highest ideals, your deepest dreams, to pull out all of the stops, to let go and to tell the world . . . SPEAK TO THE WORLD AND TELL THEM THAT YOU WANT TO LIVE!!!

Have I sufficiently taken care of your objections? If not, chances are that what remains is *fear,* and that is *your* problem. If I have taken care of your objections, then you might be asking HOW DO YOU START A REBELLION ON THE CAMPUS? That's a tough one—and you might have to get tough in order to be heard. You also know that you will need legitimate demands behind your slogans of FREEDOM NOW! THE FREEDOM TO KNOW AND TO LEARN!!

DEMANDS?

1. IMMEDIATE COMMITMENT OF THE UNIVERSITY TO THE TOTAL ELIMINATION OF THE COURSE/GRADE/UNIT SYSTEM OF UNDERGRADUATE LEARNING: IN THE SOCIAL SCIENCES AND HUMANITIES.

2. IMMEDIATE DISBANDING OF ALL UNIVERSITY DORM AND LIVING GROUP RULES WHICH PRESCRIBE HOURS AND WHICH PROVIDE FOR A SYSTEM OF STUDENT-IMPOSED DISCIPLINE, THEREBY DIVIDING STUDENTS AGAINST THEMSELVES.

3. IMMEDIATE NEGOTIATIONS ON THE ESTABLISHMENT OF A PERMANENT STUDENT VOICE WHICH IS EFFECTIVE (THAT IS, INDEPENDENT) IN RUNNING UNIVERSITY AFFAIRS.

4. IMMEDIATE EFFORTS TO BEGIN RECRUITMENT OF AN UNDERGRADUATE TEACHING FACULTY TO HANDLE UNDERGRADUATE LEARNING IN SOCIAL SCIENCES AND HUMANITIES.

5. IMMEDIATE NEGOTIATIONS REGARDING TWO METHODS OF UNDERGRADUATE LEARNING WHICH PROVIDE FOR THE BASIC FREEDOM REQUIRED IN LEARNING:

    a. A TERMINAL EXAMINATION SYSTEM WHICH WILL BE VOLUNTARY AND AN OPTION WITH "b."

    b. IMMEDIATE CREATION OF UNDERGRADUATE PROGRAMS OF A WIDE VARIETY IN WHICH THE STUDENT WILL BE GIVEN CAREFUL, BUT MINIMAL GUIDANCE, WITHOUT COURSES, GRADES, AND UNITS.

6. IMMEDIATE ESTABLISHMENT OF A UNIVERSITY COMMITTEE TO DEAL WITH THESE DEMANDS ON THE BERKELEY CAMPUS.

Go to the top. Make your demands to the Regents. If they refuse to give you an audience: start a program of agitation, petitioning, rallies, etc., in which the final resort will be CIVIL DISOBEDIENCE. In the long run there is the possibility that you will find it necessary to perform civil disobedience at a couple of major University public ceremonies. Depending on the resistance, you might consider adding the following two demands:

7. RESIGNATION OF CLARK KERR. RESIGNATION OF TOP ADMINISTRATORS WHO MIGHT EMPLOY SLICK DIVERTING TACTICS.

8. RECONSTITUTION OF THE BOARD OF REGENTS, EITHER THROUGH FIRING OR EXPANSION, PERHAPS BOTH. . . .

And if you get this far you will also have witnessed nation-wide publicity which will have exposed Berkeley for the undergraduate sham that it is. Not to say that the public in general will feel that way, what with the press "Red baiting" you, but that students all over the country will read between the lines. By this time you may also be able to call for a mass student strike . . . something which seems unthinkable at present. If a miracle occurs, or two, you might even get to say that you were the seeds of an educational revolution unlike anything which has ever occurred. Remember one thing:

> The task of genius, and man is nothing if not genius, is to keep the miracle alive, to live always in the miracle, to make the miracle more and more miraculous, to swear allegiance to nothing, but live only miraculously, think miraculously, to die miraculousy—HENRY MILLER

Questions for Discussion

1. Do you believe that Cleaveland has given a rational argument to support his contention that students should wage "an open, fierce and thoroughgoing rebellion" on the campus? If so, state it, and analyze its cogency. Or is this an issue open to rational discussion?
2. Do you agree that universities should not make contracts with public or private agencies which will further the military interests of the country? On what grounds could this principle be defended? Why should it be opposed?
3. What is the metaphor which best explains your own view of the proper relationship between a university and a society: island of refuge; ivory tower; a sword's leading edge; bomb; referee?

19   The Student As Nigger

Jerry Farber

With a direct style and—ahem—colorful language, Farber argues that teachers today treat students in the same way masters used to treat their slaves, as niggers. Is he right? His essay is followed by the comments of a California state senator.

Students are niggers. When you get that straight, our schools begin to make sense. It's more important, though, to understand why they're niggers. If we follow that question seriously enough, it will lead us past the zone of academic bullshit, where dedicated teachers pass their knowledge on to a new generation, and into the nitty-gritty of human needs and hang-ups. And from there we can go on to consider whether it might ever be possible for students to come up from slavery.

First let's see what's happening now. Let's look at the role students play in what we like to call education.

At Cal State L.A., where I teach, the students have separate and unequal dining facilities. If I take them into the faculty dining room, my colleagues get uncomfortable, as though there were a bad smell. If I eat in the student cafeteria, I become known as the educational equivalent of a niggerlover. In at least one building there are even rest rooms which students may not use. At Cal State, also, there is an unwritten law barring student-faculty lovemaking. Fortunately, this anti-miscegenation law, like its Southern counterpart, is not 100 percent effective.

Students at Cal State are politically disenfranchised. They are in an academic Lowndes County. Most of them can vote in national elections—their average age is about 26—but they have no voice in the decisions which affect their academic lives. The students are, it is true, allowed to have a toy government of their own. It is a government run for the most part by Uncle Toms and concerned principally with trivia. The faculty and administrators decide what courses will be offered; the students get to choose their own Homecoming Queen. Occasionally, when student leaders get uppity and rebellious, they're either ignored, put off with trivial concessions, or maneuvered expertly out of position.

Smiles & Shuffles

A student at Cal State is expected to know his place. He calls a faculty member "Sir" or "Doctor" or "Professor"—and he smiles and shuffles some as he stands outside the professor's office waiting for permission to enter. The faculty tell him what courses to take (in my department, English, even electives have to be approved by a faculty member); they tell him what to read, what to write, and, frequently, where to set the margins on his typewriter. They tell him what's true and what isn't. Some teachers insist that they encourage dissent but they're almost always lying and every student knows it. Tell the man what he wants to hear or he'll fail your ass out of the course.

When a teacher says "jump," students jump. I know of one professor who refused to take up class time for exams and required students to show up for tests at 6:30 in the morning. And they did, by God! Another, at exam time, provides answer cards to be filled out—each one enclosed in a paper bag with a hole cut in the top to see through. Students stick their writing hands in the bags while taking the test. The teacher isn't a provo; I wish he were. He does it to prevent cheating. Another colleague once caught a student reading during one of his lectures and threw her book against the wall. Still another lectures his students into a stupor and then screams at them in a rage when they fall asleep.

Just last week, during the first meeting of a class, one girl got up to leave after about ten minutes had gone by. The teacher rushed over, grabbed her by the arm, saying "This class is NOT dismissed!" and led her back to her seat. On the same day another teacher began by informing his class that he does not like beards, mustaches, long hair on boys, or capri pants on girls, and will not tolerate any of that in his class. The class, incidentally, consisted mostly of high school teachers.

Follow Orders

Even more discouraging than this Auschwitz approach to education is the fact that the students take it. They haven't gone through twelve years of public school for nothing. They've learned one thing and perhaps only one thing during those twelve years. They've forgotten their algebra. They're hopelessly vague about chemistry and physics. They've grown to fear and resent literature. They write like they've been lobotomized. But, Jesus, can they follow orders! Freshmen come up to me with an essay and ask if I want it folded and whether their name should be in the upper right hand corner. And I want to cry and kiss them and caress their poor tortured heads.

Students don't ask that orders make sense. They give up expecting things to make sense long before they leave elementary school. Things are true because the teacher says they're true. At a very early age we all learn to accept "two truths," as did certain medieval churchmen. Outside of class, things are true to your tongue, your fingers, your stomach, your heart. Inside class, things are true by reason of authority. And that's just fine because you don't care anyway. Miss Wiedemeyer tells you a noun is a person, place or thing. So let it be. You don't give a rat's ass; she doesn't give a rat's ass.

The important thing is to please her. Back in kindergarten, you found out that teachers only love children who stand in nice straight lines. And that's where it's been at ever since. Nothing changes except to get worse. School becomes more and more obviously a prison. Last year I spoke to a student assembly at Manual Arts High School and then couldn't get out of the goddam school. I mean there was NO WAY OUT. Locked doors. High fences. One of the inmates was trying to make it over a fence when he saw me coming and froze in panic. For a moment, I expected sirens, a rattle of bullets, and him clawing the fence.

Then there's the infamous "code of dress." In some high schools, if your skirt

looks too short, you have to kneel before the principal, in a brief allegory of fel-
latio. If the hem doesn't reach the floor, you go home to change while he, presumably, jacks off. You'd think the school board would be delighted to see all the spades
trooping to school in pointy shoes, suits, ties and stingy brims. Uh-uh. They're too
visible.

*What school amounts to, then, for white and black kids alike, is a 12-year course
in how to be slaves.* What else could explain what I see in a freshman class? They've
got that slave mentality: obliging and ingratiating on the surface but hostile and
resistant underneath.

As do black slaves, students vary in their awareness of what's going on. Some
recognize their own put-on for what it is and even let their rebellion break through
to the surface now and then. Others—including most of the "good students"—have
been more deeply brainwashed. They swallow the bullshit with greedy mouths. They
honest-to-God believe in grades, in busy work, in General Education requirements.
They're pathetically eager to be pushed around. They're like those old greyheaded
house niggers you can still find in the South who don't see what all the fuss is about
because Mr. Charlie "treats us real good."

College entrance requirements tend to favor the Toms and screen out the rebels.
Not entirely, of course. Some students at Cal State L.A. are expert con artists who
know perfectly well what's happening. They want the degree or the 2-S and spend
their years on the old plantation alternately laughing and cursing as they play the
game. If their egos are strong enough, they cheat a lot. And, of course, even the
Toms are angry down deep somewhere. But it comes out in passive rather than active
aggression. They're unexplainably thick-witted and subject to frequent spells of
laziness. They misread simple questions. They spend their nights mechanically out-
lining history chapters while meticulously failing to comprehend a word of what's
in front of them.

Inward Anger

The saddest cases among both black slaves and student slaves are the ones who
have so thoroughly introjected their masters' values that their anger is all turned
inward. At Cal State these are the kids for whom every low grade is torture, who
stammer and shake when they speak to a professor, who go through an emotional
crisis every time they're called upon during class. You can recognize them easily at
finals time. Their faces are festooned with fresh pimples, their bowels boil audibly
across the room. If there really is a Last Judgment, then the parents and teachers who
created these wrecks are going to burn in hell.

So students are niggers. It's time to find out why, and to do this, we have to take
a long look at Mr. Charlie.

The teachers I know best are college professors. Outside the classroom and taken
as a group, their most striking characteristic is timidity. They're short on balls.

Just look at their working conditions. At a time when even migrant workers have
begun to fight and win, college professors are still afraid to make more than a token
effort to improve their pitiful economic status. In California state colleges the faculties are screwed regularly and vigorously by the Governor and Legislature and yet
they still won't offer any solid resistance. They lie flat on their stomachs with their

pants down, mumbling catch phrases like "professional dignity" and "meaningful dialogue."

Professors were no different when I was an undergraduate at UCLA during the McCarthy era; it was like a cattle stampede as they rushed to cop out. And, in more recent years, I found that my being arrested in sit-ins brought from my colleagues not so much approval or condemnation as open-mouthed astonishment. "You could lose your job!"

Now, of course, there's the Vietnamese war. It gets some opposition from a few teachers. Some support it. But a vast number of professors, who know perfectly well what's happening, are copping out again. And in the high schools, you can forget it. Stillness reigns.

Forces a Split

I'm not sure why teachers are so chickenshit. It could be that academic training itself forces a split between thought and action. It might also be that the tenured security of a teaching job attracts timid persons and, furthermore, that teaching, like police work, pulls in persons who are unsure of themselves and need weapons and the other external trappings of authority.

At any rate teachers ARE short on balls. And, as Judy Eisenstein has eloquently pointed out, the classroom offers an artificial and protected environment in which they can exercise their will to power. Your neighbors may drive a better car; gas station attendants may intimidate you; your wife may dominate you; the State Legislature may shit on you; but in the classroom, by God, students do what you say— or else. The grade is a hell of a weapon. It may not rest on your hip, potent and rigid like a cop's gun, but in the long run it's more powerful. At your personal whim—and any time you choose—you can keep 35 students up for nights and have the pleasure of seeing them walk into the classroom pasty-faced and red-eyed carrying a sheaf of typewritten pages, with title page, MLA footnotes, and margins set at 15 and 91.

The general timidity which causes teachers to make niggers of their students usually includes a more specific fear—fear of the students themselves. After all, students are different, just like black people. You stand exposed in front of them, knowing that their interests, their values and their language are different from yours. To make matters worse, you may suspect that you yourself are not the most engaging of persons. What then can protect you from their ridicule and scorn? Respect for Authority. That's what. It's the policeman's gun again. The white bwana's pith helmet. So you flaunt that authority. You wither whisperers with a murderous glance. You crush objectors with erudition and heavy irony. And, worst of all, you make your own attainments seem not accessible but awesomely remote. You conceal your massive ignorance—and parade a slender learning.

White Supremacy

The teacher's fear is mixed with an understandable need to be admired and to feel superior, a need which also makes him cling to his "white supremacy." Ideally, a teacher should minimize the distance between himself and his students. He should encourage them not to need him—eventually or even immediately. But this is rarely the case. Teachers make themselves high priests of arcane mysteries. They become masters of mumbojumbo. Even a more or less conscientious teacher may be torn between the desire to give and the desire to hold them in bondage to him. I can find no other explanation that accounts for the way my own subject, Literature, is generally taught. Literature, which ought to be a source of joy, solace and enlightenment, often becomes in the classroom nothing more than a source of anxiety—at best an arena for expertise, a ledger book for the ego. Literature teachers, often afraid to join a real union, nonetheless may practice the worst kind of trade-unionism in the classroom; they do to literature what Beckmesser does to song in Wagner's *Meistersinger*. The avowed purpose of English departments is to teach literature; too often their real function is to kill it.

Finally, there's the darkest reason of all for the master-slave approach to education. The less trained and the less socialized a person is, the more he constitutes a sexual threat and the more he will be subjugated by institutions, such as penitentiaries and schools. Many of us are aware by now of the sexual neurosis which makes white man so fearful of integrated schools and neighborhoods, and which makes the castration of Negroes a deeply entrenched Southern folkway. We should recognize a similar pattern in education. There is a kind of castration that goes on in schools. It begins, before school years, with parents' first encroachments on their children's free unashamed sexuality and continues right up to the day when they hand you your doctoral diploma with a bleeding, shriveled pair of testicles stapled to the parchment. It's not that sexuality has no place in the classroom. You'll find it there but only in certain perverted and vitiated forms.

Bleeding Brains

How does sex show up in school? First of all, there's the sado-masochistic relationship between teachers and students. That's plenty sexual, although the price of enjoying it is to be unaware of what's happening. In walks the student in his Ivy League equivalent of a motorcycle jacket. In walks the teacher—a kind of intellectual rough trade—and flogs his students with grades, tests, sarcasm and snotty superiority until their very brains are bleeding. In Swinburne's England, the whipped school boy frequently grew up to be a flagellant. With us the perversion is intellectual but it's no less perverse.

Sex also shows up in the classroom as academic subject matter—sanitized and abstracted, thoroughly divorced from feeling. You get "sex education" now in both high school and college classes: everyone determined not to be embarrassed, to be very up to date, very contempo. These are the classes for which sex, as Feiffer puts it, "can be a beautiful thing if properly administered." And then, of course, there's still another depressing manifestation of sex in the classroom: the "off-color" teacher, who keeps his class awake with sniggering sexual allusions, obscene titters and academic innuendo. The sexuality he purveys, it must be admitted, is at least better than none at all.

What's missing, from kindergarten to graduate school, is honest recognition of what's actually happening—turned-on awareness of hairy goodies underneath the petti-pants, the chinos and the flannels. It's not that sex needs to be pushed in school; sex is pushed enough. But we should let it be, where it is and like it is. I don't insist that ladies in junior high lovingly caress their students' cocks (someday, maybe); however, it is reasonable to ask that the ladies don't, by example and stricture, teach their students to pretend that those cocks aren't there. As things stand now, students are psychically castrated and spayed—and for the very same reason that black men are castrated in Georgia: because they're a threat.

Once a Nigger

So you can add sexual repression to the list of causes, along with vanity, fear and will to power, that turn the teacher into Mr. Charlie. You might also want to keep in mind that he was a nigger once himself and has never really gotten over it. And there are more causes, some of which are better described in sociological than in psychological terms. Work them out, it's not hard. But in the meantime what we've got on our hands is a whole lot of niggers. And what makes this particularly grim is that the student has less chance than the black man of getting out of his bag. Because the student doesn't even know he's in it. That, more or less, is what's happening in higher education. And the results are staggering.

For one thing damn little education takes place in the schools. How could it? *You can't educate slaves; you can only train them.* Or, to use an even uglier and more timely word, you can only program them.

Dance or Dunce

I like to folk dance. Like other novices, I've gone to the Intersection or to the Museum and laid out good money in order to learn how to dance. No grades, no prerequisites, no separate dining rooms; they just turn you on to dancing. That's education. Now look at what happens in college. A friend of mine, Milt, recently finished a folk dance class. For his final he had to learn things like this: "The Irish are known for their wit and imagination, qualities reflected in their dances, which include the jig, the reel and the hornpipe." And then the teacher graded him A, B, C, D, or F, while he danced in front of her. That's not education. That's not even training. That's an abomination on the face of the earth. It's especially ironic because Milt took that dance class trying to get out of the academic rut. He took crafts for the same reason. Great, right? Get your hands in some clay? Make something? Then the teacher announced that a 20-page term paper would be required—with footnotes.

At my school we even grade people on how they read poetry. That's like grading people on how they fuck. But we do it. In fact, God help me, I do it. I'm the Adolph Eichmann of English 323. Simon Legree on the poetry plantation. "Tote that iamb! Lift that spondee!" Even to discuss a good poem in that environment is potentially dangerous because the very classroom is contaminated. As hard as I may try to turn students on to poetry, I know that the desks, the tests, the IBM cards, their own attitudes toward school, and my own residue of UCLA method are turning them off.

Another result of student slavery is equally serious. Students don't get emancipated when they graduate. As a matter of fact, we don't let them graduate until they've demonstrated their willingness—over 16 years—to remain slaves. And for important jobs, like teaching, we make them go through more years, just to make sure. What I'm getting at is that we're all more or less niggers and slaves, teachers and students alike. This is a fact you want to start with in trying to understand wider social phenomena, say, politics, in our country and in other countries.

Intimidate or Kill

Educational oppression is trickier to fight than racial oppression. If you're a black rebel, they can't exile you; they either have to intimidate you or kill you. But in high school or college, they can just bounce you out of the fold. And they do. Rebel students and renegade faculty members get smothered or shot down with devastating accuracy. In high school, it's usually the student who gets it; in college, it's more often the teacher. Others get tired of fighting and voluntarily leave the system. This may be a mistake though. Dropping out of college, for a rebel, is a little like going North, for a Negro. You can't really get away from it so you might as well stay and raise hell.

How do you raise hell? That's a whole other article. But just for a start, why not stay with the analogy? What have black people done? They have, first of all, faced the fact of their slavery. They've stopped kidding themselves about an eventual reward in that Great Watermelon Patch in the sky. They've organized; they've decided to get freedom now, and they've started taking it.

Students, like black people, have immense unused power. They could, theoretically, insist on participating in their own education. They could make academic freedom bilateral. They could teach their teachers to thrive on love and admiration, rather than fear and respect, and to lay down their weapons. Students could discover community. And they could learn to dance by dancing on the IBM cards. They could make coloring books out of the catalogs and they could put the grading system in a museum. They could raze one set of walls and let life come blowing into the classroom. They could raze another set of walls and let education flow out and flood the streets. They could turn the classroom into where it's at—a "field of action" as Peter Marin describes it. And, believe it or not, they could study eagerly and learn prodigiously for the best of all possible reasons—their own reasons.

They could. Theoretically. They have the power. But only in a very few places, like Berkeley, have they even begun to think about using it. For students, as for black people, the hardest battle isn't with Mr. Charlie. It's with what Mr. Charlie has done to your mind.

Academic Madness

John G. Schmitz, California State Senator

October 20, 1967

Those who have become, by consent or default, the leaders of our academic teaching faculty seem almost to be engaged in a contest in madness, each one striving to outdo his fellows in degrading and befouling higher education.

From "Sacramento Report," the state senator's weekly release to newspapers, included here by permission of John G. Schmitz.

We have watched them plunge from social activism through nonviolent protest to mass demonstrations to physical force and the most disgusting filth perverted minds can produce. They and the students who follow them, whom they arouse and infect with revolutionary mania, have turned campuses into battlegrounds and classrooms into political rallies.

We have just witnessed the spectacle of the Chancellor of the University of California at Berkeley publicly defending a mass meeting scheduled on his campus from which students were to march directly into the city of Oakland for a highly publicized defiance of law which could, and in fact did, lead to a riot.

Less publicized, but no less appalling, was the action of "black power" advocates on the campus of San Francisco State College last spring in threatening to use physical violence on a few less militant members of the student government there who would not agree to all their demands—and the obvious hostility of members of the faculty toward any attempt to investigate, let alone punish, those students who sought to turn the Groves of Academe into a bloody jungle.

Now I have just learned that an instructor in freshman English composition in a local state college has assigned, as required reading to a coeducational class of 24 students, an essay written by an assistant professor of English at a state college in Los Angeles whose contents and language are so vile that no newspaper in this state could print it. In a section of his essay entitled "Bleeding Brains," the assistant professor–author explains in specific detail and gutter language why he thinks that college students are resented and mistreated by older persons because the adults are jealous of the students' sexual vigor.

I recognize that almost incredible abuses such as this are the work of a minority of the teaching faculty. But the majority who seem so willing to tolerate it, and even to defend it under the tattered banner of "academic freedom," must bear a large share of the responsibility for what is happening. I will continue to urge that the legislature use its "power of the purse" to compel a complete housecleaning and I will not support the annual appropriations for state colleges and the University of California until they have taken effective action to restore common sense, common decency and the pursuit of knowledge on their campuses.

Questions for Discussion

1. The language is rough indeed. Were you offended? Should articles like this be published at all, or do you agree with Senator Schmitz's conclusions?
2. Apart from the language, is Farber's thesis about students being treated as niggers accurate? Be specific.
3. Does Farber suggest alternative ways by which teachers could relate to students? Should he? Can you offer constructive suggestions, particularly for a classroom in which you might be teaching?

20 You Have to Grow Up in Scarsdale To Know How Bad Things Really Are

Kenneth Keniston

In this thoughtful analysis of the current student revolution, the author examines two alternative hypotheses, the "Oedipal Rebellion" and the doctrine of "Historical Irrelevance," rejects both, and proposes his own explanation, identifying two different revolutions, one partially completed, the other aborning.

The recent events at Harvard are the culmination of a long year of unprecedented student unrest in the advanced nations of the world. We have learned to expect students in underdeveloped countries to lead unruly demonstrations against the status quo, but what is new, unexpected and upsetting to many is that an apparently similar mood is sweeping across America, France, Germany, Italy and even Eastern European nations like Czechoslovakia and Poland. Furthermore, the revolts occur, not at the most backward universities, but at the most distinguished, liberal and enlightened—Berkeley, the Sorbonne, Tokyo, Columbia, the Free University of Berlin, Rome and now Harvard.

This development has taken almost everyone by surprise. The American public is clearly puzzled, frightened and often outraged by the behavior of its most privileged youth. The scholarly world, including many who have devoted their lives to the study of student protest, has been caught off guard as well. For many years, American analysts of student movements have been busy demonstrating that "it can't happen here." Student political activity abroad has been seen as a reaction to modernization, industrialization and the demise of traditional or tribal societies. In an already modern, industrialized, detribalized "stable" nation like America, it was argued, student protests are naturally absent.

Another explanation has tied student protests abroad to bad living conditions in some universities and to the unemployability of their graduates. Student revolts, it was argued, spring partly from the misery of student life in countries like India and Indonesia. Students who must live in penury and squalor naturally turn against their universities and societies. And if, as in many developing nations, hundreds of thousands of university graduates can find no work commensurate with their skills, the chances for student militancy are further increased.

These arguments helped explain the "silent generation" of the nineteen-fifties and the absence of protest, during that period, in American universities, where students are often "indulged" with good living conditions, close student-faculty contact and considerable freedom of speech. And they helped explain why "super-employable" American college graduates, especially the much-sought-after ones from colleges like Columbia and Harvard, seemed so contented with their lot.

But such arguments do not help us understand today's noisy, angry and militant students in the advanced countries. Nor do they explain why students who enjoy the greatest advantages—those at the leading universities—are often found in the revolts. As a result, several new interpretations of student protest are currently being put forward, interpretations that ultimately form part of what Richard Poirier has termed "the war against the young."

Many reactions to student unrest, of course, spring primarily from fear, anger, confusion or envy, rather than from theoretical analysis. Governor Wallace's attacks on student "anarchists" and other "pin-headed intellectuals," for example, were hardly coherent explanations of protest. Many of the bills aimed at punishing student protesters being proposed in Congress and state legislatures reflect similar feelings of anger and outrage. Similarly, the presumption that student unrest *must* be part of an international conspiracy is based on emotion rather than fact. Even George F. Kennan's recent discussion of the American student left is essentially a moral condemnation of "revolting students," rather than an effort to explain their behavior.

If we turn to more thoughtful analyses of the current student mood we find two general theories gaining widespread acceptance. The first, articulately expressed by Lewis S. Feuer in his recent book on student movements, "The Conflict of Generations," might be termed the "Oedipal Rebellion" interpretation. The second, cogently stated by Zbigniew Brzezinski and Daniel Bell, can be called the theory of "Historical Irrelevance."

The explanation of Oedipal Rebellion sees the underlying force in all student revolts as blind, unconscious Oedipal hatred of fathers and the older generation. Feuer, for example, finds in all student movement an inevitable tendency toward violence and a combination of "regicide, parricide and suicide." A decline in respect for the authority of the older generation is needed to trigger a student movement, but the force behind it comes from "obscure" and "unconscious" forces in the child's early life, including both intense death wishes against his father and the enormous guilt and self-hatred that such wishes inspire in the child.

The idealism of student movements is thus, in many respects, only a "front" for the latent unconscious destructiveness and self-destructiveness of underlying motivations. Even the expressed desire of these movements to help the poor and exploited is explained psychoanalytically by Feuer: Empathy for the disadvantaged is traced to "traumatic" encounters with parental bigotry in the students' childhoods, when their parents forbade them to play with children of other races or lower social classes. The identification of today's new left with blacks is thus interpreted as an unconscious effort to "abreact and undo this original trauma."

There are two basic problems with the Oedipal Rebellion theory, however. First, although it uses psychoanalytic terms, it is bad psychoanalysis. The real psychoanalytic account insists that the Oedipus complex is universal in all normally developing children. To point to this complex in explaining student rebellion is, therefore, like pointing to the fact that all children learn to walk. Since both characteristics are said to be universal, neither helps us understand why, at some historical moments, students are restive and rebellious, while at others they are not. Second, the theory does not help us explain why some students (especially those from middle-class, affluent and idealistic families) are most inclined to rebel, while others (especially those from working class and deprived families) are less so.

In order really to explain anything, the Oedipal Rebellion hypothesis would have to be modified to point to an unusually *severe* Oedipus complex, involving especially *intense* and unresolved unconscious feelings of father-hatred in student rebels. But much is now known about the lives and backgrounds of these rebels— at least those in the United States—and this evidence does not support even the modified theory. On the contrary, it indicates that most student protesters are relatively *close* to their parents, that the values they profess are usually the ones they learned at the family dinner table, and that their parents tend to be highly educated, liberal or left-wing and politically active.

Furthermore, psychological studies of student radicals indicate that they are no more neurotic, suicidal, enraged or disturbed than are nonradicals. Indeed, most studies find them to be rather more integrated, self-accepting and "advanced," in a psychological sense, than their politically inactive contemporaries. In general, research on American student rebels supports a "Generational Solidarity" (or chip-off-the-old-block) theory, rather than one of Oedipal Rebellion.

The second theory of student revolts now being advanced asserts that they are a reaction against "historical irrelevance." Rebellion springs from the unconscious awareness of some students that society has left them and their values behind. According to this view, the ultimate causes of student dissent are sociological rather than psychological. They lie in fundamental changes in the nature of the advanced societies—especially, in the change from industrial to post-industrial society. The student revolution is seen not as a true revolution, but as a counterrevolution— what Daniel Bell has called "the guttering last gasp of a romanticism soured by rancor and impotence."

This theory assumes that we are moving rapidly into a new age in which technology will dominate, an age whose real rulers will be men like computer experts, systems analysts and technobureaucrats. Students who are attached to outmoded and obsolescent values like humanism and romanticism unconsciously feel they have no place in this post-industrial world. When they rebel they are like the Luddites of the past—workers who smashed machines to protest the inevitable industrial revolution. Today's student revolt reflects what Brzezinski terms "an unconscious realization that they [the rebels] are themselves becoming historically obsolete"; it is nothing but the "death rattle of the historical irrelevants."

This theory is also inadequate. It assumes that the shape of the future is already technologically determined, and that protesting students unconsciously "know" that it will offer them no real reward, honor or power. But the idea that the future can be accurately predicted is open to fundamental objection. Every past attempt at prophecy has turned out to be grievously incorrect. Extrapolations from the past, while sometimes useful in the short run, are usually fundamentally wrong in the long run, especially when they attempt to predict the quality of human life, the nature of political and social organization, international relations or the shape of future culture.

The future is, of course, made by men. Technology is not an inevitable master of man and history, but merely provides the possibility of applying scientific knowledge to specific problems. Men may identify with it or refuse to, use it or be used by it for good or evil, apply it humanely or destructively. Thus, there is no real evidence that student protest will emerge as the "death rattle of the historical irrelevants." It could equally well be the "first spark of a new historical era." No one today can be sure of the outcome, and people who feel certain that the future will bring the obsolescence and death of those whom they dislike are often merely expressing their fond hope.

The fact that today's students invoke "old" humanistic and romantic ideas in no way proves that student protests are a "last gasp" of a dying order. Quite the contrary: *All* revolutions draw upon older values and visions. Many of the ideals of the French Revolution, for example, originated in Periclean Athens. Revolutions do not occur because new ideas suddenly develop, but because a new generation begins to take *old* ideas seriously—not merely as interesting theoretical views, but as the basis for political action and social change. Until recently, the humanistic vision of human fulfillment and the romantic vision of an expressive, imaginative and passionate life were taken seriously only by small aristocratic or Bohemian groups. The fact that they are today taken as real goals by millions of students in many nations does not mean that these students are "counterrevolutionaries," but merely that their ideas follow the pattern of every major revolution.

Indeed, today's student rebels are rarely opposed to technology *per se*. On the contrary, they take the high technology of their societies completely for granted, and concern themselves with it very little. What they *are* opposed to is, in essence, the worship of Technology, the tendency to treat people as "inputs" or "outputs" of a technological system, the subordination of human needs to technological programs. The essential conflict between the minority of students who make up the student revolt and the existing order is a conflict over the future direction of technological society, not a counterrevolutionary protest against technology.

In short, both the Oedipal Rebellion and the Historical Irrelevance theories are what students would call "put-downs." If we accept either, we are encouraged not to listen to protests, or to explain them away or reject them as either the "acting out" of destructive Oedipal feelings or the blind reaction of an obsolescent group to the awareness of its obsolescence. But if, as I have argued, neither of these theories is adequate to explain the current "wave" of student protest here and abroad, how can we understand it?

One factor often cited to explain student unrest is the large number of people in the world under 30—today the critical dividing line between generations. But this explanation alone, like the theories just discussed, is not adequate, for in all historical eras the vast portion of the population has always been under 30. Indeed, in primitive societies most people die before they reach that age. If chronological youth alone was enough to insure rebellion, the advanced societies—where a greater proportion of the population reaches old age than ever before in history—should be the *least* revolutionary, and primitive societies the *most*. This is not the case.

More relevant factors are the relationship of those under 30 to the established institutions of society (that is, whether they are engaged in them or not); and the opportunities that society provides for their continuing intellectual, ethical and emo-

tional development. In both cases the present situation in the advanced nations is
without precedent.

Philippe Aries, in his remarkable book, *Centuries of Childhood,* points out that,
until the end of the Middle Ages, no separate stage of childhood was recognized in
Western societies. Infancy ended at approximately 6 or 7, whereupon most children
were integrated into adult life, treated as small men and women and expected to
work as junior partners of the adult world. Only later was childhood recognized as
a separate stage of life, and our own century is the first to "guarantee" it by requiring universal primary education.

The recognition of adolescence as a stage of life is of even more recent origin,
the product of the 19th and 20th centuries. Only as industrial societies became pros-
perous enough to defer adult work until after puberty could they create institutions
—like widespread secondary-school education—that would extend adolescence to
virtually all young people. Recognition of adolescence also arose from the vocational
and psychological requirements of these societies, which needed much higher levels
of training and psychological development than could be guaranteed through primary education alone. There is, in general, an intimate relationship between the way
a society defines the stages of life and its economic, political and social characteristics.

Today, in more developed nations, we are beginning to witness the recognition
of still another stage of life. Like childhood and adolescence, it was initially granted
only to a small minority, but is now being rapidly extended to an ever-larger group.
I will call this the stage of "youth," and by that I mean both a further phase of
disengagement from society and the period of psychological development that intervenes between adolescence and adulthood. This stage, which continues into the
20's and sometimes into the 30's, provides opportunities for intellectual, emotional
and moral development that were never afforded to any other large group in history.
In the student revolts we are seeing one result of this advance.

I call the extension of youth an advance advisedly. Attendance at a college or
university is a major part of this extension, and there is growing evidence that this
is, other things being equal, a good thing for the student. Put in an oversimplified
phrase, it tends to free him—to free him from swallowing unexamined the assumptions of the past, to free him from the superstitions of his childhood, to free him
to express his feelings more openly and to free him from irrational bondage to
authority.

I do not mean to suggest, of course, that all college graduates are free and liberated
spirits, unencumbered by irrationality, superstition, authoritarianism or blind adherence to tradition. But these findings do indicate that our colleges, far from crank-
ing out only machinelike robots who will provide skilled manpower for the economy,
are also producing an increasing number of highly critical citizens—young men and
women who have the opportunity, the leisure, the affluence and the educational resources to continue their development beyond the point where most people in the
past were required to stop it.

So, one part of what we are seeing on campuses throughout the world is not a
reflection of how bad higher education is, but rather of its extraordinary accomplishments. Even the moral righteousness of the student rebels, a quality both endearing
and infuriating to their elders, must be judged at least partially a consequence of the
privilege of an extended youth; for a prolonged development, we know, encourages

the individual to elaborate a more personal, less purely conventional sense of ethics.

What the advanced nations have done is to create their own critics on a mass basis —that is, to create an ever-larger group of young people who take the highest values of their societies as their own, who internalize these values and identify them with their own best selves, and who are willing to struggle to implement them. At the same time, the extension of youth has lessened the personal risks of dissent: These young people have been freed from the requirements of work, gainful employment and even marriage, which permits them to criticize their society from a protected position of disengagement.

But the mere prolongation of development need not automatically lead to unrest. To be sure, we have granted to millions the opportunity to examine their societies, to compare them with their values and to come to a reasoned judgment of the existing order. But why should their judgment today be so unenthusiastic?

What protesting students throughout the world share is a mood more than an ideology or a program, a mood that says the existing system—the power structure —is hypocritical, unworthy of respect, outmoded and in urgent need of reform. In addition, students everywhere speak of repression, manipulation and authoritarianism. (This is paradoxical, considering the apparently great freedoms given them in many nations. In America, for example, those who complain most loudly about being suffocated by the subtle tyranny of the Establishment usually attend the institutions where student freedom is greatest.) Around this general mood, specific complaints arrange themselves as symptoms of what students often call the "exhaustion of the existing society."

To understand this phenomenon we must recognize that, since the Second World War, some societies have indeed begun to move past the industrial era into a new world that is post-industrial, technological, post-modern, post-historic or, in Brzezinski's term, "technectronic." In Western Europe, the United States, Canada and Japan, the first contours of this new society are already apparent. And, in many other less-developed countries, middle-class professionals (whose children become activists) often live in post-industrial enclaves within pre-industrial societies. Whatever we call the post-industrial world, it has demonstrated that, for the first time, man can produce more than enough to meet his material needs.

This accomplishment is admittedly blemished by enormous problems of economic distribution in the advanced nations, and it is in terrifying contrast to the overwhelming poverty of the Third World. Nevertheless, it is clear that what might be called "the problem of production" *can*, in principle, be solved. If all members of American society, for example, do not have enough material goods, it is because the system of distribution is flawed. The same is true, or will soon be true, in many other nations that are approaching advanced states of industrialization. Characteristically, these nations, along with the most technological, are those where student unrest has recently been most prominent.

The transition from industrial to post-industrial society brings with it a major shift in social emphases and values. Industrializing and industrial societies tend to be oriented toward solving the problem of production. An industrial ethic—sometimes Protestant, sometimes Socialist, sometimes Communist—tends to emphasize psychological qualities like self-discipline, delay of gratification, achievement-orientation and a strong emphasis on economic success and productivity. The social, political and economic institutions of these societies tend to be organized in a way that is consistent with the goal of increasing production. And industrial societies tend to apply relatively uniform standards, to reward achievement rather than status acquired by birth, to emphasize emotional neutrality ("coolness") and rationality in work and public life.

The emergence of post-industrial societies, however, means that growing numbers of the young are brought up in family environments where abundance, relative economic security, political freedom and affluence are simply facts of life, not goals to be striven for. To such people the psychological imperatives, social institutions and cultural values of the industrial ethic seem largely outdated and irrelevant to their own lives.

Once it has been demonstrated that a society *can* produce enough for all of its members, at least some of the young turn to other goals: for example, trying to make sure that society *does* produce enough and distributes it fairly, or searching for ways to live meaningfully with the goods and the leisure they *already* have. The problem is that our society has, in some realms, exceeded its earlier targets. Lacking new ones, it has become exhausted by its success.

When the values of industrial society become devitalized, the élite sectors of youth —the most affluent, intelligent, privileged and so on—come to feel that they live in institutions whose demands lack moral authority or, in the current jargon, "credibility." Today, the moral imperative and urgency behind production, acquisition, materialism and abundance has been lost.

Furthermore, with the lack of moral legitimacy felt in "the System," the least request for loyalty, restraint or conformity by its representatives—for example, by college presidents and deans—can easily be seen as a moral outrage, an authoritarian repression, a manipulative effort to "co-opt" students into joining the Establishment and an exercise in "illegitimate authority" that must be resisted. From this conception springs at least part of the students' vague sense of oppression. And, indeed, perhaps their peculiar feeling of suffocation arises ultimately from living in societies without vital ethical claims.

Given such a situation, it does not take a clear-cut issue to trigger a major protest. I doubt, for example, that college and university administrators are in fact *more* hypocritical and dishonest than they were in the past. American intervention in Vietnam, while many of us find it unjust and cruel, is not inherently *more* outrageous than other similar imperialistic interventions by America and other nations within the last century. And the position of blacks in this country, although disastrously and unjustifiably disadvantaged, is, in some economic and legal respects, better than ever before. Similarly, the conditions for students in America have never been as good, especially, as I have noted, at those élite colleges where student protests are most common.

But this is *precisely* the point: It is *because* so many of the *other* problems of American society seem to have been resolved, or to be resolvable in principle, that students now react with new indignation to old problems, turn to new goals and propose radical reforms.

So far I have emphasized the moral exhaustion of the old order and the fact that, for the children of post-industrial affluence, the once-revolutionary claims of the industrial society have lost much of their validity. I now want to argue that we are witnessing on the campuses of the world a fusion of *two revolutions* with distinct historical origins. One is a continuation of the old and familiar revolution of the industrial society, the liberal-democratic-egalitarian revolution that started in America and France at the turn of the 18th century and spread to virtually every nation in the world. (Not completed in any of them, its contemporary American form is, above all, to be found in the increased militancy of blacks.) The other is the new revolution, the post-industrial one, which seeks to define new goals relevant to the 20th and 21st centuries.

In its social and political aspects, the first revolution has been one of universalization, to use the sociologist's awkward term. It has involved the progressive extension to more and more people of economic, political and social rights, privileges and opportunities originally available only to the aristocracy, then to the middle class, and now in America to the relatively affluent white working class. It is, in many respects, a *quantitative* revolution. That is, it concerns itself less with the quality of life than with the amount of political freedom, the quantity and distribution of goods or the amount and level of injustice.

As the United States approaches the targets of the first revolution, on which this society was built, to be poor shifts from being an unfortunate fact of life to being an outrage. And, for the many who have never experienced poverty, discrimination, exploitation or oppression, even to *witness* the existence of these evils in the lives of others suddenly becomes intolerable. In our own time the impatience to complete the first revolution has grown apace, and we find less willingness to compromise, wait and forgive among the young, especially among those who now take the values of the old revolution for granted—seeing them not as goals, but as *rights*.

A subtle change has thus occurred. What used to be utopian ideals—like equality, abundance and freedom from discrimination—have now become demands, inalienable rights upon which one can insist without brooking any compromise. It is noteworthy that, in today's student confrontations, no one requests anything. Students present their "demands."

So, on the one hand, we see a growing impatience to complete the first revolution. But, on the other, there is a newer revolution concerned with newer issues, a revolution that is less social, economic or political than psychological, historical and cultural. It is less concerned with the quantities of things than with their qualities, and it judges the virtually complete liberal revolution and finds it still wanting.

"You have to have grown up in Scarsdale to know how bad things really are," said one radical student. This comment would probably sound arrogant, heartless and insensitive to a poor black, much less to a citizen of the Third World. But he meant something important by it. He meant that *even* in the Scarsdales of America, with their affluence, their upper-middle-class security and abundance, their well-fed, well-heeled children and their excellent schools, something is wrong. Economic affluence does not guarantee a feeling of personal fulfillment; political freedom does not always yield an inner sense of liberation and cultural freedom; social justice and equality may leave one with a feeling that something else is missing in life. "No to the consumer society!" shouted the bourgeois students of the Sorbonne during May and June of 1968 — a cry that understandably alienated French workers, for whom affluence and the consumer society are still central goals.

What, then, are the targets of the new revolution? As is often noted, students themselves don't know. They speak vaguely of "a society that has never existed," of "new values," of a "more humane world," of "liberation" in some psychological, cultural and historical sense. Their rhetoric is largely negative; they are stronger in opposition than in proposals for reform; their diagnoses often seem accurate, but their prescriptions are vague; and they are far more articulate in urging the immediate completion of the first revolution than in defining the goals of the second. Thus, we can only indirectly discern trends that point to the still-undefined targets of the new revolution.

What are these trends and targets?

First, there is a revulsion against the notion of quantity, particularly economic quantity and materialism, and a turn toward concepts of quality. One of the most delightful slogans of the French student revolt was, "Long live the passionate revolution of creative intelligence!" In a sense, the achievement of abundance may allow millions of contemporary men and women to examine, as only a few artists and madmen have examined in the past, the quality, joyfulness and zestfulness of experience. The "expansion of consciousness"; the stress on the expressive, the aesthetic and the creative; the emphasis on imagination, direct perception and fantasy— all are part of the effort to enhance the quality of this experience.

Another goal of the new revolution involves a revolt against uniformity, equalization, standardization and homogenization—not against technology itself, but against the "technologization of man." At times, this revolt approaches anarchic quaintness, but it has a positive core as well—the demand that individuals be appreciated, not because of their similarities or despite their differences, but because they *are* different, diverse, unique and noninterchangeable. This attitude is evident in many areas: for example, the insistence upon a cultivation of personal idiosyncrasy, mannerism and unique aptitude. Intellectually, it is expressed in the rejection of the melting-pot and consensus-politics view of American life in favor of a post-homogeneous America in which cultural diversity and conflict are underlined rather than denied.

The new revolution also involves a continuing struggle against psychological or institutional closure or rigidity in any form, even the rigidity of a definite adult role. Positively, it extols the virtues of openness, motion and continuing human development. What Robert J. Lifton has termed the protean style is clearly in evidence. There is emerging a concept of a lifetime of personal change, of an adulthood of continuing self-transformation, of an adaptability and an openness to the revolutionary modern world that will enable the individual to remain "with it"—psychologically youthful and on top of the present.

Another characteristic is the revolt against centralized power and the complementary demand for participation. What is demanded is not merely the consent of the governed, but the involvement of the governed. "Participatory democracy" summarizes this aspiration, but it extends far beyond the phrase and the rudimentary social forms that have sprung up around it. It extends to the demand for relevance in education—that is, for a chance for the student to participate in his own educational experience in a way that involves all of his faculties, emotional and moral as well as intellectual. The demand for "student power" (or, in Europe, "co-determination") is an aspect of the same theme: At Nanterre, Columbia, Frankfurt and

Harvard, students increasingly seek to participate in making the policies of their universities.

This demand for participation is also embodied in the new ethic of "meaningful human relationships," in which individuals confront each other without masks, pretenses and games. They "relate" to each other as unique and irreplaceable human beings, and develop new forms of relationships from which all participants will grow.

In distinguishing between the old and the new revolutions, and in attempting to define the targets of the new, I am, of course, making distinctions that students themselves rarely make. In any one situation the two revolutions are joined and fused, if not confused. For example, the Harvard students' demand for "restructuring the university" is essentially the second revolution's demand for participation; but their demand for an end to university "exploitation" of the surrounding community is tied to the more traditional goals of the first revolution. In most radical groups there is a range of opinion that starts with the issues of the first (racism, imperialism, exploitation, war) and runs to the concerns of the second (experiential education, new life styles, meaningful participation, consciousness-expansion, relatedness, encounter and community). The first revolution is personified by Maoist-oriented Progressive Labor party factions within the student left, while the second is represented by hippies, the "acid left," and the Yippies. In any individual, and in all student movements, these revolutions coexist in uneasy and often abrasive tension.

Furthermore, one of the central problems for student movements today is the absence of any theory of society that does justice to the new world in which we of the most industrialized nations live. In their search for rational critiques of present societies, students turn to theories like Marxism that are intricately bound up with the old revolution.

Such theories make the ending of economic exploitation, the achievement of social justice, the abolition of racial discrimination and the development of political participation and freedom central, but they rarely deal adequately with the issues of the second revolution. Students inevitably try to adapt the rhetoric of the first to the problems of the second, using concepts that are often blatantly inadequate to today's world.

Even the concept of "revolution" itself is so heavily laden with images of political, economic and social upheaval that it hardly seems to characterize the equally radical but more social-psychological and cultural transformations involved in the new revolution. One student, recognizing this, called the changes occurring in his California student group, "too radical to be called a revolution." Students are thus often misled by their borrowed vocabulary, but most adults are even more confused, and many are quickly led to the mistaken conclusion that today's student revolt is nothing more than a repetition of Communism's in the past.

Failure to distinguish between the old and new revolutions also makes it impossible to consider the critical question of how compatible they are with each other. Does it make sense—or is it morally right—for today's affluent American students to seek imagination, self-actualization, individuality, openness and relevance when most of the world and many in America live in deprivation, oppression and misery?

The fact that the first revolution is "completed" in Scarsdale does not mean that it is (or soon will be) in Harlem or Appalachia—to say nothing of Bogotá or Calcutta. For many children of the second revolution, the meaning of life may be found in completing the first—that is, in extending to others the "rights" they have always taken for granted.

For others the second revolution will not wait; the question, "What lies beyond affluence?" demands an answer now. Thus, although we may deem it self-indulgent to pursue the goals of the new revolution in a world where so much misery exists, the fact is that in the advanced nations it is upon us, and we must at least learn to recognize it.

Finally, beneath my analysis lies an assumption I had best make explicit. Many student critics argue that their societies have failed miserably. My argument, a more historical one perhaps, suggests that our problem is not only that industrial societies have failed to keep all their promises, but that they have succeeded in some ways beyond all expectations. Abundance was once a distant dream, to be postponed to a hereafter of milk and honey; today, most Americans are affluent. Universal mass education was once a Utopian goal; today in America almost the entire population completes high school, and almost half enters colleges and universities.

The notion that individuals might be free, en masse, to continue their psychological, intellectual, moral and cognitive development through their teens and into their 20's would have been laughed out of court in any century other than our own; today, that opportunity is open to millions of young Americans. Student unrest is a reflection not only of the failures, but of the extraordinary successes of the liberal-industrial revolution. It therefore occurs in the nations and in the colleges where, according to traditional standards, conditions are best.

But for many of today's students who have never experienced anything but affluence, political freedom and social equality, the old vision is dead or dying. It may inspire bitterness and outrage when it is not achieved, but it no longer animates or guides. In place of it, students (and many who are not students) are searching for a new vision, a new set of values, a new set of targets appropriate to the post-industrial era—a myth, an ideology or a set of goals that will concern itself with the quality of life and answer the question, "Beyond freedom and affluence, what?"

What characterizes student unrest in the developed nations is this peculiar mixture of the old and the new, the urgent need to fulfill the promises of the past and, at the same time, to define the possibilities of the future.

Questions for Discussion

1. In the light of what you have read in the preceding selections and observed from your own experience, how accurately does Keniston's explanation account for what is happening?
2. Try your own hand at writing the Keniston essay. What is happening to young people today? What are the causes, and the goals, of their revolutionary activity?
3. This is the last selection from contemporary critics which you will be reading. Reflect on what you remember from Holt and Cleaveland, what you recall about A. S. Neill and Elliott Shapiro, what your impressions were of the selections on cost accounting and urban schools. Is there a common theme which runs through all these selections? If so, what does it say about the ends and means of education?

Epilogue: What's Wrong with the Old and Right with the New?

Have you been disturbed by what you have read? You should be.

These authors have been critical, possibly of ideas and values you hold, and they, too, are concerned and thoughtful about the educational process, just as the authors in Part I. Why, then, do these critics disturb you—if they do; whereas the traditional spokesmen did not—if they didn't. Answering that question can help us put the critics' comments into a perspective for proper evaluation.

After reading "The Student As Nigger," your first response might be that you are disturbed by some of the author's vulgarity. And others are, too, for many publishers have refused to print this particular piece. But this is an affront to your moral code and sense of decency, not to your educational theory, so the vulgarity, this source of your disturbance, might be important, but not particularly relevant, and certainly not of central importance, to questions involving the ends and means of the educational process.

Let us look more closely, then. Why are you disturbed? Perhaps because you have learned some things about the world and the educational process which were new? Have you ever considered before that Negro children should be taught English as a second language because the language in their homes is so different from the language in the school, and that the teacher should teach, at least initially, in their home's language? Have you thought about holding schools in abandoned storefront buildings rather than schoolhouses? Have you ever thought of educational institutions as business enterprises whose principal aim is efficiency? Perhaps these and a host of other ideas in Part II are new to you, and we all know that new ideas are disturbing, at least initially.

Or perhaps you are disturbed because, unconsciously, you have come to view your own situation in the light of these critical comments and have begun to wonder whether, in fact, the critics aren't right. Maybe, just maybe, the whole tradition of the educational process is wrong, profoundly wrong.

The chances are you are registered for a course giving X hours of credit which can be used "in partial fulfillment of the requirements for a degree"; that you are listening to lectures, reading assignments, writing papers, taking examinations; that the text and reading assignments were chosen for you; that you will complete the course in Y weeks and not have to work on this material again; that you are in school to prepare yourself for something more important later on; and that most courses you now take are pretty dull, unless a good instructor can make them interesting. How close does the description strike home?

And so you read from Holt's *How Children Fail,* and learned that the educational system itself encourages failure and creates fear, and that the bright student succeeds because he learns the name of the game. Did you stop to wonder whether he is right? And why are you succeeding? So you read the SDS statement on the need to respect every human being as an end in himself, and then you wonder whether the educational process encourages—or even recognizes—this goal. You read of Principal Elliott Shapiro's valiant efforts to keep his children from dying, and you wonder whether your own selfhood is growing or dying as the result of your own educational experiences. Maybe the critics are right, and the proof of their rightness is in your own dissatisfaction with the educational process. Maybe.

But, before we make the "maybe" into a "yes" let's explore the criticisms more closely, centering our attention on three related topics: relevance; alienation; and institutionalism.

Almost every author in Part II insists that today's educational enterprise is irrelevant to the real world. Smith says that "The schools have failed . . . the teachers have failed and those who have trained the teachers have also failed" to deal with the problems and needs of people who live in large urban areas. Neill tells us the ordinary schools are wrong because they are based on an adult conception of what a child should be and how a child should learn. Farber's indictment of the teacher-student relationship as parallel to the master-slave relationship is devastating precisely because it occurs in a society avowedly committed to the democratic and Christian ideals of freedom, equality and brotherhood. Contemporary education simply isn't relevant to the real world in which people live, so the critics say.

Notice that the claimed irrelevancies do not attach so much to the physical world of engineering, science and technology, as to the human world of needs, ideals and values. Presumably the educational system is producing engineers who can get astronauts to the moon, medical technicians who can increase longevity, and scientists who can discover the secrets of DNA, mesons and topology. But the system is not based on the ideals it proclaims for itself, and more importantly, is not producing graduates of the system who want or will do anything to make those ideals real. The educational system, then—the curriculum, the teachers, the level of financial support, everything connected with contemporary educational practice—is both hypocritical and irrelevant, and therefore should be abandoned, or at least modified drastically.

Moreover, the critics contend, the modern educational system treats people impersonally, with little concern for their individual needs or desires, and so helps to produce people with only modest human involvements, people alienated from other people and even from themselves. Let us listen to the SDS statement again:

> Our professors and administrators sacrifice controversy to public relations; their curriculums change more slowly than the living events of the world; their skills and silence are purchased by investors in the arms race; passion is called unscholastic.

Neill argues that the traditional educational system encourages similarity and uniformity rather than freedom and individuality. It encourages students to think of themselves as members of a society, parts of a crowd, rather than as freely developing human beings.

Given the system described by Neill, Smith, Cleaveland, and the Students for a Democratic Society, who will deny that the present education process tends to alienate people from each other, and from their own authentic selfhood, and to create people who have few genuinely human sensitivities or concerns?

To this existentialist argument let us add still one more dimension: The confusion of ends and means. Originally, grades were the means for determining how much one learned; now, they frequently are viewed as the purpose for learning itself. As was said in a recently overheard conversation: "What did you learn in the class?" "Oh, I got a B." Graduation requirements were intended to be a means for assuring the breadth and depth of learning—said to be characteristic of a graduate; now, most requirements are described variously as obstacles to be overcome, hurdles to be jumped or tasteless food to be taken and expelled as rapidly as possible. Unfortunately, the methods originally used by educational institutions to bring about certain purposes now have become ends in themselves. Students take courses, earn grades and complete requirements for the purpose of graduating, and maybe learn something besides. Or are the courses they take, the grades they earn and the requirements they complete an indication of what they have learned, which indicates a level of achievement worthy of graduation? Which are means and which are ends? The two are hard to distinguish, but the critics' point is that the demands of the institution have perverted, or at least obscured, its purpose, and that the educational institutions must be reconstituted so they can achieve genuinely educational purposes.

So, the critics argue, the curriculum is irrelevant to both the psychological needs and moral ideals of people, students are alienated from each other and from themselves, and the educational institutions have taken on a life of their own, irrespective of students. What should be done? Let us examine a few statements from our revolutionaries in Part II.

1. Men have unrealized potential for self-cultivation, self-direction, self-understanding and creativity. It is this potential we consider as crucial.

2. The discovery that thinking may be creative makes intellectual activity interesting, active, subtle and stimulating.

3. Our learning is not real, not complete, not accurate, above all not useful, unless we take these word strings and somehow convert them in our minds into a likeness of the world, a working mental model of the universe as we know it.

4. The only true enlargement of mind is the power of viewing many things at once as one whole, referring them severally to their true place in the universal system, of understanding their respective values, and determining their mutual dependence.

5. Given freedom from examinations I should aim at catching the children's interests and following them.

6. No doubt, he will require some guidance, but very little, and that little without his knowing it. If he goes wrong let him alone, do not correct his mistakes; hold your tongue till he finds them out for himself and corrects them, or at most arrange something, as opportunity offers, which may show Emile his mistakes.

Emile? You thought these were quotations from only the revolutionaries in Part II? Actually, only the first, third and fifth statements come from that source; the others are from Martin, Newman and Rousseau, authors we considered in Part I, "Some Traditional Views."

Examine those statements again (or for the first time if you skimmed the indented material expecting your author to summarize it in this paragraph) now in pairs, to notice the similarities between the SDS statement and Martin, Holt and Newman, Neill and Rousseau. Further, look again in Part I at Theodore Brameld's extended argument which concludes that "education is a penetrating critic, dynamic leader and imaginative re-creater," and John Dewey's contention that education "is a continuous reconstruction, moving from the child's present experience out into that represented by the organized bodies of truth that we call studies," and seriously ask yourself, perhaps for the first time, who is a traditionalist and who is a critic. Are there any real differences between Parts I and II?

The evidence suggests that a distinction is difficult to draw. You might think this is because the authors in Part I were carefully chosen to illustrate the point, but an examination of the writings of other traditionalists such as John Amos Comenius, Robert Maynard Hutchins, Aristotle, Pius XI, will demonstrate to you that they, too, are critics. The fact is that all writers on the educational process tend to be critics of the established educational order and proponents of a different educational process.

All of which suggests the context you should use for judging the validity of the critics' comments. First, what do the critics say, and what do they assume, about the ends and means of the educational process? And, just a warning, they do not all say or assume the same things. Second, do they adopt a theory of education similar to those expressed in Part I, or do they develop new theories? Notice particularly the writings of Rousseau, Dewey, Brameld and Martin in this connection, and you might find the technique of thinking in terms of metaphors particularly useful. Third, would the means they propose actually bring about the ends they desire? Do these authors have much to offer on this constructive note, or can their statements be supplemented by material from Part I?

Finally, what have their comments done to help you understand more clearly and fully the ends and means in the educational process? Do you know any more clearly what and how you would teach when you enter the classroom, and whether and why you are or are not satisfied with your own present learning situation? Ultimately, your answer to this question is the most important bit of knowledge you should have attained so far, for the degree to which you can answer it is the degree to which you are beginning to develop your own ideas on the ends and means of the educational process.

Part Three

Some Thoughts
on the Art of
Successful Teaching

Prologue: Do Students Learn What Teachers Teach?

The teaching-learning environment might be described in the following series of discernible but related concepts:

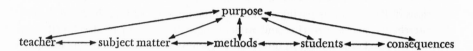

The *teacher* is a person with unique genes, experiences, problems, talents and personality, educated in a discipline, with goodwill toward students, at least initially. The *subject matter* is the body of knowledge accumulated through the patient efforts of previous generations, and added to constantly by contemporary research and rethinking. The *methods* are those mechanisms, such as books and blackboards, film strips and simulation models, lectures and discussions, computer games and tutorials, by which the teacher and student relate to each other. A *student* is a person with unique genes, experiences, problems, talents and personality, experienced but growing in a discipline, with goodwill toward teachers, at least initially. The *consequences* are those activities and behaviors which flow from the teaching-learning environment: initially, tests and grades; ultimately, changed perceptions of life and a reorientation of purposes and values. The *purpose* of the educational encounter follows from the element in this environment that is given the most weight.

As the report from the Hazen Foundation indicates, most young teachers enter the classroom very conscious of their own background. This is as it should be, for they have been learning and preparing themselves for the teaching experience, so they first enter the classroom with more enthusiasm than maturity, more knowledge than wisdom. They may know something about young people, but not about these particular students, and their knowledge of teaching techniques is untested. Given these conditions, then, their "teaching" usually consists of transferring what they now know to their students. And should the focus of their teaching continue to center on what they knew when they first entered the classroom, their teaching two decades hence will consist of well-thumbed lesson plans and lecture notes, and knowledgeable but apathetic and possibly resentful students. No educational philosophy you have read in this book advocates this position.

So the teacher's focus may shift from his own preparation to the leading edge of his discipline, and he may conceive of his purpose as exposing, indeed, involving, his students in the quest for new understandings. To teach, he must have an understanding of the subject matter, as Highet says, and some sensitivity to the excitement of the unknown, as Socrates suggests. In addition, he must know how to involve students in the romance of learning and to help them develop the ability to obtain knowledge reliably and to generalize dependably—the stages of romance, precision and generalization which Whitehead calls to our attention. If, then, a teacher holds that an exploration of the subject matter is his purpose of education, his own philosophy will tend to draw from the writings of Plato, Newman and Martin, and find expression in the manner many college-level courses are conducted.

Other theories of teaching tend to grow out of a concern for the ways in which teachers and students interrelate. Thus Highet, McKeachie and the report from the Hazen Foundation discuss the advantages of lectures, discussions and tutorials as teaching mechanisms. Skinner calls attention to the meaning and value of programmed learning. These concerns do not necessarily lead to the comprehension and coherent account of the ends and means of education which characterized the selections in Part I, but by paying attention to the question of what happens during the interchange between teacher and student, new theories can be developed, and old ones enlarged or modified. In this sense, a teaching philosophy draws its strength, sometimes its content, from the concerns of Dewey and Spencer, Loretan and Holt.

Subtly but surely, many teachers find their philosophy shifting from a concern for imparting what they know to a concern for what students do not know, or maybe even what students want to know. To experience this shift is to undergo a Copernican revolution in one's conception of the teaching situation, for the curriculum now grows out of the students' interests rather than the teacher's knowledge, testing becomes largely irrelevant rather than a measure of information retained, and the art of teaching is the act of providing resource material to answer questions of interest rather than the summary and dissemination of known information. To adopt this theory of teaching is to adopt the educational ideas of Rousseau and Montessori, Dewey and Neill, Cleaveland and SDS, and to make a classroom a place in which each student can perform the act of discovery, as Bruner suggests, perhaps even "do his own thing."

Differing theories of teaching, then, can be understood by the place at which they put the emphasis: on the teacher, the subject matter, the method of teaching, or the interests of the students. And the focal point chosen will help to shape the style of teaching and the characteristics of learning.

But, underlying the whole question of purpose is the knotty problem of whether students learn what teachers teach. Perhaps the best way for you to determine the answer to that question is to ask yourself what you have learned so far from this book and course. Have you learned what your teachers have taught? More? Less? The same? Or has your own learning been independent of the text, class and instructor? And how much was your own experience like the learning of others? Is the teaching of teachers different in rate, content, order and level than the learning of students?

This is a difficult question to answer, and perhaps should be pushed to the back of your mind where it will fester and grow, coming forward only occasionally to nag you. For the present you should read these selections with two ideas in mind: first, what specific suggestions do you find which will be useful when you first enter the classroom; and second, how does a theory about teaching relate to a concern about the ends of education? What are the proper ends—and the appropriate means —for becoming a successful teacher?

21 A Socratic Dialogue

Plato

Now we turn away from the philosophers and critics and turn to the teachers, asking ourselves what constitutes a successful teaching experience and how it might be brought about. One of the most famous teachers of all time was Socrates, whose conversations with people were recorded (and enhanced?) by his student Plato. The next selection is one of these dialogues, and you should read it for what it says and, more importantly, for the purpose of describing good teaching. Socrates' general procedure is that of giving a definition, then examining whether all instances are covered by it, then enlarging the definition to take account of the counter-examples. See if you can find examples of this procedure in this dialogue, as well as other reasoning and teaching techniques he uses.

SCENE:—*The Prison of Socrates*

Socrates. Why have you come at this hour, Crito? it must be quite early?

Crito. Yes, certainly.

Soc. What is the exact time?

Cr. The dawn is breaking.

Soc. I wonder that the keeper of the prison would let you in.

Cr. He knows me, because I often come, Socrates; moreover, I have done him a kindness.

Soc. And are you only just arrived?

Cr. No, I came some time ago.

Soc. Then why did you sit and say nothing, instead of at once awakening me?

Cr. I should not have liked myself, Socrates, to be in such great trouble and unrest as you are—indeed I should not: I have been watching with amazement your peaceful slumbers; and for that reason I did not awake you, because I wished to minimize the pain. I have always thought you to be of a happy disposition; but never did I see anything like the easy, tranquil manner in which you bear this calamity.

Soc. Why, Crito, when a man has reached my age he ought not to be repining at the approach of death.

Cr. And yet other old men find themselves in similar misfortunes, and age does not prevent them from repining.

Soc. That is true. But you have not told me why you come at this early hour.

Cr. I come to bring you a message which is sad and painful; not, as I believe, to yourself, but to all of us who are your friends, and saddest of all to me.

Soc. What? Has the ship come from Delos, on the arrival of which I am to die?

From *The Crito* and *The Phaedo* by Plato. Translated by Benjamin Jowett, 3rd ed. New York: The Macmillan Co., 1892.

Cr. No, the ship has not actually arrived, but she will probably be here to-day, as persons who have come from Sunium tell me that they left her there; and therefore to-morrow, Socrates, will be the last day of your life.

Soc. Very well, Crito; if such is the will of God, I am willing; but my belief is that there will be a delay of a day.

Cr. Why do you think so?

Soc. I will tell you. I am to die on the day after the arrival of the ship.

Cr. Yes; that is what the authorities say.

Soc. But I do not think that the ship will be here until to-morrow; this I infer from a vision which I had last night, or rather only just now, when you fortunately allowed me to sleep.

Cr. And what was the nature of the vision?

Soc. There appeared to me the likeness of a woman, fair and comely, clothed in bright raiment, who called to me and said: O Socrates,

'The third day hence to fertile Phthia shalt thou go.'[1]

Cr. What a singular dream, Socrates!

Soc. There can be no doubt about the meaning, Crito, I think.

Cr. Yes; the meaning is only too clear. But, oh! my beloved Socrates, let me entreat you once more to take my advice and escape. For if you die I shall not only lose a friend who can never be replaced, but there is another evil: people who do not know you and me will believe that I might have saved you if I had been willing to give money, but that I did not care. Now, can there be a worse disgrace than this— that I should be thought to value money more than the life of a friend? For the many will not be persuaded that I wanted you to escape, and that you refused.

Soc. But why, my dear Crito, should we care about the opinion of the many? Good men, and they are the only persons who are worth considering, will think of these things truly as they occurred.

Cr. But you see, Socrates, that the opinion of the many must be regarded, for what is now happening shows that they can do the greatest evil to any one who has lost their good opinion.

Soc. I only wish it were so, Crito; and that the many could do the greatest evil; for then they would also be able to do the greatest good—and what a fine thing this would be! But in reality they can do neither; for they cannot make a man either wise or foolish; and whatever they do is the result of chance.

Cr. Well, I will not dispute with you; but please to tell me, Socrates, whether you are not acting out of regard to me and your other friends: are you not afraid that if you escape from prison we may get into trouble with the informers for having stolen you away, and lose either the whole or a great part of our property; or that even a worse evil may happen to us? Now, if you fear on our account, be at ease; for in order to save you, we ought surely to run this, or even a greater risk; be persuaded, then, and do as I say.

Soc. Yes, Crito, that is one fear which you mention, but by no means the only one.

Cr. Fear not—there are persons who are willing to get you out of prison at no

---

[1] Homer, Il. ix. 363.

great cost; and as for the informers, they are far from being exorbitant in their demands—a little money will satisfy them. My means, which are certainly ample, are at your service, and if you have a scruple about spending all mine, here are strangers who will give you the use of theirs; and one of them, Simmias the Theban, has brought a large sum of money for this very purpose; and Cebes and many others are prepared to spend their money in helping you to escape. I say, therefore, do not hesitate on our account, and do not say, as you did in the court, that you will have a difficulty in knowing what to do with yourself anywhere else. For men will love you in other places to which you may go, and not in Athens only; there are friends of mine in Thessaly, if you like to go to them, who will value and protect you, and no Thessalian will give you any trouble. Nor can I think that you are at all justified, Socrates, in betraying your own life when you might be saved; in acting thus you are playing into the hands of your enemies, who are hurrying on your destruction. And further I should say that you are deserting your own children; for you might bring them up and educate them; instead of which you go away and leave them, and they will have to take their chance; and if they do not meet with the usual fate of orphans, there will be small thanks to you. No man should bring children into the world who is unwilling to persevere to the end in their nurture and education. But you appear to be choosing the easier part, not the better and manlier, which would have been more becoming in one who professes to care for virtue in all his actions, like yourself. And indeed, I am ashamed not only of you, but of us who are your friends, when I reflect that the whole business will be attributed entirely to our want of courage. The trial need never have come on, or might have been managed differently; and this last act, or crowning folly, will seem to have occurred through our negligence and cowardice, who might have saved you, if we had been good for anything; and you might have saved yourself, for there was no difficulty at all. See now, Socrates, how sad and discreditable are the consequences, both to us and you. Make up your mind then, or rather have your mind already made up, for the time of deliberation is over, and there is only one thing to be done, which must be done this very night, and if we delay at all will be no longer practicable or possible; I beseech you therefore, Socrates, be persuaded by me, and do as I say.

Soc. Dear Crito, your zeal is invaluable, if a right one; but if wrong, the greater the zeal the greater the danger; and therefore we ought to consider whether I shall or shall not do as you say. For I am and always have been one of those natures who must be guided by reason, whatever the reason may be which upon reflection appears to me to be the best; and now that this chance has befallen me, I cannot repudiate my own words: the principles which I have hitherto honoured and revered I still honour, and unless we can at once find other and better principles, I am certain not to agree with you; no, not even if the power of the multitude could inflict many more imprisonments, confiscations, deaths, frightening us like children with hobgoblin terrors. What will be the fairest way of considering the question? Shall I return to your old argument about the opinions of men?—we were saying that some of them are to be regarded, and others not. Now were we right in maintaining this before I was condemned? And has the argument which was once good now proved to be talk for the sake of talking—mere childish nonsense? That is what I want to consider with your help, Crito:—whether, under my present circumstances, the argument appears to be in any way different or not; and is to be allowed by me or disallowed. That argument, which, as I believe, is maintained by many persons of authority, was to the effect, as I was saying, that the opinions of some men are to be regarded, and of other men not to be regarded. Now you, Crito, are not going to die to-morrow —at least, there is no human probability of this—and therefore you are disinterested and not liable to be deceived by the circumstances in which you are placed. Tell me then, whether I am right in saying that some opinions, and the opinions of some men only, are to be valued, and that other opinions, and the opinions of other men, are not to be valued. I ask you whether I was right in maintaining this?

Cr. Certainly.

Soc. The good are to be regarded, and not the bad?

Cr. Yes.

Soc. And the opinions of the wise are good, and the opinions of the unwise are evil?

Cr. Certainly.

Soc. And what was said about another matter? Is the pupil who devotes himself to the practice of gymnastics supposed to attend to the praise and blame and opinion of every man, or of one man only—his physician or trainer, whoever he may be?

Cr. Of one man only.

Soc. And he ought to fear the censure and welcome the praise of that one only, and not of the many?

Cr. Clearly so.

Soc. And he ought to act and train, and eat and drink in the way which seems good to his single master who has understanding, rather than according to the opinion of all other men put together?

Cr. True.

Soc. And if he disobeys and disregards the opinion and approval of the one, and regards the opinion of the many who have no understanding, will he not suffer evil?

Cr. Certainly he will.

Soc. And what will the evil be, whither tending and what affecting, in the disobedient person?

Cr. Clearly, affecting the body; that is what is destroyed by the evil.

Soc. Very good; and is not this true, Crito, of other things which we need not separately enumerate? In questions of just and unjust, fair and foul, good and evil, which are the subjects of our present consultation, ought we to follow the opinion of the many and to fear them; or the opinion of the one man who has understanding? ought we not to fear and reverence him more than all the rest of the world; and if we desert him shall we not destroy and injure that principle in us which may be assumed to be improved by justice and deteriorated by injustice;—there is such a principle?

Cr. Certainly there is, Socrates.

Soc. Take a parallel instance:—if, acting under the advice of those who have no understanding, we destroy that which is improved by health and is deteriorated by disease, would life be worth having? And that which has been destroyed is—the body?

Cr. Yes.

Soc. Could we live, having an evil and corrupted body?

Cr. Certainly not.

Soc. And will life be worth having, if that higher part of man be destroyed, which is improved by justice and depraved by injustice? Do we suppose that principle, whatever it may be in man, which has to do with justice and injustice, to be inferior to the body?

Cr. Certainly not.

Soc. More honourable than the body?

Cr. Far more.

Soc. Then, my friend, we must not regard what the many say of us: but what he, the one man who has understanding of just and unjust, will say, and what the truth will say. And therefore you begin in error when you advise that we should regard the opinion of the many about just and unjust, good and evil, honourable and dishonourable.—'Well,' some one will say, 'but the many can kill us.'

Cr. Yes, Socrates; that will clearly be the answer.

Soc. And it is true: but still I find with surprise that the old argument is unshaken as ever. And I should like to know whether I may say the same of another proposition—that not life, but a good life, is to be chiefly valued?

Cr. Yes, that also remains unshaken.

Soc. And a good life is equivalent to a just and honourable one—that holds also?

Cr. Yes, it does.

Soc. From these premises I proceed to argue the question whether I ought or ought not to try and escape without the consent of the Athenians: and if I am clearly right in escaping, then I will make the attempt; but if not, I will abstain. The other considerations which you mention, of money and loss of character and the duty of educating one's children, are, I fear, only the doctrines of the multitude, who would be as ready to restore people to life, if they were able, as they are to put them to death—and with as little reason. But now, since the argument has thus far prevailed, the only question which remains to be considered is, whether we shall do rightly either in escaping or in suffering others to aid in our escape and paying them in money and thanks, or whether in reality we shall not do rightly; and if the latter, then death or any other calamity which may ensue on my remaining here must not be allowed to enter into the calculation.

Cr. I think that you are right, Socrates; how then shall we proceed?

Soc. Let us consider the matter together, and do you either refute me if you can, and I will be convinced; or else cease, my dear friend, from repeating to me that I ought to escape against the wishes of the Athenians: for I highly value your attempts to persuade me to do so, but I may not be persuaded against my own better judgment. And now please to consider my first position, and try how you can best answer me.

Cr. I will.

Soc. Are we to say that we are never intentionally to do wrong, or that in one way we ought and in another we ought not to do wrong, or is doing wrong always evil and dishonourable, as I was just now saying, and as has been already acknowledged by us? Are all our former admissions which were made within a few days to be thrown away? And have we, at our age, been earnestly discoursing with one another all our life long only to discover that we are no better than children? Or, in spite of the opinion of the many, and in spite of consequences whether better or worse, shall we insist on the truth of what was then said, that injustice is always an evil and dishonour to him who acts unjustly? Shall we say so or not?

Cr. Yes.

Soc. Then we must do no wrong?

Cr. Certainly not.

Soc. Nor when injured injure in return, as the many imagine; for we must injure no one at all?

Cr. Clearly not.

Soc. Again, Crito, may we do evil?

Cr. Surely not, Socrates.

Soc. And what of doing evil in return for evil, which is the morality of the many —is that just or not?

Cr. Not just.

Soc. For doing evil to another is the same as injuring him?

Cr. Very true.

Soc. Then we ought not to retaliate or render evil for evil to any one, whatever evil we may have suffered from him. But I would have you consider, Crito, whether you really mean what you are saying. For this opinion has never been held, and never will be held, by any considerable number of persons; and those who are agreed and those who are not agreed upon this point have no common ground, and can only despise one another when they see how widely they differ. Tell me, then, whether you agree with and assent to my first principle, that neither injury nor retaliation nor warding off evil by evil is ever right. And shall that be the premise of our argument? Or do you decline and dissent from this? For so I have ever thought, and continue to think; but, if you are of another opinion, let me hear what you have to say. If, however, you remain of the same mind as formerly, I will proceed to the next step.

Cr. You may proceed, for I have not changed my mind.

Soc. Then I will go on to the next point, which may be put in the form of a question:—Ought a man to do what he admits to be right, or ought he to betray the right?

Cr. He ought to do what he thinks right.

Soc. But if this is true, what is the application? In leaving the prison against the will of the Athenians, do I wrong any? or rather do I not wrong those whom I ought least to wrong? Do I not desert the principles which were acknowledged by us to be just—what do you say?

Cr. I cannot tell, Socrates; for I do not know.

Soc. Then consider the matter in this way:—Imagine that I am about to play truant (you may call the proceeding by any name which you like), and the laws and the government come and interrogate me: 'Tell us, Socrates,' they say; 'what are you about? are you not going by an act of yours to overturn us—the laws, and the whole state, as far as in you lies? Do you imagine that a state can subsist and not be overthrown, in which the decisions of law have no power, but are set aside and trampled upon by individuals?' What will be our answer, Crito, to these and the like words? Any one, and especially a rhetorician, will have a good deal to say on behalf of the law which requires a sentence to be carried out. He will argue that this law should not be set aside; and shall we reply, 'Yes; but the state has injured us and given an unjust sentence.' Suppose I say that?

Cr. Very good, Socrates.

Soc. 'And was that our agreement with you?' the law would answer; 'or were you to abide by the sentence of the state?' And if I were to express my astonishment at their words, the law would probably add: 'Answer, Socrates, instead of opening your eyes—you are in the habit of asking and answering questions. Tell us,—What complaint have you to make against us which justifies you in attempting to destroy us and the state? In the first place did we not bring you into existence? Your father married your mother by our aid and begat you. Say whether you have any objection to urge against those of us who regulate marriage?' None, I should reply. 'Or against those of us who after birth regulate the nurture and education of children, in which you also were trained? Were not the laws, which have the charge of education, right in commanding your father to train you in music and gymnastic?' Right, I should reply. 'Well then, since you were brought into the world and nurtured and educated by us, can you deny in the first place that you are our child and slave, as your fathers were before you? And if this is true you are not on equal terms with us; nor can you think that you have a right to do to us what we are doing to you. Would you have any right to strike or revile or do any other evil to your father or your master, if you had one, because you have been struck or reviled by him, or received some other evil at his hands?—you would not say this? And because we think right to destroy you, do you think that you have any right to destroy us in return, and your country as far as in you lies? Will you, O professor of true virtue, pretend that you are justified in this? Has a philosopher like you failed to discover that our country is more to be valued and higher and holier far than mother or father or any ancestor, and more to be regarded in the eyes of the gods and of men of understanding? also to be soothed, and gently and reverently entreated when angry, even more than a father, and either to be persuaded, or if not persuaded, to be obeyed? And when we are punished by her, whether with imprisonment or stripes, the punishment is to be endured in silence; and if she leads us to wounds or death in battle, thither we follow as is right; neither may any one yield or retreat or leave his rank, but whether in battle or in a court of law, or in any other place, he must do what his city and his country order him; or he must change their view of what is just: and if he may do no violence to his father or mother, much less may he do violence to his country.' What answer shall we make to this, Crito? Do the laws speak truly, or do they not?

Cr. I think that they do.

Soc. Then the laws will say, 'Consider, Socrates, if we are speaking truly that in your present attempt you are going to do us an injury. For, having brought you into the world, and nurtured and educated you, and given you and every other citizen a share in every good which we had to give, we further proclaim to any Athenian by the liberty which we allow him, that if he does not like us when he has become of age and has seen the ways of the city, and made our acquaintance, he may go where he pleases and take his goods with him. None of us laws will forbid him or interfere with him. Any one who does not like us and the city, and who wants to emigrate to a colony or to any other city, may go where he likes, retaining his property. But he who has experience of the manner in which we order justice and administer the state, and still remains, has entered into an implied contract that he will do as we command him. And he who disobeys us is, as we maintain, thrice wrong; first, because in disobeying us he is disobeying his parents; secondly, because we are the authors of his education; thirdly, because he has made an agreement with us that he will duly obey our commands; and he neither obeys them nor convinces us that our commands are unjust; and we do not rudely impose them, but give him the alternative of obeying or convincing us;—that is what we offer, and he does neither.

'These are the sort of accusations to which, as we were saying, you, Socrates, will be exposed if you accomplish your intentions; you, above all other Athenians.' Suppose now I ask, why I rather than anybody else? they will justly retort upon me that I above all other men have acknowledged the agreement. 'There is clear proof,' they will say, 'Socrates, that we and the city were not displeasing to you. Of all Athenians you have been the most constant resident in the city, which, as you never leave, you may be supposed to love. For you never went out of the city either to see the games, except once when you went to the Isthmus, or to any other place unless when you were on military service; nor did you travel as other men do. Nor had you any curiosity to know other states or their laws: your affections did not go beyond us and our state; we were your special favourites, and you acquiesced in our government of you; and here in this city you begat your children, which is a proof of your satisfaction. Moreover, you might in the course of the trial, if you had liked, have fixed the penalty at banishment; the state which refuses to let you go now would have let you go then. But you pretended that you preferred death to exile, and that you were not unwilling to die. And now you have forgotten these fine sentiments, and pay no respect to us the laws, of whom you are the destroyer; and are doing what only a miserable slave would do, running away and turning your back upon the compacts and agreements which you made as a citizen. And first of all answer this very question: Are we right in saying that you agreed to be governed according to us in deed, and not in word only? Is that true or not?' How shall we answer, Crito? Must we not assent?

Cr. We cannot help it, Socrates.

Soc. Then will they not say: 'You, Socrates, are breaking the covenants and agreements which you made with us at your leisure, not in any haste or under any compulsion or deception, but after you have had seventy years to think of them, during which time you were at liberty to leave the city, if we were not to your mind, or if our covenants appeared to you to be unfair. You had your choice, and might have gone either to Lacedaemon or Crete, both which states are often praised by you for their good government, or to some other Hellenic or foreign state. Whereas you, above all other Athenians, seemed to be so fond of the state, or, in other words, of us her laws (and who would care about a state which has no laws?), that you never stirred out of her; the halt, the blind, the maimed were not more stationary in her than you were. And now you run away and forsake your agreements. Not so,

Socrates, if you will take our advice; do not make yourself ridiculous by escaping out of the city.

'For just consider, if you transgress and err in this sort of way, what good will you do either to yourself or to your friends? That your friends will be driven into exile and deprived of citizenship, or will lose their property, is tolerably certain; and you yourself, if you fly to one of the neighbouring cities, as, for example, Thebes or Megara, both of which are well governed, will come to them as an enemy, Socrates, and their government will be against you, and all patriotic citizens will cast an evil eye upon you as a subverter of the laws, and you will confirm in the minds of the judges the justice of their own condemnation of you. For he who is a corrupter of the laws is more than likely to be a corrupter of the young and foolish portion of mankind. Will you then flee from well-ordered cities and virtuous men? and is existence worth having on these terms? Or will you go to them without shame, and talk to them, Socrates? And what will you say to them? What you say here about virtue and justice and institutions and laws being the best things among men? Would that be decent of you? Surely not. But if you go away from well-governed states to Crito's friends in Thessaly, where there is great disorder and licence, they will be charmed to hear the tale of your escape from prison, set off with ludicrous particulars of the manner in which you were wrapped in a goatskin or some other disguise, and metamorphosed as the manner is of runaways; but will there be no one to remind you that in your old age you were not ashamed to violate the most sacred laws from a miserable desire of a little more life? Perhaps not, if you keep them in a good temper; but if they are out of temper you will hear many degrading things; you will live, but how?—as the flatterer of all men, and the servant of all men; and doing what?—eating and drinking in Thessaly, having gone abroad in order that you may get a dinner. And where will be your fine sentiments about justice and virtue? Say that you wish to live for the sake of your children—you want to bring them up and educate them—will you take them into Thessaly and deprive them of Athenian citizenship? Is this the benefit which you will confer upon them? Or are you under the impression that they will be better cared for and educated here if you are still alive, although absent from them; for your friends will take care of them? Do you fancy that if you are an inhabitant of Thessaly they will take care of them, and if you are an inhabitant of the other world that they will not take care of them? Nay; but if they who call themselves friends are good for anything, they will—to be sure they will.

'Listen, then, Socrates, to us who have brought you up. Think not of life and children first, and of justice afterwards, but of justice first, that you may be justified before the princes of the world below. For neither will you nor any that belong to you be happier or holier or juster in this life, or happier in another, if you do as Crito bids. Now you depart in innocence, a sufferer and not a doer of evil; a victim, not of the laws but of men. But if you go forth, returning evil for evil, and injury for injury, breaking the covenants and agreements which you have made with us, and wronging those whom you ought least of all to wrong, that is to say, yourself, your friends, your country, and us, we shall be angry with you while you live, and our brethren, the laws in the world below, will receive you as an enemy; for they will know that you have done your best to destroy us. Listen, then, to us and not to Crito.'

This, dear Crito, is the voice which I seem to hear murmuring in my ears, like the sound of the flute in the ears of the mystic; that voice, I say, is humming in my ears, and prevents me from hearing any other. And I know that anything more which you may say will be vain. Yet speak, if you have anything to say.

Cr. I have nothing to say, Socrates.

Soc. Leave me then, Crito, to fulfil the will of God, and to follow whither he leads. . . .

When he had done speaking, Crito said: And have you any commands for us, Socrates—anything to say about your children, or any other matter in which we can serve you?

Nothing particular, Crito, he replied: only, as I have always told you, take care of yourselves; that is a service which you may be ever rendering to me and mine and to all of us, whether you promise to do so or not. But if you have no thought for yourselves, and care not to walk according to the rule which I have prescribed for you, not now for the first time, however much you may profess or promise at the moment, it will be of no avail.

We will do our best, said Crito: And in what way shall we bury you?

In any way that you like; but you must get hold of me, and take care that I do not run away from you. Then he turned to us, and added with a smile:—I cannot make Crito believe that I am the same Socrates who have been talking and conducting the argument; he fancies that I am the other Socrates whom he will soon see, a dead body—and he asks, How shall he bury me? And though I have spoken many words in the endeavor to show that when I have drunk the poison I shall leave you and go to the joys of the blessed,—these words of mine, with which I was comforting you and myself, have had, as I perceive, no effect upon Crito. And therefore I want you to be surety for me to him now, as at the trial he was surety to the judges for me: but let the promise be of another sort; for he was surety for me to the judges that I would remain, and you must be my surety to him that I shall not remain, but go away and depart; and then he will suffer less at my death, and not be grieved when he sees my body being burned or buried. I would not have him sorrow at my hard lot, or say at the burial, Thus we lay out Socrates, or, Thus we follow him to the grave or bury him; for false words are not only evil in themselves, but they infect the soul with evil. Be of good cheer then, my dear Crito, and say that you are burying my body only, and do with that whatever is usual, and what you think best.

When he had spoken these words, he arose and went into a chamber to bathe; Crito followed him and told us to wait. So we remained behind, talking and thinking of the subject of discourse, and also of the greatness of our sorrow; he was like a father of whom we were being bereaved, and we were about to pass the rest of our lives as orphans. When he had taken the bath his children were brought to him—(he had two young sons and an elder one); and the women of his family also came, and he talked to them and gave them a few directions in the presence of Crito; then he dismissed them and returned to us.

Now the hour of sunset was near, for a good deal of time had passed while he was within. When he came out, he sat down with us again after his bath, but not much was said. Soon the jailer, who was the servant of the Eleven, entered and stood by him, saying:—To you, Socrates, whom I know to be the noblest and gentlest and best of all who ever came to this place, I will not impute the angry feelings of other men, who rage and swear at me, when, in obedience to the authorities, I bid them drink the poison—indeed, I am sure that you will not be angry with me; for others, as you are aware, and not I, are to blame. And so fare you well, and try to bear lightly what must needs be—you know my errand. Then bursting into tears he turned away and went out.

Socrates looked at him and said: I return your good wishes, and will do as you bid. Then turning to us, he said, How charming the man is: since I have been in prison he has always been coming to see me, and at times he would talk to me, and was as good to me as could be, and now see how generously he sorrows on my account. We must do as he says, Crito; and therefore let the cup be brought, if the poison is prepared: if not, let the attendant prepare some.

Yet, said Crito, the sun is still upon the hill-tops, and I know that many a one has taken the draught late, and after the announcement has been made to him, he has eaten and drunk, and enjoyed the society of his beloved; do not hurry—there is time enough.

Socrates said: Yes, Crito, and they of whom you speak are right in so acting, for they think that they will be gainers by the delay; but I am right in not following their example, for I do not think that I should gain anything by drinking the poison a little later; I should only be ridiculous in my own eyes for sparing and saving a life which is already forfeit. Please then to do as I say, and not to refuse me.

Crito made a sign to the servant, who was standing by; and he went out, and having been absent for some time, returned with the jailer carrying the cup of poison. Socrates said: You, my good friend, who are experienced in these matters, shall give me directions how I am to proceed. The man answered: You have only to walk about until your legs are heavy, and then to lie down, and the poison will act. At the same time he handed the cup to Socrates, who in the easiest and gentlest manner, without the least fear or change of colour or feature, looking at the man with all his eyes, Echecrates, as his manner was, took the cup and said: What do you say about making a libation out of this cup to any god? May I, or not? The man answered: We only prepare, Socrates, just so much as we deem enough. I understand, he said: but I may and must ask the gods to prosper my journey from this to the other world—even so—and so be it according to my prayer. Then raising the cup to his lips, quite readily and cheerfully he drank off the poison. And hitherto most of us had been able to control our sorrow; but now when we saw him drinking, and saw too that he had finished the draught, we could no longer forbear, and in spite of myself my own tears were flowing fast; so that I covered my face and wept, not for him, but at the thought of my own calamity in having to part from such a friend. Nor was I the first; for Crito, when he found himself unable to restrain his tears, had got up, and I followed; and at that moment, Apollodorus, who had been weeping all the time, broke out in a loud and passionate cry which made cowards of us all. Socrates alone retained his calmness: What is this strange outcry? he said. I sent away the women mainly in order that they might not misbehave in this way, for I have been told that a man should die in peace. Be quiet then, and have patience. When we heard his words we were ashamed, and refrained our tears; and he walked about until, as he said, his legs began to fail, and then he lay on his back, according to the directions, and the man who gave him the poison now and then looked at his feet and legs; and after a while he pressed his foot hard, and asked him if he could feel; and he said, No; and then his leg, and so upwards and upwards, and showed us that he was cold and stiff. And he felt them himself, and said: When the poison reaches the heart, that will be the end. He was beginning to grow cold about the groin, when he uncovered his face, for he had covered himself up, and said—they were his last words—he said: Crito, I owe a cock to Asclepius; will you remember to pay the debt? The debt shall be paid, said Crito; is there anything else? There was no answer to this question; but in a minute or two a movement was heard, and the attendants uncovered him; his eyes were set, and Crito closed his eyes and mouth.

Such was the end, Echecrates, of our friend; concerning whom I may truly say, that of all the men of his time whom I have known, he was the wisest and justest and best.

Questions for Discussion

1. Did Socrates decide that he should escape from jail? What reasons did Crito give? What reasons did Socrates give? Whose reasons were better?
2. Try constructing a dialogue of your own. "Tell me, Laches, what is courage?" "Well, I say, Socrates, that courage is standing unafraid in the face of the enemy." "Ah, very good, Laches, but, aren't there examples of other kinds of courage such as . . ."
3. Can you isolate any principles of good teaching which are present in this dialogue? Be thoughtful in your answer.

22 The Art of Teaching

Gilbert Highet

This article should give you a number of practical suggestions on how to act in the classroom: how to remember the names of your students; how to handle the private counseling situation; how to relate to bright students; how to remember what you are going to teach; and so on. You might well make a list of his tips and comments, for not only should they be useful to a new teacher but they can provide a basis for his continued intellectual growth as well.

First, and most necessary of all, he must know the subject. He must know what he teaches. This sounds obvious; yet it is not always practiced. It means that, if his job is teaching chemistry, he must know chemistry. It is not enough for a chemistry teacher to know just that amount of chemistry which is taught in schools and required for the final examinations. He must really understand the science of chemistry. Its upper regions must be clear to him, at least in outline; and he should know what are the most important new discoveries made every year. If a boy shows a gift for chemistry, the master must be able to encourage him, by throwing open window after window into the future, showing him what he can learn at the university, what types of chemistry are most vital in peace and war, which big problems still remain to be solved, and (this is always **important**) how the great chemists of the past and present have lived and worked.

Therefore teaching is inseparable from learning. Every good teacher will learn more about his subject every year—every month, every week if possible. If a girl chooses the career of teaching French in school, she should not hope to commit the prescribed texts and grammars to memory and then turn her mind to other things. She should dedicate part of her life to the French language, to the superb literature of France, to French art and history and civilization. To become a good teacher of French, she will build up a growing library of her own French books, spending one year (for instance) reading Balzac, the next year reading Proust, the next with Molière, and the next with Giraudoux, Cocteau, Romains, and the other modern playwrights. She will visit France, if and when she can save up enough money to do so—which will be fearfully difficult with salaries at their present low level. She may take summer courses in French at a university. Certainly she will see every available French film, and learn to enjoy Raimu's rich Marseillais accent, to guffaw with Fernandel. For it will not all be serious work and planned self-improvement. It will be living, and therefore it will contain enjoyments, and even frivolities, like the latest records by Lucienne Boyer and Charles Trenet. But it will be learning at the same time, and it will make better teaching. . . .

The second essential is that he must like it. The two are connected, for it is almost impossible to go on learning anything year after year without feeling a spontaneous interest in it. . . .

The young dislike their elders for having fixed minds. But they dislike them even more for being insincere. They themselves are simple, single-minded, straight-forward, almost painfully naïve. A hypocritical boy or girl is rare, and is always a monster or a spiritual cripple. They know grown-ups are clever, they know grown-ups hold the power. What they cannot bear is that grown-ups should also be deceitful. Thousands of boys have admired and imitated bandits and gunmen because they felt these were at least brave and resolute characters, who had simply chosen to be spades instead of diamonds; but few boys have ever admired a forger or a poisoner. So they will tolerate a parent or a teacher who is energetic and violent, and some-times even learn a good deal from him; but they loathe and despise a hypocrite.

And the teacher who dislikes his subject or is indifferent to it always runs the risk of becoming a hypocrite. Think of the alternatives. Suppose you are teaching chemistry without thinking it worth learning. Either you can tell your pupils to learn it because you will punish them if they don't; or you can tell them to learn it because it will help to get them good jobs in the future; or you can pretend that you think it is too, too fascinating, and just watch what happens when a little H_2 is exploded along with some SO_4. In the first case they will learn grudgingly and perhaps inadequately—it depends largely on the area where you live. (A class in Germany would learn well, a class in Australia would learn badly.) In the second case some of them may believe you and learn well. In the third case none of them will believe you, and you will throw disgust into someone who might have become a good chemist.

But if you do enjoy the subject, it will be easy to teach even when you are tired, and delightful when you are feeling fresh. You will never be at a loss for a new illustration, for a topic of discussion, for an interesting point of view. Even if you do make a blunder, as every teacher does, if you forget a formula or mix up τύπτω with κρύπτω, you will not need to bluff your way out, you can admit that you have forgotten and even ask for the correct word (or, more wisely, promise to look it up), without sacrificing the respect and the attention of your class. For the young do not demand omniscience. They know it is unattainable. They do demand sin-cerity. . . .

The third essential of good teaching is to like the pupils. If you do not actually like boys and girls, or young men and young women, give up teaching.

It is easy to like the young because they are young. They have no faults, except the very one which they are asking you to eradicate: ignorance, shallowness, and inexperience. The really hateful faults are those which we grown men and women have. Some of these grow on us like diseases, others we build up and cherish as though they were virtues. Ingrained conceit, calculated cruelty, deep-rooted coward-ice, slobbering greed, vulgar self-satisfaction, puffy laziness of mind and body—these and the other real sins result from years, decades of careful cultivation. They show on our faces, they ring harsh or hollow in our voices, they have become bone of our bone and flesh of our flesh. The young do not sin in those ways. Heaven knows they are infuriatingly lazy and unbelievably stupid and sometimes detestably cruel—but not for long, not all at once, and not (like grown-ups) as a matter of habit or policy. They are trying to be energetic and wise and kind. When you remember this, it is difficult not to like them.

A teacher must not only like the young because they are young. He must enjoy their company in groups. There is a famous American definition of a good education. It consists, says the epigram, of Mark Hopkins on one end of a bench and the student on the other. Mark Hopkins was a fine teacher, but he did better when he put ten students on the bench and stood in front of them. Later we shall discuss the advantages of man-to-man teaching and of classes of various kinds. Meanwhile it is enough to point out that there are many more pupils than teachers in the world, so that the average teacher must spend several hours a day with a collection of ten to thirty youngsters. Unless he likes groups of young people, he will not teach them well. It will be useless for him to wish that there were only two or three, or that they were all more mature. They will always be young, and there will always be lots of them.

In certain institutions, and given certain rather special conditions, someone who hates large groups and is nervous among young people can still be accepted and admitted as a teacher. A scholar, for instance, who has spent a generation learning a difficult subject may not know how to teach it, and may be embarrassed or repelled by having a youthful audience. But if his reputation and his knowledge are distinguished enough, they will hold the attention of a class even when he himself is dull and inaudible. Many of his hearers will go away stimulated, not by his teaching, but by the excitement of contact, however remote, with a distinguished mind. Many of the world's great universities contain such scholars. Usually they are shocking bad teachers during the first twenty or thirty years, and continue to be bad teachers when they reach their peak; but by the time they have mastered genetics or iconography, most of the work of teaching is done for them, by the accumulated power of their knowledge. Their classes sit silent, attentive, eager. Their thin flat voices are magnified by the attention of their pupils. Incomplete ideas are filled in, obscure trains of thought are illuminated, by the keenness of the audience. I have never heard Dr. Einstein speak, I do not believe he would put much vital energy into teaching, and I do not understand astrophysics; but I should go to hear him lecture, and I know I should learn something from it.

But for most of us, who cannot reasonably count on being savants with a self-illuminating reputation, it is essential to enjoy the conditions of teaching, to feel at home in a room containing twenty or thirty healthy young people, and to make our enjoyment of this group-feeling give us energy for our teaching. Every profession has its atmosphere, its setting, and those who practice it must feel at home there. It is silly to become an actor if you want a settled home and time to think. Do not enter journalism unless you like the bustle of a large noisy office, welcome travel and the unexpected, and hope to like it all the rest of your life. If you do not enjoy the prospect of facing the young in large groups, if you would always prefer working in a laboratory or reading in a library, you will never be a good teacher.

Of course nobody can bear young people all the time. One of the pleasures and the necessities of the teacher's life is to escape—into a cool library or a little garden —away from their noise and their devilish energy. Among the most difficult jobs in the profession are those which give very little respite and condemn the dean to be always on call, the housemaster to spend every day of his working life among the boys. Still, those jobs are not thrust upon us, but taken by choice. Those who hold them usually relish them. Remember, you must not armor yourself against the energies of the young. You must not be the policeman watching the mob. You must be the leader of a group—something higher than the actor with his audience, something lower than the priest with his congregation, something kindlier than the officer with his unit. You must always feel what the orator feels when he addresses an audience partly friendly and partly docile, and senses after a little that they are with him. Such a man is borne upwards and swept onwards by energy which flows into him from outside, from the group of which he is the heart and the voice. The good teacher feels that same flow of energy, constantly supplied by the young. If he can canalize it, he will never be tired. At least, not while he is teaching. . . .

We have seen, then, that the third essential of teaching in ordinary schools and colleges is to like the pupils. Is it also essential to know the pupils?

It depends largely on the method of teaching that is being used—class instruction, lecturing, laboratory work, or tutoring. The distinction between these methods will be discussed later. Here it is enough to say that there is only one of them in which it is genuinely necessary to know every individual pupil well: the tutorial system.

In the other systems, how much must the teacher know of his pupils?

To begin with, he must know the young. They are quite unlike adults. They are so different that it would be easier to understand them if they looked like animals. You know how a baby, before it is born, passes through the main stages of evolution. It begins by looking like an amœba, goes on to look like a fish, resembles a big-headed monkey for some time, and ends up at birth still looking remarkably like a little red blind clutching grimacing ape. I have often thought that in its first fifteen years of life it passes through another series of animal existences. Boys of nine and ten, for instance, are very like dogs. Watch a pack of them hot on the scent, yapping, running and jumping, bouncing aimlessly around full of unexpendable energy, kicking one another or breaking down a door as carelessly as a dog nips at its neighbor's flanks or bursts through a hedge. When they are really enjoying the chase, all their teeth and eyes gleam and their breath and laughter go "huh, huh, huh, huh" like a leash of fox-terriers. Girls in their middle teens are like horses, strong, nervous, given to sudden illnesses and inexplicable terrors, able to work remarkably hard if they are kept firmly in hand, but really happiest when they are thinking of nothing in particular and prancing about with their manes flying. Both dogs and horses are amiable creatures and can be domesticated, but it is a mistake to treat them as though they were human. It is also a mistake to treat horses as though they were dogs, or dogs like horses.

So, if you are interested in teaching, do not even expect the young to be like yourself and the people you know. Learn the peculiar patterns of their thought and emotions just as you would learn to understand horses or dogs—or other animals (for there are all kinds of different animals implicit in children: the very small ones are often more like birds)—and then you will find that many of the inexplicable things they do are easy to understand, many of the unpardonable things easy to forget.

How can you learn this? Chiefly by experience. Watch them and talk to them. Mix with them sometimes off duty. Give them a party now and then, or play games with them. Listen to them, not to eavesdrop, but to understand, by learning the random careless rhythm of their chatter, how their emotions and minds really work. But as well as doing this, you can learn a great deal about them by remembering your own youth. The more intensely you can think yourself back into those parts of it which seem furthest away from your present adult life, the better you can understand the young. . . .

The teacher, then, must know the young as such. Next, he must know the names and faces of his pupils. Some people find this easy, some very difficult, but it is a *must*. I do it so badly myself that I cannot advise anyone how to do it. Still, I know it must be done. One of the gravest mistakes made by A. E. Housman as a teacher at London University was to boast of his inability to recognize his pupils. The girls hated it, particularly because he would put what felt like really personal venom and vitality into correcting their blunders, and would pass them on the street next day. In his farewell address, before departing for Cambridge, he told them he was sorry, adding: "If I had remembered all your faces, I might have forgotten more important things" —meaning that if he had burdened his memory with the distinction between Miss Jones and Miss Smith, he might have forgotten the difference between the second and the fourth declension. You can imagine how this bogus humility and pedantic arrogance was welcomed by the young women he had snubbed. There was of course a certain amount of truth in it. He meant that it would have been an extra expenditure of time and energy for him to learn the names of his pupils; but he also implied that the effort was unnecessary, and not really part of his job. And there, since he was taking money for teaching, he was wrong. The young are trying desperately hard to become real people, to be individuals. If you wish to influence them in any way, you must convince them that you know them as individuals. The first step towards this is memorizing their faces and their names.

But the teacher will find that, beyond that, it is seldom feasible to treat all his pupils as individuals. Even if it were possible, it would be unwise. For it would mean that the problem presented by each young man or girl would have to be approached as though it were unique. This would make it very difficult to solve, would be exhausting for the teacher, and would waste the profits of experience. The art of teaching, like the art of healing, consists partly in recognizing, within each individual, a particular type or combination of types. . . .

Similarly, the best way to know one's pupils is to divide them into types. This is a skill which the teacher can learn only by experience. He will begin, early in his career, by thinking they are all different. Then he will observe that Clark is rather like Johansen, and that Verney and Lennox react in very much the same way to difficulties, and even write similar essays. Then, after four or five years' teaching, he will notice another Clark in his class—a youth who looks the same (except that he has red hair) and laughs at the same kind of jokes and writes the same big square hand . . . only this boy is called Macdonald and comes from a different part of the country. Next year another Verney will turn up. And so on, until the teacher, if he learns well, will in ten or fifteen years assemble a little gallery of types which, singly or combined, will account for eighty-five per cent of the average class.

It is a complicated business, typing one's pupils. It must not be oversimplified. It would be frankly impossible in a very broad sampling of humanity. For instance, it was extremely difficult in the army, where one had great strong farmers, quick little city boys, grave youths from the small towns, and dozens of unexpected blends of character and background and physique, all in the same unit. But schools and universities do not function in mid-air. They are each attached to one group of traditions and supplied chiefly by two or three localities; also, schools and local society and youth itself do a great deal of uniformizing, so that a teacher can usually count on a fairly even distribution and recurrence of types.

But after he has learnt the main types and subspecies, some unclassifiable individuals will always remain. These are the joys, the sorrows, and the horseflies of the teacher's life.

Rebels are not necessarily individuals. At certain times and in certain schools it is orthodox to be a rebel; and in general it is a very poor class that does not contain at least three pupils who can be counted on to oppose the teacher's authority and loudly and persistently to question everything he says. No, the individuals are those who go neither with the stream nor against it, but dart violently from side to side, spin slowly round in a backwater, bury themselves in the mud at the bottom, or, occasionally, take wings and soar in the air above. They may show up in any classroom, and come from any section of society. Their eccentricity may take any form; it may be so excessively complicated that it cannot be understood for years afterwards or so extreme that it is actively dangerous. They may be quiet, noisy, stupid, clever, sociable or solitary, handsome, hideous, or mousy, dim or dazzling, it is impossible to foresee them and unwise to overlook them. Often one eccentric will cause more trouble than all the rest of a class, and occasionally one will prove to be more rewarding than a thousand ordinary pupils. But the danger of all classifications is that they fail to prepare you for the eccentric. They may even make you mistreat him, by implying that if he does not fit into one of the accepted categories he does not really exist. On the contrary, he usually exists more intensely than his more typical classmates.

Since the eccentrics are all individuals, it is difficult to offer any general rules for treating them. But a few suggestions for the teacher himself are worth remembering.

First, always expect that one or two of your pupils will be eccentrics, even if they do not show at first. Never assume that you are addressing a group of types. That calm, fair-haired girl with the cheerful smile may turn out to be a cruel satirist with a bite like a rattlesnake. The plump short-sighted youth who seems to be bored and sleepy may be weighing and memorizing every word you say in the hope of proving you are an atheist, a Jesuit, a fascist, a Communist, or a vivisectionist. The earnest, pimpled hobbledehoy who writes down everything rather slowly may be three or four years ahead of the rest of the class. Watch them all. Human beings are infinitely complex.

Then, when you have discovered the eccentrics, treat them with extreme care. They are explosive mixtures. Some of them are sensitive as those fulminates which can be detonated by a falling leaf. Others are fitted with a slow-burning, delayed-action fuse. You do not necessarily want to neutralize them. But you do want to employ all that force in a useful way—to economize and direct it instead of allowing it to blow itself to smithereens, perhaps taking your hand and arm with it.

These are the students whom you must learn to know as individuals. You must find out as many ingredients of the unstable compound as possible. The attempt to analyze may itself provoke an explosion. The risk, however, is worth taking, for the investigation is justifiable, and sometimes it relieves the dangerous tension. . . .

For dealing with these cases, there is one sovereign rule. *Keep the relationship impersonal.* Never step outside the bounds of your profession. If they want private interviews at which they can "really tell you all their problems," beware. Give them an interview in your study at a fixed hour, for a fixed time; take notes; and leave the door open as though you expected a colleague in ten minutes. If their personality swells up and becomes inflamed, make yourself into a cool, dry administrator who has a reasonable precedent for everything he does. Commit no dramatic personal gestures.

A colleague of mine once had a graduate student who came to his office and threatened to jump out of the window unless he revised her mark from C "to at least a B." I asked him what he did then. He said: "I opened the window for her. She didn't do it."

But he was taking a terrible risk. He was betting the woman's life against her sanity—not to mention his own career. I have often thought over this story, and the only way I can explain it is this. He himself was a quiet, hard-headed New Englander; and he knew that such a gesture, *from him,* would bring the woman to her senses. From nearly anyone else, it would have been a dangerous, a murderous provocation.

They are not uncommon, these people; and even quite normal pupils will, under a combination of strains, sometimes begin to behave strangely, whinnying, kicking, and shying at shadows. However, six such fits are amply compensated by the appearance of one really brilliant pupil. He, or she, will be difficult to handle also, but infinitely rewarding. To train him or her properly is one of the chief functions for which the teacher should prepare; suggestions for this preparation will therefore emerge from the whole of this book, but a few general hints can be given here.

Most important of all is a negative. Do not try to make the brilliant pupil a replica of yourself. To begin with, that would be impossible, because individuals differ and brilliant individuals diverge widely. Even if it were possible, it would be stupid: because much of a man's creative energy flows from his knowledge of his own uniqueness and originality, whereas anyone who has been molded to fit the pattern of another personality usually spends the rest of his life *either* trying to conform and crushing out spontaneous and creative impulses, *or* rebelling in that dreary uncreative way which consists in saying "I don't care what I do, I just want to deny everything X stands for." (For X, read "my father," "my mother," or "my teacher."

On the other hand, do not hesitate to train him in your skills and give him your experience. Many teachers tend to forget how valuable the wide reading and accumulated experience of a mature man or woman can be, to a pupil who is still groping around helplessly among untried experiments and unread books. If you can send him on into the world with frames of reference suggested by you and tricks of craftsmanship which he could get only from you, you will have made him your pupil, as much as he will ever be, and earned a right to his permanent gratitude.

Next, give him plenty of work, plenty to think about. Provided you are sure he is brilliant and his health is normally good, you should pile on as much as the traffic will bear. Even if he does not do all the work, he will know that it is there to be done some day. Unknown to you, after you have asked him if he has ever read Rousseau, he will buy a second-hand copy of *The Social Contract,* he will make notes saying *Mem. read Rousseau* THIS WEEK, and he will, first in experimental dips and then in a splashing plunge of activity, read *The Social Contract,* and the *Confessions* too, and *The New Héloïse,* and *Émile.*

If he gets enough work to do and his health holds up, the chief danger for him will be wasting his energy. He will be apt to rush at everything he sees, jump every fence, climb every hill, race down every valley, and then retain nothing but a feeling of exhaustion and disillusionment. . . .

The best way to avoid wasting the powers of a good pupil is to plan his work for him. You need not necessarily tell him that it is all laid out some distance ahead. Better not. Sometimes that discourages him. But you must arrange matters so that, at the end of a three-month or a six-month period, you will be able to make him look back over the journey he has made and be pleased and surprised at its extent. Make him keep records. Make him write. Extract from him groups of notes on the successive experiments he makes, or get him to put down a weekly summary of the period he has been studying, or set him a series of essays carefully designed to guide him through every sector of an important field. Then, at the end of three months, give him a rest and congratulate him, and while he is still elated, take him rapidly over his whole achievement. This gives him a sense of unexpected power; fixes the broad outlines of his work much more firmly in his mind; allows grand general ideas time to germinate in him; and often stimulates him to suggest further work in a direction that would not have occurred to you. It is also a valuable insurance against those fits of depression that often afflict the brilliant. When he comes to you haggard and sullen after being baffled by a new set of problems, and says he is convinced all his effort has been wasted, then you will produce the solid collection of work he has already done, show him how far he pushed ahead during that period, persuade him that his profits there are inalienable, and, if you feel it wise, explain how the present period of work will dovetail into the earlier. Usually he will appear unconsoled. The young are easily changed, therefore they like to pose as being immutable. But after going away he will look back over the immediate past—his own, hand-made, unique, indestructible past, the work that has become part of himself—and he will start again with new energy to hammer out his future.

Such pupils you must know. You must know the geniuses, the loonies, and the weaklings, all the eccentrics. You must know some of them for your own protection— in the same way as a wise physician with a new paranoiac patient telephones his previous doctor to get a complete history of his weaknesses and treatment. Others you must learn in order to draw the maximum out of them, and put the maximum in. The rest, the typical students, you need hardly know as separate persons.

But—one last word—never let them feel that they are only types: that would be quite wrong. If they ask for personal advice, it is your duty to give it freely and pleasantly. If they have special inclinations, they will be delighted to hear you discuss them. You should not, however, feel it your responsibility to know every single one of your pupils as well as you know the special individuals whom we have been dis-cussing—since average youngsters, being easier to educate in a class and more friendly to the rest of their group, do not need such particular attention.

Now we have listed the main things that a good teacher will know and like. But what kind of man or woman will the good teacher be? Are there any abilities which are absolutely essential?

Not many. But there are certainly three.

The first is memory. A teacher with a poor memory is ridiculous and dangerous. He is like a musician who announces an ambitious concert and plays innumerable wrong notes; or an actor who begins: "It is the cause, it is the cause, my soul," and then blows up; or a doctor who gives one gram of digitalis instead of one grain; or a policeman who directs three lines of traffic into one another; or a merchant who cannot find the goods his customers want ("I know they were in here somewhere; just a moment, it'll come to me where I left them, let me see now . . ."); or a painter who puts both eyes on the same side of the nose—no, no, hush, for Picasso is still alive and distinguished; but certainly those others. Of course he must remember all the essentials of his subject. So much we have already said; although if he now and then forgets a detail, the class will understand and sympathize. (Let him look it up freely and openly—preferably in his own notes, not in a book.) But his memory is also important in covering what is said in class. If a question is raised and discussed, let him remember it and bring it back a week or two later in another context. If a pupil volunteers a good illustration from his own reading, or from a hobby, let the teacher remember to ask him for another one later. If one little group find a problem unusually hard, let him give special attention to them when the next such problem appears. Memory is as important for the teacher as for other professional men. A creative memory is one of the qualities that differentiate the good lawyer, doctor, or teacher from the mediocre.

A display of good creative memory by a teacher helps the young in one of their most difficult jobs. Their attention is lively and their perception is keen, but they find it very hard to correlate. Many of the facts they learn merely drop into their minds like blocks of metal, and lie there. At examinations they take out the blocks, polish them, and show them to us. Then they put them back, or sometimes throw them away. If the facts simply remain on deposit, however neatly packed and highly polished, their possessors are not educated. The business of the teacher is to pass currents of interest and energy through the facts, while they are being learnt and afterwards, so that they melt, fuse, become interconnected, acquire life, and grow into vital parts of the minds which hold them. One excellent way to do this is to demonstrate *how* apparently remote facts are organically linked, and that can some-times be done more happily as improvisation than as a prepared part of a lesson. When it comes off, the teacher's reward is there: he sees face after face light up as two blank areas of the brain, with the connections flashing between them, come alive.

Second to memory comes will-power. A good teacher is a determined person. This was widely known in the nineteenth century. That was a time of strong-

willed parents and tough teachers. Sometimes they were merely tyrants. But sometimes they were wise, firm, and efficient educators; and even if the children they
produced did often rebel, they became well-educated rebels. This necessity is not so
well known nowadays—at least in the schools of the Western democracies. It was
recognized in Germany during the National Socialist regime, when will-power was
classed as one of the essential qualifications of a schoolmaster and as one of the
essential qualities he had to develop in his pupils. Teachers in America and Britain,
France and Italy and elsewhere, often avoid the display of will, and prefer to be
"nice"—which often means being cheery and indulgent and evasive on difficulties.
On the whole, they do not teach so well as their resolute predecessors.

Yet it is obvious that a teacher needs will-power. Everyone who has ever faced a
class and seen thirty pairs of eyes turned upon him knows that. Some nervous ladies
stand behind their desks, as though they were hunting leopards from a hide, while
there are men teachers who stride up and down among their pupils, catching every
gaze and holding it, barking out short urgent phrases, lacking only the chair and
whip to be lion-tamers. Still, it seems that some teachers do not know why they
must have a strong will and exercise it: they are perhaps a little ashamed of the
necessity, even afraid of it; they feel that in a perfect society no display of will-power
would be needed in the schools. But it would.

Consider how many different kinds of resistance the teacher has to overcome. To
begin with, the young do not like work. They would rather be playing football, or
sitting in the movies eating chocolate. But they must learn to work, because they
will assuredly have to work all the rest of their lives; and to teach them that work
is unnecessary or avoidable is to deform their characters. (It is odd, by the way, that
the word "school" means "leisure" or "pastime." When that name was coined, people felt that a boy was lucky to be in school, because if he weren't he would be
sweeping out his father's shop or milking his father's cows: that was real work, and
"school" was "play.")

Nor do the young like authority. They are natural anarchists. They would prefer
a world of unpredictable disorder, without duties or responsibilities. Such a world
is impracticable now. So the young must be taught to respect the principle of
authority; and if they do not learn it in school they will find it very bitter to
learn later. A subsequent duty of their teachers will be to teach them to distinguish
between different types of authority, to choose the good and reject the bad. Only
a determined teacher can teach them the first lesson. If he is both determined and
wise, he can teach them both.

Also, the young hate concentration. It is an effort, an unfamiliar and painful effort.
Watch a boy doing his home-work when he thinks he is not observed. He will read
ten lines, then draw a funny face in the margin, then try to read ten lines more and
give up, then stop to whistle two bars of "Blood on the Saddle," then rearrange all
the books on his table and sharpen all his pencils, then make a dash at the book and
read twenty-five lines, and then sit panting and vacant-eyed for at least three minutes
before beginning the struggle once more. Even his moments of true attention are
accompanied by all kinds of waste motion and diversion: he taps both heels rhythmi-
cally on the ground, bites his nails, shifts his position as though he were sitting in a
red-hot torture-seat, and usually keeps the radio on full blast. All this side-effort

means that he finds concentration to be so painful that he must mitigate the agony by every possible means. He is pretending to escape.

Yet he learns. By the time he gets to college he will be able to concentrate oftener and keep it up for longer periods. If he enters one of the professions, he will have to increase his ability until he can follow and reproduce nearly every stage of a complex operation, or summarize the essentials of six leading judicial decisions in one evening. If he goes to work on leaving school, life will teach him concentration —or else it will make him a nonentity, the sort of man who hops from job to job and has a constant struggle to keep alive in a world where the bees outnumber the butterflies.

Concentration must be learnt. It should be learnt in school. A good teacher can teach it to his pupils. It should not be imagined as nothing but an effort of the will. Concentration is also an intellectual process. It is choice. Take the same boy who reads his book slowly, grudgingly, five lines at a time, and increase the urgency of his study—somehow, anyhow—make the choice clearer to him, and the importance of his study paramount—put him to work on the prize essay—and then watch. "Turn that radio off!" he shouts. He clears the table, except for one photograph. He sits fixed in one position till he is cramped. Sometimes, when he is really intent, he will miss meals and forget about sleep. All this because he has chosen one aim and discarded others. And that, after all, is what we learn to do throughout life. . . .

Memory, then, and will-power are two of the qualities that make a good teacher. The third is kindness. It is very difficult to teach anything without kindness. It can be done, of course, by the exercise of strong compulsion—as lion-tamers teach their beastly pupils—but there are not many types of pupil on which such compulsion can be exercised. Lions are imprisoned, and partially cowed by hot irons and guns. Boys learning religious texts like the Koran and the Talmud are caged within generations of previous examples and prodded on by their own (and their families') ambition. Pupils at officers' schools, and certain other institutions where attendance is a guarded privilege, will drive themselves on within the tight disciplinary mechanism of the school even if the master hates them as much as they hate him. But in nearly all other kinds of learning the pupils should feel that the teacher wants to help them, wants them to improve, is interested in their growth, is sorry for their mistakes and pleased by their successes and sympathetic with their inadequacies. Learning anything worth while is difficult. Some people find it painful. Everyone finds it tiring. Few things will diminish the difficulty, the pain, and the fatigue like the kindness of a good teacher.

This kindness must be genuine. Pupils of all ages, from careless children up to hard-working graduates, easily and quickly detect the teacher who dislikes them, as easily as a dog detects someone who is afraid of him. It is useless to feign a liking for them if you do not really feel it.

On the other hand, it is not at all necessary to show it by pats on the shoulder, by nods and becks and wreathed smiles. A serious-faced lecturer, who seldom addresses a pupil by name and thinks only about the job of making the basic principles of economics or the powers of the Supreme Court absolutely clear and memorable, will often be recognized as a teacher genuinely interested in the job of teaching and anxious for the welfare of his classes. It is not enough for him to be interested in the subject. Many a man is interested in a subject without wanting to teach it to anyone else. But if he is really interested in making the subject better known and more correctly understood, and if he does not expect all his pupils to grasp its elements at the first attempt but will help the slow and correct the confused, then he will be counted kind, although his face remains immovably grave and his manner unemotional and impersonal.

Still, the kindness must be there. It may be the kindness of an elder brother or sister, even of a parent. It can well be the kindness of a fellow-student. Sometimes it is a sympathy based on local patriotism, where the teacher feels he is helping the younger generation of his own fellow-citizens to grow and prosper. (This is at the basis of the admirable plan for conquering illiteracy in Mexico, by getting every Mexican who can read to teach one other of his countrymen.) But if the teacher feels none of these emotions, nor anything like them, if he or she regards the students merely as a necessary evil, in the same way as he regards income-tax forms, then his or her job will be far more difficult to do, far more painful for the pupils, and far less effectively done. Every teacher dislikes *some* pupils—the cheeky lip-sticked adolescent girls, the sullen hangdog youths, the cocky vulgar little comedians, how loathsome they can be, all the more so because they do it deliberately! But if any teacher finds hmself disliking *all* his pupils, he should change his character, and if that fails, change his job.

Fathers and mothers, husbands and wives, managers and foremen, doctors and psychiatrists, clergymen, advertisers, propagandists, politicians, artists, and authors: all these, in one way or another, are teachers. Their methods will vary as widely as their jobs and characters, so that we can point out only a few general principles to make their teaching more effective.

The first is *clarity*. Whenever you are teaching, make it clear. Make it as firm as stone and as bright as sunlight. Not to yourself—that is easy. Make it clear to the people you are teaching—that is difficult. The difficulty lies partly in subject-matter, and partly in language. You must think, not what you know, but what they do not know; not what you find hard, but what they will find hard; then, after putting yourself inside their minds, obstinate or puzzled, groping or mistaken as they are, explain what they need to learn. And you must be sure they understand your words. A strange name, a phrase only vaguely understood, will blur an explanation badly. Abstract words mean little on first hearing. Illustrate them. Give pictures and examples. And whenever possible, make sure you have been understood, by talking over what you have been trying to teach. A good pupil is seldom silent.

The second is *patience*. Anything worth learning takes time to learn, and time to teach. It is a mistake often made by great scholars and distinguished statesmen, to assume that their audiences have thought deeply about their problems and are only a few steps behind them in any discussion—so that they treat as partially solved problems which the majority of their audience have scarcely envisaged, or dart rapidly from one obscure question to another without attempting to show the connection. Real teaching is not simply handing out packages of information. It culminates in a conversion, an actual change of the pupil's mind. An important change takes a long time to carry through, and should therefore be planned carefully and approached in slow stages with plenty of repetition disguised by variation. It is particularly important to keep out emotion, or rather to control it carefully. Fathers and mothers, husbands and wives, and people in authority very often forget this. When they explain, they shout. Their faces become distorted with anger or urgency. They make violent gestures. They *feel* that they are explaining things more forcibly. But in fact their emotion makes them difficult to understand. A wife screaming at her husband, a sergeant roaring at a platoon, a father bellowing at his son, create fear, and even hatred, but they do not manage to explain what they want done and persuade their hearers to do it. Whenever we sink to believing that the more emotion we display, the more effect we shall produce, we are reverting to our animal ancestry and forgetting that conscious reason is what makes us men.

The third principle is *responsibility*. It is a serious thing to interfere with another man's life. It is hard enough to guide one's own. Yet people are easily influenced for good or evil, particularly when they are young or when their teacher speaks with authority. The effects of bad teaching, of glib and shallow advice, of money-grubbing or publicity-hunting declarations to a trusting public are quite incalculable. Every now and then the papers mention that a man has been arrested for selling a Cancer Cure composed of bread pills flavored with saccharin. He gets ten years; but how can that compare with the tortures he has inflicted on his "patients"? In the same way, it is hard to see how any politician who has once offered to teach the public what was right on a vital issue, and who has been proved wrong, can ever venture to open his mouth again. But they are seldom punished, and sometimes praised as versatile and constructive thinkers. It must be a fearful thing to write a series of plays or novels, rapidly and irresponsibly, in order to gain a reputation and make money; and then, late in life, to realize that they express foolish or wicked ideas, and to be ashamed of your own words. The surest safeguard against that is to ask how your ideas could possibly be misused or misunderstood, and to think, not of yourself, but of your friends and brothers whom you are trying to teach.

Questions for Discussion

1. Report at least ten different principles of good teaching mentioned in this selection. Evaluate them in regard to their advantages, disadvantages, and ways in which they can be applied to a classroom situation.
2. Do you really believe that teaching and learning are inseparable; that you cannot have one without the other? The principle, if true, is easily understood for the classroom teacher, but what does it imply for the student? And for the principal?
3. Do you agree that a teacher should "keep the relationship impersonal" with his students? Before you answer, first be certain you understand what Highet means.
4. Measured against Highet's standards would Socrates qualify as a good teacher? Be specific.

23 The Rhythmic Claims of Freedom and Discipline

Alfred North Whitehead

Unlike Highet, who provides practical advice and tips for effective teaching, this is a selection of high generalization which pictures the learning process as a movement from "romance" to "precision" to "generalization." Notice how Whitehead describes each stage and the ways in which a teacher can use each effectively. Notice, also, Whitehead's conception of a university and its faculty, and compare his conception to your own experience with the institution you are now attending.

The fading of ideals is sad evidence of the defeat of human endeavour. In the schools of antiquity philosophers aspired to impart wisdom, in modern colleges our humbler aim is to teach subjects. The drop from the divine wisdom, which was the goal of the ancients, to text-book knowledge of subjects, which is achieved by the moderns, marks an educational failure, sustained through the ages. I am not maintaining that in the practice of education the ancient were more successful than ourselves. You have only to read Lucian, and to note his satiric dramatizations of the pretentious claims of philosophers, to see that in this respect the ancients can boast over us no superiority. My point is that, at the dawn of our European civilisation, men started with the full ideals which should inspire education, and that gradually our ideals have sunk to square with our practice.

But when ideals have sunk to the level of practice, the result is stagnation. In particular, so long as we conceive intellectual education as merely consisting in the acquirement of mechanical mental aptitudes, and of formulated statements of useful truths, there can be no progress; though there will be much activity, amid aimless re-arrangement of syllabuses, in the fruitless endeavour to dodge the inevitable lack of time. We must take it as an unavoidable fact, that God has so made the world that there are more topics desirable for knowledge than any one person can possibly acquire. It is hopeless to approach the problem by the way of the enumeration of subjects which every one ought to have mastered. There are too many of them, all with excellent title-deeds. Perhaps, after all, this plethora of material is fortunate; for the world is made interesting by a delightful ignorance of important truths. What I am anxious to impress on you is that though knowledge is one chief aim of intellectual education, there is another ingredient, vaguer but greater, and more dominating in its importance. The ancients called it "wisdom." You cannot be wise without some basis of knowledge; but you may easily acquire knowledge and remain bare of wisdom.

Reprinted with permission of The Macmillan Company from *The Aims of Education*, by Alfred North Whitehead. Copyright 1929 by The Macmillan Company, renewed 1957 by Evelyn Whitehead. Also reprinted with the permission of George Allen & Unwin Ltd.

Now wisdom is the way in which knowledge is held. It concerns the handling of knowledge, its selection for the determination of relevant issues, its employment to add value to our immediate experience. This mastery of knowledge, which is wisdom, is the most intimate freedom obtainable. The ancients saw clearly—more clearly than we do—the necessity for dominating knowledge by wisdom. But, in the pursuit of wisdom in the region of practical education, they erred sadly. To put the matter simply, their popular practice assumed that wisdom could be imparted to the young by procuring philosophers to spout at them. Hence the crop of shady philosophers in the schools of the ancient world. The only avenue towards wisdom is by freedom in the presence of knowledge. But the only avenue towards knowledge is by discipline in the acquirement of ordered fact. Freedom and discipline are the two essentials of education, and hence the title of my discourse to-day, "The Rhythmic Claims of Freedom and Discipline."

The antithesis in education between freedom and discipline is not so sharp as a logical analysis of the meanings of the terms might lead us to imagine. The pupil's mind is a growing organism. On the one hand, it is not a box to be ruthlessly packed with alien ideas: and, on the other hand, the ordered acquirement of knowledge is the natural food for a developing intelligence. Accordingly, it should be the aim of an ideally constructed education that the discipline should be the voluntary issue of free choice, and that the freedom should gain an enrichment of possibility as the issue of discipline. The two principles, freedom and discipline, are not antagonists, but should be so adjusted in the child's life that they correspond to a natural sway, to and fro, of the developing personality. It is this adaptation of freedom and discipline to the natural sway of development that I have elsewhere called The Rhythm of Education. I am convinced that much disappointing failure in the past has been due to neglect of attention to the importance of this rhythm. My main position is that the dominant note of education at its beginning and at its end is freedom, but that there is an intermediate stage of discipline with freedom in subordination: Furthermore, that there is not one unique threefold cycle of freedom, discipline, and freedom; but that all mental development is composed of such cycles, and of cycles of such cycles. Such a cycle is a unit cell, or brick; and the complete stage of growth is an organic structure of such cells. In analysing any one such cell, I call the first period of freedom the "stage of Romance," the intermediate period of discipline I call the "stage of Precision," and the final period of freedom is the "stage of Generalisation."

Let me now explain myself in more detail. There can be no mental development without interest. Interest is the *sine qua non* for attention and apprehension. You may endeavour to excite interest by means of birch rods, or you may coax it by the incitement of pleasurable activity. But without interest there will be no progress. Now the natural mode by which living organisms are excited towards suitable self-development is enjoyment. The infant is lured to adapt itself to its environment by its love of its mother and its nurse; we eat because we like a good dinner: we subdue the forces of nature because we have been lured to discovery by an insatiable curiosity: we enjoy exercise: and we enjoy the unchristian passion of hating our dangerous enemies. Undoubtedly pain is one subordinate means of arousing an organism to action. But it only supervenes on the failure of pleasure. Joy is the normal

healthy spur for the *élan vital*. I am not maintaining that we can safely abandon ourselves to the allurement of the greater immediate joys. What I do mean is that we
should seek to arrange the development of character along a path of natural activity,
in itself pleasurable. The subordinate stiffening of discipline must be directed to
secure some long-time good; although an adequate object must not be too far below
the horizon, if the necessary interest is to be retained.

The second preliminary point which I wish to make, is the unimportance—indeed
the evil—of barren knowledge. The importance of knowledge lies in its use, in our
active mastery of it—that is to say, it lies in wisdom. It is a convention to speak of
mere knowledge, apart from wisdom, as of itself imparting a peculiar dignity to its
possessor. I do not share in this reverence for knowledge as such. It all depends on
who has the knowledge and what he does with it. That knowledge which adds greatness to character is knowledge so handled as to transform every phase of immediate
experience. It is in respect to the activity of knowledge that an over-vigorous discipline in education is so harmful. The habit of active thought, with freshness, can
only be generated by adequate freedom. Undiscriminating discipline defeats its own
object by dulling the mind. If you have much to do with the young as they emerge
from school and from the university, you soon note the dulled minds of those whose
education has consisted in the acquirement of inert knowledge. Also the deplorable
tone of English society in respect to learning is a tribute to our educational failure.
Furthermore, this overhaste to impart mere knowledge defeats itself. The human
mind rejects knowledge imparted in this way. The craving for expansion, for activity, inherent in youth is disgusted by a dry imposition of disciplined knowledge. The discipline, when it comes, should satisfy a natural craving for the wisdom
which adds value to bare experience.

But let us now examine more closely the rhythm of these natural cravings of the
human intelligence. The first procedure of the mind in a new environment is a
somewhat discursive activity amid a welter of ideas and experience. It is a process
of discovery, a process of becoming used to curious thoughts, of shaping questions,
of seeking for answers, of devising new experiences, of noticing what happens as
the result of new ventures. This general process is both natural and of absorbing
interest. We must often have noticed children between the ages of eight and
thirteen absorbed in its ferment. It is dominated by wonder, and cursed be the dul-
lard who destroys wonder. Now undoubtedly this stage of development requires help,
and even discipline. The environment within which the mind is working must be
carefully selected. It must, of course, be chosen to suit the child's stage of growth,
and must be adapted to individual needs. In a sense it is an imposition from without;
but in a deeper sense it answers to the call of life within the child. In the
teacher's consciousness the child has been sent to his telescope to look at the stars, in
the child's consciousness he has been given free access to the glory of the heavens.
Unless working somewhere, however obscurely, even in the dullest child, there is this
transfiguration of imposed routine, the child's nature will refuse to assimilate the
alien material. It must never be forgotten that education is not a process of packing
articles in a trunk. Such a simile is entirely inapplicable. It is, of course, a process
completely of its own peculiar genus. Its nearest analogue is the assimilation of food
by a living organism: and we all know how necessary to health is palatable food

under suitable conditions. When you have put your boots in a trunk, they will stay there till you take them out again; but this is not at all the case if you feed a child with the wrong food.

This initial stage of romance requires guidance in another way. After all the child is the heir to long ages of civilisation, and it is absurd to let him wander in the intellectual maze of men in the Glacial Epoch. Accordingly, a certain point-ing out of important facts, and of simplifying ideas, and of usual names, really strengthens the natural impetus of the pupil. In no part of education can you do without discipline or can you do without freedom; but in the stage of romance the emphasis must always be on freedom, to allow the child to see for itself and to act for itself. My point is that a block in the assimilation of ideas inevitably arises when a discipline of precision is imposed before a stage of romance has run its course in the growing mind. There is no comprehension apart from romance. It is my strong belief that the cause of so much failure in the past has been due to the lack of care-ful study of the due place of romance. Without the adventure of romance, at the best you get inert knowledge without initiative, and at the worst you get contempt of ideas—without knowledge.

But when this stage of romance has been properly guided another craving grows. The freshness of inexperience has worn off; there is general knowledge of the groundwork of fact and theory: and, above all, there has been plenty of independent browsing amid first-hand experiences, involving adventures of thought and of action. The enlightenment which comes from precise knowledge can now be understood. It corresponds to the obvious requirements of common sense, and deals with familiar material. Now is the time for pushing on, for knowing the subject exactly, and for retaining in the memory its salient features. This is the stage of precision. This stage is the sole stage of learning in the traditional scheme of education, either at school or university. You had to learn your subject, and there was nothing more to be said on the topic of education. The result of such an undue extension of a most neces-sary period of development was the production of a plentiful array of dunces, and of a few scholars whose natural interest had survived the car of Juggernaut. There is, indeed, always the temptation to teach pupils a little more of fact and of precise theory than at that stage they are fitted to assimilate. If only they could, it would be so useful. We—I am talking of schoolmasters and of university dons—are apt to forget that we are only subordinate elements in the education of a grown man; and that, in their own good time, in later life our pupils will learn for themselves. The phenomena of growth cannot be hurried beyond certain very narrow limits. But an unskilful practitioner can easily damage a sensitive organism. Yet, when all has been said in the way of caution, there is such a thing as pushing on, of getting to know the fundamental details and the main exact generalisations, and of acquiring an easy mastery of technique. There is no getting away from the fact that things have been found out, and that to be effective in the modern world you must have a store of definite acquirement of the best practice. To write poetry you must study metre; and to build bridges you must be learned in the strength of material. Even the Hebrew prophets had learned to write, probably in those days requiring no mean effort. The untutored art of genius is—in the words of the Prayer Book—a vain thing, fondly invented.

During the stage of precision, romance is the background. The stage is dominated by the inescapable fact that there are right ways and wrong ways, and definite truths to be known. But romance is not dead, and it is the art of teaching to foster it amidst definite application to appointed task. It must be fostered for one reason, because romance is after all a necessary ingredient of that balanced wisdom which is the goal to be attained. But there is another reason: The organism will not absorb the fruits of the task unless its powers of apprehension are kept fresh by romance. The real point is to discover in practice that exact balance between freedom and discipline which will give the greatest rate of progress over the things to be known. I do not believe that there is any abstract formula which will give information applicable to all subjects, to all types of pupils, or to each individual pupil; except indeed the formula of rhythmic sway which I have been insisting on, namely, that in the earlier stage the progress requires that the emphasis be laid on freedom, and that in the later middle stage the emphasis be laid on the definite acquirement of allotted tasks. I freely admit that if the stage of romance has been properly managed, the discipline of the second stage is much less apparent, that the children know how to go about their work, want to make a good job of it, and can be safely trusted with the details. Furthermore, I hold that the only discipline, important for its own sake, is self-discipline, and that this can only be acquired by a wide use of freedom. But yet—so many are the delicate points to be considered in education—it is necessary in life to have acquired the habit of cheerfully undertaking imposed tasks. The conditions can be satisfied if the tasks correspond to the natural cravings of the pupil at his stage of progress, if they keep his powers at full stretch, and if they attain an obviously sensible result, and if reasonable freedom is allowed in the mode of execution.

The difficulty of speaking about the way a skilful teacher will keep romance alive in his pupils arises from the fact that what takes a long time to describe, takes a short time to do. The beauty of a passage of Virgil may be rendered by insisting on beauty of verbal enunciation, taking no longer than prosy utterance. The emphasis on the beauty of a mathematical argument, in its marshalling of general considerations to unravel complex fact, is the speediest mode of procedure. The responsibility of the teacher at this stage is immense. To speak the truth, except in the rare case of genius in the teacher, I do not think that it is possible to take a whole class very far along the road of precision without some dulling of the interest. It is the unfortunate dilemma that initiative and training are both necessary, and that training is apt to kill initiative.

But this admission is not to condone a brutal ignorance of methods of mitigating this untoward fact. It is not a theoretical necessity, but arises because perfect tact is unattainable in the treatment of each individual case. In the past the methods employed assassinated interest; we are discussing how to reduce the evil to its smallest dimensions. I merely utter the warning that education is a difficult problem, to be solved by no one simple formula.

In this connection there is, however, one practical consideration which is largely neglected. The territory of romantic interest is large, ill-defined, and not to be controlled by any explicit boundary. It depends on the chance flashes of insight. But the area of precise knowledge, as exacted in any general educational system, can be, and should be, definitely determined. If you make it too wide you will kill interest and defeat your own object: if you make it too narrow your pupils will lack effective grip. Surely, in every subject in each type of curriculum, the precise knowledge required should be determined after the most anxious inquiry. This does not now seem to be the case in any effective way. For example, in the classical studies of boys destined for a scientific career—a class of pupils in whom I am greatly interested— What is the Latin vocabulary which they ought definitely to know? Also what are the grammatical rules and constructions which they ought to have mastered? Why not determine these once and for all, and then bend every exercise to impress just these on the memory, and to understand their derivatives, both in Latin and also in French and English. Then, as to other constructions and words which occur in the reading of texts, supply full information in the easiest manner. A certain ruthless definiteness is essential in education. I am sure that one secret of a successful teacher is that he has formulated quite clearly in his mind what the pupil has got to know in precise fashion. He will then cease from half-hearted attempts to worry his pupils with memorising a lot of irrelevant stuff of inferior importance. The secret of success is pace, and the secret of pace is concentration. But, in respect to precise knowledge, the watchword is pace, pace, pace. Get your knowledge quickly, and then use it. If you can use it, you will retain it.

We have now come to the third stage of the rhythmic cycle, the stage of generalisation. There is here a reaction towards romance. Something definite is now known; aptitudes have been acquired; and general rules and laws are clearly apprehended both in their formulation and their detailed exemplification. The pupil now wants to use his new weapons. He is an effective individual, and it is effects that he wants to produce. He relapses into the discursive adventures of the romantic stage, with the advantage that his mind is now a disciplined regiment instead of a rabble. In this sense, education should begin in research and end in research. After all, the whole affair is merely a preparation for battling with the immediate experiences of life, a preparation by which to qualify each immediate moment with relevant ideas and appropriate actions. An education which does not begin by evoking initiative and end by encouraging it must be wrong. For its whole aim is the production of active wisdom.

In my own work at universities I have been much struck by the paralysis of thought induced in pupils by the aimless accumulation of precise knowledge, inert and unutilised. It should be the chief aim of a university professor to exhibit himself in his own true character—that is, as an ignorant man thinking, actively utilising his small share of knowledge. In a sense, knowledge shrinks as wisdom grows: for details are swallowed up in principles. The details of knowledge which are important will be picked up *ad hoc* in each avocation of life, but the habit of the active utilisation of well-understood principles is the final possession of wisdom. The stage of precision is the stage of growing into the apprehension of principles by the acquisition of a precise knowledge of details. The stage of generalisations is the stage of shedding details in favour of the active application of principles, the details retreating into subconscious habits. We don't go about explicitly retaining in our own minds that two and two make four, though once we had to learn it by heart. We trust to habit for our elementary arithmetic. But the essence of this stage is the emergence from the comparative passivity of being trained into the active free-dom of application. Of course, during this stage, precise knowledge will grow, and more actively than ever before, because the mind has experienced the power of definiteness, and responds to the acquisition of general truth, and of richness of illustration. But the growth of knowledge becomes progressively unconscious, as being an incident derived from some active adventure of thought.

So much for the three stages of the rhythmic unit of development. In a general way the whole period of education is dominated by this threefold rhythm. Till the age of thirteen or fourteen there is the romantic stage, from fourteen to eighteen the stage of precision, and from eighteen to two and twenty the stage of generali-sation. But these are only average characters, tinging the mode of development as a whole. I do not think that any pupil completes his stages simultaneously in all subjects. For example, I should plead that while language is initiating its stage of precision in the way of acquisition of vocabulary and of grammar, science should be in its full romantic stage. The romantic stage of language begins in infancy with the acquisition of speech, so that it passes early towards a stage of precision; while science is a late comer. Accordingly a precise inculcation of science at an early age wipes out initiative and interest, and destroys any chance of the topic having any richness of content in the child's apprehension. Thus, the romantic stage of science should persist for years after the precise study of language has commenced.

There are minor eddies, each in itself a threefold cycle, running its course in each day, in each week, and in each term. There is the general apprehension of some topic in its vague possibilities, the mastery of the relevant details, and finally the putting of the whole subject together in the light of the relevant knowledge. Unless the pupils are continually sustained by the evocation of interest, the acquirement of technique, and the excitement of success, they can never make progress, and will certainly lose heart. Speaking generally, during the last thirty years the schools of England have been sending up to the universities a disheartened crowd of young folk, inoculated against any outbreak of intellectual zeal. The universities have sec-onded the efforts of the schools and emphasised the failure. Accordingly, the cheerful gaiety of the young turns to other topics, and thus educated England is not hos-pitable to ideas. When we can point to some great achievement of our nation—let us hope that it may be something other than a war—which has been won in the class-room of our schools, and not in their playing-fields, then we may feel content with our modes of education.

So far I have been discussing intellectual education, and my argument has been cramped on too narrow a basis. After all, our pupils are alive, and cannot be chopped into separate bits, like the pieces of a jig-saw puzzle. In the production of a mechanism the constructive energy lies outside it, and adds discrete parts to dis-crete parts. The case is far different for a living organism which grows by its own impulse towards self-development. This impulse can be stimulated and guided from outside the organism, and it can also be killed. But for all your stimulation and guidance the creative impulse towards growth comes from within, and is intensely characteristic of the individual. Education is the guidance of the individual towards a comprehension of the art of life; and by the art of life I mean the most complete achievement of varied activity expressing the potentialities of that living creature in the face of its actual environment. This completeness of achievement involves an artistic sense, subordinating the lower to the higher possibilities of the indivisible personality. Science, art, religion, morality, take their rise from this sense of values within the structure of being. Each individual embodies an adventure of existence. The art of life is the guidance of this adventure. The great religions of civilisation include among their original elements revolts against the inculcation of morals as a set of isolated prohibitions. Morality, in the petty negative sense of the term, is the deadly enemy of religion. Paul denounces the Law, and the Gospels are vehement against the Pharisees. Every outbreak of religion exhibits the same intensity of antagonism—an antagonism diminishing as religion fades. No part of education has more to gain from attention to the rhythmic law of growth than has moral and religious education. Whatever be the right way to formulate religious truths, it is death to religion to insist on a premature stage of precision. The vitality of religion is shown by the way in which the religious spirit has survived the ordeal of religious education.

The problem of religion in education is too large to be discussed at this stage of my address. I have referred to it to guard against the suspicion that the principles here advocated are to be conceived in a narrow sense. We are analysing the general law of rhythmic progress in the higher stages of life, embodying the initial awakening, the discipline, and the fruition on the higher plane. What I am now insisting is that the principle of progress is from within: the discovery is made by ourselves, the discipline is self-discipline, and the fruition is the outcome of our own initiative. The teacher has a double function. It is for him to elicit the enthusiasm by resonance from his own personality, and to create the environment of a larger knowledge and a firmer purpose. He is there to avoid the waste, which in the lower stages of existence is nature's way of evolution. The ultimate motive power, alike in science, in morality, and in religion, is the sense of value, the sense of importance. It takes the various forms of wonder, of curiosity, of reverence, or worship, of tumultuous desire for merging personality in something beyond itself. This sense of value imposes on life incredible labours, and apart from it life sinks back into the passivity of its lower types. The most penetrating exhibition of this force is the sense of beauty, the aesthetic sense of realised perfection. This thought leads me to ask, whether in our modern education we emphasise sufficiently the functions of art. . . .

Mere literary knowledge is of slight importance. The only thing that matters is, how it is known. The facts related are nothing. Literature only exists to express and develop that imaginative world which is our life, the kingdom which is within us. It follows that the literary side of a technical education should consist in an effort to make the pupils enjoy literature. It does not matter what they know, but the enjoyment is vital. The great English Universities, under whose direct authority school-children are examined in plays of Shakespeare, to the certain destruction of their enjoyment, should be prosecuted for soul murder.

Now there are two kinds of intellectual enjoyment: the enjoyment of creation, and the enjoyment of relaxation. They are not necessarily separated. A change of occupation may give the full tide of happiness which comes from the concurrence of both forms of pleasure. The appreciation of literature is really creation. The written word, its music, and its associations, are only the stimuli. The vision which they evoke is our own doing. No one, no genius other than our own, can make our own life live. But except for those engaged in literary occupations, literature is also a relaxation. It gives exercise to that other side which any occupation must suppress during the working hours. Art also has the same function in life as has literature.

To obtain the pleasure of relaxation requires no help. The pleasure is merely to cease doing. Some such pure relaxation is a necessary condition of health. Its dangers are notorious, and to the greater part of the necessary relaxation nature has affixed, not enjoyment, but the oblivion of sleep. Creative enjoyment is the outcome of successful effort and requires help for its initiation. Such enjoyment is necessary for high-speed work and for original achievement.

To speed up production with unrefreshed workmen is a disastrous economic policy. Temporary success will be at the expense of the nation, which, for long years of their lives, will have to support worn-out artisans—unemployables. Equally disastrous is the alternation of spasms of effort with periods of pure relaxation. Such periods are the seed-times of degeneration, unless rigorously curtailed. The normal recreation should be change of activity, satisfying the cravings of instincts. Games afford such activity. Their disconnection emphasises the relaxation, but their excess leaves us empty.

It is here that literature and art should play an essential part in a healthy organised nation. Their services to economic production would be only second to those of sleep or of food. I am not now talking of the training of an artist, but of the use of art as a condition of healthy life. It is analogous to sunshine in the physical world.

When we have once rid our minds of the idea that knowledge is to be exacted, there is no especial difficulty or expense involved in helping the growth of artistic enjoyment. All school-children could be sent at regular intervals to neighbouring theatres where suitable plays could be subsidised. Similarly for concerts and cinema films. Pictures are more doubtful in their popular attraction; but interesting representations of scenes or ideas which the children have read about would probably appeal. The pupils themselves should be encouraged in artistic efforts. Above all the art of reading aloud should be cultivated. The Roger de Coverley essays of Addison are perfect examples of readable prose.

Art and literature have not merely an indirect effect on the main energies of life. Directly, they give vision. The world spreads wide beyond the deliverances of material sense, with subtleties of reaction and with pulses of emotion. Vision is the necessary antecedent to control and to direction. In the contest of races which in its final issues will be decided in the workshops and not on the battlefield, the victory will belong to those who are masters of stores of trained nervous energy, working under conditions favourable to growth. One such essential condition is Art.

If there had been time, there are other things which I should like to have said: for example, to advocate the inclusion of one foreign language in all education. From direct observation I know this to be possible for artisan children. But enough has been put before you to make plain the principles with which we should undertake national education.

In conclusion, I recur to the thought of the Benedictines, who saved for mankind the vanishing civilisation of the ancient world by linking together knowledge, labour, and moral energy. Our danger is to conceive practical affairs as the kingdom of evil, in which success is only possible by the extrusion of ideal aims. I believe that such a conception is a fallacy directly negatived by practical experience. In education this error takes the form of a mean view of technical training. Our forefathers in the dark ages saved themselves by embodying high ideals in great organisations. It is our task, without servile imitation, boldly to exercise our creative energies. . . .

The universities are schools of education, and schools of research. But the primary reason for their existence is not to be found either in the mere knowledge conveyed to the students or in the mere opportunities for research afforded to the members of the faculty.

Both these functions could be performed at a cheaper rate, apart from these very expensive institutions. Books are cheap, and the system of apprenticeship is well understood. So far as the mere imparting of information is concerned, no university has had any justification for existence since the popularisation of printing in the fifteenth century. Yet the chief impetus to the foundation of universities came after that date, and in more recent times has even increased.

The justification for a university is that it preserves the connection between knowledge and the zest of life, by uniting the young and the old in the imaginative consideration of learning. The university imparts information, but it imparts it imaginatively. At least, this is the function which it should perform for society. A university which fails in this respect has no reason for existence. This atmosphere of excitement, arising from imaginative consideration, transforms knowledge. A fact is no longer a bare fact: it is invested with all its possibilities. It is no longer a burden on the memory: it is energising as the poet of our dreams, and as the architect of our purposes.

Imagination is not to be divorced from the facts: it is a way of illuminating the facts. It works by eliciting the general principles which apply to the facts, as they exist, and then by an intellectual survey of alternative possibilities which are consistent with those principles. It enables men to construct an intellectual vision of a new world, and it preserves the zest of life by the suggestion of satisfying purposes.

Youth is imaginative, and if the imagination be strengthened by discipline this energy of imagination can in great measure be preserved through life. The tragedy of the world is that those who are imaginative have but slight experience, and those who are experienced have feeble imaginations. Fools act on imagination without knowledge; pedants act on knowledge without imagination. The task of a university is to weld together imagination and experience. . . .

Imagination is a contagious disease. It cannot be measured by the yard, or weighed by the pound, and then delivered to the students by members of the faculty. It can only be communicated by a faculty whose members themselves wear their learning with imagination. In saying this, I am only repeating one of the oldest of observations. More than two thousand years ago the ancients symbolised learning by a torch passing from hand to hand down the generations. That lighted torch is the imagination of which I speak. The whole art in the organisation of a university is the provision of a faculty whose learning is lighted up with imagination. This is the problem of problems in university education; and unless we are careful the recent vast extension of universities in number of students and in variety of activities—

of which we are so justly proud—will fail in producing its proper results, by the mishandling of this problem.

The combination of imagination and learning normally requires some leisure, freedom from restraint, freedom from harassing worry, some variety of experiences, and the stimulation of other minds diverse in opinion and diverse in equipment. Also there is required the excitement of curiosity, and the self-confidence derived from pride in the achievements of the surrounding society in procuring the advance of knowledge. Imagination cannot be acquired once and for all, and then kept indefinitely in an ice box to be produced periodically in stated quantities. The learned and imaginative life is a way of living, and is not an article of commerce.

It is in respect to the provision and utilisation of these conditions for an efficient faculty that the two functions of education and research meet together in a university. Do you want your teachers to be imaginative? Then encourage them to research. Do you want your researchers to be imaginative? Then bring them into intellectual sympathy with the young at the most eager, imaginative period of life, when intellects are just entering upon their mature discipline. Make your researchers explain themselves to active minds, plastic and with the world before them; make your young students crown their period of intellectual acquisition by some contact with minds gifted with experience of intellectual adventure. Education is discipline for the adventure of life; research is intellectual adventure; and the universities should be homes of adventure shared in common by young and old. For successful education there must always be a certain freshness in the knowledge dealt with. It must either be new in itself or it must be invested with some novelty of application to the new world of new times. Knowledge does not keep any better than fish. You may be dealing with knowledge of the old species, with some old truth; but somehow or other it must come to the students, as it were, just drawn out of the sea and with the freshness of its immediate importance.

It is the function of the scholar to evoke into life wisdom and beauty which, apart from his magic, would remain lost in the past. A progressive society depends upon its inclusion of three groups—scholars, discoverers, inventors. Its progress also depends upon the fact that its educated masses are composed of members each with a tinge of scholarship, a tinge of discovery, and a tinge of invention. I am here using the term "discovery" to mean the progress of knowledge in respect to truths of some high generality, and the term "invention" to mean the progress of knowledge in respect to the application of general truths in particular ways subservient to present needs. It is evident that these three groups merge into each other, and also that men engaged in practical affairs are properly to be called inventors so far as they contribute to the progress of society. But any one individual has his own limitation of function, and his own peculiar needs. What is important for a nation is that there shall be a very close relation between all types of its progressive elements, so that the study may influence the market place, and the market place the study. Universities are the chief agencies for this fusion of progressive activities into an effective instrument of progress. Of course they are not the only agencies, but it is a fact that to-day the progressive nations are those in which universities flourish.

It must not be supposed that the output of a university in the form of original ideas is solely to be measured by printed papers and books labeled with the names of their authors. Mankind is as individual in its mode of output as in the substance of its thoughts. For some of the most fertile minds composition in writing, or in a form reducible to writing, seems to be an impossibility. In every faculty you will find that some of the more brilliant teachers are not among those who publish. Their originality requires for its expression direct intercourse with their pupils in the form of lectures, or of personal discussion. Such men exercise an immense influence; and yet, after the generation of their pupils has passed away, they sleep among the innumerable unthanked benefactors of humanity. Fortunately, one of them is immortal—Socrates.

Thus it would be the greatest mistake to estimate the value of each member of a faculty by the printed work signed with his name. There is at the present day some tendency to fall into this error; and an emphatic protest is necessary against an attitude on the part of authorities which is damaging to efficiency and unjust to unselfish zeal.

But, when all such allowances have been made, one good test for the general efficiency of a faculty is that as a whole it shall be producing in published form its quota of contributions of thought. Such a quota is to be estimated in weight of thought, and not in number of words.

This survey shows that the management of a university faculty has no analogy to that of a business organisation. The public opinion of the faculty, and a common zeal for the purposes of the university, form the only effective safeguards for the high level of university work. The faculty should be a band of scholars, stimulating each other, and freely determining their various activities. You can secure certain formal requirements, that lectures are given at stated times and that instructors and students are in attendance. But the heart of the matter lies beyond all regulation.

Questions for Discussion

1. Briefly describe each of the stages in learning Whitehead mentions. Is his description accurate? Is it complete? Is it applicable to every subject? Is it applicable every day?

2. There are a number of provocative sentences in this selection which might elicit comments from you. Among them are: 1) "A university professor should exhibit himself in his own true character—that is, as an ignorant man thinking." 2) "Knowledge shrinks as wisdom grows: for details are swallowed up in principles." 3) "Imagination is a contagious disease." 4) "A certain ruthless definiteness is essential in education." 5) "Undiscriminating discipline defeats its own object by dulling the mind." Do you agree with them?

3. Specifically, how would you apply Whitehead's ideas if you were teaching a semester-long course in American history?

4. Do you see any relationship between Whitehead's thoughts and any of the traditional theories of education you examined in Part I? Look carefully at the selections from Newman and Martin, or is that too big a hint?

24 The Act of Discovery

Jerome Bruner

*In recent years, the questions of how and when students learn have oc-
cupied the attention of many psychologists and educators. The next three
selections present the conclusions of some of the most distinguished investigators. One of America's leading psychologists, Bruner, has turned his
interests and talents toward educational psychology, and has long advocated
that good teaching requires students to engage in the act of discovering
knowledge for themselves. He holds there is nothing mysterious about this
act, for it is "a matter of rearranging or transforming evidence in such a
way that one is enabled to go beyond the evidence so reassembled to new
insights." As you read this selection, notice what arguments he uses to
support his conclusion, and also begin to ask yourself what, if any, the role
of a teacher, a textbook, a grade, and a classroom would be if you were to
adopt Bruner's ideas on learning in your own teaching.*

Maimonides, in his *Guide for the Perplexed,* speaks of four forms of perfection that men might seek.[1] The first and lowest form is perfection in the acquisition of worldly goods. The great philosopher dismisses this on the ground that the
possessions one acquires bear no meaningful relation to the possessor: "A great king
may one morning find that there is no difference between him and the lowest person." A second perfection is of the body, its conformation and skills. Its failing is
that it does not reflect on what is uniquely human about man: "he could (in any
case) not be as strong as a mule." Moral perfection is the third, "the highest degree
of excellency in man's character." Of this perfection Maimonides says: "Imagine a
person being alone, and having no connection whatever with any other person; all
his good moral principles are at rest, they are not required and give man no perfection whatever. These principles are only necessary and useful when man comes
in contact with others." The fourth kind of perfection is "the true perfection of
man; the possession of the highest intellectual faculties. . . ." In justification of his
assertion, this extraordinary Spanish-Judaic philosopher urges: "Examine the first
three kinds of perfection; you will find that if you possess them, they are not your
property, but the property of others. . . . But the last kind of perfection is exclusively
yours; no one else owns any part of it."

Without raising the question of whether moral qualities exist without reference to
others, it is a conjecture much like the last of Maimonides' that leads me to examine the act of discovery in man's intellectual life. For if man's intellectual excel-

[1] Maimonides, *Guide for the Perplexed* (New York: Dover Publications, 1956).

lence is the most his own among his perfections, it is also the case that the most personal of all that he knows is that which he has discovered for himself. How important is it, then, for us to encourage the young to learn by discovery? Does it, as Maimonides would say, create a unique relation between knowledge and its possessor? And what may such a relation do for a man—or, for our purposes, a child?

The immediate occasion for my concern with discovery is the work of the various new curriculum projects that have grown up in America during the last few years. Whether one speaks to mathematicians or physicists or historians, one encounters repeatedly an expression of faith in the powerful effects that come from permitting the student to put things together for himself, to be his own discoverer.

First, I should be clear about what the act of discovery entails. It is rarely, on the frontier of knowledge or elsewhere, that new facts are "discovered" in the sense of being encountered, as Newton suggested, in the form of islands of truth in an uncharted sea of ignorance. Or if they appear to be discovered in this way, it is almost always thanks to some happy hypothesis about where to navigate. Discovery, like surprise, favors the well-prepared mind. In playing bridge, one is surprised by a hand with no honors in it and also by one that is all in one suit. Yet all particular hands in bridge are equiprobable: to be surprised one must know something about the laws of probability. So too in discovery. The history of science is studded with examples of men "finding out" something and not knowing it. I shall operate on the assumption that discovery, whether by a schoolboy going it on his own or by a scientist cultivating the growing edge of his field, is in its essence a matter of rearranging or transforming evidence in such a way that one is enabled to go beyond the evidence so reassembled to new insights. It may well be that an additional fact or shred of evidence makes this larger transformation possible. But it is often not even dependent on new information.

Very generally, and at the risk of oversimplification, it is useful to distinguish two kinds of teaching: that which takes place in the *expository mode* and that in the *hypothetical mode*. In the former, the decisions concerning the mode and pace and style of exposition are principally determined by the teacher as expositor; the student is the listener. The speaker has a quite different set of decisions to make: he has a wide choice of alternatives; he is anticipating paragraph content while the listener is still intent on the words; he is manipulating the content of the material by various transformations while the listener is quite unaware of these internal options. But in the hypothetical mode the teacher and the student are in a more cooperative position with respect to what in linguistics would be called "speaker's decisions." The student is not a bench-bound listener, but is taking a part in the formulation and at times may play the principal role in it. He will be aware of alternatives and may even have an "as if" attitude toward these, and he may evaluate information as it comes. One cannot describe the process in either mode with great precision of detail, but I think it is largely the hypothetical mode which characterizes the teaching that encourages discovery.

Consider now what benefits might be derived from the experience of learning through discoveries that one makes oneself. I shall discuss these under four headings: (1) the increase in intellectual potency, (2) the shift from extrinsic to intrinsic rewards, (3) the learning of the heuristics of discovering, and (4) the aid to conserving memory.

Intellectual potency. I should like to consider the differences among students in a highly constrained psychological experiment involving a two-choice machine.[2] In order to win chips, they must depress a key either on the right or the left side of the apparatus. A pattern of payoff is designed so that, say, they will be paid off on the right side 70 percent of the time, on the left 30 percent, but this detail is not important. What is important is that the payoff sequence is arranged at random, that there is no pattern. There is a marked contrast in the behavior of subjects who think that there is some pattern to be found in the sequence—who think that regularities are discoverable—and the performance of subjects who think that things are happening quite by chance. The first group adopts what is called an "event-matching" strategy in which the number of responses given to each side is roughly commensurate to the proportion of times that it pays off: in the present case, 70 on the right to 30 on the left. The group that believes there is no pattern very soon settles for a much more primitive strategy allocating *all* responses to the side that has the greater payoff. A little arithmetic will show that the lazy all-and-none strategy pays off more if the environment is truly random: they win 70 per cent of the time. The event-matching subjects win about 70 percent on the 70-percent payoff side (or 49 percent of the time there) and 30 percent of the time on the side that pays off 30 percent of the time (another 9 percent for a total take-home wage of 58 percent in return for their labors of decision).

But the world is not always or not even frequently random, and if one analyzes carefully what the event matchers are doing, one sees that they are trying out hypotheses one after the other, all of them containing a term that leads to a distribution of bets on the two sides with a frequency to match the actual occurrence of events. If it should turn out that there is a pattern to be discovered, their payoff could become 100 percent. The other group would go on at the middling rate of 70 percent.

What has this to do with the subject at hand? For the person to search out and find regularities and relationships in his environment, he must either come armed with an expectancy that there will be something to find or be aroused to such an expectancy so that he may devise ways of searching and finding. One of the chief enemies of search is the assumption that there is nothing one can find in the environment by way of regularity or relationship. In the experiment just cited, subjects often fall into one of two habitual attitudes: either that there is nothing to be found or that a pattern can be discovered by looking. There is an important sequel in behavior to the two attitudes.

We have conducted a series of experimental studies on a group of some seventy schoolchildren over a four-year period.[3] The studies have led us to distinguish an interesting dimension of cognitive activity that can be described as ranging from *episodic empiricism* at one end to *cumulative constructionism* at the other. The two attitudes in the above experiments on choice illustrate the extremes of the dimension. One of the experiments employs the game of Twenty Questions. A child

[2] J. S. Bruner, J. J. Goodnow, and G. A. Austin, *A Study of Thinking* (New York: John Wiley, 1956).

[3] J. S. Bruner and others, *Studies in Cognitive Growth* (New York: John Wiley, 1966).

—in this case he is between ten and twelve—is told that a car has gone off the road and hit a tree. He is to ask questions that can be answered by "yes" or "no" to discover the cause of the accident. After completing the problem, the same task is given him, though this time he is told that the accident has a different cause. In all, the procedure is repeated four times. Children enjoy playing the game. They also differ quite markedly in the approach or strategy they bring to the task. In the first place, we can distinguish clearly between two types of questions asked: one is intended to locate constraints in the problem, constraints that will eventually give shape to an hypothesis; the other is the hypothesis as question. It is the difference between, "Was there anything wrong with the driver?" and "Was the driver rushing to the doctor's office for an appointment and the car got out of control?" There are children who precede hypotheses with efforts to locate constraint and there are those who are "potshotters," who string out hypotheses noncumulatively one after the other. A second element of strategy lies in the connectivity of information gathering: the extent to which questions asked utilize or ignore or violate information previously obtained. The questions asked by children tend to be organized in cycles, each cycle usually given over to the pursuit of some particular notion. Both within cycles and between cycles one can discern marked differences in the connectivity of the children's performances. Needless to say, children who employ constraint location as a technique preliminary to the formulation of hypotheses tend to be far more organized in their harvesting of information. Persistence is another feature of strategy, a characteristic compounded of what appear to be two factors: sheer doggedness and a persistence that stems from the sequential organization that a child brings to the task. Doggedness is probably just animal spirits or the need to achieve. Organized persistence is a maneuver for protecting the fragile cognitive apparatus from overload. The child who has flooded himself with disorganized information from unconnected hypotheses will become discouraged and confused sooner than the child who has shown a certain cunning in his strategy of getting information— a child who senses that the value of information is not simply in getting it but in being able to carry it. The persistence of the organized child stems from his knowledge of how to organize questions in cycles and how to summarize things to himself.

Episodic empiricism is illustrated by information gathering that is unbound by prior constraints, that is deficient in organizational persistence. The opposite extreme, what we have called cumulative constructionism, is characterized by sensitivity to constraint, by connective maneuvers, and by organized persistence. Brute persistence seems to be one of those gifts from the gods that make people more exaggeratedly what they are.

Before returning to the issue of discovery and its role in the development of thinking, there is a word more to say about the ways in which the problem solver may transform information he has dealt with actively. The point arises from the pragmatic question: what does it take to get information processed into a form best designed to fit some future use? An experiment by R. B. Zajonc in 1957 suggests an answer.[4] He gave groups of students information of a controlled kind, some groups being told that they were to transmit the information later on, others that they

[4] R. B. Zajonc, personal communication (1957).

were merely to keep it in mind. In general, he found more differentiation of the information intended for transmittal than of information received passively. An active attitude leads to a transformation related to a task to be performed. There is a risk, to be sure, in the possible overspecialization of information processing. It can lead to such a high degree of specific organization that information is lost for general use, although this can be guarded against.

Let me convert the foregoing into an hypothesis. Emphasis on discovery in learning has precisely the effect on the learner of leading him to be a constructionist, to organize what he is encountering in a manner not only designed to discover regularity and relatedness, but also to avoid the kind of information drift that fails to keep account of the uses to which information might have to be put. Emphasis on discovery, indeed, helps the child to learn the varieties of problem solving, of transforming information for better use, helps him to learn how to go about the very task of learning. So goes the hypothesis; it is still in need of testing. But it is an hypothesis of such important human implications that we cannot afford not to test it—and the testing will have to be in the schools.

Intrinsic and extrinsic motives. Much of the problem in leading a child to effective cognitive activity is to free him from the immediate control of environmental rewards and punishments. Learning that starts in response to the rewards of parental or teacher approval or to the avoidance of failure can too readily develop a pattern in which the child is seeking cues as to how to conform to what is expected of him. We know from studies of children who tend to be early overachievers in school that they are likely to be seekers after the "right way to do it" and that their capacity for transforming learning into viable thought structures tends to be lower than that of children achieving at levels predicted by intelligence tests.[5] Our tests on such children show them to be lower in analytic ability than those who are not conspicuous in overachievement. As we shall see later, they develop rote abilities and depend on being able to "give back" what is expected rather than to make it into something that relates to the rest of their cognitive life. As Maimonides would say, their learning is not their own.

The hypothesis I would propose here is that to the degree that one is able to approach learning as a task of discovering something rather than "learning about" it, to that degree there will be a tendency for the child to work with the autonomy of self-reward or, more properly, be rewarded by discovery itself.

To readers familiar with the battles of the last half-century in the field of motivation, this hypothesis will be recognized as controversial. For the traditional view of motivation in learning has been, until very recently, couched in terms of a theory of drives and reinforcements: learning occurs because a response produced by a stimulus is followed by the reduction in a primary drive. The doctrine is greatly but thinly extended by the idea of secondary reinforcement: anything that has been "associated" with such a reduction in drive or need can also serve to reinforce the connection between a stimulus and the response that it evokes. Finding a steak will do for getting a food-search act connected with a certain stimulus, but so will the sight of a nice restaurant.

[5] See Note 3 above.

In 1959 there appeared a most searching and important criticism of this ancient hedonistic position, written by Robert White, reviewing the evidence of recently published animal studies, of work in the field of psychoanalysis, and of research on the development of cognitive processes in children. Professor White comes to the conclusion, quite rightly I think, that the drive-reduction model of learning runs counter to too many important phenomena of learning and development to be either regarded as general in its applicability or even correct in its general approach. Let me quote some of his principal conclusions and explore their applicability to the hypothesis stated above.

> I now propose that we gather the various kinds of behavior just mentioned, all of which have to do with effective interaction with the environment, under the general heading of competence. According to Webster, competence means fitness of ability, and the suggested synonyms include capability, capacity, efficiency, proficiency, and skill. It is therefore a suitable word to describe such things as grasping and exploring, crawling and walking, attention and perception, language and thinking, manipulating and changing the surroundings, all of which promote an effective—a competent—interaction with the environment. It is true, of course, that maturation plays a part in all these developments, but this part is heavily overshadowed by learning in all the more complex accomplishments like speech or skilled manipulation. I shall argue that it is necessary to make competence a motivational concept; there is *competence motivation* as well as competence in its more familiar sense of achieved capacity. The behavior that leads to the building up of effective grasping, handling, and letting go of objects, to take one example, is not random behavior that is produced by an overflow of energy. It is directed, selective, and persistent, and it continues not because it serves primary drives, which indeed it cannot serve until it is almost perfected, but because it satisfies an intrinsic need to deal with the environment.[6]

I am suggesting that there are forms of activity that serve to enlist and develop the competence motive, that serve to make it the driving force behind behavior. I should like to add to White's general premise that the *exercise* of competence motives has the effect of strengthening the degree to which they gain control over behavior and thereby reduce the effects of extrinsic rewards or drive gratification.

In 1934 the brilliant Russian psychologist Vygotsky characterized the growth of thought processes as starting with a dialogue of speech and gesture between child and parent.[7] Autonomous thinking, he said, begins at the stage when the child is first able to internalize these conversations and "run them off" himself. This is a typical sequence in the development of competence. So too in instruction. The narrative of teaching is of the order of Vygotsky's conversation. The next move in the development of competence is the internalization of the narrative and its "rules of generation" so that the child is now capable of running off the narrative on his own. The hypothetical mode in teaching, by encouraging the child to participate in "speaker's decisions," speeds this process along. Once internalization has occurred,

[6] R. W. White, "Motivation Reconsidered: The Concept of Competence," *Psychological Review*, no. 66 (1959), pp. 317–318.

[7] L. S. Vygotsky, *Thinking and Speech* (Moscow, 1934).

the child is in a vastly improved position from several obvious points of view—notably that he is able to go beyond the information he has been given to generate additional ideas that either can be checked immediately from experience or can, at least, be used as a basis for formulating reasonable hypotheses. But over and beyond that, the child is now in a position to experience success and failure not as reward and punishment but as information. For when the task is his own rather than a prescribed matching of environmental demands, he becomes his own paymaster in a certain measure. Seeking to gain control over his environment, he can now treat success as indicating that he is on the right track, failure as indicating that he is on the wrong one.

In the end, this development has the effect of freeing learning from immediate stimulus control. When learning leads only to pellets of this or that in the short run rather than to mastery in the long run, then behavior can be readily "shaped" by extrinsic rewards. But when behavior becomes more extended and competence-oriented, it comes under the control of more complex cognitive structures and operates more from the inside out.

The position of Pavlov is interesting. His early account of the learning process was based entirely on a notion of stimulus control of behavior through the conditioning mechanism in which, through contiguity, a new conditioned stimulus was substituted for an old unconditioned stimulus. But even he recognized that his account was insufficient to deal with higher forms of learning. To supplement it, he introduced the idea of the "second signalling system," with central importance placed on symbolic systems, such as language, in mediating and giving shape to mental life. Or as Luria put in 1959, the first signal system is "concerned with directly perceived stimuli, the second with systems of verbal elaboration." Luria, commenting on the importance of the transition from first to second signal system, says:

> It would be mistaken to suppose that verbal intercourse with adults merely changes the contents of the child's conscious activity without changing its form. . . . The word has a basic function not only because it indicates a corresponding object in the external world, but also because it abstracts, isolates the necessary signal, generalizes perceived signals and relates them to certain categories; it is this systematization of direct experience that makes the role of the word in the formation of mental process so exceptionally important.[8]

It is interesting too that the final rejection of the universality of the doctrine of reinforcement in direct conditioning came from some of Pavlov's own students. Ivanov-Smolensky and Krasnogorsky published papers showing the manner in which symbolized linguistic messages could take over the place of the unconditioned stimulus and of the unconditioned response (gratification of hunger) in children.[9] In all

[8] A. L. Luria, "The Directive Function of Speech in Development and Dissolution," *Word*, no. 15 (1959), p. 12.

[9] A. G. Ivanov-Smolensky, "The Interaction of the First and Second Signal Systems in Certain Normal and Pathological Conditions," *Physiological Journal of the USSR*, XXXV, no. 5 (1949); Ivanov-Smolensky, "Concerning the Study of the Joint Activity of the First and Second Signal Systems," *Journal of Higher Nervous Activity*, I, no. 1 (1951); N. I. Krasnogorsky, *Studies of Higher Nervous Activity in Animals and in Man*, I (Moscow, 1954).

instances, they speak of these as *replacements* of lower first-system mental or neural processes by higher second-system controls. A strange irony, then, that Russian psychology, which gave us the notion of the conditioned response and the assumption that higher-order activities are built up out of colligations of such primitive units, has rejected this notion while much of the American psychology of learning until quite recently has stayed within the early Pavlovian fold—as, for example, a 1959 article by Spence in the *Harvard Educational Review,* reiterating the primacy of conditioning and the derivative nature of complex learning.[10] It is even more noteworthy that Russian pedagogic theory has become deeply influenced by this new trend and is now placing much stress upon the importance of building up a more active symbolical approach to problem solving among children.

In this matter of the control of learning, then, my conclusion is that the degree to which the desire for competence comes to control behavior, to that degree the role of reinforcement or "outside rewards" wanes in shaping behavior. The child comes to manipulate his environment more actively and achieves his gratification from coping with problems. As he finds symbolic modes of representing and transforming the environment, there is an accompanying decline in the importance of stimulus-response-reward sequences. To use the metaphor that David Riesman developed in a quite different context, mental life moves from a state of outer-directedness, in which the fortuity of stimuli and reinforcement are crucial, to a state of inner-directedness in which the growth and maintenance of mastery become central and dominant.

The heuristics of discovery. Lincoln Steffens, reflecting in his *Autobiography* on his undergraduate education at Berkeley, comments that his schooling paid too much attention to learning what was known and too little to finding out about what was not known.[11] But how does one train a student in the techniques of discovery? Again there are some hypotheses to offer. There are many ways of coming to the arts of inquiry. One of them is by careful study of its formalization in logic, statistics, mathematics, and the like. If one is going to pursue inquiry as a way of life, particularly in the sciences, certainly such study is essential. Yet whoever has taught kindergarten and the early primary grades or has had graduate students working with him on their theses—I choose the two extremes for they are both periods of intense inquiry—knows that an understanding of the formal aspect of inquiry is not sufficient. Rather, several activities and attitudes, some directly related to a particular subject and some fairly generalized, appear to go with inquiry and research. These have to do with the *process* of trying to find out something and, though their presence is no guarantee that the *product* will be a great discovery, their absence is likely to lead to awkwardness or aridity or confusion. How difficult it is to describe these matters—the heuristics of inquiry. There is one set of attitudes or methods that has to do with sensing the relevance of variables—avoiding immersion in edge effects and getting instead to the big sources of variance. This gift partly comes from intuitive familiarity with a range of phenomena, sheer "knowing the stuff." But it also comes out of a sense of what things among many "smell right," what things are of the right order of magnitude or scope or severity.

[10] K. W. Spence, "The Relation of Learning Theory to the Technique of Education," *Harvard Educational Review,* no. 29 (1959), pp. 84–95.
[11] *Autobiography of Lincoln Steffens* (New York: Harcourt, Brace, 1931).

Weldon, the English philosopher, describes problem solving in an interesting and picturesque way. He distinguishes among difficulties, puzzles, and problems. We solve a problem or make a discovery when we impose a puzzle form on a difficulty to convert it into a problem that can be solved in such a way that it gets us where we want to be. That is to say, we recast the difficulty into a form that we know how to work with—then we work it. Much of what we speak of as discovery consists of knowing how to impose a workable kind of form on various kinds of difficulties. A small but crucial part of discovery of the highest order is to invent and develop effective models or "puzzle forms." It is in this area that the truly powerful mind shines. But it is surprising to what degree perfectly ordinary people can, given the benefit of instruction, construct quite interesting and what, a century ago, would have been considered greatly original models.

Now to the hypothesis. It is my hunch that it is only through the exercise of problem solving and the effort of discovery that one learns the working heuristics of discovery; the more one has practice, the more likely one is to generalize what one has learned into a style of problem solving or inquiry that serves for any kind of task encountered—or almost any kind of task. I think the matter is self-evident, but what is unclear is the kinds of training and teaching that produce the best effects. How, for instance, do we teach a child to cut his losses but at the same time be persistent in trying out an idea; to risk forming an early hunch without at the same time formulating one so early and with so little evidence that he is stuck with it while he waits for appropriate evidence to materialize; to pose good testable guesses that are neither too brittle nor too sinuously incorrigible? And so on and on. Practice in inquiry, in trying to figure out things for oneself is indeed what is needed —but in what form? Of only one thing am I convinced: I have never seen anybody improve in the art and technique of inquiry by any means other than engaging in inquiry.

Conservation of memory. I have come to take what some psychologists might consider a rather drastic view of the memory process. It is a view that in large measure derives from the work of my colleague, George Miller.[12] Its first premise is that the principal problem of human memory is not storage but retrieval. In spite of the biological unlikeliness of it, we seem to be able to store a huge quantity of information—perhaps not a full tape recording, though at times it seems we even do that, but a great sufficiency of impressions. We may infer this from the fact that recognition, the ability to recall with maximum promptings, is so extraordinarily good in human beings and that spontaneous recall, with no promptings, is so extraordinarily bad. The key to retrieval is organization or, in even simpler terms, knowing where to find information that has been put into memory.

Let me illustrate with a simple experiment. We present pairs of words to twelve-year-olds. The children of one group are told only to remember the pairs and that they will be asked to repeat them later. Others are told to remember the pairs by producing a word or idea that will tie them together in a way that will make sense. The word pairs include such juxtapositions as "chair-forest," "sidewalk-square," and the like. One can distinguish three styles of mediators, and children can be

12 G. A. Miller, "The Magical Number Seven, Plus or Minus Two," *Psychological Review,* no. 63 (1956), pp. 81–97.

scaled in terms of their relative preference for each: generic mediation, in which a pair is tied together by a superordinate idea: "chair and forest are both made of wood"; thematic mediation, in which the two terms are imbedded in a theme or a little story: "the lost child sat on a chair in the middle of the forest"; and part-whole mediation, in which "chairs are made from trees in the forest" is typical. Now the chief result, as you would predict, is that children who provide their own mediators do best—indeed, one time through a set of thirty pairs, they recover up to 95 percent of the second words when presented with the first ones of the pairs, whereas the uninstructed children reach a maximum of less than 50 percent recovered. Also, children do best in recovering materials tied together by the form of mediator they most often use.

One can cite a myriad of findings to indicate that any organization of information that reduces the aggregate complexity of material by imbedding it into a cognitive process a person has constructed for himself will make that material more accessible for retrieval. We may say that the process of memory, looked at from the retrieval side, is also a process of problem solving: how can material be "placed" in memory so that it can be obtained on demand?

We can take as a point of departure the example of the children who developed their own technique for relating each word pair. The children with the self-made mediators did better than the children who were given ready-made ones. Another group of children were given the mediators developed by this group to aid them in memorizing—a set of "ready-made" memory aids. In general, material that is organized in terms of a person's own interests and cognitive structures is material that has the best chance of being accessible in memory. It is more likely to be placed along routes that are connected to one's own ways of intellectual travel. Thus, the very attitudes and activities that characterize figuring out or discovering things for oneself also seem to have the effect of conserving memory.

Questions for Discussion

1. Why does Bruner say that learning through discovery leads to an increase in "intellectual potency" and is an aid to "conserving memory"?
2. Have you ever examined the processes by which you learn? Try it, introspectively, by identifying a bit of knowledge you now have and attempting to reconstruct the process by which you arrived at that knowledge. Does your account of your own learning correspond with Bruner's?
3. What does this account of the learning process imply for the classroom? How would you teach if you adopted these ideas? Be specific.
4. Do you see any relationships between Bruner's ideas and those of Rousseau, Holt, Neill and Farber? You should!

25 Thoughts on Teaching and Learning

Carl R. Rogers

The thoughts are personal, stated rather than argued, and provocative. Do you agree with him that "the only learning which significantly influences behavior is self-discovered, self-appropriated learning?" If so, what does this imply for the role of the teacher in a classroom?

I wish to present some very brief remarks, in the hope that if they bring forth any reaction from you, I may get some new light on my own ideas.

I find it a very troubling thing to *think,* particularly when I think about my own experiences and try to extract from those experiences the meaning that seems genuinely inherent in them. At first such thinking is very satisfying because it seems to discover sense and pattern in a whole host of discrete events. But then it very often becomes dismaying because I realize how ridiculous these thoughts, which have much value to me, would seem to most people. My impression is that if I try to find the meaning of my own experience it leads me, nearly always, in directions regarded as absurd.

So in the next three or four minutes, I will try to digest some of the meanings which have come to me from my classroom experience and the experience I have had in individual and group therapy. They are in no way intended as conclusions for someone else, or a guide to what others should do or be. They are the very tentative meanings, as of April 1952, which my experience has had for me, and some of the bothersome questions which their absurdity raises. I will put each idea or meaning in a separate lettered paragraph, not because they are in any particular logical order, but because each meaning is separately important to me.

(a) I may as well start with this one in view of the purposes of this conference. My experience has been that I cannot teach another person how to teach. To attempt it is for me, in the long run, futile.

(b) It seems to me that anything that can be taught to another is relatively inconsequential, and has little or no significant influence on behavior. That sounds so ridiculous I can't help but question it at the same time that I present it.

(c) I realize increasingly that I am only interested in learnings which significantly influence behavior. Quite possibly this is simply a personal idiosyncrasy.

(d) I have come to feel that the only learning which significantly influences behavior is self-discovered, self-appropriated learning.

(e) Such self-discovered learning, truth that has been personally appropriated and assimilated in experience, cannot be directly communicated to another. As soon as an individual tries to communicate such experience directly, often with a quite natural enthusiasm, it becomes teaching, and its results are inconsequential. It was some relief recently to discover that Soren Kierkegaard, the Danish philosopher, had found this too, in his own experience, and stated it very clearly a century ago. It made it seem less absurd.

(f) As a consequence of the above, I realize that I have lost interest in being a teacher.

(g) When I try to teach, as I do sometimes, I am appalled by the results, which seem a little more than inconsequential, because sometimes the teaching appears to succeed. When this happens, I find that the results are damaging. It seems to cause the individual to distrust his own experience and to stifle significant learning. Hence, I have come to feel that the outcomes of teaching are either unimportant or hurtful.

(h) When I look back at the results of my past teaching, the real results seem the same—either damage was done or nothing significant occurred. This is frankly troubling.

(i) As a consequence, I realize that I am only interested in being a learner, preferably learning things that matter, that have some significant influence on my own behavior.

(j) I find it very rewarding to learn, in groups, in relationships with one person as in therapy, or by myself.

(k) I find that one of the best, but most difficult, ways for me to learn is to drop my own defensiveness, at least temporarily, and to try to understand the way in which his experience seems and feels to the other person.

(l) I find that another way of learning for me is to state my own uncertainties, to try to clarify my puzzlements, and thus get closer to the meaning that my experience actually seems to have.

(m) This whole train of experiencing, and the meanings that I have thus far discovered in it, seem to have launched me on a process which is both fascinating and at times a little frightening. It seems to mean letting my experience carry me on, in a direction which appears to be forward, toward goals that I can but dimly define, as I try to understand at least the current meaning of that experience. The sensation is that of floating with a complex stream of experience, with the fascinating possibility of trying to comprehend its ever changing complexity.

I am almost afraid I may seem to have gotten away from any discussion of learning, as well as teaching. Let me again introduce a practical note by saying that by themselves these interpretations of my own experience may sound queer and aberrant, but not particularly shocking. It is when I realize the implications that I shudder a bit at the distance I have come from the common-sense world that everyone knows is right. I can best illustrate that by saying that if the experiences of others had been the same as mine, and if they had discovered similar meanings in it, many consequences would be implied.

Questions for Discussion

1. Do you agree that bringing about a change in behavior is the purpose of education? What is "behavior"?
2. Would Rogers' ideas, if applied consistently, result in the abolition of formal classrooms and schools? Why?
3. You already know quite a bit about alternative ways of viewing the educational enterprise. Which of the previous authors have stated a similar educational philosophy? Do you tend to view yourself as an exponent of this general view?

26 On Teaching Thinking

B. F. Skinner

A longtime advocate of programmed learning, Skinner holds that thinking should be identified with behavioral changes, and that learning occurs as successful behavior is reinforced. In this selection he develops this general theory, further distinguishing between covert and overt behavior, defining carefully the meaning of self-instructional learning and commenting on the ways in which problem solving is to be equated with learning. As you read, try to determine what the implications of his theory are for the classroom.

The early history of programmed instruction has led to some misunderstanding. Programming has been most quickly adopted in industry, where objectives can be clearly defined and methods easily changed and where the resulting gains, often expressed in dollars and cents, naturally lead to administrative action. In schools, colleges, and graduate schools it is much more difficult to define goals and to change practices, and gains from improvement are often too vague or remote to affect administrators. The more rapid adoption by industry has suggested that the scope of programmed instruction is limited, and the conclusion seems to be confirmed by the fact that most of the programs suitable for school or college use are designed either to transmit verbal knowledge or to develop basic motor and perceptual skills. These are the subjects most often taught, and for practical and commercial reasons programs have been constructed to teach them. The emphasis comes from the educational establishment, not from the nature of programming, but programming has suffered from guilt by association. It is widely believed that it is useful only in the transmission of knowledge and simple skills.

Some critics have gone further. They have argued that its very success works against the attainment of special objectives. If traditional methods are less efficient in teaching some things, it is because they are designed to teach other things as well —things which are not only out of reach of programmed instruction but somehow threatened by it. Any kind of effective teaching can be criticized in this way. The student who is well taught has no opportunity to learn how to learn—an opportunity enjoyed by those who are badly taught or not taught at all. Every problem solved with the help of a teacher is one problem less for the student to learn how to solve by himself. The more successfully the teacher spreads knowledge before the student as *terra cognita,* the fewer the chances to learn to explore the unknown. In full possession of conclusions reached and decisions taken, he has no chance to learn how to conclude or decide. The better his acquaintance with the established methods and views of others, the poorer his opportunity to be original or creative. If there is any one word for what seems to be missing when teaching is too successful, it is the chance to learn to *think.*

It is important that the student should learn without being taught, solve problems by himself, explore the unknown, make decisions, and behave in original ways, and these activities should, if possible, be taught. But when? The traditional strategy has been to teach thinking while teaching subject matter, and some sort of conflict is then inevitable. Instruction designed simply to transmit what is already known has often neglected the teaching of thinking. Some recent reforms have swung to the other extreme: in making sure that the student learns how to think, they neglect the transmission of what is known. It may appear that the problem is to find some sort of balance, but only if the assignments are carried out at the same time. If thinking can be analyzed and taught separately, the already-known can be transmitted with maximal efficiency.

This alternative has not been thoroughly explored because it is not compatible with traditional views of thinking. When we say that we want students to think, what do we really want them to do? It is as important to define the terminal behavior in teaching thinking as in teaching knowledge. How can it be done?

The traditional view is that thinking is an obscure, intellectual, "cognitive" activity—something which goes on in the mind and requires the use of rational powers and faculties. It leads to action when the thoughts to which it gives rise are expressed, but it is not itself behavior. It can sometimes be observed by the thinker, but it can also be unconscious, and introspective accounts are therefore not very consistent or helpful. Outstanding instances of thinking seem especially likely to arise from obscure intuitions or insights, and great thinkers seldom have great thoughts about thinking. This is particularly unfortunate because thinking in this sense is never observed by anyone except the thinker. (If we believe that others think as we do, it is only because they arrive at the same expressed conclusions, given the same public premises.)

So defined, thinking is hard to study. Cognitive psychologists tend to confine themselves to the structure of expressed thoughts—to the outcomes of thinking rather than thinking itself. The variables to which structure is most commonly related cannot be manipulated. Time is perhaps the best example: the products of various cognitive activities are studied as a function of age, as in the work of Piaget. The investigator can then turn from the shadowy processes of thinking to the conspicuous processes of development and growth. Sex, race, cultural history, and personality are other variables which are said to affect thinking in this sense but which are either uncontrollable or not substantially controlled in the research at hand.

Those who study thinking experimentally may not suffer greatly from the limitations imposed by variables of this sort, but that is not true of the teacher. He needs to control his conditions. He can take little satisfaction in simply waiting for his students to grow older. He cannot change their sex or race, and their personalities and cultural histories are practically out of reach. How, then, can he bring about the changes in behavior which are said to show that his students are learning to think? Possessing no clear-cut description of the behavior he is to set up and having no apparent access to controllable variables, he is forced back upon the notion of exercise. He sets problems to be solved and reinforces the student when he solves them or punishes him when he does not. In this way he "strengthens rational powers" in a sort of intellectual muscle-building.

He may go somewhat further by arranging tasks in order of increasing difficulty: the student strengthens his mental muscles on an easy problem before moving on to a harder one. This rudimentary programming is possible because it does not require any knowledge of thinking. One might teach high-jumping with the same technique —setting the bar at a given height, inducing the student to jump, and moving the bar up or down as the outcome dictates. It is not necessary to know anything about jumping. The student will learn to clear the bar at a respectable height, but he will almost certainly not jump well, for he cannot profit from what others have learned about good form. Similarly, a student may learn to think when the teacher simply poses problems and reinforces solutions, but he will almost always think inefficiently rather than with the good form which others have discovered before him.

Exercising rational powers is a sink-or-swim technique, and it is no more successful in teaching thinking than in teaching swimming. If we throw a lot of children into a pool, some of them will manage to get to the edge and climb out. We may claim to have taught them to swim, although most of them swim badly. Others go to the bottom, and we rescue them. We do not see those who go to the bottom when we teach thinking, and many of those who survive think badly. The method does not teach; it simply selects those who learn without being taught. Selection is always more wasteful than instruction and is especially harmful when it takes its place. Schools and colleges have come to rely more and more on selecting students who do not need to be taught, and in doing so they have come to pay less and less attention to teaching. Among current proposals for reform, programmed instruction is almost unique in focusing on the learning process and in suggesting practices which actually teach rather than select those who learn without being taught. The issue is crucial in teaching thinking.

The good high-jumping coach is less concerned with whether the bar is cleared than with form or style. Clearing the bar usually sustains good form in an accomplished jumper, but it produces it only by accident. Special reinforcers must be made contingent on the topography of the behavior rather than its outcome. Only under rare circumstances will the ultimate advantages of thinking teach a student to think. The teacher must arrange effective contingencies which respect the topography of thinking. Scientific help is needed. Research on the structure of expressed thoughts, relevant perhaps to evaluating the outcomes of thinking, has little to say about techniques. A more helpful formulation can be derived from the experimental analysis of behavior.

Thinking as Behavior

"To think" often means simply to behave. In this sense we are said to think verbally or nonverbally, mathematically, musically, socially, politically, and so on. In a slightly different sense, it means to behave with respect to stimuli. A man may think it is raining when he has been wet by a lawn sprinkler beyond a hedge. No special problem arises in teaching the repertoires which are exhibited as we think in either of these senses.

Thinking is also identified with certain behavioral processes, such as learning, discriminating, generalizing, and abstracting. These are not behavior but changes in behavior. There is no action, mental or otherwise. When we teach a child to press a button by reinforcing his response with candy, it adds nothing to say that he then responds because he "knows" that pressing the button will produce candy. When we teach him to press a red button but not a green, it adds nothing to say that he now "discriminates" or "tells the difference between" red and green. When we teach him to press a red button and then discover that he will press an orange button as well, though with a lower probability, its adds nothing to say that he has "generalized" from one color to another. When we bring the response under the control of a single property of stimuli, it adds nothing to say that the child has formed an "abstraction." We bring about the changes which define processes of this sort, but we do not teach the processes, and no special techniques are needed to teach thinking in this sense.

Certain kinds of behavior traditionally identified with thinking must, however, be analyzed and taught as such. Some parts of our behavior alter and improve the effectiveness of other parts in what may be called intellectual self-management. Faced with a situation in which no effective behavior is available (in which we cannot emit a response which is likely to be reinforced), we behave in ways which make effective behavior possible (we improve our chances of reinforcement). In doing so, technically speaking, we execute a "precurrent" response which changes either our environment or ourselves in such a way that "consummatory" behavior occurs.

Attending

A rather simple example of precurrent behavior which illustrates the difference between leaving the student to discover techniques for himself and giving him instruction in self-management is *attention*. If we were to respond with the same speed and energy to every aspect of the world around us, we should be hopelessly confused. We must respond only to selected features. But how are they selected? Why do we look at one thing rather than another? How do we observe the shape of an object while paying no attention to its color? What is happening when we listen only to the cello in a recorded string quartet?

Some selective mechanisms are, of course, genetic. We respond only to those energies which affect our receptors, and even though we possess both sensitive eyes and ears, we may nevertheless be "ear-minded" or "eye-minded." Some stimuli elicit or release reflex or instinctive responses, as when we are alerted by a loud or unusual noise. Stimuli of this sort are used to get attention. The teacher induces the student to look at an object by isolating it from other attention-getting things or by showing it suddenly or moving it about. He induces him to listen to what he is saying by speaking loudly or varying his speed or intonation. So-called audio-visual materials—for example, brightly colored textbooks and animated films—are made attractive on the same principles. None of this teaches the student to pay attention, and it may actually make him less likely to pay attention to things which are not on their face interesting.

The student can be induced to act selectively to special features of the environment by arranging contingencies of reinforcement. Roughly speaking, he can be taught that some features of the environment are "worth responding to." The central process is discrimination, and instruction consists simply in arranging appropriate contingencies. (When we appear to short-circuit the process by pointing to a stimulus or otherwise calling attention to it, we are actually taking advantage of similar, if more complex, contingencies in the student's history.) There is no special problem in teaching the student to pay attention in this sense.

To attend to something as a form of self-management is to respond to it in such a way that subsequent behavior is more likely to be reinforced. The precurrent behavior may be learned or unlearned. When we turn our eyes toward an object and focus upon it, or sniff an odor, or move a liquid about on the tongue, or slide our fingers over a surface, we make a stimulus more effective. There are two stages: (1) attending to a given state of affairs and (2) responding to it in some other way. In the normal course of events the reinforcement of the second stage strengthens the first.

In sink-or-swim instruction reinforcement is also contingent on the second stage. We set tasks which demand attention and reinforce the student when he is successful or punish him when he is not, presumably because he has or has not paid attention. He is left to discover how to pay attention for himself. The method often works. A child can be taught to match colors [on a device] . . . if he is reinforced when he presses the panel which is of the same color as the sample panel. He must, of course, look at the sample. He will probably learn to do so if he is reinforced when he presses the matching panel and mildly punished when he presses other panels. But a better technique is to teach the precurrent behavior directly. For example, if the machine requires him to press the sample panel before the other panels are illuminated, looking at the sample (in the act of pressing it) will be immediately reinforced by the illumination of the other panels. We achieve the same result when we warn a child to "stop and look" when he starts to respond without having done so.

In a simple example of this sort the gain from direct instruction may not be great, but some techniques of attending to a stimulus are learned only slowly, if at all, when reinforcement is confined to the second stage. Very few people learn to look slightly to one side of an object in order to respond to it more effectively in night vision unless they are specifically taught to do so. Specific contingencies may be needed to teach a baseball batter to "keep his eye on the ball," particularly because natural contingencies are opposed to the behavior (it is dangerous to look at a ball at the moment of impact, and the flight of the ball a moment later is the principal reinforcing consequence). Simply reinforcing a child when he reads a text correctly may be much less effective than special contingencies which induce him to read from left to right or to read a block of words at a glance. Another way to attend to stimuli so that one may respond to them more effectively is to construct supplemental stimuli. We do this when we point to words we are reading or follow a voice in a recorded fugue by singing or beating time with it or by moving our eyes along a score. Techniques of this sort are not likely to be learned simply because behavior which presupposes them is reinforced.

In short, much of the elaborate art of looking and listening cannot be taught simply by reinforcing the student when he responds in ways which show that he has previously looked and listened carefully. Direct instruction is needed.

Covert Behavior

Before turning to kinds of self-management which are more likely to be called thinking, it will be well to note a special characteristic responsible for much confusion in the field. Since precurrent behavior operates mainly to make subsequent behavior more effective, it need not have public manifestations. Any behavior may recede to the private or covert level so long as the contingencies of reinforcement are maintained, and they are so maintained when reinforcement is either automatic or derived from the effectiveness of subsequent overt behavior. As a result, much of the precurrent behavior involved in thinking is not obvious. It is therefore easily assumed to have nonphysical dimensions and likely to be neglected by the teacher.

The behavior most easily observed at the covert level is verbal. We speak to ourselves as we speak aloud and respond as we respond to the behavior of others or to ourselves when we speak aloud. What we say is sometimes immediately and automatically reinforcing—for evample, when we silently recite a poem we like—but reinforcement is more often deferred—for example, when we talk to ourselves while solving a problem but are reinforced only when the solution has been made public. The special conspicuousness of covert verbal behavior led John B. Watson to hazard the guess that all thought was subvocal speech, but nonverbal behavior may be covert. It is perhaps easier to talk to oneself about riding a bicycle than to "ride a bicycle to oneself," but nonverbal behavior may be automatically reinforcing or reinforced because of its role in intellectual self-management. The ultimate dimensions of covert behavior are not of interest here, beyond the requirement that the behavior be self-stimulating. The main issue is accessibility to instructional contingencies. When we teach simply by reinforcing successful outcomes, it does not matter whether precurrent behavior is private or public, but in direct instruction we cannot dispose of the problem that way.

The solution is simply to teach the behavior at the overt level. Although a child eventually speaks to himself silently, we teach him to speak by differentially reinforcing his audible behavior. Although he later reads books and recites passages to himself, we teach him as he reads and recites aloud. We teach mathematical problem solving in overt form, though much of it eventually recedes to the covert level. Covert behavior makes fewer demands on the current environment and is easy, quick, and secret, but so far as we know, there is no kind of thinking which must be covert. On the other hand, there are times when the overt form is preferred or required. A thinker returns to the overt level, for example, when covert self-stimulation is inadequate; he may begin a mathematical calculation privately but start speaking aloud or making notes when the work grows difficult or distractions arise. We eventually insist that a child think silently most of the time, and material which is automatically reinforcing is helpful in encouraging recession to the covert level. External contingencies may be withdrawn gradually so that automatic reinforcement can take over.

Covert *perceptual* behavior is an especially difficult subject. How does a child learn to "see things which are not really there"? Traditional formulations of visualizing or imagining are not very satisfactory. In general it is assumed that a person first somehow constructs an "image" and then looks at it. We can avoid this duplication by assuming that when a visual object is automatically reinforcing, the behavior of seeing it may become so strong that it occurs in the absence of the object. . . . It is learned when the object is present. The child who sees the objects and events described by a storyteller does so only because he has been exposed to complex contingencies involving actual events, pictured or otherwise. (Such contingencies are not as common as they once were. With audio-visual aids and devices the modern child is not often required to "see things which are not really there." He does not visualize very much when being read to from books with pictures in four colors on every page. Moving pictures and television remove practically all occasions for covert seeing. This is education for *Life* or the comics, but it does not prepare the student to read unillustrated materials.)

Covert perceptual behavior in intellectual self-management is usually taught, if at all, by reinforcing successful outcomes. We reinforce a student when he correctly describes or copies a picture he has seen some time before. He may find it helpful to see the picture again covertly, but we have not taught him to do so. A problem in "mental arithmetic" may require a good deal of covert seeing, but reinforcement is usually reserved for the overt solution. The student who is asked to "bound" a country may see a map, although he is reinforced only for naming contiguous countries. These forms of instruction are also becoming less common.

We may program covert seeing by setting problems of increasing difficulty. We ask the student to describe or copy something at first while he is looking at it but then only after increasing intervals of time. According to Winston Churchill, Whistler used a technique of this sort. He put his model in the basement and his students with their canvases and brushes on the first floor. The students went to the basement, looked at the model, and returned to the first floor to paint. When they improved, they were moved to the second floor. According to Churchill, some of them eventually reached the sixth floor. Another kind of programming in terms of difficulty consists in differentially reinforcing the delayed copying of progressively more subtle features.

Though this is in a sense programmed instruction, the reinforcement is still contingent on outcome. The nature of covert perceptual behavior may lead us to conclude that nothing else is possible, but overt techniques of observing are relevant. So far as we know, nothing is ever seen covertly which has not already been seen overtly at least in fragmentary form. Covert seeing may therefore be taught as overt seeing. Some ways of looking are especially effective. In describing or copying an object we move the eyes along salient features, look back and forth to gauge distances, look quickly from one feature to another to emphasize differences, view from different angles, gesture or otherwise create supplemental stimuli which emphasize lines and curves. Versions of such behavior may survive in covert form. The change in level may be facilitated by gradually weakening the external stimulus—as in teaching the student to see forms which are slightly out of focus, or crudely sketched, or presented as parts of puzzle pictures.

In summary, then, the self-management exemplified by paying attention, and by the more characteristic forms of thinking to which we now turn, is hard to observe and teach at the covert level. Skillful thinkers may internalize their behavior to the point at which even the thinker himself **cannot see** what he is doing. Nevertheless, we can teach relevant techniques at the overt level, and we can to some extent facilitate the recession to the covert level if this is desirable.

Learning How to Learn

"To study" often means simply to pay close attention: we study a situation carefully so that we can then act more effectively. A different kind of studying, particularly important to student and teacher, has the effect of facilitating recall. It is more than close observation. A book we are reading for pleasure may command our full attention, but we nevertheless forget it quickly. We read light fiction, as we listen to most music, because of its immediate effects. It often happens that we find such a book or piece of music familiar when we encounter it again and when asked about it may even be able to say it was enjoyable or exciting, although we cannot describe the plot or characters, or hum, sing, or play the music. Even a detective story which depends for its effect on the reader's ignorance of the outcome can often be reread with pleasure after a few years. To study is to read in a special way. We are concerned here with the fact that we may not have a chance to learn to study when material has been prepared so that it is easily remembered.

The standard practice, again, is to teach studying indirectly. An assignment is followed by a test; students who do well, presumably because they have studied effectively, are reinforced, and those who do not, possibly because they do not know how to study, are punished or "failed." The student reads carefully as a form of avoidance. He studies to avoid not-knowing. The aversive contingencies may be fine-grained. Materials designed to teach "reading with comprehension" often consist of passages to be read and questions about them to be answered. Pestalozzi, in his unpublished *The Instruction of Children in the Home*, offers an early example. The student is to read a page or two beginning as follows:

> There is one woman in Bonal who brings up her children better than all the others. Her name is Gertrude (1); her husband, who is a Mason (2), is called Leonard (3). They have (4) seven children. . . .

He is then to answer questions, such as:

> (1) What is the name of the woman in Bonal who brings up her children better than all the rest? (3) What is her husband's name? (2) What is he? . . .

These are obviously not facts worth remembering; the material is designed to teach ways of reading which lead to remembering. Some help may be given by grading such material in terms of difficulty. The material itself may be made more complex, students may be asked to read more before questions are answered, or the time for answering questions may be postponed.

These practices are not incompatible with programmed instruction. The student may begin by reading a brief text and recall it in working through a program; he then reads a longer text and recalls it in another program; and so on. In doing so he may discover how to learn from unprogrammed material. But this is still the standard assign-and-test pattern. The student may discover how to study, but he is not being taught.

To teach a student to study is to teach him techniques of self-management which increase the likelihood that what is seen or heard will be remembered. Word for-word memorizing is a special case. A student usually remembers some part of a page he has read. If he reads it again, he remembers more. After reading it many times, he may be able to reproduce it all. If he has done nothing more than read the page repeatedly, however, he has not studied it in any important sense. He has learned it simply by piling up small gains. To study a page so that it can be recalled word by word, he must respond to it in ways which increase the chances that he will speak as if he were reading the page when it is not actually present. The page must actually be recalled—though not necessarily all at once. Its effectiveness as a stimulus must be progressively reduced as the response of "reading it in its absence" gains strength. The student can probably repeat a short sentence he has just read. By waiting a moment before repeating it, he weakens the control exerted by the text. (He recalls the page bit by bit just because too much time would otherwise elapse to make recall of the first part possible when he has reached the end.) The student who knows how to study knows how much to recall at a time and how long to wait before trying. . . . Learning appears to be maximal if the response is emitted just before it grows too weak to be recalled.

Another way of weakening a stimulus is to reduce its clarity, duration, or extent The student who knows how to study glances quickly at a text to expose a necessary word or two briefly and possibly only in peripheral vision, or he uncovers parts of the text as needed. (There are strong opposing contingencies. The student is usually reinforced, by himself or others, for responding adequately at the moment, and he may therefore take steps which permit him to do so even though he does not then increase the probability that he will respond in the future. It is difficult to resist getting too much help—studying too small a section at a time, recalling it too soon, or reading the whole text rather than glimpsing only a small part of it as a prompt.)

Learning "what a page is about" is, of course, different from learning it word for word. We say that the student is to paraphrase the text or state a few of its points, but these are elliptical expressions. Linguistic and psycholinguistic formulations of verbal knowledge almost always appeal to meanings or ideas: the student is to discover the propositions expressed by a text so that he can express them himself, quite possibly in other words. This is far from an objective description of what happens, and it is not surprising that the long history of concepts like idea and meaning has not been marked by the discovery of better methods of instruction.

An analysis of verbal behavior throws some light on this difficult subject. When a student learns a page word for word (possibly without understanding it), the text functions as a formal stimulus evoking a textual response and as a series of formal prompts as the page is memorized. Eventually the student acquires a string of intra-verbal responses which permit him to reproduce the page. When he learns what a page is about, the text supplies thematic stimuli, many of which evoke intraverbal responses. He uses parts of the text as thematic rather than formal prompts. The final result is also a set of intraverbal responses, but not all of them are to be found in the text. Good programmed instruction builds thematic relations of this sort. The student may help himself in studying unprogrammed material by, for example, underlining important thematic stimuli and arranging them in outlines or summaries. Even when summaries are memorized word for word, they still function as thematic prompts which permit the student to construct a paraphrase.

Mnemonic devices play a role in studying. By definition a mnemonic is easier to learn than the material it helps to recall. By reproducing a mnemonic, verbal or perceptual, the student generates stimuli, usually as formal or thematic prompts, which aid in either word-for-word or paraphrased recall. Some mnemonics are constructed on the spot while studying, others are learned in advance and connected with current material. Fragmentary mnemonics probably play a more substantial role in studying than is commonly supposed.

Techniques of studying are particularly likely to recede to the covert level, where they may be maintained through their contribution to effective recall or other use. They must be taught at the overt level, however, if instructional contingencies are to respect topography rather than mere outcome.

Solving Problems

Thinking is often called problem solving. The term can be applied to the examples we have considered: we pay attention to something in order to solve the problem of dealing with it more effectively, and we study something in order to solve the problem of recalling it at a later date. The term is usually reserved, however, for precurrent activities which facilitate behavior under a much greater variety of circumstances. We face a problem when we cannot emit a response which, because of some current state of deprivation or aversive stimulation, is strong. If we are inclined to eat lobster, we face a problem if no lobster is available. If the room is hot, we face a problem if we cannot open the window. We solve such problems either by changing the situation so that the response can occur (we find some lobster or a way of opening the window) or by changing the deprivation or aversive stimulation (we eat something else or cool the room in some other way). . . .

Almost everything we do is relevant to solving one sort of problem or another, and we cannot learn problem solving, as we learn to pay attention or study, by acquiring a few special techniques. There are many ways of changing a situation so that we are more likely to respond to it effectively. We can clarify stimuli, change them, convert them into different modalities, isolate them, rearrange them to facilitate comparison, group and regroup them, "organize" them, or add other stimuli. These practices can be classified without too much trouble, but specific techniques depend upon the problems to be solved and show a very wide range. A teacher usually confines instruction to a small area—he teaches problem solving in mathematics, for example, or logic, or mechanical invention, or personal relations—and appropriate techniques can then be specified and taught.

Faced with a given kind of problem, the student learns to behave in ways which maximize the probability that he will find a solution. It is not quite correct, then, to say that no effective response is available. A *solution* is not available, but if the problem is soluble, a response which will produce a solution is. Solving the problem is one step removed from the solution—from emitting the response which causes the problem to disappear. Roughly speaking, the student must learn to recognize the kind of problem with which he is faced and to select an appropriate technique.

A particular difficulty arises when the problem can be solved only through a sequence of steps, for it is then necessary to learn a response appropriate to each step, and many of these may be a long way from the ultimate solution.

The standard sink-or-swim technique is to set problems of a given type, possibly graded according to difficulty, and to reinforce the student when he solves them. When this method is used in its crudest form, the teacher need know nothing of problem solving. A knowledge of the outcome—whether the student's solution is correct or not—is sufficient. Direct instruction depends upon the type of problem. In a familiar example, the student is taught to translate the prose statement of a problem into algebraic symbols, to arrange or rearrange these in standard ways, to convert one expression into another by transposing, clearing fractions, extracting roots, and so on, and to proceed in this fashion until an expression appears which can be solved in some way already learned. The entire repertoire is essentially verbal and is easily represented and taught with the help of available systems of notation. Nonverbal problem solving—as in inventing a mechanical device having a given effect—is not so easily described and, possibly for the same reason, not so easily taught. Both verbal and nonverbal problem-solving repertoires may recede to the covert level, where analysis becomes difficult, but they are taught at the overt level.

When teachers turn to direct instruction in problem solving, they are often misled by what may be called the Formalistic Fallacy. To get the student to execute problem-solving behavior it is tempting simply to show him what to do. The student imitates what the teacher says, or reads what he has written, and in doing so engages in behavior which solves the problem. The probability that he will engage in similar behavior in the future is not necessarily increased. Mathematics is often "taught" by taking the student through a proof. The student does indeed engage in the behavior which solves the problem, but if the behavior is entirely under the control of the printed page or the teacher's voice, it is probably not being brought under the control of stimuli which will be encountered in similar problems. "Giving the student reasons" why a step is taken may bring the behavior under useful control, but it is not necessarily the most effective way of doing so.

Productive Thinking

When a student has learned to recognize various kinds of problems and apply relevant techniques, he does not seem to be "thinking" at all. His behavior is perhaps one remove from reinforcement, but it is still nothing more than a set of responses of specified topographies evoked by specified occasions. The cognitive processes seem to have vanished. When the student has learned how to attend to the environment, he has no further need for mental screening or selection. When he has learned how to study, he can dispense with inner processes of coding, storing, and retrieving information. The precurrent behavior with which he solves problems seems to become "thoughtless." Only instruction via the outcome of thinking may seem to preserve some mental life, but it does this only because it does not directly teach any alternative.

Those who insist that thinking is something more than behaving will point to as yet unanalyzed problems. Algorithmic problem solving is perhaps not necessarily mental, but what about heuristics? There must be problematic situations which evoke not only no response which proves to be a solution but no precurrent behavior generating such a response. "Productive" thinking then seems to be required. But it survives only so long as it remains unanalyzed. Far from offering scope for a special kind of mental activity, heuristics may be treated simply as a set of techniques designed to solve the problem of solving problems.

Polya's *How to Solve It* is significantly titled. The author is concerned with teaching students how to solve, not first-order problems, but the second-order problem of discovering first-order techniques. As an accomplished problem-solver, he can recommend helpful moves. For example, he suggests that the student ask himself, "What is the unknown?" In answering that question, the student may convert a problem which has not seemed soluble into one to which an available first-order technique applies. Similarly, if he will ask himself, "Do I know a related problem?" the answer may suggest a useful first-order technique.

The occasions upon which heuristic techniques are useful are by definition harder to specify than those to which first-order, algorithmic techniques apply. Moreover, the behavior which solves the problem of solving problems is one further remove from ultimate reinforcement. But appropriate techniques can nevertheless be analyzed and taught. Solving the problem of solving problems then becomes as mechanical as first-order problem solving, and there is no room left for "productive" thinking.

If no previously learned technique of any sort applies, the problem must be attacked by trial-and-error, which is not really a behavioral process at all. As we have seen, it was once common to study learning by putting an organism into a complex situation (what we should now call a set of terminal contingencies) and watching the adaptive behavior emerge. The organism was under strong deprivation or aversive stimulation and hence not inactive. Most of its responses suffered extinction, but some were reinforced. When repeatedly subjected to the same contingencies, it usually came to respond in an effective way. But its responses were in no important sense trials, nor were they errors because they proved not to be solutions. Trial-and-error is at best a process of selection in which some of the responses evoked by a given situation prove effective. When the same terminal contingencies are programmed, the organism may reach the same terminal behavior without errors.

Questions for Discussion

1. Describe what Skinner means by: 1) thinking as behavior; 2) attending and paying attention to; 3) covert and overt behavior; and 4) studying.
2. What do you know about programmed learning? Do you approve if it?
3. Do you think programmed learning increases or decreases the development of a student's imaginative life?
4. After reading Bruner, Rogers, and Skinner, do you think that psychologists present important information which is useful to a teacher?

27 The Carnegie Tech Management Game

K. J. Cohen et al.

This selection presents one version of programed learning: the use of games for instructional purposes. This particular game is used in a business management course and consists of situations in which the consequence of the students' decisions can be determined by the computer and so their successes and failures as managers can be known by themselves and others in the class. Can the principles of this game be used in other types of instruction?

Business games, in general, consist of two parts—external environment and internal decisions. The games have usually been built around some given market in which the players making up the several teams are competing. The teams or firms generally are required to make such decisions as setting price, determining output, etc. The environment, which is normally programed on an electronic computer, contains the various functions, such as the demand curve, which determine the outcome for each firm of the decisions made. The firms usually receive some form of income statement and balance sheet, and the outcome of their decisions can be traced in the ebb and flow of the accounts on the financial statements.

The environment is designed to simulate, at least to some degree, the real world. The decisions that must be made by the members of the firms are modeled on the types of decisions actually made in business firms. The level of the decision varies, but most games concentrate on decisions at a high executive level. The development of the computer has stimulated the growth of business games by making it possible to devise environments which are faithful simulations of segments of the economy. As the simulation of the environment becomes more realistic, so also can the decisions that must be made become closer to the decisions of an actual business firm.

It was, in fact, a basic article of faith of the development group of the Carnegie game that if the realism of business games could be increased, a more effective educational and research tool than previously existed would be created. After a period of development and experimental trials we now have a game which we feel has achieved the kind of complexity and realism desired. It is the purpose of this article to explain the game in some detail and then to discuss the education and research possibilities of the game.

I. Description of the Game

The packaged detergent industry has served as a general model for the industry of the game. The selection of this industry for our model was primarily one of con-

From "The Carnegie Tech Management Game" by K. J. Cohen, R. M. Cyert, W. R. Dill, A. A. Kuehn, M. H. Miller, T. A. Van Wormer, and P. R. Winters, *The Journal of Business*, October 1960, pp. 303–321. Used by permission of the authors and the University of Chicago Press.

venience. Its advantages included the existence of a national market, a small number of firms, and a set of differentiated products. In addition, some members of the development group had an intimate knowledge of the industry. The game is not, however, an exact simulation of the detergent industry. Only those features deemed useful in terms of the purposes of the game were used.

There are three companies in the game. The players have the role of executives in the three competing companies. Each firm consists of one factory, located in one of the four geographical territories that comprise the total detergent market. At this factory, there are the following facilities: (1) a raw-materials warehouse, (2) production facilities that can be used to produce different mixes of product, (3) a factory warehouse for the storage of finished product, and (4) offices and facilities for new-product research and development.

The firm maintains, in addition, a district warehouse for finished products in each of the four regions. These facilities, in contrast with the facilities at the central-plant location, are leased rather than owned.

At the beginning of the game, each firm is "given" one product neither very good nor very bad in terms of its basic characteristics, washing power, sudsing power, and gentleness. By expenditures for new-product research, teams can generate new products. If, on the basis of laboratory reports or market test data, a team wants to put a new product into production, it can do so, as long as the total number of brands in production does not exceed three.

The factory makes all products with the same equipment, using the same work force. In other words, during the month the work force divides its time among products which are scheduled in sequence for production on the same equipment. The team of managers is not concerned, therefore, with detailed scheduling of products among men or machines, and they can regard equipment and work force as homogeneous.

All products in the game are developed from a basic set of seven available raw materials. The team must order raw materials from suppliers in advance of their use in production, but teams can assume that deliveries will be made on schedule. Lead times vary for different materials, and prices will fluctuate seasonally and with general economic conditions. All suppliers of raw materials are assumed to offer a discount of 3 per cent if the team pays its bills within 1 month of delivery of the materials. Payment is required within 2 months of delivery.

Production within each 1-month operating period is scheduled by the players, but the actual monthly output does not necessarily meet their schedule. The computer is programed to impose realistic constraints on the attainment of production goals. Rules in the machine determine how output is affected by raw-material run-outs, by expenditures for maintenance, by limits to plant capacity and to the utilization of overtime, by limits to the rate at which the work force can be expanded, and by undertime and overtime effects on employee productivity. Production costs, as well as output, will be affected by these factors, and costs, in addition, will depend on longer-run decisions of the team to expand capacities for production and for inventory storage.

We should also like to thank the members of the Carnegie Tech faculty, the members of the Ford Seminar at Denver, and the graduate students at Carnegie who served as guinea pigs for the original plays of the game.

All production for a given month is presumed available at the warehouse to which it has been consigned at the beginning of the following month. Realistic shipping times and costs are associated with shipments from factory warehouse to district warehouses or from one district warehouse to another. Sales lost because of inventory run-outs over 1 week old cannot be regained, and run-outs carry penalties for future demand.

As sales, the company counts shipments from the factory or district warehouses to its customers who are wholesalers or retail chains. All products which the firm has or can develop are presumed to be distributed at the retail level through supermarkets and grocery stores for use in the home. The firm sets one price for each product in each region, and retail prices may vary considerably by region and by individual store.

In any month, sales for the company depend on the total retail demand for soaps and detergents, which is sharply seasonal, and on the relative effectiveness of the company, vis-à-vis its competitors, in influencing consumer behavior by advertising, by pricing decisions, by outlays for sales force and promotional efforts, and by product characteristics. Consumer response to these variables may vary in the different regions.

To develop new products or to improve existing products, the team must spend money for product research and development. The amount spent determines the probability of generating new-product ideas. As in real life, most new-product ideas will not be worth very much; and even when a good product is developed, its superiority need not be immediately apparent. Laboratory reports on new products will describe the composition (in terms of the seven raw materials), the requirements for them in quantity, their characteristics (washing power, etc.) as revealed by laboratory tests, and the raw material cost per case at current raw-material prices.

If the players think a product idea is worth further study, they can spend money to draw a sample of consumers and to test their product preference. From such test studies, the team will have to decide whether or not to put the product into full-scale production.

Each company is a "going concern" at the beginning of the game. It will have, as noted, a product and a plant to produce the product. The financial condition with which the firm begins the game can be made to vary, depending on the educational objectives of the particular play. Normally, however, we start with each team in reasonably sound financial condition with a modest liquid reserve and an established dividend policy.

The firm can obtain additional funds during play in most of the ways that would be open to a real management group, but they must anticipate their needs for funds. Except for emergency measures, which are described below, the quickest means of financing—a 3-month bank loan—requires a month between the filing of an application and the release of funds to the firm. To qualify for a short-term bank loan, the company must meet specific requirements with respect to liquidity prior to and throughout the life of the loan. The size of loan is limited by the firm's current assets and recent income.

The players can also apply for permission to issue various kinds of marketable debentures. It takes 6 months from the time of application before funds from the issuing of bonds are available, and substantial negotiation and flotation costs are incurred. These forms of financing must be for minimum amounts, and neither can exceed realistic maxima in terms of assets and income. Long-term debt financing also involves realistic restrictive covenants on current ratios, working capital, dividend payments, and sinking funds; but firms can avoid some of these restrictions if they are willing to pay higher coupons.

The players will begin the game with an authorization to issue some additional common stock. If the market value of the stock is adequate, the players may get additional authorization to issue common stock. Funds from new flotations will be available 6 months after the team applies to market the shares at the price then ruling. Flotation costs are substantially higher than in the case of debentures. The market price of the stock of each firm is computed and posted each month. The function, based on recent research findings, makes price vary in the long run according to the growth potential of the industry, to other investment opportunities available to the shareholders in the market, and to the demonstrated efficiency of the players in managing the shareholders' investment. In the short run, price may also vary in response to changes in dividend policy. . . .

If the firm gets into financial difficulties, there will be provisions for temporary relief. The team can sell government bonds to get immediate access to extra cash. Players can delay 1 month, at the cost of their discount, on settling accounts with suppliers. If the firm meets minimal requirements, the due dates for short-term bank loans can be extended.

Plans that the players make for each operating period will be checked by the computer for financial feasibility. If they are not feasible, the players may have to redo the plans and will incur the realistic penalties of improvising, some immediate and some delayed.

The players may wish to expand their plant at one or more points during the game, particularly since there are costs associated with overutilization of facilities. They are permitted to expand production and storehouse facilities at the same localities, but not to add new locations. The capacity of district warehouses may be expanded simply by leasing new space, but the capacity of all other facilities can be expanded only by capital investment. The players may enter into contracts to enlarge the raw-materials warehouse, production plant and equipment, or the factory warehouse. Expenditures for each of these three purposes must be unitary; that is, they cannot specify expenditures for particular kinds of storage space or for particular kinds of equipment. After a period of 6 months, when construction is completed, the costs of production and storage will be adjusted to reflect the additions to capacity. . . .

This, then, summarizes the main characteristics of the companies and of the industry in which they operate. Companies can be differentiated from each other in many ways. Each, of course, will eventually have products with different characteristics. The computer can be programed easily so that they will differ in cost structure, in initial financial position, in plant capacity, in access to markets, or in a variety of other ways.

Players' Actions

The basic actions of the players must be oriented around two activities. They must analyze the output of the computer, and, on the basis of this analysis, they must make decisions. The output of the computer is detailed and varied and is designed to be complete enough to allow modern mathematical techniques to be utilized. It will be necessary for the firms to develop a system of accounting as well as a system for processing the information received. The magnitude of the problem can be better appreciated by looking at the kind of information received in the areas of production, marketing, and finance. Production men will receive forms that summarize the following:

1. The raw-materials situation: stocks on hand, quantities on order, deliveries during past month, usage during past month, and current prices
2. Factory performance: actual quantities produced and shipped (by product and destination), raw-material and labor usage by product, employment levels, amount of overtime, maintenance expenditures, equipment downtime
3. Warehouse transactions: opening and closing inventories, receipts from other warehouses, shipments to other warehouses, sales, and receipts from factory

The production men will also get, at the beginning of the game and later at irregular intervals, information about the following:

1. Raw-material requirements for each product
2. Required lead times for raw-material orders
3. Space requirements for raw-materials storage
4. Estimates of "normal" worker productivity for each product
5. Current hiring and firing costs
6. Current wage rates (straight time and overtime)
7. Space requirements for storing finished goods
8. Charges for excess inventory storage
9. Shipping costs and required shipping times from factory to warehouses
10. Storage costs at district warehouses
11. Price changes for various raw materials

They will get less explicit "reports of past experience" about plant capacity, about the impact of maintenance expenditures, raw-material shortages, overtime, and undertime on production, and about the rules for rescheduling shipments to warehouses if actual production differs from scheduled production.

The marketing men will know, after each operating period, the following information about their firms:

1. Expenditures by product and by region for advertising and for sales force and promotional efforts and total expenditures for market research, sales office and administration, and product research and development
2. Information about the environment, such as current and forecasted annual rates of gross national product, salesmen's reports on brands introduced and dropped by competitors in each region
3. Sales by brand and by district warehouse

In proportion to specific expenditures on market research, they will receive estimates of what competitors have spent on advertising and research activity and free predictions of approximately the usual reliability on gross national product for the coming 5 years. As the occasion warrants, they will receive laboratory reports on new products. These reports will scale the product on sudsing, washing power, and gentleness. They will tell raw-material requirements and raw-material and production costs. There will also be estimates of expected productivity in making the new product.

The company can pay to get additional marketing data on brand preferences of consumers and on market variables, such as share of market, or competitors' advertising, distribution, and prices to wholesalers.

Initially, the marketing men will start with some specific data about such things as (1) the costs of market studies on various scales and (2) the characteristics of the company's given products (and, to a lesser extent, of competitors' products).

They will have less explicit "experiential" data on the potential gains from different kinds of marketing and research expenditures, about the structure of the market, and about the firm's position vis-à-vis competitors.

The finance men will receive at the end of each month the following kinds of information:

1. A balance sheet, with special reports on inventory position, plant and equipment accounts, construction obligations outstanding, and status of loans and securities outstanding
2. Summary of receipts and disbursement during the month
3. Statement of financial commitments for next and future months
4. Current information on the availability of financing
5. General information on money and capital markets
6. An income statement, with special reports on cost of goods sold and cost of materials used
7. At the end of every quarter a balance sheet and an income statement for each competitor issued to each firm

As the occasion warrants, they will receive notice of violations of loan covenants.

In addition, they will have detailed initial reports on the way in which accounts are kept and on the way in which various cash receipts and disbursements do—or can—occur. The conditions under which they can obtain various forms of financing will be spelled out in detail, along with explanations of the length of time before funds become available, of the conditions for extending a loan, and of the penalties for failing to meet commitments.

This information then becomes the basis for a whole complex of decisions. In the area of production, the players must regularly

1. Order raw materials
2. Decide on size of labor force
3. Decide how much overtime to authorize
4. Plan how much to spend for maintenance of plant and equipment
5. Schedule the total quantity of production for the month by product
6. Decide how to allocate production among warehouses
7. Decide what transshipments of existing inventories need to be made from factory to district warehouses or among district warehouses

In the marketing area, the players must regularly

1. Set prices by product and by region
2. Determine advertising expenditures by product and by region
3. Decide distribution expenditures (for sales force and promotion) by product and by region

In the financial area, the players must regularly

1. Estimate net cash requirements for operations in the coming month
2. Authorize total receipts and disbursements for the coming month
3. Arrange for payments of funds for taxes, for interest, for construction, for retirement of debt, and for purchase of government bonds
4. Decide what share of profits should be allocated as dividends to stockholders
5. Decide (in the case of inadequate cash reserves) what steps should be taken to cut expenditures

Most of these decisions bind the company only in the short run. The decisions on dividend payments need be made only quarterly, and some of the others might also be, but most will need to be reviewed and remade every month. These are the decisions which the computer must have in satisfactory form before it can produce operating results for the next period.

In addition, to survive and grow in the face of competition from one or more other firms, the players must be prepared to consider at frequent intervals the following:

1. Expenditures for research on new products and for test market studies on consumer acceptance of the products
2. Expenditures for general market research into the nature of consumer preferences, into the patterns of retail sales, or into the performances of competitors
3. The desirability of dropping, changing, or adding products or of extending marketing efforts into a new territory
4. Investment in new facilities for the storage of raw materials or finished goods
5. Investment in new plant and equipment for production
6. The advisability of applying for
   a) Renegotiation of current debt
   b) Additions to working capital by short-term bank loans
   c) Long-term additions to capital by issuing stock or by selling bonds

Decisions on these matters may not be made very often, and, when made, they will frequently take the nature of long-term commitments. But the players must be continually alert to their long-run interests and must anticipate their requirements while they still have time to act. Specific instructions about how much to spend or about what to do must be fed to the computer.

In developing the Carnegie game, we had as our objective a game that would be useful both as a teaching device and as a research tool. In the next two sections we shall discuss the potential of the game as we see it in each of these directions.

II. Uses of the Game in Education

Our educational objectives in designing the Carnegie Tech management game were more ambitious than the goals of designers of the simpler games. Ben R. Faden has said that the educational purpose of the IBM game is "to help us to discard emotional blocks and to use our best judgment."[1] In a similar vein, an executive writes of his experience with the AMA games:

> The complex problems of running a business are presented in such a way that seems to facilitate rapid comprehension, active participation, and intense involvement in the process of planning, review, and analysis.[2]

The emphasis is not on teaching managers specific skills; it is limited to reminding experienced specialists that the functions—and people—of a business are interdependent and that many decisions must be made under time pressure by the cooperative judgments of several individuals.[3]

The undergraduate or graduate student of business (or sometimes even the seasoned executive), though, does not become a manager simply by discarding emotional blocks or participating intensely in an absorbing, but grossly oversimplified, substitute for a real management environment. We began work on the Carnegie Tech game with the hope of doing more—of developing an environment in which players could test and develop some of the positive skills which a manager must employ. This concern is reflected both in the design of the game and in the arrangements we have adopted for its administration.

What must a manager do well to be effective? We do not pretend, of course, to have anything like the whole answer to this, but we believe that the following skills, at least, will be universally recognized as important.

1. *An ability to abstract, organize, and use information from a complex and diffuse environment.* Managers live in a world which lavishes information on them but which affords them little time and little guidance about how to use it. A key function of management is to discover the pertinence of various data to the organization's objectives, to isolate the problems which deserve immediate attention, and to identify the constraints which must be observed in seeking a solution.

The way in which the game is currently being administered seems also to add to its utility as an environment for sharpening information-processing skills. Two features of the administrative arrangements are particularly important—team size and the subordination of each team to a board of directors.

The Carnegie Tech game is complex enough to permit ten-man teams whose members have clearly differentiated functions to perform. Because no one man consistently has time to absorb the information made available to the team, players must

---

[1] From the *Proceedings of the National Symposium on Management Games, University of Kansas, May, 1959,* pp. iv–11.

[2] Clifford Craft, "Competitive Management Simulation," *Journal of Industrial Engineering,* September–October, 1959, p. 363.

[3] We are speaking here of the simpler "general management" games which have received most of the attention and publicity in the last year or two. There are a number of games —some which James Lubin at the University of Pennsylvania has developed, for example —whose purpose is more didactic: to persuade clerks of the superiority of a new method of production scheduling or to demonstrate the efficacy of modern inventory-control techniques.

learn to interpret and summarize incoming results in a way that helps their team-mates as well as themselves. The financial officers must be able to talk to the pro-duction officers about relevant aspects of the company's financial condition without discussing all the details of cost trends, current cash position, stock prices, or nego-tiations with outside lenders. The marketing officers must be able to translate their detailed marketing experience into a sales forecast on which the finance officers can base their cash budgets and projected income statements and on which the produc-tion officers can base orders for raw materials, production schedules, and schedules for shipment of finished goods to district warehouses.

In the first extended play of the game, boards of three to four faculty members were appointed for each firm. The director's job was essentially to test the players' understanding of their environment, to force them to communicate information about their positions and plans, and to direct their attention—when appropriate—to particular problems and goals. Regular meetings of the boards of directors with the members of their firms were held at the end of every (simulated) quarter or half-year of play. At these meetings the officers of the firms had to review the results of their past operations and to present their plans for future operations.

At the end of every (simulated) year of play, each firm was required to present a written annual report to their stockholders. This report had to include financial statements for the current and recent years; a review of developments in production, sales, finance, new products, plant facilities, and organization during the current year; an evaluation of the present competitive position of the firm; and a review of plans for changes in operations and for new investments in products, market development, and new-plant or warehouse facilities for the future, with an explanation of the reasons behind these plans.

2. *An ability to forecast and to plan.* The complexity of modern business opera-tions and the time lags that occur before the effects of decisions are realized put a premium on the manager's ability to look ahead. The student of management needs to recognize at an early stage not only the immediate, but the cumulative, effects of his actions (or lack of action). He should also practice forecasting consequences of his decisions so that he can measure what he accomplishes against what he planned to achieve.

Over and above the presence of directors and of time pressure on the officers, though, the game itself is designed to encourage planning and to penalize lack of attention to future needs. The finance officers, for example, must make sure that sufficient funds are available to carry out the planned operating decisions and to pay the firm's debts when due, developing and applying to that end techniques of cash-flow forecasting and cash budgeting. If the funds available in any period are not sufficient to meet the firm's immediate financial obligations and to carry out its currently programed operating decisions, the machine will reject the move. The team will then have to improvise a new program consistent with its resources, a process which will involve costs, some immediate and visible, such as loss of discounts, and some subtle and delayed, such as loss of continuity in programs whose results depend on the cumulated level of expenditures.

3. *An ability to combine the role of generalist and specialist.* The image which simple management games present of managers as a team of generalists, all con-

cerned with over-all company policy, seems to have a limited basis in real life. Most managers, as individuals, are as much specialists as generalists. Even in the top positions of organizations, men are committed by experience, expertise, loyalties and job responsibilities to subareas like production, marketing and finance. Their commitments as specialists affect their behavior on top policy decisions; and, at the same time, their identification with the enterprise as a whole requires them to co-operate at lower levels in the planning of many detailed operating decisions.

More than the simpler games, the Carnegie Tech game may lure the careless player into the trap of excessive specialization. But in real life, too, the manager must learn to be a generalist under conditions where the temptations are strong to remain a specialist. Here we rely primarily on the unsatisfactory income statements and balance sheets of teams which do not plan and co-ordinate their activities to draw their attention to the needs for considering the firm as a whole. The boards of directors can also be expected to comment on the lack of integration in what various groups from the firm are doing. Through these devices we have tried to emphasize interdepartmental co-operation both on short-term actions and on broad policy questions.

4. *An ability to work effectively with other people.* Managers must effectively maintain three kinds of co-operative working relationships with other people in an organizational setting. In relation to their own superiors—who may be other managers, directors, stockholders, or others who have influence on company goals and on the evaluation of managerial performance—managers are required to negotiate about the objectives toward which they are working and about the impact of these objectives for decisions about operating the company. Second, when goals have been established or inferred, managers must work together to produce good decisions with the resources that they have at their disposal. Third, managers must work through a subordinate organization to elaborate and implement their policies and decisions.

Our objective in designing the Carnegie Tech management game was to provide an environment in which these abilities might be developed. We do not expect that a game, any more than any other single teaching technique, can take over the whole task of molding men into managers; but we expect that complex management games will earn an important role in such efforts.

Questions for Discussion

1. What do you see as the chief educational advantages and disadvantages to the use of the game as an instructional technique?
2. Could you apply the principles used in game theory to teach a course in history? Reading? Chemistry?
3. This type of teaching provides immediate feedback for students to use in judging their achievements. What are the advantages of this? Any disadvantages?

28 Research in Teaching: The Gap Between Theory and Practice

W. J. McKeachie

When you enter the classroom you will have to decide whether you want to lecture or conduct a discussion, use audiovisual materials or programed learning. Which is the most effective method for teaching? Teaching what? Perhaps different types of subject matter suggest different styles of presentation. This selection will tell you what researchers have learned about different methods for arranging the teaching-learning environment.

Gilbert Highet writes in the Preface to his *The Art of Teaching,* [This book] . . . is called *The Art of Teaching* because I believe teaching is an art, not a science. It seems very dangerous to me to apply the aims and methods of science to human beings as individuals. . . . Teaching is not like inducing a chemistry reaction: it is much more like painting a picture, or making a piece of music, or on a lower level like planting a garden or writing a friendly letter. You must throw your heart into it, you must realize that it cannot all be done by formulas, or you will spoil your work, and your pupils and yourself.[1]

One cannot help cheering Professor Highet's call for commitment to teaching, but in practice the "art of teaching" is all too often based on naïve assumptions about students, teaching methods, and the nature of the student-teacher relationship. Art based on sound knowledge and well-honed skills is more effective in promoting student learning.

Teaching is like art in that it involves value judgments, and the means for achieving these values are complex. Research has revealed that many variables interact in determining teaching effectiveness. But it is the very complexity of the teaching situation that makes every bit of empirical information the more precious.

The basic question researchers have tried to answer is: What kind of teaching-learning situation is educationally most effective? This implies that the goals of education can be defined precisely enough to permit judgments about which of two teaching methods is more effective. Unfortunately, statements about goals are often so general that opinions about teaching effectiveness can only be impressionistic. The ultimate criteria of teaching effectiveness are *changes in students*—learning; movement toward educational objectives.

Author's note: Preparation of this paper was greatly facilitated by my participation in research sponsored by the U.S. Office of Education, Research Contract OE No. 4/10/001 with W. J. McKeachie, J. E. Milholland, and Robert L. Isaacson.

An excellent review of recent work in this field is found in Ruth E. Eckert and D. C. Neale, "Teachers and Teaching," *Review of Educational Research,* 1965, *35,* 304–17.

[1] G. Highet, *The Art of Teaching* (New York: Alfred A. Knopf, 1950).

In thinking about college teaching, we professors have usually been most concerned about content. The Ph.D. has been the teacher's certificate for working at the college level. It seems obvious that knowledge of subject should be necessary (but not sufficient) for effective teaching. This assumption, however, has never been checked, and, conceivably, students might become better educated by a confused or ill-informed instructor who motivated his students to clear up the confusions than by a professor with great depth of knowledge.

The emphasis on content has led to a distorted view of the role of the professor.[2] This view is that the professor's most important qualification is his knowledge and that the process of teaching involves communicating the professor's knowledge to students. This notion of the professor as a source of information—a walking encyclopedia—is really a carry-over from the times when books were scarce and expensive, and oral transmission of culture was necessary.

Today the importance of the Ph.D. degree is as a symbol that the holder has achieved some degree of expertness in *learning* a scholarly field. His role in teaching should be as an expert guiding novices in developing the skills of learning his field. The professor's knowledge is a concomitant of his skill as a learner rather than the *sine qua non* for teaching.

What is the relationship between the instructor's learning skills and his ability both to teach these learning skills to students and to motivate students to learn? The whole area of content has been neglected in research on teaching.[3] We do not know the effects of misinformation, amount of information presented, level of abstraction, emphasis upon cognition versus motivation, analysis versus synthesis, didactic versus problem-solving approaches, or deductive versus inductive styles. Fortunately, programed instruction is beginning to give some attention to these variables.[4]

One can imagine that proposals for research on "professors' knowledge of subject matter" would not be greeted with enthusiasm by professors. It is thus not surprising that the beginnings of research on teaching have been in areas that are less personally threatening.

Class Size

The earliest research on teaching was on class size. Are small classes really more effective for teaching than large classes? The answer of the professor has generally been "yes." But the refreshing empiricism of the 1920's looked hard at many "self-evident truths" about human behavior. Among them was the assumption that class size has something to do with educational effectiveness.

Among the first investigators were Edmondson and Mulder,[5] who compared the

[2] My conception of college teaching is largely derived from the ideas of Roger Heyns.

[3] This point was stimulated by N. L. Gage's "Psychological Conceptions of Teaching," paper presented Feb. 14, 1966, at New York University.

[4] For example, J. D. Krumboltz and W. W. Yabroff, "The Comparative Effects of Inductive and Deductive Sequences in Programed Instruction," *American Education Research Journal*, 1965, *2*, 223–35, found that inductive and deductive methods were not differentially effective.

[5] J. B. Edmondson and F. J. Mulder, "Size of Class as a Factor in University Instruction," *Journal of Educational Research*, 1924, *9*, 1–12.

performance of students matched for intelligence enrolled in a 109-student class with students enrolled in a 43-student class in the same course in education. Achievement of the two groups was approximately equal, with a slight edge for the small class on an essay and the mid-semester tests and for the large class on quizzes and the final examination. Students reported a preference for small classes. The Edmonson and Mulder results at Michigan encouraged the Committee on Research of the University of Minnesota to begin the most comprehensive studies of class size ever undertaken. Fifty-nine well-controlled experiments, reported by Hudelson,[6] involved such widely varying subject matter as psychology, physics, accounting, law, and education. In 46 of the experiments, results favored the large classes. Although only eight differences were large enough to be statistically significant at the 5 percent level, six of the eight favored large classes.

Support for small classes, however, came from studies in the teaching of French conducted by Cheydleur[7] at the University of Wisconsin between 1919 and 1943. With hundreds of classes ranging in size from nine to 33, Cheydleur found a consistent superiority on departmental examinations for the smaller classes. Mueller[8] found similar results in an experiment comparing elementary psychology classes of 20 and 40 students. More recent experiments are also less favorable to large classes. Nachman and Opochinsky[9] found a small class to be superior to a large class on surprise quizzes, but the two classes were not significantly different on the final examination. In the Macomber and Siegel experiments at Miami University[10] significant differences favoring small classes were found on measures of change in misconceptions in psychology, on a case test of problems in a course in marketing, and on the measures of student attitudes toward all the courses. When retention of knowledge was measured one to two years after completion of the courses, in eight of the nine courses compared, small differences favored the small class.[11] Differences were also revealed in the more subtle and persisting outcomes in Feldhusen's[12] study showing that a small class in educational psychology produced more change in attitudes toward teaching than a large class.

Few of us are satisfied with achievement of knowledge if it is not remembered, if the student is unable to use it in solving problems, or if he fails to relate the knowledge to attitudes. If one takes the more basic outcomes of retention, problem

---

[6] E. Hudelson, *Class Size at the College Level* (Minneapolis: University of Minnesota Press, 1928).

[7] F. S. Cheydleur, "Criteria of Effective Teaching in Basic French Courses," *Bulletin of the University of Wisconsin*, August 1945.

[8] A. D. Mueller, "Class Size as a Factor in Normal School Instruction," *Education*, 1924, *45*, 203–27.

[9] M. Nachman and S. Opochinsky, "The Effects of Different Teaching Methods: A Methodological Study," *Journal of Educational Psychology*, 1958, *49*, 245–49.

[10] F. G. Macomber and L. Siegel, "A Study of Large Group Teaching Procedures," *Educational Research*, 1957, *38*, 220–29; *Experimental Study in Instructional Procedures*, Progress Report No. 2 (Oxford, Ohio: Miami University, 1957); *Final Report of the Experimental Study in Instructional Procedures* (Oxford, Ohio: Miami University, 1960).

[11] L. Siegel, J. F. Adams, and F. G. Macomber, "Retention of Subject Matter as a Function of Large Group Instructional Procedures," *Journal of Educational Psychology*, 1960, *51*, 9–13.

[12] J. F. Feldhusen, "The Effects of Small and Large Group Instruction on Learning of Subject Matter, Attitudes, and Interests," *Journal of Psychology*, 1963, *55*, 257–62.

solving, and attitude differentiation as ends, the evidence clearly favors small classes. Moreover, in almost all studies, students and faculty members tend to prefer small classes; other things being equal, high student and faculty morale is an asset.

As in most areas of research on college teaching, the initial interest in class size was empirical, and theoretical considerations came to the fore later. Social psychologists Thomas and Fink[13] reviewed research on face-to-face groups; they suggest that two types of input increase with increasing group size—*resource input* (skills, knowledge, and the like) and *demand input* (needs).

It is clear that the more members in the group, the greater the likelihood that some members will have resources of knowledge, intelligence, or other skills needed for the educational purposes of the group. It seems likely, however, that the amount of relevant knowledge and skills is limited, so that beyond some point additional students will contribute little that is not already in the group's resources. The group's utilization of its resources is constrained by the simple fact that (1) in large groups, a smaller proportion of group members can participate verbally, and (2) the larger the group, the less likely a given person will feel free to volunteer his contribution. As the size of the class is increased, the number of different demands or needs of members also increases. But it is unlikely that the instructor and class can meet increased, different expectations proportionately, since class time usually cannot be extended. As Stephan and Mishler[14] have shown, larger groups are more likely to be dominated by the leader, and the teacher can give less individual attention to each member. The research of McKeachie *et al.*[15] indicates that men high in the need for affiliation achieve well for teachers who take a personal interest in students; we might, then, expect such students to fare better in the smaller classes. Likewise, we might expect more frustration and dissatisfaction in larger classes unless they are relatively homogeneous.

In order to apply these general propositions to teaching, we need to ask such questions as:

In what teaching situations is amount of information in the group important? One might, for example, hypothesize that in most courses in which knowledge is the primary goal, the relevant information is contained in books and the instructor's head, and the amount added by students is likely to be inconsequential. On the other hand, if application is an important goal, amount of knowledge of application situations and of the conditions governing application contributed by students may well be significant; therefore, if Thomas and Fink's principles are valid, there may be groups too small, as well as too large, to be maximally effective.

In most courses there are several levels of goals—knowledge, critical thinking, attitudes toward learning, and so on. The teacher's task is to find a combination of methods that will achieve an optimal balance of all these. Unfortunately most teaching research has studied the effect of one method versus another painfully repeated

[13] E. J. Thomas and C. F. Fink, "The Effects of Group Size," *Psychological Bulletin*, 1963, *60*, 371–85.

[14] F. F. Stephan and E. G. Mishler, "The Distribution of Participation in Small Groups: An Experimental Approximation," *American Sociological Review*, 1952, *17*, 598–608.

[15] W. J. McKeachie, Yi-Guang Lin, John Milholland, and Robert Isaacson, "Student Affiliation Motives, Teacher Warmth, and Academic Achievement," *Journal of Personality and Social Psychology*, In press.

day after day for a semester; thus little evidence is available on the relative effectiveness of differing combinations or degrees of flexibility in teaching methods. (Some studies on lecture-discussion combinations are reviewed in the next section.)

While many teaching methods can be used in large groups, probably teaching is confined more to lecturing than in smaller classes. The large class often reduces the teacher's sense of freedom in choosing teaching methods, assigning papers, and testing to achieve various objectives. Assuming that teachers have some repertoire of skills, anything that handcuffs them is likely to be educationally damaging. This is how education is likely to be sabotaged by large classes.

What can we say about class size? It is a commonplace that the effect of size depends on the method used, and probably true that group size is less critical for success of lectures than of discussion. But analysis also suggests that the importance of size depends on educational goals. In general, large classes are simply not as effective as small classes for retention, critical thinking, and attitude change.

Lecturing

Lecture versus Discussion

Research on the lecture method is almost as hoary as that on class size. In 1925 Bane published "The Lecture vs. the Class-Discussion Method of College Teaching."[16] In five experiments, he found little difference between the methods on measures of immediate recall, but on tests given one to six months later consistent differences favored discussion. Later studies similarly have found little effect on end-of-course achievement.[17] Ruja,[18] however, found that the lecture was superior to discussion as measured by a test of subject-matter mastery in a general psychology course. In the other two courses included in his experiment, no significant differences appeared in achievement or in changes in adjustment in any of the courses. When we turn to measures of more complex outcomes, the results favor discussion. Hirschman[19] compared the effectiveness of presenting material by dictation with presenting written materials followed by discussion and rereading. The reading-discussion method resulted in superior ability to identify examples of the concepts presented.

[16] C. L. Bane, "The Lecture vs. the Class-Discussion Method of Teaching," *School and Society*, 1925, *21*, 300–302.

[17] R. B. Spence, "Lecture and Class Discussion in Teaching Educational Psychology," *Journal of Educational Psychology*, 1928, *19*, 454–62; H. H. Remmers, "Learning, Effort, and Attitudes as Affected by Three Methods of Instruction in Elementary Psychology," *Purdue University Studies in Higher Education*, 1933, *21*; R. W. Husband, "A Statistical Comparison of the Efficacy of Large vs. Smaller Recitation Sections upon Achievement in General Psychology," *Journal of Psychology*, 1951, *31*, 297–300; A. Eglash, "A Group Discussion Method of Teaching Psychology," *Journal of Educational Psychology*, 1954, *45*, 257–67; D. A. Leton, "An Evaluation of Course Methods in Teaching Child Development," *Journal of Educational Research*, 1961, *55*, 118–22.

[18] H. Ruja, "Outcomes of Lecture and Discussion Procedures in Three College Courses," *Journal of Experimental Education*, 1954, *22*, 385–94.

[19] C. S. Hirschman, "An Investigation of the Small Group Discussion Classroom Method on Criteria of Understanding, Pleasantness, and Self-confidence Induced" (Master's thesis, University of Pittsburgh, 1952).

Barnard[20] compared the effectiveness of a lecture-demonstration teaching method with that of a problem-solving developmental discussion in a college science course. In this experiment the lecture-demonstration method proved superior on a test of specific information, but the discussion method proved superior on measures of problem solving and scientific attitude. Likewise, Dawson[21] found problem-solving recitation and lecture-demonstration methods to be equally effective in a course in elementary soil science as measured by a test of recall of specific information, but the problem-solving method was significantly superior as measured by tests of problem-solving abilities.

Other evidence favoring discussion emerged from the experiment of Elliott,[22] who found that students in his discussion groups in elementary psychology became more interested in electing additional courses in psychology than were students in a large lecture. Similarly Casey and Weaver[23] found no differences in knowledge of content but superiority in attitudinal outcomes (as measured by the Minnesota Teacher Attitude Inventory) for small-group discussions as compared to lectures.

What can we say about lectures versus discussion? Since discussion offers the opportunity for a good deal of student activity and feedback, it could be (according to theory) and is (according to research results) more effective than typical lectures in developing concepts and problem-solving skills. However, because the rate of transmission of information is slow in discussion classes, we would expect lecture classes to be superior in attaining the objective of teaching knowledge. Research results tend to support this generalization and probably are not more convincing largely because the knowledge tested on course examinations usually can be learned by reading the textbook.

The Role of Lectures

The lecture continues to be the most commonly used method of teaching in colleges and universities. Although it has been severely criticized, it still should not be rejected, for research has not dealt specifically with the strongest aspects of lecturing.[24] For example, although normally one should assign reading rather than lecture when the material is available in printed form, books or printed materials are not always readily available in an appropriate form. The lecturer may be able to choose from a book those elements most needed by his class and save student time by a concise presentation.

[20] J. D. Barnard, "The Lecture-Demonstration versus the Problem-solving Method of Teaching a College Science Course," *Science Education*, 1942, *26*, 121–32.

[21] M. D. Dawson, "Lectures versus Problem-solving in Teaching Elementary Soil Sections," *Science Education*, 1956, *40*, 395–404.

[22] Elliott, reported in D. Beardslee and R. Birney, "Summary of Conference on Research in Classroom Processes" (unpublished MS, Department of Psychology, University of Michigan, 1951).

[23] J. E. Casey and B. E. Weaver, "An Evaluation of Lecture Method and Small Group Method of Teaching in Terms of Knowledge of Content, Teacher Attitude, and Social Status," *Journal of Colorado-Wyoming Academy of Science*, 1956, (4), 54.

[24] But reading's advantage of speed may be challenged by "speeded speech"—time compression of tape-recorded lectures. H. L. Fridman and D. B. Orr, "Comprehension of Speeded Speech as a Function of Practice," paper presented at American Psychological Association meeting, Sept. 3, 1965.

Moreover, a lecturer can be an effective guide to reading. By indicating the most important points, by posing questions with which students can approach their reading, by his own appreciation and interpretation of what has been assigned, the instructor can help his students develop the ability to read in his field. Presumably this role of the instructor is particularly important early in a student's entrance into a field. As the student gains experience, the lecturer can rely more and more on the student to get information from reading and cut down the proportion of time devoted to lecturing. Unfortunately in most courses the size of class and characteristics of the classroom lock us in so that such flexibility is difficult to realize.

As reading materials carry an increasing portion of the task of communication of knowledge, the lecturers' role becomes that of presenting new materials not yet in print. The lecture is the newspaper or journal of teaching; it, more than any other teaching, must be up to date.

Distribution of Lecture and Discussion Time

Many universities and large colleges use a method of distributing class meetings between lectures and discussions. This administrative arrangement is supported by studies in psychology[25] and physics.[26] In general, the more course time devoted to recitations in proportion to lectures, the better is student achievement. The conclusion to be drawn from these studies seems to be that a combination of large lecture and small discussion sections is preferable to the common arrangement of several sections of unwieldy medium size.

To summarize: What is the role of the lecturer in higher education? The research results cited provide little basis for an answer. Nevertheless, they do not contradict and sometimes support the notion that the lecture is a useful way of communicating information, particularly in classes where the use of printed materials is impractical. A good deal of evidence, however, sugests that discussion is more effective than lecturing in achieving the more complex cognitive and attitudinal objectives.

Discussion Methods

The chief alternative to lecture is discussion. What theoretical concepts are apposite to the relative effectiveness of various types of discussion methods both alone and in combination with other teaching methods?

Active versus passive learning: Lectures usually place the learner in a passive role,

25 N. Lifson, P. Rempel, and J. A. Johnson, "A Comparison Between Lecture and Conference Methods of Teaching Psychology," *Journal of Medical Education,* 1956, *31,* 376–82; M. J. Eash and C. M. Bennett, "The Effect of Class Size on Achievement and Attitudes," *American Educational Research Journal,* 1964, *1,* 229–39; H. H. Remmers, "Learning, Effort, and Attitudes as Affected by Three Methods of Instruction in Elementary Psychology," *Purdue University Studies in Higher Education,* 1933, *21.*
26 O. E. Lancaster, K. V. Manning, M. W. White, and other members of the Physics Department, Pennsylvania State University, "The Relative Merits of Lecture and Recitation in Teaching College Physics," *Journal of Engineering Education,* 1961, *51,* 425–53; R. Warren, "A Comparison of Two Plans of Study in Engineering Physics" (doctoral dissertation, Purdue University, 1954 [*Dissertation Abstracts,* 1954, *14,* 1648–49]).

and passive learning is generally less efficient than active learning. Bloom and his colleagues at the University of Chicago used recordings of classes to stimulate students to recall their thoughts during class.[27] As predicted, they found that more active thinking was stimulated by discussion than by lecture classes.

Practice and feedback: If students are to achieve application, critical thinking, or some higher cognitive outcomes, a reasonable assumption is that they should have an opportunity to practice application and critical thinking and to receive feedback on the results. Although teaching machines and mock-ups may also be programed to provide prompt and realistic feedback, group discussion permits presentation of a variety of problems that allow a number of people to gain experience in integrating facts, formulating hypotheses, amassing relevant evidence, and evaluating conclusions. In fact, the prompt feedback from the teaching machine may actually be less effective than a method in which students are encouraged to discover solutions for themselves with less step-by-step guidance.[28]

Motivation: A decade or two ago psychologists discussing motivation would have talked about reward and punishment and suggested that teachers look at the rewards for learning in the classroom. Rewards and punishments do play an important role in determining what we learn. But the revolution in motivation research and theory lies in new evidence that Man is naturally curious. He seeks new experiences; he enjoys learning new things; he finds satisfaction in solving a puzzle or developing a skill.

How does this generalization apply to learning in college? It is tempting to answer in vague phrases such as: "varied teaching methods," "posing new, but soluble problems," or "setting realistic standards of achievement." But we can go beyond this. One hint comes from studies by Berlyne.[29] He found that asking students questions, rather than presenting statements of fact, not only improves learning but also increases interest in learning more about the topic. Questions, he found, are particularly effective in arousing curiosity about things that are already familiar, and the most successful questions are those that are most unexpected. This checks with the finding that National Merit scholars describe the classes which influenced their choice of field to be ones where they didn't know what to expect next.[30] The interplay between familiar and novel may thus be a very significant factor in developing curiosity. Thus, the unsettling lack of certainty about "where we're going" may be one of the assets of the discussion method.[31]

[27] B. S. Bloom, "Thought Processes in Lectures and Discussions," *Journal of General Education*, 1953, *7*, 160–69.

[28] G. M. Della-Piana, "Two Experimental Feedback Procedures: A Comparison of Their Effects on the Learning of Concepts" (doctoral dissertation, University of Illinois, 1956 [*Dissertation Abstracts*, 1956, *16*, 910–11]).

[29] D. E. Berlyne, *Conflict, Arousal, and Curiosity* (New York: McGraw-Hill Book Co., 1960).

[30] D. L. Thistlethwaite, "College Press and Changes in Study Plans of Talented Students" (Evanston, Ill.: National Merit Scholarship Corp., 1960).

[31] Having everything wrapped up neatly by the instructor may reduce motivation for further thought and work. See R. C. Craig, "Discovery, Task Completion, and the Assignment as Factors in Motivation," *American Educational Research Journal*, 1965, *2*, 217–22.

Group Variables

A final theory to be considered in discussion methods derives from social and clinical psychological studies of attitudinal and personality change. Failure to achieve some goals of learning may not be due to lack of intelligence or deficiencies in the materials presented but rather to emotional barriers in the learner. For example, a student of literature may fail to see the essential elements of a novel because it comes too close to his own problems; a mathematics student may have a block against mathematics; a history student may resist materials counter to his concept of American idealism; a potentially creative student may inhibit his intuitions because of insecurity.

Psychotherapists and social psychologists believe that expressing one's attitude in a non-threatening situation may help "unfreeze" the attitude. Group discussion may provide opportunities for such expression as well as give opportunities for members to express other attitudes that may be instrumental to meeting the individual's needs. Most attitudes influencing learning have some interpersonal antecedents and are stabilized by one's perception of the attitudes of other liked persons. Group discussion may facilitate a high degree of liking for the instructor and for other group members. It also permits more accurate assessment of group norms than is likely to occur in other techniques of instruction. In fact, while individual instruction is advantageous for many teaching purposes, group processes provide a real advantage in bringing about changes in motivation and attitudes. Lewin[32] showed in his classic experiments on group decision that sometimes change is easier for a group than for an individual.

Whether or not discussions actually are superior in these theoretical respects cannot be easily determined, for discussions range from monologues, in which occasional questions are interposed, to bull sessions in which the instructor is an interested (or bored) observer. Nevertheless, a good deal of research has attempted to compare the effectiveness of various discussion techniques.

Student-Centered versus Instructor-Centered Teaching

A wide variety of teaching methods are described by labels: "student-centered," "non-directive," "group-centered," and "democratic" discussion. They have in common the desire to break away from the traditional instructor-dominated classroom and to encourage greater student participation and responsibility.

Theoretically, student-centered teaching in its more extreme forms might be expected to have some serious weaknesses, at least in achieving lower-level cognitive goals. With the instructor's role as information-giver reduced, his role as source of feedback virtually eliminated, and his opportunity to provide organization and structure curtailed, it is apparent that a heavy burden falls upon the group member to carry out any of these functions that are necessary. Since student-centered teaching attempts to reduce dependence upon the instructor, it would be expected to

---

[32] K. Lewin, "Group Decision and Social Change," *Readings in Social Psychology*, ed. G. E. Swanson, T. M. Newcomb, and E. L. Hartley (2d ed.; New York: Henry Holt & Co., 1952), pp. 330–44.

diminish his influence as a prestige figure. However, this may be more than compensated for by increased freedom of expression and increased potency of group norms as sources of influence. I have reviewed the research on student-centered teaching elsewhere.[33] The results are not conclusive, but tend to support this theory. There seem to be few instances of loss in achievement of knowledge in student-centered classes. Students apparently can get information from textbooks as well as from the instructor.

In eleven studies, significant differences in ability to apply concepts, in attitudes, in motivation, and in group membership skills have been found between discussion techniques emphasizing freer student participation compared with discussion with greater instructor dominance. In ten of these the differences favored the student-centered method. The eleventh[34] had mixed results. Thistlethwaite[35] found that National Merit scholars check as one of the outstanding characteristics of the teachers who contributed most to their desire to learn, "allowing time for classroom discussion." Other characteristics mentioned included "modifying course content to meet students' needs and interests," "treating students as colleagues," and "taking a personal interest in students." However, in line with the earlier discussion of feedback, another trait mentioned was "providing evaluations reassuring the student of his creative or productive potentialities."

A recently completed, and as yet unpublished, study by a University of Michigan research group has also shown that psychology instructors whose students do best on tests of psychological thinking (with intelligence controlled) tend to be described as follows:

He listened attentively to what class members had to say.
He was friendly.
He was permissive and flexible.
He explained the reasons for criticism.
Things are explained clearly.
He is skillful in observing student reactions.

Both the Thistlethwaite and the Michigan results support the value of student-centered teaching for motivation and critical thinking.

The choice of instructor-centered versus student-centered discussion thus appears to depend upon one's goals. The more highly one values outcomes going beyond knowledge acquisition, the more likely that student-centered methods will be preferred.

Reading, Programed Learning, and Independent Study

One of the newest developments in higher education which has received much less publicity than television and teaching machines but probably will have more

[33] W. J. McKeachie, *Teaching Tips: A Guide-Book for the Beginning College Teacher* (Ann Arbor Mich.: George Wahr Publishing Co., 1965).

[34] H. Guetzkow, E. L. Kelly, and W. J. McKeachie, "An Experimental Comparison of Recitation, Discussion, and Tutorial Methods in College Teaching," *Journal of Educational Psychology*, 1954, 45, 193–209.

[35] D. L. Thistlethwaite, "College Press and Changes in Study Plans of Talented Students" (Evanston, Ill.: National Merit Scholarship Corp., 1960).

long-term significance for higher education is the revolution in the use of printed materials, such as paperback books, off-prints of journal articles, facsimile or micro-film copies, and other duplicated materials. Not only is the student now able to own a richer variety of resources, but, in addition, the new open-stack libraries invite him to go beyond his assignments to books and journals giving other viewpoints and additional information.

In discussions of the remarkable values of bringing "master teachers" to all learn-ers through television, we often overlook the fact that through books and printed materials the student can follow the teaching of a master teacher and, further, can choose from among a number of master teachers the one who best communicates to him.

An early study[36] found that students learned as thoroughly from reading material as from listening to it. The better students, moreover, profited more from reading than from listening. A number of other studies have compared printed materials with lectures, with results favoring print, at least with difficult materials.[37] However, the amount of research on books and articles as teaching media is small, considering their widespread use. There have, however, been studies of size of print, readability, and the effectiveness of illustrations. (Illustrations apparently don't contribute much to learning as measured by conventional tests.)

Programed Instruction

One of the newest developments in textbooks is the programed textbook, an in-structional book that uses the learning-in-small-steps sequence of the teaching machine. Such books and pamphlets are often designed as adjuncts to conventional teaching materials.

The teaching machine is a device for presenting questions in a predetermined sequence and providing immediate knowledge of results to an active learner. The questions proceed in tiny steps from the simple to the complex and permit the learner to proceed at his own rate. With some machines, the student may, if he makes a series of correct responses, adjust the machine to skip some steps; if he fails items, they are repeated.

There have been two general approaches to the use of teaching machines. In the early investigations of Pressey and his students, the teaching machine was used primarily as a device to provide prompt knowledge of results of conventional testing procedures. As a testing machine, it was simply a supplement to conventional teach-ing methods such as lectures, discussion, and textbook assignments. The second approach, originated by Skinner and his followers, substitutes the teaching machine for other teaching methods: it is used either as the sole instrument of instruction or at least as a major method to be supplemented by the teacher. In some cases the

[36] E. B. Greene, "Relative Effectiveness of Lecture and Individual Reading as Methods of College Teaching," *Genetic Psychology Monographs*, 1928, *4*, 457–563.
[37] For a review of these studies, see F. R. Hartman, "Single and Multiple Channel Com-munication: A Review of Research and a Proposed Model," *Audio-Visual Communication Review*, 1961, *9*, 235–62.

"program" (the series of questions or statements presented to the student) is presented in a text or workbook, and "programed instruction" is now used to refer to any carefully sequenced presentation, whether by teaching machine, book, lecture, film, or television.

Some of the research evidence supports the use of teaching-testing machines as supplements to conventional instruction. In addition to Pressey's early work, Angell,[38] Peterson and Peterson,[39] and Stephens[40] found that knowledge of results on a quiz or special answer sheets was more effective when it was immediate than when delayed until the next class meeting. The research with Skinnerian types of programs has been less encouraging. Students do learn from the programs, but learning is generally slower than with conventional printed materials (but faster than lectures).[41] In some cases, achievement is higher for the programed learners,[42] and one must judge whether the extra investment in time is justified by the gain in learning. In other cases learning from programs is less than learning from conventional sources.[43]

The controversy about whether the student needs to make a response has largely abated. If the response itself must be learned, as in the teaching of typewriting or a new vocabulary, an overt response is required, but in most college courses the responses required are already in the student's repertoire and he learns more rapidly by not stopping to fill in blanks.[44]

Little research has been done to determine what kinds of students learn well or poorly from programs and what types of objectives can be achieved most efficiently. It might be expected that programs written so that every question is answered cor-

38 G. W. Angell, "Effect of Immediate Knowledge of Quiz Results on Final Examination Scores in Freshman Chemistry," *Journal of Educational Research*, 1949, *42*, 391–94.

39 H. J. and J. C. Peterson, "The Value of Guidance in Reading for Information," *Transactions of the Kansas Academy of Science*, 1931, *34*, 291–96.

40 A. L. Stephens, "Certain Special Factors Involved in the Law of Effect," *Abstracts of Doctoral Dissertations*, No. 64 (Columbus: Ohio State University, 1953).

41 N. H. Smith, "The Teaching of Elementary Statistics by the Conventional Classroom Method versus the Method of Programmed Instruction," *Journal of Educational Research*, 1962, *55*, 417–20.

42 For example, see Joanna P. Williams, "Comparison of Several Response Modes in a Review Program," *Journal of Educational Psychology*, 1963, *54*, 253–60.

43 For example, J. J. Wulff and D. L. Emeson, "The Relationship between 'What Is Learned' and 'How It Is Taught,'" *Student Response in Programmed Learning: A Symposium*, ed. A. A. Lumsdaine (Washington: National Academy of Sciences—National Research Council, 1961); chap. 30 reported that in learning the names of electrical circuits, students did better by studying alone than in learning from a structured program. Also see C. G. Zuckerman, G. R. Marshall, and S. Groesberg, *Research in the Automation of Teaching*, NAVTRADEVCEN 666-1 (Port Washington, N.Y.: U.S. Naval Training Device Center, February 1961); J. F. Follettie, "Effects of Training Response Mode, Test Form, and Measure on Acquisition of Semi-ordered Factual Materials," Research Memorandum 24 (Mimeographed; Fort Benning, Ga.: U.S. Army Infantry Human Research Unit, April 1961); M. E. Feldman, "Learning by Programmed and Text Format at 3 Levels of Difficulty," *Journal of Educational Psychology*, 1965, *56*, 133–39.

W. H. Bartz and C. L. Darby, "A Study of Supervised and Nonsupervised Programmed Instruction in the University Setting," *Journal of Educational Research*, 1965, *58*, 208–11, found that *supervised* programed instruction was not inferior to formal instruction even though unsupervised programed instruction was inferior.

44 A. A. Lumsdaine and M. A. May, "Mass Communication and Educational Media," *Annual Review of Psychology*, 1965, *16*, 475–534.

rectly by almost every student would bore most students, particularly those with strong achievement motivation, and this is affirmed by Moore, Smith, and Teevan.[45] A study by Lublin[46] found that performance was better with variable reinforcement or without reinforcement as compared with consistent reinforcement. A less expected but reasonable finding is that students scoring high on a sociability test do poorly with programed instruction.[47]

The furore about teaching machines and programed learning is subsiding, and research is beginning to clarify effective and ineffective uses.[48] Present programs are not panaceas for the problems of American higher education. For a while it appeared that programed materials might give educators a shortcut in the difficult problems of curriculum and course organization, but now it is recognized that writing a good program requires just as much scholarship as writing a good textbook.[49] Programing is hard work, and so far scholars seem less willing to write programs than books. As of now the number of good programs for college use is very limited, and programs adapted to computer-assisted instruction are almost nonexistent.

Programing has also suffered from a lack of evaluation. To many advocates of programed instruction, it has seemed self-evident that anyone who completes a program successfully has learned—he has achieved the goals of the program. Professors like to make this same assumption about their lectures; yet most of them have had the disheartening experience of finding that points made crystal clear in a brilliant lecture have not sunk into the awareness of their students sufficiently to be used in responding to an examination question. One of the problems for programers of college materials is that, in general, they are working at a level of conceptualization where the required response is only one of the class of related responses to a group of stimuli. Sometimes the programer provides irrelevant cues, to which the student learns to make the desired response; at other times the response required is irrelevant to the goals—simply indicates that the student read the frame, as when he is asked to fill in a trivial word.

Some program writers have recognized the importance of a separate testing of learning, but such tests frequently contain items or paraphrases of items from the program. Correct answers then are not accurate measures since a high score might be

[45] J. W. Moore, W. I. Smith, and R. Teevan, "Motivational Variables in Programmed Learning: The Role of Need Achievement, Fear of Failure, and Student Estimate of Achievement as a Function of Program Difficulty," Final Report: USOE, Title VII, Grant No. 7-48-0070-149.1.

[46] Shirley Lublin, "Reinforcement Schedules, Scholastic Aptitude, Autonomy Need, and Achievement in a Programmed Course," *Journal of Educational Psychology*, 1965, *56*, 295–302.

[47] Barbara and L. A. Doty, "Programmed Instructional Effectiveness in Relation to Certain Student Characteristics," *Journal of Educational Psychology*, 1964, *55*, 334–38.

[48] An excellent review of this literature appears in A. A. Lumsdaine and M. A. May, "Mass Communication and Educational Media," *Annual Review of Psychology*, 1965, *16*, 475–534, and in more length in A. A. Lumsdaine, "Instruments and Media of Instruction," *Handbook of Research on Teaching*, ed. N. L. Gage (Chicago: Rand McNally & Co., 1963), pp. 583–682.

[49] For example, see J. D. Krumboltz, "The Nature and Importance of the Required Response in Programmed Instruction," *American Educational Research Journal*, 1964, *1*, 203–9.

obtained by someone who has learned to respond to irrelevant cues or who has learned only the specific responses taught without grasping the principle or concept. Ideally, achievement should be measured by a test as different as possible from the program items.

The programed learning movement has had the healthy effect of forcing clarification of educational objectives. But after obtaining a precise list, the programed learning protagonists have tended to dismiss as unreal any objectives that were not specified at a level appropriate for programing and have, instead, prepared programs that had trivial objectives. Disillusionment with the movement has arisen in part when, once a program has been written, educators have too often discovered that what it taught was not really what their students needed to learn.

Despite these problems, programed learning is here to stay and will make a real contribution to higher education. Few teachers enjoy the role of drill master; yet drill seems necessary if students are to master certain necessary facts, schemata, and responses. Here, at least, is a task programs can perform, freeing the instructor for other functions. More than this is also possible. Computers can individualize instruction as printed programs do not. With computers, the motivational value of unexpectedness can be retained. Frase[50] has even experimented with the effects of varying praise and reproof upon programed learning for students differing in aggression, deference, and other personality characteristics. The Socratic dialogue, which was the rallying cry of teaching machine salesmen, can become reality. We have not yet explored the full potential of programing, for it is, in essence, simply careful, systematic educational planning.

Independent Study

One of the advantages of programed materials is that they can be used with relatively little teacher supervision; they force the student to read carefully and actively. Thus the programed learning movement has looked for allies among the proponents of independent study. If one goal of education is to help the student develop the ability to continue learning after his formal education is complete, it seems reasonable that he should have supervised experience in learning independently—experience in which the instructor helps the student learn how to formulate problems, find answers, and evaluate his own progress.

Independent study has a strong kinship with the project method, which became popular a generation ago. The results of research are not particularly encouraging. One of the first "independent study" experiments was that of Seashore.[51] His course consisted primarily of guided individual study with written reports on eight projects, each of which took about a month to complete. Final examination scores, however, were no different for these students than for students taught by the usual lecture-

50 L. T. Frase, "The Effect of Social Reinforcers in a Programed Learning Task," Nonr. 1834 (36), Technical Reports, No. 11 (Urbana, Ill.: Training Research Laboratory, University of Illinois, 1963).

51 C. E. Seashore, "Elementary Psychology: An Outline of a Course by the Project Method," Aims and Progress Research, No. 153 (Iowa City: University of Iowa, 1928).

discussion method.[52] In a study in a college botany course, Novak found[53] that students in conventional classes learned more facts than did those taught by the project method. Similarly, Goldstein[54] reports that students taught pharmacology by a project method did not learn more than those taught in a standard laboratory.

Unfortunately, measures of achievement such as those just noted are probably insufficient measures of the purported objectives of project instruction. Presumably the real superiority of the project method should be revealed in measures of motivation and resourcefulness. One morsel of support is Thistlethwaite's[55] finding that National Merit scholars checked requirement of a term paper or laboratory project as one characteristic of their most stimulating course, but most research on independent study has failed to find expected gains in motivation, learning, or even independence.[56]

As yet few studies have attempted to assess the unique learning of each group from classroom lectures and discussion or from additional reading.

The most favorable results on independent study were obtained in the experiments at the University of Colorado by Gruber and Weitman.[57] In a course in freshman English in which the group met only about 90 percent of the regularly scheduled hours and had little formal training in grammar, the self-directed study group was significantly superior to control groups on a test of grammar. In a course in physical optics, groups of students who attended class without the instructor (but were free to consult him) remembered fewer facts and simple applications, yet were superior to students in conventional classes in difficult applications and learning new material. Moreover, the latter difference was maintained in a retest three months later, although the difference in factual knowledge had disappeared.[58] An experimental class in educational psychology which met once a week with the instructor and twice a week in groups of five or six students without the instructor was equal or superior to a conventional three-lectures-a-week class in mastery of content, did more serious reading after the course, and tended to be superior on

[52] Norma V. Scheidemann, "An Experiment in Teaching Psychology," *Journal of Applied Psychology*, 1929, *13*, 188–91.

[53] J. D. Novak, "An Experimental Comparison of a Conventional and a Project Centered Method of Teaching a College General Botany Course," *Journal of Experimental Education*, 1958, *26*, 217–30.

[54] A. Goldstein, "A Controlled Comparison of the Project Method with Standard Laboratory Teaching in Pharmacology," *Journal of Medical Education*, 1956, *31*, 365–75.

[55] D. L. Thistlethwaite, "College Press and Changes in Study Plans of Talented Students" (Evanston, Ill.: National Merit Scholarship Corp., 1960).

[56] See W. J. McKeachie, "Research on Teaching at the College and University Level," *Handbook of Research on Teaching*, ed. N. L. Gage (Chicago: Rand McNally & Co., 1963), pp. 1118–72. Also see R. E. Ulrich and S. I. Pray, "Comparison of Directed Self-study versus Lecture in Teaching General Psychology," *Psychology Reports*, 1965, *16*, 278, and P. W. Caro, "The Effect of Class Attendance and 'Time Structured' Content on Achievement in General Psychology," *Journal of Educational Psychology*, 1962, *53*, 76–80.

[57] H. E. Gruber and M. Weitman, "Cognitive Processes in Higher Education: Curiosity and Critical Thinking," Paper read at Western Psychological Association, San Jose, Calif., April 1960.

[58] M. Weitman and H. E. Gruber, "Experiments in Self-directed Study: Effects on Immediate Achievement, Permanence of Achievement and Educational Values," Paper read at Western Psychological Association, San Jose, Calif., April 1960.

measures of curiosity. Beach[59] found similar results for self-directed student groups at Whitworth College: as compared with classroom groups, the self-directed groups were superior in quantity and quality of study, amount of required and non-required reading, and publications consulted in writing term papers. These are the kinds of results that are the objectives of independent study.

The experiment reported by McKeachie, Lin, Forrin, and Teevan[60] also involved contact with the instructor, in this case at least biweekly. The results suggest that the "tutorial" students did not learn as much from the textbook as did students taught in conventional lecture and discussion section classes, but did develop stronger motivation both for course work and for continued learning after the course.

Typically, knowledge of specific facts is not the major objective of an independent study program: what we are hoping for is greater integration, increased purposefulness, and more intense motivation for further study. That independent study can achieve these ends is indicated by the Colorado, Whitworth, and Michigan experiments. But the paucity of positive results suggests that we need more research on methods of selecting and training students for independent study, arranging the independent study experience, and measuring outcomes.

Laboratory Methods

The activity of the student and the frequent individualization of laboratory instruction should, theoretically, contribute positively to learning. However, information usually cannot be obtained as rapidly by direct experience as from abstractions presented orally or by printing. Films, demonstrations, ready-made drawings, and labeled photomicrographs may also short-cut some of the trial and error of the laboratory.[61] Thus, laboratory teaching would not likely have an advantage over other teaching methods in information gained; rather, the differences should be revealed in retention, in ability to apply learning, or in skill in observation or manipulation of materials. Unfortunately, little research has attempted to tease out these special types of outcome.

In experiments in physics and engineering, Kruglak[62] and White[63] found that

59 L. R. Beach, "Self-directed Groups and Student Learning," *Approach to Independent Study*, compiled by W. R. Hatch and Alice Richards, New Dimensions in Higher Education, No. 13, OE–50041 (Washington: Government Printing Office, 1965). Also see L. R. Beach, "Sociability and Achievement in Various Types of Learning Situations," *Journal of Educational Psychology*, 1960, *51*, 208–12.

60 W. J. McKeachie, Yi-Guang Lin, B. Forrin, and R. Teevan, "Individualized Teaching in Elementary Psychology," *Journal of Educational Psychology*, 1960, *51*, 285–91.

61 For example, see W. T. Stickley, "The Evaluation of a Film Program Technique for Self-instruction in Medical Pharmacology," *Dissertation Abstracts*, 1966, *26*, 4462; L. E. Taylor, "Ready Made Drawings with Relation to Student Achievement," *School and Society*, 1930, *32*, 371–74; and J. D. Novak, "The Use of Labeled Photomicrographs in Teaching College General Botany," *Science Education*, 1961, *45*, 119–31.

62 H. Kruglak, "Experimental Outcomes of Laboratory Instructions in Elementary College Physics," *American Journal of Physics*, 1952, *20*, 136–41.

63 J. R. White, "Methods in Engineering Laboratory Instruction," *Journal of Engineering Education*, 1945, *36*, 50–54.

students taught by individual or group laboratory methods achieved more than those taught by lecture-demonstration. In contrast, in studies by Balcziak,[64] Dearden,[65] and Trotter,[66] individual laboratory was combined with (1) lecture-demonstration, (2) combined demonstration and laboratory, (3) workbook, and (4) term paper in physical science, general biology, and home economics courses, and no significant differences were found between the methods as measured by tests of information, practical application, scientific attitude, and laboratory performance. Also earlier experiments[67] found no significant loss resulting from reduction of laboratory time or assigning one cadaver to four students rather than to two.

Bainter[68] found that a problem-solving method was superior to traditional laboratory manual methods in teaching students to apply principles of physics in interpreting phenomena. Lahti[69] also found problem solving to be superior to more conventional procedures in developing ability to design experiments. Because many laboratory teachers have been interested in teaching problem-solving methods, this may also be an appropriate place to note Burkhardt's finding[70] that students who are taught the calculus with an emphasis on the understanding of concepts learn concepts better than students taught with conventional emphasis upon solving problems. Although this finding appears to controvert the results of Kruglak, Bainter, and Lahti, actually all of them point to the importance of developing understanding rather than teaching solution of problems by routine steps. Whether or not laboratory is superior to lecture-demonstration in developing understanding and problem-solving skills probably depends upon the amount of emphasis placed on understanding of concepts and on general problem-solving procedures.

[64] L. W. Balcziak, "The Role of the Laboratory and Demonstration in College Physical Science in Achieving the Objectives of General Education" (Doctoral dissertation, University of Minnesota, 1953 [*Dissertation Abstracts*, 1955, *15*, 2485–86]).

[65] D. M. Dearden, "An Evaluation of the Laboratory in a College General Biology Course," *Journal of Experimental Education*, 1960, *28*, 241–47.

[66] Virginia Trotter, "A Comparison of the Laboratory and the Lecture Demonstration Methods of Teaching Survey of Food Preparation for Freshman Home Economics Students at the University of Vermont," abstract of research done for the doctoral dissertation at Ohio State University, 1960.

[67] R. E. Downing, "Methods in Science Teaching," *Journal of Higher Education*, 1931, *2*, 316–20; A. W. Hurd, *Problems of Science Teaching at the College Level* (Minneapolis: University of Minnesota Press, 1929); also, C. M. Jackson, "Experiment in Methods of Teaching Gross Human Anatomy," *Problems of College Education* by E. Hudelson (Minneapolis: University of Minnesota Press, 1929), pp. 444–49; V. H. Noll, *Laboratory Instruction in the Field of Inorganic Chemistry* (Minneapolis: University of Minnesota Press, 930); V. H. Noll, "The Optimum Laboratory Emphasis in College Chemistry," *School and Society*, 1930, *32*, 300–303.

[68] Monica Bainter, "A Study of the Outcomes of Two Types of Laboratory Techniques Used in a Course in General College Physics for Student Planning To Be Teachers in the Elementary Grades" (Doctoral dissertation, University of Minnesota, 1953 [*Dissertation Abstracts*, 1954, *14*, 502–3]).

[69] A. M. Lahti, "The Inductive-deductive Method and the Physical Science Laboratory," *Journal of Experimental Education*, 1956, *24*, 149–63.

[70] Sara Burkhardt, "A Study in Concept Learning in Differential Calculus" (Doctoral dissertation, Columbia University, 1956).

Simulation

As remote terminals of computers begin to sprout throughout the campus, I predict that simulation will replace television, independent study, and programed instruction as the glamour method in the 1970's. Simulation does not necessitate the use of a computer, but computers can provide rapid calculations and prompt feedback on the results of decisions. According to theory, the active participation, uncertainty about outcome, and prompt feedback should be motivating and effective for learning.

Presumably simulation can be used in almost any subject matter. For example, in science courses, the variables and equations of a theory can be programed into a computer and students given the task of designing experiments to run on the computer to test their hypotheses about "nature" as represented in the computer.[71] However, simulation is currently most used in teaching political science and business courses, although there are some educational games in courses in education and other fields.

"Games" or simulations are ordinarily intended to develop skills in making decisions, to give students understanding of the principal parameters of a field and of the complexity of interactions, and to develop motivation for learning. Although millions of dollars have been spent in developing simulations, I can find only two college-level studies evaluating their effectiveness.[72] In neither study was simulation more effective than other methods. This should not lead to the conclusion that the method should be abandoned. As we have seen in our evaluation of other teaching methods, the gap between theory and research findings has narrowed only as one was able to view the results of a number of studies. The studies to date should dampen the uncritical enthusiasm that often accompanies innovations, but the findings contain enough glimmerings of pay dirt to justify further research.

Audio-visual Devices

Most higher education is verbal and conceptual. Words are wonderfully efficient substitutes for direct sensory experiences, but on occasion visual identification, discrimination, or eye-hand responses are important goals of education. In such cases, audio-visual aids may substitute for direct experience.

71 This technique was developed by the late Paul Fitts who used it in teaching his course Principles of Research Design in the Department of Psychology, University of Michigan.

72 In the study by G. L. Hershey, L. V. Shepard, and J. D. Krumboltz, "Effectiveness of Classroom Observation and Simulated Teaching in an Introductory Educational Psychology Course," *Journal of Educational Research*, 1965, *58*, 233–36, participation in simulated teaching experiences was not significantly different in effect on knowledge, attitudes, and career plans from actual classroom observation (presumably a plus for simulation). In J. A. Robinson, R. C. Snyder, L. F. Anderson, and Margaret Hermann, "A Comparison of Simulation, Case Studies, and Problem Papers in Teaching Decision-making," Cooperative Research Project No. 1568 (Evanston, Ill.: Northwestern University, 1964), simulation was compared with case studies in a sophisticated study. Women high in need for power in the simulation groups developed more interest in the subject and read more than similar women in case study, and simulation tended to develop more interest generally according to three criteria; learning of facts or principles was not significantly different.

Television

The most widely publicized solution to teaching greater numbers of college students has been the use of closed-circuit television to bring a single teacher to several classrooms. Although some experiments were not sufficiently well designed to permit evaluation, there are probably more good comparisons of television and live instruction than of any other teaching methods. The results are also much more consistent than are any other comparisons. Of the 33 experiments at the college level in which controls were reasonably adequate, 27 produced greater learning in the "live" classes than in those taught by television.[73] Most of these differences were not statistically significant by themselves but their consistency is statistically significant. One can thus conclude that television is generally not as effective as face-to-face instruction.

The conclusion, however, isn't this simple. In the first place, goals of instruction are important. While television instruction seems to be inferior, on the basis of results on the types of measures used, there is still a hidden criterion problem that troubles most research on teaching. Television should be at its best in teaching visual recognition and form discrimination. The tests of achievement, however, are almost entirely verbal. Therefore, the results do not disclose whether television students are better able to recognize or evaluate some visual properties because these outcomes have not been measured. Where there are courses in which visual skills are important objectives, television might be expected to be superior to conventional instruction.

A second condition upon the simplicity of the conclusion that television is inefficient is the instructor. There is some evidence in both Army and college studies that certain instructors blossom before the TV cameras and actually are more effective than in their ordinary classes. Others, however, freeze when the camera red light goes on.

A third variable is the student, and a fourth is the instructional methods used. Complex interactions of these variables occur.[74]

Films

Like the advocates of television and teaching machines, educational film experts have been frustrated by lack of acceptance by college faculties. The only difference is that for the audio-visual aid protagonists the frustration has now subsided into a dull pain; after some forty years of experience they no longer cherish a vision of leading a revolution that will topple existing teaching methods. Films have found a modicum of acceptance; good films are available in most fields, and most professors

---

[73] For a detailed review, see W. J. McKeachie, "Research on Teaching at the College and University Level," *Handbook of Research on Teaching*, ed. N. L. Gage (Chicago: Rand McNally & Co., 1963), pp. 1118–72. See also W. Schramm, "What We Know about Learning from Instructional Television," *Educational Television: The Next Ten Years* (Stanford, Calif.: Institute for Communication Research, 1962); Schramm reports 13 significant differences favoring live teaching versus three favoring television.

[74] L. and Lila Siegel, "The Instructional Gestalt: A Conceptual Framework and Design for Educational Research," *Audio-Visual Communication Review*, 1964, *12*, 16–45.

are willing to accept their educational value (when used sparingly; the professor who uses many films still is assumed to be shirking his work).

Most of the research on educational films has been carried out by the Armed Forces or in elementary schools. Although it is not appropriate to review this research in detail, certain emerging principles seem relevant to our purposes.[75]

1. Students can learn from films, and usually do learn at least as much as from a poor teacher.[76]

2. Such learning is not confined to details, but may include concepts and attitudes.[77]

3. Outline material such as titles and commentary increase learning if a film is not well organized.[78]

4. For less intelligent students, repeating the film increases learning.[79]

5. Students learn how to learn from films; that is, students with previous experience with instructional films learn more than students without previous experience, especially students with little previous knowledge of the film subject matter.[80]

6. Presenting pictures is more effective than presenting words as stimuli in rote association tasks such as learning a foreign language.[81]

7. Participation increases learning.[82] In this study, active response with prompting and feedback was most effective on the most difficult material with the least moti-

[75] For a more complete analysis, see N. M. Miller, "Scientific Principles of Maximum Learning from Motion Pictures," *Audio-Visual Communication Review, Graphic Communication*, 1957, 5, 61–113. Air Force research is summarized and integrated with concepts from programmed learning in A. A. Lumsdaine (ed.), *Student Response in Programmed Instruction: A Symposium* (Washington: National Academy of Sciences—National Research Council, 1961).

[76] A. W. VanderMeer, *Relative Effectiveness of Instruction by Films Exclusively, Films Plus Study Guides, and Standard Lecture Methods, Instructional Film Research Report* SDC 269-7-12 (Special Devices Center, Office of Naval Research, July 1950).

[77] J. P. Kishler, "The Effects of Prestige and Identification Factors on Attitude Restructuring and Learning from Sound Films," Technical Report SDC 269-7-10 (Port Washington, N.Y.: U.S. Naval Training Device Center, Office of Naval Research, 1950); Marjorie S. Mertens, *The Effects of Mental Hygiene Films on Self Regarding Attitudes*, Pennsylvania State University Instructional Film Research Program, Technical Report No. SDC 269-7-22 (Port Washington, N.Y.: U.S. Naval Training Device Center, Office of Naval Research, July 1951); C. F. Hoban, Jr., and E. B. Van Ormer, *Instructional Film Research, 1918–1950*, Pennsylvania State University Instructional Film Research Program, Technical Report No. SDC 269-7-19 (Port Washington, N.Y.: U.S. Naval Training Device Center, Office of Naval Research, 1950).

[78] D. S. Northrop, *Effects on Learning of the Prominence of Organizational Outlines in Instructional Films*, Pennsylvania State University Instructional Film Research Program, Human Engineering Report SDC 269-7-33 (Port Washington, N.Y.: U.S. Naval Training Device Center, Office of Naval Research, October 1952).

[79] C. L. McTavish, *Effect of Repetitive Film Showings on Learning*, Pennsylvania State University Instructional Film Research Program, Technical Report No. SDC 269-7-12 (Port Washington, N.Y.: U.S. Naval Training Device Center, Office of Naval Research, November 1949).

[80] A. W. VanderMeer, *Effect of Film-viewing Practice on Learning from Instructional Films*, Pennsylvania State University Instructional Film Research Program, Technical Report No. SDC 269-7-20 (Port Washington, N.Y.: U.S. Naval Training Device Center, Office of Naval Research, November 1951).

[81] F. F. Kopstein and S. M. Roshal, "Learning Foreign Vocabulary from Pictures vs. Words," *American Psychologist*, 1954, 9, 407–8.

[82] C. I. Hovland, A. A. Lumsdaine, and F. D. Sheffield, *Experiments in Mass Communication* (Princeton, N.J.: Princeton University Press, 1949).

vated, least able students—a finding which probably has wide generality in teaching.[83] However, Ash and Carlton[84] found that note taking during a film was not effective. Snow, Tiffin, and Seibert[85] found that active, assertive students and students low in responsibility learn less well from films than live demonstration. It may be that such students especially need participation devices.

Language Laboratories and Tape Recorders

Tape recorders are now convenient and relatively inexpensive tools available for teaching. Their original and most common use has been in language laboratories. Developed in the Army intensive language training programs of World War II, language laboratories multiplied rapidly in the postwar years and boomed under the financial impetus of the National Defense Education Act of 1958. The core of the language laboratory is the tape recorder, and, as Carroll[86] has noted, "This device can present foreign language sounds and utterances with accuracy, fidelity, and endless patience and do so with great flexibility and ease of handling."

With its emphasis upon prepared recorded sequence of stimuli with frequent opportunities for student responses, the language laboratory has close kinship to the programed learning movement. Language laboratories are now an accepted part of the college scene, and I was amazed to find no experimental tests of their value in college as I prepared this paper. One study of a senior high school class found that students who had the benefit of a language laboratory did less well in reading, vocabulary, and grammar than those without the laboratory experience.[87] On the other hand, the use of undergraduate student assistants to conduct laboratory sessions including films, acetate visuals, and language has been successful in saving instructor time with no loss and some possible gain in achievement at Antioch College.[88]

[83] D. N. Michael and N. Maccoby, "Factors Influencing the Effects of Student Participation on Verbal Learning from Films under Varying Conditions of Audience Participation," *Journal of Experimental Psychology*, 1953, *46*, 411–18; D. N. Michael and N. Maccoby, "Factors Influencing the Effects of Student Participation on Verbal Learning from Films: Motivating versus Practice Effects, Feedback, and Overt versus Covert Responding," *Student Response in Programmed Instruction: A Symposium*, ed. A. A. Lumsdaine (Washington: National Academy of Sciences—National Research Council, 1961).

[84] P. Ash and B. J. Carlton, *The Value of Note-taking during Film Learning*, Pennsylvania State University Instructional Film Research Program, Technical Report No. SDC 269-7-21, November 1951).

[85] R. E. Snow, J. Tiffin, and W. F. Seibert, "Individual Differences and Instructional Film Effects," *Journal of Educational Psychology*, 1965, *56*, 315–26.

[86] J. B. Carroll, "Research on Teaching Foreign Languages," *Handbook on Research on Teaching*, ed. N. L. Gage (Chicago: Rand McNally & Co., 1963), pp. 1060–101.

[87] J. B. Carroll et al. *Annual Report, Committee on Foreign Languages, School and University Program for Research and Development* (Cambridge, Mass.: Graduate School of Education, Harvard University, 1960).

[88] "Experiment in French Language Instruction," Antioch College Reports (Yellow Springs, Ohio: Office of Educational Research, Antioch College, 1960).
The use of undergraduates to teach small groups proved spectacularly successful at Pennsylvania State University. Results were among the most consistently favorable of any experiment I have reviewed. See C. R. Carpenter, "The Penn State Pyramid Plan: Interdependent Student Work Study Groupings for Increasing Motivation for Academic Develop-

Other imaginative uses of tape recorders are in presenting oral questions in programed teaching,[89] in dictating comments about student papers,[90] in lecture-poster or slide presentation,[91] in an automated taped lecture programed question–filmstrip presentation,[92] and in recording lectures prepared by students as a technique for developing student motivation and active integration of material.[93]

Telephones

Cutler, McKeachie, and McNeil[94] and Davis[95] have shown that instruction can be effectively carried out over telephone circuits. The most imaginative use of the telephone has been to enable students to listen to and question a distinguished guest. The use of the telephone hour for students to interview the guest rather than to listen to him lecture maintains a high level of student interest and provides needed feedback to the guest.[96] In Hilgard's terms,[97] this is an example of successful invention in which the actual practice of education is probably ahead of theory, for theory alone would probably not have suggested this technique or predicted the high level of interest generated.

---

ment," paper read at the Fourteenth National Conference on Higher Education, Chicago, March 1959. Also, R. H. Davage, "The Pyramid Plan for the Systematic Involvement of University Students in Teaching-Learning Functions" (University Park: Division of Academic Research and Services, Pennsylvania State University, 1958), and R. H. Davage, "Recent Data on the Pyramid Project in Psychology" (University Park: Division of Academic Research and Services, Pennsylvania State University, 1959).

89 H. C. Mahan, "Adjunct Programming of the Basic Psychology Course for Oral Presentation via Tape Recorder" (Abstract of paper presented at the Western Psychological Association, spring meeting, 1966).

90 Reported by John Moore at faculty fall conference, Kalamazoo College, September 1965.

91 R. E. Johnston, "Magnetic Recordings and Visual Displays as Aids in Teaching Introductory Psychology to College Students," *Audio-Visual Communication Review*, 1961, *9*, 1–46; students in this experiment who were taught by the taped lectures achieved less than those taught conventionally. Also see W. J. Popham, "Tape Recorded Lectures in the College Classroom," *Audio-Visual Communication Review*, 1961, *9*, A28–A29. The same technique has also been used at the Technical University of Berlin.

92 K. U. Smith, "Audiovisumatic Teaching: A New Dimension in Education and Research," *The Behavior of Man*, by K. U. and W. M. Smith (New York: Henry Holt & Co., 1958).

93 N. J. Webb, "Student Preparation and Tape Recording of Course Lectures as a Method of Instruction," *Psychological Reports*, 1965, *16*, 67–72.

94 R. L. Cutler, W. J. McKeachie, and E. B. McNeil, "Teaching Psychology by Telephone," *American Psychologist*, 1958, *13*, 551–52.

95 K. E. Davis, "Do Students Learn from a Telephone Lecture?" Paper presented at the American Psychological Association meetings, September 1963.

96 There are hints of these reactions in both the Davis paper and the Stephens College experience: J. A. Burkhart, "An Experiment to Determine the Values of Using Amplified Classroom Telephone Interviews with Significant Individuals to Enrich Certain College Courses," Final Report, Registry Form Title VII, File 250, Sponsored under the Provisions of the National Defense Education Act of 1958 (P.L. 85–864).

97 E. R. Hilgard, "Learning Theory and Its Applications," *New Teaching Aids for the American Classroom* (Stanford, Calif.: Institute for Communication Research, Stanford University, 1960).

Conclusions

Where do we stand today with respect to teaching methods? Clearly, no one method is best for all goals, students, or teachers. Rather, what is the best method is a function of each of these variables.

When one looks at current learning theory, the gap between it and current educational practice appears tremendous. But this is neither the fault of the learning theorist nor the educator.[98] Educators *are* applying learning theory; the empirical wisdom of good teachers is generally consistent with learning theory so far as comparisons can be made, but learning theory cannot dictate educational practice because no learning theory deals with the complex interactions of the many variables affecting classroom learning. The very constraints necessary for laboratory experimentation limit the applicability of the research to the classroom. The programed learning movement failed to reach its goals as rapidly as had been hoped because the jump from laboratory to school gave rise to motivational and social-psychological variables that were controlled in laboratory studies. Notwithstanding, the research on programed learning is proving highly productive for education. No other stream of educational research has produced so many findings on issues both of theoretical and practical importance to education. As we have seen, theory is also beginning to have an impact on the direction of research on traditional problems of college teaching. The generalization that psychological theory has dictates for teaching that can be applied immediately with great profit seems to me about as true as that theoretical chemistry has rules useful to a good cook; nevertheless psychological theory can provide concepts that help college teachers analyze and interpret their experience.

Moreover, we do know more from theory and research on classroom teaching than we are usually given credit for.[99] We have seen fairly convincing evidence that differing teaching methods do make a difference in learning if one analyzes the different goals of education. Other things being equal, small classes are probably more effective than large, discussions than lectures, and student-centered discussions more effective than instructor-centered discussions for goals of retention, application, problem solving, attitude change, and motivation for further learning. Factual learning and these other kinds of learning are not positively correlated across teaching methods; thus the teacher must make value decisions about what he wants to aim for as well as strategic decisions about his means to these goals.

One implication of this finding is that one should expect to find a variety of teaching methods used in a college and that teachers should develop a repertoire of

[98] See E. R. Hilgard, Chairman, Yearbook Committee, *Theories of Learning*, 63rd Yearbook, National Society for the Study of Education (Chicago: University of Chicago Press, 1964), Pt. I, p. 404; A. Melton, "The Science of Learning and the Technology of Educational Methods," *Harvard Educational Review*, 1959, *29*, 96–106; and A. A. Lumsdaine (ed.), *Student Response in Programmed Instruction: A Symposium* (Washington: National Academy of Sciences—National Research Council, 1961).

[99] And we have some promising analytic frameworks. For example, see L. and Lila Siegel, "The Instructional Gestalt: A Conceptual Framework and Design for Educational Research," *Audio-Visual Communication Review*, 1964, *12*, 16–45.

skills. With increasing knowledge about their particular strengths, we should be better able to match means and ends.

Further, more and more evidence shows that different teaching methods work well for different types of students. A direct implication is that a variety of methods be used in a college and in a course. One would hope that each student will be "turned on" somehow, somewhere during the course even though aspects of it remain relatively unprofitable for him. As I suggested in my discussion of class size, large classes constrain a teacher's ability to use the most effective methods. Another constraint is facilities. The nature of the classroom, the unavailability of audio-visual services, or the inadequacy of the library resources limits the instructor's flexibility.

With freedom to adapt teaching to achieve goals with the infinite variety of students, teaching becomes an art—an art that builds upon knowledge and skill. The very complexity of the teaching process is the source of its challenge to creative minds. Research can help to lay bare the deepest properties of our teaching while revealing to us more wonderful intricacies. As we gain in our understanding, our teaching will be illumined with new insight, delight, and mastery.

Questions for Discussion

1. Briefly describe and explain what can and cannot be done effectively by the following ways of arranging the teaching-learning environment: (a) lecture; (b) discussion; (c) programed learning; (d) independent study; (e) television; and (f) laboratories.
2. Can you find examples in your own experience where the methods used were not appropriate to the stated purposes of the instructor? What would you have done to correct the situation?
3. Note the extensive footnotes in this article, and examine those references for further information on research findings. Pay particular attention to the methods used when conducting this research. Do you really believe we can obtain reliable research information on the effectiveness of various teaching methods?

29 On First Entering the Classroom

The Hazen Foundation

This selection deals with a college teacher entering the classroom for the first time, but the problems he confronts and the options he has for solving them are universal. Notice that this article advises the new teacher to prepare for the class and to study his students as well, to share his knowledge and yet encourage independent thought, to both stimulate and be stimulated by his students. It also discusses the advantages and disadvantages of various teaching techniques, and as you read you might make comparisons with the research conclusions reported in the selection you have just read.

The Opportunities and Roles of the Undergraduate Teacher

Teaching is a process much broader than the techniques employed in lecture hall, classroom, laboratory, or studio. It is broader than the preparation a teacher must make, or than any specific tasks required of the student. At its best, teaching entails the planning of a whole educational program, and of a specific course or other learning activity in that program. It involves the skillful evaluation of learning, not for the purpose of grading alone, but principally for assisting the student. At the foundation of all teaching, good or bad, lies some concept of what must be learned, of how best learning takes place, of the role both the teacher and the student have in this process. Let us begin by considering the foundation concepts and work our way toward the equally important subject of the specific techniques and skills required for the carrying out of these concepts.

There is a widely practiced tendency to regard undergraduate education as merely the transmission of culture. This conventional concept at its worst implies passivity on the part of the student and a "laying out of the subject" by the professor. In whatever setting, lecture or discussion or laboratory, the student can become a mere receptor for facts and interpretations set forth at the morning class by the authors of the books he reads, in the manual he uses. Beginning teachers seldom approach the task in this negative manner because of their own high motivation. When they do, it may be because of such preoccupation with their own efforts that they fail to perceive that learning is an active process in which both the student and the teacher must play roles, the teacher hopefully a diminishing one. Far from merely transmitting culture, the task of faculty is to invoke what Gordon Allport has termed the distinctive goal of higher education, "to inspect and criticize, to improve and increase this cultural cumulation." Beyond piquing the students' interest and filling their heads, therefore, the perceptive young professor will wish at the same time to help them improve their learning capacities and skills. He will try to help them carry on their own investigations, generate plausible hypotheses, verify, disprove or modify these in a scientific manner, reach warranted conclusions. He will

From *The Importance of Teaching* (New Hazen: Foundation, n.d.). Reprinted by permission of The Hazen Foundation.

help them improve their capacities for intelligent criticism, extend their perspectives, deepen their perceptions, heighten their sensitivities, release their creative impulses.

In describing the special task of the undergraduate college, Daniel Bell has said provocatively:

> As between the secondary school, with its emphasis upon primary skills and factual data, and the graduate or professional school, whose necessary concern is with specialization and technique, the distinctive function of the college is to deal with the grounds of knowledge. . . . The college can be the unique place where students acquire self-consciousness, historical consciousness, methodological consciousness.[1]

Good undergraduate education, therefore, means much more than any passive transmission of culture. It means the active involvement of students, on and off campus, in the process of learning. It means the stirring of motivation, one of the most crucial elements in learning. It means sufficient attention to the student to assist him in cultivating his individual style of learning, precisely as the young professor himself is cultivating his own style of teaching. Morris Keeton has summed it up in this manner:

> If we gave up "covering material" as our objective, in the interest of maximum motivation; if we provided as convenient as possible access to knowledge *when needed by the students;* if we permitted the role of individuality and individual style in learning and teaching to be what it needs to be; if we respected the different modes of intellection . . . ; and if we provided a really active interplay between direct experience of the world and reflection upon that world—we would have a revolution in the way we teach.[2]

When the learning process is regarded passively, and even sometimes when it is not, the program of undergraduate education tends to be viewed as an aggregation or succession of courses. There is then a tendency among faculty to place much greater emphasis upon the subject taught than upon the learning desired. If the objective is a student possessed of usable knowledge and understanding in reasonable depth, of disciplined intellect and cultivated taste, of the capacity for creative expression, and of sufficient initiative to keep on growing, curricula and courses can be built, and indeed have been built to attain that object. The roles of the teacher then begin to emerge more clearly as facilitating ones. This implies no derogation of the young professor's scholarly capacities or aspirations. On the contrary, it can enhance them, as we shall attempt to show.

Let us view the young college teacher in four of the roles he inevitably plays: student of his students, exemplar of the educated man, expert in his discipline and special area of study, and master of teaching approaches calculated to achieve the "object desired," as we have just defined it.

[1] Bell, Daniel, *The Reforming of General Education* (New York: Columbia University Press, 1966), p. 12.
[2] Morris Keeton, "Is There a Future for Our Alma Mater?" *Mills Quarterly* (August, 1967), p. 12.

Studying One's Students

The wise young teacher of undergraduates will quickly recognize that he must give some time and attention to the study of his students. In the carrying out of his primary purpose, which is to bring about among them an intelligent understanding of the course he teaches and of his discipline, he will very soon be confronted with one of the elementary laws of learning, that the building of new comprehension must always start with what the student brings to the teaching situation. In conference with students, or through their papers, he will discover how far he may have misapprehended their backgrounds. He may at first be disillusioned when he learns that what he had regarded as an illuminating metaphor was taken literally by a good portion of the class, or that an illustration was remembered by nearly everyone in neglect of the principle it was intended to clarify. Or he may discover, as did one young professor, that his students were bored with his lectures and discussions because he was repeating materials to which they had already been exposed in secondary school, a circumstance that will be increasingly common as our high schools continue to improve. If he is sufficiently sensitive to the human beings with whom he is working, he will soon learn that it is a far greater sin to talk down to them than to talk over their heads. And gradually, as he watches their faces and listens to their impulsive comments, he will begin to find the level at which he must approach them, and the range on either side of that level necessary to accommodate the spread of capacities and backgrounds in his class. In some situations it is possible to discover these things by tests properly constructed. As a result of diagnostic tests, for example, many chemistry departments have found it not only possible but necessary to elevate the levels of freshman instruction.

Not infrequently the beginning college teacher rightly considers himself at an advantage over his older colleagues in being closer to the age of his students. This may produce some shock as he discovers that during his immersion in graduate studies he has lost touch with the freshman or sophomore in late adolescence. He may actually have to begin afresh to learn who and what his students are, what brings them to college and keeps them there. He must discover what their problems are and which of the great problems of society are meaningful to them.

Fortunately we are gaining greater insight into the college undergraduate through numerous studies of his being and his behavior. In one study, Nevitt Sanford has characterized college freshmen as being typically "authoritarian personalities," at least in a mild sense. Though they may seem relatively stable and happy, they are apt to be stereotyped in their thinking, intolerant of ambiguity, submissive toward the powerful and dominant toward the weak, unsure of their own abilities, given to depression when faced with reverses, and well organized and well behaved. Such students tend to change considerably by the time they are seniors, losing much of their compulsiveness, and becoming both more tolerant and more rebellious, more liberal, more unconventional, but also perhaps less stable and happy. The freshman stands in need of adult models, particularly young adults who show themselves to him not simply as classroom teachers but also as human beings.[3]

The study of students is not restricted, however, to finding out what is the level

[3] Sanford, Nevitt, "The Developmental Status of the Entering Freshman," in *The American College* (New York: John Wiley & Sons, 1962), p. 253–282.

of their maturity or the depth of their knowledge and perception. As the young man or woman moves from high school to the new styles and techniques of learning expected at the college level (granted that the range of difference is steadily narrowing), he or she can be greatly helped by the discerning professor. Many students remember with gratitude those professors who taught them something important about how, and how not, to write a paper, or frame a bluebook answer, or separate the parts of a complex question. Many also appreciate suggestions about such fundamental things as the taking of notes, the intelligent use of reference tools in the library, methods of going about research. Almost invariably the student will be grateful for special help in understanding a perplexing concept, a baffling problem. The study of the student, a rewarding process in terms of teaching result, never ceases to be necessary. It is practiced by professors who with frequency find themselves on the lists of men and women singled out by college students for their teaching competence.

Serving as Exemplar

Let us look next at the teacher as exemplar. In this role, the teacher is saying, frequently without being conscious of it, "Watch how I work and do likewise in your own way." This is common enough in mathematics, where the professor often works through a proof, not just to show the outcome but to reveal the procedure, the way he makes derivations, and to exemplify elegance rather than cumbersomeness in the style of the proof. The teacher of painting may sit at his student's canvas and paint a while, not just to help him over a rough spot, but to show how an experienced artist goes about tackling such a problem. The scientist continually shows how he uses laboratory equipment to conduct an experiment, to refine an observation. The teacher of literature may analyze a poem or read one of his own, the philosopher may work through the central concepts in a paragraph, or the anthropologist may describe how he went about gaining essential information about a village, all as means of bringing to the student examples of the professional at work.

One eminent historian talking about another, Carl Lotus Becker on his teacher, Frederick Jackson Turner, reveals clearly this sense of exemplification:

> From the moment Turner ceased to figure in my mind as a teacher, I began to learn something from him. Not "teacher" but "historian" he was, better still "author," whose main occupation it was, not to teach us, but to be deeply engaged in research preliminary to the writing of notable books.
>
> *   *   *   *   *   *
>
> An ordered body of information I could get, and did afterwards get, for myself; but from no other man did I ever get in quite the same measure that sense of watching a first-class mind at work on its own account, and not merely rehearsing for the benefit of others; the most delightful sense in the world of sitting there waiting for ideas to be born; expectantly waiting for secret meanings, convenient explanatory hypotheses to be discovered, lurking as like as not under the dullest mass of drab facts ever seen.[4]

[4] *Great Teachers,* ed. Houston Peterson (New Brunswick, N.J.: Rutgers University Press, 1946), pp. 233, 236.

Another observer lauds the well-conceived and well-delivered lecture on the grounds that the student learns not necessarily or solely because a certain body of material is taught, but more because of the valuable human intellectual effort being made and observed. He cites James Russell Lowell's reaction to an Emerson lecture at Harvard: "We do not go to hear what Emerson says so much as to hear Emerson."[5] As in the case of David Starr Jordan whose introductory course on "Evolution" was always taken by great numbers of Stanford students in order to obtain a "course on Jordan," the man, the mind and the scholar at work are both model and inspiration.

Specifically, the great teacher at his best moments exemplifies much more than his knowledge and his methods of work. He shows not only how he attacks a problem, what tools he uses and how he uses them, but also where he looks for help from those who have gone before him. He displays also, perhaps unconsciously, the special concerns of his discipline, as revealed in what he looks for and what he can, for his purposes, ignore. He manifests an attitude of profound inquiry, perhaps surprising his students by taking seriously some things that they had regarded as trivial. By the standards he displays toward evidence and his rigorously disciplined handling of data, he may help his students to sense and share the contempt in which the scholar holds any dishonesty in research. He may also infect his students with his own delight in even small discoveries, in the beauty of a comprehensive explanation, in the freshness of an ingenious hypothesis.

Not all fields lend themselves equally well to exemplification in its several forms. Yet no field by its very nature forbids teaching by exemplification. And there can be no doubt that the exemplar carries much more conviction when he is being most true to the dictates of his own inquiring or creative mind, and to the most fundamental demands of his discipline. William Arrowsmith puts the need for exemplary teaching in vivid language:

> It is *men* we need now, not programs. . . . The humanities stand or fall according to the human worth of the man who professes them. . . . Charisma in a teacher is not a mystery or nimbus of personality, but radiant exemplification to which the student contributes a correspondingly radiant hunger for becoming.[6]

What Professor Arrowsmith says about humanists can readily be adapted to every major field of learning and endeavor. What he implies is essential for effective exemplification, is to surmount any inclination to contrive to be exemplary, and instead to carry out one's intellectual or creative task so effectively that its performance is inherently a compelling example. Whitehead gave the same intrinsic meaning to the exemplary function of the teacher, though in slightly different concept: "It should be the chief aim of a university professor to exhibit himself in his own true character—that is, as an ignorant man thinking, actively utilizing his small share of knowledge."[7]

---

[5] Rothstein, A. M., "The Lecture and Learning," *AAUP Bulletin* (June, 1966), p. 218.
[6] Arrowsmith, William, "The Future of Teaching," in *Improving College Teaching* (Washington: American Council on Education, 1967), p. 60.
[7] Whitehead, A. N., *The Aims of Education* (New York: New Library, a Mentor Book, 1953), p. 48.

Being the Expert

We shall have more to say about the example of "man thinking" as we examine now in greater depth the relation between teaching and research. This leads us to the role of the teacher as expert in his discipline and in his special field of study.

Expertness can be the source of great good in undergraduate teaching, or it can detract from teaching, depending upon the values and interests of the professor and the manner in which he uses his expertise. We yield to none in our conviction that profound knowledge in a field of learning, coupled with the capacity for creative exploration and expression in that field, can contribute centrally to the finest teaching. The teacher who brings these attributes to the undergraduate classroom in the right way not only informs; he equips his students to learn with full effectiveness at the next higher level. The extent to which he does so depends in some measure upon elusive qualities of intellect and personality. Even college freshmen, however, are capable of sensing genuine worth and of thrusting aside extraneous factors for the purpose of learning better how to learn.

But the influence of great knowledge and creative capacity in the undergraduate class can be diminished in more than one way. It will be lessened obviously if the professor downgrades or neglects his teaching for the sake of other things for which his expertness qualifies him: research, writing, consultation, frequent service away from the campus, and related activities. The extent to which these things do injury varies, of course, from field to field and likewise from person to person. As we have indicated earlier in this memorandum, the neglect or downgrading need not be a consequence. On the contrary, research, writing, consultation at home or abroad can lend new dimensions of motivation and effectiveness to teaching.

As we have also suggested, the professor, whatever the level of his expertness, can dissipate his teaching effectiveness by the manner in which he approaches his students. When he views his teaching task as that of "laying out" his subject, when he sees his role as that of consciously benefiting a student audience, the benefits of his expertness are diminished, regardless of student capacity to separate the gold from the dross. Such is human weakness that some teachers cherish, consciously or subconsciously, the authority over students which is bequeathed upon them in the classroom. They treasure grading as an arm of that authority. They avoid endangering their prestige as experts by any sharing of learning that might equip students to challenge their authority. Fortunately, such extreme pettiness is infrequent. Hopefully, it is a phenomenon that appears even less frequently among beginning undergraduate teachers.

Sharing with Learners

Fine teaching will happen when the expert, or better, the learned or artistically competent man, approaches his students in the spirit of one thinking or one creating, to paraphrase Whitehead. It will happen when the teacher achieves, without artificiality, the spirit of learning as an enterprise shared between senior and junior colleague. It will happen when the professor carries forward his research or the development of his artistic concepts before his student public in such a way as gradually to be able to benefit from the participation of that public in his own labors.

Admittedly, this approach to teaching has about it something of the ideal. Yet it has been practiced by some of the greatest of college and university professors. It is a demonstrably effective way to bridge the commonly perceived canyon between teaching and research, with reciprocal benefits to each. It is offered as a norm or model for the beginning undergraduate teacher. To the extent that he and his students can see their common task as that of bringing the resources of a discipline to bear upon important and unsolved problems, all will be conscious of learning as a shared undertaking. In saying this we do not intend to shrug off the most elementary and inescapable parts of the professor's job. The basic learning, the long hours of preparation, the tedious but unavoidable paper work in all teaching, the difficult evaluation of student performance; all of these must be acknowledged and respected. But they must also be put into the context of the shared learning which is their consummation.

Perhaps the concept of shared learning should be more concretely illustrated. Let us suppose that an English professor has become interested in the possibility that Shakespeare's *Henry the Eighth* was in fact written by someone else. If this professor wished to play the role of undisputed expert, he might overwhelm his students with his evidence and subsequently obtain bluebook reiterations, often garbled and incomplete, of what he has said, although this kind of uncritical response is occurring with less frequency in this generation of students. Or the professor could ignore both the play and his own theory, thus keeping his classroom and his study quite separate. On the other hand, he might decide that his class, even an elementary class, could provide a laboratory for the testing of his hypothesis. In doing so, he must be at some pains to prevent his students becoming premature converts by pointing the way to writings supportive of Shakespeare's authorship. He will want to sensitize them to stylistic analysis so that they can initiate their own direct comparisons, even though he may know that only the ablest students can make noticeable progress on this front. He will surely raise the question of ideational congruities between this play and others certainly by Shakespeare. It is then by no means unlikely that a point or two will emerge from the apprentice critics in support or refutation of his thesis. It may be taken as certain that the teacher, having successfully armed his own junior critics, will be forced into a deeper consideration of the subject as he defends his hypothesis. When this happens, there can be no question of the irrelevance of research to teaching or of interference of research with teaching.

Admittedly the example is a simplified one, and one must of course ask whether this approach to teaching is feasible in other fields. Within the humanities there appears to be no question. Outside them, the problem may be harder, although it takes no great amount of imagination to think of possibilities in sociology, economics, political science, psychology, anthropology, and geography. Perhaps the greater the extent to which a subject seems to require a particular order of learning, as in mathematics, the likelier some students are to let themselves be scared off, believing there is no room for considerations of value, for aesthetic judgments, and for basic issues on which novices can speak up. Under any circumstances and in any field, however, these foundations are necessary to the development of those advanced students who will carry on, both now and in the future, the essential disciplines.

To recapitulate, we are not advocating a teacher who teaches only a set of skills. The beginning undergraduate teacher will more quickly and more readily attain the role of the senior scholar sharing the satisfactions of intellectual discovery with his junior "partners" if he begins by viewing his class as a group of persons between 18 and 22 years of age, with varied abilities and interests. His task is to establish a relationship with them whereby in three or four months they will have acquired not only a certain amount of knowledge, but also certain skills and interests. During those months, he must draw himself into their inquiry, and them into his. Out of this relationship must grow within the students a sense of intellectual or aesthetic challenge. Out of it must emerge a desire to continue the study of the subject or the discipline. One must applaud the young teacher who enters his undergraduate class with a determination to emerge from the quarter or semester with as many continuing and independent learners as possible. And one must also applaud the young teacher who comes from an encounter with his students feeling "I am the better historian (or whatever) for this."

Fostering Independence

Let us consider in conclusion two other roles of the young undergraduate teacher. Whether he has sought to do so or not, he exerts a moral influence upon his students. This is especially true today, and perhaps most especially of the young professor, not far removed from the age group of his students. In ways he may not wholly perceive, the young teacher influences the feelings, attitudes, and values of his students, probably less because of his words than of what the students observe him to feel and be. They are quick to recognize the young teacher who is as much interested in them as in his subject. In him they find a bridge to relevance between the intellectual enterprise of the class or seminar, and the world beyond the classroom, beyond the campus.

This relationship between teacher and student can be intense and deeply satisfying without being personal in any usual sense. What some students want and need is to relate to a unique human being, one who has feelings and values and holds to a distinctive standpoint about the world. He is a person, not just a teacher-in-general or a mouthpiece for a discipline, no matter how learned he may be. What the student seeks is of the same essence as what Professor Carl L. Becker found gratifying in the intellectual relationship he established with Frederick Jackson Turner. It is akin to what another distinguished scholar once described as the sense of discipleship which the budding student develops toward the person and the mind of an outstanding professor, a discipleship which should be the first step toward ultimate maturity and mastery.

The reference to discipleship that gives way to mastery leads us to the consideration of one of the most difficult roles a teacher must play. It is the role which requires that he so teach as to make himself less and less important in the learning process. The teacher, as George Herbert Palmer said long ago, must be willing to be forgotten. His task is to help the student internalize the goals of his education and thus to free himself from any need for external motivation. It is to help the student sharpen the tools of his inquiry or of his creative effort so that he can proceed with ever greater independence. But teaching so conceived is by no means a self-negating effort. In the measure that he accomplishes these tasks, the great teacher becomes in the minds of his students one of the rare landmarks of intellectual and creative growth. And the student, in turn, is set more surely on the road toward continuous learning and toward some of the satisfactions of mastery itself when the wise teacher makes him a contributor to and not just a beneficiary of the teaching process. Whitehead puts it this way:

> The justification for a university is that it preserves the connection between knowledge and the zest of life, by uniting the young and the old in the imaginative consideration of learning. . . . A university which fails in this respect has no reason for existence. This atmosphere of excitement, arising from imaginative consideration, transforms knowledge. A fact is no longer a bare fact: it is invested with all its possibilities. It is no longer a burden on the memory: it is energizing as the poet of our dreams, and as the architect of our purposes.[8]

Teaching Procedures and Strategies

One function of the young professor which merits extended attention is his role as a master of teaching procedures and strategies. This role, in combination with his role as scholar, is at the heart of his professional performance. What he does in the role will reflect the philosophy with which he approaches teaching and will also be influenced, of course, by the way in which he performs as exemplary and expert. The teaching procedures he employs are necessarily his own; they are shaped by his style. The selection of these procedures, however, offers a wide range of alternatives, among which the young teacher has considerable free choice if he will equip himself.

Course Planning

The actual conduct of teaching is something done in the lecture hall, the class or seminar room, the laboratory, the field location; but it is also much more. It is the subtle, intimate meeting of minds in conference or counseling session, or in informal conversation. It is the fitting of educational means to ends on a larger scale through the curriculum, the individual course, the combination of the experiences offered the student, and the system of evaluation of student performance and development. In a measure that varies from institution to institution according to size and kind, the young professor will "teach" in each and all of these ways, and perhaps in others.

Curriculum revision has become almost a continuous way of life in many colleges and universities sensitive to the growth of knowledge and changing societal needs and responsive to the insistent requests of students and many faculty. The chances

---

[8] *Ibid.,* p. 97.

are, therefore, increased that the beginning undergraduate teacher will have some share in this important function. He will have opportunity, not merely to reshuffle courses as sometimes happens in presumed curriculum revision, but rather to consider with his colleagues what the results of undergraduate education should be and to devise a program for attaining them. Among other things, this will involve consideration of the scope of knowledge to be presented in four years, the sequence of presentation, the range of choice permitted to the student, the skills to be cultivated and the manner of fostering them. It will also involve consideration of attitudes and values which the student may achieve, among these the desire and capacity to work independently, and the intellectual curiosity to sustain that work. While helping to plan the curriculum, the young professor will also be engaged with his colleagues in setting scholarly norms for the institution, in fixing standards for disciplinary adequacy, in planning cross-disciplinary ventures. While doing these things, he will almost inevitably be responding to the current student quest for relevance. He will be able to view the curriculum as a means for enabling the student to relate what he learns of the human heritage to himself, and to his role in the world around him. Needless to say, curriculum building in these ways can be an exciting adventure.

The young professor will also have opportunity to plan at least one and probably more of the courses he teaches. He will do so most effectively when he is able to see his own course in the perspective of the total educational program of the college or university, even the total program of his department. He will also build a better course when he has achieved that awareness of what his students are, what they seek, and how they propose to attain their goals, of which we have spoken. Whether the beginning teacher is planning and teaching his own course or whether he is working with others on a staff course, he must meet the same criteria of effectiveness, the same questions as to content and method. In responding to those criteria and questions, he is able to exercise one of the most precious opportunities of the teacher, the freedom to choose among a wide range of alternatives.

The most important relationship a teacher must decide as he plans his course is that between ends and means, between what he proposes to accomplish in the course and the procedures he employs to attain his purposes. Before the relationship can be ascertained, of course, the young professor must first have thought through the course purposes. One wonders how often college teachers do sufficiently particularize, even for themselves, the ends they espouse. What kinds of knowledge do they want the students to gain? How organized? What skills? How are the knowledge and skills to be related to attitudes and values? What would the teachers have remain after the details are forgotten?

Having thought about the purposes of a course, the teacher must next determine what procedures are most likely to fulfill those purposes. To put the question in the language of the behavioral scientist, what do given results mean operationally; or, to put it another way, what steps specifically must be taken to bring about what changes in student intellectual and attitudinal behavior? For example, in what ways should the students experience inquiry or research? Until the young teacher answers these questions in a manner that becomes reflected in his teaching, there may be serious discrepancies between what he professes or believes is happening and what is actually taking place.

It is not uncommon for teachers, who think of themselves as aiming at the improvement of the problem-solving skills of their students, unconsciously to conduct their classes in such a way that they are mainly dispensing information. Sometimes a teacher, while professing his belief that students should grow in their ability to express themselves orally and learn, through the give and take of class discussion, some of the skills of reasonable and disciplined conversation, nevertheless defeats his purpose by his own inability to stop talking long enough to give the students a chance. The observation is not simply the familiar one of a discrepancy between preachment and practice, among all too human professors, but the assertion that educational purposes in particular too seldom get carried out systematically.

One may, of course, dispute the wisdom of any particular set of aims, no matter how carefully they may be specified in terms of changed student behavior. In fact, the vital teacher usually keeps questioning and modifying his aims, as situations and students change. To have formulated desirable outcomes, however, is a long step toward satisfying accomplishment. Not only is one able to choose means with ends clearly in mind, but possibly more important, he is able to change those means—in mid-course or in subsequent course—if they seem to be failing.

Let us examine some of the procedures that may be available to the beginning teacher and explore their relative advantages. As we do so it is important to recognize two things. The option among procedures may be less in staff courses, or even in courses assigned to beginning college teachers where the classes are large and the approaches somewhat weighted by tradition. Secondly, we must recognize the difficulty and the danger of generalizing about any procedure. As in any other human enterprise, the most effective way to do the job must be determined by pragmatic variation from general principles and previous experience.

Lectures

Teaching approach and class size are, of course, closely related, but the relationship is by no means a fixed one. There is a normal tendency in very large classes to use the lecture approach, probably in combination with some discussion each week in sections. It is also usual for the amount of lecturing to decrease and that of discussion to increase in proportion to the diminishing size of the classes. As the teaching groups shrink to seminar size or to the very few students manageable in the tutorial, lecturing is often completely replaced by discussion or even by the individual conference. Yet there are important exceptions to these generalizations. In both the universities and the colleges some professors choose to lecture even when the classes are of fifty or fewer students. In fact, the lecture is not infrequently carried into the small seminar on an informal basis.

Generalizations about the teaching approaches in given institutions must also be used with care. To be sure, there are many lecture courses with from 300 to 500 students in the larger universities. Within the same university, where the stigma of impersonality is engendered by the large lecture course, however, it may be true that much of the undergraduate teaching is done less formally in classes of fifty or fewer, possibly some of it by design in groups of seminar size, even in the freshman year.

Overall there tends to be in American institutions a prevalence of lecturing. And there is continuing controversy concerning the relative merits of lecture and discussion. Those who are dubious of the lecture as a teaching approach often cite Boswell's quotation from Dr. Johnson:

> Lectures were once useful; but now, when all can read, and books are so numerous, lectures are unnecessary. If your attention fails, and you miss part of the lecture, it is lost; you cannot go back as you do upon a book.[9]

This general attitude continues to prevail in England where lecturing has never been the favored teaching approach among either students or professors. It is not wholly unexpected that the Hale report on *University Teaching Methods* (1964) should conclude that: "Overindulgence in lectures should be classed as drug addiction on the part of both giver and receiver." It is more notable that an able American critic, now chancellor of a large university, should state as strongly as he does:

> Using talented manpower as "talking books" is a shameful waste in most of our colleges and universities today, and tends to keep the student a permanent adolescent. The student's umbilical cord must be severed at graduation in any event, and we should take the responsibility of playing midwife at an earlier stage.[10]

Without wishing to detract from the truth in these criticisms as they apply to much lecturing, we would redress the balance by emphasizing that both giving lectures and listening to them can be, and often has proved to be, both an active and a creative process, stimulating and freeing the minds of both lecturer and listener, rather than indenturing them in perpetual adolescence. Giving lectures and listening to them, moreover, continues to be a prevalent means of adult communication, amplified on both sides of the Atlantic by radio and television. Education in these arts would seem, therefore, to have a proper place in our colleges and universities.

In actual practice, there is not in any kind of institution of higher learning as sharp a polarization between lecturing and alternative methods of teaching as might be suggested by this discussion. Rather they tend to be used in some combination to augment one another. Research surveys and studies reported by McKeachie disclose a trend in preference, unfavorable to the lecture, however. They show that a majority of students as well as many professors have a strong preference for discussion, and many of these professors in fact practice it. The same research also shows, however, that the lecture and the discussion tend to accomplish different results. The lecture is the better vehicle for the transmission of information, whereas discussion can more readily yield the subtler goals of learning: the understanding of new concepts, deeper and more lasting motivation, greater capacity for change, for example. On the basis of his survey, McKeachie concludes:

9 Hill, G. B., ed., *Boswell's Life of Johnson,* revised and enlarged edition by L. F. Dowell (Oxford, 1934), Vol. IV, p. 92.
10 Alan Cartter, *Improving College Teaching, op. cit.,* p. 155.

Other things being equal, small classes are probably more effective than large, discussion than lectures, and student-centered discussions more effective than instructor-centered discussions for goals of retention, application, problem solving, attitude change, and motivation for further learning.[11]

Lecturing varies along a continuum from formal to informal, the most formal consisting of the memorized address and the read paper, neither of which is common today. However, another kind of formal lecture, the highly organized, uninterrupted speech by the professor, usually from notes, continues to hold an important place in higher education, especially in large classes.

In the light of comments critical of the lecture, the young professor may wish to resolve in his mind two kinds of questions about this approach. He may ask whether what he proposes to say in the lecture is not covered adequately, or possibly better, in some combination of texts and other sources, including the rich variety of paper backs now available. He may conclude that he is, in fact, placing the information which the student can get from printed sources in a new context by means of his lecture, and thus lending perspective to the readings. Or if the lecture is in the field of his own scholarly concerns, he may find ample justification for it in the presentation of data and conclusions not elsewhere available.

Beyond this, the beginning lecturer may ask himself whether his students would be better served by a mimeographed copy of his speech, which most of them can read in less time than the delivery takes. The question becomes especially pertinent today when the formal lecturer has to compete not only with the mimeograph machine, but also with the tape recorder, brought to the lecture. He may still decide in favor of the oral lecture, recognizing that to put everything he has to say into a series of fully written manuscripts would be a formidable task, would deprive him of the opportunities for interpretation and interpolation which speaking from notes makes possible, and, moreover, would not serve the interests of his ear-minded students. He may recognize that the carefully prepared, well-delivered lecture can be a potent means of exemplification. And he may be aware that his own style of oral presentation, his flair for dramatization, can bring alive what he has to say.

Nearly everyone knows that an exciting speech may come off tame in written form. This suggests that a man's thought may become better than it is through his exceptional powers of presentation. The reverse may also be true. Irwin Edman has told of the somnolent quality of John Dewey's lectures, and their seeming lack of organization, an impression given the lie by a perusal of notes taken from the lecture, which revealed subtle but powerful arrangement of the points. Presumably these virtues would also have been discoverable in a transcription. Dewey's ponderous qualifications would have been there in either case.

McKeachie argues that the peculiar values of the lecture are seldom actualized. Yet nearly everyone has listened to lecturers who by their ability to emphasize points of importance, to pose searching questions and to organize complex material with clarity if not brilliance have made listening an active process in which the student is genuinely involved. Such a lecture may bring wholly new insights. It cannot only stimulate the student's reading, but also assist it. It can awaken interest and provide motivation.

[11] W. J. McKeachie, "Research in Teaching: The Gap Between Theory and Practice" in *Improving College Teaching, op. cit.,* p. 230.

When lecturing is done in this manner, it tends to approach the informal end of the lecture continuum. The informal lecture that combines in varying measure speaking and discussion is, in fact, much more common than the formal. Some informal lecturers are very skillful in presenting the "unfinished" lecture that leaves many questions showing. Some interrupt the lecture to make explicit the question with which they are wrestling and to invite or provoke comment. In some lectures it is understood that students may interrupt with questions or comments, and that the professor's presentation will be liberally interspersed with discussion. The advantages of informality flow mainly from the more overtly active role of the students, and from the change of pace possible for the professor. The possible disadvantage is the lesser degree of organization that can result from student participation, something which the skilled teacher can not only keep in bounds but can even use as a stimulus to thought.

Discussion

There is clearly no sharp line between informal lecturing and the class conducted entirely on a discussion basis. In either case, the size of the class will be a conditioning factor with which the teacher must cope. In the very large group, significant discussion is hard to achieve, if for no other reason than the difficulties of real communication. In such situations, the division of the large group for discussion purposes is a device often resorted to. As has been suggested where the lecture prevails, one frequently used procedure is to break the very large class into sections for discussions once or twice a week under the leadership of teaching assistants. Another device for obtaining more discussion in a large group is to entrust a portion of the class, from time to time, to more advanced students, or even to a pair of students from the class itself provided, of course, another room is available. Sometimes a large lecture hall will permit groupings of ten to twelve students in—if the name can be forgiven—"buzz sessions" assigned the responsibility of reporting questions or comments back to the meeting as a whole. Another, somewhat unusual system has been employed with success: the professor designates, in advance or at the time, some twenty-five students as his discussants and proceeds to carry on the discussion with that group, everyone else acting as eavesdroppers, perhaps with instructions about what to note or watch for as the discussion proceeds.

Many a professor has said, "I prefer discussion to lecture, but what are you going to do with forty (sixty, seventy-five, one hundred) students?" With classes of more than fifty, some combination of lecture and discussion may be both unavoidable and desirable. When the groups are under fifty, however, one may very well ask of the professor: "Are you sure you cannot hold a discussion with a class of that size?" It will be more difficult than with a group of twenty-five, and it may be impossible to involve every student, but many a teacher conducts a lively discussion with classes of forty to fifty and gets at least two-thirds active participation. Moreover, the teacher frequently discovers that even the students not directly involved have profited at least as much, if not more, from the give and take of discussion than they would have from the most informal mode of lecturing.

The conduct of an effective discussion requires careful planning and a high order of skill in leading the discussants. These requisites are important because the discussion, if successful, frequently becomes so student-centered, as compared with the informal lecture, that the professor will talk much less than the class members. Although some professors are made uneasy by any procedure that seems to diminish their expertness before the class, some of the most effective discussion leaders like to confine their participation principally to the asking of questions, the sorting out of the answers that are elicited, and the posing of new questions that have emerged.

Many professors have difficulty in establishing their roles as discussion leaders because they have never had opportunity to participate in an expertly handled discussion, and so have no model ready at hand. In consequence, they tend to commit common errors that reduce the usefulness of discussion. Pace learned, for example, from university and liberal arts college students alike that lively discussions were rare in their experience.[12]

The leading of discussion differs in actual practice according to how tightly the reins are held, or—to put it another way—according to how narrowly or widely "relevance" is interpreted. At one extreme, everything goes: free association, sudden changes of subject, personal reminiscence, and other permissive practices. At the opposite extreme, a strong attempt is made to get the group to arrive at positions decided upon by the teacher in advance. Neither of these extremes can be called a genuine discussion. The former more nearly resembles a "bull session," while the latter is a disguised lecture or recitation. Good discussion, by contrast, is purposeful but involves much student initiative and creative interaction between students and professor.

Most experienced teachers would agree that discussion is not normally an economic way of presenting facts and that this cannot be its highest purpose, as McKeachie's studies have suggested. Rather there is good evidence that it can be a powerful means for inducing thoughtfulness about problems to which neither the teacher nor anyone else may have satisfactory answers. It can, that is, if the teacher, employing the Socratic approach, involves the students in the common task of exploration.

Other procedures

The seminar, which in recent years many institutions have shown to be a workable type of course, even at the freshman level, needs little explanation to the beginning undergraduate teacher who has usually had ample seminar experience.[13] If he is in the sciences, he has similarly had ample experience with laboratory teaching. Both the seminar and the laboratory can gain greatly in effectiveness if— or to the extent that—the teacher brings in his own research. Many an established scholar has testified that the best teaching he ever knew was when he was allowed to share in his own teacher's specific research.[14]

The basic principle for the seminar, as for the laboratory, is that it is not a way

---

12 Pace, C. R., "Perspectives on the Student and His College," in *The College and the Student*, ed. L. E. Dennis and J. F. Kauffman (Washington: American Council on Education, 1966), p. 84 and *passim*.

13 Cf. Taylor, W. R., "The Wisconsin Laboratory Course in American History," *AHA Newsletter*, February, 1968.

14 Merton, R. K., "The Matthew Effect in Science," *Science*, 159 (1968), pp. 60–61.

for the teacher to get out of work. Careful preparation can make the laboratory exercises bear freshly on the difficulties and rewards being experienced in the course. In the first meetings of a seminar, by informal lectures or group discussion the teacher can astutely lay the groundwork for stimulating consideration of the several student papers as they are successively completed and presented. If he fails to do so, he may justify the frequent saying among students that seminars are a waste of time, except for what goes into writing one's own paper.

The beginning undergraduate teacher will undoubtedly remember also that the value of the seminar or laboratory depends in addition upon the care with which the teacher counsels the student during the preparation of the paper or performance of the exercise and the thoroughness with which he evaluates what is done.

Tutorials may be thought of as small seminars which allow for a more intensive analysis and evaluation of student papers. They are probably more effective in an informal setting with from three to six students. One-to-one tutorials can produce superb results. They may be impractical and uneconomic in large institutions, and they are always dependent for best results upon a favorable match between tutor and tutee. Some professors, nevertheless, prefer this kind of opportunity for intimate work with the student. Under their tutelage, learning may be intense.

Consideration of the one-to-one tutorial brings us to the alternative of independent study. In general, independent study for merely filling out one's store of information, or for practicing insecure skills, is neither new nor on a par with learning under a good teacher. Yet the large number of laboratory guides on audiovisual film, and of other programed aids, now makes possible a form of independent study that relies both on such materials and on interdependence with colleague students, while the student himself takes the initiative in a new sense as learner.

The case method of teaching has a long and successful history in schools of law and schools of business administration. Some have argued recently that it may be employed to good advantage in many courses in the social and behavioral sciences and in other professional schools. Much depends, of course, upon the ingenuity and imagination that go into the construction of the cases. At their best, they can present an exceptionally strong challenge to the student to bring his theoretical knowledge to bear upon concrete problems. They cultivate judgment and the capacity for wise decision.

Experience has disclosed difficulties in the case method, however. Students frequently make two salutary discoveries during the early part of their study:

> One is that each of them sees something different in each case, and that this difference is due not to what is in the case but to what each of them brings to the case from his own background. The other is that trying to understand one another is more difficult than conducting monologues designed to catch the teacher's attention. . . .[15]

Another approach that calls upon the students to make decisions as a means of learning is the "simulation technique." In this approach, the student is confronted with a simulated problem closely resembling actual problems, past or present. He is

[15] Andrews, K. R., *The Case Method of Teaching Human Relations and Administration* (Cambridge: Harvard University Press, 1953), p. 34.

asked to clarify the problem, assemble the data that bears upon it, and map out alternative strategies of solution, estimating the risks and probable outcomes of each. This technique, together with more structured game-playing, is being used with frequency in the field of international relations, sometimes with the aid of a computer. It aims to develop skills in the rendering of judgment and decision too often neglected in liberal arts education.

Yet another way to induce learning has been used and advocated by "group dynamics" psychologists. It is sensitivity training or the formation of "T-groups." The proponents of this approach make the point that truly meaningful learning emerges when students confront their own problems in a setting that permits and even encourages openness of social response. Consequently, when a class is organized as a "T (training) group," time will be spent identifying problems, acknowledging prejudices and other blocks to learning, and identifying feelings and attitudes to clear the way for more cognitive inquiry. Thus far, this technique has been employed mainly in courses in clinical psychology, social work, theology, and other fields centering around human relations. Its proponents advocate, however, wider experimentation.

We have very briefly described a number of alternative teaching approaches usable in the classroom. The inquiring undergraduate teacher will have no difficulty, however, in extending the discussion, either through consultation with his colleagues or by means of the selective bibliography appended to this report.

Before we leave the subject of classroom procedures, it is desirable to stress again one underlying requirement of any approach. This is the necessity for a sense of purpose that is clear to both the students and the professor. A clear sense of purpose is more important, indeed, than complete explicitness as to what the teacher expects from the students as their part in the attainment of these purposes in the common learning adventure. Most students will tolerate a fair amount of ambiguity on almost every academic subject except "What exactly do you expect of me?" The average class member insists on knowing explicitly what readings will be required and what will be the range of his optional reading, what laboratory experiments he must complete, how many papers he must write and of what character, what will be the nature of the examinations, and what will be the ingredients of his grade. The wise teacher will be judicious in meeting these demands for explicitness, so as to lead the student toward a greater measure of independence in his approach to learning. He will work toward the latter goal through his attitudes in class, in his counseling of individual students, which hopefully will be frequent, and in the actual formulation of the requirements of his course. Perhaps the most important thing the teacher can make explicit as the course proceeds is what he values in learning and how he will estimate with his students their progress toward those goals of value.

The wise teacher will also remind himself that the learning process, even in his own course, will by no means be confined to his classroom, laboratory, or office. If he teaches well, it will go forward in informal meetings of his students over coffee, in the residence halls, or on the bus. In some courses—urban sociology for example, or botany—the most significant learning may take place in the field, either on a formal trip, or through individual inquiry. Some part of the learning may take place at another institution, during a quarter or semester away, or simultaneously if the institution is near. And the teacher may also hope that the learning begun in his class will never cease, either with the final examination or at the boundaries of the campus. His professional concern may ignite sparks of motivation, and may even prove contagious.

Technological aids

Let us turn, for a moment, to the place in the learning process of teaching aids or "substitutes" for teaching, subjects of much controversy among faculty. We refer to all aspects of teaching technology from the simple device of the blackboard to such teaching media as flannel boards, slides, films, recordings, audio and video tapes, television, teaching machines and all the rest of the burgeoning battery of learning aids. Nowhere is faculty conservatism so manifest as in the stout refusal of many professors to believe that some or all of these devices have any relevance to their own teaching. This rather widespread belief requires critical scrutiny. On the side of the skeptical, Alan Cartter may be quoted:

> . . . however effective these technical improvements are for purely informational and routinized aspects of learning, they may be called diabolically illiberal. . . . Given the will and the desire, one can obtain knowledge from the book, the television screen, the magnetic tape, but wisdom, understanding, and tolerance —the essential aims of liberal learning—are attainable only through personal confrontation of teacher and student. Interest, individualism, and integrity cannot be mass-produced; they result from the personal interaction of man with man.[16]

On the other hand, the teaching of art history without a slide projector, of elementary foreign language without the facilities of the language laboratory, or of music appreciation without a phonograph is today almost inconceivable. Experience has demonstrated, moreover, that the televised or telephoned lecture is not limited to the mere transmission of information. Frequently they bring into intimate settings distinguished personalities who would not otherwise be available. As used at Stephens College and other colleges, the tele-lecture also permits discussion between the lecturer and the students. In some subjects the guest lecture being heard by telephone may be coordinated with locally projected slides or film strips. Or, by means of closed circuit television, a scientific demonstration, or a panel discussion, may be piped to fifty classrooms instead of being presented live but impersonally and less perceptibly in an auditorium. The advantages of intimate viewing through either motion picture or television have long since been recognized in medical education.

Many advocates of instructional television argue that it is no more sensible to consider this medium as simply a reproduction of a regular classroom presentation than it is to consider a motion picture film simply a photograph of a stage play. If television is to be employed for teaching, it is wasteful not to use the medium distinctively for presentations that would be difficult or unfeasible live, such as the showing of objects or events not otherwise available in the classroom that illustrate concepts under consideration.

[16] Cartter, *op. cit.*, p. 159–160.

The new media, mechanical though they are, provide the teacher with many resources with which to supplement his live teaching. The English or drama professor may wish to have his students compare the interpretations of Hamlet, by Olivier and Burton, on film. The biologist, of all undergraduate teachers, has perhaps had most experience in organizing lectures in terms of slides, to explain difficult phenomena clearly. The linguist is experienced in having his students hear on tape or record a variety of dialects. A teacher in almost any field may do well to seek out such experienced advice on how to improve the quality of conceptual learning by combining both visual and verbal presentations.

Furthermore, technological aids may permit an individualization of instruction that would otherwise be unfeasible. Thus, students may help to diagnose and remove their own deficiencies by having access to film strips, tapes, records, or information stored in a computer; and they may use teaching machines of one kind or another to facilitate drill on important factual material. Rather than dehumanizing teaching, some maintain, the teaching machine used under proper direction relieves the teacher of certain mechanical chores, such as the conducting of repetitive drills, and thus releases energies and time for those things which the live teacher can do better than any machine.

Some persons say that the time has come to transcend piecemeal reliance upon help from the media, and to program whole courses or even series of courses as systems wherein live instruction and a battery of technical aids are all carefully tied together in such a way as to maximize learning, even taking into account the well-established fact that students differ considerably with respect to the ways in which they learn.

Numerous evaluations of instructional television have shown both advantages and disadvantages as compared with live teaching. It is plain that at the college level televised teaching is generally inferior to live teaching, although there are certainly some situations where television is advantageous. There is furthermore some resistance among college students to televised teaching. Principally, students complain about the one-way communication, an objection that can be minimized by alternating televised programs with live discussion, or by such further technological sophistication as the provision of "feed-back" through radio, telephone, or even the pushing of buttons to indicate to the lecturer agreement or disagreement on various points.

Teachers will continue, of course, to differ in finding such mechanisms compatible or incompatible with their own teaching styles. It seems increasingly clear, however, that at least they should acquaint themselves with the resources of the modern audiovisual center before deciding whether or not to make use of its technology.

Aim of intellectual growth

The ultimate result of good teaching will be found, of course, in the student—in the growth of his knowledge, the extension of his skills, the lengthening of his perspectives, the shifts in his attitudes, the conscious re-examination of his values, the maturing of his intellectual or creative discipline. Does the professor give these sufficient attention as he performs the functions of measurement and counseling so integral to his teaching? It stands to reason that the closer he is to the student, in the tutorial or seminar, in the small class, the better is his opportunity to observe growth in its more subtle as well as obvious form. Yet even in these situations, many professors fail to gain adequate or accurate insight into what the student has accomplished, principally because they have not given sufficient thought to the goals of the course, or have not made themselves sensitive to changes that are not always disclosed in testing. Sometimes the tests the student takes do not measure what the professor himself has specified as the purposes of his teaching.

Tests and examinations are often, indeed, the most eloquent statement of what the professor values as learning. They fix the goals of the course, in the students' practical understanding. The construction of good tests, therefore, requires skill and experience fitted to the full purposes of the course, and these purposes must help decide whether those tests be "objective" or "essay" in form, whether the questions are given the student at the moment of writing or in advance of it, whether or not the examination is of the "open book" variety.

In large courses, and particularly in very large lecture courses, where testing is crucial because it may be the only means of measuring what the student has gained, the construction of adequate examinations becomes even more difficult and too often is given insufficient attention. And for this reason it fails, not merely as a measuring instrument, but as a means of teaching. The carefully thought-out examination, on the other hand, whether for large class or small, and no matter how difficult it may be, will evoke from the discerning student not only new insights, but also genuine satisfactions.

Evaluation is essentially for the purpose of estimating and stimulating growth, of disclosing where special help may be necessary, of revealing to the teacher where the intent of the course may have gone astray, what additional emphases are needed. Used in this way, it is both positive and creative. It can benefit the student as much as the teacher, provided only the latter finds time and occasion for some counseling.

The same observations apply, of course, to grading, which is simply a stated measure of evaluation. Grades may be used judiciously to spur learning. On the other hand, they are often used as a whip, as a means of placing students in categories, as ends in themselves. As a result, the student's first question too frequently is "What did you get in the course?" rather than "What did you get from the course?" or "What is your G.P.A.?" rather than "What have you learned this year?"

For this distortion of emphasis, we teachers must take some responsibility. But so must the admissions officers and committees of most colleges and universities, and those of the graduate schools. The habit of working for grades, acquired in high school or earlier by students aspiring to college, is sustained through the undergraduate years as an ever larger proportion of the students aspire to graduate school. When this happens, it is detrimental to genuine liberal learning.

Teaching styles

Beyond the teaching procedures, methods of learning, and media of learning we have considered, there are teaching styles. In the last analysis, teaching as well as learning must be individualized.

A person's peculiar teaching style is in large measure a function of his temperament and personality. Some teachers have a flair for vivid phrasing, while others are
slow, painstaking, and analytic. Some are highly systematic, while others are impulsive and spontaneous. Some are lighthearted, while others are consistently serious.
Some are almost always the same, in a large class or small, with beginners or sophis-
ticates, early in the morning or late in the afternoon, while others are mercurial.

There have been great teachers who frightened, ridiculed, and badgered their
students. There have been other great teachers, like William James, who were
always gentle, kind, and considerate to their students.

There is, of course, no one right style in teaching, any more than in painting or
writing, and therefore it is unfair and unrealistic to set for oneself or for another
a model distant from what is consonant with one's own distinctive being. Yet there
remains a vast difference between the teacher who has sought and found his own
style or voice, perhaps after protracted experimentation and modification, and one
who uncritically settles for the way he happens first to teach. Teaching is a personal
but not a private act, and somehow the teacher's immediate public will provide him
clues for indicated revisions of his performance. Only in the rare and fortunate
instance will a teacher discover his mature style between the gaining of his last
degree and the teaching of his first course.

It may be hoped that when a teacher has begun to discover the style most consonant with his own temperament, it will be a style that exemplifies to students the
learner at work. In the fullness of years, Carl Jung said that he had never had a
patient from whom he had not learned. One teaches best what it is like to be a
learner by visibly and impressively being one.

Questions for Discussion

1. How can you study your students? What can you learn from them?
2. Are the research findings reported by McKeachie compatible with the advice
   given in this selection in regard to (a) lectures, (b) discussions, (c) independent
   study, (d) television, and (e) programmed learning?
3. Describe as many techniques as you can by which a teacher can obtain information for self-evaluation. Are some more effective—or reliable—than others?
4. What have you learned about the art of teaching as the result of your study of
   this part? Write an essay answering this question both to help you summarize
   your own thoughts and to provide the basis for your further thinking on the
   subject.

Epilogue: And So to the Classroom

Your reading on the subject of the educational process is now coming to an end, and sometime in the not too distant future you may be walking into your own classroom and asking students to invest their time and energy (and their parents to invest their money) in your talents and skills. What words will you use to keep your heart from popping out of your mouth? Will you stand up or sit down, lecture or discuss, test objectively or assign committee reports? And what else do you need to learn between now and that first day to justify your students', and their parents', investment in you?

Obviously you need to have something to talk about. At the minimum, you must know as much about a body of knowledge as the certification requirements demand and a personnel officer is likely to ask. But that is a minimum. Beyond that you must have an interest in what you have learned, a desire to continue learning in that discipline, and above all, a profound and moving conviction that what you have learned and are teaching is worth learning and teaching. Your students will know very soon if you lack this conviction, in the same way you, perhaps, have learned this about some of your own teachers. Knowledge, interest, conviction: without these, no teacher is worth his salt.

But even with these, you still might not be an effective teacher, for you may not communicate effectively with your students. Therefore, you also need to learn something about the learning process which is occurring in your students, and something about the techniques which lead to effective teaching.

When is a student learning? When are you learning? What physical conditions are conducive to learning—or do they matter? What social and mental conditions are necessary? Is there a "normal" development in the learning enterprise so that certain skills or subjects can be taught better at different ages? If so, which is appropriate to what age? How does a teacher's personality—and idiosyncracies—affect the learning environment?

These are the sort of questions you should consider in your study of educational psychology, but you might have noticed, also, that your present authors have a number of comments on this subject. Whitehead tells us that there is a rhythm to the learning process moving from the stage of romance to the stage of precision to the stage of generalization, from freedom to discipline and back to a different kind of freedom. Skinner tells us that learning is the act of behaving appropriately. Bruner reminds us that all learning requires a predisposition to learn.

Keep these ideas, as well as the other thoughts you have encountered in Part III, in mind as you develop your understanding of psychology, but in that study keep uppermost in your own mind the question "What is learning?" Is a student learning when he can repeat factual knowledge? Is he learning when he scores well on an examination? Is he learning when he is thinking creatively? Are you learning when your face looks attentively at your teacher? Have you learned something when you behave differently? Learning theory is an important subject for you to study more deeply, if for no other reason that that it, too, leads you directly to the central question in the educational process: "What is the purpose of education?"

These authors have also given you some valuable comments on techniques you might use to be an effective teacher. Read Highet again on the way a teacher relates effectively to his students, and how he remembers their names and abilities. The Hazen Foundation report contains useful discussions on the techniques and effectiveness of teaching by lectures, discussions and tutorials, and McKeachie tells you the results of the research studies on each. The Carnegie Tech game portrays one of the recent teaching innovations, and should help you to decide when simulation models, instructional media or programed learning can be used most advantageously.

Beyond these resource ideas, you need to watch yourself in the classroom. How do you use your desk? To hide behind? To sit on casually? Or do you ignore it? And does such a simple matter as the way you use your desk say the same thing to your students as your mouth is saying? How do you use the blackboard? To outline a lecture? To spell difficult words? To preserve epigrams? And what does your way of using it say about your teaching purposes? What do you do with your lecture notes? Read from them? Refer to them frequently, or occasionally? Maybe you don't have any. And what are you saying to your class by the way in which you use them? What are you saying to your students with your style of dress? What are you saying to them by the way you arrange the chairs in your classrooms? What do you say with your hands? What do you do while your class is taking an examination, and what are you saying to them by your actions? Or will you give examinations? All of these little details are part of the teaching-learning process, too; in fact, some educators believe that students learn more from a teacher's attitude, as expressed in these subtle ways, than from anything he may say.

So subject matter, learning theory, and teaching techniques are three of the four major concerns you must investigate more thoroughly before you enter that classroom for the first time. And the fourth is that question which has occupied our attention during the whole course of this book: "What are the proper ends and appropriate means of education?" Today you should be coming to grips with that question, for soon you will have to act on whatever answers you give, or assume.

You may agree with Dewey that the purpose of education is to help children become intelligent problem solvers. You may be attracted to Rousseau's and Neill's ideal of the nondirected, freely developing child. Smith's notion that both white and black cultures ought to have their own educational systems might be appealing to you, as is Newman's concept of disciplining the mind. Or you may be attracted to the suggestion offered in the epilogue to Part I that different subjects and types of students suggest different purposes and styles of teaching.

But regardless of the alternative you choose, always try to make your means compatible with your purposes. Do not lecture to your students unless you know something they don't know, but they want to know; only then can you disseminate knowledge effectively. Recognize that any discussion will be less effective if your students are looking at the backs of each other's heads than if they can see each other's faces; in a circle the give and take of individual expression is more genuine than in any other seating arrangement. Do not encourage creative thinking during the class period and then test your students on their ability to remember the text. Ends suggest means, and teaching techniques imply purposes; the teaching-learning process should be viewed as an integral whole.

All of which suggests that the ancient saw "Good teachers are born not made" is one of those pleasant epigrams which is, at best, but partially true, and which prevents serious thinking about the teaching process. If the analysis of this epilogue is accurate, effective teaching can be taught, and can be learned.

In conclusion, then, develop your knowledge and interest in a subject, and as you develop, your commitment to that subject's value will make itself known to your students. You cannot be a successful teacher if you treat your subject matter in a desultory and pedestrian way. Learn more about the learning process, the abilities of different age groups, the effect of the environment on learning, etc., and you will be able to relate more meaningfully to your students. Reflect on your own teaching experiences, and notice how you use blackboards and desks, lecture notes and examinations, and you will understand more clearly what ends you hope to achieve and whether you are using appropriate means. This is to say that good teaching, in large part, is a matter of extensive and continuous self-study, careful observation and the wise use of knowledge. Even the teacher's personality should be a part of that study, for a thoughtful and effective teacher will make his personality an integral part of his teaching purposes and techniques.

And so you're going into the classroom for the first time. What are you going to say? How are you going to act? What are you going to do? Do the questions sound forbidding and ominous, or challenging and exciting? Hopefully the latter, for the chances that you will be an effective teacher are better if your anticipations reflect enthusiasm rather than fear. And as you go in, go with the recognition that you do not know everything about successful teaching yet, that you still are a student, in this case learning how to be a good teacher. Do not be afraid to try different styles of teaching and experimental approaches to your topic, learning from your experience what you do well. Do not be afraid to see yourself in a micro–teaching unit, and to ask the more experienced teachers in your school to exchange observations in the classroom. Seek the counsel of those whose opinions you respect, recognizing that cynicism and weariness are as likely to appear with age as wisdom. Above all, watch your students; they will tell you in a thousand ways whether you are effective and successful.

All the elements in your classroom will not be pleasant, or even rewarding. You will have to put up with reports, unpredictable intercoms, confusion, unexpected visits, bureaucracy, changing time schedules, lost books and all the other vagaries of human beings and their institutions. Moreover, you will quickly discover that teaching—even ineffective, but especially effective teaching—is hard work, very hard work indeed. Not only is a forty-hour work week an ideal most teachers might like to work down to, but teaching also makes both mental demands to discuss clearly and intelligently the subject at hand, and also emotional and psychic demands to observe and evaluate your own performance, repeat or modify your judgments, argue or explain the subject more carefully. You must not only teach but also observe the results of your teaching—and do both at the same time, and that is no easy task. This is why you must learn to use your energies and talents efficiently as well as effectively.

But if you can come to that first day with some knowledge and some skill, some enthusiasm and some commitment, and if you can begin to develop patience and tenacity, forebearance and insight, wisdom and thoughtfulness on the second day, then succeeding days, and even years, will pass unnoticed as you engage in one of the most richly rewarding and humanizing experiences of man, the art of teaching.

Index